THE POLICE IN AMERICA

AN INTRODUCTION

FOURTH EDITION

Samuel Walker

University of Nebraska at Omaha

Charles M. Katz

Arizona State University West

Mc
Graw
Hill

Boston   Burr Ridge, IL   Dubuque, IA   Madison, WI   New York
San Francisco   St. Louis   Bangkok   Bogotá   Caracas   Kuala Lumpur
Lisbon   London   Madrid   Mexico City   Milan   Montreal   New Delhi
Santiago   Seoul   Singapore   Sydney   Taipei   Toronto

McGraw-Hill Higher Education

A Division of The McGraw-Hill Companies

THE POLICE IN AMERICA: AN INTRODUCTION

Published by McGraw-Hill, an imprint of The McGraw-Hill Companies, Inc. 1221 Avenue of the Americas, New York, NY, 10020. Copyright © 2002, 1999, 1992, 1983 by The McGraw-Hill Companies, Inc. All rights reserved. No part of this publication may be reproduced or distributed in any form or by any means, or stored in a database or retrieval system, without the prior written consent of The McGraw-Hill Companies, Inc., including, but not limited to, in any network or other electronic storage or transmission, or broadcast for distance learning.
Some ancillaries, including electronic and print components, may not be available to customers outside the United States.

This book is printed on acid-free paper.

1 2 3 4 5 6 7 8 9 0 FGR/FGR 0 9 8 7 6 5 4 3 2 1

ISBN   0-07-241491-X

Editorial director: *Phillip A. Butcher*
Senior sponsoring editor: *Carolyn Henderson*
Editorial assistant: *Julie Abodeely*
Senior marketing manager: *Daniel M. Loch*
Project manager: *Scott Scheidt*
Production supervisor: *Debra R. Sylvester*
Designer: *Damian Moshak*
Associate supplement producer: *Vicki Laird*
Media producer: *Shannon Rider*
Photo research coordinator: *Jeremy Cheshareck*
Photo researcher: *PoYee Oster*
Cover design: *Damian Moshak*
Interior design: *Kiera Cunningham*
Typeface: *10/12 Times Roman*
Compositor: *GAC Indianapolis*
Printer: *Quebecor World Fairfield Inc.*

Library of Congress Cataloging-in-Publication Data

Walker, Samuel, 1942-
    The police in America : an introduction / Samuel Walker.—4th ed.
      p. cm.
    Includes bibliographical references and index.
    ISBN 0-07-241491-X (alk. paper)
      1. Police—United States. 2. Police administration—United States. I. Title.
HV8138.W3418 2002
363.2'0973—dc21   2001044534

www.mhhe.com

ABOUT
THE AUTHOR

DR. SAMUEL WALKER is Isaacson Professor of Criminal Justice at the University of Nebraska at Omaha. He is the author of eleven books and numerous articles on policing, criminal justice, and civil liberties. He is currently engaged in research on police accountability systems. This includes a recent book on citizen oversight of police and a national evaluation of early warning systems for problem police officers. He has also completed a study of the mediation of citizen complaints against police officers for the U.S. Justice Department.

DR. CHARLES KATZ is an Assistant Professor in the Administration of Justice Department at Arizona State University West. He currently serves as the director of the department's graduate program. Dr. Katz earned his Ph.D. in Criminal Justice from the University of Nebraska at Omaha in 1997. Dr. Katz is responsible for teaching Introduction to Administration of Justice, Police and Society, Police and Culture, and Gangs to undergraduate students and Seminar in Criminal Justice and Seminar in Criminal Justice Organizations to graduate students at Arizona State University West. Dr. Katz is currently involved in several federally funded research projects. He is the project director for a National Institute of Justice study examining the police response to gangs in four cities: Phoenix, Albuquerque, Las Vegas, and Inglewood (California); and he is currently serving as a local evaluator for the Mesa, Arizona, component of "The Comprehensive Community-Wide Approach to Gang Prevention, Intervention, and Suppression Program" sponsored by the Office of Juvenile Justice and Delinquency Prevention (JODI). Dr. Katz is also currently a consultant for three nationwide projects examining the implementation of community policing and problem solving in local police departments, and he is the Site Coordinator for Maricopa and Pima County for the Arrestee Drug Abuse Monitoring (ADAM) Project funded by the National Institute of Justice. His work has recently appeared in *Criminology, Justice Quarterly,* and *Police Quarterly.*

CONTENTS IN BRIEF

CONTENTS

PART THREE   POLICE PROBLEMS

PREFACE

The Police in America: An Introduction provides a comprehensive presentation of the foundations of policing in the United States today. Descriptive and analytical, the text is designed to offer undergraduate students a balanced and up-to-date overview of who the police are and what they do, the problems they face, and the many reforms and innovations that have taken place in policing. The book is designed primarily for undergraduate students enrolled in their first police or law enforcement course such as Introduction to Policing, Police and Society, Police Function, or Law Enforcement Systems.

THE FOURTH EDITION

The Police in America, fourth edition, has undergone extensive revision. In response to reviewer feedback, the fourth edition not only includes coverage of the latest research and practices in policing but also contains updated statistical information throughout. Among the most important changes we have made to the fourth edition are the following:

- Chapter 2, "The History of the American Police," now includes new historical perspectives on community policing and police relations with racial and ethnic minorities.
- In Chapter 4, "Patrol: The Backbone of Policing," we eliminated discussion of outdated police strategies and technologies and have included data on "hot spots" patrolling, innovations such as 311 nonemergency numbers, new information on patrol supervision, and the latest data on patrol activity under community policing.
- Chapter 5, "Peacekeeping and Order Maintenance," has been expanded to include state-of-the-art strategies that the police are using to respond to the homeless, the mentally ill, and people with HIV/AIDS. The chapter also has been expanded to include a discussion of curfew laws and the effectiveness of these laws on juvenile disorder and crime.
- Chapter 6, "The Police and Crime," was substantially expanded to include sections on gun crime and hate crime as well as the police response to gang crime, school crime, terrorism, and computer-related crime.

- Chapter 7, "Innovations in Policing," was almost entirely rewritten. We eliminated much of the material related to outdated policing strategies and added coverage of the most up-to-date strategies used in departments across the country—such as community-oriented, problem-oriented, and zero-tolerance policing.
- Chapter 8, "Police Discretion," has been expanded to include the most recent research on the police use of force and the impact of policies designed to control officer abuse of authority.
- Chapter 9, "Police–Community Relations," has up-to-date coverage of the racial profiling controversy and programs designed to help officers respond effectively to racial and ethnic minorities who do not speak English.
- Chapter 10, "Police Corruption," features many of the new developments that have occurred since the last edition, including the Rampart scandal in Los Angeles and a series of police misconduct incidents in New York City.
- Chapter 11, "Accountability of the Police," has been expanded to include coverage of important new accountability measures such as early warning systems, officer use of force reporting systems, and the latest developments in citizen oversight of the police.
- Chapter 12, "Police Officers I: Entering Police Work," has been expanded to include new material on Latino/Hispanic officers and the latest data on women in policing.
- Chapter 13, "Police Officers II: On the Job," has been revised to include new material on the changing police subculture and how backgrounds and attitudes affect officer behavior, along with new material on performance evaluation systems under community policing.
- Chapter 14, "Police Organizations," has been expanded to include organizational theory and its applicability toward understanding police organizations. The chapter also now includes coverage of how police organizations have changed with the implementation of community policing and problem-oriented policing.

OVERVIEW OF THE CONTENTS

Part One, "Foundations," provides students with an introduction to policing in America. It explains the role of the police in the United States along with the realities of police work and the many factors that shape policing. It also traces the history of the police from the creation of the first modern police department through the many new developments that can be found in policing today. The section concludes with a discussion of the characteristics of the contemporary law enforcement industry.

Part Two, "Police Work," includes explanations of what the police do and how they do it. Among the subjects covered are the function of patrol, the delivery of services, and the effectiveness of traditional policing strategies. This section also discusses the various problems that the police face while on the job and the strategies that they use to respond to these problems. The section closes with a discussion of innovations in policing such as community-oriented policing, problem-oriented policing, and zero-tolerance policing.

Part Three, "Police Problems," covers the various problems that police officers and police organizations encounter. The chapter on police discretion explains the nature of police discretion, sources of discretion, and how police organizations have attempted to control discretion. The section also includes a chapter on police–community relations.

Attention is placed on citizen perception of the police, police perceptions of citizens, and sources of police–community relations problems—with special emphasis on race and ethnicity and its implications for policing in the United States. A chapter on police corruption is also included in this section, which discusses the different types of corruption and the different strategies that are used to control it. The section concludes with a chapter on police accountability.

Part Four, "Officers and Organizations," includes an explanation of police recruitment, selection, and training practices as well as a discussion of the characteristics of American police officers. The section also includes coverage of the reality shock that officers encounter when beginning their job, the concept of police culture, and the relationship between the attitudes of the police and police behavior. The section ends with an explanation of the characteristics of police organizations, the role and influence of police unions, and a discussion of the theoretical rationales for why police organizations behave the way they do.

LEARNING AIDS

A number of new pedagogical aids have been added to the fourth edition of *The Police in America* to make the text easier to teach and learn from, and to make the material come alive with practical, concrete examples and applications. In response to feedback from adopters of the third edition, we have added the following learning aids to the fourth edition:

- Opening "Chapter Outlines" to guide students through the chapter
- "Key Terms and Concepts" sections at the start of each chapter to help focus the students' attention on the important issues found within each chapter
- "Sidebars" in every chapter to expound upon important concepts and highlight contemporary issues related to the chapter discussion
- An end-of-chapter "Case Study"—a real-world example highlighting a major concept or idea from the chapter—to enable students to begin applying what they have read
- "For Discussion" questions following the "Case Study" to stimulate classroom discussion of the case
- "Internet Exercises" at the end of each chapter that can be used by students for further Web-based study

SUPPLEMENTS

As a full-service publisher of quality educational products, McGraw-Hill does much more than just sell textbooks. The publisher creates and publishes an extensive array of print, video, and digital supplements for students and instructors. This edition of *The Police in America* is accompanied by a comprehensive supplements package.

For the Student

- Online Learning Center— this free Web-based student supplement includes a self-quiz for each chapter (with feedback, so that students can better prepare for exams), interactive chapter summaries, PowerPoint lecture notes, FAQs, links, and Power-Web, a unique collection of current articles on policing that have been carefully selected by educators. PowerWeb also features daily and weekly updates, online quizzing and assessment, annotated links organized by course topic, interactive glossaries with self-tests, and more.

For the Instructor

- Instructor's Manual/Testbank—chapter outlines, key terms, overviews, lecture notes, discussion questions, a complete testbank, and more.
- Computerized Testbank—easy-to-use computerized testing program for both Windows and Macintosh computers.
- PowerPoint Slides—complete chapter-by-chapter slide shows featuring text, tables, and illustrations.
- Instructor's Online Learning Center—password-protected access to important instructor support materials and additional resources.
- PageOut—easy-to-use tool that allows the instructor to create his or her own course Web page and access all material on *The Police in America* Online Learning Center.

All of the above supplements are provided free of charge to students and instructors. Orders of new (versus used) textbooks help us defray the cost of developing such supplements, which is substantial. Please contact your local McGraw-Hill representative for more information on any of the above supplements.

ACKNOWLEDGMENTS

We would both like to thank the reviewers of the third edition of this text for their many contributions in helping us revise the book in its fourth edition:

Donna Sherwood, Macomb Community College
William E. Kelly, Auburn University
Dennis Stevens, University of Massachusetts–Boston
Ellen Cohn Odza, Florida International University
Cliff Roberson, Washburn University

Sam Walker would like to thank his colleagues at the University of Nebraska at Omaha, and in particular chairperson Bob Meier, for creating a supportive academic environment. He also wishes to thank several of his graduate students who have not only helped to track down particular bits of information from time to time but also provided a sounding board for how particular issues should be covered in this book. These students include Carol Archbold, Mark Foxall, Leigh Herbst, and Dawn Irlbeck. Sam would especially like to thank former student and current coauthor Chuck Katz for agreeing to share the work on producing this fourth edition. For Sam, it has been as much a pleasure to work with Chuck as a colleague as it was to work with him as a student just a few years ago.

Charles Katz would like to thank the many people who have contributed to the completion of this edition and to acknowledge his colleagues at Arizona State University

West, who have always been supportive and have been willing to lend a helpful hand when asked. Gratitude is particularly owed to Vincent Webb, the chair of the department, for always being a strong advocate for the department and for fostering an environment that is conducive for creative work. With regard to the production of the book, Charles would like to thank Carolyn Henderson, whose editorial expertise improved the quality of this book and who always provided helpful suggestions on how to present material in an innovative way. Special thanks, too, to three people in particular: To Charles' parents, who have always been loving and supportive; this book, and his other work, is just as much a result of their dedication and efforts as his own. And to his coauthor Sam Walker, who asked Charles to join him on the fourth edition of this book; Sam has always been supportive, whether it be professional or personal, and has been one of the most influential persons in Charles' life.

THE POLICE IN AMERICA

PART **ONE**

FOUNDATIONS

CHAPTER ONE

Police and Society

CHAPTER OUTLINE

INTRODUCTION: WHY POLICE?

More than 30 years ago, Jerome Skolnick posed the fundamental question, "For what social purpose do police exist?"[1] Why do we have police? What purpose do they serve? What do we want them to do? What do they do that other government agencies do not do? How do we want them to do these things? These are basic questions related to the police role in society.

Too often the answers to these questions are vague and simplistic. People say the police should "protect and serve," or "enforce the law." Such answers, however, avoid all the important issues. Policing is extremely complex, involving difficult questions

3

KEY TERMS AND CONCEPTS

about the police role, treating citizens fairly, police organizations, and the recruitment, training, and supervision of police officers.

The Goals of This Book

Several new innovations in policing such as community-oriented policing, problem-oriented policing, and zero-tolerance policing have raised new questions about the police role. These new strategies represent a different role for the police compared with the "professional" style of policing that prevailed as a result of the professionalization movement (1900–1980).[2] It reopens all of the basic questions about how we should organize and deliver police services, whom we should recruit, and how we should evaluate them.

The purpose of this book is not to argue for or against any one of these new innovations in policing. It is to provide the necessary background information about policing to help you, the reader, discuss these innovations intelligently. It seeks to describe what police do (Chapter 4), the many problems that arise such as the exercise of discretion (Chapter 8), police–community relations (Chapter 9), how police officers are selected and who police officers are (Chapters 12 and 13), and how police organizations operate (Chapter 14). It seeks to describe what policing has been in the past (Chapter 2), what it is like today, and what it could be in the future (Chapter 7).

Myths, Realities, and Possibilities

At the outset it is necessary to sort out the myths, realities, and possibilities of policing. The myths include the many erroneous ideas about what the police do and what they should do. The realities include what the police in fact do on a day-to-day basis, and the role they play in society. The possibilities include the ways in which policing could be different from what it is today.

MYTHS ABOUT POLICING

Policing is surrounded by many myths and stereotypes.[3] One of the enduring myths is that police are primarily crime fighters. According to this view, police devote most of their efforts to enforcing the criminal law: patrolling to deter crime, investigating crimes, and arresting criminals. Some people believe that this is what the police *should* do. A lot of the rhetoric about the police reflects the crime-fighter image: the idea of the police as a "thin blue line," fighting a war on crime.[4]

The crime-fighter image, however, is not an accurate description of what the police do. Only about one-third of a patrol officer's activities are devoted to criminal law enforcement (Chapter 4). The typical police officer rarely makes a felony arrest, and almost never fires a weapon in his or her entire career. Most police work is best described as peacekeeping, or order maintenance, or problem solving (Chapter 5).

Sources of the Crime-Fighter Image

The myth of the crime fighter endures for many reasons. The entertainment media play a major role in popularizing it. Movies and television police shows feature crime-related stories because they offer drama, fast-paced action, and violence. Think for a moment about the latest Hollywood cop movie: How many car chases were there? How many shoot-outs? The typical domestic disturbance, which in real life is a common police situation, does not offer the same kind of dramatic possibilities.

The news media are equally guilty of overemphasizing police crime fighting. A recent study of crime and the news media concluded that "crime stories are frequently presented and prominently displayed," and the number of these stories is "large in comparison with other topics."[5] A serious crime is a newsworthy event. There is a victim who engages our sympathies, a story, and then an arrest that offers dramatic visuals of the suspect in custody. A typical night's work for a patrol officer, by way of contrast, does not offer much in the way of dramatic news.

The police perpetuate the crime-fighter image themselves. Official press releases and annual reports emphasize crime and arrests. Crime fighting is a way for the police to tell the public they are doing something and doing something important. Peter Manning argues that the police deliberately adopted the crime-fighter role image as a way of staking claim to a domain of professional expertise that they, and they alone, could control.[6]

Consequences of the Crime-Fighter Image

Because it does not present an accurate picture of what the police do, the crime-fighter image creates a number of serious problems.[7] Most important, it ignores the order maintenance and peacekeeping activities that consume most police time and effort (Chapters 4 and 5). This prevents us from intelligently evaluating police performance. The emphasis on crime fighting also creates unrealistic public expectations about the ability of the police to prevent crime and catch criminals. Movies and TV shows strengthen the impression that the police are highly successful in solving crimes, when in fact only 21 percent of all reported Index crimes are solved (Chapter 6).

The police themselves suffer from this distorted image. Police chiefs cannot effectively manage their departments when so much attention is given to only one small part of their activities. The crime-fighter image also creates role conflict for individual police officers. By placing a premium on detective work and devaluing patrol work it creates a contradiction between what patrol officers value and what they actually do.[8]

THE REALITIES OF POLICING

The reality of policing is that the police play an extremely complex role in today's society. This role involves many different tasks. Herman Goldstein warns that "anyone attempting to construct a workable definition of the police role will typically come away with old images shattered and a new-found appreciation for the intricacies of police work."[9]

Many studies of police work document the complexity of the police role. The Police Services Study (PSS), for example, examined 26,418 calls for service to the police in three metropolitan areas.[10] As the data in Table 1-1 indicate, only 19 percent of the calls involve crime, and only 2 percent of the total involve violent crime.

The data in Table 1-1 also illustrate how ambiguous police work is. The situations in the category of interpersonal conflict, for example, may involve a potential crime (e.g., assault), or pose a serious risk to the officer or another person (e.g., a mentally disturbed person with a gun), or merely be an argument and some noise.

One of the most important aspects of policing is that officers exercise enormous discretion in handling these situations (Chapter 8). Take, for example, the case of Mr. and Mrs. Jones. One night the neighbors overhear the couple arguing and call the police. After the police arrive and are faced with the dispute, should they warn Mr. and Mrs. Jones, ask one of them to leave the premises, arrest one of them, or try to mediate the dispute? These are difficult choices, requiring good judgment and human relations skills. It is not a simple matter of making an arrest, as the crime-fighter image suggests.

The American Bar Association's *Standards Relating to the Urban Police Function* illustrates the complexity of the police role by identifying eleven different police responsibilities (Figure 1-1).[11]

The ABA list illustrates three ways in which the police role is extremely complex. First, it involves a wide variety of tasks. Only a few deal with criminal law enforcement.

Second, many of the tasks are extremely vague. Resolving conflict, for example, raises a number of difficult questions. What kinds of situations represent conflicts that require police intervention? What is the best response to a conflict situation? Should officers always make arrests in domestic disputes, for example? If not, what should they do?

Third, different responsibilities often conflict with each other. Police are responsible for both maintaining order and protecting constitutional liberties, for example. In the case of a large political demonstration, the police have to balance the First Amendment rights of the protesters and the need to maintain order and protect the rights of other people to use the streets and sidewalks.

As Goldstein points out, "The police, by the very nature of their function, are an anomaly in a free society."[12] On the one hand, we expect them to exercise coercive

TABLE 1-1 CITIZEN CALLS FOR POLICE SERVICES, BY GENERAL PROBLEM TYPES AND SUBCATEGORIES

Type of Problem	Number of Calls	Percent of Total	Percent of Category
Violent Crimes	642	2	
1. Homicide	9		1
2. Sexual attack	26		4
3. Robbery	118		18
4. Aggravated assault	74		12
5. Simple assault	351		55
6. Child abuse	38		6
7. Kidnapping	26		4
Nonviolent Crimes	4,489	17	
1. Burglary and break-ins	1,544		34
2. Theft	1,389		31
3. Motor vehicle theft	284		6
4. Vandalism, arson	866		19
5. Problems with money/credit/documents	209		5
6. Crimes against the family	29		1
7. Leaving the scene	168		4
Interpersonal Conflict	1,763	7	
1. Domestic conflict	694		39
2. Nondomestic arguments	335		19
3. Nondomestic threats	277		16
4. Nondomestic fights	457		26
Medical Assistance	810	3	
1. Medical assistance	274		34
2. Death	38		5
3. Suicide	34		4
4. Emergency transport	203		25
5. Personal injury, traffic accident	261		32
Traffic Problems	2,467	9	
1. Property damage, traffic accident	1,141		46
2. Vehicle violation	543		22
3. Traffic-flow problem	322		13
4. Moving violation	292		12
5. Abandoned vehicle	169		7
Dependent Persons	774	3	
1. Drunk	146		19
2. Missing persons	318		41
3. Juvenile runaway	121		16
4. Subject of police concern	134		17
5. Mentally disordered	55		7
Public Nuisances	3,002	11	
1. Annoyance, harassment	980		33
2. Noise disturbance	984		33
3. Trespassing, unwanted entry	302		10

TABLE 1-1   CONTINUED

Type of Problem	Number of Calls	Percent of Total	Percent of Category
Public Nuisances (continued)			
4. Alcohol, drug violations	130		4
5. Public morals	124		4
6. Juvenile problem	439		15
7. Ordinance violations	43		1
Suspicious Circumstances	1,248	5	
1. Suspicious person	674		54
2. Suspicious property condition	475		38
3. Dangerous person or situation	99		8
Assistance	3,039	12	
1. Animal problem	755		24
2. Property check	616		20
3. Escorts and transports	86		3
4. Utility problem	438		14
5. Property discovery	240		8
6. Assistance to motorist	154		5
7. Fires, alarms	112		4
8. Crank calls	114		4
9. Unspecified requests	425		14
10. Other requests	99		3
Citizen Wants Information	5,558	21	
1. Information, unspecified	248		5
2. Information, police related	1,262		23
3. Information about specific case	1,865		34
4. Information, nonpolice related	577		10
5. Road directions	189		3
6. Directions, nontraffic	55		1
7. Requests for specific unit	1,362		25
Citizen Wants to Give Information	1,993	8	
1. General information	1,090		55
2. Return of property	156		8
3. False alarm	176		9
4. Complaint against specific officer	105		5
5. Complaint against police in general	350		18
6. Compliments for police	20		1
7. Hospital report to police	96		5
Internal Operations	633	2	
1. Internal legal procedures	63		10
2. Internal assistance request	134		21
3. Officer wants to give information	298		47
4. Officer wants information	132		21
5. Other internal procedures	6	—	—
Total calls	26,418	100	1

Source: Eric J. Scott, *Calls for Service: Citizen Demand and Initial Police Response* (Washington, DC: Government Printing Office, 1981), pp. 28–30.

FIGURE 1-1   POLICE ROLES AND RESPONSIBILITIES

1 Identify criminal offenders and criminal activity and, when appropriate, apprehend offenders and participate in subsequent court proceedings.
2 Reduce the opportunities for the commission of some crimes through preventive patrol and other measures.
3 Aid individuals who are in danger of physical harm.
4 Protect constitutional guarantees.
5 Facilitate the movement of people and vehicles.
6 Assist those who cannot care for themselves.
7 Resolve conflict.
8 Identify problems that are potentially serious law enforcement or government problems.
9 Create and maintain a feeling of security in the community.
10 Promote and preserve civil order.
11 Provide other services on an emergency basis.

Source: American Bar Association, *Standards Relating to the Urban Police Function*, 2nd ed. (Boston: Little, Brown, 1980), pp. 1–31 to 1–32, Standard 1–2.2, "Major Current Responsibilities of Police."

force: to restrain people when they are out of control, to arrest them when they break the law, and in some extreme cases to use deadly force. At the same time, however, we expect the police to protect the individual freedoms that are the essential part of a democratic society. The tension between freedom and constraint is one of the central problems in American policing.[13]

Factors That Shape the Police Role

Several factors contribute to the complexity of the police role. Most important is the fact that police services are available 24 hours a day. The telephone makes it possible to call the police at any hour and for any problem. The police, moreover, have encouraged people to call and have promised to respond to those calls. Goldstein argues that the police end up handling many problems "because no other means has been found to solve them. They are the residual problems of society."[14] Policing involves society's "dirty work": the tasks that no one else wants to do.[15] People call the police when everything else has failed.

The public wants a general-purpose emergency service, available to handle problems that arise. This job falls to the police. It would be extremely expensive to maintain a number of additional specialized agencies, for example, one that deals only with domestic disturbances, or one that responds only to mental illness situations. The 24-hour availability of the police gives them an extremely heavy workload. Many calls do not necessarily require a sworn police officer with arrest power. Also, some of these calls require someone with professional expertise (some mental health incidents, for example). As a result, the police are generalists, expected to handle a wide range of situations, but with only limited training and expertise in family problems, mental illness, or alcohol and drug abuse.

The complexity of the police role was not really planned. For the most part, it just happened. The police acquired many responsibilities simply because they were the only

---

SIDEBAR 1-1   THE PRINCIPLES OF DEMOCRATIC POLICING

As a result of the conflict in Bosnia and Herzegovina, the warring factions and several other interested parties came together in Youngstown, Ohio, to discuss the principles to guide the development of a new police force in the country. As part of what was later called the "Youngstown Accord," seven principles were established to guide policing in both established and emerging democracies across the world. These seven principles were:

1   The police must operate in accordance with democratic principles.
2   The police as recipients of public trust should be considered as professionals whose conduct must be governed by a professional code.
3   The police must have as their highest priority the protection of life.
4   The police must serve the community and consider themselves accountable to the community.
5   The police must recognize that protection of life and property is the primary function of police operations.
6   The police must conduct their activities with respect for human dignity and basic human rights.
7   The police are expected to discharge their duties in a nondiscriminatory manner.

1   In groups of four or five, discuss whether you think American policing is characterized by democratic principles.
2   Discuss which principles you believe are more closely adhered to in American policing.
3   Should these principles be adopted by all law enforcement agencies in the United States?

Source: Adapted from Jeremy Travis, 2000, "Policing in Transition," *Police Practice & Research: An International Journal,* 1(1): 31–40.

---

agency available. The telephone made it convenient for people to call the police, and so they did (Chapter 2). The debate over the police role today raises basic questions about whether we really want the police to do all these things.

The Authority to Use Force

The authority to use force is one of the most important factors shaping the police role. In this crucial respect, the police are different from other professionals: teachers, social workers, doctors. In one of the most important essays on policing, Egon Bittner argues that the capacity to use coercive force is the defining feature of the police.[16] Force includes the power to take someone's life (deadly force), the use of physical force, and the power to deprive people of their liberty through arrest.

Bittner quickly adds that the authority to use force is not unlimited. First, it is limited by law. The police cannot lawfully shoot to kill anyone. The power to arrest is also limited by the law. Second, officers may use force only in the performance of their job.

They may not use force, for example, to settle a private dispute. Third, officers may not use force maliciously or frivolously. They may not arrest, harass, or abuse citizens for personal spite or amusement.

The authority to use force has implications that go far beyond its actual use. Bittner argues that it is latent and ever present, defining relations between officers and citizens. He observes: "There can be no doubt that this feature of police work is uppermost in the minds of people who solicit police aid." [17] People call the police because they want an officer to settle a problem: to arrest someone, to get someone to calm down, or to have someone removed from the home. People generally defer to police authority. In the vast majority of situations, citizens comply with police officer requests, suggestions, or threats. [18]

The Police and Social Control

The police are part of the system of social control. Morris Janowitz defines social control as "the capacity of a society to regulate itself according to desired principles and values." [19] Control, in this sense, is not the same as repression or enforced conformity. The distinguishing feature of a democratic society is the existence of mechanisms for peaceful political change. Constitutional guarantees of freedom of speech, press, and assembly facilitate peaceful change by allowing new and controversial ideas to be heard. As the ABA list of police tasks indicates (Figure 1-1), preserving constitutional rights is part of the police role.

The police contribute to social control through both their law enforcement and order maintenance responsibilities. Their task is to preserve the norms of society by deterring crime and arresting people who violate the criminal law, which embodies those norms. The police presence in society is also intended to preserve order by serving as a deterrent to misconduct and by providing a quick-response mechanism for potential or low-level problems.

The capacity of the police to exercise complete social control is extremely limited, however. As we will learn in Chapter 4, routine patrol has only a limited effect on crime, and as we will see in Chapter 5, the ability of the police to identify and arrest criminal suspects is extremely limited.

Experts now recognize that the police are heavily dependent on citizens in carrying out their responsibilities. Police depend on people to report crimes, to provide information about suspects, to cooperate in investigations, and so on. For this reason, many experts refer to citizens as "coproducers" of police services. [20]

In the colonial era (1600–1840s), before we had the modern police, citizens were the primary agents of social control. Behavior was regulated by comments, warnings, or rebukes by family, friends, and neighbors. [21] The creation of the modern police, as a large professional bureaucracy, transferred that responsibility away from citizens (Chapter 2). The community-policing movement is an attempt to restore and develop the role of citizens as coproducers of police services.

In important respects, the police are the last resort in the system of social control. We call the police when everything else has failed. The primary social control mechanism is the family. Peer groups, community groups, religious institutions, and the schools are also important. When these mechanisms fail and a person breaks the law, we call the police.

The Police and Social Control Systems

The police are part of several different systems of social control. First, and most important, they are the "gatekeepers" of the criminal justice system. The decision by a police officer to make an arrest initiates most criminal cases. The decision not to arrest keeps the incident out of the system.[22] Thus, the police determine the workload for the criminal justice system. At the same time, police efforts are deeply affected by the actions of other criminal justice agencies.

Second, the police are an important part of the social welfare system. They are often the first contact that official agencies have with social problems such as delinquency, family problems, drug abuse, and alcoholism. The police often refer individuals to social service agencies. The police are also an important part of the mental health system. Patrol units are routinely called to situations where someone is believed to be mentally ill. The officer has the responsibility of determining whether the person is in fact mentally ill and requires hospitalization. Goldstein argues that we need to recognize the fact that this is what police actually do, and we should develop alternatives to the criminal justice system for dealing with these situations.[23]

Third, the police are an important part of the political system. In a democratic society, the political system ensures public control and accountability of the police: The people, acting through their elected representatives, determine police policy, such as community policing, or not? Aggressive enforcement of traffic laws, or not? In the case of the sheriff, the people directly elect the top law enforcement official (Chapter 3).

Political control of law enforcement agencies represents one of the central dilemmas of policing a democratic society. On the one hand, the people have a fundamental right to control their government agencies. At the same time, however, politics has historically been the source of much corruption and abuse of law enforcement powers (Chapter 2). Striking the balance between popular control and professional standards is another one of the basic tensions in American policing.

In important respects, the police are symbols of the political system. They are the most visible manifestation of power and authority in society. The badge, the gun, and the billy club are potent visual reminders of the ultimate power of the police in maintaining the existing social and political system. As a result, attitudes toward the police are influenced by people's attitudes toward the political system generally. Arthur Niederhoffer describes the police officer as "a 'Rorschach' in uniform." People project upon the officer their attitudes about a wide range of issues.[24]

POSSIBILITIES

The form of policing we currently have is not the only one that is possible. The idea that the police do not and cannot change is a myth. The history of the police indicates that they have changed dramatically over the years (Chapter 2).[25] In *Police for the Future*, David H. Bayley argues that we have a choice—a political choice about different possibilities for policing.[26] The real question is, "What kind of policing do we want to create?"

Bayley argues that we should take the crime prevention role of the police seriously. He believes the police, as traditionally organized, cannot effectively prevent crime. But he does see the possibility of more effective crime prevention if we choose to decentralize police departments and give more responsibility to neighborhood police officers (NPOs). This approach takes police departments and stands them on their heads, giving more decision-making responsibility to the officers at the bottom of the organization. Executives at the top of the organization would coordinate rather than command, as they do in the traditional quasi-military-style organization.[27]

Is Bayley's proposal sound? Would it achieve its goals without doing more harm to society? The purpose of this book is not to provide prescriptive yes or no answers to these questions. Instead, our purpose is to provide a factual, up-to-date description of policing today so that we can make informed decisions about the choices that are available—choices that are based on evidence, not subjective beliefs.

Let's consider some of the alternative possibilities for the police.

Functional Specialization

In 1967 the President's Crime Commission proposed dividing current police tasks among three different specialties within police agencies. Community service officers (CSOs), apprentices between the ages of 17 and 21, would work under the supervision of a regular police officer. They would be responsible for nonemergency calls for service. Police officers would perform most of the patrol, investigation, and enforcement tasks currently handled by the police. Police agents would concentrate on criminal investigation, with subspecialties focusing on homicide, rape, and so on.[28]

The Crime Commission's proposal represents a functional specialization approach. Most other professions operate in this way. Professional educators, for example, specialize in preschool, elementary, and secondary education, and college and university teaching. Within levels of education, moreover, there are area specialties: mathematics, biology, history, and so on. Lawyers specialize in criminal defense, tax law, personal injury, and the like. Also, most professions delegate less critical tasks to paraprofessionals, such as teaching assistants, law clerks, and nurses.[29]

Some police departments have experimented with part of the Crime Commission's proposal, using police cadets or aides for nonemergency tasks. An evaluation of a CSO-type program in Worcester, Massachusetts, found it to be highly effective. The officers, called police service aides (PSAs), handled "cold" crimes—those that are not discovered or reported until after they have been committed. The PSAs took crime reports, transported suspects, and provided information and miscellaneous nonemergency service to the public. The evaluation found that the PSAs handled 24.7 percent of all citizen calls directly and assisted in another 8.2 percent. Citizens, PSAs, and regular police officers expressed satisfaction with their performance.[30]

The Crime Commission's full proposal has not been adopted by police departments, however. The basic problem is that it does not resolve the issues surrounding the complexity of the police role. Police officers would still be called to many situations where they would have to determine what is happening and make difficult discretionary decisions about the best response.

Problem-Oriented Policing

Herman Goldstein's concept of problem-oriented policing (POP) represents a different approach to the complexity of the police role. He argues that the police should disaggregate their workload, identify recurring problems, and develop strategies to reduce or eliminate those problems. Instead of thinking in terms of general categories of crime and disorder, the police should identify particular kinds of crime (drug dealing, drunk driving) and disorder (rowdy juveniles, chronic alcoholics in the neighborhood) and develop appropriate responses. POP represents a proactive approach, very different from the reactive approach of simply responding to 911 calls. It involves research and planning, and a shift from individual calls for service to a concern with underlying problems. The category of disorder, for example, would be disaggregated into separate problems: domestic disturbances, juvenile rowdiness, and chronic alcoholism on the street. A different strategy would be developed for each one.[31]

One of the first experiments in problem-oriented policing occurred in Newport News, Virginia, in the mid-1980s. The program focused on burglaries in the New Briarfield apartments, one of the worst low-income housing units in the city. The project began by analyzing crime patterns in the area and conducting an opinion survey of apartment complex residents. The survey discovered that deteriorated buildings contributed to many burglaries: windows and doors were easily broken into, vacant apartments created havens for criminals, and deteriorated conditions created an atmosphere of despair and powerlessness among the residents.[32]

Police officers assigned to New Briarfield responded by attempting to improve the physical condition of the buildings. One officer negotiated the settlement of a dispute with the private trash hauler that resulted in the removal of accumulated garbage. Abandoned refrigerators and other dangers to children were also removed. The police department organized a meeting of government agencies that had some responsibility for the housing project: the fire department, the Department of Public Works, the Redevelopment and Housing Authority, and so on. The purpose of the meeting was to develop a coordinated strategy to improve conditions in the complex. One officer organized a tenants' group to pressure city officials into making short-term improvements in the apartments.

POP in Newport News represented a new role for the police. Officers functioned as community organizers and brokers of government services, mediating between citizens and other agencies.

Today, police departments around the world practice problem-oriented policing. To facilitate its practice the San Diego police department and the Police Executive Research Forum (PERF) have cohosted the International Problem-Oriented Policing (POP) Conference every year since 1990. At the conference are hundreds of representatives from police agencies and academic institutions who come together to discuss the direction of problem-oriented policing and to share information about problem-oriented policing strategies.[33] Each year the Herman Goldstein Award is presented at the conference to recognize the most innovative and successful problem-oriented policing project implemented by a police agency. Recent award winners have been the Boston police department (1998), the Green Bay police department (1999), and the San Diego police department (2000). The award was created to honor Herman Goldstein, who developed the concept of problem-oriented policing.[34]

Community Policing

The most popular new approach to policing today is community policing. Community policing alters the basic philosophy of policing. It holds that the police should work closely with community residents, instead of being an inward-looking bureaucracy; that they should emphasize crime prevention, as opposed to law enforcement; and that they should decentralize the decision-making authority to rank-and-file officers, as opposed to the top-down military-style organization.[35]

Community-policing programs take many different forms.[36] Some emphasize disorder and quality-of-life issues, while others focus on serious crime. Some primarily address drug-related crime.

In Chicago, the police department has instituted CAPS (Chicago Alternative Policing Strategy). At the root of the CAPS plan is the idea that the whole police department, and not just a specialized unit, should become intimately involved with and partner with the community. As part of this strategy officers are permanently assigned to neighborhoods to enhance their knowledge about the community in which they work and to allow the officers and the neighborhood residents to get to know one another on a personal level. Under CAPS the police department requires officers to meet with neighborhood residents regularly to discuss problems in the community and to develop strategies to solve them. Once neighborhood residents identify problems, officers mobilize the necessary resources to address them. While there are a number of obstacles to implementing CAPS, independent research is beginning to show that the strategy has been successful in reducing crime and fear of crime and is successful in building a stronger relationship between the police and the community.[37]

In Oakland, California, the SMART (Specialized Multi-Agency Response Team) program involved many different government agencies working closely with the police to tackle drug-related problems. City housing inspectors, for example, cited suspected drug houses for building code violations, landlords were encouraged or coerced into cleaning up blighted properties, while the police engaged in standard law enforcement tactics. Lorraine Green's evaluation of SMART found that it not only reduced drug activity but also diffused the positive benefits to surrounding areas.[38] SMART is an example of the community-policing philosophy of the police working closely with other agencies and using noncriminal justice system strategies.

Zero-Tolerance Policing

New York City adopted a policy of zero-tolerance policing in the 1990s. This approach concentrates on relatively minor quality-of-life issues, such as urinating in public and "fare-beating" (jumping over the subway turnstiles to avoid paying the fare). George

Kelling and Catherine Coles argue that tough enforcement on minor crimes directly contributes to a significant reduction in serious crime. Some fare-beaters, for example, were found to be carrying weapons in violation of the law. The weapons were then seized and the persons were arrested on more serious gun charges. The crime rate in New York City began to fall dramatically in 1992, and by 1997 it was at the lowest level in 30 years.[39]

Critics of the zero-tolerance policy, however, argue that it encourages police abuse of citizens. And, in fact, complaints against New York City police officers increased in the 1990s. From 1994 through 1996 the police department paid out over $70 million for police misconduct.[40] These allegations raise the question of whether it is possible to have tough law enforcement while at the same time respecting the rights of citizens.

Honest Law Enforcement

One of the options identified by Bayley in *Police for the Future* is "honest law enforcement." Under this approach, the police would continue to do what they now do well, but be honest with themselves and the public about it. They would continue to patrol neighborhoods, answer calls for service, intervene in problem situations, and try to apprehend offenders; but they would not claim that they are preventing crime. This approach represents low expectations for what the police can do, but it does have the virtue of being honest about it. As Bayley points out, too much of contemporary policing involves "dishonest law enforcement," making unjustified claims for effective crime prevention.[41]

THE IMPLICATIONS OF CHANGE

It is easy to talk about dramatic changes in policing. For example, advocates of community policing believe that it represents a new era in American policing. Translating ideas into practice is extremely difficult, however. Consider, for example, the case of team policing. It was a radical innovation in the early 1970s, involving restructuring police operations along neighborhood lines and decentralizing decision-making authority. At one point a large number of police departments said they were doing team policing.[42] And then, suddenly, the team-policing movement collapsed and it vanished.[43] Obviously, something went wrong. Most analysts conclude that team-policing experiments were poorly planned, with little attention given to important operational details.[44]

No matter what a police department decides to do—community policing, problem-oriented policing, zero-tolerance policing, or traditional-style policing—a number of basic issues must be faced.

• **Mission.** What is the primary mission of the department? Law enforcement, order maintenance, service, crime prevention, or some combination of all four? How is that mission expressed? How do citizens know what it is? How do officers know what it is? Does the department have a written mission statement? If so, what does it say?

• **Patrol Operations.** What is the place of basic preventive patrol operations in the mission of the department? Is it the central aspect of departmental activities? Or is it only one part of a multitasked mission? If it is central, how efficiently is it currently being operated? What improvements need to be made? These issues are covered in Chapter 4.

• **Calls for Service.** Does the department respond to each and every call for service? Does the department attempt to manage the call for service workload through differential response? These issues are also covered in Chapter 4.

• **Discretion.** What policies does the department maintain to control police officer discretion? What is the current policy on use of deadly force? Is there a written policy on handling domestic violence incidents? Is there a written policy on dealing with mentally ill citizens? These issues are covered in Chapter 8.

• **Police–Community Relations.** How are the department's relations with racial and ethnic minority communities? Is there a high level of tension and conflict? What kinds of programs does the department maintain to improve police–community relations? These issues are covered in Chapter 9.

• **Corruption.** Does the department have a reputation for corruption? If it does, what evidence is there to support this reputation? Does the department have a specific anti-corruption program? These issues are covered in Chapter 10.

• **Accountability.** What accountability mechanisms exist in local law enforcement agencies? Is there a citizen review board? Does the police chief have civil service protection, or can he or she be fired at will? What kind of data are published in the annual report? Does this report provide information that allows you to make a meaningful judgment about the performance of the department? See Chapter 11 for a discussion of these issues.

• **Personnel.** What are the minimum recruitment standards for a law enforcement agency? What is the educational level for the department as a whole? How long is the preservice training program? Does the curriculum contain a section on ethics? Is there a field training component? Is the training program consistent with the stated mission of the department? What is the racial, ethnic, and gender composition of the different departments? Does the composition of particular departments match the composition of the local population? Personnel issues are covered in Chapters 12 and 13.

• **Organization.** What is the organizational structure of the department? Is it consistent with recommended standards? If there is a community-policing program, is it departmentwide or carried out by a special unit? Does a recognized police union represent the rank-and-file officers? How powerful is the union? What influence does it have over department policy? These issues are covered in Chapter 14.

SUMMARY

Why do we have police? Jerome Skolnick's question, with which we opened this chapter, cannot be avoided. As this chapter has indicated, we cannot be satisfied with simplistic answers like "protect and serve." The police role is extremely complex. First, we must decide which tasks we want the police to emphasize: law enforcement? crime prevention? order maintenance? Second, we need to decide how we want the police to carry out those tasks. Third, we need to decide what kind of officers we want for these tasks, including what selection criteria we want to use, what kind of training they will receive, and how they will be supervised. We need to decide how we are going to hold the police accountable for the tasks we ask them to carry out.

All of these questions are extremely complex. This book is designed to provide a basic introduction to the police in America so that we can discuss policing in an informed manner.

CASE STUDY: REALITY-BASED POLICE TELEVISION: DOES "REALITY TELEVISION" DISTORT REALITY?

Beginning in 1989 with the television debut of *Cops,* reality-based police shows have been in the forefront of "reality" television, paving the way for other live action, uncensored documentary programs. These in-depth programs look into law enforcement—with their use of real-time video footage, featuring real cops and criminal suspects—and appeal to many viewers, as indicated by their consistently high ratings. Some proponents of these programs contend that they help the public to understand police work and the criminal justice system. However, some critics believe that reality-based police shows are more interested in high ratings than pursuing a journalistic truth and that they present violent, one-dimensional depictions of law enforcement.

The National Television Violence Study found that for three straight television seasons (1994–1998), every reality-based police show contained visual violence. Today, these programs continue to show live footage or dramatic reenactments of violent events, which leave many researchers concerned about the effects this content has on viewers. In addition, the number of reality specials that combine unusually violent video clips under sensationalistic program topics has risen, and they often feature fatal police car chases and police shoot-outs that highlight the dangerous, and often tragic, elements of police work. Murder, aggravated assault, and robbery are also depicted on police programs at a much higher rate than they actually occur in real life.

Reality-based police programs have been criticized for distorting the truth by offering a one-sided view of events to television audiences, usually from the police officer's standpoint. Although police programs feature real stories and use live footage, critics argue that the editing process produces overly positive portrayals of law enforcement officers and their work. For example, studies show that reality police programs overrepresent the percentage of crimes that are cleared or solved by law enforcement personnel. More than 60 percent of crime stories featured on shows are solved, but success rates for police departments are typically much lower. Police work is also portrayed as continually exciting; rarely does television depict the job's day-to-day tedium, such as paperwork and other office duties. Audiences are only afforded a look into dramatic moments captured during active duty while in the squad car, receiving radio calls, or at a suspect's home ready to execute a search/arrest warrant.

Some people are skeptical about the portrayals of officers featured on reality police programs, claiming that they are acutely aware of being filmed and may conduct themselves accordingly. Their meticulously professional and solicitous behavior can be perceived as an act, rather than a true representation. Furthermore, reality-based police shows depend on police departments' voluntary participation, so the programs have an interest in maintaining favorable relationships with the police. Casting officers in a negative light would jeopardize that rapport.

Others criticize police shows for how they portray certain ethnic groups. Studies have found that programs tend to underrepresent African Americans and overrepresent whites as police officers. Minority groups are also portrayed as committing a greater share of crime on television than they do in real life, while white people are rarely portrayed as criminal suspects. Such ethnic representations may contribute to and perpetuate racial stereotyping.

Source: Adapted from *Reality-Based Police Programs.* 2000. Issue Briefs. Studio City, CA: Mediascope Press; or it can be viewed at **http://www.mediascope.org/pubs/ibriefs/rbpp.htm.**

FOR DISCUSSION

1 Divide into groups and discuss the various functions/roles that the police play in communities. Which functions should the police continue to perform and which functions should be eliminated? How much time should the police devote to each function?

2 Discuss the question raised by Jerome Skolnick: "Why do we have police?"

3 Discuss how the police are part of the system of social control.

4 Discuss how the myths of policing impact the public's expectations of police work.
5 What factors influence the police role?

INTERNET EXERCISES

Exercise 1 Many police departments have placed their mission statements on the Web. Locate the websites for several departments. Which ones have mission statements? How do they compare?

Exercise 2 Check out the websites **www.officer.com** and **www.leolink.com.** They offer a number of resources to the public and police officers on issues relating to policing, including information on your local police department, police associations, and employment opportunities. Examine the sites closely; they will provide you with a number of Web links that you will need to use over the course of the semester.

REFERENCES

1 Jerome H. Skolnick, *Justice without Trial: Law Enforcement in a Democratic Society*, 3rd ed. (New York: Macmillan, 1994), p. 1.

2 George L. Kelling and Mark H. Moore, *The Evolving Strategy of Policing*, "Perspectives on Policing," No. 4 (Washington, DC: Government Printing Office, 1988); Samuel Walker, *A Critical History of Police Reform* (Lexington, MA: Lexington Books, 1977).

3 David H. Bayley, *Police for the Future* (New York: Oxford University Press, 1994), Ch. 1.

4 Egon Bittner, *The Functions of the Police in Modern Society* (Cambridge, MA: Olgeschlager, Gunn, and Hain, 1980).

5 Steven M. Chermak, *Victims in the News: Crime and the American News Media* (Boulder, CO: Westview Press, 1995), p. 47.

6 Peter Manning, *Police Work* (Cambridge, MA: MIT Press, 1977).

7 Herman Goldstein, *Policing a Free Society* (Cambridge, MA: Ballinger, 1977), pp. 29–31.

8 J. Milton Yinger, *Toward a Field Theory of Behavior* (New York: McGraw-Hill, 1965), pp. 99–100.

9 Goldstein, *Policing a Free Society*, p. 21.

10 Eric J. Scott, *Calls for Service: Citizen Demand and Initial Police Response* (Washington, DC: Government Printing Office, 1981).

11 American Bar Association, *Standards Relating to the Urban Police Function*, 2nd ed. (Boston: Little, Brown, 1980), pp. 1–31 to 1–32.

12 Goldstein, *Policing a Free Society*, p. 1.

13 The classic discussion is Skolnick, *Justice without Trial*.

14 Herman Goldstein, "Improving Policing: A Problem-Oriented Approach," *Crime and Delinquency*, 25 (1979): 236–258.

15 William A. Westley, *Violence and the Police* (Cambridge, MA: MIT Press, 1970), pp. 18–19.

16 Egon Bittner, "The Capacity to Use Force as the Core of the Police Role," in Bittner, *The Functions of the Police in Modern Society*, pp. 36–47.

17 Bittner, p. 40.

18 Stephen D. Mastrofski, Jeffrey B. Snipes, and Anne E. Supina, "Compliance on Demand: The Public's Response to Specific Police Requests," *Journal of Research in Crime and Delinquency*, 33 (August 1996): 269–305.

19 Morris Janowitz, "Sociological Theory and Social Control," *American Journal of Sociology*, 81 (July 1975): 82–85.

20 Wesley G. Skogan and George E. Antunes, "Information, Apprehension, and Deterrence: Exploring the Limits of Police Productivity," *Journal of Criminal Justice*, 7 (Fall 1979): 217–241.

21 Samuel Walker, *Popular Justice: A History of American Criminal Justice*, 2nd ed. (New York: Oxford University Press, 1998), Ch. 1.

22 Wayne LaFave, *Arrest* (Boston: Little, Brown, 1965).

23 Goldstein, *Policing a Free Society*, Ch. 4.

24 Arthur Niederhoffer, *Behind the Shield: The Police in Urban Society* (Garden City, NY: Anchor Books, 1969), p. 1.

25 Walker, *Popular Justice*.

26 Bayley, *Police for the Future*, Part II, "Possibilities," pp. 77–120.

27 Bayley, *Police for the Future*, pp. 143–161.

28 President's Commission on Law Enforcement and Administration of Justice, *The Challenge of Crime in a Free Society* (Washington, DC: Government Printing Office, 1967), pp. 108–109.

29 Wilbert E. Moore, *The Professions: Roles and Rules* (New York: Russell Sage Foundation, 1970).

30 James N. Tien and Richard C. Larson, "Police Service Aides: Paraprofessionals for Police," *Journal of Criminal Justice,* 6 (Summer 1978): 117–131.

31 Herman Goldstein, "Improving Policing: A Problem-Oriented Approach," *Crime and Delinquency*, 25 (April 1979): 236–258; Herman Goldstein, *Problem-Oriented Policing* (New York: McGraw-Hill, 1990).

32 John E. Eck and William Spelman, *Problem-Solving: Problem-Oriented Policing in Newport News* (Washington, DC: Police Executive Research Forum, 1987).

33 Tara O'Connor Shelly and Anne C. Grant, *Problem-Oriented Policing: Crime-Specific Problems, Critical Issues, and Making POP Work* (Washington DC: Police Executive Research Forum, 1999).

34 http://www.policeforum.org/popcall2001.html

35 Jack R. Greene and Stephen D. Mastrofski, eds., *Community Policing: Rhetoric or Reality* (New York: Praeger, 1991).

36 Dennis P. Rosenbaum, ed., *The Challenge of Community Policing: Testing the Promises* (Thousand Oaks, CA: Sage Publications, 1994).

37 Wesley G. Skogen and Susan M. Hartnett, *Community Policing: Chicago Style* (New York: Oxford University Press, 1997).

38 Lorraine Green, "Cleaning Up Drug Hot Spots in Oakland, California: The Displacement and Diffusion Effects," *Justice Quarterly*, 12 (December 1995): 737–754.

39 George L. Kelling and Catherine Coles, *Fixing Broken Windows* (New York: Free Press, 1996).

40 Bernard Harcourt, "Reflecting on the Subject: A Critique of the Social Influence Conception of Deterrence, the Broken Windows Theory, and Order Maintenance Policing New York Style," *Michigan Law Review*, 97 (1998): 291–389.

41 Bayley, *Police for the Future*, pp. 124–130.

42 John F. Heaply, *Police Practices: The General Administrative Survey* (Washington, DC: The Police Foundation, 1978).

43 Samuel Walker, "Does Anyone Remember Team Policing?" *American Journal of Police*, XXII, no. 1 (1993): 33–55.

44 Lawrence W. Sherman et al., *Team Policing: Seven Case Studies* (Washington, DC: The Police Foundation, 1973).

CHAPTER TWO

The History of the American Police

CHAPTER OUTLINE

INTRODUCTION

The police today are the product of their history. Many basic police practices and procedures are rooted in the past. At the same time, a number of important problems have long histories. Finally, many important changes have occurred in policing. A knowledge of police history helps to put contemporary policing in context. It helps us to understand why the police are organized and operate the way they do, what has changed and what has not changed over the years, and what reforms have succeeded in improving policing. This chapter examines the history of the American police, from its roots in England and colonial America down to present-day issues related to community policing and racial and ethnic tensions. (See Figure 2-1.)

KEY TERMS AND CONCEPTS

THE RELEVANCE OF HISTORY

The history of the American police can help us understand policing today. The idea that the police do not change is a myth. In fact, American policing has changed tremendously, even in the last few years. David Bayley argues that "the last decade of the twentieth century may be the most creative period in policing since the modern police officer was put onto the streets of London in 1829."[1]

The study of history helps us understand how and why these changes occur. It can illuminate the social and political forces affecting the police, as well as the impact of different reforms.

• The police–community relations problem has a long history, and it is useful to understand why it continues despite major efforts to eliminate it.

• Police corruption has a long history, and it is useful to understand its origins and why it has been so difficult to eliminate.

• The patrol car revolutionized police work, and it is important to understand both its positive contributions and its unintended consequences.

• Controls over police use of deadly force have significantly reduced the number of citizens shot and killed by the police. It is useful to analyze how and why this reform has succeeded.

• An understanding of police history can help explain the origins and impact of community policing.

THE ENGLISH HERITAGE

American policing is a product of its English heritage. The English colonists brought a criminal justice system as part of their cultural baggage. This heritage included the English common law, the high value placed

SIDEBAR 2-1   THE RELEVANCE OF HISTORY

The study of police history can:

1 Dramatize the fact of change.
2 Put current problems into perspective.
3 Help us understand what reforms have worked.
4 Alert us to the unintended consequences of reforms.

on individual rights, the court system, various forms of punishment, along with different law enforcement agencies.[2]

The English heritage contributed three enduring features to American policing. The first is a tradition of limited police authority. The Anglo-American legal tradition places a high premium on protecting individual liberty, and to that end places limits on governmental authority.[3] In the United States, these limits are embodied in the Bill of Rights. Continental European countries, by contrast, give their law enforcement agencies much broader powers. German citizens, for example, are required to carry identity cards and report changes of address to police authorities.

The second feature inherited from England is a tradition of local control of law enforcement agencies.[4] Countries in Europe, Asia, Africa, and South America, by contrast, have centralized, national police forces.

Local control contributes to the third feature, a highly decentralized and fragmented system of law enforcement. The United States is unique in having about 18,000 separate law enforcement agencies, subject only to minimal coordination and very little national control or regulation.[5]

Formal law enforcement agencies emerged in England in the thirteenth century, and over the years evolved in an unsystematic fashion. Responsibility for law enforcement and keeping the peace was shared by the constable, the sheriff, and the justice of the peace. Private citizens, however, retained much of the responsibility for law enforcement, pursuing offenders on their own and initiating criminal cases. This approach was brought to America and persisted into the nineteenth century.[6]

Creation of the Modern Police: London, 1829

More than any other single person, Robert Peel deserves credit as the "father" of modern policing. A member of England's elite social and political class, he fought for over 30 years to improve the basic structure of law enforcement in the country. By the early nineteenth century the old system of law enforcement in England began to collapse. London had grown into a large industrial city, with problems of poverty, disorder, ethnic conflict, and crime. The 1780 Gordon riots, a clash between Irish immigrants and English citizens, triggered a 50-year debate over the need for better public safety. Peel took up the issue and after many years of political effort finally persuaded the English Parliament to create the London Metropolitan Police in 1829. The new police reflected

FIGURE 2-1   THREE ERAS OF AMERICAN POLICING

I. The political era: 1830s–1900
II. The professional era: 1900–1960s
III. The era of conflicting pressures: 1960s–present

his vision of an efficient, proactive police force, and officers soon became known as "Bobbies" in honor of Sir Robert Peel.[7]

The London police introduced three new elements that became the basis for modern policing: mission, strategy, and organizational structure.

The mission of the new police was crime prevention. This reflected the utilitarian idea that it was better to prevent crime than to respond after the fact. Crime prevention, or deterrence, was to be achieved through a strategy of preventive patrol. Officers would maintain a visible presence throughout the community by continuously patrolling fixed "beats." Peel borrowed the organizational structure of the London police from the military, including uniforms, rank designations, and the authoritarian system of command and discipline. This quasi-military style prevails in American police administration to this day.

In a comparative study of the development of policing around the world, David Bayley argues that the essential features of the modern police are that they are "public, specialized, and professional."[8] They are public in the sense that government agencies have primary responsibility for maintaining public safety. They are specialized in the sense that they have a distinct mission of law enforcement and crime prevention. Finally, they are professional in the sense that they are full-time, paid employees.

The continual presence of the police throughout the community was part of a general growth of government regulation in all aspects of social and economic life. Allan Silver argues that this presence reflected a "demand for order" in the emerging urban industrial society.[9] Bayley cautions that these characteristics did not appear all at once. Although 1829 is traditionally cited as the date the London police were created, in reality it represented a consolidation of features that had been developing for centuries.[10]

LAW ENFORCEMENT IN COLONIAL AMERICA

The first English colonists in America created law enforcement institutions as soon as they established organized communities. Although borrowed from England, the sheriff, the constable, and the watch evolved in the new environment and eventually acquired distinctive American features.[11]

The sheriff, appointed by the colonial governor, was the chief local government official. In addition to criminal law enforcement, the sheriff's responsibilities included collecting taxes, conducting elections, maintaining bridges and roads, and other duties.[12] The constable also had some responsibility for enforcing the law and maintaining order. Initially an elective position, the constable gradually evolved into a semiprofessional appointed office. In Boston and several other cities, the office of constable became a desirable and often lucrative position.[13]

The watch resembled the modern-day police in some respects. Watchmen patrolled the city to guard against fires, crime, and disorder. At first there was only a night watch.

Gradually, however, as towns grew larger, they created a day watch. Boston created a watch in 1634. Following the English tradition, all adult males were expected to serve as watchmen. Many men tried to avoid this duty, either by outright evasion or by paying others to serve in their place. Eventually, the watch evolved into a paid professional position.[14]

The slave patrol was a distinctly American form of law enforcement. In southern states where slavery existed, it was intended to guard against slave revolts and capture runaway slaves. In some respects, the slave patrols were the first modern police forces in this country. The Charleston, South Carolina, slave patrol had about 100 officers in 1837 and was far larger than any northern city police force.[15]

The Quality of Colonial Law Enforcement

Colonial law enforcement was inefficient, corrupt, and subject to political interference. There was never a "golden age" of efficiency and integrity in American policing.

With respect to crime control, the sheriff, the constable, and the watch had little capacity to either prevent crime or apprehend offenders.[16] The sheriff and constable were reactive agencies, responding to complaints brought to them, and did not engage in preventive patrol. Moreover, they did not have enough personnel to investigate many crimes. Crime victims had no convenient way to report crimes. Finally, officials were paid through a system of fees that reimbursed them for particular duties. As a result, they had greater incentive to work on their civil responsibilities, which offered more certain payment, than on criminal law enforcement. Members of the watch patrolled city streets—checking taverns for drunks, for example—but were not much of a deterrent to crime. They were few in number, patrolled on foot, and had no way of communicating with one another in case of serious trouble.

With respect to order maintenance, colonial agencies were also ill-equipped to provide the kind of service that we expect today. There were simply too few watchmen on duty to be effective in the case of major problems. Disorder was a serious problem in colonial cities. Public drunkenness was a constant problem, particularly among sailors in seaport cities. Riots were common as well.[17] Citizens could not readily report disturbances, and neither the sheriff nor the constable could respond effectively.

Finally, providing both routine and emergency service to the public, as today's police do, was not a regular part of the sheriff's or the constable's job. There were not enough officers, there was no way for citizens to efficiently contact the sheriff or constable, and there was no tradition of providing such services.

In practice, ordinary citizens played a major role in maintaining social control through informal means: a comment, a warning, or a rebuke from friends or neighbors, or a "trial" by the church congregation for misbehavior. This system worked because communities were small and homogeneous; there was much face-to-face contact, and people shared the same basic values. The system eventually broke down as communities grew into larger, diverse towns and cities.[18]

If policing was ineffective in cities and towns, it was almost nonexistent on the frontier. Organized government did not appear in many areas for decades. Even then, the courts operated only once or twice a year. Settlers had to rely on their own resources and often took the law into their own hands. This tradition of vigilantism persisted into the twentieth century and represented some of the worst aspects of American criminal justice. Frequently, mobs drove out of town or even killed people whom they did not like. The lynching of African Americans was used to maintain the systems of racial segregation in the South.[19]

Corruption appeared very early. The criminal law was even more moralistic than today, with restrictions on drinking, gambling, and sexual practices. But as is the case today, people wanted to engage in these activities and tried to bribe law enforcement officials to not enforce the law.

THE FIRST MODERN AMERICAN POLICE

Modern police forces were established in the United States in the 1830s and 1840s. As in England, the old system of law enforcement broke down under the impact of urbanization, industrialization, and immigration. In the 1830s, a wave of riots struck American cities. Boston had major riots in 1834, 1835, and 1837.[20] Philadelphia, New York, Cincinnati, Detroit, and other cities all had major disturbances. In 1838, Abraham Lincoln, then a member of the Illinois state legislature, warned of the "increasing disregard for law which pervades the country."[21]

Many riots were clashes between different ethnic groups: Irish or German immigrants against native-born English Protestants. Other riots were economic in nature. During economic crises, for example, angry depositors often stormed and destroyed banks. Moral issues also produced violence. People objecting to medical research on cadavers attacked hospitals; residents of Detroit staged several "whorehouse riots," attempting to close down houses of prostitution. Finally, pro-slavery whites attacked abolitionists and free black citizens in northern cities.[22]

Despite the breakdown in law and order, Americans moved very slowly in creating new police forces. New York City did not create a new police force until 1845, 11 years after the first outbreak of riots. Philadelphia followed a more erratic course. Between 1833 and 1854, it created and abolished several different forms of law enforcement before finally creating a consolidated, citywide police force on the London model.[23]

These delays reflected deep public uncertainty about how to maintain public safety. The idea of a continual police presence throughout the community was something radically new. For many Americans, it brought back memories of the hated British colonial army. Others were afraid that their political opponents would control the police and use them to their advantage. Finally, many people were not prepared to pay the cost of a public police force.

Many of the early American police departments were little more than expanded versions of the existing watch system. The Boston police department had only nine officers in 1838.[24] The first American police officers did not wear uniforms, but were identified only by a distinctive hat and badge. They also did not carry firearms. Weapons did not become standard police equipment until the late nineteenth century, in response to rising levels of crime and violence.

Americans borrowed most of the London model of modern policing: the mission of crime prevention, the strategy of visible patrol over fixed beats, and the quasi-military organizational structure. The structure of political control of the police, however, was very different. The United States was a far more democratic country than Britain.

American voters—only white males with property until the latter part of the nineteenth century—exercised direct control over all government agencies. London residents, by contrast, had no direct control over their police. As a result, American police departments were immediately immersed in local politics, a situation that led to many serious problems. The commissioners of the London police, freed from political influence, were able to maintain high personnel standards.[25]

AMERICAN POLICING IN THE NINETEENTH CENTURY, 1834–1900

In the United States, however, politics influenced every aspect of American policing in the nineteenth century. Inefficiency, corruption, and lack of professionalism were the chief results.[26]

Personnel Standards

Police departments in the nineteenth century had no personnel standards as we understand them today. Officers were selected entirely on the basis of their political connections. Men who had no education, bad health, and criminal records were hired as officers. There were a few female matrons but no female sworn officers until the early twentieth century. In New York City, a $300 payment to the Tammany Hall political machine was the only requirement for appointment to the force.[27]

Only a few departments offered recruits any formal preservice training. New officers were generally handed a badge, a baton, and a copy of the department rules (if one existed), and were sent out on patrol duty. Cincinnati created a police academy in 1888, but it lasted only a few years. New York City established a School of Pistol Practice in 1895, but offered no training in any other aspect of policing until 1909. Even then, a 1913 investigation found it gave no tests and all recruits were automatically passed.[28]

Police officers had no job security and could be fired at will. In some instances, almost the entire police force was dismissed after an election. Nonetheless, it was an attractive job because salaries were generally higher than those for most blue collar jobs. In 1880 officers in most big cities earned $900 a year, compared with $450 for factory workers.

Jobs on the police force were a major form of patronage, which local politicians used to reward their friends. Consequently, the composition of departments reflected the ethnic and religious makeup of the cities. When Irish Americans began to win political power, they appointed their friends as police officers. When Barney McGinniskin became the first Irish American police officer in Boston in 1851, it provoked major protests from the English and Protestant establishment in the city. Many German Americans served as police officers in Cleveland, Cincinnati, Milwaukee, and St. Louis, where German immigration was heavy. After the Civil War, some African Americans were appointed police officers in northern cities where the Republicans were in power.[29]

Patrol Work

Routine police patrol was hopelessly inefficient. Officers patrolled on foot and were spread very thin. In Chicago, beats were three and four miles long. In many cities entire areas were not patrolled at all. The lack of communications systems made it impossible to respond to crime and disorder.

Supervision was weak or nonexistent. Officers easily evaded duty and spent much of their time in saloons and barber shops. Rain, snow, and extremely hot weather were powerful incentives for officers to avoid patrolling. Sergeants also patrolled on foot and found it nearly impossible to keep track of the officers under their command.

The first primitive communications systems involved a network of call boxes that allowed patrol officers to call precinct stations. Officers learned to sabotage them: They left receivers off the hook, which took the early systems out of operation, or lied about where they were.[30] The lack of an effective communications system made it difficult if not impossible for citizens to contact the police. In the event of a crime or disturbance, someone had to personally locate an officer, who would then have to walk to the scene.

The Police and the Public

Many people today have a romanticized image of the nineteenth-century police officer. The myth is that officers were friendly, knowledgeable about the neighborhood, and helpful. If their methods were often rough, they did maintain order. This image is highly inaccurate. It is unlikely that police officers had close relations with many people on their beats. They were few in number, personnel turnover was high, and people moved more often than today. Official records, moreover, indicate that many police officers had serious drinking problems and frequently used excessive physical force. There is considerable evidence that police officers enjoyed little citizen respect and often faced open hostility from the public. Juvenile gangs, for example, made a sport of throwing rocks at the police or taunting them. People who were arrested often fought back.[31]

SIDEBAR 2–2   THE DIARY OF A POLICE OFFICER: BOSTON, 1895

We know very little about what police officers actually did in the early years. Most of the evidence comes from reformers or journalists seeking to expose corruption and inefficiency. Their reports are inherently biased. The recently discovered 1895 diary of Boston police officer Stillman S. Wakeman provides a revealing glimpse into actual police work 100 years ago.

Officer Wakeman was "an officer of the neighborhood." He spent most of his time on patrol responding to little problems that neighborhood residents brought to him: disputes, minor property crimes, and so on. He spent relatively little time on major offenses: murder, rape, robbery. He resolved most of the problems informally, acting as a neighborhood magistrate.

Officer Wakeman's role was remarkably similar to that of contemporary patrol officers. He was reactive and a problem solver. The major difference was the absence of modern police technology: the patrol car and the 911 telephone system.

Source: Alexander von Hoffman, "An Officer of the Neighborhood: A Boston Patrolman on the Beat in 1895," *Journal of Social History,* 26 (Winter 1992): 309–330.

In a provocative study of the police in London and New York City, Wilbur Miller argues that in London a high level of mutual respect emerged between citizens and police. Through their restrained and civil conduct, the police overcame initial public hostility. The commissioners of the London Metropolitan Police maintained high personnel standards and exercised strict supervision. In the United States, however, the lack of adequate supervision allowed police officers to respond to public hostility with physical force. The result was a complete lack of professionalism.[32]

Citizen violence eventually caused American police officers to begin carrying firearms. As late as 1880 the police in Brooklyn (then an independent city of 500,000 people) were unarmed. In some cities weapons were optional or carried at the discretion of a sergeant. Firearms did not become standard equipment for police officers until the late nineteenth century, in response to rising levels of crime and violence.

The police were a major social welfare institution in the nineteenth century. Precinct stations offered lodging to the homeless. The Philadelphia police lodged over 100,000 people a year during the 1880s. After 1900, care for the poor became the responsibility for professional social work agencies and the police concentrated more on crime.[33]

Corruption and Politics

George W. Plunkitt represented everything that was wrong with American policing in the nineteenth century. Plunkitt was a district leader for Tammany Hall, the social club that controlled New York City politics for several generations. He was unique in that he not only explained in writing exactly how corruption worked but offered a philosophy to justify it. Corruption, according to Plunkitt, was the essence of democracy. His Tammany Hall organization "always stood for rewardin' the men that won the victory." Jobs on the police department were one of the major rewards he and other political leaders had to offer. Running a political organization was expensive, of course, and Tammany Hall funded itself through kickbacks from people it rewarded or payoffs from gamblers and prostitutes. Why did police corruption last so long? Plunkitt explained that the people "knew just what they were doin'": They liked the rewards they received and were not offended by the illegal activity.[34]

Police corruption was epidemic in the nineteenth century. Historian Mark Haller argues that corruption was one of the main functions of local government, and the police were only one part of the problem.[35] The police took payoffs for not enforcing laws on drinking, gambling, and prostitution. The money was divided among officers at all ranks. Corruption extended to personnel decisions. Officers often had to pay bribes for promotion. The cost of obtaining a promotion was compensated for by the greater opportunities for graft. The New York City police commissioner, forced to resign in 1894, admitted that he had amassed a personal fortune of over $350,000.[36]

Corruption served important social and political ends. Alcohol was an important symbolic issue in American politics. Protestant Americans saw sobriety as a badge of respectability and self-discipline. They sought to impose their morality on immigrant groups, especially the Irish and Germans, by controlling or outlawing drinking. For immigrant and blue collar Americans, meanwhile, the neighborhood saloon was an important social institution and often the base of operations for political machines. Thus, the attack on drinking was also an attack on working-class political power. Working-class immigrants fought back by controlling the police through their political machines and effectively nullified laws intended to control drinking.[37]

The Failure of Police Reform

Political reformers made police corruption a major issue during the nineteenth century. Their efforts were generally unsuccessful. The reformers concentrated on changing the formal structure of control of police departments, usually by creating a board of police commissioners appointed by the governor or the legislature. This struggle for control reflected divisions along the lines of political parties, ethnic groups, and urban and rural perspectives. New York created the first state-controlled police commission in 1857.[38] In many cities, the battle for control of the police was endless. Cincinnati underwent ten major changes in the form of police control between 1859 and 1910.[39]

Even when the reformers won, however, they did not succeed in improving the quality of policing. Their reform agenda emphasized replacing "bad" people (their political opponents) with "good" people (their own supporters). They did not have any substantive ideas about police administration and made no significant changes in recruitment standards, training, or supervision. By today's standards, what is most notable about the reform agenda of the nineteenth century is what it did *not* include. There was no attention given to police use of excessive force or race discrimination—two issues that are of paramount concern today.

Theodore Roosevelt, who served as President of the United States from 1901 to 1908, is one of the most famous people in American history. Yet few are aware that earlier in his career he served as a police commissioner of New York City between 1895 and 1897. As commissioner he fought against everything that Tammany Hall's George Plunkitt represented. He was outraged by both the systematic police corruption and the inefficiency of the NYPD. His career also dramatizes the failure of the reformers in the nineteenth century. Roosevelt waged a vigorous and at times flamboyant effort to raise recruitment standards, discipline officers guilty of misconduct, and ensure enforcement of laws prohibiting the sale of liquor on Sundays. He went out on the streets at night, catching officers who were not at their posts or sleeping on the job. While Roosevelt made headlines (which, of course, advanced his political career), he made no lasting changes in the NYPD. Corruption and inefficiency continued long after he resigned in 1897.[40]

The Impact of the Police on Society

Did the police reduce crime and disorder? Did a young man in the slums of Cincinnati or Baltimore refrain from committing a burglary or robbery because he was afraid of being caught? Did the presence of patrol officers on the street help to maintain order? Probably not. Historians debate the impact of the police on society. Some argue that the police did help to maintain order. Cities became more orderly as the nineteenth century progressed, but it is not clear that the police were primarily responsible for this. Other historians argue that the police were so few in number that they could not possibly have deterred crime. Orderliness may have been the result of a more general adaptation to urban life. The daily routine of urban life—reporting to work every day at the same hour—cultivated habits of self-discipline and order. The police, according to this view, played a supporting role at best.[41]

The role of the police in labor relations during the nineteenth century is also a matter of debate among historians. Sid Harring and other Marxist historians argue that the police served the interests of business and were used to harass labor unions and break strikes.[42] American labor relations during these years were extremely violent. Management adamantly resisted unions, and many strikes led to violence. In some communities, particularly those with coal and steel industries, strikes were virtual civil war. In many cities, however, the police were friendly to organized labor, mainly because they came from the same blue collar communities.[43]

The modern police were created to deal with the problems of crime and disorder, but they succeeded primarily in becoming a social and political problem themselves. The rampant corruption and inefficiency set in motion generations of reform efforts that continue today.

THE TWENTIETH CENTURY: THE ORIGINS OF POLICE PROFESSIONALISM, 1900–1930

American policing underwent a dramatic change in the twentieth century. There were two principal forces for change: an organized movement for police professionalism and the introduction of modern communications technology.

The Professionalization Movement

If Robert Peel was the father of the modern police, August Vollmer was the father of American police professionalism. Vollmer served as chief of police in Berkeley, California, from 1905 to 1932 and, more than any other person, defined an agenda of police reform that continues to influence policing even today. He is most famous for advocating higher education for police officers. He hired college graduates in Berkeley and organized the first college-level police science courses at the University of California in 1916. In that respect, he is also the father of modern criminal justice education. Vollmer also served as a consultant to many local police departments and national commissions. In 1923 he took a year's leave from Berkeley to serve as chief of the Los Angeles police department. When the year was up, he returned home very pessimistic about the chances of reforming the corrupt and inefficient LAPD. Vollmer also wrote the 1931 Wickersham Commission *Report on Police*, which summarized the reform agenda of modern management for police departments and higher recruitment standards for officers. He trained a number of students who went on to become reform police chiefs in California and other states.[44]

Vollmer was one of a new generation of leaders at the turn of the century who launched an organized effort to professionalize the police. Police reform was part of a much broader political movement known as progressivism between 1900 and 1917. Progressive reformers sought to regulate big business, eliminate child labor, improve social welfare services, reform local government, as well as professionalize the police.[45]

The Reform Agenda

The professionalization movement developed an agenda that dominated police reform through the 1960s (see Figure 2-2).[46] First, the reformers sought to define policing as a profession. This meant that the police should be public servants with a professional obligation to serve the entire community on a nonpartisan basis. Second, they sought to eliminate the influence of politics on policing. Third, they argued in favor of hiring qualified chief executives to head police departments. The reformers believed that the police needed chief executives who had proven abilities to manage a large organization. Arthur Woods, a prominent lawyer, served as police commissioner in New York City from 1914 to 1917, while Philadelphia hired Marine Corps General Smedley Butler to head its police department from 1911 to 1915.[47]

Fourth, the reformers tried to raise personnel standards for rank-and-file officers. This included establishing minimum recruitment requirements of intelligence, health, and moral character. New York City created the first permanent police training academy in 1895, although it was initially restricted to firearms training. In most cities the process of reform was painfully slow. Some cities did not offer any meaningful training until the 1950s.

Fifth, professionalism meant applying modern management principles to police departments. This involved centralizing command and control and making efficient use of personnel. Until then, police chiefs had exercised little real control; captains in neighborhood precincts and politicians had the real power. Reformers closed precinct stations and used the new communications technology to control both middle management personnel and officers on the street.

Finally, reformers created the first specialized units such as traffic, juvenile, and vice. Previously, police departments had only patrol and detective units. Specialization, meanwhile, increased the size and complexity of the police bureaucracy, complicating the problem of managing departments.

Juvenile units led to a historic innovation: the first female sworn officers. Until then, policing had been an all-male occupation. The Portland (Oregon) police hired the first policewoman, Lola Baldwin, as a juvenile specialist in 1905.

Alice Stebbins Wells soon emerged as the real leader of the policewomen's movement. She joined the Los Angeles police department in 1910, and eventually became active at the national level. She organized the International Association of Policewomen in 1915 and gave many talks around the country about the role of policewomen. By 1919

**FIGURE 2-2   THE REFORM AGENDA OF THE
PROFESSIONALIZATION MOVEMENT**

1 Define policing as a profession.
2 Eliminate political influence from policing.
3 Appoint qualified chief executives.
4 Raise personnel standards.
5 Introduce principles of scientific management.
6 Develop specialized units.

over sixty police departments employed female officers. Wells shared the dominant values of her time, however, particularly related to the role of women. While the idea of women as police officers seemed very radical in those years, Wells's agenda appears very conservative and limited by today's standards. The first policewomen did not perform regular patrol duty, usually did not wear uniforms, and did not carry weapons. Most had only limited arrest powers. Policewomen advocates argued that women were specially qualified to work with children, and that they should not handle regular police duties.[48]

The Impact of Professionalization

Police reform progressed very slowly. By 1920 Milwaukee, Cincinnati, and Berkeley had emerged as leaders in the field. Most other departments, however, remained mired in corruption and inefficiency. August Vollmer spent the year 1924 attempting to reform the Los Angeles police, but gave up in despair and returned to Berkeley. Chicago seemed to resist all efforts at reform. In some cities, the police made notable steps forward, only to slide backward a few years later. Philadelphia made considerable strides under a reform mayor and police commissioner between 1911 and 1915, only to have all progress wiped out when the city's political machine regained control.[49] Despite these failures, the reformers could claim one great success: They firmly established the idea of professionalism as the goal for modern policing and had defined a specific agenda for reform.

The reformers increased the military ethos of police departments, adding parades, close-order drills, and military-style commendations. Until that time, American police departments had in fact been extremely unmilitary-like: undisciplined and inefficient.[50]

The New Police Subculture

Professionalization also introduced a number of new problems in policing. The rank-and-file police officer remained a forgotten person. Most reformers did not respect ordinary officers and placed all of their hopes on strong administrators. As a result, the rank and file retreated into an isolated and alienated police subculture that opposed most reforms.[51]

The most dramatic expression of this development was the emergence of police unions. As policing became a profession and officers thought in terms of the job as a career, they demanded better salaries and a voice in decisions affecting their jobs. The problem reached crisis proportions during World War I, as increases in the cost of living eroded the value of police salaries. This set the stage for the 1919 Boston police strike, one of the most famous events in police history. Salaries for Boston police officers had not been raised in nearly 20 years. When their demand for a 20 percent raise was rejected, they voted to form a union. Police Commissioner Edwin U. Curtis then suspended the union leaders, and 1,117 officers went out on strike, leaving only 427 on duty. Violence and disorder erupted throughout the city. Governor Calvin Coolidge called out the state militia and won national fame for his comment, "There is no right to strike against the public safety by anybody, anywhere, at any time." The strike quickly collapsed and all the strikers were fired.[52]

Because of the violence in Boston, a national backlash against police unions set in, and other police unions across the country disappeared. Police unionism was dead for the next 20 years, but the problem of an alienated rank and file remained.

Professionalism also created new problems in police administration. As departments grew in size and created new specialized units, they became increasingly complex bureaucracies, which required increasingly sophisticated management. Managing police organizations continued to be a major challenge into the 1990s.

Police and Racial Minorities

Conflict between the police and the African American community also appeared during the World War I years. Major race riots erupted in East St. Louis, Illinois (1917), and in Chicago and other cities in 1919. Investigations of these riots found race discrimination by the police prior to and during the riots. In some cases, officers joined in the rioting themselves. The Chicago riot commission recommended several steps to improve police–community relations, but virtually nothing was done to either hire more African American officers or eliminate race discrimination in police work.[53]

Some police departments in northern and western cities hired a few African American officers, but almost all were assigned to the black community. Southern police departments were rigidly segregated. Many hired no African American officers at all. Others hired some in a second-class category: assigned to the black community and not allowed to arrest whites.[54] Conflict between the police and the African American community remained a serious problem in all parts of the country. It did not receive any serious attention until the riots of the 1960s.

New Law Enforcement Agencies

Two important new law enforcement agencies appeared in the years before World War I: the state police and the Federal Bureau of Investigation.

Several states created state-level law enforcement agencies in the nineteenth century, but they remained relatively unimportant. The Texas Rangers were established in 1835. The Pennsylvania State Constabulary, created in 1905, was the first modern state police force, but was not typical of most others. It was a highly centralized, militaristic agency that concentrated on controlling strikes. Business leaders felt that local police and the militia were unreliable during strikes. Organized labor bitterly attacked the constabulary, denouncing its officers as "cossacks."[55]

Other states soon created their own agencies. About half were highway patrols, limited to traffic control, and the other half were general law enforcement agencies. While business interests sought the creation of Pennsylvania-style agencies, in several states organized labor was able to limit their powers or block their creation altogether.[56]

The Bureau of Investigation was established in 1908 by executive order of President Theodore Roosevelt. (Its name was changed to the Federal Bureau of Investigation in 1935.) Until then, the federal government had no full-time criminal investigation agency. Private detective agencies were sometimes used under contract on an as-needed basis. The new Bureau of Investigation was immediately involved in scandal. Some agents were caught opening the mail of one senator who had opposed creation of the agency. In 1919 and 1920 the bureau conducted a massive roundup of suspected radicals, accompanied by gross violations of due process. More scandals followed in the 1920s.[57]

THE NEW COMMUNICATIONS TECHNOLOGY

Some of the most important changes in policing were the result of modern communications technology. The patrol car, the two-way radio, and the telephone transformed patrol work, the nature of police–citizen contacts, and police management (see Figure 2-3).[58]

The patrol car first appeared just before World War I, and by the 1920s, it was in widespread use. In certain respects, the police had to keep up with citizens and criminals who were now driving cars. Police chiefs also believed that the patrol car would make possible efficient patrol coverage that would effectively deter crime and allow the police to respond quickly to crimes and other problems. American police departments steadily converted from foot to motor patrol, and by the 1960s, only a few major cities still relied primarily on foot patrol.

The patrol car had important unintended consequences that created new problems. By removing the officer from the street, it reduced informal contact with law-abiding citizens. Racial minorities increasingly saw the police as an occupying army. This problem remained hidden until the police–community relations crisis of the 1960s.

The two-way radio became widespread in the late 1930s and had two important consequences. First, it completed the communications network and allowed departments to dispatch officers in response to citizen calls. Second, it revolutionized police supervision by allowing the department to maintain continuous contact with patrol officers.

The telephone was invented in 1877, but it did not have a great impact on policing until it was linked with the patrol car and the two-way radio in the mid-twentieth century. Together, the three pieces of technology completed a communications link between citizens and the police. The telephone allowed citizens to contact the police easily and to request service; the two-way radio enabled the police department to dispatch a patrol officer to the scene; the patrol car, in turn, allowed the patrol officer to reach the scene quickly.

FIGURE 2–3 THE TECHNOLOGICAL REVOLUTION IN POLICING

New Technology	Impact
Telephone	Facilitates citizen calls for service
Two-way radio	Quick dispatch of police to calls Constant supervision of patrol officers
Patrol car	Quick response to citizen calls Efficient patrol coverage Isolation of patrol officers

Police departments encouraged people to call, promising an immediate response. Gradually, citizens became socialized into the habit of "calling the cops" to handle even the smallest problems.[59] As a result, citizens developed higher expectations about the quality of life, and the call workload steadily increased. When the rising number of calls overloaded the police, they responded by adding more officers, more patrol cars, and more sophisticated communications systems. More resources, however, only encouraged more calls, and the process repeated itself.

Telephone-generated calls for service altered the nature of police–citizen contacts. Previously, police officers rarely entered private dwellings. Patrolling on foot, they had no way of learning about problems in private areas. Nor did citizens have any way of summoning the police. The new communications technology made it possible for citizens to invite the police into their homes. The result was a complex and contradictory change in police–citizen contacts. While the patrol car isolated the police from people on the streets, the telephone brought police officers into people's living rooms, kitchens, and bedrooms. There, officers became involved in the most intimate domestic problems: husband–wife disputes, alcohol abuse, parent–child conflicts, and other issues.[60]

NEW DIRECTIONS IN POLICE ADMINISTRATION, 1930–1960

The Wickersham Commission Report

In 1929 President Herbert Hoover created the Wickersham Commission, officially the National Commission on Law Observance and Enforcement, to conduct the first national study of the American criminal justice system. The commission published fourteen reports in 1931, but the most important was the *Report on Lawlessness in Law Enforcement*.[61] The report shocked the country with its conclusion that "the third degree—the inflicting of pain, physical or mental, to extract confessions or statements—is extensively practiced." The report found that police routinely beat suspects, threatened them with worse punishment, and held them illegally for protracted questioning. It cited examples of a suspect who was held by the ankles from a third-story window, and another who was forced to stand in the morgue with his hand on the body of a murder victim. The chief of police in Buffalo, New York, openly declared that he would violate the Constitution if he felt he had to.[62]

Professionalization Continues

Under the influence of August Vollmer, California police departments took the lead in professionalization from the 1920s through the 1960s. Vollmer's protégés became police chiefs throughout the state, spreading the reform agenda of professionalization. The first undergraduate law enforcement program was established at San Jose State College in 1931. California also developed a system of regional training for police officers in the late 1930s.[63]

O. W. Wilson was August Vollmer's most famous protégé, and he was the most prominent leader of the professionalization movement from the late 1930s through the end of the 1960s. Wilson served as chief of police in Wichita, Kansas, from 1928 to 1935; as dean of the University of California School of Criminology from 1950 to 1960; and as superintendent of the Chicago police from 1960 to 1967.[64] His greatest influence came through his two textbooks on police management: the International City Management Association's *Municipal Police Administration* and his own *Police Administration* (1950). The latter book became the informal "bible" of police administration and, with new coauthors, is still in print today.[65]

Wilson's major contribution to police management involved the efficient management of personnel, particularly patrol officers. In 1941 he developed a formula for assigning patrol officers on the basis of a workload formula that reflected reported crime and calls for service. This formula, refined and updated through modern management information systems, is still used by police departments today. Wilson's emphasis on efficiency was the major influence in the basic shift of American policing from foot patrol to automobile patrol.

J. Edgar Hoover and the War on Crime

The most important new figure in American law enforcement in the 1930s was the director of the Bureau of Investigation, J. Edgar Hoover. He was appointed director of the bureau in 1924 after a series of scandals. Capitalizing on public fears about a national crime wave in the 1930s, he increased the size and scope of the bureau's activities. In 1930 he won control of the new Uniform Crime Reports (UCR) system. In 1934 a set of new federal laws gave the FBI increased jurisdiction, including authority to arrest criminals who crossed state lines in order to avoid prosecution. The following year the FBI opened its National Police Academy, which trained bureau agents and, by invitation, some local police officers.[66]

Hoover was a master at public relations, skillfully manipulating the media to project an image of the FBI agent as the paragon of professionalism: dedicated, honest, trained, and relentlessly efficient.[67] Some of Hoover's reputation was deserved. FBI agents were far better educated and trained than local police officers. But there was an ugly underside to Hoover's long career (1924–1972) as leader of the bureau. He exaggerated the FBI's role in several famous cases such as that of Pretty Boy Floyd and manipulated crime data to create an exaggerated impression of the bureau's effectiveness. He concentrated on small-time bank robbers, while ignoring organized crime, white collar crime, and violations of federal civil rights laws. Even worse, Hoover systematically violated the constitutional rights of citizens, spying on political groups and compiling secret files on elected officials. His misuse of power did not become known until after his death in 1972.[68]

Hoover's leadership of the FBI had a significant impact on local police. His emphasis on education and training established a model for personnel standards. The introduction of the UCR, the development of the Ten Most Wanted list, and the creation of the FBI crime lab all served to emphasize crime fighting at the expense of other aspects of policing.

THE POLICE CRISIS OF THE 1960S

The Cops and the Supreme Court

Ernesto Miranda was just an ordinary career criminal. Between the ages of 14 and 18 he had been arrested six times and imprisoned four times. He also had an undesirable discharge from the army, where he served more time in detention as a result of going AWOL and a "peeping tom" offense. On the evening of March 2, 1963, Miranda raped a young woman in Phoenix, Arizona. When he was arrested 11 days later, he was on his way to becoming one of the most famous individuals in American criminal justice history. The U.S. Supreme Court decision overturning his conviction, *Miranda v. Arizona* (1966), required police officers to advise criminal suspects of their rights before being interrogated.

Miranda himself was eventually convicted for the March 1963 rape and sentenced to prison. After he was paroled, he returned to Phoenix and worked as a deliveryman. On the night of January 31, 1976, at age 34, he got into a fight while playing poker in a bar and was stabbed to death. When one of his two assailants was arrested, the police officers followed the law and read him his *Miranda* rights.[69]

In the 1960s the police were at the center of a national crisis over race, crime, and justice (see Figure 2-4). The Supreme Court, reflecting new public expectations about due process and the conduct of government agencies, issued a series of landmark decisions placing constitutional limits on police practices. The 1961 *Mapp v. Ohio* decision held that evidence gathered in an illegal search and seizure could not be used against the defendant. In the even more controversial *Miranda v. Arizona* (1966) decision, the Court held that police officers were required to advise suspects that they had a right to remain silent, that anything they said could be used against them, that they had the right to an attorney, and that, if they could not afford one, a lawyer would be appointed. The *Miranda* warning was designed to ensure the suspect's protection against self-incrimination.[70]

FIGURE 2–4   CONFLICTING PRESSURES OF THE POLICE, 1960 TO PRESENT

Intervention of the courts
High crime rates; fear of crime; political reaction
Riots/PCR crisis; PCR programs
Research and experimentation
Traditional professionalization (recruitment standards, patrol management)
Team policing
Affirmative action (race and gender)
Administrative control of discretion (deadly force, domestic violence, pursuits)
Community policing
Problem-oriented policing
Citizen oversight

Mapp, *Miranda*, and other decisions provoked an enormous political controversy. The police and their supporters claimed that the Court had "handcuffed" them in the fight against crime. Conservative politicians accused the Court of favoring the rights of criminals over the rights of victims and law-abiding citizens.[71]

The Cops and Civil Rights

Meanwhile, the civil rights movement entered a new militant phase in the 1960s, challenging race discrimination in all areas of American life. African American college students launched sit-ins to protest segregated stores in the South, and civil rights groups challenged job and housing discrimination in northern states. Civil rights groups also attacked race discrimination and physical brutality by the police.[72] The white police officer in the black ghetto became a symbol of white power and authority. Studies of deadly force found that police officers shot and killed African American citizens about eight times as often as white citizens. As a result of employment discrimination, meanwhile, African Americans were seriously underrepresented as police officers.[73]

Tensions between the police and the black community exploded in a nationwide wave of riots between 1964 and 1968. Almost all were sparked by an incident involving the police. The 1964 New York City riot began after a white off-duty officer shot and killed a black teenager. The 1965 riot in the Watts district of Los Angeles was sparked by a simple traffic stop. The Kerner Commission counted over 200 disorders in 1967 alone.[74]

Police departments responded to the crisis by establishing police–community relations (PCR) units. PCR programs included speaking to community groups and schools, "ride-along" programs that allowed citizens to view police work from the perspective of the police officer, and neighborhood storefront offices to facilitate communication with citizens. These programs, however, had little impact on day-to-day police work and, therefore, did little to improve police–community relations.[75]

Civil rights leaders demanded the hiring of more African American officers and the creation of citizen review boards to investigate citizen complaints of excessive force. Although the 1964 Civil Rights Act outlawed race discrimination in employment, minority employment made little progress until the 1980s. The demand for civilian review was also unsuccessful. The Philadelphia Police Advisory Board (PAB), created in 1958, was abolished in 1967 under pressure from the police union. The police union in New York City succeeded in abolishing a citizen-dominated Civilian Complaint Review Board (CCRB) in 1966.[76] By the end of the 1960s, even though the riots had stopped, relations between the police and minority communities remained tense.

The Police in the National Spotlight

As a result of rising public concern about crime, riots, and the police–community relations crisis, there was a new interest in research on the police. Previously, the police had been almost completely neglected by social scientists, and little was known about even basic operations such as patrol work. In addition, a series of national commissions examined the police and made recommendations for change.

In the 1950s, the American Bar Foundation (ABF) conducted the first field observations of police work and found that police officers exercised broad discretion and that most police work involved noncriminal activity.[77]

In 1965 President Lyndon Johnson appointed the President's Commission on Law Enforcement and Administration of Justice (known as the President's Crime Commission). The commission's report, *The Challenge of Crime in a Free Society* (1967), endorsed most of the traditional agenda of professionalization: higher recruitment standards, more training, and better management and supervision. The commission sponsored pioneering research, including Albert Reiss and Donald Black's observation of patrol officers at work, and made important recommendations for the control of police discretion.[78] The first two chapters of the commission's *Task Force Report: The Police* included a thoughtful analysis of the complexity of the police role and the fact that only a relatively small part of police work was devoted to criminal law enforcement.[79]

The National Advisory Commission on Civil Disorders, popularly known as the Kerner Commission, was created after the riots of 1967 to study the national crisis in race relations. Its report found "deep hostility between police and ghetto communities as a primary cause of the disorders." It recommended that routine police operations be changed "to ensure proper individual conduct and to eliminate abrasive practices," that more African American police officers be hired, and that police departments improve their procedures for handling citizen complaints.[80]

The Kerner Commission raised serious questions about the traditional assumptions of professionalization. It noted that "many of the serious disturbances took place in cities whose police are among the best led, best organized, best trained, and most professional in the country."[81] The patrol car removed the officer from the street and alienated the police from ordinary citizens, and aggressive crime-fighting tactics, such as frequent stops and frisks, were a particular source of tension.

Chief William Parker of the Los Angeles Police Department (LAPD) illustrated the commission's point. Parker was nationally recognized for turning the LAPD into what was then widely regarded as the most professional department in the country. Parker took command of a notoriously corrupt LAPD in 1950 and quickly asserted authoritarian control over it. He instituted high personnel standards, modern management principles, and an aggressive anticrime approach to policing. Like J. Edgar Hoover, Parker was a master of public relations. He developed a close working relationship with Jack Webb, whose television program "Dragnet" not only became one of the top-rated programs but projected an image of the LAPD as flawlessly professional and efficient.

Parker's style of policing came at a price, however. The aggressive law enforcement tactics aggravated conflict with minority communities, and the LAPD's famous disciplinary system overlooked officer use of excessive force. Civil rights groups protested, but Parker tolerated no criticism and accused the NAACP and the ACLU of supporting the criminal element.[82] Parker's legacy lived on in the LAPD long after he retired. The LAPD generated national controversy as a result of the 1991 beating of Rodney King and again in 1999 with the Rampart scandal. In both cases the LAPD was accused of tolerating excessive use of force, particularly against racial and ethnic minorities, and of failing to discipline its officers.

In 1973 the American Bar Association (ABA) published its *Standards Relating to the Urban Police Function*. The standards reflected a growing body of research on the police and a new understanding of the complex role that police departments play. The emerging view recognized the fact that police officers were primarily peacekeepers rather than crime fighters: They spent most of their time maintaining order rather than fighting crime. The ABA standards also emphasized the need to control the exercise of discretion by police officers.[83]

The Research Revolution

These reports were accompanied by an explosion of research on the police. Much of this research was funded by the Law Enforcement Assistance Administration (LEAA) (1968–1976), and later the National Institute of Justice (NIJ). In 1970 the Ford Foundation established the Police Foundation with a grant of $30 million. The foundation sponsored some of the most important police research, including the Kansas City Preventive Patrol Experiment. Later, the Police Executive Research Forum (PERF), a professional association of big-city police managers, emerged as the leader of innovation in policing.

The Kansas City Preventive Patrol Experiment was one of the most important pieces of police research ever conducted (1972–1973). The experiment tested the effect of different levels of patrol and found that increased patrol did not reduce crime and had no significant effect on public awareness about police presence. At the same time, reduced patrol did not lead to an increase in crime or in public fear of crime. Challenging the basic assumptions about the effect of patrol on crime, the experiment had a profound effect on thinking about the police.[84]

Research also questioned the value of rapid police response. Faster response time did not lead to more arrests. Few calls involved crimes in progress, and most crime victims did not call the police immediately.[85] The Rand Corporation study of criminal investigation, meanwhile, shattered traditional myths about the detective. Follow-up investigations are very unproductive, most crimes are solved through information obtained by the first officer on the scene, and most detective work is boring, routine paperwork.[86]

There was also much research on police officers' attitudes and behavior. William Westley identified a distinct police subculture, characterized by hostility toward the public, group solidarity, and secrecy.[87] Jerome Skolnick found that policing has a distinct working environment, dominated by danger and exercise of authority. The pressure to achieve results in the form of arrests and convictions, moreover, encouraged officers to violate legal procedures.[88] Most studies indicated that police officers' attitudes were shaped by the nature of police work, including the culture of the organization, and not by their individual background characteristics.

The rapidly accumulating body of research had a significant effect on reform efforts. Much of the important new research shattered traditional assumptions about policing (e.g., the deterrent effect of patrol, the value of quick response time). The Kerner Commission suggested that many aspects of professionalism had adverse consequences for police–community relations. According to historian Robert Fogelson, police reform was "at a standstill" by the early 1970s.[89] Reform efforts were eventually revitalized in the 1980s with the emergence of community policing and problem-oriented policing.

NEW DEVELOPMENTS IN POLICING, 1970–2000

The crisis of the 1960s stimulated a burst of police reform. Some of these efforts represented a continuation of the traditional reform agenda, while others reflected very different ideas about policing.[90]

The Changing Police Officer

The profile of the American police officer changed significantly between the 1960s and 1990. The employment of racial and ethnic minority officers increased slowly but steadily. Underrepresentation of African American officers on big-city police departments was one of the major complaints raised by civil rights groups. The Kerner Commission found that in 1967 African Americans represented 34 percent of the population of Cleveland but only 7 percent of the police officers; in Oakland, they were 31 percent of the population and 4 percent of the officers.[91] By the 1990s African American officers were a majority in Detroit, Washington, and Atlanta. In Miami, Hispanic officers constituted 47.7 percent of the police force in 1993, while African Americans made up another 17.4 percent.[92] African Americans served as police chief in New York City, Los Angeles, Atlanta, Chicago, Houston, and many other cities.

Felicia Shpritzer made history in breaking down the barriers against women in policing. She joined the New York City police department in 1942 and, following the model established by Alice Stebbins Wells and the other pioneer policewomen, served almost 20 years in the juvenile unit. In 1961, however, she and five other female officers applied for promotion to sergeant. Their applications were rejected, and in fact they were not even allowed to take the promotional exam. They sued, and in 1963 the courts declared the NYPD policy illegal and ordered the department to allow them to take the exam. The following year, 126 policewomen took the exam; Shpritzer and one other woman passed. The other woman, Gertrude Schimmel, became the first female captain in the NYPD in 1971. Shpritzer died in December 2000 at age 87.[93]

Traditional barriers to the employment of women in policing crumbled under the impact of the 1964 Civil Rights Act, which barred discrimination on the basis of sex, and the women's movement. By the mid-1990s, the percentage of female officers in most big-city departments was about 13 percent.[94] Female officers were assigned to routine patrol duty for the first time, while departments eliminated barriers to the recruitment of women. Evaluations of female officers on patrol in Washington, DC, and New York City found their performance to be as effective as that of comparable groups of male officers.[95]

Police departments began to recruit college students. Between 1968 and 1976, the federal Law Enforcement Education Program (LEEP) provided nearly $200 million in financial assistance to students in college criminal justice programs. While only 20 percent of all sworn officers had any college education in 1960, the figure had risen to 65 percent by 1988.[96]

The length of preservice training increased from an average of about 300 hours in the 1960s to over 1,000 hours in many departments by the 1990s. The more professional departments added a field training component to the traditional academy program. Police academy curricula added units on race relations, domestic violence, and ethics.

New York and California had introduced mandatory training for all police officers in 1959, and by the 1970s every state had a similar requirement. Previously, many small police and sheriffs' departments offered no preservice training whatsoever.[97]

The Control of Police Discretion

As a result of Supreme Court decisions on police practices, minority community protests about misconduct, and a rising tide of lawsuits, police departments instituted procedures to control on-the-street police behavior.[98] This mainly involved written policies covering search and seizure, interrogations, and other aspects of police work. Particularly important were the policies on the use of deadly force, handling domestic violence, and high-speed pursuits. These policies were collected in the standard operating procedure (SOP) manual, which became the basic tool of police management. They were part of a general movement to control the exercise of discretion in the criminal justice system.[99]

The control of deadly force was one of the most important reforms. Research indicated that police shot eight African Americans for every white citizen. The disparity was especially great with respect to unarmed citizens. Many of the 1960s riots were sparked by a shooting incident. Most police departments at that time either had no policy on deadly force or relied on state statutes that permitted the shooting of unarmed suspects under the fleeing-felon rule. In the early 1970s, they began to adopt a more restrictive "defense-of-life" rule. Pioneering research by James J. Fyfe found that the New York City police department's new policy (1972) reduced firearms discharges by 30 percent.[100] As other departments adopted similar policies, the number of citizens shot and killed by the police nationwide dropped by 50 percent between 1970 and 1984. At the same time, the ratio of blacks to whites shot and killed fell by 50 percent.[101]

Rising public concern about domestic violence led to a revolution in police policy in that area as well. Women's groups sued the police in New York, Oakland, and other cities for failing to arrest men who had committed domestic assault. These suits produced departmental policies prescribing mandatory arrest. Soon, other departments across the country adopted similar policies. This trend received a strong boost when a Police Foundation study found that arrest deterred future violence more effectively than either mediation or separation. Although subsequent studies failed to confirm this effect, mandatory arrest policies remained popular.[102]

The cost of lawsuits against the police led to the creation of the Commission on Accreditation in Law Enforcement (CALEA) in 1979. CALEA published its first set of standards in 1983, and by 2001 about 500 law enforcement agencies had been accredited.[103] Although accreditation was entirely voluntary, it represented an important step forward in terms of professional self-regulation.

Police Unions

Police unions, which had been denied the right to exist in 1919 and again in the 1940s, spread rapidly in the 1960s, and by the 1970s they had established themselves as a powerful force in American policing. Police officers were angry and alienated over Supreme

Court rulings, criticisms by civil rights groups, poor salaries and benefits, and arbitrary disciplinary practices by police chiefs.[104]

Unions had a dramatic impact on police administration. They won significant improvements in salaries and benefits for officers, along with grievance procedures that protected the rights of officers in disciplinary hearings. They also produced a revolution in police management. Police chiefs were no longer all-powerful and now had to negotiate with unions over many management issues. Many reformers were alarmed about the growth of police unions. Unions tended to resist innovations and were particularly hostile to attempts to improve police–community relations.

Citizen Oversight of Police

Another important development in the 1980s and 1990s was the growth of citizen oversight of the police. Citizen review of complaints was one of the major demands of civil rights groups since the 1960s. By the year 2000 there were over 100 citizen oversight procedures across the country, covering almost all of the big cities. The term *citizen oversight* most accurately described the variety of agencies that existed. Some, like the Minneapolis Civilian Review Authority, had full responsibility for investigating all citizen complaints. The San Jose Independent Police Auditor, on the other hand, audited or monitored the handling of complaints by the police department. The more effective oversight agencies engaged in a process known as policy review: examining the underlying causes of complaints and recommending changes in police department policy.[105]

The idea that citizen input into the complaints process was an important mechanism of accountability was, in fact, an international phenomenon. Citizen review procedures were universal in England, Canada, Australia, and New Zealand, and growing in other countries as well.[106]

Community Policing and Problem-Oriented Policing

The most important new development in policing in the 1980s and 1990s was the advent of community policing and the closely related concept of problem-oriented policing.

Community policing is a philosophy holding that police departments should develop partnerships with neighborhood residents, develop programs tailored for specific problems, and give rank-and-file officers more decision-making freedom with regard to how best to deal with particular problems. In the seminal article "Broken Windows," James Q. Wilson and George L. Kelling summed up the recent research on policing: that patrol had only limited deterrent effect on crime, that faster response times did not increase arrests, and that the capacity of detectives to solve crimes was limited. This research suggested two important points: that the police could not fight crime by themselves, but were very dependent upon citizens, and that the police could reduce fear by concentrating on less serious quality-of-life problems.[107]

The most ambitious community policing program was in Chicago where Chicago Alternative Policing Strategy (CAPS) was a citywide effort. The core element of CAPS was a series of regular neighborhood meetings between police and residents for the purpose of identifying neighborhood problems and developing solutions. An evaluation of CAPS found that it did result in greater citizen involvement with the police, improved cooperation between the police and other government agencies (e.g., sanitation), a decline in neighborhood problems, and improved public perceptions of the police department.[108]

The concept of problem-oriented policing holds that instead of thinking in terms of global concepts such as "crime" and "disorder," the police should address particular problems and develop creative responses to each one. Instead of crime fighters, officers should function as problem solvers, planners, and community organizers.[109] In the first POP experiment, officers in Newport News, Virginia, attacked crime in a deteriorated housing project by helping the residents organize to improve conditions in the project itself. This included pressuring both government agencies and private companies to fulfill their responsibilities regarding building conditions and sanitation.[110]

Advocates of community policing hailed it as a new era in policing. As early as 1988 Kelling argued that "a quiet revolution is reshaping American policing."[111] By the year 2000, however, it was still too early to assess the impact of community policing. The U.S. Justice Department encouraged the growth of community policing through the Office of Community Oriented Policing Services (informally known as the COPS office), which distributed the money for hiring 100,000 new officers. Many police departments received federal funds for additional officers and established community policing programs. The extent to which they fully implemented community policing was difficult to assess, however. Many programs were traditional anticrime, antidrug efforts. In some departments there was little more than rhetoric.

Serious crime fell substantially in the 1990s. In New York City and San Diego, as well as elsewhere, serious crime returned to levels not seen since the 1960s. It was not possible, however, to say with certainty that either community policing or the addition of police officers under the 1994 Violent Crime Control Act was responsible for this important development. Many social indicators began moving in a positive direction in the early 1990s. By 2000, unemployment and teenage pregnancies were at levels not seen since the early 1960s.

Whatever the impact of community policing, by the late 1990s the American police were in the midst of an extraordinary period of innovation. Police chiefs across the country were open to experimentation and evaluation. David Bayley argues that "the last decade of the twentieth century may be the most creative period in policing since the modern police officer was put onto the streets of London in 1829."[112]

Race and Ethnic Conflict Continues

Despite the many positive gains made by the police in the previous 30 years, tensions between the police and racial and ethnic minority groups reemerged as a serious problem in the late 1990s. A report by Human Rights Watch in 1998 concluded that "race continues to play a central role in police brutality in the United States."[113] The 1991 beating of Rodney King by Los Angeles police officers provided dramatic visual evidence of police use of excessive force. Massive riots broke out in Los Angeles and other cities in 1992 when four officers involved in the beating were acquitted of criminal charges (three were subsequently convicted on federal criminal charges).[114]

In New York City, a vicious assault on Abner Louima in 1997 and the fatal shooting of the unarmed Amadou Diallo inflamed the police–community relations problem. Many observers blamed the race relations crisis in New York City on its zero-tolerance policing policy that involved aggressive enforcement of laws against minor crimes such as public urination and graffiti. Serious crime in the city dropped significantly through the 1990s, and by 2000 the murder rate had returned to the level of the 1960s. Critics of the police department argued that the aggressive style of policing created a sense of harassment among racial and ethnic minorities, particularly young men.[115]

The Los Angeles Police Department, meanwhile, was hit by one of the most serious corruption and brutality scandals. In 1999 it was revealed that officers assigned to the Rampart station had brutalized and framed a number of citizens. One person, for example, was shot and left paralyzed by LAPD officers and then prosecuted on false criminal charges. Over the next 12 months, more than 100 prior criminal convictions were overturned because of misconduct by LAPD officers. Officials estimated that the city would face lawsuits in excess of $100 million brought by victims of police misconduct. An internal LAPD Board of Inquiry report on the Rampart scandal found that the department's own accountability mechanisms had broken down and allowed the scandal to occur. The report, for example, concluded that the LAPD's standard personnel evaluations were regarded as worthless by people in the department itself.[116] The Rampart scandal had racial and ethnic overtones, as virtually all of the victims were Hispanics and African Americans. Most were suspected gang members and many were immigrants. There was widespread suspicion that Rampart officers regarded these individuals as vulnerable because of these factors.

On the morning of May 8, 1992, Robert Wilkins was driving on Interstate 95 in Maryland with three members of his family. They were returning to Washington, DC, from the funeral of a family member in Chicago. They were stopped by an officer of the Maryland State Police who told them to get out of the car and then asked for permission to search the car. Wilkins, an attorney and a graduate of Harvard Law School, informed the officer that without an arrest of the driver a search would be illegal. The officer ignored this advice and made the four family members stand in the rain while they waited for the agency's drug dog to arrive. The dog eventually found no trace of drugs, and Wilkins was finally given a $105 speeding ticket. Wilkins believed not only that the traffic stop was illegal but that he was stopped only because he is African American. This traffic stop eventually led to a major lawsuit (*Wilkins v. Maryland*) that sparked national controversy over the practice of racial profiling.[117]

The most important new issue in the late 1990s was the controversy over "driving while black" (or DWB, as it was known). Civil rights leaders charged that the police stopped African American drivers solely on the basis of their race and not on the basis of any suspected criminal activity. This practice was also referred to as racial profiling. Data produced as part of an ACLU lawsuit against the Maryland State Police indicated that while African Americans represented only 17 percent of all drivers on Interstate 95 and 18 percent of all observed traffic law violators, they represented 72.9 percent of all drivers stopped by the state police. Additionally, among those drivers stopped, 81.3 percent of those subsequently searched were African American. Many observers argued that racial profiling, particularly on interstate highways, was a result of the national "war on drugs," and that police officers stereotyped both African Americans and Hispanics as drug dealers.[118]

By 2000 efforts to combat racial profiling had become a national movement. Civil rights groups focused on traffic stop data collection for the purpose of documenting the problem and providing a basis for corrective action. A bill to require all law enforcement agencies to collect traffic stop data by race was introduced in Congress. Meanwhile, by mid-2000 seven states had passed laws requiring agencies to collect data. Finally, a growing number of law enforcement agencies began collecting traffic stop data voluntarily. The San Diego (California) Police Department is believed to have been the first to take this step. Many other departments soon followed.

Experts on policing faced the task of explaining how the national controversy over racial profiling and other forms of police misconduct could exist despite the many reforms that had occurred in policing over the previous three decades. One explanation is that some police departments had taken positive steps in the direction of accountability while others allowed misconduct to persist. Walker argues that police problems are highly contextual; that is, they are concentrated in certain police departments, certain police practices, and certain officers.[119] Another explanation is that even though the police have generally made significant improvements since the 1960s, public expectations have risen even faster. As a result, police departments are held to a higher standard than in the past, and incidents of misconduct that were silently accepted in the past were now met with protest and demands for change.

SUMMARY: THE LESSONS OF THE PAST

American policing has changed dramatically throughout its history. Viewed from the perspective of 300 years, the major change was the creation of the modern police: a large, specialized bureaucratic agency devoted to crime control and order maintenance. From the perspective of 100 years, American police departments have changed from inefficient and corrupt political organizations to enterprises with a nonpartisan professional mission.

From the perspective of the last 30 years we can see vast improvements in personnel standards and systems of accountability, including the values of due process and equal protection. The research revolution has produced an impressive body of knowledge about policing. There is a new candor about police discretion and about the limits of the police's ability to control crime. And, as David Bayley argues, the police are remarkably open to innovation and experimentation.[120]

The legacy of the past continues to weigh heavily on the police, however. Problems of abuse of authority—excessive force, corruption—continue to plague many departments. Conflict between the police and racial and ethnic minority communities remains a problem in nearly every city. And despite the many community policing experiments, routine police work in most cities has not changed that much in 30 years: Officers patrol in cars and answer their 911 calls. In a comprehensive review of recent developments in policing, Stephen Mastrofski concludes that "the patrol officers of today can be expected to do their job by and large as they did a decade ago and as they will do a decade hence."[121]

History offers many lessons about the American police. It dramatizes the fact that policing is always changing. Some of these changes are the result of planned innovation, while others are the result of external social changes. At the same time, history illustrates the extent to which many aspects of policing, including some serious problems, endures.

CASE STUDY: POLICE PATROL PRACTICES

Although police administrators may take steps to attempt to eliminate misconduct by individual police officers, many departments have adopted patrol practices which, in the words of one commenter, have "replaced harassment by individual patrolmen with harassment by entire departments."

These practices, sometimes known as *"aggressive preventative patrol,"* take a number of forms, but invariably they involve a large number of police–citizen contacts initiated by police rather than in response to a call for help or service. *One such practice utilizes a roving task force,* which moves into high crime districts without prior notice and conducts intensive, often indiscriminate, street stops and searches. A number of persons who might legitimately be described as suspicious are stopped. But so also are persons who the beat patrolman would know are respected members of the community. Such tasks forces are often deliberately moved from place to place making it impossible for its members to know the people with whom they come in contact.

In some cities aggressive patrol is not limited to special task forces. The beat patrolman himself is expected to participate and to file a minimum number of stop-and-frisk or field interrogation reports for each tour of duty. This pressure to produce, or a lack of familiarity with the neighborhood and its people, may lead to widespread use of these techniques without adequate differentiation between genuinely suspicious behavior and behavior which is suspicious to a particular officer merely because it is unfamiliar.

Police administrators, pressed by public concern about crime, have instituted such patrol practices often without weighing their tension-creating effects and the resulting relationship to civil disorder.

Motorization of police is another aspect of patrol that has affected law enforcement in the ghetto. The patrolman comes to see the city through a windshield and hear about it over a police radio. To him, the area increasingly comes to consist only of lawbreakers. To the ghetto resident, the policeman comes increasingly to be only an enforcer.

Loss of contact between the police officer and the community he serves adversely affects law enforcement. If an officer has never met, does not know, and cannot understand the language and habits of the people in the area he patrols, he cannot do an effective police job. His ability to detect truly suspicious behavior is impaired. He deprives himself of important sources of information. *He fails to know those persons with an "equity" in the community*—homeowners, small businessmen, professional men, persons who are anxious to support proper law enforcement—and thus sacrifices the contributions they can make to maintaining community order.

Source: Excerpt from the Kerner Commission Report, 1968, pp. 304–305. Emphasis added.

FOR DISCUSSION

The 1968 Kerner Commission Report on urban riots identified a number of police practices that created problems with racial and ethnic minority communities. Has anything changed in the past 33 years? Specifically:

1 Do some police departments still engage in "aggressive preventative patrol"? Can you identify any departments that do? Is the New York City zero-tolerance anti-

crime program the same thing with just a different name? Find some articles on zero tolerance and examine the similarities.

2 Do some departments use roving anticrime task forces? What about the Street Crime Unit in the New York City police department? Did the policies of the SCU lead to the controversial shooting of Amadou Diallo in 1999? Find some articles on the Diallo case and discuss whether there are any similarities.

3 The Kerner Commission concluded that automobile patrol alienated officers from the community. Have any departments taken steps to overcome this problem? How? Do some departments use more foot patrol than they did in the 1960s? Is it effective in improving police–community relations? Find an evaluation of a foot patrol program. Did it make a difference in terms of citizen attitudes toward the police?

4 Are community-policing programs effective in improving police–community relations? Can you find specific examples? Find some material on community policing in San Diego. What, exactly, does it consist of? Is there persuasive evidence that it is effective in both controlling crime and maintaining good police–community relations?

INTERNET EXERCISES

Many police departments include material on the history of the department in their annual report and/or on their website.

Exercise 1 Go to **www.officer.com** and click on "Agencies." Select several police departments and check their websites for historical material.

Exercise 2 Check the San Diego Police Historical Association, through either **www.officer.com** or **www.ci.san-diego.ca/us.** Locate the information on the first African American, Hispanic, and female officers. When was the first female officer assigned to patrol duty? Check some other police department websites for similar information.

Exercise 3 Check the Miami–Dade police department website: **www.mdpd.com** or through **www.officer.com.** Trace the history of the department: How many times has it been reorganized and renamed? How have its responsibilities changed over the years? Can you find some other county law enforcement agencies that have been reorganized in a similar fashion?

REFERENCES

1 David Bayley, *Police for the Future* (New York: Oxford University Press, 1994), p. 126.
2 Samuel Walker, *Popular Justice: A History of American Criminal Justice*, 2nd ed. (New York: Oxford University Press, 1998), Ch. 1.
3 Bayley, *Police for the Future*, p. 126.
4 T. A. Critchley, *A History of Police in England and Wales*, 2nd ed. (Montclair, NJ: Patterson Smith, 1972).

5 Bureau of Justice Statistics, *Local Police Departments, 1997* (Washington, DC: Government Printing Office, 2000).

6 Allen Steinberg, *The Transformation of Criminal Justice, Philadelphia, 1800–1880* (Chapel Hill: University of North Carolina Press, 1989).

7 Critchley, *A History of Police in England and Wales*, Ch. 2.

8 David Bayley, *Patterns of Policing: A Comparative International Analysis* (New Brunswick, NJ: Rutgers University Press, 1985), p. 23.

9 Allan Silver, "The Demand for Order in Civil Society: A Review of Some Themes in the History of Urban Crime, Police, and Riot," in David J. Bordua, ed., *The Police: Six Sociological Essays* (New York: John Wiley, 1967), pp. 12–13.

10 Bayley, *Patterns of Policing*.

11 Walker, *Popular Justice*, Ch. 1.

12 Julian P. Boyd, "The Sheriff in Colonial North Carolina," *North Carolina Historical Review*, 5 (1928): 151–181.

13 Roger Lane, *Policing the City* (New York: Atheneum, 1971), Ch. 1.

14 Lane, *Policing the City*.

15 Robert F. Wintersmith, *Police and the Black Community* (Lexington, MA: Lexington Books, 1974), pp. 17–21.

16 Douglas Greenberg, *Crime and Law Enforcement in the Colony of New York, 1691–1776* (Ithaca, NY: Cornell University Press, 1976).

17 Richard Hofstadter and Michael V. Wallace, *American Violence: A Documentary History* (New York: Vintage Books, 1971).

18 Walker, *Popular Justice*, Ch. 1.

19 Richard Maxwell Brown, *Strain of Violence: Historical Studies of American Violence and Vigilantism* (New York: Oxford University Press, 1975).

20 Lane, *Policing the City*, Ch. 3.

21 Quoted in Brown, *Strain of Violence*, p. 3.

22 Hofstadter and Wallace, eds., *American Violence*.

23 James F. Richardson, *The New York Police: Colonial Times to 1900* (New York: Oxford University Press, 1970); Steinberg, *The Transformation of Criminal Justice*, pp. 119–149.

24 Lane, *Policing the City*, p. 37.

25 Wilbur R. Miller, *Cops and Bobbies: Police Authority in New York and London, 1830–1870* (Chicago: University of Chicago Press, 1977).

26 Samuel Walker, *A Critical History of Police Reform* (Lexington: Lexington Books, 1977); Robert Fogelson, *Big City Police* (Cambridge, MA: Harvard University Press, 1977).

27 Jay Stuart Berman, *Police Administration and Progressive Reform: Theodore Roosevelt as Police Commissioner of New York* (New York: Greenwood Press, 1987), p. 71.

28 Walker, *A Critical History of Police Reform*, pp. 71–72.

29 W. Marvin Dulaney, *Black Police in America* (Bloomington: Indiana University Press, 1996), Ch. 3.

30 Jonathan Rubenstein, *City Police* (New York: Ballantine Books, 1974), pp. 15–22.

31 Walker, *A Critical History of Police Reform*, pp. 14–19.

32 Miller, *Cops and Bobbies*.

33 Eric H. Monkkonen, *Police in Urban America, 1860–1920* (Cambridge, England: Cambridge University Press, 1981).

34 William L. Riordan, ed., *Plunkitt of Tammany Hall* (New York: Dutton, 1963).

35 Mark Haller, "Historical Roots of Police Behavior: Chicago, 1890–1925," *Law and Society Review*, 10 (Winter 1976): 303–324.

36 Berman, *Police Administration and Progressive Reform*, p. 51.

37 Ibid.

38 Richardson, *The New York Police*.

39 Walker, *A Critical History of Police Reform*.

40 Berman, *Police Administration and Progressive Reform*.

41 Roger Lane, *Violent Death in the City* (Cambridge, MA: Harvard University Press, 1979); Walker, *Popular Justice*, pp. 66–69.

42 Sidney L. Harring, *Policing a Class Society: The Experience of American Cities, 1865–1915* (New Brunswick, NJ: Rutgers University Press, 1983).

43 Walker, *A Critical History of Police Reform*.

44 Gene E. Carte and Elaine H. Carte, *Police Reform in the United States: The Era of August Vollmer* (Berkeley: University of California Press, 1975).

45 Ibid.

46 Walker, *A Critical History of Police Reform*.

47 Ibid., pp. 61–66.

48 Dorothy Moses Schulz, *From Social Worker to Crimefighter: Women in United States Municipal Policing* (Westport, CT: Praeger, 1995).

49 Walker, *A Critical History of Police Reform*.

50 Walker, *A Critical History of Police Reform*, pp. 63, 66–67; Berman, *Police Administration and Progressive Reform*.

51 Ibid.

52 Francis Russell, *A City in Terror—1919—The Boston Police Strike* (New York: Viking Press, 1975).

53 Chicago Commission on Race Relations, *The Negro in Chicago* (Chicago: University of Chicago Press, 1922).

54 Dulaney, *Black Police in America*.

55 Walker, *Popular Justice*, p. 140.

56 H. Kenneth Bechtel, *State Police in the United States: A Socio-Historical Analysis* (Westport, CT: Greenwood, 1995).

57 Curt Gentry, *J. Edgar Hoover: The Man and the Secrets* (New York: W. W. Norton, 1991).

58 Samuel Walker, "Broken Windows and Fractured History: The Use and Misuse of History in Recent Police Patrol Analysis," *Justice Quarterly*, I (March 1984): 77–90.

59 Malcolm K. Sparrow, Mark H. Moore, and David M. Kennedy, *Beyond 911: A New Era for Policing* (New York: Basic Books, 1990).

60 Walker, "Broken Windows and Fractured History."

61 National Commission on Law Observance and Enforcement, *Report on Lawlessness in Law Enforcement* (Washington, DC: Government Printing Office, 1931).

62 Ibid.
63 Carte and Carte, *Police Reform in the United States*.
64 William J. Bopp, *O. W.: O. W. Wilson and the Search for a Police Profession* (Port Washington, NY: Kennikat Press, 1977).
65 O. W. Wilson, *Police Administration* (New York: McGraw-Hill, 1950).
66 Gentry, *J. Edgar Hoover: The Man and the Secrets*.
67 Richard Gid Powers, *G-Men: Hoover's FBI in American Popular Culture* (Carbondale: Southern Illinois University Press, 1983).
68 Athan G. Theoharis and John Stuart Cox, *The Boss: J. Edgar Hoover and the Great American Inquisition* (Philadelphia: Temple University Press, 1988).
69 Liva Baker, *Miranda* (New York: Atheneum, 1983).
70 Richard A. Leo and George C. Thomas III, *The Miranda Debate: Law, Justice, and Policing* (Boston: Northeastern University Press, 1998).
71 Fred P. Graham, *The Self-Inflicted Wound* (New York: Macmillan, 1970); Walker, *Popular Justice*, Ch. 6.
72 Paul Chevigny, *Police Power* (New York: Vintage Books, 1969).
73 National Advisory Commission on Civil Disorders, *Report* (New York: Bantam Books, 1968), pp. 315–316, 321–322.
74 Ibid.
75 Department of Justice, *Improving Police/Community Relations* (Washington, DC: Government Printing Office, 1973).
76 Samuel Walker, *Police Accountability: The Role of Citizen Oversight* (Belmont, CA: Wadsworth, 2001), Ch. 2.
77 Samuel Walker, "Origins of the Contemporary Criminal Justice Paradigm: The American Bar Foundation Survey, 1953–1969," *Justice Quarterly*, 9 (March 1992): 47–76.
78 President's Commission on Law Enforcement and Administration of Justice, *The Challenge of Crime in a Free Society* (Washington, DC: Government Printing Office, 1967).
79 President's Commission on Law Enforcement and Administration of Justice, *Task Force Report: The Police* (Washington, DC: Government Printing Office, 1967).
80 National Advisory Commission on Civil Disorders, *Report*.
81 Ibid., p. 301.
82 Lou Cannon, *Official Negligence* (New York: Times Books, 1997), Ch. 3.
83 American Bar Association, *Standards Relating to the Urban Police Function*, 2nd ed. (Boston: Little, Brown, 1980).
84 George L. Kelling et al., *The Kansas City Preventive Patrol Experiment* (Washington, DC: The Police Foundation, 1974).
85 Department of Justice, *Response Time Analysis* (Washington, DC: Government Printing Office, 1978).
86 Peter Greenwood, *The Criminal Investigation Process* (Santa Monica, CA: Rand, 1975).
87 William A. Westley, *Violence and the Police* (Cambridge, MA: MIT Press, 1970).
88 Jerome Skolnick, *Justice without Trial: Law Enforcement in a Democratic Society*, 3rd ed. (New York: Macmillan, 1994).

89 Robert M. Fogelson, *Big City Police* (Cambridge, MA: Harvard University Press, 1977), pp. 269–295.

90 Samuel Walker, "Between Two Worlds: The President's Crime Commission and the Police, 1967–1992," in John A. Conley, ed., *The 1967 President's Crime Commission Report: Its Impact 25 Years Later* (Cincinnati, OH: Anderson Publishing, 1994), pp. 21–35.

91 National Advisory Commission on Civil Disorder, *Report*, pp. 321–322.

92 Samuel Walker and K. B. Turner, *A Decade of Modest Progress* (Omaha: University of Nebraska at Omaha, 1992); Bureau of Justice Statistics, *Law Enforcement Management and Administrative Statistics, 1997* (Washington, DC: Government Printing Office, 1999).

93 "Felicia Shpritzer Dies at 87; Broke Police Gender Barrier," *The New York Times,* December 31, 2000.

94 Susan E. Martin, *Women on the Move: The Status of Women in Policing* (Washington, DC: The Police Foundation, 1990); Walker and Turner, *A Decade of Modest Progress.*

95 Peter B. Bloch and Deborah Anderson, *Policewomen on Patrol: Final Report* (Washington, DC: The Police Foundation, 1974).

96 David L. Carter et al., *The State of Police Education* (Washington, DC: PERF, 1989).

97 International Association of Directors of Law Enforcement Standards and Training, *Sourcebook of Standards and Training Information* (Charlotte: University of North Carolina at Charlotte, 1993); Bureau of Justice Statistics, *Law Enforcement Management and Administrative Statistics, 1997.*

98 Samuel Walker, "Historical Roots of the Legal Control of Police Behavior," in David Weisburd and Craig Uchida, eds., *Police Innovation and the Rule of Law* (New York: Springer, 1991), pp. 32–55.

99 Samuel Walker, *Taming the System: The Control of Discretion in Criminal Justice, 1950–1990* (New York: Oxford University Press, 1993).

100 James J. Fyfe, "Administrative Interventions on Police Shooting Discretion: An Empirical Analysis," *Journal of Criminal Justice,* 7 (Winter 1979): 309–323.

101 William A. Geller and Michael Scott, *Deadly Force: What We Know* (Washington, DC: Police Executive Research Forum, 1992).

102 Lawrence W. Sherman, *Policing Domestic Violence* (New York: The Free Press, 1992).

103 Commission on Accreditation for Law Enforcement, *Standards for Law Enforcement Agencies,* 4th ed. (Fairfax, VA: CALEA, 1999).

104 Hervey A. Juris and Peter Feuille, *Police Unions* (Lexington, MA: Lexington Books, 1973).

105 Samuel Walker, *Police Accountability: The Role of Citizen Oversight* (Belmont, CA: Wadsworth, 2001).

106 Andrew Goldsmith, *Complaints against the Police: The Trend to External Review* (Oxford, England: Clarendon Press, 1991).

107 James Q. Wilson and George L. Kelling, "Broken Windows: The Police and Neighborhood Safety," *Atlantic Monthly,* 249 (March 1982): 29–38.

108 Wesley G. Skogan and Susan M. Hartnett, *Community Policing, Chicago Style* (New York: Oxford University Press, 1997).

109 Jack R. Greene and Stephen D. Mastrofski, eds., *Community Policing: Rhetoric or Reality* (New York: Praeger, 1991).

110 John E. Eck and William Spelman, *Problem-Solving: Problem-Oriented Policing in Newport News* (Washington, DC: PERF, 1987).

111 George L. Kelling, "Police and Communities: The Quiet Revolution," *Perspectives in Policing* (Washington, DC: Government Printing Office, 1988).

112 David H. Bayley, *Police for the Future*, p. 101.

113 Human Rights Watch, *Shielded from Justice: Police Brutality and Accountability in the United States* (New York: Human Rights Watch, 1998), p. 39.

114 Lou Cannon, *Official Negligence;* Jerome H. Skolnick and James J. Fyfe, *Above the Law* (New York: Free Press, 1993).

115 George L. Kelling and Catherine M. Coles, *Fixing Broken Windows* (New York: Free Press, 1996).

116 Los Angeles Police Department, *Board of Inquiry Report on the Rampart Incident* (Los Angeles: LAPD, 2000).

117 Details of the case are in David Harris, "'Driving While Black' and All Other Traffic Offenses: The Supreme Court and Pretextual Traffic Stops," *Journal of Criminal Law and Criminology*, 87, no. 2 (1997): 563–564.

118 ACLU, *Driving While Black* (New York: ACLU, 1999).

119 Samuel Walker, *Police Interactions with Racial and Ethnic Minorities: Assessing the Evidence and Allegations* (Washington, DC: Police Executive Research Forum, 2000).

120 Ibid.

121 Stephen D. Mastrofski, "The Prospects of Change in Police Patrol: A Decade in Review," *American Journal of Police*, IX, no. 3 (1990): 62.

CHAPTER THREE

The Contemporary Law Enforcement Industry

CHAPTER OUTLINE

INTRODUCTION

Basic Features of American Law Enforcement

Law enforcement in the United States is a large and extremely complex enterprise. There are almost 18,000 federal, state, and local agencies, along with a private security industry that employs over a million additional people.

Several basic features characterize the law enforcement industry. Most important is the tradition of local political control. The primary responsibility for police protection rests with local governments: cities and counties. This tradition was inherited from England during the colonial period (see Chapter 2).

As a result, American policing is highly fragmented.[1] There is no formal, centralized system for coordinating or regulating all the different agencies. There are some mechanisms for federal and state regulation of local police. They are discussed later in this chapter.

Fragmentation produces tremendous variety. Police services are provided by four different levels of government: city, county, state, and federal. Agencies at each level have very different roles and responsibilities. Within each category, moreover, there is tremendous variety. The six largest police departments—New York City, Chicago, Los Angeles, Houston, Philadelphia, and Detroit—are very different from the 10,580 police departments with fewer than twenty-five officers.[2]

As a result of this variety, it is very difficult to generalize about American policing. All police departments have some characteristics in common, but most generalizations about the "typical" police department are extremely risky. Writing about the county sheriff, David N. Falcone and L. Edward Wells reject the common assumption that "policing is policing" and argue that the sheriff "represents a historically different mode of policing that needs to be distinguished more clearly from municipal policing."[3]

An "Industry" Perspective

Because of its fragmentation and variety, it is useful to take an industry perspective on American law enforcement. This approach provides a comprehensive picture of all the different producers of police services in a particular area.[4]

The industry approach also provides a consumer's perspective on policing. On a typical day, the average citizen receives police services from several different agencies. Consider the

> **SIDEBAR 3-1**   BASIC SOURCES ON LAW ENFORCEMENT
> AGENCIES
>
> The most comprehensive source of data on American law enforcement agencies
> is the report from the Bureau of Justice Statistics (BJS), *Law Enforcement
> Management and Administrative Statistics.* The most recent report is for 1999.
> BJS intends to conduct new surveys every two or three years. You should look
> for a new report in 2003 or 2004.
>
> Additional data can be found in the FBI's Uniform Crime Reports (UCR), pub-
> lished annually.
>
> Many law enforcement agencies now maintain their own website, which pro-
> vides information about organizational structure and current programs.

case of Mr. and Mrs. Smith. The small local police department patrols their suburban neighborhood. Mrs. Smith works downtown where she is served by the big-city police department. Mr. Smith is a sales representative and drives through small towns and areas patrolled by the county sheriff. The office building where Mrs. Smith works hires private security guards. On her way home, Mrs. Smith drives on the interstate highway, which is patrolled by the state patrol. Meanwhile, the Federal Bureau of Investigation (FBI), the Drug Enforcement Agency (DEA), and other federal agencies are at work investigating various violations of federal law.

Figure 3–1 indicates the various components of the law enforcement industry.

An International Perspective

A quick look at law enforcement in other countries provides a useful perspective on the decentralization and fragmentation of American law enforcement.

England, with a population one-fourth that of the United States, has forty-three police departments: forty-one provincial departments and two police forces in London. This is half the number of law enforcement agencies in the state of Nebraska (total of ninety-three). All forty-three agencies are administered by the home secretary, who is one of the top officials in the national government (and in some respects the equivalent of the attorney general in the United States). Each provincial department also answers to a local police commission. The home secretary has the power to issue administrative regulations on personnel and police operations. Additionally, each of the forty-three police departments receives 51 percent of its annual budget from the home secretary's office, giving it the power to enforce regulations.[5]

The Japanese police system also balances central coordination with local control. The National Police Agency is responsible for coordinating the operations of the forty-seven prefectural police. Each prefecture is officially independent, but the National Police Agency can recommend operational standards and, as in England, provides a significant part of each local agency's budget.[6]

A DEFINITION OF TERMS

What Is a Law Enforcement Agency?

What do we mean when we talk about a police or law enforcement agency? The question is not as simple as it might seem. Many different kinds of government agencies have some responsibility for enforcing the law and/or providing protection: state game and parks departments, federal agencies such as the U.S. Supreme Court Police, some college campus police.

This book focuses only on *general service* law enforcement agencies: those that are regularly engaged in (1) preventing crime, (2) investigating crimes and apprehending criminals, (3) maintaining order, and (4) providing other miscellaneous services.

This definition excludes many government regulatory agencies whose personnel often have law enforcement powers. It excludes investigatory and prosecutorial agencies, such as state bureaus of criminal investigation, coroner's offices, and constables. It also excludes correctional agencies even though in many states their officers are legally peace officers with arrest power.

Who Is a Police Officer?

The term *police officer* is often used interchangeably with *peace officer.* There is an important distinction, however. All police officers are peace officers, but all peace officers are not police officers. The legal status of peace officers is defined by statute.

FIGURE 3–1   COMPONENTS OF THE AMERICAN LAW ENFORCEMENT INDUSTRY

Government Agencies
Local
  Municipal police
  County police
  County sheriffs
State
  State police
  Bureaus of criminal investigation
Federal
  Federal law enforcement agencies
  Military law enforcement
Special district police
  Public schools
  Transit police
  College and university police
Native American tribal police
Private Security
  Private security firms
  Security personnel

Iowa law, for example, designates eight categories of peace officer, the last coming under the catchall phrase "all other persons so designated." California law gives peace officer status to more than thirty different occupations.

Peace officer status grants certain powers and provides certain legal protections that ordinary citizens do not have. Under the English common-law standard, all citizens have the power to make a "citizen's arrest." Private citizens can also shoot to kill under certain limited circumstances. Sworn peace officers, however, have broader power in taking these actions and have somewhat greater protection from liability when they are acting "in good faith" in carrying out an official duty.

SIZE AND SCOPE OF THE LAW ENFORCEMENT INDUSTRY

The Number of Law Enforcement Agencies

There are over 18,000 law enforcement agencies in the United States. This includes 13,578 local police, 3,088 sheriff's departments, 49 state police agencies, 1,316 special police agencies, and 16 federal agencies that employ 500 or more sworn officers (Table 3–1).[7]

The Myth of 40,000 Agencies For many years there was great controversy over exactly how many law enforcement agencies exist in the United States. In 1967 the President's Crime Commission incorrectly reported that there were 40,000 agencies,

TABLE 3–1	EMPLOYMENT BY STATE AND LOCAL LAW ENFORCEMENT AGENCIES IN THE UNITED STATES, 1997*						
		Number of Employees					
		Full-Time			**Part-Time**		
Type of Agency	**Number of Agencies**	**Total**	**Sworn**	**Civilian**	**Total**	**Sworn**	**Civilian**
Total	18,760	940,275	695,378	244,897	99,191	46,884	52,307
Local police	13,540	531,496	420,152	111,345	62,373	31,079	31,294
Sheriff	3,088	263,427	174,673	88,754	20,025	10,633	9,392
State police	49	82,261	54,206	28,055	895	70	825
Special police	1,332	61,022	44,509	16,513	15,234	4,502	10,732
Texas constable	751	2,068	1,838	230	664	600	64

*Data are for the pay period that included June 30, 1997. Consolidated police–sheriff agencies are included under local police category. Detail may not add to total because of rounding.

repeating an unconfirmed figure that had been used for years.[8] The correct figure is about 18,000 state and local agencies.

The typical police department is very small. As Table 3–2 indicates, over half (52.9 percent) have nine or fewer sworn officers. The eighty-four largest departments, which represent less than 1 percent of the departments, employ about 40 percent of all full-time sworn officers.[9]

The Number of Law Enforcement Personnel

In 1996 there were 663,535 full-time sworn law enforcement officers employed by local and state law enforcement agencies (Table 3–1). In addition there were 74,500 federal law enforcement officers authorized to carry firearms and make arrests (this figure, however, does not include military law enforcement personnel).[10] The number of state and local officers has grown significantly since 1993. The 1994 Violent Crime Control Act provided federal funds to hire 100,000 new officers. By 1997 there were about 45,000 (12 percent) more sworn officers than in 1993.[11]

Understanding Law Enforcement Personnel Data

There is often much confusion about law enforcement personnel data. The important question is, "How much police protection does a community receive?" The *total number of employees* includes clerical staff and civilian specialists in computers, criminalistics, and so on. The *number of sworn officers* refers to those employees who are legally recognized as police officers, with full arrest power and the like.

TABLE 3–2 LOCAL POLICE DEPARTMENTS, BY NUMBER OF SWORN PERSONNEL, 1997				
Number of Sworn Personnel*	Agencies		Full-Time Sworn Personnel	
	Number	Percentage	Number	Percentage
Total	13,540	100%	420,152	100%
1,000 or more	41	0.3	139,961	33.3
500–999	43	0.3	30,645	7.3
250–499	90	0.7	30,998	7.4
100–249	367	2.7	53,431	12.7
50–99	752	5.6	49,750	11.8
25–49	1,666	12.3	51,395	12.2
10–24	3,416	25.2	42,026	10.0
5–9	3,364	24.8	15,675	3.7
2–4	3,001	22.2	5,647	1.3
1	799	5.9	625	0.1

*Includes both full-time and part-time employees. Detail may not add to total because of rounding.

It is also important to distinguish between an agency's authorized strength and the number of sworn officers *currently employed.* Because of retirements, resignations, and terminations, most departments are below their authorized strength. The annual average attrition rate is about 5 percent.[12] Hiring is often delayed as a way of allowing the city or county to cope with a budget shortfall.[13]

Thus, if you want to know the level of police protection in Cleveland, for example, you need to determine the number of full-time sworn officers currently employed.

Civilianization

Civilianization is the process of replacing sworn officers with nonsworn personnel for certain positions. In 1997, 28.6 percent of all local police department employees were civilians. This represents an increase from 11.1 percent in 1960 and 18.4 percent in 1980. Nonsworn personnel have been increasingly used as dispatchers, research and planning specialists, crime data analysts, and computer technicians (see Figure 3–2).[14]

There are several reasons for utilizing civilians in police work. First, they free sworn officers for critical police work that requires a trained and experienced officer. Second, they possess needed expertise in such areas as computers or data analysis. Third, in many cases they are less expensive than sworn officers, thereby representing a cost saving.[15] For these reasons, a number of experts use the proportion of civilian employees within a police agency as an indicator of departmental professionalism.[16]

The Police–Population Ratio

The standard measure for the level of police protection in a community is the *police–population ratio.* This is usually expressed as the number of sworn officers per

FIGURE 3–2
TRENDS IN CIVILIANIZATION IN POLICE DEPARTMENTS BETWEEN 1955 AND 1997

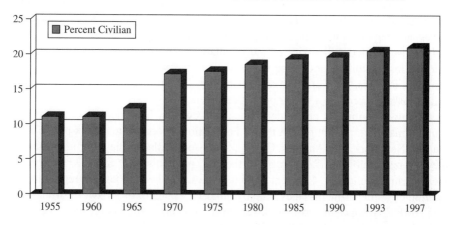

Source: William King and Edward Maguire, "Police Civilianization, 1950–2000: Change or Continuity?" presented at the American Society of Criminology, November 2000.

thousand population. In 1996 the national average for local agencies was 1.5 sworn officers per thousand. The ratio for large cities with populations of 250,000 or more was 4.0. Small cities (population 50,000 to 99,999) had the lowest ratio (2.3 per thousand).[17]

There is tremendous variation in the police–population ratios among big cities. Washington, DC, has a ratio of 6.7 per thousand residents, compared with 4.1 in Detroit and 1.7 in San Diego.[18] There is no clear relationship between the police–population ratio and the crime rate. In many respects, instead of higher levels of police protection producing lower crime rates, higher crime rates lead to the employment of more police.[19] The relationship of the police–population ratio to the crime rate is discussed in detail in Chapter 4.

The Cost of Police Protection

Law enforcement is an extremely expensive enterprise. In 1994, local government agencies spent a total of $46 billion on police services. This represented about 45 percent of all criminal justice system expenditures. These figures do not, however, include the cost of private security. The cost of police protection increased about 300 percent between 1980 and 1994. Expenditures for corrections increased almost twice as fast (500 percent) in the same period, mainly as a result of the soaring prison population.[20]

Law enforcement is a labor-intensive industry. Personnel costs, including salaries and fringe benefits, consume about 85 to 90 percent of an agency's budget. For this reason, the efficiency of a police department depends heavily on how well it manages its personnel and what percentage of officers it places in patrol and investigative units (see Chapter 4).

MUNICIPAL POLICE

Municipal or city police are the most important component of American law enforcement. In 1996 they represented 72 percent of all law enforcement agencies and employed 62 percent of all sworn officers.[21]

Even more important, municipal police play a more complex role than any other type of law enforcement agency. The external environment heavily influences all agencies.[22] Cities, and big cities in particular, represent the most complex environments, particularly in terms of the diversity of the population. City police departments have the heaviest responsibility for dealing with serious crime, which is disproportionately concentrated in cities. They are also responsible for difficult order maintenance problems and are asked to provide a wide range of emergency services.[23]

Among all municipal police departments, a few very large departments play a disproportionately important role. A Police Foundation report on the big six police departments—New York, Los Angeles, Chicago, Houston, Philadelphia, Detroit—found that they are responsible for 7.5 percent of the U.S. population but face 23 percent of all violent crime, including 34 percent of all robberies.[24] Although these six represent a tiny fraction of all departments, they employ almost 13 percent of all sworn officers. The New York City police department towers over all others, with 38,000 sworn officers in 1997. Chicago is second with 13,000 officers.[25]

The big departments dominate public thinking about the police. Events in New York or Los Angeles—the Rodney King case, for example—are reported by the national news media. Moreover, a disproportionate amount of the research on policing has been conducted in New York, Chicago, Los Angeles, Philadelphia, Boston, and Washington. Much less is known about medium-sized police departments, and almost no research has been done on small departments, even though they are more representative of policing in America.

The typical municipal police department is in a small town. Slightly more than half (52.9 percent) employ fewer than ten sworn officers.[26] Small-town and rural police operate in a very different context than big-city police. There is less serious crime than in urban areas. The majority of calls for police service involve noncriminal events and minor disturbances.[27] In one study, traffic problems accounted for 25 percent of all calls, public disturbances accounted for 19 percent, family disturbances represented 18 percent, and stray dogs another 11 percent. (The remaining 27 percent were miscellaneous calls.)[28]

County Police

A few areas are served by county police departments. They are essentially municipal police that operate on a countywide basis, but do not have any of the nonlaw enforcement roles of the county sheriff (see below). Only about 1 percent of all local departments are county police. The largest are the Nassau County Police (2,935 sworn officers) and the Suffolk County police (2,711 sworn).[29]

THE COUNTY SHERIFF

There are 3,088 sheriff's departments in the United States.[30] The county sheriff's office is unique among American law enforcement agencies, in terms of both its legal status and its role.[31]

The legal status of the sheriff is unique because in thirty-seven states it is a constitutional office, whose responsibilities are defined in the state constitution. Also, sheriffs are elected in all but two states. (In Rhode Island they are appointed by the governor; in Hawaii they are appointed by the chief justice of the state supreme court.) As elected officials, sheriffs are directly involved in partisan politics in ways that municipal police chiefs are not. Historically in rural areas the sheriff was the most powerful politician in the county.[32]

The Role of the Sheriff

Sheriffs have a unique role in that they serve all three components of the criminal justice system: law enforcement, courts, and corrections. As Table 3–3 indicates, almost all sheriff's departments perform the basic law enforcement functions of receiving calls for service, patrolling, and investigating crimes. Almost all serve the courts by process serving (subpoenas, etc.) and providing security for the courts. In many urban areas, sheriffs spend more time on civil court duties than on criminal law enforcement.

Only 84 percent of all sheriff's departments still maintain the county jail. In most big cities the jail is operated by a separate department of corrections.[33]

Lee Brown identified four different models of sheriff's departments, according to their responsibilities: (1) Full-service model sheriff's departments carry out law enforcement, judicial, and correctional duties; (2) law enforcement model agencies carry out only law enforcement duties, with other responsibilities assumed by separate agencies; (3) civil-judicial model agencies handle only court-related duties (e.g., counties in Connecticut and Rhode Island); and (4) correctional-judicial model agencies (e.g., San Francisco County) handle all responsibilities except law enforcement.[34]

The distribution of sheriff's departments resembles that of the municipal police. There are a few very large departments and many small ones. The largest is the Los Angeles County sheriff's department, which had 8,021 sworn officers in 1997. About 28 percent of all sheriff's departments, however, have fewer than ten sworn officers.[35]

OTHER LOCAL AGENCIES

The American law enforcement picture is complicated by the existence of other local agencies that have some law enforcement responsibilities.

The Constable

Like the sheriff, the constable is an office whose roots can be traced back to colonial America (see Chapter 1). Urbanization and the consequent growth of city departments have stripped the constable's office of most of its functions. The Advisory Commission on Intergovernmental Relations found it to be "of minor importance" and recommended its abolition.[36]

The Coroner

The office of the coroner, or medical examiner, is often considered a law enforcement agency because it has the responsibility to investigative crimes. A Department of Justice survey found a total of 1,683 coroners or medical examiners.[37]

TABLE 3–3 RESPONSIBILITIES OF SHERIFF'S DEPARTMENTS, 1997	
Function	**Percentage of Agencies**
Routine patrol	98%
Responding to calls for service	95
Crime investigation	91
Enforcement of traffic laws	84
Process serving	98
Court security	95
Jail operations	80
Dispatching calls for service	75
Fingerprint processing	65
Search and rescue	58

Source: Adapted from Bureau of Justice Statistics, *Sheriff's Departments, 1997* (Washington, DC: Government Printing Office, 2000), p. 14.

Special District Police

Special district police agencies serve particular government agencies. The Los Angeles School District, for example, has its own police force. Some urban transit systems maintain separate law enforcement agencies.[38] The Metropolitan Transit Police Force in the Washington, DC, subway system overlaps three different political jurisdictions: the District of Columbia, Virginia, and Maryland.[39] The New York City transit police were merged with the New York City police department several years ago, and the Los Angeles police have acquired responsibility for policing the city's buses and subways.

Campus Police

College and university campus police are an important example of special district police.[40] About three-fourths of the campus security forces at colleges and universities with 2,500 or more students are state certified law enforcement agencies. Their officers have general arrest powers, are certified by the state, and participate in the FBI's Uniform Crime Reports (UCR) system. In 1995 they employed about 11,000 full-time sworn officers. The other colleges and universities use private security or their own nonsworn security officers.[41]

NATIVE AMERICAN TRIBAL POLICE

A unique aspect of American criminal justice is that many Native American tribes maintain their own separate criminal justice systems, including tribal police departments, on their reservations. Native American tribes are separate nations, which signed treaties with the United States government and retain a significant degree of legal autonomy. In a number of important respects, tribes and reservations are not subject to federal or state law.[42]

SIDEBAR 3–2   GETTING TO KNOW YOUR CAMPUS POLICE

1 Is your campus police agency a certified law enforcement agency?
2 If so, what state-mandated training do they receive? How many hours of training? What is the content of the curriculum? Who provides the training?
3 If it is not, what are the recruitment standards? What kind of training do officers receive? Who provides the training?
4 If your campus police agency is a certified law enforcement agency, does it file the required UCR report?
5 If not, does it file an annual crime report anyway?
6 Are your campus police officers armed? What kind of training in firearms use do they receive? What kind of retraining or recertification are the officers required to receive?
7 Does your campus police agency have a written deadly force policy? What does that policy say? (See Chapter 11 on deadly force policies.)

There are over 500 Native American tribes, which include about 1.9 million enrolled members. The exact number of tribal police departments is not known. Tribal affairs have historically been the responsibility of the Bureau of Indian Affairs (BIA), which is located in the U.S. Department of the Interior. The BIA has maintained its own police force. The number of tribal police is growing, mainly as a result of the 1994 Tribal Self-Government Act. In 1995 the U.S. Department of Justice established the Office of Tribal Justice to coordinate relations between tribal governments and the various federal agencies with respect to criminal justice issues.[43]

STATE LAW ENFORCEMENT AGENCIES

State law enforcement agencies fall into three categories: state police, highway patrols, and state investigative agencies. This book will focus on the first two, since they are regarded as general service law enforcement agencies.[44]

State police are defined as agencies "having statewide police powers for both traffic regulation and criminal investigations." Highway patrols are defined as agencies having "statewide authority to enforce traffic regulations and arrest non-traffic violators under their jurisdiction."[45]

There are forty-nine general service state law enforcement agencies in the United States; Hawaii is the only state without one. These agencies are divided about equally between state police and highway patrol. Several states have more than one law enforcement agency. California, for example, maintains both the California Highway Patrol and the California Division of Law Enforcement; in Ohio there is both the Ohio Highway Patrol and the Ohio Bureau of Criminal Identification and Investigation. The roles and missions of state law enforcement agencies are defined by state law, and hence vary widely from state to state.

There is considerable variation in the administrative structure of state law enforcement agencies. One report found that "almost every possibility" exists. Several states have an umbrella agency containing a number of different departments responsible for various services. The New Jersey Department of Public Safety includes eight divisions: Division of Law, State Police, Division of Motor Vehicles, Division of Alcoholic Beverage Control, Division of Criminal Justice, Division of Consumer Affairs, Police Training Commission, and State Athletic Commissioner.

Roles and Responsibilities

State police and highway patrol provide a variety of law enforcement services. In terms of patrol, state police have concurrent or shared responsibility with local police agencies. In about half of the states, the state police or highway patrol agency has the primary responsibility for enforcing traffic laws on the main highways.[46]

State laws vary regarding responsibility for criminal investigation. In some states, the state police have general responsibility; in others, the investigative powers are limited. About half of all state agencies provide crime lab services (ballistics, drug testing) for local police departments. Finally, 77.6 percent of state police agencies operate a training academy. In some states, they are responsible for training recruits from local police departments.[47]

FEDERAL LAW ENFORCEMENT AGENCIES

The federal component of the law enforcement industry is relatively small but more complex than generally recognized. In 1996 there were an estimated 74,500 full-time federal law enforcement employees. This figure includes all personnel "authorized to carry firearms and make arrests." It does not include military police, however.[48]

There is no agreement about the exact size of federal law enforcement activities. The confusion is due to the fact that many federal agencies have enforcement or regulatory powers. Most are not general service agencies, as defined above. They do not provide the basic services of protection and criminal investigation.

Sixteen federal law enforcement agencies employ 500 or more sworn officers. The Immigration and Naturalization Services and the Federal Bureau of Prisons are the largest, each with over 11,000 officers in 1996. The Federal Bureau of Investigation (FBI) and U.S. Customs Service are the next largest with about 10,000 officers each. The Drug Enforcement Agency (DEA) employs 2,946 officers. The complexity and variety of federal law enforcement are indicated by the fact that the largest agencies include the U.S. Fish and Wildlife Service (869 officers) and the U.S. Forest Service (619 officers).[49]

Roles and Responsibilities

The role of each federal agency is specified by federal statute. In important respects, federal agencies have a far less complex role than that of municipal agencies. Federal agents do not have the ambiguous and difficult order maintenance responsibilities, do not maintain 911 emergency telephone services, and are not asked to handle vague "disturbance" calls.

The role of the FBI has historically been shaped by administrative and political factors. Under J. Edgar Hoover (1924–1972), the FBI concentrated its efforts on investigating alleged "subversives" and apprehending bank robbers and stolen cars. Critics charged that the FBI ignored white collar crime, organized crime, and violations of the civil rights of minorities. After Hoover's death it was discovered that, under his direction, the FBI had committed many violations of citizens' constitutional rights: It was guilty of spying on individuals and groups because of their political beliefs, conducting illegal wiretaps, and even burglarizing the offices of groups it was spying on.[50]

Since Hoover's death, subsequent FBI directors have reoriented the bureau's mission, putting more emphasis on white collar crime, organized crime, and political corruption. The bureau has been more responsive to the general law enforcement policies of current presidential administrations.[51]

THE PRIVATE SECURITY INDUSTRY

Private security is an important part of American law enforcement. Its exact size is difficult to determine because it involves many small, private agencies, part-time employees, and security personnel that are employed by private businesses. It is estimated that there are over 2 million people employed in private security. This figure includes the following jobs: proprietary (in-house) security, guard and patrol services, alarm services, private investigators, armored car services, the manufacturers of security equipment, locksmiths, and consultants and engineers. Brian Forst points out that Sears corporation employs about 6,000 security guards, which is significantly more personnel than almost all metropolitan police departments.[52]

The size of the private security industry raises a number of important issues. The first is the quality of private security personnel. Requirements for employment are minimal, and in many cases, training is nonexistent. One survey found that the typical guard receives between 4 and 6 hours of training.[53] Private security is often a last resort for people unable to find other jobs.

Several states have adopted minimum recruitment and training standards and guidelines for private security personnel. Most state laws, however, cover only firearms training and certification. There has been a movement toward enacting laws to require training and certification.

Second, there are problems related to cooperation between public and private police. The Philadelphia Center City District, established in 1990, represents a unique collaboration between the municipal police and private security to improve the quality of life in the downtown business district of the city.[54]

Third, there are equity problems. Wealthy neighborhoods are able to purchase additional protection while poor neighborhoods receive less protection because financially strapped city governments are unable to hire more police.

Finally, there are issues of civil liberties. Supreme Court decisions such as *Miranda* apply to public police. A Department of Justice report, however, points out that private security officers are not bound by these decisions, and that many employers do not provide their security officers with adequate training in complex legal issues.[55]

THE FRAGMENTATION ISSUE

In 1967 the President's Crime Commission concluded that "a fundamental problem confronting law enforcement today is that of fragmented crime repression efforts resulting from the large number of uncoordinated local governments and law enforcement agencies."[56]

The commission published a map of the Detroit metropolitan area indicating the eighty-five agencies in the area. As Figure 3–3 indicates, almost half of these agencies had twenty or fewer officers ("men," in the now outdated language of the times).

The major problem, according to the critics, is a lack of coordination between agencies in the same geographic area. Criminals do not respect political boundaries. In a large metropolitan area, a burglar may commit crimes in several different communities, each with its own police force. Auto-theft rings are often multistate operations. Detectives in one police department may have information that would help solve a series of crimes in a neighboring jurisdiction. In many instances, agencies compete rather than cooperate with one another.

Second, fragmentation of responsibility can also lead to crime displacement, especially with respect to vice crimes. One community may adopt a policy of strict enforcement of laws against gambling or prostitution. This often has the effect of driving vice activities to a neighboring jurisdiction, where different community standards exist.

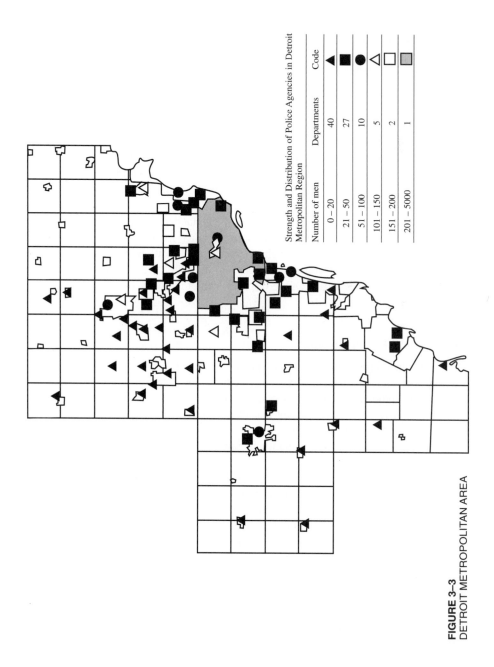

Strength and Distribution of Police Agencies in Detroit Metropolitan Region

Number of men	Departments	Code
0 – 20	40	◀
21 – 50	27	■
51 – 100	10	●
101 – 150	5	◁
151 – 200	2	□
201 – 5000	1	▨

FIGURE 3-3
DETROIT METROPOLITAN AREA

SIDEBAR 3-3   EXERCISE: STUDYING THE FRAGMENTATION PROBLEM IN YOUR AREA

1 Prepare a map and accompanying table indicating the number of law enforcement agencies in your metropolitan area, the names of these agencies, and the number of sworn officers in each.
2 Research the nature of any contract or collaborative arrangements between these agencies (e.g., shared communications systems, jail services, etc.).

Third, many experts believe there is a serious problem of duplication of services, with the resulting increase in costs. A city police department and the local sheriff's department may both operate their own 911 telephone systems and their own training academies. Several agencies in the same area may operate their own crime laboratories.

Fourth, fragmentation leads to inconsistent standards. Law enforcement agencies in the same area may have very different recruitment standards, training programs, and salary scales. In countries with a single national police force, uniform standards are established at the national level. In England, which has a tradition of local control of the police, minimum national standards are achieved through a process of inspection and financial incentives. The Home Office inspects each of the forty-five local police constabularies annually.

Alternatives to Fragmentation

The fragmentation problem is not easily solved. The independence of local governments is deeply rooted in American history. The principle of local control, not just of police but of schools and other government services, is deeply rooted in American political culture. There has always been a very strong fear of a national police force and suspicion of federal control of schools and police.

The major remedies for fragmentation include the following.

Consolidation   Some experts argue that small agencies should be consolidated into larger ones.[57] The National Advisory Commission on Criminal Justice Standards and Goals recommended the consolidation of all agencies with ten or fewer sworn officers (or more than half of the current total).[58] In a few urban areas, the city police and the sheriff's department have been merged. The Charlotte, North Carolina, and the Mecklenburg County Sheriffs' Department, for example, were merged in the early 1990s. Some cities, meanwhile, have combined police and fire departments into a single agency.[59]

Consolidation of police and sheriff's departments has made little progress, however. Both are large bureaucracies that do not want to give up their autonomy. Also, there are practical problems related to merging different entrance requirements, salary schedules, and pension systems.

Contracting   A second alternative to fragmentation is for small agencies to contract with larger agencies for specific services. About half of all cities and counties contract with other governmental units for various services. These contracts cover everything from sewage disposal to tax assessment and water supply. The most common criminal justice services include jails and detention facilities and police-fire communications systems.[60] In many cases, the county sheriff maintains the 911 service for small towns in the area. In other cases, small towns contract with the sheriff for all police services. The Los Angeles County Sheriff's Department, for example, contracts with forty separate towns. Because of consolidation, the number of police departments has been declining. Nearly a thousand disappeared in the 1970s.[61]

The Fragmentation Problem Reconsidered

Some experts believe the fragmentation problem may not be as serious as others have argued. The Police Services Study (PSS) undertook the first systematic research on the issue in the 1970s, examining the activities of 1,827 law enforcement agencies in eighty medium-sized metropolitan areas. Contrary to the traditional image of fragmentation, the study found that "informal interagency assistance is common," and "strict duplication of services is almost nonexistent in the production of direct police services."[62]

With respect to patrol, for example, informal arrangements involving coordination, sharing, or alternating responsibility were common. No areas were left completely unpatrolled; nor were areas being patrolled by two or more agencies. With respect to auxiliary services, small police departments routinely had access to crime laboratories, training academies, communications systems, and other services provided by larger agencies.

Even more important, the PSS concluded that small police departments were not necessarily less efficient than large departments. Small departments put a higher percentage of their officers on the street, performing direct police services. Larger departments did not necessarily achieve any advantages of scale.[63] Larger agencies had more complex bureaucratic structures, with the result that a smaller percentage of officers are available for direct police services. Gary Cordner found that among Maryland agencies, the complexity of the community social structure, not the size of the agency, was most important in determining the effectiveness of criminal investigation: The less complex the community, the more effective the police.[64]

Finally, the emphasis on decentralized policing under community policing suggests that small local law enforcement agencies might be preferable to large consolidated agencies.[65]

MINIMUM STANDARDS: AMERICAN STYLE

Unlike most other countries, the United States does not have a national police system. There is no federal agency responsible for supervising local agencies or ensuring minimum standards. In England each local department receives half of its budget from the national government and undergoes a regular inspection as part of the process.[66] Nonetheless, there are some minimum standards for law enforcement agencies in the

United States required by federal and state governments. The process for developing and enforcing these standards, however, is not systematic.

The Role of the Federal Government

The most important set of national standards are the decisions of the U.S. Supreme Court related to police procedures. Decisions such as *Mapp v. Ohio, Miranda v. Arizona,* and *Tennessee v. Garner* set minimum national standards based on provisions of the U.S. Constitution. Beginning in the 1960s, these and other Supreme Court decisions were a major instrument of reform, forcing departments to significantly improve personnel standards and management and supervision.[67]

Relying on the Supreme Court to define minimum standards for police has serious limitations, however. First, most aspects of policing do not raise issues of constitutional law—for example, the length of police academy training or the content of that training. Second, enforcing Supreme Court decisions is extremely difficult. A police department may systematically violate the *Miranda* requirement; it is enforced only when someone is convicted and then appeals that conviction on the basis of the *Miranda* decision.[68]

Congress has passed a number of laws that directly apply to state and local law enforcement agencies. Most important is the 1964 Civil Rights Act, which prohibits discrimination on the basis of race, color, national origins, religion, or sex. Local and state agencies are forbidden to discriminate in recruitment, promotion, or assignment of officers.[69] The law, however, does not cover many police personnel issues. It does not, for example, establish minimum standards for recruitment or training. No federal law specifies a minimum level of education for police recruits. Nor does any law require a minimum police–population ratio or set standards for patrol operations.

The U.S. Department of Justice also uses grants to encourage changes in policing. The 1994 Violent Crime Control Act provided funds for 100,000 officers. The program is administered through the Office of Community Oriented Police Services (COPS), and money is granted only if the local agency develops a plan for community policing.[70]

The Role of State Governments

State governments also set minimum standards for police in a number of areas. State supreme courts rule on issues under their state constitutions. State codes of criminal procedure also define what police must do and what they may not do.

The most important role of state governments has been to require the licensing or certification of all sworn officers. In particular, this includes mandatory preservice training. New York and California were pioneers in this area in 1959, and by the 1970s every other state had some kind of certification requirement. Prior to this time, it was not uncommon in small departments for officers to have no preservice training whatsoever.[71]

In a further development of this approach, some states have adopted procedures for delicensing or decertifying police officers. In Florida, for example, when an officer's license is revoked by the state, that person is not eligible to be employed by any other law enforcement agency in the state.[72] In most states, however, it is possible for an officer to be fired by one police department and then hired by another.

Accreditation

A final approach to establishing minimum national standards in policing is through accreditation.[73] Accreditation is a process of professional self-regulation, similar to those that exist in medicine, law, education, and other occupations. The Commission on Accreditation of Law Enforcement Agencies (CALEA) was established in 1979. The fourth edition of its *Standards for Law Enforcement* includes 439 separate standards. Some standards are mandatory, while others are only recommended.[74]

The major weakness with accreditation is that it is a voluntary process. There is no penalty for a police department not being accredited. By comparison, a nonaccredited educational institution is not eligible for certain federal funds, and graduates from nonaccredited institutions find that their credits are not accepted by other schools.[75]

The process of becoming accredited is expensive, in terms of both the formal CALEA fees and the staff time required to meet the various standards.[76] By mid-2000, CALEA had accredited 479 agencies. While the number of state and local agencies accredited is relatively small (less than 2 percent of the total), forty of the largest sixty-three state and local agencies are in CALEA, leading to about 19 percent of all full-time state and local law enforcement officers working in a CALEA certified agency.[77]

Critics question the impact of accreditation on police work. Mastrofski suggests that accreditation standards "add[s] to the proliferation of rules in already rule-suffused bureaucracies, without appreciably affecting patterns of police behavior."[78] Others, however, have found that accreditation has a positive impact on police organizations. For example, McCabe and Fajardo reported in 2001 that accredited agencies, when compared to nonaccredited agencies, are more likely to require more training, higher minimum educational requirements for new officers, and are twice as likely to require drug testing for sworn officers. Agencies that are accredited were also found to be more likely to have specialized units to respond to child abuse and to enforce drug laws.[79]

In short, American law enforcement agencies must meet *some* minimum standards. These standards cover only a limited range of issues, and there is no system for developing and implementing a comprehensive set of standards.

SUMMARY

Law enforcement is an extremely complex activity in the United States. The delivery of police services is fragmented among thousands of city, county, state, special district, federal, and private security agencies. There are tremendous differences in the size, role, and activities of these different agencies. Consequently, it is extremely difficult to generalize about the police in America.

CASE STUDY: SPECIAL DISTRICT POLICE: THE NEW YORK CITY TRANSIT POLICE

Rapid transit has played an integral part in the lives of New Yorkers for well over 100 years. The first trains ran at grade level and on elevated structures. Underground trains were added on October 27, 1904, when, after taking 4½ years to build, the Interborough Rapid Transit (IRT) line opened to the public. Since both the IRT and the competing

BMT (Brooklyn–Manhattan Transit) lines were privately financed and built, they had no police but only their own private security personnel. The new IND (Independent) lines, however, which began operating in 1932, were owned by New York City and run by the Board of Transportation. These lines originally had station supervisors employed to police them, their names having been taken from the NYC police department's hiring list.

On November 17, 1933, six men were sworn in as New York State railway police. They were unarmed but were still responsible for the safety of the passengers on the IND line, as well as guarding the system's property. Two years later, twenty-six station supervisors, class B were added for police duty. Responsible for assisting in the opening and closing of doors and announcing destinations, these twenty-six "specials" were soon given powers of arrest, but only on the IND line. And thus the New York City transit police department was born.

In 1937, 160 more men were added to this police force. Additionally, three lieutenants, one captain, and one inspector from the NYPD were assigned as supervisors. When the privately run IRT and BMT lines were taken over by New York City in 1940, the small patrol force on the IND line nearly doubled in size. Now part of the civil service system, more transit supervisors were needed. In 1942, the first promotional exam was given for the title of special patrolman, grade 2—or what is now known as a sergeant.

The Code of Criminal Procedure was changed in 1947 granting transit patrolmen peace officer status, and by 1950, the number of "specials" reached 563. The following year, exams were held for both transit sergeants and lieutenants. In 1953, the New York City Transit Authority came into being and assumed control over all the subway lines from the old Board of Transportation.

Beginning in 1949, the question as to who should supervise the transit police department was one that was carefully scrutinized over the next 5 years by various city officials. The issue being considered was, "Should transit be taken over by the NYPD?" In 1955, the decision was made that the transit police department would become a separate and distinctly different department, ending almost two decades of rule by the NYPD. The Civil Service Commission established a new test for transit recruits, and on April 4, the first appointments from the list were made. An NYPD lieutenant, Thomas O'Rourke, was also designated as the first commanding officer of the transit police department. Soon after, Lieutenant O'Rourke, along with nine others, passed the captain's exam. Captain O'Rourke was appointed as the first chief of the new department.

With crime on the rise, the number of transit officers increased, so that by 1966, the department had grown to 2,272 officers. That year, Robert H. Rapp was appointed chief by the NYC Transit Authority. Under Chief Rapp, and at the direction of the mayor, an ambitious new anticrime program got under way. The program had a goal of assigning an officer to each of New York City's subway trains between the hours of 8 P.M. and 4 A.M. The transit police department continued to grow and, by early 1975, consisted of nearly 3,600 members.

In 1975, a former NYPD chief inspector and sometime city council president, Sanford D. Garelik, was appointed chief of the transit police department. Determined to reorganize the department, Chief Garelik was also successful in instilling a new sense of pride and professionalism among the ranks. However, the fiscal crisis which began that year was an unexpected blow—especially to transit cops. Over the next 5 years, layoffs and attrition reduced their numbers to fewer than 2,800. New officers would not be hired until 1980. By the early 1990s, however, the transit police department had regained all of its former strength and had increased even further. In 1994, there were almost 4,500 uniformed and civilian members of the department, making it the sixth largest police force in the United States.

Over time, however, the separation between the NYPD and the NYC transit police department created more and more problems. Redundancy of units, difficulty in communications, and differences in procedures all created frustration and inefficiency. As part of his mayoral campaign, candidate Rudolph Giuliani pledged to end the long unresolved discussion and merge all three of New York City's police departments (the NYPD, the transit police, and the NYC Housing Authority police department) into a single, coordinated force. Mayor Giuliani took office on January 1, 1994, and immediately undertook to fulfill his promise to end a problem that had defied final solution for almost half a century. Discussions between the City of New York and the New York City Transit Authority produced a memorandum of understanding, and on April 2, 1995, the NYC transit police was consolidated with the New York City police department to become a new bureau within the NYPD. After a reorganization of the department in February 1997, the Transit Bureau became the Transit Division within the newly formed Transportation Bureau. The Transportation Bureau dissolved in the spring of 1998, and in July 1999, the Transit Division once again became the Transit Bureau. The Transit Bureau has entered the new millennium and shall continue to provide dedicated police protection to the nation's largest rapid transit system in the twenty-first century.

Source: Adapted from **http://www.ci.nyc.ny.us/html/nypd/html/transportation/tpd.html**

FOR DISCUSSION

1 Go to your campus law enforcement agency's headquarters and request a copy of last year's campus crime statistics. Ask the desk attendant how many full-time employees work for the agency. Ask how many are sworn officers and how many are nonsworn officers. As a class, discuss whether you think there are too many or too few personnel working for your campus law enforcement agency in light of the campus's reported crime problem.

2 What are some of the advantages and disadvantages of civilianization?

3 What are the strengths and weaknesses of leaving the primary responsibility for police protection to local governments versus the federal or state government?

4 The military has rarely been used for local crime control. When, if ever, would the use of the military be acceptable to address local crime problems?

INTERNET EXERCISES

Exercise 1 Go to a website of an agency in your region and find out (*a*) the total number of employees who are authorized to work for the agency, (*b*) the total number of sworn officers authorized to work for the agency, and (*c*) the total number of employees who are currently employed by the agency.

Exercise 2 Go to the website **www.calea.org**. Examine the process that a police department must go through to become accredited by CALEA.

Exercise 3 Go to the websites of both your police and sheriff's department and find out what services are duplicated by the two agencies.

REFERENCES

1 Elinor Ostrom, Roger Parks, and Gordon P. Whitaker, *Patterns of Metropolitan Policing* (Cambridge, MA: Ballinger, 1978).
2 Bureau of Justice Statistics, *Local Police Departments, 1997* (Washington, DC: Government Printing Office, 2000).
3 David N. Falcone and L. Edward Wells, "The County Sheriff as a Distinctive Policing Modality," *American Journal of Police,* XIV, no. 3/4 (1995): 123–124.
4 Ostrom, Parks, and Whitaker, *Patterns of Metropolitan Policing.*
5 Richard J. Terrill, *World Criminal Justice Systems: A Survey,* 3rd ed. (Cincinnati, OH: Anderson, 1997), pp. 12–13.
6 Ibid., pp. 246–248.
7 Bureau of Justice Statistics, *Census of State and Local Law Enforcement Agencies, 1996* (Washington, DC: Government Printing Office, 1998); Bureau of Justice Statistics, *Federal Law Enforcement Officers, 1996* (Washington, DC: Government Printing Office, 1997).
8 President's Commission on Law Enforcement and Administration of Justice, *The Challenge of Crime in a Free Society* (Washington, DC: Government Printing Office, 1967).
9 Bureau of Justice Statistics, *Local Police Departments, 1997.*
10 Bureau of Justice Statistics, *Census of State and Local Law Enforcement Agencies, 1996;* Bureau of Justice Statistics, *Federal Law Enforcement Officers, 1996.*
11 Bureau of Justice Statistics. *Local Police Departments, 1997.*
12 President's Commission on Law Enforcement and Administration of Justice, *Task Force Report: The Police* (Washington, DC: Government Printing Office, 1967), p. 9.
13 James J. Fyfe, "Police Personnel Practices, 1986," *Municipal Yearbook, 1987* (Washington, DC: ICMA, 1987), Table 3/2, p. 17.
14 Bruce L. Heininger and Janine Urbanek, "Civilianization of the American Police: 1970–1980," *Journal of Police Science and Administration,* 11 (1983): 200–205; William King and Edward Maguire, "Police Civilianization, 1950–2000: Change or Continuity?" presented at the American Society of Criminology (November 2000).
15 Alfred I. Schwartz, Alease M. Vaughn, John D. Waller, and Joseph S. Wholey, *Employing Civilians for Police Work* (Washington, DC: Urban Institute, 1975).
16 Neal A. Milner, *The Court and Local Law Enforcement* (Beverly Hills, CA: Sage, 1971), pp. 250–251.

17 Bureau of Justice Statistics. *Sourcebook of Criminal Justice Statistics—1998* (Washington, DC: Government Printing Office, 1999).

18 Bureau of Justice Statistics, *Local Police Departments, 1997.*

19 Thomas B. Marvell and Carlisle E. Moody, "Specification Problems, Police Levels, and Crime Rates," *Criminology,* 34 (November 1996): 609–646.

20 Bureau of Justice Statistics, *Sourcebook of Criminal Justice Statistics—1998.*

21 Bureau of Justice Statistics, *Census of State and Local Law Enforcement Agencies, 1996.*

22 John P. Crank and Robert Langworthy, "An Institutional Perspective on Policing," *Journal of Criminal Law and Criminology,* 83, no. 2 (1992): 341–346.

23 Herman Goldstein, *Policing a Free Society* (Cambridge, MA: Ballinger, 1977).

24 Anthony Pate and Edwin E. Hamilton, *The Big Six: Policing America's Largest Cities* (Washington, DC: The Police Foundation, 1991).

25 Bureau of Justice Statistics, *Local Police Departments, 1997.*

26 Ibid.

27 Ralph A. Weisheit, David N. Falcone, and L. Edward Wells, *Crime and Policing in Rural and Small-Town America: An Overview of the Issues* (Washington, DC: Government Printing Office, 1995).

28 John F. Galliher et al., "Small-Town Police: Troubles, Tasks, and Publics," *Journal of Police Science and Administration,* 3 (March 1975): 19–28.

29 Bureau of Justice Statistics, *Law Enforcement Management and Administrative Statistics, 1997* (Washington, DC: Government Printing Office, 1998), p. vii.

30 Bureau of Justice Statistics, *Sheriffs' Departments, 1997* (Washington, DC: Government Printing Office, 2000).

31 Falcone and Wells, "The County Sheriff as a Distinctive Policing Modality."

32 National Sheriff's Association, *County Law Enforcement: Assessment of Capabilities and Needs* (Washington, DC: National Sheriff's Association, 1976).

33 Bureau of Justice Statistics, *Law Enforcement Management and Administrative Statistics, 1997.*

34 Lee P. Brown, "The Role of the Sheriff," in Alvin W. Cohn, ed., *The Future of Policing* (Beverly Hills, CA: Sage, 1978), pp. 227–228.

35 Bureau of Justice Statistics, *Sheriffs Departments, 1997.*

36 U.S. Advisory Commission on Intergovernmental Relations, *State and Local Relations in the Criminal Justice System* (Washington, DC: Government Printing Office, 1971), p. 28.

37 Department of Justice, *Justice Agencies in the United States: Summary Report 1980* (Washington, DC: Government Printing Office, 1980).

38 Department of Justice, *Policing Urban Mass Transit Systems* (Washington, DC: Government Printing Office, 1979).

39 Martin Hannon, "The Metro Transit Police Force: America's First Tri-State, Multi-Jurisdictional Police Force," *FBI Law Enforcement Bulletin,* 47 (November 1978): 16–22.

40 John J. Sloan, "The Modern Campus Police: An Analysis of Their Evolution, Structure, and Function," *American Journal of Police,* XI, no. 2 (1992): 85–104.

41 Bureau of Justice Statistics, Campus Law Enforcement Agencies, 1995 (Washington, DC: Government Printing Office, 1996).

42 Ken Peak, "Criminal Justice, Law, and Policy in Indian Country: A Historical Perspective," *Journal of Criminal Justice,* 17, no. 5 (1989): 393–407.

43 Jacob Clark, "Complex Job in Changing Times," *Law Enforcement News* (April 15, 1996), p. 1.

44 Donald A. Torres, *Handbook of State Police, Highway Patrols, and Investigative Agencies* (New York: Greenwood Press, 1987).

45 Ibid., p. 12.

46 Department of Justice, *Profile of State and Local Law Enforcement Agencies 1987* (Washington, DC: Government Printing Office, 1989).

47 Ibid.

48 Bureau of Justice Statistics, *Federal Law Enforcement Officers, 1996.*

49 Ibid.

50 Curt Gentry, *J. Edgar Hoover: The Man and the Secrets* (New York: Norton, 1991).

51 Tony Poveda, *Lawlessness and Reform: The FBI in Transition* (Pacific Grove, CA: Brooks/Cole, 1990).

52 Brian Forst, "The Privatization and Civilianization of Policing," in Charles Friel, ed., *Criminal Justice 2000,* 2 (2000): 19–79.

53 These 1976 data are cited in Ibid., p. 3.

54 Jack R. Greene, Thomas M. Seamon, and Paul R. Levy, "Merging Public and Private Security for Collective Benefit: Philadelphia's Center City District," *American Journal of Police,* XIV, no. 2 (1995): 3–20.

55 Marcia Chaiken and Jan Chaiken, *Public Policing—Privately Provided* (Washington, DC: Government Printing Office, 1987).

56 President's Commission on Law Enforcement and Administration of Justice, *Task Force Report: The Police* (Washington, DC: Government Printing Office, 1967), p. 68.

57 Terry W. Koepsell and Charles M Girard, *Small Police Agency Consolidation: Suggested Approaches* (Washington, DC: Government Printing Office, 1979).

58 National Advisory Commission on Criminal Justice Standards and Goals, *Police* (Washington, DC: Government Printing Office, 1973), pp. 73–76.

59 International City Management Association, *Public Safety Departments: Combining the Police and Fire Functions* (Washington, DC: ICMA, July 1976).

60 International City Management Association, "Intergovernmental Service Arrangements and the Transfer of Functions," *Baseline Data Report,* 16 (June 1984).

61 Department of Justice, *Justice Agencies in the United States: Summary Report 1980.*

62 Ostrom, Parks, and Whitaker, *Patterns of Metropolitan Policing.*

63 Ibid., pp. xxi, 101.

64 Gary W. Cordner, "Police Agency Size and Investigative Effectiveness," *Journal of Criminal Justice,* 17, no. 1 (1989): 153.

65 Weisheit, Falcone, and Wells, *Crime and Policing in Rural and Small-Town America,* pp. 69–73.

66 Terrill, *World Criminal Justice Systems,* pp. 9–25.

67 Samuel Walker, "Historical Roots of the Legal Control of Police Behavior," in David Weisburd and Craig Uchida, eds., *Police Innovation and Control of the Police* (New York: Springer, 1993), pp. 32–55.

68 Anthony Amsterdam, "Perspectives on the Fourth Amendment," *Minnesota Law Review,* 58 (1974): 428.

69 Susan E. Martin, *On the Move: The Status of Women in Policing* (Washington, DC: The Police Foundation, 1990), pp. 11–24.

70 Department of Justice, *COPS Office Report* (Washington, DC: Government Printing Office, 1997).

71 International Association of Directors of Law Enforcement Standards and Training, *Sourcebook of Standards and Training Information* (Charlotte: University of North Carolina at Charlotte, 1993).

72 Roger Goldman and Stephen Puro, "Decertification of Police: An Alternative to Traditional Remedies for Police Misconduct," *Hastings Constitutional Law Quarterly,* 15 (Fall 1987): 45–80.

73 Jack Pearson, "National Accreditation: A Valuable Management Tool," in James J. Fyfe, ed., *Police Management Today: Issues and Case Studies* (Washington, DC: ICMA, 1985), pp. 45–48.

74 www.calea.org. Commission on Accreditation for Law Enforcement Agencies, *Standards for Law Enforcement Agencies,* 4th ed. (Fairfax, VA: CALEA, 1999).

75 Stephen D. Mastrofski, "Police Agency Accreditation: The Prospects of Reform," *American Journal of Police,* VI, no. 2 (1986): 45–81.

76 W. E. Eastman, "National Accreditation: A Costly, Unneeded Make-Work Scheme," in Fyfe, ed., *Police Management Today,* pp. 49–54.

77 http://www.calea.org; CALEA Update (1999, No. 71): 1–3; CALEA Update (1999, No. 70): 1–4.

78 Stephen D. Mastrofski, "The Prospects of Change in Police Patrol: A Decade in Review," *American Journal of Police,* IX, no. 2 (1990): 25.

79 Kimberly McCabe and Robin Fajardo, "Law Enforcement Accreditation: A National Comparison of Accredited vs. Nonaccredited Agencies," *Journal of Criminal Justice,* 29, 2001: 127–131.

TWO

POLICE WORK

CHAPTER FOUR

Patrol: The Backbone of Policing

CHAPTER OUTLINE

INTRODUCTION

Patrol is the backbone of policing, the central aspect of police operations. This chapter examines the nature of patrol work in contemporary American policing: how patrol is organized and delivered, the nature of citizen calls for service, the effectiveness of patrol in deterring crime, and programs designed to improve patrol services.

THE CENTRAL ROLE OF PATROL

Patrol is the center of police activity for several reasons. First, the majority of police officers are assigned to patrol and in that capacity deliver the bulk of police services to the

KEY TERMS AND CONCEPTS

public. According to the 1997 LEMAS report, municipal police departments assign an average of 63 percent of all officers to patrol duty.[1] The marked patrol car and the uniformed patrol officer are the visible symbols of the police in the eyes of the public.

Second, patrol officers are also the most important decision makers in policing and the gatekeepers of the entire criminal justice system. James Q. Wilson points out that police departments are unique in that discretion increases as one moves down the organizational hierarchy.[2] In deciding whether or not to make an arrest, or how to handle a domestic disturbance, patrol officers are the real policymakers in policing. As government officials who make important decisions affecting people's lives, and who work on the street, the police have been characterized as "street-level bureaucrats."[3]

Third, experience on patrol is a formative part of a police officer's career. In virtually all American police departments, assignments are based on seniority. New officers start out on patrol duty, usually on the evening shift and in the highest crime neighborhoods. This street experience becomes an important part of the police officer subculture, forging a bond of common experience among officers.

Despite its central role in policing, patrol duty has generally been considered the least desirable assignment, and career advancement usually means promotion or assignment to something more desirable, especially detective work. The National Advisory Commission on Criminal Justice Standards and Goals comments that "the patrolman is usually the lowest-paid, least-consulted, most taken-for-granted member of the force. His duty is looked on as routine and boring."[4] One element of community policing has been to enlarge the role of patrol officers to give them more decision-making authority as problem solvers able to respond to specific neighborhood problems (see Chapter 7).[5]

THE FUNCTIONS OF PATROL

Robert Peel, creator of the modern police, was very clear about the purpose of police patrol. In his first instructions to the new London Metropolitan Police in 1829 he wrote, "It should be understood at the outset, that the object to be obtained is the prevention of crime."[6] Since Peel's time, visible patrol over fixed beats has been the core of the police mission. Patrol has three distinct functions: (1) to deter crime, (2) to enhance feelings of public safety, and (3) to make officers available for service.

O. W. Wilson, for decades the leading expert on police management, explained that patrol is designed to deter crime by creating "an impression of omnipresence" that will eliminate "the actual opportunity (or the belief that the opportunity exists) for successful misconduct."[7] The effectiveness of traditional patrol in deterring crime is examined in detail below.

The second function of patrol is to maintain feelings of public safety. The visible presence of patrol officers is designed to assure law-abiding citizens that they are being protected against crime. Most people believe that patrol deters crime. When asked to suggest improvements in policing, most citizens call for more police and/or more patrol in their neighborhood.[8]

The third function of patrol is to be available for service. This is accomplished by dispersing patrol officers throughout the community. Albert Reiss observes that "no other professional operates in a comparable setting."[9] The clients of other professions— doctors, lawyers, and dentists—must go to the professionals' offices. The police may be the last profession to make house calls.

THE ORGANIZATION AND DELIVERY OF PATROL

Visit different police departments and you will find that patrol is carried out in very different ways. New York City uses a lot of foot patrol: 39 percent of all patrol units, according to the 1997 LEMAS data. The San Jose police department, meanwhile, uses no foot patrol units. In Florida, one-third of all patrol units in St. Petersburg involve officers on motorcycles, compared with only 5 percent in Miami.[10]

The manner in which patrol services are delivered to the public is affected by a number of different community and organizational factors. Except in the very small departments, patrol is housed in a separate unit of the police organization, often referred to as the uniform field bureau. In many departments this also includes the traffic enforcement unit. Municipal police departments assign about 63 percent of all sworn officers to patrol duty.[11]

The number or percentage of all officers assigned to patrol does not tell us whether a police department is carrying out patrol functions efficiently or effectively. The following factors need to be considered when evaluating how good a job a police department is doing.

Number of Sworn Officers

Some cities have a lot of police officers, while others have relatively few. In Washington, DC, the nation's capital, there are 6.7 sworn officers for every 1,000 people. In San Jose, California, however, there are only 1.6 per 1,000. The traditional measure of the level of

TABLE 4-1	POLICE-POPULATION RATIOS, SELECTED CITIES, 1999
City	Sworn Officers per 1,000 Residents
Washington, DC	6.3
New York City	5.3
Baltimore	4.4
Detroit	4.0
Boston	4.0
Denver	2.9
Dallas	2.7
San Diego	1.7
San Jose	1.6
Miami-Dade	1.4

Source: Bureau of Justice Statistics, *Law Enforcement Management and Administrative Statistics, 1999* (Washington, DC: Government Printing Office, 2001), Table 1a.

police protection in a community is the police–population ratio. The national average is 2.3 officers per 1,000 population; for large cities the figure is somewhat higher.[12] Table 4–1 indicates the enormous variations in the police–population ratios of different cities.

One of the most important questions to be considered is whether a higher police–population ratio means that a city receives better police protection. Although widely used as a measure of the amount of police service, the police–population ratio has little relationship to the crime rate or even to calls for service. Cities with more police per population do not necessarily have lower crime rates. More often, the reverse is true: Cities with high crime rates often have more police officers, as high crime rates produce public demand for more police.[13] Washington, DC, with the highest police–population ratio, does not have a correspondingly low crime rate.

Allocation and Distribution of Officers to Patrol

Officers assigned to patrol need to be allocated and distributed in a rational way, based on the department's workload. The standard workload formula, based on citizen calls for service and reported crimes, was first developed by O. W. Wilson in 1941.[14]

First, patrol officers need to be allocated to different shifts according to the workload. Most serious crimes occur at night, as do the majority of disturbances (family disputes, bar fights, and so on). Figure 4–1 indicates the distribution of 911 calls for service and the assignment of officers by shift in Omaha, Nebraska.[15] The data indicate that the assignment of officers is reasonably related to the workload. All police departments do not operate in a rational manner, however. A 1987 investigation of the Philadelphia police found that "the same number of officers are on the street at all times—during the early morning, when there is practically no activity, and on weekend evenings, when the calls for service are heaviest."[16]

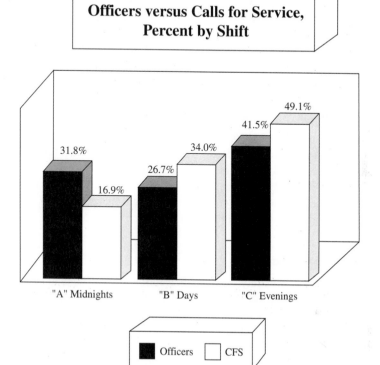

FIGURE 4–1
DISTRIBUTION OF 911 CALLS, OMAHA, NEBRASKA

Some departments utilize a fourth patrol shift, beginning in the late afternoon and ending in the early morning (e.g., 6 P.M. to 2 A.M.).[17] This approach provides additional officers on the evening shift, when the number of calls is highest, and avoids over-staffing in the early morning hours, when the number of calls is at its lowest.

In his study of deadly force by New York City police officers, James J. Fyfe found that the police department gave precincts different experience ratings. The A precincts were classified as high experience assignments because they were high crime areas. B precincts were medium experience assignments, and C precincts were low experience. Fyfe described C precincts as "residential 'country clubs' that place comparatively few demands on their police."[18]

The New York City example illustrates the point that the patrol workload varies by location. Crime and disorder are not evenly distributed throughout the community. Crime is more prevalent in poorer neighborhoods, and low-income people are the heaviest users of police services for order maintenance and community assistance. National Crime Victimization Survey reports that the household burglary rate for the poorest households (income of $7,500 or less) was 78.7 per 1,000, compared with 40 per 1,000 for households with incomes over $50,000.[19] Low-income people are also the heaviest users of police services for noncrime events: medical emergencies and other types of situations requiring assistance. And because a disproportionate number of racial and ethnic minorities live in low-income neighborhoods, more police are generally assigned to minority neighborhoods.

Some departments fail to redraw beat boundaries regularly in order to adjust for social change. Neighborhoods grow or decline in population. Some deteriorate economically; as a neighborhood shifts from middle income to low income, crime and calls for service generally increase. Some cities expand geographically, incorporating outlying suburban areas. The 1987 report on Philadelphia found that the department had not redrawn its boundaries in 16 years. Partly as a result, officers in the Thirty-Fifth District handled an average of 494 calls, while officers in the Fifth District handled only 225. The disparity in workload was even greater in terms of serious crime: Officers in the Thirty-Fifth District handled an average of thirty-eight major offenses per year compared with only eight for officers in the Fifth District.[20]

Assignment to Shifts and Areas

Police departments use a variety of methods for assigning officers to particular shifts and patrol areas. Some assign officers on the basis of a strict seniority system and permit bidding for new assignments every 6 months or annually. Some departments, meanwhile, rotate officers through different shifts every month, or on an even shorter time frame.[21] A PERF report concludes that frequent change in shift "is deleterious to the physical and psychological health of the individual and to the well-being of the organization."[22] Problems include loss of sleep, cardiovascular and other health problems, on-the-job accidents, disrupted family lives, and low morale. The report recommends steady shift assignments, based primarily on seniority with some managerial discretion in assignment based on performance and workload needs.

"Hot Spots"

Patrol Beat 144 in Kansas City was one of the most dangerous areas in the nation. In 1991 the homicide rate was 177 per 100,000, about twenty times the national rate. Partly for this reason, the beat was chosen as the site for the Kansas City Gun Experiment, an innovative program to remove guns from the streets.[23]

Beat 144 is a classic example of a "hot spot": an area that receives a disproportionate number of calls for police service and/or has a very high crime rate. A study of calls for service to the Minneapolis police department found that only 5 percent of the addresses in the city accounted for 64 percent of all calls. Meanwhile, 60 percent of the addresses never called the police for any reason. Routine police work is heavily skewed: A relatively small number of citizens in a community are extremely high consumers of police services.[24] Focusing police activities on "hot spots" is one of the most important innovations in policing, particularly in community policing and problem-oriented policing programs (see Chapter 7).

Types of Patrol

Most (84 percent) police patrol in the United States today involves automobile patrol. Only 4 percent of all patrol is done on foot; 5 percent is done on motorcycle and another 5 percent on bicycles.[25] Automobile patrol provides more efficient coverage than foot patrol. A patrol car can cover more area, pass each point more often, return to particular spots in an unpredictable manner if necessary, and respond quickly to calls for service. The efficiency of the patrol car in this regard is the reason why police departments converted from foot patrol to car patrol between the 1920s and the 1950s (see Chapter 2).

Efficiency comes at a price, however. When an officer patrols a neighborhood by car, he or she loses a lot of direct contact with citizens, especially law-abiding people. As a result, some people begin to see the police as an occupying army. William A. Westley was probably the first expert to notice this effect of automobile patrol. In his 1950 study of Gary, Indiana, he noted that "in contrast to the man on the beat, the man in the car is isolated from the community."[26] A decade and a half later, when riots were erupting across the country, no one could ignore the problem. The President's Crime Commission observed in 1967 that "the most significant weakness in American motor patrol operations today is the general lack of contact with citizens except when an officer has responded to a call. Forced to stay near the car's radio, awaiting an assignment, most patrol officers have few opportunities to develop closer relationships with persons living in the district."[27]

Foot Patrol

In response to the police–community relations crisis of the 1960s, many police departments experimented with restoring foot patrol in selected neighborhoods. Foot patrol has also been incorporated into some community policing programs (see Chapter 7). Because a patrol officer on foot can cover only a very limited area, foot patrol is extremely expensive. The inefficiency in patrol coverage, however, is offset by anticipated gains in police–community relations. Most police departments have some foot patrol units (94 percent of the very largest departments), but only 4 percent of all patrol officers in the country work on foot.[28]

One-Officer versus Two-Officer Cars

The outcry from patrol officers was predictable. One angrily accused the mayor of "jeopardizing the lives of cops." The cause of this outburst was a 1996 proposal in New York City to convert from two-officer to one-officer patrols in low-crime districts.[29] Many rank-and-file officers have opposed one-officer patrol assignments on the grounds that this approach endangers their safety.

Most patrol units involve single police officers—89 percent of all patrols in municipal police departments. One-officer patrols are more efficient than two-officer patrols: Two one-officer cars can patrol twice as much area and be available for twice as many calls as one two-officer car. Some police departments, however, still rely primarily on two-officer patrols: 90 percent of all patrol units in Buffalo, New York, for example, involve two officers.[30]

Although some rank-and-file officers favor two-officer cars, believing that they are safer, a Police Foundation study of patrol staffing in San Diego found that officers in one-officer units were assaulted less often and were less involved in resisting arrest incidents than those in two-officer units. The one-officer patrol units, moreover, made more arrests and wrote more crime reports than two-officer units. Police officer concern about safety appears to be exaggerated. In 56.5 percent of the incidents where backup officers were dispatched in San Diego, it was later determined that they were not needed. Meanwhile, only 2.8 percent of the incidents were underdispatched, in the sense that the officers responding to the call had to request backup after they had arrived at the scene.[31]

Staffing Patrol Beats

When investigators for a mayor's Task Force in Philadelphia went out on a randomly selected Saturday night, they were shocked at the actual level of police patrol. Less than half (47 percent of all patrol sectors: 190 out of 450) were fully staffed with the assigned number of patrol officers.[32]

Police patrol is an extremely expensive, labor-intensive enterprise. Staffing a single patrol beat around the clock, seven days a week, requires almost five (4.8) officers.[33] In addition to the three officers assigned to each shift, almost two others are needed because of days off, vacations, illness, and injuries. In practice, police departments are often shorthanded and have a difficult time fully staffing patrol beats. The Newark Foot Patrol Experiment found that an average of 19 percent of all beat assignments were not covered during the year. Coverage ranged from a low of 64 percent to a high of 91 percent.[34]

STYLES OF PATROL

Individual Styles

How much work do patrol officers do? A New York City police officer explained that "it depends on what [you] want to make of it. . . . You can make it as easy or difficult as you want. If it's done the way it's probably supposed to be done, it's probably not easy at all. But, it's the type of assignment you can also 'skate' in."[35]

In short, the actual amount of police work done by patrol officers depends on their work style. Some officers initiate more activity than others. Officer-initiated actions include stopping, questioning, and frisking suspicious citizens; making informal contacts with law-abiding citizens; stopping vehicles for possible violations; writing traffic tickets; checking suspicious events; and making arrests. The amount of officer-initiated contact with citizens varies considerably from department to department. The Project on Policing Neighborhoods reports that in one department 50 percent of all citizen contacts were officer initiated, compared with only 20 percent in another department.[36] These variations reflect differences in organizational style and management (see below).

In citizen-initiated calls for service, some officers initiate more activity than others. Bayley and Garofalo found that some officers were likely to simply observe the situation and leave, while others took control over the situation, asked probing questions, and had citizens explain themselves.[37] The National Crime Victimization Survey (NCVS) found that in 20 percent of all reported property crimes, police officers only "looked around." They took a report in only about half of all property crimes.[38]

Supervisors' Styles

The level of an officer's activity can also be shaped by his or her supervisor's style. Some sergeants engage in close supervision, maintaining regular contact with their officers, and demand specific levels of output: arrests, field interrogations, and so on. Other sergeants may use a more detached form of supervision, maintaining only limited contact with their officers and letting individual officers set their own work levels.

Organizational Styles

Patrol officer activity is also affected by different departmental styles of policing. James Q. Wilson identified three distinct organizational styles. The watchman style emphasizes peacekeeping, without aggressive law enforcement and few controls over rank-and-file officers. The legalistic style emphasizes aggressive crime fighting and attempts to control officer behavior through a rule-bound by-the-book administrative approach. The service style emphasizes responsiveness to community expectations and is generally found in suburban police departments where there is relatively little crime.[39] The Los Angeles police department has traditionally had an organizational culture that emphasizes aggressive police work, including high rates of officer-initiated contacts with citizens and high arrest rates.[40]

Some departments attempt to influence the work activity of patrol officers through quotas for traffic tickets, arrests, or field interrogations. Most experts, however, believe that numerical quotas are not related to the quality of police work.[41]

PATROL SUPERVISION

The Role of the Sergeant

Some New York City police officers preferred the department's community-policing program (CPOP) because you "have more freedom . . . [you] aren't monitored by the radio and have only one sergeant who spends most of his time doing administrative work."[42] Standard police management texts call for close supervision of patrol officers by their sergeants. Community policing (see Chapter 7), on the other hand, generally involves less direct supervision and more discretion and control over time for officers on the street.

The style of supervision affects the amount of work performed by patrol officers. The basic unit of police patrol consists of a sergeant and a crew of patrol officers. The principle of the *span of control* holds that a supervisor can effectively manage only a limited number of people.[43] The optimum crew size must strike a balance between the higher cost of small crews and the danger of loss of discipline if crews are too large. The recommended span of control is one sergeant for about eight or ten patrol officers.

Like patrol officers, sergeants have different work styles. Active sergeants have more contact with the officers under their command and are more likely to communicate specific instructions or patrol objectives.[44] The Project on Policing Neighborhoods study found that supervisors spend about 30 percent of their time in encounters with other officers and citizens. They spend slightly more time (about one-third of the total) in general patrol. In one department a supervisor was present in 7 percent of all patrol officer encounters with citizens. It was estimated that an officer could expect to have a supervisor present at an average of about 11 public encounters with citizens every 20 working days. Supervisors were present at 34 percent of all arrests of two or more persons and 75 percent of all assaults on officers.[45] When supervisors were present at the scene of encounters with citizens, they did not discuss the incident with the officer at any time during the work shift. This is not surprising, given the fact that most encounters are routine and problem-free. When supervisors did discuss an encounter, their comments were nearly always in the form of a suggestion rather than an order.

Not having the proper span of control can have a tremendous impact on the quality of police work. The Special Counsel to the Los Angeles Sheriff's Department (LASD) found that a high rate of shootings by officers assigned to the Century Station was due in part to the fact that the span of control in that station was at times as high as 20 or 25 officers per sergeant, far in excess of the department's own recommended standard of 8 to 1.[46]

Although supervision by sergeants is one of the most important aspects of policing, sergeants are one of the least studied aspects of policing. We don't know that much about different styles of supervision, of how sergeants interact with patrol officers, and how departments supervise sergeants. Much more research is needed on this subject. The role of supervision by sergeants as a mechanism of accountability is discussed in Chapter 11.

HOW MUCH ACTUAL POLICE PROTECTION? A SUMMARY

The previous sections illustrate the important point that the number of sworn officers in a police department (as expressed by the police–population ratio) does not reflect the actual amount of police protection a community receives. As a result of inefficiency and poor management, a department with a large number of officers may actually deliver relatively little in the way of protection. The impact of inefficient allocation and distribution of officers is illustrated in Table 4–2. City A has a police–population ratio 50 percent larger than City B (which means that it is paying 50 percent more in taxes for police). And yet, through more efficient management, City B provides its citizens with more patrol units during the busy and high-crime evening shift.

THE COMMUNICATIONS CENTER

The Nerve Center of Policing

Peter Manning's visit to a police 911 communications center was a powerful experience: "My impressions of the communications center remain vivid and powerful. It was a smelly, smoky, poorly lit room reeling under the glare of harsh flickering fluorescent lights. Windowless, stuffy, with restricted exit and entry, few amenities. Nervous anxiety

TABLE 4–2	DEPLOYMENT OF PATROL OFFICERS IN TWO HYPOTHETICAL CITIES	
	City A	**City B**
Population	500,000	500,000
Sworn officers	900	600
Percentage of officers assigned to patrol	50%	70%
Officers assigned to patrol	450	420
Percentage of patrol officers assigned to 4 PM–12 AM shift	33%	50%
Patrol officers, 4 PM–12 AM shift	148	210
One-officer patrols	20	190
Two-officer patrols	64	10
Total patrols, 4 PM–12 AM	84	200

and worry was the prevalent tone. . . . I have rarely endured such an unpleasant field work experience."[47]

The communications center is the real nerve center of the modern police department. Patrol work, in fact, is dominated by modern communications technology: the telephone, the two-way radio, and the patrol car. Contemporary 911-driven police work is (1) citizen-dominated, (2) reactive, and (3) incident-based. Critics call this system "dial a cop" and argue that the 911 system runs the police department, preventing any rational planning and proactive police response to problems.[48] As explained above, there are considerable variations in the amount of officer-initiated contacts with citizens from department to department, ranging from a high of 50 percent to a low of 20 percent of all contacts.[49] In short, police departments vary tremendously in terms of their working style of patrol. More research is needed on the factors that shape a department's patrol style.[50] Nonetheless, even in a department where there is a high level of officer-initiated contacts, the 911 communications center plays a major role in patrol operations.

The communications center receives incoming calls from citizens, makes a series of discretionary decisions about how to handle those calls, and in many but not all cases dispatches police cars to the scene of the incident. The decisions by communications center personnel play a major role in shaping police work.[51] Antunes and Scott argue that the operator is "the key decision maker in the police bureaucracy."[52]

Figure 4–2 offers a schematic diagram of a police communications center. In most large police departments today, the communications system is staffed by civilians rather than sworn officers. In many departments they are not employed by the police department itself. Some states have only recently considered legislation to require training and licensing of communications center personnel.[53]

911 Systems

The 911 emergency number was introduced by the American Telephone and Telegraph (AT&T) Company in 1968. By 1993, over 90 percent of all local police departments in cities with populations over 50,000 participated in a 911 system. Because of their

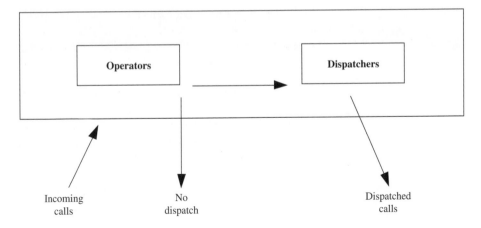

FIGURE 4–2
911 COMMUNICATIONS CENTER

convenience, and because police departments advertise the number, 911 systems have contributed to the great increase in calls for service. Some departments experienced increases of over 50 percent in the first 12 months after the 911 system was installed.[54]

Processing Calls for Service

It is useful to think of the 911 system as an information processing system. The operators, dispatchers, and patrol officers are "information brokers" who receive citizen calls and translate them into official bureaucratic responses.[55] The operator obtains information from the caller and then makes a decision about the appropriate response. If he or she decides that the call requires a police response, the call is communicated to the dispatcher. The dispatcher then communicates information about the call to a patrol officer.

Manning illustrates the processing of calls with a description of a call reporting an alleged kidnapping. The operator has available four different kidnapping-related codes, but "there are no rules given to determine selection among these options." The operators have a 300-page procedure manual, but it "is virtually never used" because it is too large and there is no room for it on the operators' consoles.[56]

Only about half of all calls received by 911 communications centers result in the dispatch of a police officer. The Police Services Study (PSS) found that 17 percent of all calls are referred to another agency. The operator takes information from the citizen in 16 percent of all calls and gives information to the citizen in 9 percent. In the remaining 14 percent of the calls, the citizen is told that the police cannot handle the call, the call is transferred, or some other response is given.[57]

Obtaining information from citizen callers is often difficult. Callers frequently provide vague, incomplete, or inaccurate information. Many are confused or frightened. Some are intoxicated or mentally disturbed. A situation that a caller describes as a "disturbance" could range from a party with only loud noise to an armed or mentally disordered person.

The information is often incorrect. Bayley and Garofalo, for example, found that a weapon was actually present in only 25 percent of the reported "weapon present" calls.[58] Gilsinan observed 911 operators in a large Midwestern city handling 265 calls over one 24-hour period. He found that operators interpret incoming information from callers and translate it into a category that fits an established bureaucratic response. Operators interact with callers in a problem-solving process, especially asking for more details, to reach the final determination.[59]

The dispatcher also makes important decisions. The basic decision involves which patrol unit to dispatch. The unit assigned to a particular beat is often not available: either "out of service" handling another call or not on duty at all that day. Consequently, officers are routinely assigned to calls outside their beat.[60] The most critical decision is whether the situation is an emergency and requires an expedited patrol response. Reiss found that 18 percent of dispatches received an urgent response.[61] Manning found that dispatchers can ignore the formal coded classification they receive about a call and "act as if the event has another priority informally," including adding his or her own comments when communicating to patrol officers.[62]

Patrol officers process the information they receive from dispatchers, which is limited and often inaccurate. Thus, patrol officers respond to calls in the context of great uncertainty. They are dependent upon the information as given by the caller, interpreted by the operator, communicated to the dispatcher, communicated to the patrol officer, and interpreted by the patrol officer. In most departments, patrol officers are not required to provide detailed records of how they handle calls. Reports are often limited to "service rendered" or "no police action required."[63]

THE SYSTEMATIC STUDY OF POLICE PATROL

Patrol work is the most important aspect of policing. It is where the police have the most contact with citizens and where the most serious problems in police–citizen interactions occur. Understanding how patrol officers operate, therefore, is extremely important. But because of the decentralized nature of the job, studying patrol systematically is extremely difficult and expensive.[64]

There have been four major observational studies of police patrol over the past 50 years. They are listed below in terms of their title, year, methodology, principal findings, and major publications from or about the project.

American Bar Foundation Survey, 1956–1957
Methodology: direct observation, qualitative
Sites: Kansas, Michigan, Wisconsin
Major findings: exercise of discretion; complexity of police role; use of criminal law for purposes other than prosecution
Publications: J. Goldstein, 1960; LaFave, 1966; Walker, 1992

President's Crime Commission, 1965-1967
Methodology: direct observation, qualitative
Sites: Boston, Chicago, Washington, DC
Major findings: quantitative analysis of patrol activities and exercise of discretion; situational factors in the exercise of discretion; officer use of force
Publications: Black, 1980; President's Crime Commission, 1967; Reiss, 1971

Police Services Study, 1977
Methodology: direct observation, quantitative
Sites: metropolitan areas in St. Louis, MO; Rochester, NY; St. Petersburg, FL
Major findings: 911 call workload; race and gender in exercise of discretion
Publications: Whitaker, 1981; Smith, Visher, and Davidson, 1984; Visher, 1983;
    Worden, 1995

Project on Policing Neighborhoods, 1996–1997
Methodology: direct observation, quantitative
Sites: Indianapolis, St. Petersburg
Major findings: activities of community-policing versus non-community-policing officers;
    citizen compliance with officer requests
Publications: Mastrofski et al., 1998; Parks and Mastrofski, 1990

THE CALL SERVICE WORKLOAD

The Volume of Calls

They are called the "twin cities," but the 911 workloads of Minneapolis and St. Paul patrol officers are very different. According to the 1997 LEMAS data, Minneapolis patrol officers handle twice as many calls per year as St. Paul officers: 550 versus 221 per year. The Chicago police, meanwhile, handle 282 calls per officer compared with 489 in the San Francisco police department.[65] In short, even though the basic technology of 911 systems is the same, the workload they produce varies tremendously.

Types of Calls

"When you're in [patrol] you handle all kinds of jobs—maybe ones that just happened," explained a New York City patrol officer. Also, "you don't get to stay at a job for very long . . . the job is over in 15 minutes."[66] Routine patrol work involves handling "anything and everything" that comes in over the 911 system. Each call is an isolated incident that the officer handles as quickly as possible before moving on.

Studies of the 911 call workload have given us a comprehensive picture of routine police patrol work. The most important finding is that only 20 to 30 percent of all calls for service involve criminal law enforcement. Most calls involve order maintenance or service incidents. Table 4–3 presents the Police Services Study (PSS) data on calls for service to twenty-four police departments in three metropolitan areas. Other studies of 911 calls have found a similar distribution of calls. In Minneapolis (1985–1986), about 30 percent of all calls were crime-related (1.9 percent crimes against persons, 28.4 percent property crimes), 32.5 percent involved conflict management, and 13.2 percent were service calls.[67]

Several basic points emerge from these data. First, criminal law enforcement represents a minority of all calls for service. The police are not primarily crime fighters but are peacekeepers and problem solvers.

Second, the vast majority of crime-related calls involve property crimes. Only 2 percent of all calls in Table 4–3 involve a violent crime. Thus, the media image of

TABLE 4–3 CRIME AND NONCRIME INCIDENTS AND THEIR DISTRIBUTION IN POLICE SERVICES STUDY	
	Percentage of All Encounters
Crime incidents	
Violent crimes. Murder, robbery, assault, kidnapping, rape, child abuse	3.0
Nonviolent crimes. Theft, selling or receiving stolen goods, breaking and entering, burglary, vandalism, arson, fraud, leaving the scene, false report, nonsupport	15.0
Morals crimes. Drug violations, gambling, prostitution, obscene behavior, pornography	1.3
Suspicious circumstances. Reports or observations of prowlers, gunshots, screams, suspicious persons or conditions	9.8
Total	29.1
Noncrime incidents	
Traffic (regulation and enforcement). Violation of traffic laws, traffic-flow problem, accidents, abandoned vehicles	24.1
Disputes. Fights, arguments, disturbances involving interpersonal conflict	8.6
Nuisances. Annoyance, harassment, noise disturbance, trespassing, minor juvenile problem, ordinance violation	10.7
Dependent persons. Drunks, missing persons, juvenile runaway, mentally disordered, other person unable to care for self	3.4
Medical. Injured accident victims, suicide and attempts, deaths, others needing medical attention	1.9
Information request. Road directions, referral, police or government procedures, miscellaneous requests where no additional police action mentioned	4.0
Information offer. Return property, missing or stolen property, false alarm report, complaint or compliment about police, general information provision	2.8
General assistance. Animal problem, lost or damaged property, utility problem, fire or other disaster, assist motorist, lockouts, companionship, irrational or crank call, house check, escort, transportation	9.2
Miscellaneous. Internal legal procedures, assistance request, officer wants to give information, officer wants information, officer assists, courier	4.4
Gone on arrival. Dispatched calls where parties to the problem are not at the scene	1.8
Total	70.9

Source: Stephen Mastrofski, "The Police and Noncrime Services," in G. Whitaker and C. Phillips, eds., *Evaluating the Performance of Criminal Justice Agencies* (Beverly Hills, CA: Sage, 1983), p. 40.

policing that emphasizes the crime-fighting role, with a particular emphasis on violent crime and dangerous criminals, is a distortion of routine police work.

Third, most police work involves order maintenance, or conflict management, and service. For this reason, policing is best characterized as peacekeeping (see Chapter 1). Cumming, Cumming, and Edell characterize the police officer as "a philosopher, guide, and friend."[68]

Fourth, many situations are ambiguous and require the exercise of discretion by the officers. It is not clear what the best response should be to situations classified as interpersonal conflict or public nuisance. Many calls that citizens characterize as crime-related do not necessarily involve an actual criminal incident. The caller may believe that a crime has been committed, but there may not be sufficient evidence to support that belief. Reiss found that citizens defined 58 percent of all incidents as a criminal matter, but responding police officers recorded only 17 percent as crime-related. Reiss argues that "many citizens have only a vague understanding of the difference between civil, private, and criminal matters."[69] Officers need to use their judgment based on the particular circumstances of each situation. Police discretion is examined in detail in Chapter 8.

Fifth, many of the order maintenance and service calls involve family problems that occur in private homes. The 911 system allows people to invite the police into their homes, which the police would normally not have a legal right to enter.[70] As a result, the police encounter, firsthand, the most intimate human problems: family disputes, mental illness, alcoholism, and so on.

Sixth, calls for service do not come from a representative sample of the community. Some people are very heavy users of police services; others rarely, if ever, call the police. Low-income people are the heaviest users of police services.[71] A study of calls for service in Minneapolis during one 12-month period found that 5 percent of the addresses accounted for 64 percent of all the calls. These areas are now referred to as "hot spots." Some individuals or households have chronic problems and call the police repeatedly within a period of a few months. Meanwhile, 60 percent of the addresses in the Minneapolis study never called the police.[72]

ASPECTS OF PATROL WORK

Response Time

Getting to the scene of a crime quickly has traditionally been a top police priority. Quick response to calls is a part of the folk wisdom of policing. Both police and citizens believe that it will (1) increase the probability of an arrest and (2) increase public satisfaction. Under the traditional style of policing, professionalism was defined in large part by the fastest possible response to all calls for service.

Unfortunately, research has not supported the folk wisdom about rapid response time. Several studies have found that response time has little effect on clearance rates.[73] The total amount of time between the commission of a crime and the moment a police officer arrives on the scene includes separate parts:

1 **Discovery Time.** The interval between the commission of the crime and its discovery.
2 **Reporting Time.** The interval between discovery and when the citizen calls the police.
3 **Processing Time.** The interval between the call and the dispatch of a patrol car.
4 **Travel Time.** The length of time it takes patrol officers to reach the scene.

A Police Foundation study found that processing time took an average of 2 minutes and 50 seconds, while travel time averaged 5 minutes and 34 seconds.[74] Cordner, Greene, and Bynum found similar times in a study of calls to the Pontiac, Michigan, police department.[75]

Items 1, 2, and 3 of the total response time are beyond the control of the police. A PERF study found that 75 percent of all reported crimes are discovery or cold crimes, and only 25 percent are involvement crimes (e.g., a confrontation between the victim and the offender). Most burglaries, for example, are not discovered until hours after they occurred. Cordner, Greene, and Bynum found that the discovery delay, the interval between the time the crime occurred or was discovered and reported, was measured in hours for property crimes and about 30 minutes for personal crimes of violence. In this context, the police travel time (item 4) is largely irrelevant in terms of catching the offender on the premises.[76]

In involvement crimes, the PERF study found that victims took an average of 4.0 to 5.5 minutes to call the police. Of these involvement crimes, 13 percent were reported while the crime was in progress and 14 percent were reported within the first minute after it was committed. Victim delay in calling the police undermines any potential gain by a faster police travel time. The study concluded that between 80 and 90 percent of serious crimes were reported to the police "too slowly for a response-related arrest to be made, even if the police response time was zero."[77]

Citizens delay calling the police for many reasons. In some cases they want to verify that a crime has actually occurred. In others, they try to cope with the problems created by the crime, by waiting to regain their composure or by calling a friend or family member. In a small number of cases a telephone is not available (e.g., a street robbery). Some people may not know the police phone number, or the citizen may have trouble communicating the problem to the police.

Citizen satisfaction with police service is affected by response time. Furstenburg and Wellford found that citizens who had to wait more than 15 minutes for the police to arrive were significantly less satisfied than those who obtained a faster response. For both black and white citizens, satisfaction dropped steadily as response time increased from 5 to more than 15 minutes.[78] Satisfaction is a function of citizen expectations about how soon the police will arrive. Citizens are most likely to be dissatisfied when they expect a quick response but do not receive it. The PSS data indicate that callers were informed of how long they would have to wait for a police unit in only 1 percent of all calls.[79] Experiments with differential response to calls (see below) found that citizens were satisfied if they were informed that the police would not be there immediately.[80]

Officer Use of Patrol Time

One of the traditional negative stereotypes about police officers involves the donut shop: that officers spend all their time eating donuts instead of patrolling and doing police work. This stereotype raises the crucial question of how patrol officers use their time. What does a typical patrol officer do during a typical 8-hour shift? How much "real" police work does he or she do? Another stereotype about policing is that the job is highly stressful, and that officers are continually rushing from one call to another. Is that stereotype valid?

How officers spend their time is also important from a cost standpoint. Personnel costs consume 80 to 90 percent of a police department's budget. Therefore, maximizing the productivity of a police department requires getting patrol officers to do as much work as possible.

Mastrofski's observations of patrol in St. Petersburg and Indianapolis found that regular patrol officers spend about 25 percent of their time on face-to-face encounters with citizens (in St. Petersburg, 120 minutes or 2 hours out of each 8-hour shift). Indianapolis officers spend about 2 hours on general patrol and slightly more than an hour en route (i.e., traveling from one place to another for some specific purpose). Regular patrol officers in both cities spent about an hour of each shift on personal matters.[81]

Time spent handling calls for service is often characterized as committed time. Officers devote the remaining uncommitted time to a number of different activities. In the Kansas City patrol experiment, uncommitted time was almost equally divided between regular patrol, non-police-related activity (eating, personal business), stationary police-related activities (report writing), and residual time (traveling to and from police stations, etc.).[82] In certain respects, there is no practical difference between some of the categories of uncommitted time. When a citizen sees a patrol car driving down the street, it makes no difference whether the officer is delivering a report to headquarters, on his or her way to a lunch break, or engaged in routine patrol. The patrol car's visible presence is the same no matter what.

Arrests have a major impact on patrol officers' use of time. An arrest can take 1.5 to 2 hours to process. Many arrests require at least two officers, depending on a department's standard operating procedures.[83] Each arrest removes the patrol officer from the street, thereby reducing the amount of time available for preventive patrol and for responding to calls.

Evasion of Duty

Despite the fact that the two-way radio allows direct communication with patrol officers, officers are still able to avoid work. The easiest way is to delay reporting the completion of a call. A dispatcher assumes that an officer is still busy with a call (committed) until the officer reports that the call has been completed. Officers can create free time for themselves by simply delaying that call.[84]

High-Speed Pursuits

High-speed pursuits are a major problem in police patrol. A pursuit is defined as a situation where a police officer attempts to stop a vehicle and the suspect knowingly flees at a high rate of speed. Pursuits are fairly common and pose serious risks to police officers, the persons being pursued, and other drivers and bystanders.[85]

Alpert and Dunham's study of pursuits by the Metro-Dade, Florida, police found that 33 percent resulted in accidents and 17 percent resulted in injuries. Slightly less than 1 percent resulted in the death of the suspect.[86] Other studies have found even higher accident rates (44 percent in one study, but 18 percent in another). Studies have found injury rates that range from a high of 24 percent to a low of 5 percent of all pursuits.[87]

Studying and attempting to control high-speed pursuits is made difficult because all pursuits may not be reported by officers. In most departments, officers are required to complete an official report on every pursuit. Yet, many pursuits are of very short duration, and it is possible that officers do not report some of these. Officers may also not report pursuits where they know they have violated the department's pursuit policy (e.g., pursuing when road conditions are hazardous).

Until recently, patrol officers had complete discretion to initiate a pursuit. Most police departments today, however, attempt to control pursuits through written policies. These policies fall into three general categories. In 1997, 60 percent of all departments had *restrictive* policies limiting discretion by specifying the conditions under which pursuits may or may not be initiated. Another 6 percent had *discouraging* policies that advise officers against pursuits in certain situations but are not as limiting as restrictive policies. Finally, 23 percent of all departments had *discretionary* or *judgmental* policies that give officers broad discretion about whether to engage in pursuits.[88]

The Miami–Dade police department policy prohibits pursuits in less serious crimes: traffic offenses, misdemeanors, and nonviolent felonies where the identity of the violator is known.[89] Many experts argue that the potential risks involved are not justified in the case of minor offenses. Other departments restrict pursuits where bad weather creates unsafe driving conditions or where pedestrians are present.

THE EFFECTIVENESS OF PATROL

Initial Experiments

Since the time of Robert Peel, the basic assumption of policing has been that a visible police presence deters crime. A related assumption is that increasing the number of officers on patrol will increase the deterrent effect. Until the early 1970s, however, there were no scientific experiments testing these assumptions.

Initial experiments designed to test the effectiveness of patrol in the 1950s and 1960s did not meet contemporary standards of scientific research. In Operation 25, the New York City police department doubled the number of patrol officers in the Twenty-Fifth Precinct for 4 months during 1954. The department claimed that the increased patrol reduced muggings (street robberies) by 90 percent over the same period a year before, and that auto thefts declined by two-thirds.[90]

The Operation 25 experiment was methodologically flawed, however. It was not independently evaluated, raising the possibility that department officials manipulated the Uniform Crime Reports (UCR) figures on reported crime to achieve the desired results. The research design did not control for the possible displacement of crime to other areas, or for other variables that might have affected criminal activity.

In another New York City experiment, the city more than doubled the number of police officers on the subways (from 1,200 to 3,100) between 8 P.M. and 4 A.M. After a short-term decline, crime began to increase rapidly. By 1970 there were six times as many subway robberies as in 1965, before the additional police were deployed. Moreover, it was later discovered that the transit police deliberately manipulated the crime reports to lower the number of reported crimes during the experimental period.[91]

The Kansas City Preventive Patrol Experiment

In 1972 Kansas City Police Chief Clarence M. Kelley decided to take a dangerous gamble. No chief had ever been willing to experiment with different levels of police patrol over a long period of time. And most dangerously, from a political standpoint, no chief had ever been willing to endorse an experiment where some patrol beats would receive *less* than the normal amount of patrol. There was always the possibility of a public backlash that could cost the chief his job. The experiment was also professionally risky: What if the experiment found that routine police patrol made no difference in the crime rate? Kelley was willing to take the risks, however. He was a strong chief who had brought many reforms to the Kansas City police department. In recognition of his leadership qualities, he was appointed director of the FBI in 1972, before the patrol experiment was completed.

The Kansas City Preventive Patrol Experiment (1972–1973) was a landmark event in American policing. It was the first experiment testing the effectiveness of patrol that met minimum standards of scientific research. The Police Foundation, a private and independent organization, funded the experiment, provided the expertise in research design, and ensured that the evaluation was independent and objective.[92]

The research design involved fifteen of the twenty-four beats in the South Patrol Division (nine were eliminated as unrepresentative of the area). They were matched on the basis of crime data, number of calls for service, ethnic composition, median income, and transiency of population into five groups of three each. Beats were assigned one of three levels of patrol: (1) Reactive beats received "no preventive patrol" as such; police vehicles assigned to these beats entered them only in response to calls for service; noncommitted time was spent patrolling other beats; (2) proactive beats received two or three times the normal level of patrol; (3) control beats were assigned the normal level of patrol (one car per beat).

The experiment measured the impact of different levels of patrol on (1) criminal activity, (2) community perceptions and attitudes, and (3) police officer behavior and police department practices. Criminal activity was measured through official UCR data on reported crime and arrest, and through a victimization survey. This was one of the first important applications of the relatively new victimization survey technique. The victimization survey was used to measure criminal victimization, citizen fear of crime, protective measures taken by citizens, protective measures taken by businesses, and citizen attitudes toward the police. Data were also gathered on police response time, arrest practices, police officer use of time, and officer attitudes. No previous police experiment had investigated such a wide range of issues, used such a variety of data sources, or relied on data independent of official departmental records. The experiment began in July 1972 but was suspended within a month when it was discovered that the experimental conditions were not being maintained. After being reorganized, it was resumed in October 1972 and ran for 12 months.

Findings and Implications

The findings of the experiment were first reported on national television. One night in late 1973 the evening news carried the sensational story that increased patrol did not reduce crime. The experiment found that variations in the level of patrol had no significant effect on either criminal activity or citizen feelings of safety. The victimization survey found no statistically significant differences in crime in any of the sixty-nine comparisons made among reactive, control, and proactive beats. It also found that citizen fear of crime was not significantly affected by changes in the level of patrol. Nor were citizen attitudes toward police significantly affected by the level of patrol.

The Kansas City experiment challenged traditional assumptions about routine patrol. More patrol did not reduce crime, and lower levels of patrol did not lead to an increase in crime. Nor did citizens notice the different levels of police patrol. Since there was never any area that had absolutely no police presence, the experiment did not prove that routine patrol has no effect on crime. Patrol cars entered the reactive beats in response to calls, and marked police cars from other units also entered these areas.

There are several reasons why different levels of patrol had no impact on either crime or public perceptions. First, as Sherman and Weisburd point out, patrol is spread so thin under normal conditions that doubling it is not likely to have any additional impact.[93] A separate analysis of data from both Kansas City and San Diego concludes that patrol is spread so thin that, for example, any increases in "perceived patrol visibility" resulting from a shift from two-officer to one-officer patrols are "likely [to] occur only on paper."[94]

Second, many crimes are not likely to be deterred by patrol because they occur indoors and are often impulsive acts. NCVS data indicate that 33.7 percent of all sexual assaults occur at home while another 21.3 percent occur at, in, or near someone else's house. More assaults occur inside a home, restaurant, or commercial building than occur on the street.[95] About 60 percent of all murders, meanwhile, are between people who know each other. Crimes that occur indoors are not likely to be suppressed by the level of patrol on the street. Moreover, many of the offenders in these crimes do not rationally calculate the risk of arrest and punishment and, in particular, do not assess the level of police patrol in the area. In short, the traditional approach to police patrol has grossly exaggerated the extent to which many crimes are suppressible, or capable of being deterred by patrol.[96]

Third, people did not perceive the different levels of patrol coverage in Kansas City in part because of the "phantom effect," or what criminologists call residual deterrence.[97] Many (and perhaps most) people believe the police are present even when there is no patrol in the area. They have seen the police at some other time or place (e.g., the day before or in another area) and assume that the police are patrolling their area at the present moment. The initial perception has a residual effect, carrying over to other times and places.

Fourth, the Kansas City experiment tested only the level of police patrol. It measured only the number of patrol units assigned to different areas and did not study patrol officer activities. Thus, it did not investigate whether certain patrol activities are more effective than others. Community policing and problem-oriented policing (see Chapter 7) are important innovations primarily because they emphasize police activities that are different from traditional patrol.

Critics found a number of flaws in the Kansas City experiment. Larson points out that police vehicles from other specialized units (which were not part of the experiment) operated in the reactive beats, thus adding to a visible police presence. Officers in the reactive beats engaged in more self-initiated activities (such as vehicle stops) and used their sirens and lights more often in responding to calls. There was also a higher incidence of two or more cars responding to a call for service in those beats. All of these actions may have created the perception of a greater police presence than actually existed.[98]

One of the most important implications of the data was that officers' uncommitted time (about 60 percent of their time on duty) might be used more effectively. Anthony Pate argues that since reduced patrol levels do not result in increased crime, "patrol can be removed, at least temporarily, without incurring negative consequences" and officers can be redeployed to other areas for specific purposes.[99] The implications of this observation are discussed below.

The Newark Foot Patrol Experiment

The Kansas City experiment involved officers patrolling in cars. The findings quickly stimulated questions about whether they could be generalized to foot patrol. Is foot patrol fundamentally different from automobile patrol with regard to its impact on crime and public attitudes? These questions led to the Newark Foot Patrol Experiment (1978–1979), which tested the effect of foot patrol on crime and public perceptions. The design of the experiment was similar to the Kansas City experiment. Some beats received additional foot patrol, others received less foot patrol, and others served as control beats. The experiment tested the effect of different levels of foot patrol on crime, arrest rates, and community attitudes.[100]

The Newark Foot Patrol Experiment found that additional foot patrol did not reduce serious crime: "Generally, crime levels . . . are not affected by foot patrol for residents or commercial respondents at a significant level." Different levels of foot patrol did, however, have a significant effect on citizen attitudes. Citizens were "acutely aware" of the different levels of foot patrol, and residents in beats with added foot patrol consistently saw "the severity of crime problems diminishing in their neighborhoods at levels greater than other areas studied."[101]

Reduced fear of crime was also associated with more positive attitudes toward the police, including other police activities unrelated to foot patrol. At the same time, foot patrol officers reported more positive attitudes about citizens, believing them to be more supportive of the police. Foot patrol officers ranked "helping the public" as the second most important part of their job, while motor patrol officers ranked it fifth. The data suggest that the positive benefits of foot patrol on attitudes are a two-way street.

New Questions, New Approaches

The Kansas City and Newark patrol experiments were major watersheds in thinking about the police. The findings indicated that while some police presence probably had some deterrent effect (remember, they did not test the effect of no patrol whatsoever), simply adding more patrol does not reduce crime. By questioning the traditional assumptions about patrol, the experiments encouraged some creative new thinking. The finding that foot patrol reduced fear was encouraging. Also, as some observers pointed out, the experiments only tested the amount of patrol and did not examine what patrol officers actually did while on duty. This new thinking directly contributed to the new idea of community policing (see Chapter 7).[102]

IMPROVING PATROL

The traditional approach to improving patrol accepted the old assumptions that patrol deterred crime and that the police should respond to all calls for service as quickly as possible. To this end, police departments, following the management principles of O. W. Wilson, attempted to maximize the efficient use of patrol officers: converting from foot patrol to automobile patrol, using one-officer rather than two-officer cars, distributing patrol cars throughout the community on the basis of a workload formula, and improving the communications system to reduce response time.[103] Police executives also sought more sworn officers, more patrol cars, and more sophisticated communications equipment.

Recent innovations, however, have built upon the research on patrol and have operated on different assumptions about what patrol can accomplish and what is important in policing.

Differential Response to Calls

Do the police really have to respond immediately to every call for service? As patrol officers have always known, many calls involve trivial matters. In addition to the proverbial "cat in a tree" call, most property crimes are cold crimes where the responding officer just takes a crime report. Given the huge volume of 911 calls and the burden they place on the police, is there a better way of providing service to the public?

Some police departments have responded to this issue by attempting to manage the calls-for-service workload more effectively. This approach rejects the traditional assumption that the police should respond as quickly as possible to every call. Differential response involves screening incoming 911 calls and providing different responses depending on the nature of the call.

Differential response programs classify calls according to their seriousness. Calls receive either (1) an immediate response by a sworn officer; (2) a delayed response by a sworn officer; or (3) no police response, with reports taken over the telephone, by mail, or by having the person come to a police station in person. Implementing differential response requires written guidelines and careful training for communications center personnel.[104]

An evaluation of differential response experiments found it to be successful. In Greensboro, North Carolina, only about half (53.6 percent) of all calls received an immediate dispatch of a police officer; 19.5 percent received no dispatched officer at all (most were cold larcenies where a report was taken over the telephone), and another 26.9 percent received a delayed response.[105] Both police officers and citizens were satisfied with differential response. Greensboro citizens expressed satisfaction with 90 percent of the alternative responses, except for walk-in reports. In the case of delayed police response, citizen satisfaction was directly related to "whether the caller was informed that a delay might occur."[106] This finding confirmed earlier research suggesting that citizen expectations are not a fixed entity but are dependent on what the police tell people to expect.[107]

The evaluation also found that differential response improved the overall quality of the call-for-service system. The new procedures "(1) increased the amount of information obtained from callers; (2) provided callers with more accurate information on what to expect in terms of response to their calls; and (3) provided patrol officers with more detailed information on calls prior to arrival at the scene."[108]

Robert Worden's study of differential response in Lansing, Michigan, found that it was both efficient and equitable. Cold crimes and other low-priority calls received a delayed response, with a median response time of 16 minutes. Over 90 percent of the citizens were satisfied with this service. Other calls were handled by taking reports over the telephone (almost all were larceny and vandalism incidents). Over 90 percent of the citizens were satisfied with this service. Differential response was equitable in the sense that whites and racial and ethnic minorities were just as likely to be satisfied (although there was some variation in intensity: satisfied versus very satisfied).[109]

Telephone Reporting Units

Some departments have established telephone reporting units (TRUs) to handle calls where a citizen is reporting a crime but no immediate police response is necessary. Almost half of all reported crimes are larcenies and almost all of those are cold crimes in which the patrol officer would do nothing more than take a report. Many TRUs are staffed by officers on light duty due to injury. The TRUs handle anywhere from 10 to 20 percent of all calls on some shifts and up to 35 percent of all crime reports. One department found that TRUs took only half as long to take reports as patrol officers (16 versus 34 minutes).[110]

311 Nonemergency Numbers

Another innovation is the addition of a separate 311 telephone number for nonemergency calls. In early 1997, at the request of the COPS office, the Federal Communications Commission reserved the 311 number for national nonemergency use. By 1997, 6 percent of all municipal police departments had 311-type systems.[111] The Baltimore, Maryland, police department launched a 311 pilot project in 1996. The department determined that 60 percent of the 1.3 million calls to the 911 number every year were nonemergencies. Under the 311 system, citizens could call the 311 number directly, or if their call was determined to be a nonemergency, it would be transferred from 911 to 311. If a call to 311 was determined to be an emergency, it would be transferred to 911. After the first year of operation, the 311 number was handling one-third of the combined 911/311 total.[112] The differential response, TRU, and 311 innovations suggest that police departments are not necessarily trapped by an unmanageable call-for-service workload. That workload was, in fact, something the police themselves created, by adopting the technology that made it possible and promising quick response to all calls. These recent innovations, however, suggest that police departments can resocialize the public about what to expect from the police and manage the call workload.

Non-English 911 Call Services

The face of America is changing. Immigration continues to bring to this country people from many different countries and cultures. A growing number of people in America do not speak English or have only weak command of English. This creates a major problem for the police. In order to serve all members of the community, it is necessary for police departments to be able to receive and respond to calls from non-English speakers. Language barriers are one of the reasons why Hispanic Americans are less likely to call the police for service. In response to this situation, police departments may subscribe to translation services through a national telephone number. These services are provided by private firms, and local police departments pay a fee for the services.

Reverse 911

New communications and crime mapping technology has created reverse 911 systems. Instead of citizens calling the police, a reverse 911 system allows the police to call citizens. If a police department has important information about an event in a particular neighborhood, the system can identify telephone numbers in that area and call the residents. In Beech Grove, Indiana, for example, the system alerted businesses about a series of burglaries in their neighborhood. In another city a missing child was located within 30 minutes by alerting people in the area. A reverse 911 system can be activated within 5 minutes following a reported incident and can flood the affected area with hundreds of calls an hour.[113]

Computers and Video Cameras in Patrol Cars

To enhance the efficiency of patrol operations, police departments are placing computers in patrol cars. Computer terminals allow officers to both obtain information and file reports efficiently. In 1997, 78 percent of all city police departments had some type of computer in patrol cars and 59 percent had equipped cars with laptop computers.[114]

Police departments are also placing video cameras in patrol cars, primarily as an accountability measure. Videotapes of controversial incidents document the behavior of both citizens and officers and can help to resolve controversies over, for example, whether an officer used excessive force. By 1997, 41 percent of city police departments had video cameras in police cars.[115]

Police Aides or Cadets

An alternative method of handling low-priority calls is to use nonsworn personnel. Not all police tasks involve the need for a sworn police officer. The President's Crime Commission recommended the creation of a community service officer (CSO) to handle many of these routine assignments, thus freeing sworn officers for more critical tasks.[116] This approach is similar to the way other professions operate: delegating routine tasks to subprofessionals in training (e.g., lawyers use law clerks, college professors use graduate assistants).

In an experiment in Worcester, Massachusetts, police service aides (PSAs) handled 24.7 percent of all calls and assisted in another 8.2 percent. These were nonemergency calls that did not require the presence of a sworn police officer. Citizens expressed satisfaction with the service they received from the PSAs and did not object to not having a sworn officer respond.[117] A Seattle CSO program was established in 1971 and by 1993 employed seventeen CSOs supervised by a sworn sergeant and a sworn lieutenant. CSOs were specially trained in social services and worked primarily with street people. CSOs patrolled the downtown area on foot and referred homeless people to agencies providing shelter, food, clothing, and alcohol or drug abuse treatment.[118]

Despite the potential for utilizing aides or police cadets, the idea has not been widely adopted. The major obstacle appears to be opposition from police unions, which fear loss of sworn police officer positions.

Directed Patrol and "Hot Spots"

Directed patrol is a program that provides patrol officers with specific duties to perform during a specified time period during which they are freed from normal 911 dispatches. Traditional patrol gives officers only a general mandate to patrol their beats and to respond to calls for service. A directed patrol program might, for example, involve instruction to look for specific persons or types of crimes, or to patrol certain areas intensively.[119]

Cordner's evaluation of directed patrol in Pontiac, Michigan, found mixed results. There was some evidence that aggressive anticrime activities under the program may have reduced or displaced some kinds of criminal activity. The exact nature of this effect was difficult to determine conclusively, however. Cordner argues that the evidence does lend support to the view that what police officers actually do is more important than the number of officers on patrol.[120]

A more recent version of directed patrol focuses on "hot spots," or those areas that receive a very high volume of calls for service. An experiment in Minneapolis used a crack-down–back-off technique in which patrol officers would intensively patrol hot spots for short periods of time. The underlying assumption was that the impact of a short-term police presence would carry over because of residual deterrence.[121]

Beyond Traditional Patrol

There have been a number of experiments and innovations in police patrol in the last 25 years. Overall, however, the extent of change has been fairly limited. Reviewing developments in police patrol in the 1980s, Stephen Mastrofski concludes that the net effect was "changes in patrol practice of only modest increments in the short run."[122] Traditional preventive patrol and calls for service remain the central aspect of American police departments. The most important innovations in policing look beyond traditional patrol. Advocates of community policing and problem-oriented policing argue that 911-driven policing is reactive and limited to isolated incidents. They argue that the police should be more proactive and, working closely with community residents, focus on underlying problems. Community policing and problem-oriented policing are covered in detail in Chapter 7.

SUMMARY

Patrol is the backbone of policing. Despite many recent innovations in community policing, most police work involves patrol officers who patrol their assigned beats and respond to citizen calls for service. The patrol workload is dominated by calls for service and primarily involves noncriminal incidents. Thus, police work is best described as peacekeeping rather than crime fighting. The evidence suggests that increases in the level of patrol do not deter crime more effectively than lower levels of patrol. Innovations in patrol emphasize making more efficient use of patrol personnel and reducing the high volume of calls for service.

CASE STUDY: KANSAS CITY (MO) GUN EXPERIMENT (EXCERPT)

Program Type or Federal Program Source. Program to deter gun carrying in high crime hotspot areas; Offices of Weed and Seed.
Program Goal. To reduce crime by seizures of illegal guns.
Specific Groups Targeted by the Strategy. Violent perpetrators carrying guns.
Geographical Area Targeted by the Strategy. Eighty-block area of Kansas City, Missouri.

The Kansas City Gun Experiment used intensive police patrols directed to an 80-block hotspot area where the homicide rate was 20 times the national average. Patrol officers seized guns by frisking individuals who were arrested and by making plain view sightings of firearms during routine traffic violation or safety stops. Traffic stops were most effective in locating illegal guns, with 1 gun found per 28 stops. Gun crimes, including drive-by shootings and homicides, declined significantly during the 29-week experimental period between July 1992 and January 1993. Drive-by shootings dropped from 7 to 1 in the target area, while increasing from 6 to 12 in a comparison area. Overall gun crimes dropped 49 percent (169 to 86) and criminal homicide declined 67 percent (30 to 10) from the 29 weeks before the patrols to the 29-week experiment period. However, there was no effect on other crime indicators, including calls for police service, calls about violence, property or disorder crimes, and total offense reports within the target area. Significantly, there did not appear to be a displacement effect (i.e., gun crimes did not increase in any of the seven surrounding patrol beats).

Evaluated by: Department of Criminology, University of Maryland; Department of Criminal Justice, University of Texas. Years of Operation: 1992–1993

FOR DISCUSSION

1 The Kansas City Gun Experiment represented a unique approach to crime prevention through patrol. Discuss how this approach is different from traditional
patrol. What are the key elements of the experiment? What do patrol officers in this
experiment do that is different from what basic patrol officers do? What is the relationship between the officers in this experiment and other patrol officers?

2 This experiment was a one-time special project. Discuss how this approach could be
integrated into a police department on a permanent basis. What problems would you
anticipate? How could those problems be overcome through careful planning and
administration?

3 Imagine that you are the chief of police. Write a General Order implementing a permanent gun reduction program modeled after the Kansas City Gun Experiment.

INTERNET EXERCISES

What kinds of innovative patrol programs are currently operating around the country?
Do a Web search of police departments using **www.officer.com** as your starting point.
Divide the class into teams and assign each team a different group of departments to
research. For example, you might assign teams different regions, or different size
departments, or a range of departments of different sizes within particular regions.

Identify specific innovative patrol programs. Are there any programs listed on
department websites? Describe the programs you find. Are they similar to programs
described in this chapter? Or are they different in important ways? How are they different? Do the websites provide much detail about them? Are there any obvious patterns
related to where these programs exist? Big departments versus small departments? One
region of the country rather than others?

REFERENCES

1 Bureau of Justice Statistics, *Law Enforcement Management and Administrative
Statistics, 1997* (Washington, DC: Government Printing Office, 1999), p. xiii.

2 James Q. Wilson, *Varieties of Police Behavior* (New York: Atheneum, 1973), p. 7.

3 Michael Lipsky, *Street-Level Bureaucracy* (New York: Russell Sage, 1980).

4 National Advisory Commission on Criminal Justice Standards and Goals, *Police*
(Washington, DC: Government Printing Office, 1973), p. 189.

5 Wesley G. Skogan and Susan M. Hartnett, *Community Policing, Chicago Style*
(New York: Oxford University Press, 1997), Ch. 4.

6 Quoted in T. A. Critchley, *A History of Police in England and Wales,* 2nd ed.
(Montclair, NJ: Patterson Smith, 1972), p. 52.

7 O. W. Wilson and Roy C. McLaren, *Police Administration,* 4th ed. (New York:
McGraw-Hill, 1977), p. 320.

8 U.S. Department of Justice, *The Police and Public Opinion* (Washington, DC:
Government Printing Office, 1977), pp. 39–40.

9 Albert Reiss, *The Police and the Public* (New Haven, CT: Yale University Press, 1971), p. 3.

10 Bureau of Justice Statistics, *Law Enforcement Management and Administrative Statistics, 1997* (Washington, DC: Government Printing Office, 1999), Table 8a.

11 Bureau of Justice Statistics, *Law Enforcement Management and Administrative Statistics, 1997*, p. xiii.

12 Ibid.

13 Thomas B. Marvell and Carlisle E. Moody, "Specification Problems, Police Levels, and Crime Rates," *Criminology,* 34 (November 1996): 609–646.

14 The original workload formula was developed by O. W. Wilson in 1941. See O. W. Wilson, *Distribution of Police Patrol Force* (Chicago: Public Administration Service, 1941). Excerpts are found in Wilson and McLaren, *Police Administration,* 4th ed., pp. 633–655, Appendix J.

15 Police Executive Research Forum, *Organizational Evaluation of the Omaha Police Division* (Washington, DC: PERF, 1992).

16 Philadelphia Police Study Task Force, *Philadelphia and Its Police* (Philadelphia: The City, 1987), p. 49.

17 Police Executive Research Forum and the Police Foundation, *Survey of Police Operational and Administrative Practices—1981* (Washington, DC: PERF, 1981), pp. 428–432.

18 James J. Fyfe, "Who Shoots? A Look at Officer Race and Police Shooting," *Journal of Police Science and Administration,* 9 (December 1981): 373.

19 Bureau of Justice Statistics, *Criminal Victimization in the United States, 1994* (Washington, DC: Government Printing Office, 1997).

20 Philadelphia Police Study Task Force, *Philadelphia and Its Police,* pp. 48–49.

21 James L. O'Neill and Michael A. Cushing, *The Impact of Shift Work on Police Officers* (Washington, DC: Police Executive Research Forum, 1991), Appendix C.

22 Ibid., p. 66.

23 Lawrence W. Sherman, James W. Shaw, and Dennis P. Rogan, *The Kansas City Gun Experiment* (Washington, DC: Government Printing Office, 1995).

24 Lawrence W. Sherman, Patrick R. Gartin, and Michael E. Buerger, "Hot Spots of Predatory Crime: Routine Activities and the Criminology of Place," *Criminology,* 27, no. 2 (1989): 27–55.

25 Bureau of Justice Statistics, *Law Enforcement Management and Administrative Statistics, 1997,* p. xv.

26 William A. Westley, *Violence and the Police* (Cambridge, MA: MIT Press, 1970), p. 35.

27 President's Commission on Law Enforcement and Administration of Justice, *Task Force Report: The Police* (Washington, DC: Government Printing Office, 1967), p. 54.

28 Bureau of Justice Statistics, *Local Police Departments 1997* (Washington, DC: Government Printing Office, 2000); Bureau of Justice Statistics, *Law Enforcement Management and Administrative Statistics, 1997,* p. xv.

29 "Officers Denounce Proposal for One-Person Patrol Cars," *The New York Times* (February 16, 1996).

30 Bureau of Justice Statistics, *Law Enforcement Management and Administrative Statistics, 1997,* Table 8a.
31 John E. Boydstun, Michael E. Sherry, and Nicholas P. Moelter, *Police Staffing in San Diego: One- or Two-Officer Units* (Washington, DC: The Police Foundation, 1977).
32 Philadelphia Police Task Force, *Philadelphia and Its Police,* p. 48.
33 Wilson and McLaren, *Police Administration,* p. 663.
34 The Police Foundation, *The Newark Foot Patrol Experiment* (Washington, DC: The Police Foundation, 1981), p. 36.
35 Quoted in Jerome E. McElroy, Colleen A. Cosgrove, and Susan Sadd, *Community Policing: The CPOP in New York* (Newbury Park, CA: Sage, 1993), p. 133.
36 Stephen D. Mastrofski, Roger B. Parks, Albert J. Reiss, Jr., Robert E. Worden, Christina DeJong, Jeffrey B. Snipes, and William Terrill, *Systematic Observation of Public Police* (Washington, DC: Government Printing Office, 1998), p. 25.
37 David H. Bayley and James Garofalo, "The Management of Violence by Police Patrol Officers," *Criminology,* 27 (February 1989): 1–25.
38 Bureau of Justice Statistics, *Criminal Victimization in the United States, 1994,* p. 100.
39 Wilson, *Varieties of Police Behavior.*
40 Christopher Commission, *Report of the Independent Commission on the Los Angeles Police Department* (Los Angeles: The Commission, 1991); Erwin Chermerinsky, *An Independent Analysis of the Los Angeles Police Department's Board of Inquiry Report on the Rampart Scandal* (Los Angeles: Police Protective League, 2000).
41 Bureau of Justice Statistics, *Performance Measures for the Criminal Justice System* (Washington, DC: Government Printing Office, 1993), pp. 109–140.
42 McElroy, Cosgrove, and Sadd, *Community Policing: The CPOP in New York City,* p. 138.
43 Wilson and McLaren, *Police Administration,* p. 83.
44 John van Maanen, "The Boss: First-Line Supervision in an American Police Agency," in Maurice Punch, ed., *Control in the Police Organization* (Cambridge, MA: MIT Press, 1983), pp. 275–317.
45 Mastrofski et al., *Systematic Observation of Public Police,* p. 29.
46 Special Counsel to the Los Angeles Sheriff's Department, *9th Semiannual Report* (Los Angeles: Special Counsel, June 1998), p. 23.
47 Peter K. Manning, *Symbolic Communication: Signifying Calls and the Police Response* (Cambridge, MA: MIT Press, 1988), p. xiii.
48 Malcolm K. Sparrow, Mark H. Moore, and David M. Kennedy, *Beyond 911: A New Era for Policing* (New York: Basic Books, 1990).
49 Roger B. Parks, Stephen D. Mastrofski, Christina DeJong, and M. Kevin Gray, "How Officers Spend Their Time with the Community," *Justice Quarterly,* 16 (September 1999): 497.
50 Mastroski et al., *Systematic Observation of Public Police.*
51 Manning, *Symbolic Communication: Signifying Calls and the Police Response.*
52 George Antunes and Eric J. Scott, "Calling the Cops: Police Telephone Operators and Citizen Calls for Service," *Journal of Criminal Justice,* 9, no. 2 (1981): 167.
53 "Licensing May Loom for 911 Dispatchers in Pa.," *Law Enforcement News* (May 15, 1995), p. 1.

54 Kent W. Colton, Margaret L. Brandeau, and James M. Tien, *A National Assessment of Police Command, Control, and Communications Systems* (Washington, DC: Government Printing Office, 1983); Bureau of Justice Statistics, *Local Police Departments, 1993* (Washington, DC: Government Printing Office, 1996), p. 11.

55 Peter K. Manning, "Information Technologies and the Police," in Michael Tonry and Norval Morris, eds., *Modern Policing* (Chicago: University of Chicago Press, 1992), pp. 349–398.

56 Manning, *Symbolic Communication,* p. 145.

57 Eric J. Scott, *Calls for Service: Citizen Demand and Initial Police Response* (Washington, DC: Government Printing Office, 1981).

58 Bayley and Garofalo, "The Management of Violence," 7.

59 James F. Gilsinan, "They Is Clowning Tough: 911 and the Social Construction of Reality," *Criminology,* 27 (May 1989): 329–344.

60 Ibid., p. 99.

61 Reiss, *The Police and the Public,* p. 6.

62 Manning, *Symbolic Communication,* p. 168.

63 Manning, "Information Technologies and the Police," p. 371.

64 Mastrofski et al., *Systematic Observation of Public Police.*

65 Bureau of Justice Statistics, *Law Enforcement Management and Administrative Statistics, 1997,* Table 9a.

66 McElroy, Cosgrove, and Sadd, *Community Policing: The CPOP in New York City,* pp. 132–133.

67 Sherman, Gartin, Buerger, "Hot Spots of Predatory Crime."

68 Elaine Cumming, Ian Cumming, and Laura Edell, "Policeman as Philosopher, Guide, and Friend," *Social Problems,* 12 (Winter 1965): 276–286.

69 Reiss, *The Police and the Public,* p. 73.

70 Arthur L. Stinchcombe, "Institutions of Privacy in the Determination of Police Administrative Practice," *American Journal of Sociology,* 69 (September 1963): 150–160.

71 Reiss, *The Police and the Public,* p. 63.

72 Sherman, Gartin, and Buerger, "Hot Spots of Predatory Crime."

73 William Spelman and Dale K. Brown, *Calling the Police: Citizen Reporting of Serious Crime* (Washington, DC: Government Printing Office, 1984).

74 Kansas City Police Department, *Response Time Analysis: Executive Summary* (Washington, DC: Government Printing Office, 1978), p. 6.

75 Gary W. Cordner, Jack R. Greene, and Tim S. Bynum, "The Sooner the Better: Some Effects of Police Response Time," in Richard R. Bennett, ed., *Police at Work* (Beverly Hills, CA: Sage, 1983), pp. 145–164.

76 Cordner, Greene, and Bynum, "The Sooner the Better."

77 Spelman and Brown, *Calling the Police,* p. 74.

78 Frank F. Furstenburg, Jr., and Charles F. Wellford, "Calling the Police: The Evaluation of Police Service," *Law and Society Review,* 7 (Spring 1973): 393–406.

79 Antunes and Scott, "Calling the Cops," 175–176.

80 J. Thomas McEwen, Edward F. Connors III, and Marica Cohen, *Evaluation of the Differential Police Response Field Test* (Washington, DC: Government Printing Office, 1986).

81 Parks, Mastrofski, DeJong, and Gray, "How Officers Spend Their Time with the Community."

82 George L. Kelling et al., *The Kansas City Preventive Patrol Experiment: A Summary Report* (Washington, DC: The Police Foundation, 1974).

83 Herman Goldstein, *The Drinking Driver in Madison: Project on the Development of a Problem-Oriented Approach to the Improvement of Policing,* V. 2 (Madison: University of Wisconsin Law School, 1982), pp. 67–68.

84 Jonathan Rubenstein, *City Police* (New York: Ballantine, 1974), pp. 117–119.

85 National Institute of Justice, *Restrictive Policies for High-Speed Police Pursuits* (Washington, DC: Government Printing Office, 1989), p. 1.

86 Geoffrey P. Alpert and Roger D. Dunham, *Police Pursuit Driving: Controlling Responses to Emergency Situations* (New York: Greenwood Press, 1990), p. 37.

87 L. Edward Wells and David N. Falcone, "Organizational Variables in Vehicle Pursuits by Police: The Impact of Policy of Practice," *Criminal Justice Policy Review,* 6, no. 4 (1992): 317.

88 Ibid., 324–325; Bureau of Justice Statistics, *Local Police Departments 1997,* p. 22.

89 Alpert and Dunham, *Police Pursuit Driving,* p. 80.

90 Experiments regarding the effectiveness of patrol are reviewed in University of Maryland, *Preventing Crime: What Works, What Doesn't, What's Promising* (Washington, DC: Government Printing Office, 1997), Ch. 8, "Policing for Crime Prevention"; see also John Eck and Edward Maguire, "Have Changes in Policing Reduced Violent Crime?" in A. Blumstein and J. Wallman, eds., *The Crime Drop in America* (New York: Cambridge University Press, 2000), Ch. 7.

91 Ibid.

92 Kelling et al., *The Kansas City Preventive Patrol Experiment.*

93 Lawrence W. Sherman and David Weisburd, "General Deterrent Effects of Police Patrol in Crime 'Hot Spots': A Randomized Controlled Trial," *Justice Quarterly,* 12 (December 1995): 627–628.

94 Edward H. Kaplan, "Evaluating the Effectiveness of One-Officer versus Two-Officer Patrol Units," *Journal of Criminal Justice,* 7 (Winter 1979): 339.

95 Bureau of Justice Statistics, *Criminal Victimization in the United States, 1994* (Washington, DC: Government Printing Office, 1997), p. 59.

96 Wesley G. Skogan and George E. Antunes, "Information, Apprehension, and Deterrence: Exploring the Limits of Police Productivity," *Journal of Criminal Justice,* 7 (Fall 1979): 229.

97 Lawrence W. Sherman, "Police Crackdowns: Initial and Residual Deterrence," in Michael Tonry and Norval Morris, eds., *Crime and Justice: A Review of Research* (Chicago: University of Chicago, 1990), pp. 1–48.

98 Richard C. Larson, "What Happened to Patrol Operations in Kansas City?" *Journal of Criminal Justice,* 3, no. 4 (1975): 273.

99 Anthony M. Pate, "Experimenting with Foot Patrol: The Newark Experience," in Dennis P. Rosenbaum, ed., *Community Crime Prevention: Does It Work?* (Beverly Hills, CA: Sage, 1986), p. 155.

100 The Police Foundation, *The Newark Foot Patrol Experiment;* Pate, "Experimenting with Foot Patrol."

101 The Police Foundation, *The Newark Foot Patrol Experiment,* pp. 4–5.

102 James Q. Wilson and George L. Kelling, "Broken Windows: The Police and Neighborhood Safety," *Atlantic Monthly,* 249 (March 1982): 29–38.

103 Wilson and McLaren, *Police Administration.*

104 J. Thomas McEwen, Edward F. Connors III, Marcia I. Cohen, *Evaluation of the Differential Police Response Field Test* (Washington, DC: Government Printing Office, 1986).

105 Ibid.

106 Ibid.

107 Scott, *Calls for Service,* p. 97.

108 McEwen, Connors, and Cohen, *Evaluation of the Differential Police Response Field Test,* p. 8.

109 Robert E. Worden, "Toward Equity and Efficiency in Law Enforcement: Differential Police Response," *American Journal of Police,* XII, no. 1 (1993): 1–32.

110 Margaret J. Levine and J. Thomas McEwen, *Patrol Deployment* (Washington, DC: Government Printing Office, 1985), p. 40–41.

111 Bureau of Justice Statistics, *Law Enforcement Management and Administrative Statistics, 1997,* p. xv.

112 National Institute of Justice, *Reducing Non-Emergency Calls to 911: Four Approaches to Handling Citizen Calls for Service* (Washington, DC: Government Printing Office, 1998).

113 Mike Johnson, "A New Twist on 911 Capability," *American City and County,* 112 (December 1997): 10.

114 Bureau of Justice Statistics, *Law Enforcement Management and Administrative Statistics, 1997,* p. xix.

115 Bureau of Justice Statistics, *Law Enforcement Management and Administrative Statistics, 1997,* p. xvii.

116 President's Commission on Law Enforcement and Administration of Justice, *The Challenge of Crime in a Free Society* (Washington, DC: Government Printing Office, 1967), pp. 108–109.

117 James M. Tien and Richard C. Larson, "Police Service Aides: Paraprofessionals for Police," *Journal of Criminal Justice,* 6 (Summer 1978): 117–131.

118 Martha R. Plotkin and Ortwin A. "Tony" Narr, *The Police Response to the Homeless: A Status Report* (Washington, DC: Police Executive Research Forum, 1993), pp. 116–117, Appendix C, pp. 85–90.

119 Department of Justice, *Improving Patrol Productivity* (Washington, DC: Government Printing Office, 1977), Ch. 4.

120 Gary W. Cordner, "The Effects of Directed Patrol: A Natural Quasi-Experiment in Pontiac," in James J. Fyfe, ed., *Contemporary Issues in Law Enforcement* (Beverly Hills, CA: Sage, 1981), pp. 37–58.

121 Lawrence W. Sherman and David Weisburd, "General Deterrent Effects of Police Patrol in Crime 'Hot Spots': A Randomized, Controlled Trial," *Justice Quarterly,* 12 (December 1995): 625–648.

122 Stephen D. Mastrofski, "The Prospects of Change in Police Patrol: A Decade in Review," *American Journal of Police,* IX, no. 3 (1990): 66.

CHAPTER FIVE

Peacekeeping and Order Maintenance

CHAPTER OUTLINE

INTRODUCTION

Most police work involves peacekeeping and order maintenance, rather than crime fighting. People call the police for an infinite range of problems: arguments, fights, and domestic disputes; medical emergencies, including deaths, suicides, and injuries; assistance for dependent persons, including drunks, missing persons, and juvenile runaways; public nuisances, including noise, trespassing, and suspicious persons. Table 4–3 in the previous chapter (p. 101) provides the PSS data on the frequency of these various calls for service. Many order maintenance situations involve what are referred to as "special populations": the mentally ill, public inebriates, and the homeless.[1]

KEY TERMS AND CONCEPTS

This chapter examines the peacekeeping and order maintenance activities of the police. It gives special attention to several specific situations that frequently arise and looks at the different police responses to them.

The Police Role

Order maintenance calls raise important questions about the police role. As we discussed in Chapter 1, some people view the police as crime fighters and think the noncrime calls are unimportant. Many police officers adopt this view and regard order maintenance calls as "garbage," "social work," or "bullshit."[2] This conflict between what the police actually do and what they value produces role conflict.

Some people, meanwhile, believe that noncrime calls are important but primarily because they contribute to effective crime fighting. Stephen Mastrofski identifies four different ways that noncrime calls for service can help improve police effectiveness in dealing with crime: (1) The "crime prophylactic" model holds that police intervention can defuse potentially violent situations and prevent them from escalating into criminal violence. (2) The "police knowledge" model holds that noncrime calls give officers a broader exposure to the community with the result that they have more knowledge that will help them solve crimes. (3) The "social work model" holds that the latent coercive power of the police can help to steer potential lawbreakers into law-abiding behavior. (4) The "community cooperation" model holds that effective responses to noncrime calls can help the police to establish greater credibility with the public.[3]

All of these models, however, assume that crime fighting is the central part of the police role and that noncrime calls are subordinate

SIDEBAR 5–1   POLICE POLICY TOWARD COMPLEX PROBLEMS

In his book on domestic violence, Lawrence W. Sherman advises that the problem "should be approached with the premise that new information will continue to appear, and that police policy should remain flexible enough to adapt to it."

His advice applies to every aspect of policing. All the issues the police deal with are complex. There are no easy answers. We should continually seek new information and be willing to reexamine our assumptions and the policies we support.

Source: Lawrence W. Sherman, *Policing Domestic Violence* (New York: The Free Press, 1992), p. 252.

to it. Most experts on policing today, however, argue that order maintenance is at least as important as crime fighting, if not more important.[4] It is a legitimate role for the police to resolve problems that people believe exist. An orderly and peaceful society is a better society. If the police did not respond to these problems, someone else would have to. Community policing, problem-oriented policing, and zero-tolerance policing (see Chapter 7) are based on the idea that the police should focus on community problems, not all of which are crime-related.[5]

CALLING THE POLICE

Public Expectations

In a classic analysis, Egon Bittner describes police work in terms of situations involving "something-that-ought-not-to-be-happening-and-about-which-someone-had-better-do-something-now!"[6] In short, a citizen believes there is a problem and wants something done about it. The modern police communications technology encouraged this expectation by creating the possibility that someone could respond to problems (see Chapter 2). The police encouraged people to call, and over time, people were socialized into the habit of "calling the cops."[7]

Citizens have different reasons for calling the police in noncrime situations. John C. Meyer identified four specific expectations.[8]

1 To Maintain a Social Boundary. People often want the police to remove someone they believe does not belong there. The victim of domestic violence, for example, may call the police to remove the assailant. Homeowners may want the police to disperse a group of teenagers from the front of their homes.

In many of these situations, no actual crime has occurred: It is no crime to assemble peacefully on the street. In response, police officers often ask, suggest, or order people to leave. To a great extent, people comply with such requests even when they are not legally required to.

2 To Relieve Unpleasant Situations. In many situations, someone calls the police because of noise, an argument, a family problem, or a dispute with neighbors. The role of the police is to restore order and keep the peace.

3 Counterpunching. In some disputes, someone calls the police about another person as a way of diverting attention away from his or her own behavior.

4 To Obtain an Emergency Service. People frequently call the police for emergency services: missing children, medical crises, suicide attempts, being locked out of their car or home, and so on.

Police Response

Police officers exercise great discretion in handling noncrime incidents. Typically, they handle situations informally and take no official action (e.g., arrest). Informal responses include a wide variety of verbal and nonverbal tactics. In their observation of New York City police officers, Bayley and Garofalo identified twenty different tactics that officers use in handling situations (Table 5–1).[9]

Some officers are more active than others. Bayley and Garofalo found that the passive officers did nothing more than observe and take notes. The more active officers took control of the situation by asking questions, giving advice or information, or warning the persons involved. Some officers accepted the complainant's definition of the situation, while others rejected it.

Citizens generally comply with specific police requests. Mastrofski, Snipes, and Supina found that citizens comply with police requests in 80 percent of all encounters.

TABLE 5–1 SPECIFIC ACTIONS TAKEN DURING CONTACT STAGE BY ESOs AND CSOs—311 NONTRAFFIC ENCOUNTERS

Action*	ESOs		CSOs	
	%	#	%	#
Observed, stood by, took notes	4.4	20	14.6	26
Sought identity, relationships of parties	15.4	70	19.1	34
Questioned to elicit nature of problem	30.8	140	30.9	55
Asked citizens to "explain themselves"	16.0	73	7.3	13
Stated problem as police saw it	3.5	16	3.4	6
Verbally tried to defuse, "cool out" situation	11.0	50	4.5	8
Verbally restrained citizens (gave controlling orders)	5.9	27	2.8	5
Physically restrained citizens	2.2	10	0.6	1
Threatened physical force	1.1	5	2.2	4
Separated disputants in a nonphysical manner	2.9	13	4.5	8
Physically separated disputants	1.1	5	0.0	0
Requested dispersal of citizens	1.1	5	0.6	1
Ordered dispersal of citizens	0.7	3	2.8	5
Other	3.9	18	6.8	11
Total	100.0	455	100.0	177

*Up to five actions were coded for each officer.

These incidents include requests to leave other people alone, to calm down and cease creating a disorder, to stop illegal behavior, and other miscellaneous requests. Compliance varied with the nature of the situation, the behavior of the officer, and the condition of the citizen. The more serious the situation, the less likely citizens are to comply. They are also less likely to comply with officers who approach the situation with a high degree of authoritativeness and/or who are disrespectful. Citizens are also more likely to comply in situations occurring in public rather than private places.[10]

TRAFFIC ENFORCEMENT

Traffic enforcement activity is perhaps the most common type of order maintenance activity carried out by the police. Whereas citizen-initiated calls for service are heavily skewed toward a relatively small segment of any community, virtually all adult citizens drive cars, and minor violations of traffic laws are common. Traffic stops are the source of low-level but significant friction between the police and the public. Citizens resent being stopped, asked to produce identification, and ticketed. For their part—because of citizen resentment—police officers generally find traffic enforcement a distasteful task.[11] Traffic stops are also one of the most dangerous police tasks, in terms of officers killed or injured on duty, because some stops involve armed and dangerous criminals.[12]

All patrol officers are responsible for traffic law enforcement, but departments with more than 200 sworn officers generally maintain a separate traffic unit. An average of about 7 percent of all officers are allocated to these units.[13]

The enforcement of traffic law violations varies widely from department to department. For example, in Dallas, Texas, police officers write twenty times as many tickets as officers in Boston, even though both cities are approximately the same size.[14] James Q. Wilson found similar variations in traffic law enforcement in his study of police organizations.[15]

Traffic enforcement policy is generally the result of formal or informal department policies. In some instances, community pressure dictates vigorous enforcement. In others, it is the decision of the top police administrator. Some departments have formal or informal quotas on traffic tickets for officers.[16]

Police departments occasionally engage in highly publicized traffic enforcement crackdowns. There is mixed evidence about whether such efforts effectively reduce traffic accidents or other crimes. For example, in Dayton, Ohio, the police department intensified enforcement in one high-traffic precinct over a 6-month period. Officers were instructed to write many traffic tickets and to make frequent and highly visible traffic stops. This particular precinct was compared with another comparable precinct where no crackdown occurred in terms of crime, arrests, and traffic accidents; the department found that the crackdown had no significant impact on any of these areas.[17]

There are three possible reasons why the crackdown had no effect. First, it is possible that there is no relationship between enforcement effort and crime. That is to say, increased enforcement has no deterrent effect. Second, it is possible that the increased level of enforcement was too small to make any difference. (The same issue arose with respect to the Kansas City patrol experiment discussed in Chapter 4.) Third, it is possible that some effect occurred but that the methods used in the evaluation lacked sufficient statistical power to detect it.[18] Similar problems arise in other studies of police law enforcement programs.

Drunk-Driving Crackdowns

In the 1980s, public concern led to a national crusade against drunk driving. Most states increased the penalties for drunk driving, federal regulations forced states to raise the legal drinking age to 21,[19] and local police departments intensified enforcement efforts. Drunk-driving crackdowns included such tactics as random stops of drivers and road-blocks to stop all drivers. The goals were to apprehend actual drunk drivers and deter potential drunk drivers.

There is considerable debate over whether enforcement crackdowns reduce drunk driving. Evaluations of crackdowns in England and Scandinavia found short-term reductions in traffic fatalities followed by a return to previous levels.[20] Several factors appear to contribute to this phenomenon. The publicity surrounding a tough enforcement effort may cause changes in people's behavior: People drink less, or ask someone else to drive them home, or a friend stops them from driving. As the publicity surrounding the crackdown wears off, however, people return to their previous behavior patterns and drunk-driving fatalities increase.

The actual risk of arrest for drunk driving is extremely low. The probability of a police officer spotting a drunk driver is limited by several factors. First, a very small percentage of all drivers are drunk: an estimated 5 percent of all drivers on an average evening, with a higher percentage on weekends. Second, there are relatively few police officers on duty at any given moment relative to the number of cars on the road. Third, not all drivers who are in fact drunk exhibit impaired driving.[21]

Each arrest, meanwhile, sharply reduces the probability of catching other drunk drivers. An arrest is an extremely time-consuming event, involving one or more officers for anywhere from 1 to 4 hours. For the duration, each officer is out of service, unable to make further arrests or to deter drunk driving through patrol. Finally, crackdowns are difficult to sustain. Police officers, like drinkers, slip back into their normal routine and reduce their level of arrest activity.

The rate of alcohol-related traffic fatalities (based on the number of licensed vehicles and/or drivers) has declined steadily since the 1920s. Experts believe that several factors have contributed to this trend: safer cars, better roads and traffic safety measures, seat belts, air bags, and most recently the increase in the legal drinking age. The tough anti-drunk-driving enforcement programs have made, at best, some contribution to this trend, but they are only one part of a larger social control effort.[22]

POLICING DOMESTIC DISPUTES

Domestic disputes are an important order maintenance situation. Domestic incidents represented 4.5 percent of all calls in the PSS data (see Table 4–3).[23] Police response to domestic incidents has been a matter of great controversy over the past 25 years. A revolution in public attitudes about domestic violence has led to new laws and policies, including increased criminal penalties, the development of treatment programs for batterers, and changes in police department policies.[24]

Defining Our Terms

There is much confusion about the police response to domestic incidents in part because many people fail to distinguish between disputes and violent incidents. The police handle many situations that are labeled *disturbances*. These include bar fights, arguments between neighbors, and many other kinds of problems. A *domestic* disturbance is one involving two or more people engaged in an intimate relationship. This includes married or divorced couples, live-in lovers, or people who are on a first date. It includes problems between adults and their children, or adults and their elderly parents. It also includes same-sex relationships. Only some of those—an estimated 30 percent—involve actual or threatened *violence*. The violence is usually an assault. Depending on the degree of seriousness, it is either a felony or a misdemeanor. About two-thirds of all domestic assaults are misdemeanors, and one-third are felonies.[25]

Donald Black studied 317 disputes involving "two or more people who were related in some way" and where there was some request that the police "exercise their authority." Thirty-one percent involved a physical fight, injury to someone, or the threat of injury. Another 30 percent involved noise or some other disturbance; 14 percent involved a dispute over property, and 12 percent involved a request that someone leave the premises.[26]

The Prevalence of Domestic Violence

The National Crime Victimization Survey (NCVS) estimated that in 1998 1 million violent crimes were committed against persons by their spouses, ex-spouses, boyfriends, or girlfriends.[27] Murray Straus and Richard Gelles, the two leading experts on the subject, have conducted a number of national surveys on domestic violence. They estimate that about 13 percent of all wives have experienced some form of domestic violence, and one-third of these have experienced severe violence.[28] An earlier survey of married women in Kentucky found that 10 percent of all married women in the state had been victims of domestic violence in the previous year and that 20 percent had suffered some domestic violence at some point in their marriage.[29]

The Bureau of Justice Statistics reported that in 1997 intimate partner violence made up 22 percent of all violent incidents against women. They also reported that intimate partner violence had decreased substantially from 1993 to 1997. In particular, they found that intimate partner violence against women decreased by 21 percent during this time period, with 1.1 million women being victimized in 1993 compared with 848,480 in 1997. Victimization rates for women also declined during this period, falling from 9.8 per 1,000 women victimized to 7.5 per 1,000 women victimized.[30]

Calling the Police

Many domestic violence victims do not call the police. NCVS data show that female victims called the police only about 50 percent of the time.[35] The reporting of domestic violence varies by the status of the victim. Low-income people call the police most frequently. In the Omaha domestic violence study 50 percent of the victims and 31 percent of the suspects were unemployed at the time of the police call. Only 7.4 percent of all calls to the police came from the western half of the city, which includes the middle- and

The domestic violence issue is generally defined in terms of male violence against females. Yet, Gelles and Straus found that 4.4 percent of the husbands had experienced violence at the hands of their wives (a rate slightly higher than male-to-female violence). When their colleague Suzanne K. Steinmetz first published these findings, an enormous controversy erupted. Some critics accused her of distracting attention from male-on-female violence.[31] Several explanations have been offered to explain husband beating. Much of it is self-defense or retaliatory. Female violence against men is probably even more highly unreported than male-on-female violence. Gelles and Straus found that "men are least likely to call a friend, neighbor, or the police."[32]

The National Crime Victimization Survey (NCVS) data, however, present a somewhat different picture of male versus female victimization. The rate of intimate partner violence directed against females (7.7 per 1,000) was more than five times that of violence against men (1.5 per 1,000).[33]

The phenomenon of husband beating has important implications for the police. In many domestic disturbance calls, the police arrive to find that both people have committed (or are alleged to have committed) some violent act. The officers face the challenge of determining exactly what happened and assessing responsibility. The Iowa mandatory arrest law, for example, directs the police to arrest the "primary aggressor."[34]

upper-middle-class residential neighborhoods.[36] In Kentucky, working women were three times more likely to call the police than nonworking women (21 percent versus 8 percent).[37] The NCVS survey found that nonwhite female victims are approximately 34 percent more likely to call the police than white female victims.[38]

Middle-class women are more likely to turn to private sources for help: a friend, a family member, a religious counselor, or a social worker. They are also more likely to be embarrassed about calling the police and worried about what neighbors or friends might think. The Kentucky Commission on the Status of Women concluded that "the poor become part of the official police record; the middle class conceals its family violence from public and official view."[39] Finally, the middle-income woman is more likely to be economically dependent upon her spouse (especially if she is a housewife and he is the sole source of income). The low-income woman is more likely to have relatively more economic equality to her husband or male friend.[40]

There are several reasons why victims of domestic violence do not call the police. According to an NCVS report on *Intimate Partner Violence,* 35 percent of women did not report the incident to the police because they regarded it as a private matter. Meanwhile, 19 percent did not call because they feared reprisal; 7 percent thought that it was a minor crime; and another 6 percent thought the police would not want to be bothered.[41]

Domestic violence is concentrated in certain families and nonexistent in most families. Consequently, repeat calls to the same address are a common occurrence. An Ann

Arbor study found that 36 percent of all the domestic disturbance calls in one 6-month period involved repeat calls. Six residences had 4 calls, six had 5 calls, and three had 6 calls in that period.[42] In the Omaha study, 65 percent of the suspects had previously been arrested for some offense; 11 percent had been arrested for a past offense against the victim; and 3 percent had been arrested for an offense against the victim in the previous 6 months.[43] Gelles and Straus found the average female victim was battered three times a year.[44]

Danger to Police?

There is considerable controversy over the extent to which domestic disturbance calls pose a danger to police officers. Joel Garner and Elizabeth Clemmer's analysis of FBI data on officers killed or assaulted in the line of duty found that domestic disturbance calls ranked very low in terms of officers killed. Robbery and burglary were consistently the most dangerous kinds of incidents. There was mixed evidence with respect to assaults on officers. Some data indicate that domestic calls are the most dangerous situations, while others indicate that they rank third or lower.[45] Uchida, Brooks, and Kopers analyzed assault and injury rates relative to the frequency of domestic disturbance calls. They found that "domestics present a high risk of danger to police," ranking first in one analysis and third (out of twenty) in another.[46]

Domestic disturbances are more often frustrating than dangerous. The police are frequently able to resolve the immediate dispute, but they cannot do anything about the underlying cause—unemployment, alcohol or drug abuse, or psychological trouble. Black found that some officers deliberately drove slowly to a domestic disturbance, hoping the dispute would resolve itself before they arrived.[47]

POLICE RESPONSE TO DOMESTIC DISTURBANCES

Police officers exercise great discretion in handling domestic disturbances. The alternative responses include (1) arrest, (2) mediation, (3) separating the parties, (4) referral to a social service agency, or (5) no action at all.

Arrest is not the most common response. As Mastrofski, Snipes, and Supina's study of police encounters (including all types of situations) found, police officers often ask a person to cease illegal behavior rather than make an arrest.[48] Studies have found arrest rates ranging from a high of about 40 percent of all incidents to a low of about 12 percent. (Some studies, however, have not distinguished between violent incidents and disturbances, where no law has been broken and arrest is not an option.) The Kentucky domestic violence study found arrests in 41 percent of all violent incidents, but Donald Black's earlier study found arrests in only 25 percent of all violent felonies and 20 percent of all violent misdemeanors.[49]

Mediation includes a variety of kinds of verbal responses: talking sympathetically, talking in an unsympathetic or hostile manner, asking the complainant what she or he would like done, ordering the parties to be quiet, threatening arrest.

Officers often separate the parties to a dispute by asking one of them to leave the premises. If a person is the legal resident of the house or apartment, the police have no legal right to force him or her to leave. Again, to a great extent, people comply with police requests that they leave. In the Omaha domestic violence study, virtually all people left the premises when asked; moreover, couples remained apart an average of 3 days (70 hours), and 87 percent of the victims reported that the police intervention helped resolve the problem they were having.[50]

Police officers may also refer one or more of the parties to the dispute to social services: marriage counseling, alcohol or drug treatment, or legal aid (for those contemplating separation, divorce, and other legal matters). Many departments provide officers with a list of social agencies. One study, however, found that officers choose this alternative in only 4 percent of all incidents. A police officer has no legal power to compel someone to seek professional help. A study of referrals in Ann Arbor found that only 1 percent of those referred actually contacted the social agency. An experiment designed to increase contacts through follow-up telephone calls succeeded in increasing the rate to only 7 percent of all those referred.[51]

A police officer can also take no action whatsoever. Donald Black found that in about 5 percent of the cases (13 out of 317) the police left the scene almost immediately after listening to one or more of the parties involved.[52]

Factors Influencing the Arrest Decision

Several studies have explored the factors that influence the police officer decision to arrest in domestic violence situations. Generally, the decision is influenced by the same factors that influence arrest in all situations: the seriousness of the crime, the victim's preference for arrest, the relationship between the victim and the suspect (with arrest less likely the closer the relationship), and whether the suspect is disrespectful toward the police.[53] Studies by Berk and Loeske and by Worden and Pollitz found that the probability of arrest in domestic violence situations increased if the woman was willing to sign an arrest warrant, if there was evidence that the man had been drinking, and where there was an allegation of violence against the woman.[54]

Several factors have traditionally discouraged officers from making arrests. First, some officers regard domestic violence as a private matter. Some may hold the sexist belief that a husband has a *right* to beat his wife. Second, many officers have learned from experience that domestic violence arrests are often dismissed because the victim refuses to pursue the case. A Police Foundation survey of officers found that the tendency of victims to drop charges was the second most frequently cited reason for not making arrests.[55]

Third, in the past police departments officially discouraged arrest for domestic violence. The International Association of Chiefs of Police (IACP) training materials in the 1960s advised that arrest should be a "last resort" in domestic disputes.[56] One of the most famous reforms of the 1960s, Morton Bard's Family Crisis Intervention (FCI) project, trained officers in alternatives to arrest.[57]

Fourth, an arrest is work. It requires the officer to perform many tasks (taking the suspect into custody, writing reports), some of which are potentially dangerous. An arrest also raises the visibility of the officer's work, bringing it to the attention of other officials who might find it improper. If an officer does not make an arrest, on the other hand, the situation remains hidden from others. As is true in other occupations, police officers often try to reduce their workload.[58] Moreover, police departments have traditionally not valued domestic violence arrests (which are regarded as order maintenance activities), placing a higher value on arrests for murder, rape, robbery, or narcotics.

A Revolution in Policy: Mandatory Arrest

A revolution in public attitudes toward domestic violence began in the 1970s. The women's movement identified spouse abuse as a major problem and demanded protection for victimized women. In two important lawsuits, women's groups in New York City and Oakland sued the local police departments, charging that they had denied women equal protection of the law by failing to arrest persons who had committed domestic assaults. The suits led to new department policies on police handling of domestic violence.[59] In *Bruno v. Codd* (1978) the New York City police agreed to adopt a written policy mandating arrest in cases of felonious assault (Figure 5–1). The *Scott v. Hart* (1979) suit against the Oakland police resulted in a similar policy.[60]

Mandatory arrest policies represent one of the first attempts to control officer arrest discretion. The strategy of using written policies is called administrative rulemaking, and it has also been used to control officer discretion in the use of deadly force, high-speed pursuits, and other areas of policing.[61] The control of police discretion is covered in detail in Chapter 8.

FIGURE 5–1 SUMMARY POLICY STATEMENT ON DOMESTIC VIOLENCE BY THE OAKLAND POLICE

OFFICE OF CHIEF OF POLICE
OAKLAND POLICE DEPARTMENT

SPECIAL ORDER NO. 3853

November 1, 1979

Domestic Violence

1. It is the policy of the Oakland Police Department to treat complaints of domestic violence as alleged criminal conduct. For the purposes of this order, "domestic violence" refers to offensive or harmful physical conduct of one spouse or cohabitant, or former spouse or cohabitant, towards the other.
2. The Police Department will not employ an arrest avoidance policy in response to incidents of alleged domestic violence. Although officers shall exercise discretion and shall utilize less punitive options when appropriate (e.g., citation, dispute mediation, referral, citizen's arrest), arrest shall be presumed to be the most appropriate response in domestic violence cases which involve an alleged felony, physical violence committed in the presence of an officer, repeated incidents, or violation of a restraining order.
3. Departmental policy and procedures regarding domestic violence cases are set forth in detail in Training Bulletin III–J, DOMESTIC VIOLENCE AND DOMESTIC DISPUTES.

The Impact of Arrest on Domestic Violence

Many people believe that arrest deters future domestic violence. The Minneapolis Domestic Violence Experiment (1981–1982) sought to determine the relative deterrent effect of arrest, mediation, and separation in misdemeanor domestic violence incidents. Cases were randomly assigned to one of the three treatments. Each officer carried a color-coded pad of report forms and handled each case according to the approach indicated by the top form. Investigators measured repeat violence over the next 6 months through follow-up interviews with victims and police department records of calls to the same address.[62]

The Minneapolis study found that arrest produced lower rates of repeat violence than separation or mediation. Rearrest occurred in 10 percent of the arrest cases, compared with 19 percent of the mediation incidents and 24 percent of the separation incidents. The experiment received considerable national attention and had a major impact on public policy. Between 1984 and 1986 the percentage of big-city police departments with "arrest preferred" policies increased from 10 to 46 percent.[63] By 1997, 97 percent of all municipal police departments had a written policy on domestic disputes (although not necessarily a mandatory arrest policy) and 46 percent had a special domestic violence unit.[64]

Critics have raised a number of serious questions about the Minneapolis experiment. Some police officers violated the integrity of the experiment by failing to handle the cases as directed, thereby undermining the random assignment of cases. A very small percentage of the participating officers produced the majority of the arrests. They were also more likely to follow the rules of the experiment. When only their cases were examined, the deterrent effect disappeared.[65] There was also a great deal of attrition among the subjects. Only 62 percent of the victims (205 out of 330) could be located for an initial interview, and only 49 percent completed all twelve of the interviews.

Some critics argue that Sherman, the director of the experiment, had "prematurely and unduly publicized" the results. It is unwise, they argue, to recommend major changes in public policy on the basis of only one study that had not yet been replicated.[66] The lack of replications is a general problem in police research. Many of the most important experiments, such as the Kansas City Preventive Patrol Experiment (see Chapter 4), have not been replicated at all. It is dangerous to base public policy on one or even a small number of experiments.[67]

Replications of the Minneapolis experiment in other cities, in fact, failed to find a consistent deterrent effect of arrest. In Omaha, Charlotte, and Milwaukee there was no deterrent effect found for arrest, whereas in Colorado Springs arrest was found to deter domestic violence. Some of the findings of the Omaha, Milwaukee, and Colorado Springs experiments were particularly disturbing (see Table 5–2). Arrest appeared to *escalate* violence among unemployed persons compared with those who were employed. These data clearly indicate that arrest—at least for domestic violence—has different effects on different kinds of people.[68]

Impact of Mandatory Arrest Laws and Policies

The full impact of mandatory arrest laws and policies is still not known. One important question is whether officers actually carry out mandatory arrest policies. Data on arrest

TABLE 5–2 SUMMARY RESULTS OF SIX ARREST EXPERIMENTS FOR REPEAT VIOLENCE AGAINST THE SAME VICTIM

Finding	Minneapolis	Omaha	Charlotte	Milwaukee	Colorado Springs	Miami
6-month deterrence, official measures	Yes	No	No	No	No	1 or 2
6-month deterrence, victim interviews	Yes	Border	No	No	Yes	Yes
6- to 12-month escalation, official measures	No	Yes	Yes	Yes	No	No
6- to 12-month escalation, victim interviews	*	No	No	No	No	No
30- to 60-day deterrence, official measures (any or same victim)	Yes	No	Border	Yes	No	1 or 2
Escalation effect for unemployment	*	Yes	*	Yes	Yes	*
Deterrence for employment	*	Yes	*	Yes	Yes	*

* = Relationship not reported.

Source: Lawrence Sherman, Janell Schmidt, and Dennis Rogan, *Policing Domestic Violence: Experiments and Dilemmas* (New York: Free Press, 1992).

trends suggest, but do not necessarily prove, that they do. Between 1971 and 1994 arrests for aggravated assault increased 140 percent. During the same time period, arrests for rape increased only 33.6 percent, arrests for robbery increased 8.2 percent, yet arrests for burglary declined by 24 percent. Arrests for misdemeanor assault, meanwhile, also increased at a far higher rate than for other Part II crimes.[69]

The implementation of mandatory arrest laws raises a number of important questions that may have serious implications. First, some commentators have warned that mandatory arrest may discourage calls by persons who only want the police to calm the immediate situation. For example, Martin reports that following the implementation of a mandatory arrest statute in Connecticut a dual arrest (meaning arresting both the offender and victim) was made in 33 percent of all police contacts for domestic violence. Accordingly, mandatory arrest laws may have the unintended impact of deterring people from calling the police for fear that they themselves may be arrested.[70] Second, mandatory arrest is likely to have a disproportionate impact on lower-class men, and

---

SIDEBAR 5-3 STUDYING YOUR LOCAL POLICE

Do the major law enforcement agencies in your area have written domestic violence policies? Obtain copies of those policies and compare them. Are they
mandatory arrest or arrest *preferred* policies? How much discretion do they leave
to the officer? Do any of the agencies have special domestic violence units or
programs? What do these programs involve?

---

poor African American men in particular.[71] On the other hand, the traditional no-arrest
approach had a negative effect primarily on poor, African American women by denying
them equal protection of the law.

Other Laws and Policies

In addition to mandatory arrest policies, many departments have added special training
for their officers in how to handle family violence situations. Surveys of victims,
however, have failed to find greater satisfaction among those victims served by specially
trained officers compared with officers who have not received special training.[72]

At the same time, many states have revised their laws on domestic violence. For
example, Iowa law directs the officer to identify and arrest the primary aggressor. At least
eight states now require law enforcement agencies to develop written policies on the handling of domestic violence. Several other states expanded the arrest power, allowing the
police to arrest in the case of misdemeanor assaults that did not occur in their presence.[73]
Traditionally, police did not have power to arrest in these situations. Eighteen states
mandate police officers to make an arrest for violation of a protection order. Traditionally,
police did not have the power to arrest in these situations, with the result that many
women's advocates regarded protection orders as worthless pieces of paper.[74]

The Future of Domestic Violence Policy

The future of police policy toward domestic disturbances and domestic violence is not
clear. Mandatory arrest policies remain extremely popular, but the full impact of these
policies is uncertain. In a comprehensive review of domestic violence policies, Jeffrey
Fagan concludes that there is "weak or inconsistent evidence" on the deterrent effect of
arrest, prosecution, protection orders, and batterer treatment.[75] Lawrence W. Sherman,
who directed the original Minneapolis experiment, no longer supports mandatory arrest
in all situations.[76]

POLICING VICE

Crimes of vice—involving prostitution, gambling, and narcotics—present special
enforcement problems because they are "victimless crimes," with no complaining
party.[77] First, the police must initiate investigations on their own. Wiretaps, informants,

SIDEBAR 5-4 DOMESTIC VIOLENCE BY POLICE OFFICERS

A 1996 federal law (known as the Lautenberg Amendment) prohibits anyone with a conviction for domestic violence from owning a firearm. The law has serious implications for both the police and the military, since possession and possible use of a weapon is an essential part of the job. Police departments have been wrestling with how to respond to this law.

The law presents several questions for consideration:

1 Is the law good social policy? Is it appropriate to deny firearms to people with a record of domestic violence?
2 Is it fair, or even constitutional, for a law to be applied retroactively?
3 Should a person with any kind of criminal conviction be employed as a police officer?

undercover work, and other covert investigative techniques raise a number of difficult legal and moral questions. Second, victimless crimes involve behavior that many people regard as legitimate, or at least a private matter. The result is conflicting public attitudes about how vigorously the laws should be enforced. Enforcement, consequently, is often selective, inconsistent, and arbitrary.[78]

Prostitution

Prostitution takes two different forms, each presenting the police with a different law enforcement problem.[79] Streetwalkers represent the lower end of the social and economic scale of prostitution. Prostitutes themselves are generally low-income people. Prostitution is often a last-resort source of income for the poor.[80] Because they solicit on the streets, they are highly visible to both the police and the general public. Streetwalkers also include male prostitutes soliciting male customers.[81] In many cities, a low level of streetwalking is tolerated by the police. It is usually confined to certain parts of the central business district where it is not seen by most of the public.

For instance, prostitution in Phoenix, Arizona, is primarily restricted to a two-mile strip of a major thoroughfare in the central part of the city. The police have reported that the area is fairly well organized in terms of the services offered by the prostitutes: One area of the strip consists of female prostitutes, a second area consists of male prostitutes, and a third area consists of transvestites. Historically, prostitution has been somewhat tolerated by the community as long as it is restricted to this area of the city and is not too obvious.

As such, for the patrol officer, streetwalking is essentially an order maintenance problem similar to the policing of skid row (discussed later in this chapter). The primary police objectives are (1) to keep streetwalking confined to a limited area (containment) and (2) to prevent related disorders from breaking out (keep the peace).[82]

Prostitution is often accompanied by an ancillary crime: a more serious offense that results from prostitution. "Johns" may be robbed, or prostitutes may be assaulted by their pimp or manager.

Arrests of prostitutes typically involve different motives. Conviction and punishment is not always the primary goal. Many arrests are designed to control streetwalking, either by confining it to a certain area or deterring it altogether. Convictions are usually for misdemeanors, with a sentence of, at most, several hundred dollars in fines and a few weeks or months in the county jail. The prostitutes themselves regard this as a routine business expense. In some instances, police attack prostitution by citing the pimps for numerous traffic violations.[83]

Periodically, streetwalking increases to the point where it becomes more visible to the public. The resulting public outcry leads to a police crackdown: sweep arrests of all prostitutes. Like crackdowns related to other crimes, they have a short-term impact after which things return to normal.

Call girls represent the upper end of the economic scale of prostitution (and male prostitutes also fall into this category). They cater to a more affluent customer and generally make their arrangements over the telephone. Because they are not on the street, their activities are not visible to either the public or the police. Prostitution of this sort may, however, come to the public's attention if the prostitutes are working out of a motel or apartment complex in a way that causes other people to notice, take offense, and complain.

Prostitution arrests pose a number of legal problems for the police. The most difficult is the issue of entrapment, which occurs if the police officer initiates the idea of payment for sex. Also, equal protection problems are raised by the traditional police practice of arresting only the prostitute (usually female) and ignoring the customer (usually male), even though both are guilty of violating the law against commercialized sex. Finally the informal practice of confining streetwalking to a certain area of a city involves an illegal form of selective enforcement: enforcing the law in some areas but not others.[84]

Gambling

The status of gambling in the United States has changed dramatically in the last 25 years. Many states have established lotteries, a number have legalized casino gambling, while many Native American tribes operate casinos on reservations.

Despite the spread of opportunities for legal gambling, much illegal gambling continues to exist. Nonetheless gambling represents a difficult problem in law enforcement because it is a victimless crime and an activity that many Americans regard as a legitimate form of recreation.[85] Illegal gambling has traditionally been the major source of revenue for organized crime and a factor in police corruption.[86]

Gambling enforcement often involves covert investigative techniques. Detectives must initiate investigations proactively, often using informants, undercover officers, or wiretaps. Similar tactics are often necessary for drug enforcement. All three tactics involve difficult legal questions. They are discussed in Chapter 6.[87]

POLICING THE HOMELESS

Homeless people represent another order maintenance problem for the police. Because of changes in the nature of homelessness, it is important to distinguish between the old and the new homeless problems.

The Old Homeless Problem

The classic study of the police response to the old homeless problem is Egon Bittner's article on policing skid row.[88] Skid row is the name given to the part of the city where the homeless congregate. It is usually located in a warehouse or industrial area near the central business district. The old homeless population consisted primarily of adult males who were unemployed, often with chronic alcoholic abuse problems, and who had fallen through society's safety nets: not eligible for unemployment insurance or welfare benefits and with no family support. They survived through temporary work, panhandling, scavenging, and selling blood. The skid row area contains various private and public agencies that serve the homeless: soup kitchens, shelters, cheap hotels, liquor stores, temporary employment agencies, and blood plasma centers.

Bittner characterized the traditional police response to the homeless as a classic example of peacekeeping. He found that police officers develop "an immensely detailed factual knowledge" about the area and a have a good feel for its normal routine. Officers have two principal objectives in policing skid row. The first is maintaining the boundaries: keeping homeless people in the skid row area. Business owners in other areas complain when the homeless engage in aggressive panhandling and expect the police to remove them. Homeless people almost always comply, even though not legally required to do so.

The second objective is keeping the peace, which means intervening when a homeless person's behavior exceeds certain informally established limits. This includes extremely loud and disruptive behavior, overly aggressive panhandling, or anything else that offends other nonhomeless people. Urinating in public or sleeping in doorways not only violates these rules but also is a crime in most jurisdictions and tends to cause the police to respond by arresting the offenders.

Even when homeless people are arrested, the purpose is not to convict and punish but to control the immediate situation. Officers sometimes arrest people for their own protection: chronic alcoholics who are in danger of death through exposure to bad weather; helpless people who are easy prey for muggers.

Bittner found that police officer attitudes toward the homeless are complex. On the one hand, many officers take a tolerant and even parental attitude, regarding them as children who cannot care for themselves. On the other hand, many officers view the homeless with contempt, seeing them as weak and morally flawed people.

The New Homeless Problem

The homeless problem increased significantly in the 1980s. There has been much controversy over the actual number of homeless people. In the best study of the subject, Christopher Jencks estimated the total at about 400,000 people in 1998 (far less than the numbers used by some homeless advocates, but more than some government estimates).[89] The new homeless population includes more families than in the past, including more women and children. Some observers also believe there are more mentally ill persons among the homeless than in the past because of changes in mental health services.

Skid row in Los Angeles in the 1990s included a designated "sleeping zone," an area of fifty square blocks where the homeless are allowed to sleep on the streets. A newspaper account found on one night a 69-year-old grandmother and a 32-year-old woman, pregnant with twins, struggling to get into their cardboard boxes for the night. An estimated 12,000 people live in the neighborhood, most in single-room occupancy hotels, although no one knows exactly how many homeless people sleep on the streets.[90]

The new homeless problem created a number of new challenges for the police. Homeless people established semipermanent camps in public parks, resisted transport to homeless shelters, and slept in bus stations and subways in some cities. Advocates for the homeless have filed lawsuits challenging both police actions and local ordinances designed to restrict the homeless. Some but not all of these suits have been successful.[91]

Members of the new homeless population are more likely to commit predatory crime. In the past, the homeless were more likely to be victims than offenders. The Santa Monica, California, police department reported that the homeless accounted for 27 percent of all calls for service in 1990 and a steadily increasing percentage of arrests: from 25 percent of all burglary arrests in 1985 to 53 percent in 1990; from 19 to 49 percent of all robbery arrests from 1985 to 1990.[92]

The Police Executive Research Forum (PERF) surveyed police departments in 1996 to determine how they were responding to the new homeless problem. Over 70 percent of the departments located in large metropolitan areas reported that homeless people posed a major or moderate problem in the community.[93]

The current police response to the homeless problem, however, is little different than it was in the past. First, it is reactive, with the police responding to calls for service about a problem with a homeless person. This has led to a police strategy that places primary emphasis on addressing complainant concerns rather than proactively working on behalf of the homeless to prevent problems from occurring in the first place. Second, the current police strategy is based on the idea of containment. Police attempt to contain the homeless problem to one area of a community to minimize disorder and to keep the homeless out of public view.[94]

However, some police agencies have begun to use proactive strategies to address problems related to the homeless. For example, the Seattle police department uses community service officers (CSOs) to handle many of the homeless-related situations. A CSO street team refers homeless persons to shelters, alcohol and drug abuse treatment programs, and financial assistance services. During extremely cold weather CSOs distribute clothes and sleeping bags that have been donated, and patrol alleys looking for people who are in danger of death through exposure.[95]

Police and the Chronic Alcoholic

Many homeless people suffer from chronic alcohol abuse problems. In the past, the police responded by arresting them on charges of public intoxication, vagrancy, or for violating some other ordinance. Police departments conducted occasional "sweep" arrests, picking up all vagrants and chronic alcoholics to clean up the streets. In some instances, the police escorted men to the city limits and ordered them not to return. In St. Louis the police dumped men on the banks of the Mississippi River, calling the area "detox east."[96] Such practices have been severely limited as many states have decriminalized public intoxication, and advocates for the poor have challenged illegal police practices.

In the 1960s many experts argued that arrest of these people is inappropriate. First, it overloads the criminal justice system and diverts police time and resources from more serious crimes. Second, it fails to deal effectively with the underlying social and medical problems of the chronic alcoholic.[97] Following a recommendation by the President's Crime Commission, many states decriminalized public intoxication and a number of cities developed detoxification centers as alternatives to criminal prosecution.[98] St. Louis established a pioneering detoxification center in 1966. Police officers could offer persons arrested for public intoxication the alternative of either entering the 7-day treatment program or being prosecuted through the courts. In effect, the program was a form of diversion.

Detoxification programs introduce new problems, however. First, where states have decriminalized public intoxication, it is not clear that the police have the authority to compel someone to enter a treatment program. Second, detoxification programs are expensive. The St. Louis program actually increased total expenditures: It saved $64,000 in court costs, but had a budget of $200,000, resulting in a net increase in total costs of $140,000 per year.[99] Third, there is no clear evidence that short-term treatment programs solve the underlying problems of chronic alcoholics. Fourth, many officers do not regard public drunkenness as an important part of their role and, consequently, use their discretion to ignore drunken individuals.

Changes in the law and public attitudes about drunkenness produced changes in police arrest activity. In 1960 police arrested 1.2 million people for drunkenness, representing 38 percent of all arrests. By 1999 there were only 437,153 drunkenness arrests, representing only 4.8 percent of all arrests.[100] Arrests also declined because police chose to concentrate their efforts on more serious crimes.

POLICING THE MENTALLY ILL

Mentally ill persons represent another important order maintenance problem for the police. The police usually become involved because someone defines the situation as a problem and there is no other solution available. The exact frequency of mental illness incidents is difficult to determine precisely because of different definitions of mental illness. One study of 1,072 police–citizen encounters (not including traffic stops) found that 7.3 percent were related to mentally ill persons. In this study, a person was defined as mentally disordered if he or she exhibited one or more of the following behavior patterns: "confusion/disorientation, withdrawal/unresponsivity, paranoia, inappropriate or bizarre speech and/or behavior, and self-destructive behavior."[101] In another study of recently booked arrestees in Cook County, Illinois, Teplin found that about 10 percent of arrestees had experienced a serious mental disorder such as schizophrenia, mania, or major depression at some time in their life, compared with 4.4 percent for the general population.[102]

Police Response to the Mentally Ill

The police come into contact with the mentally ill in a number of ways. The most common way is in response to calls from family members (32 percent). Family members often try to handle problems by themselves, and when the situation becomes uncontrollable, they call the police. Businesspersons and landlords calling the police account for about one-third of cases involving police contact with mentally ill persons. Because mentally ill persons often live in and around the central business district, businesspersons often call the police to "shoo away" a mentally ill person who may be interfering with business.[103]

Typically the police are called to the scene because a mentally ill person is seen as threatening. In one study, almost half of all incidents involving a mentally ill person involved the person having a weapon of some kind. Property damage also occurred in about 33 percent of police contacts with mentally ill persons.[104] Because of the complexities of handling problems associated with mentally ill persons, a great amount of time is often required. Pogrebin found that the average length of time for handling a mental health call was 74 minutes, which is significantly longer than other order maintenance calls.[105]

Police officers exercise great discretion in handling the mentally ill. The basic options include (1) hospitalization, (2) arrest, and (3) informal disposition. An examination of eighty-five police contacts with mentally disordered persons found that 11.8 percent were hospitalized, 16.5 percent were arrested, and 71.8 percent were handled informally.[106] However, the police response may largely be a consequence of the resources available to them. If the appropriate resources are available to police officers, they may be more likely to use those resources as an alternative to arrest or handling the situation informally. For example, in one jurisdiction researchers found that of ninety police encounters with mentally disordered persons 21.1 percent were arrested, 47.7 percent (including some arrestees) were taken to a psychiatric facility, and 43 percent were taken to a medical facility.

Several institutional and legal factors have an impact on the police response. First, the law limits the ability of the police to commit someone to a mental health facility involuntarily. A person can be committed only if he or she is a danger to self or to others. The paperwork required to meet this standard discourages officers from trying to commit people except in the most extreme cases.[108]

Second, mental health services are highly fragmented, consisting of a variety of hospitals, homeless shelters, and detoxification facilities. Most have their own admission criteria and refuse to accept people the police bring to them. In some instances, police officers go from one agency to another looking for one that will accept the mentally disordered person.

Arrest of the mentally ill is also infrequent. Arrest is used when a person's behavior is too bizarre to ignore, but the person is not sufficiently mentally ill to be accepted by a hospital. The factors influencing the decision to arrest include (1) the seriousness of the person's apparent illness, (2) the presence of another person who is greatly offended by the individual's behavior and is willing to sign a formal complaint, (3) refusal by a medical facility to accept the person, and (4) the officer's belief that the individual would continue to be a problem.[109]

The vast majority of the mentally ill are handled informally. These people fall into three general categories: neighborhood characters, troublemakers, and quiet, unobtrusive "mentals." Neighborhood characters are well known to the police and others in the community and are often referred to by nicknames such as "Crazy Harry" and "Mailbox Molly." Police officers know from previous contact that they are not dangerous. Informal methods for dealing with them include "cooling them out," which generally means talking with them to make certain they are not dangerous, to calm them down, and to reduce their more bizarre behavior. Troublemakers include people the police regard as too difficult to handle through formal means. Though their behavior might warrant arrest or hospitalization, the police decide that it would not be worth the effort. The unobtrusive "mentals" include people who have obvious signs of mental disturbance but whose behavior does not offend anyone to a serious degree.[110]

An important question is, "How accurate are police officers in identifying seriously mentally ill persons?" A report by PERF found that police recruits receive an average of only 4.3 hours of training in mental health problems.[111] Yet, a study of Toronto police officers found that their judgments about people correlated with those individuals' prior record of violence and were generally consistent with the clinical diagnoses by mental health professionals.[112]

Old Problems/New Programs

A report by PERF cited three model programs for handling the mentally ill. In Madison, Wisconsin, officers receive over 20 hours of training on mental health problems. Officers faced with difficult cases are able to confer with a 24-hour emergency mental health center run by the county. The Galveston County (Texas) sheriff's department dispatches six specially trained officers to all known mental health calls. The Birmingham (Alabama) police department sends social workers with police officers to the scene of mental health calls.[113]

A Justice Department report, meanwhile, emphasizes the importance of police departments establishing networks with social service agencies. The Los Angeles police department, for example, has a written agreement with the County Department of Mental Health to maintain a 24-hour unit available to police officers for consultation on difficult cases. The police department also created a special mental health evaluation unit, staffed by trained officers who screen all mental health cases.[114]

POLICING PEOPLE WITH AIDS

In the 1980s acquired immunodeficiency syndrome (AIDS) presented the police with a new set of problems. Because police officers often handle people with AIDS (PWAs), there is some risk of infection. Infected bodily fluids can be transmitted through biting, scratching, or spitting, or through throwing infected blood, urine, or feces at an officer. AIDS cannot be transmitted through casual physical contact such as touching, however.[115]

The Centers for Disease Control (CDC) estimates that 413,924 individuals in the United States are living with HIV or AIDS.[116] While the spread of the disease has been declining in general, it has been increasing in some populations such as minorities and females. While no studies to date have systematically assessed the risk of police officers being exposed to HIV, recent research examining HIV/AIDS among arrestees—a group of individuals with whom the police have frequent contact—shows that the potential for exposure to the police is higher than many other occupations. This is largely a consequence of the shift in policy toward more aggressive enforcement of substance abusers. In most cities across the country about 60 to 70 percent of those who are arrested by the police are current drug users, many of whom are injection drug users, placing them at higher risk for HIV infection.[117]

While the concern among police officers about contracting AIDS is high, few if any officers have contracted the disease. A survey by the FBI reports that between 1981 and 1991 seven police officers contracted HIV from a work-related exposure. However, recent research conducted by the Centers for Disease Control (CDC) found that not a single officer in the United States has ever contracted HIV/AIDS as a result of a work-related exposure.[118]

Flavin points out that even though the risk of contracting HIV/AIDS is low for police officers, it poses a unique threat. First, HIV/AIDS is contracted through a small microbe rather than a readily observable threat, such as a person or situation. Second, if an officer is exposed to HIV, it takes 3 to 6 months to know whether or not the officer has contracted the virus. Third, unlike most threats that the police are exposed to, HIV/AIDS is an incurable and deadly disease.[119]

As a consequence of the fear of contracting HIV/AIDS a number of officers have become reluctant to render medical assistance. In a study of one police department 30 percent of officers stated that they avoid helping people because of their fear of contracting HIV/AIDS.[120] In other studies researchers have found that most police officers attempt to take precautions to minimize their chances of contracting the disease, such as wearing latex gloves when assisting someone who is bleeding. However, with this said, precautions are not always possible, and as a result, officers sometimes do not render assistance and instead wait for medical personnel to take care of any medical problems.[121]

The fear of contracting HIV/AIDS has also led a number of police agencies to unofficially keep records of infected individuals. When the police agency receives a call for service, the dispatcher will notify the responding officer if the individual with whom the officer will be coming into contact is HIV positive. This practice is intended to protect officers from unknowingly placing themselves at risk. However, the collection of such information may lead to the violation of a person's right to privacy. Persons with HIV/AIDS are often the subject of prejudice and discrimination. For example, in Kokomo, Indiana, a waiter lost his job as a consequence of a police officer informing the restaurant's management that the waiter was HIV positive—information that the officer had obtained while working on the job. The waiter later sued the City of Kokomo and was awarded $60,000, and the police department was ordered to educate its officers on issues of confidentiality.[122]

A Justice Department report recommended that all law enforcement agencies provide HIV/AIDS-related education and training for their officers, and develop formal policies for the handling of HIV-positive individuals in routine encounters, arrest situations, and police lock-ups.[123] By 1996 approximately 86 percent of state police departments offered HIV/AIDS training to recruits during basic training and 78 percent offered it through in-service training.[124] Almost half of all agencies are required to offer such training to meet state legal requirements. A study of sheriffs' deputies in Durham, North Carolina, found that officers who had better knowledge about HIV/AIDS and its transmission were less fearful of contracting the disease themselves.[125]

POLICING JUVENILES

Juveniles represent a special set of problems for the police. First, the police have a high level of contact with people under the age of 18. Young people are more likely to be out on the street than adults, where the police observe them. "Hanging out" on the corner or "cruising" in cars often produces citizen conflict over the proper use of public spaces.

Second, young people consistently express more negative attitudes toward the police than older people. In a 1995 survey, 72 percent of people between the ages of 18 and 29 expressed favorable attitudes with respect to the fairness of the police, compared with 90 percent for people in the 40- to 49-year-old age group.[126]

Third, juveniles represent a significant aspect of the crime problem in the United States: 18.7 percent of all arrests, 30.3 percent of all index crime arrests, and 35 percent of all property crime arrests. Juveniles are involved in three crimes at a particularly high rate: 52.2 percent of all arson arrests, 47.7 percent of all vandalism arrests, and 34.1 percent of all motor vehicle theft arrests.[127] Even more serious, homicides by juveniles soared between the mid-1980s and the early 1990s, while homicides by adults were declining.[128] Moreover, there was a sharp increase in firearms-related homicides by juveniles. Part of the murder and firearms problem is due to the increase in gang activity by juveniles.

Controversy over the Police Role

There is significant controversy over the proper police role toward juveniles. Some people favor a strict law enforcement role, emphasizing the arrest of offenders. Others prefer a crime prevention role, arguing that the police should emphasize helping young people who are at risk with advice, counseling, and alternatives to arrest.[129] The International Association of Chiefs of Police (IACP) recommends a middle-of-the-road approach: "Most police departments operate juvenile programs that combine the law enforcement and delinquency prevention roles, and the police should work with the juvenile court to determine a role that is most suitable for the community."[130]

Uncertain or conflicting department policies regarding juveniles often cause role conflict in police officers on the street. One report on police–juvenile operations pointed out that "crime prevention can be viewed as 'social work,' a role that police often see as taking time away from what they consider to be their primary role—the apprehension of criminals."[131]

Police response to juveniles is complicated by conflicting police responsibilities (see Chapter 1). The case of kids hanging out on the streets illustrates the problem. On the one hand, the police are expected to maintain order. To this end, a number of cities have passed curfews for juveniles and/or "gang loitering" ordinances. At the same time, however, the police have a responsibility to respect the rights of citizens. Young people have a First Amendment right to assemble in public.

Because of increased public fear of crime and violent juvenile crime in particular, police departments have given greater emphasis to the law enforcement role in recent years. With the exception of programs such as D.A.R.E. (see below), traditional crime prevention programs have been deemphasized.

Specialized Juvenile Units

Most police contacts with juveniles are divided between two units within the department: patrol and specialized juvenile units. Patrol officers have the most contact with juveniles as part of their normal patrol duty. They regularly see and have contact with groups of kids hanging out on the street corner, people they suspect to be gang members, and so on.

Most large police departments have special juvenile units. They are often referred to by such names as the juvenile division, the youth division, or the crime prevention bureau. In 1997, 67 percent of all municipal police departments had a special juvenile unit. Many departments also had special child abuse and missing children units. The D.A.R.E. (Drug Abuse Resistance Education) program, where police officers provide drug education in the schools, is extremely popular. Currently, about 81 percent of all police departments have a special unit for drug education in the schools.[133]

The responsibilities of traditional juvenile units typically include (1) investigating reports of juvenile crime, (2) arresting delinquents, (3) preparing cases for court, and (4) appearing in court. However, some juvenile units have other responsibilities as well. For example, in the Ross, Pennsylvania, police department the juvenile unit is responsible not only for investigating juvenile criminal behavior and the processing of cases but also

---

SIDEBAR 5–5   DO JUVENILE CURFEW LAWS WORK?

Today 80 percent of large-sized cities (cities with a population of 100,000 or more) and 75 percent of medium-sized cities (cities with a population between 10,000 and 100,000) have juvenile curfew laws. These laws are intended to decrease the opportunity for youths to commit delinquency by prohibiting them from being in public areas in the evening and at night unless an adult accompanies them. The idea is that curfew laws will lead to the reduction of delinquency by decreasing youth access to environments associated with delinquency and by increasing the amount of parental supervision. However, research has found curfew laws to be ineffective in reducing delinquency. Most of the research has indicated that curfew laws have no impact on victimization or juvenile arrests or that crime is displaced to time periods that are not impacted by curfew laws.[132]

These findings present several questions for consideration:

1 Why are these laws popular?
2 Why are these laws ineffective?
3 Does your city have a curfew law? If so, how many youths a year are arrested for a curfew violation?

for (1) investigating offenses against children, including abuse, neglect, or exploitation; (2) acting as a liaison to juvenile justice agencies (e.g., courts and probation) and schools; and (3) maintaining all juvenile records within the police department.[134]

Juvenile units tend to be small and, according to one study, are declining in significance. Bittner, however, found that police juvenile units occupied low status in most police departments and officers regarded most juvenile-related incidents as trivial.[135]

On-the-Street Encounters

Black and Reiss found that 72 percent of all encounters between police and juveniles were initiated by a telephone call. Officers appear to initiate contacts with juveniles at a slightly higher rate (28 percent of all contacts) than with adults.[136] This is due to the fact that young people are more likely to be out on the street than adults, and the police are more likely to regard juveniles as criminal suspects.

As is the case with all other police activities, officers exercise great discretion in dealing with juveniles on the street (see Chapter 8). The alternative police responses include the following.[137]

1 Taking no official action. This is the most common outcome. As is the case with domestic disputes and allegedly mentally disturbed people, the police dispose of situations informally, mainly just by talking with people. Talking may involve advising, warning, mediating disputes, or simply listening. In many instances no arrest is made even though there are sufficient legal grounds to make an arrest.

2 Taking a juvenile into custody but releasing him or her to a parent or guardian. An estimated 30 percent of all juveniles taken into custody are released in this fashion.[138]

3 Taking the juvenile into custody and releasing him or her to another law enforcement or social service agency. About 3 percent of all juveniles taken into custody are released in this fashion.[139]

4 Arresting the juvenile and referring him or her to juvenile court. About two-thirds of all juveniles are referred to juvenile court. Some (about 7 percent of the total) are referred to criminal court for prosecution as adults.[140]

Arrest discretion involving juveniles is influenced by the same situational factors that affect encounters with adults. These factors include the seriousness of the offense, the preference of the victim or complaining party, the relationship between complainant and suspect, and the demeanor of the suspect.[141]

The Issue of Race Discrimination

The police arrest proportionately far more African American juveniles than white. Several factors account for this disparity. First, police departments generally assign more patrol officers to minority neighborhoods than white neighborhoods (see Chapter 4) and, consequently, observe minority youths more frequently.[142]

Second, minority youths are stopped and questioned at a higher rate than whites. The San Diego Field Interrogation study found that minorities were stopped for questioning at rates disproportionate to their presence in particular neighborhoods.[143]

Third, the racial disparity in arrests is associated with other factors that influence arrest decisions. Black and Reiss found that the higher arrest rate was explained in large part by greater African American involvement in serious crime. When seriousness of the suspected offense was controlled, blacks and whites were arrested at similar rates.[144] Lundman, meanwhile, found that black adults are more likely to ask the police to arrest the suspect than are white adults. Since most complainant–suspect situations are intraracial, black juveniles are arrested at a higher rate.[145] Smith, Visher, and Davidson, in a study of arrests involving persons of all ages, found that police are slightly more likely to arrest when the victim is white rather than African American. Other studies have also suggested that the police are more likely to arrest a juvenile when an adult is the complaining party.[146]

The demeanor of the suspect also influences police arrest decisions. In separate studies, Black and Reiss and also Piliavin and Briar found that African American juveniles expressed hostility toward the police more often than did whites and, as a consequence, were arrested at higher rates. Piliavin and Briar described the phenomenon as the "self-fulfilling consequences of the original set of police attitudes and behavior toward black youth." The police expect black juveniles to engage in more law breaking, stop and question them at a higher rate, and as a consequence create the perception of harassment and generate more hostile reactions.[147] David Klinger, however, has raised new questions about the role of demeanor in arrests, arguing that these earlier studies did not control for hostile behavior that occurred after the arrest and therefore could not have influenced the arrest itself.[148]

Crime Prevention Programs

Police crime prevention efforts have traditionally involved programs designed to steer juveniles away from criminal activity through education, counseling, or role modeling. The basic idea is for the police to present themselves as friends and helpers rather than as law enforcers.

Some current crime prevention programs are part of community policing. The Spokane police department, for example, ran a COPY Kids program in 1992. About 300 youths, both male and female, with a median age of 13, spent a week in the program. Police officers and volunteers conducted drug education and other information programs, led the kids in neighborhood clean-up and graffiti eradication, and supervised recreation programs. The officers wore plainclothes at the beginning of the week, but wore their uniforms at the end when they felt they had established rapport with the kids. The purpose of the program was to establish positive relations between the police and at-risk juveniles, to provide information on specific topics such as drugs, and to reinforce the idea that hard work and productivity are rewarded. Follow-up interviews with the kids, the staff, and parents found positive results. The evaluation did not, however, survey either drug use or involvement in crime before and after the program.[149]

The most popular current crime prevention programs are D.A.R.E. and G.R.E.A.T., which attempt to prevent drug use, delinquency, and gang participation and activity. These police prevention strategies will be covered in Chapter 6.

SUMMARY

Order maintenance and peacekeeping is an important part of policing for the simple reason that most calls for service fall in this category. How the police respond to these calls raises the basic issues about the police role that we discussed in Chapter 1. How do we think about the police? What do we want them to do?

Traditionally, police officers regarded order maintenance calls as garbage and social work, placing a higher value on crime fighting. Most experts today, however, argue that maintaining order and keeping the peace is a central aspect of policing. Community policing, problem-oriented policing, and zero-tolerance policing place a high value on dealing with noncrime problems. Many order maintenance situations, moreover, involve special populations: the homeless, the mentally ill, the chronic alcoholic. If we think of the police in terms proposed by Herman Goldstein, as a general service agency providing a wide range of services to the public, it becomes important for police departments to develop special programs and procedures to improve the handling of these problem situations.[150]

CASE STUDY: WESTMINSTER, CALIFORNIA, POLICE DEPARTMENT'S SHIELD PROGRAM

The SHIELD program is designed to accomplish two primary goals. First, it uses the contacts that police officers make in the course of their normal duties to identify youth who they think are likely to become involved in violent behavior, substance abuse, and gang activities. At-risk youth are identified as those who are exposed to family risk factors such as domestic violence and other criminal activities in the home. Second, SHIELD provides youth with services that are tailored to meet their individual needs by using a multidisciplinary team of representatives from the community, schools, and service agencies.

The primary mechanism that supports these goals is the youth referral process. At the outset of the SHIELD program, all officers in Westminster were given the following orders as part of the youth referral protocol.

Police personnel are required to obtain the name, age, and school attended of any minor youth living in a home where a report is filed involving the following police activity: family violence of any type, neglect or abandonment, gang activity, drug sales or usage, arrests made associated with alcohol abuse, or any other call for service where the welfare of minor youth is at risk due to the behavior of older siblings or adults living in, or frequenting, the home.

Whenever an officer responds to an incident or makes an arrest, he or she completes a standard report to document the details of the contact. If the officer identifies a youth as having been exposed to risk factors, he or she marks a box on the police report and forwards a full copy of the report through departmental channels to the SHIELD resource officer (SRO).

On receiving a report, the SRO assumes responsibility for administering the SHIELD program and screens the case to determine whether the circumstances make the youth appropriate for SHIELD intervention. In the early stages of the program, the SRO simply used the family risk factors that were noted in the youth referral protocol to verify that the reporting officer had correctly identified a youth from the target population. These instruments are used to strengthen the screening process and prioritize access to services based on the level of risk each youth faces. The risk assessment instruments enable the SRO to place youth in low-, medium-, or high-risk categories for both general delinquency and gang involvement.

If the SRO deems a case appropriate for SHIELD intervention, he or she creates a student referral report, which contains a short synopsis of the incident as it pertains to the youth, demographic information about the youth and his or her family, contact information for the parents, and information from the assessments of both risk and protective factors. The SRO then sends the student referral report to the Youth and Family Resource Team. This multidisciplinary team includes officials from the local school district, such as the pupil personnel administrator, the district nurse, a specialist in drug abuse prevention, and school principals; counseling staff from a community service provider; a county social worker; the Westminster Community Services Recreation Supervisor; the SRO; and a second officer formerly assigned to Drug Abuse Resistance Education (D.A.R.E.). Beyond the core group of members who attend regular weekly meetings, the team may invite additional members, such as teachers and school counselors, who are familiar with a given youth. The disclosure of confidential information to such a multidisciplinary team for use in prevention and intervention is authorized by the State of California's Welfare and Institutions Codes, sections 827–830.

When they receive the student referral report, the members of the Youth and Family Resource Team consider a range of school- and community-based treatment options and make recommendations for treatment. However, treatment recommendations are often enhanced by information that goes beyond the original student referral report. Team members familiar with the youth frequently provide additional information that allows the team to understand the youth's circumstances more fully. This sharing of information leads to better informed treatment recommendations than would be provided by any agency or service provider working alone.

Depending on the recommendation, treatment may or may not require parental consent. For example, if the Youth and Family Resource Team recommends that a youth receive individual counseling from a community treatment provider, parental consent generally is necessary. However, in cases where the team recommends informal school-based monitoring of the youth, no parental consent is required. Treatment providers such as school counselors and community-based service providers are generally responsible for getting parental consent when it is necessary. In the early stages of the program, treatment providers were also responsible for notifying parents of their child's referral to the SHIELD program. Some parents were upset when they learned that the police department had referred their child to the program. Because many youth in this program are exposed to domestic violence, the parent who is in the position to provide consent for treatment may also be the one who created the risk factors in the home or allowed them to exist in the first place. Therefore, the process of obtaining parental consent is often delicate. In response to this issue, the SRO now contacts parents directly when their child is referred to the program. During this contact, the SRO describes the program and addresses any questions or concerns that the parents have. The SRO will make two attempts to contact a parent by telephone and will resort to sending a letter only if these two attempts are unsuccessful.

In some cases, the SRO makes home visits. The Youth and Family Resource Team reassesses the treatment recommendations and progress of each youth 3 weeks after the initial recommendation. While a youth is involved in treatment, the service providers send monthly progress reports to the SHIELD staff at the Westminster police department. These reports allow for ongoing tracking and reassessment of the services provided to program youth.

It should be noted that SHIELD relies on services that are already in the community. The program works closely with all of the local schools and the local Boys & Girls Club. During the first year of the program, 60 percent of youth who were referred to SHIELD received services in some form. Individual and group counseling were commonly used in both school and community settings. Issues covered in counseling varied based on the circumstances of the individual youth, but common themes included anger management, goal setting, pregnancy prevention, conflict resolution, and other coping skills. In some cases, treatment plans for youth were more specialized. For example, one youth who had a history of drug involvement and exposure to family violence served as an assistant instructor for a summer program on drug use prevention and received individual counseling related to setting and achieving goals.

Informal school-based monitoring is also frequently included in treatment plans. Informal monitoring may be used in conjunction with other treatment or as a stand-alone treatment when the youth shows a low level of risk in conjunction with many protective factors or when parental consent for more intensive treatment is not granted. When teachers and administrators are aware of the risk factors that a student faces outside the classroom and they are actively monitoring that student, they are more likely to detect and respond to early signs of problem behavior, abuse, or neglect.

Source: The above was adapted from Phelan Wyrick, *Law Enforcement Referral of At-Risk Youth: The SHIELD Program* (Washington DC: Office of Juvenile Justice and Delinquency Prevention: 2000).

FOR DISCUSSION

1 Describe four reasons why the public calls the police in situations not involving a crime.
2 Briefly explain why deaths involving drunken driving have declined over the past 50 years.
3 Explain how domestic violence policies evolved in local police departments across the United States.
4 Discuss the research findings on the impact of mandatory arrest for misdemeanor domestic violence.
5 Explain the difference between streetwalkers and call girls, and discuss how each might have an impact on order maintenance and peacekeeping.
6 Why are specialized juvenile units becoming less popular in police departments?

INTERNET EXERCISES

Exercise 1 How many people in your community have HIV/AIDS? Check with your department of public health or check **http://www.hivsite.ucsf.edu/map** for local and national statistics.

Exercise 2 Check out the website **http://www.ojp.usdoj.gov/vawo/.** This site has a number of resources regarding domestic violence.

Exercise 3 The National Task Force on Prostitution (NTFP) was founded in 1979 to act as an umbrella organization for prostitutes and prostitutes' rights organizations in different parts of the United States. In 1994, its purpose was expanded to involve organizations and individuals who support the rights of prostitutes and other sex workers. Go to the website **http://www.bayswan.org/NTFP.html** to understand the activities of the organization. As a class discuss what you think about the organization and its possible impact on communities and prostitution as a profession.

Exercise 4 Go to the website **http://www.nlchp.org** to find information related to the homeless problem in the United States. The site is filled with information about why people are homeless, how the homeless live, and laws and policies regarding the homeless.

REFERENCES

1 Peter E. Finn and Monique Sullivan, *Police Response to Special Populations* (Washington, DC: Government Printing Office, 1988).
2 Albert Reiss, *The Police and the Public* (New Haven, CT: Yale University Press, 1971).
3 Stephen Mastrofski, "The Police and Non-crime Services," in G. Whitaker and C. Phillips, eds., *Evaluating the Performance of Criminal Justice Agencies* (Beverly Hills, CA: Sage, 1983), pp. 44–47.
4 Herman Goldstein, *Policing a Free Society* (Cambridge, MA: Ballinger, 1977), pp. 21–44.
5 Herman Goldstein, *Problem-Oriented Policing* (New York: McGraw-Hill, 1990); James Q. Wilson and George L. Kelling, "Broken Windows: The Police and Neighborhood Safety," *Atlantic Monthly,* 249 (March 1982): 29–38.
6 Egon Bittner, "Florence Nightingale in Pursuit of Willie Sutton: A Theory of the Police," in Herbert Jacob, ed., *The Potential for Reform of Criminal Justice* (Beverly Hills, CA: Sage, 1974), pp. 1–25.
7 Samuel Walker, *Popular Justice: A History of American Criminal Justice,* 2nd ed. (New York: Oxford University Press, 1998), pp. 165–167.
8 John C. Meyer, "Patterns of Reporting Noncriminal Incidents to the Police," *Criminology,* 12 (May 1974): 70–83.
9 David H. Bayley and James Garofalo, "The Management of Violence by Police Patrol Officers," *Criminology,* 27 (February 1989): 1–25.

10 Stephen D. Mastrofski, Jeffrey B. Snipes, and Anne E. Supina, "Compliance on Demand: The Public's Response to Specific Requests," *Journal of Research in Crime and Delinquency,* 33 (August 1996): 269–305; John McCluskey, Stephen Mastrofski, and Roger Parks, "To Acquiesce or Rebel: Predicting Citizen Compliance with Police Requests," *Police Quarterly,* 2, no. 4 (1999): 389–416.

11 William Westley, *Violence and the Police* (Cambridge, MA: MIT Press, 1970), p. 57.

12 Federal Bureau of Investigation, *Law Enforcement Officers Killed and Assaulted, 1994* (Washington, DC: Government Printing Office, 1995).

13 PERF, *Survey of Police Operational and Administrative Practices—1981.* (Washington, DC: PERF, 1981), pp. 22–23.

14 John A. Gardiner, *Traffic and the Police: Variations in Law Enforcement Policy* (Cambridge, MA: Harvard University Press, 1969).

15 James Q. Wilson, *Varieties of Police Behavior* (New York: Atheneum, 1973), pp. 95–99.

16 Ibid.

17 Alexander Weiss and Sally Freels, "The Effects of Aggressive Policing: The Dayton Traffic Enforcement Experiment," *American Journal of Police,* XV, no. 3 (1996): 45–64.

18 Ibid.

19 James B. Jacobs, *Drunk Driving: An American Dilemma* (Chicago: University of Chicago Press, 1989); H. Laurence Ross, *Confronting Drunk Driving: Social Policy for Saving Lives* (New Haven, CT: Yale University Press, 1992).

20 Ross, *Confronting Drunk Driving.*

21 Ross, *Confronting Drunk Driving*; Jacobs, *Drunk Driving.*

22 Ibid.

23 Eric J. Scott, *Calls for Service: Citizen Demand and Initial Police Response* (Washington, DC: Government Printing Office, 1981); Craig D. Uchida, Laure Brooks and Christopher S. Kopers, "Danger to Police during Domestic Encounters: Assaults on Baltimore County Police, 1984–1986," *Criminal Justice Policy Review,* 2 (1987): 357–371.

24 Jeffrey Fagan, *The Criminalization of Domestic Violence: Promises and Limits* (Washington, DC: Government Printing Office, 1996); Lawrence W. Sherman, *Policing Domestic Violence: Experiments and Dilemmas* (New York: The Free Press, 1992).

25 Donald Black, "Dispute Settlement by the Police," in Black, *The Manners and Customs of the Police* (New York: Academic Press, 1980), pp. 109–192.

26 Ibid., p. 112.

27 Callie Rennison and Sarah Welchans, *Intimate Partner Violence* (Washington, DC: Bureau of Justice Statistics, 2000).

28 Murray A. Straus and Richard J. Gelles, *Physical Violence in American Families: Risk Factors and Adaptation to Violence in 8,145 Families* (New Brunswick, NJ: Transaction, 1990).

29 Mark A. Schulman, *A Survey of Spousal Violence against Women in Kentucky* (Washington, DC: Government Printing Office, 1979).

30 Rennison and Welchans, *Intimate Partner Violence.*

31 Suzanne K. Steinmetz, "The Battered Husband Syndrome," *Victimology,* 2, no. 3/4 (1978): 499–509.

32 Richard Gelles and Murray Straus, *Intimate Violence: The Causes and Consequences of Abuse in the American Family* (New York: Touchstone Books, 1988), p. 150.

33 Bureau of Justice Statistics, *Intimate Partner Violence* (Washington, DC: Government Printing Office, 2000).

34 *Code of Iowa* (1997), V. II, Sec. 236.11.

35 Rennison and Welchans, *Intimate Partner Violence.*

36 Franklyn W. Dunford, David Huizinga, Delbert S. Elliot, "The Role of Arrest in Domestic Assault: The Omaha Police Experiment," *Criminology,* 28 (May 1990): 183–206. Some of these data appear in the unpublished technical report.

37 Schulman, *A Survey of Spousal Violence.*

38 Rennison and Welchans, *Intimate Partner Violence.*

39 Schulman, *A Survey of Spousal Violence.*

40 Black, "Dispute Settlement by the Police," pp. 125–126.

41 Bureau of Justice Statistics, *Intimate Partner Violence.*

42 Wayne Hanewicz et al., "Improving the Linkages between Domestic Violence Referral Agencies and the Police," *Journal of Criminal Justice,* 10, no. 6 (1982): 493–503.

43 Dunford, Huizinga, and Elliott, "The Role of Arrest in Domestic Assault."

44 Gelles and Straus, *Intimate Violence,* p. 104.

45 Joel Garner and Elizabeth Clemmer, *Danger to Police in Domestic Disturbances—A New Look* (Washington, DC: Government Printing Office, 1986).

46 Uchida, Brooks, and Kopers, "Danger to Police during Domestic Encounters."

47 Black, "Dispute Settlement by the Police," p. 146.

48 Mastrofski, Snipes, and Supina, "Compliance on Demand."

49 Ibid., p. 181.

50 Dunford, Huizinga, and Elliott, "The Role of Arrest in Domestic Assault."

51 Hanewicz et al., "Improving the Linkages between Domestic Violence Referral Agencies and the Police."

52 Donald Black, "Dispute Settlement by the Police," p. 129.

53 Donald Black, "The Social Organization of Arrest," in Black, *The Manners and Customs of the Police* (New York: Academic Press, 1980).

54 Sara Fenstermaker Berk and Donileen R. Loeske, " 'Handling' Family Violence: Situational Determinants of Police Arrest in Domestic Disturbances," *Law and Society Review,* 15 (1980–1981): 317–346; Robert E. Worden and Alissa A. Pollitz, "Police Arrest in Domestic Disturbances: Another Look," in Gordon P. Whitaker, ed., *Understanding Police Agency Performance* (Washington, DC: Government Printing Office, 1984), pp. 77–92.

55 Nancy Loving, *Responding to Spouse Abuse and Wife Beating: A Guide for Police* (Washington, DC: Police Executive Research Forum, 1980), p. 42.

56 International Association of Chiefs of Police, *Training Key #16,* "Handling Disturbance Calls" (Gaithersburg, MD: IACP, 1977).

57 Morton Bard, *Training Police as Specialists in Family Crisis Intervention* (Washington, DC: Government Printing Office, 1970).

58 Albert Reiss, *The Police and the Public* (New Haven, CT: Yale University Press, 1971), p. 14.

59 Loving, *Responding to Spouse Abuse and Wife Beating: A Guide for Police;* Laurie Woods, "Litigation on Behalf of Battered Women," *Women's Rights Law Reporter,* 5 (Fall 1978): 7–34.

60 Loving, *Responding to Spouse Abuse and Wife Beating.*

61 Samuel Walker, *Taming the System: The Control of Discretion in Criminal Justice, 1950–1990* (New York: Oxford University Press, 1993).

62 Lawrence W. Sherman and Richard A. Berk, "The Specific Deterrent Effect of Arrest for Domestic Assault," *American Sociological Review,* 49, no. 2 (1984): 261–272; Sherman, *Policing Domestic Violence,* pp. 95–91.

63 Sherman, *Policing Domestic Violence,* p. 110.

64 Bureau of Justice Statistics, *Law Enforcement Management and Administrative Statistics, 1997* (Washington, DC: Government Printing Office, 1999).

65 Patrick R. Gartin, "Examining Differential Officer Effects in the Minneapolis Domestic Violence Experiment," *American Journal of Police,* XIV, no. 3/4 (1995): 93–110.

66 Richard E. Lempert, "From the Editor," *Law and Society Review,* 18, no. 4 (1984): 505–513; Lawrence W. Sherman and Ellen G. Cohn, "The Impact of Research on Legal Policy: The Minneapolis Domestic Violence Experiment," *Law and Society Review,* 23, no. 1 (1989): 117–144; Richard Lempert, "Humility as a Virtue: On the Publicization of Policy-Relevant Research," *Law and Society Review,* 23, no. 1 (1989): 145–161; Sherman, *Policing Domestic Violence,* pp. 92–124.

67 University of Maryland, *Preventing Crime* (Washington, DC: Government Printing Office, 1997), Ch. 8.

68 Lawrence Sherman, Janell Schmidt, and Dennis Rogan, *Policing Domestic Violence: Experiments and Dilemmas* (New York: Free Press, 1992).

69 Bureau of Justice Statistics, *Sourcebook of Criminal Justice Statistics—1995* (Washington, DC: Government Printing Office, 1996), p. 403.

70 M. Martin, "Double Your Trouble: Dual Arrest in Family Violence," *Journal of Family Violence,* 12, no. 2 (1997): 139–157.

71 Susan L. Miller, "Unintended Side Effects of Pro-Arrest Policies and Their Race and Class Implications for Battered Women: A Cautionary Note," *Criminal Justice Policy Review,* 3, no. 3 (1989): 299–317.

72 National Institute of Justice, *Evaluation of Family Violence Training Programs* (Washington, DC: Government Printing Office, 1995).

73 Joan Zorza, "The Criminal Law of Misdemeanor Domestic Violence, 1970–1990," *Journal of Criminal Law and Criminology,* 83 (1992): 240–279.

74 Barbara J. Hart, *State Codes on Domestic Violence* (Reno, NV: National Council of Juvenile and Family Court Judges, 1992); Eve Buzawa and Carl Buzawa, *Domestic Violence: The Criminal Justice Response* (Newbury Park, CA: Sage, 1990), pp. 110–135.

75 Fagan, *The Criminalization of Domestic Violence,* p. 1.

76 Sherman, *Policing Domestic Violence,* p. 253.
77 Robert F. Meier and Gilbert Geis, *Victimless Crime?* (Los Angeles: Roxbury, 1997).
78 Wayne R. LaFave, *Arrest* (Boston: Little, Brown, 1965).
79 Jerome Skolnick, *Justice without Trial,* 3rd ed. (New York: Macmillan, 1994), pp. 94–104.
80 Diana Lewis, *The Prostitute and Her Clients* (Springfield, IL: Charles C. Thomas, 1985).
81 Cudore L.Shell, *Young Men in the Street* (Westport, CT: Praeger, 1994); Robert P. McNamara, *The Times Square Hustler* (Westport, CT: Praeger, 1994).
82 Egon Bittner, "The Police on Skid Row: A Study of Peacekeeping," in Bittner, *Aspects of Police Work* (Boston: Northeastern University Press, 1990), pp. 30–62.
83 LaFave, "Arrest to Control the Prostitute," in *Arrest,* pp. 450–464.
84 Ibid.
85 Department of Justice, *Gambling Law Enforcement in Major American Cities* (Washington, DC: Government Printing Office, 1978).
86 President's Commission on Law Enforcement and Administration of Justice, *The Challenge of Crime in a Free Society* (Washington, DC: Government Printing Office, 1967), pp. 187–210.
87 LaFave, *Arrest,* pp. 471–482.
88 Egon Bittner, "The Police on Skid Row: A Study in Peacekeeping," *American Sociological Review,* 32 (October 1967): 694–715.
89 Christopher Jencks, *The Homeless* (Cambridge, MA: Harvard University Press, 1994).
90 "Redevelopment Plans May Hem in Skid Row," *The New York Times* (October 23, 1997), p. 1.
91 George L. Kelling and Catherine M. Coles, *Fixing Broken Windows* (New York: The Free Press, 1996).
92 Barney Melekian, "Police and the Homeless," *FBI Law Enforcement Bulletin* (November 1990).
93 Colleen Cosgrove and Anne Grant, *National Survey of Municipal Police Departments on Urban Quality of Life Initiatives, in Problem Oriented Policing,* Tara O'Connor Shelley and Anne Grant, eds. (Washington, DC: PERF, 1998).
94 David Snow and Leon Anderson, *Down on Their Luck* (Berkeley, CA: University of California Press, 1993).
95 Martha R. Plotkin and Ortwin A. Narr, *The Police Response to the Homeless: A Status Report* (Washington, DC: Police Executive Research Forum, 1993), Appendix, C-85–C-116.
96 David E. Aaronson, C. Thomas Dienes, and Michael C. Musheno, *Public Policy and Police Discretion* (New York: Clark Boardman, 1984), pp. 311–314.
97 President's Commission on Law Enforcement and Administration of Justice, *Task Force Report: Drunkenness* (Washington, DC: Government Printing Office, 1967).
98 Raymond T. Nimmer, *Two Million Unnecessary Arrests* (Chicago: American Bar Foundation, 1971).
99 Ibid., p. 96.

100 Aaronson, Dienes, and Musheno, *Public Policy and Police Discretion,* pp. 311–314; Federal Bureau of Investigation, *Crime in the United States, 1999* (Washington DC: Government Printing Office, 2000).

101 Linda Teplin, *Keeping the Peace: Parameters of Police Discretion in Relation to the Mentally Disordered* (Washington, DC: Government Printing Office, 1986).

102 Linda Teplin, "The Prevalence of Severe Mental Disorder among Male Urban Jail Detainees: Comparison with the Epidemiological Catchment Area Program," *American Journal of Public Health,* 80, no. 6 (1990): 663–669.

103 Robert Panzarella and Justin Alicea, "Police Tactics in Incidents with Mentally Disturbed Persons," *Policing: International Journal of Police Strategies and Management,* 20, no. 2 (1997): 339–356.

104 Ibid.

105 M. Pogrebin, "Police Responses for Mental Health Assistance," *Psychiatric Quarterly,* 58, no. 1 (1986–87): 66–73.

106 Teplin, *Keeping the Peace.*

107 Panzarella and Alicea, "Police Tactics in Incidents with Mentally Disturbed Persons."

108 Teplin, *Keeping the Peace.*

109 Ibid.

110 Ibid.

111 Police Executive Research Forum, *Special Care: Improving Police Response to the Mentally Disabled* (Washington, DC: PERF, 1988).

112 Robert J. Menzies, "Psychiatrists in Blue: Police Apprehension of Mental Disorder and Dangerousness," *Criminology,* 25 (August 1987): 429–453; Henry J. Steadman et al., "Psychiatric Evaluations of Police Referrals in a General Hospital Emergency Room," *International Journal of Law and Psychiatry,* 8, no. 1 (1986): 39–47.

113 Police Executive Research Forum, *Special Care.*

114 Peter E. Finn and Monique Sullivan, *Police Response to Special Populations* (Washington, DC: Government Printing Office, 1988).

115 Theodore M. Hammett, *AIDS and the Law Enforcement Officer: Concerns and Policy Responses* (Washington, DC: Government Printing Office, 1987).

116 CDC-NCHSTP-DHAP: HIV/AIDS Surveillance Report, Vol. 12, No. 1. **http://www.cdc.gov/hiv/stats/hasr1201/table1.htm**

117 National Institute of Justice, *1999 Annual Report on Drug Use among Adult and Juvenile Arrestees* (Washington, DC: National Institute of Justice, 1999).

118 R. Alan Thompson and James Marquart, "Law Enforcement Responses to the HIV/AIDS Epidemic," *Policing: An International Journal of Police Strategies and Management,* 21, no. 4 (1998): 648–665; Jeanne Flavin, "Police and HIV/AIDS: The Risk, the Reality, the Response," *American Journal of Criminal Justice,* 23, no. 1 (1998): 33–58.

119 Flavin, "Police and HIV/AIDS: The Risk, the Reality, the Response."

120 C. Herlitz and B. Brorsson, "Facing AIDS: Reactions among Police Officers, Nurses and the General Public in Sweden," *Social Science Medicine,* 30 (1990): 913–918.

121 Flavin, "Police and HIV/AIDS: The Risk, the Reality, the Response."

122 Ibid.

123 Theodore M. Hammett, *AIDS and the Law Enforcement Officer: Concerns and Policy Responses.*

124 Terry Edwards and Richard Tewksbury. "HIV/AIDS: State Police Training Practices and Personnel Policies," *American Journal of Police,* 15, no. 1 (1996): 45–62.

125 Douglas Yearwood, "Law Enforcement and AIDS: Knowledge, Attitudes, and Fears in the Workplace," *American Journal of Police,* 11, no. 2 (1992): 65–83.

126 W. S. Wilson Huang and Michael S. Vaughn, "Support and Confidence: Public Attitudes toward the Police," in Timothy J. Flanagan and Dennis R. Longmire, eds., *Americans View Crime and Justice: A National Public Opinion Survey* (Newbury Park, CA: Sage Publications, 1996), p. 40.

127 Bureau of Justice Statistics, *Sourcebook of Criminal Justice Statistics—1998* (Washington, DC: Government Printing Office, 1999).

128 James Alan Fox, *Trends in Juvenile Violence* (Washington, DC: Government Printing Office, 1996).

129 National Institute for Juvenile Justice and Delinquency Prevention, *Police-Juvenile Operations: A Comparative Analysis of Standards and Practices,* V. 2 (Washington, DC: Government Printing Office, nd), pp. 3–10.

130 R. Kobetz and B. Borsage, *Juvenile Justice Administration* (Gaithersburg, MD: International Association of Chiefs of Police, 1973), p. 112.

131 National Institute for Juvenile Justice, *Police-Juvenile Operations,* V. 2, p. 3.

132 K. Michael Reynolds, Ruth Seydlitz, Pamela Jenkins, "Do Juvenile Curfew Laws Work? A Time-Series Analysis of the New Orleans Law," *Justice Quarterly,* 17, no. 1 (2000): 205–230.

133 Bureau of Justice Statistics, *Law Enforcement Management and Administrative Statistics, 1997* (Washington, DC: Government Printing Office, 1999).

134 http://trfn.clpgh.org/rosspd

135 Egon Bittner, "Policing Juveniles: The Social Context of Common Practice," in M. K. Rosenheim, ed., *Pursuing Justice for the Child* (Chicago: University of Chicago Press, 1976), p. 80.

136 Donald Black and Albert J. Reiss, "Police Control of Juveniles," *American Sociological Review,* 35 (February 1970: 63–77).

137 Adapted from Office of Juvenile Justice and Delinquency Prevention, *Police-Juvenile Operations,* V. 2, p. 57.

138 OJJDP, *Juvenile Offenders and Victims: A National Report* (Washington, DC: Government Printing Office, 1995).

139 Ibid.

140 Ibid.

141 Black and Reiss, "Police Control of Juveniles."

142 Samuel Walker, Cassia Spohn, and Miriam DeLone, *The Color of Justice,* 2nd ed. (Belmont, CA: Wadsworth, 2000), Ch. 4.

143 John E. Boydstun, *San Diego Field Interrogation: Final Report* (Washington, DC: The Police Foundation, 1975).

144 Black and Reiss, "Police Control of Juveniles."

145 Richard J. Lundman, "Police Control of Juveniles: A Replication," *Journal of Research in Crime and Delinquency,* 15 (1978): 74–91.

146 Douglas A. Smith, Christy A. Visher, and Laura A. Davidson, "Equity and Discretionary Justice: The Influence of Arrest on Police Arrest Decisions," *Journal of Criminal Law and Criminology,* 75 (Spring 1984): 234–249.

147 Carl Werthman and Irving Piliavin, "Gang Members and the Police," in David J. Bordua, ed., *The Police: Six Sociological Essays* (New York: Jorn Riley, 1968), pp. 58–59.

148 David Klinger, "Demeanor or Crime?: Why 'Hostile' Citizens Are More Likely to Be Arrested," *Criminology,* 32 (1994): 475–493.

149 Quint C. Thurman, Andrew Giacomazzi, and Phil Bogen, "Cops, Kids, and Community Policing—An Assessment of a Community Policing Demonstration," *Crime and Delinquency,* 39 (October 1993): 554–564.

150 Goldstein, *Policing a Free Society.*

CHAPTER SIX

The Police and Crime

CHAPTER OUTLINE

INTRODUCTION

Crime control is one of the major responsibilities of the police (see Chapter 1, Figure 1–1). This involves several specific activities: preventing crime, responding to criminal incidents, conducting criminal investigations, and arresting offenders.

This chapter examines the crime control activities of the police. It describes what the police do and gives special attention to the popular myths that surround the subject of the police and crime.

THE POLICE AND CRIME

People usually think about the subject of the police and crime in terms of patrol and arrests. The subject is actually far more complex, involving a number of different assumptions and strategies.

Crime Control Strategies

Lawrence W. Sherman provides the most systematic classification of the different crime control strategies used by the police, or potentially available to them.[1]

Proactive versus Reactive Some police anticrime strategies are proactive, in the sense that the police themselves initiate them. This reflects the police department's own sense of priorities. Most drug enforcement, for example, is proactive. Other strategies are reactive, in the sense that they occur in response to a citizen request for service. Citizen calls to report crimes involve a reactive police response.

General versus Specific Some police activities are general in the sense that they are directed at the community at large and not at any particular crime. Routine preventive patrol is the most important general crime control strategy. Specific crime control activities, on the other hand, are directed at particular crimes, places, offenders, or victims.

Particular Crimes Routine patrol and the 911 system are general service activities that respond to any and all types of crimes. Other programs are directed at particular crimes. These include drunk-driving crackdowns, drug or gang crackdowns, sting operations, or stakeouts designed to catch robbers.

Specific Places Routine patrol serves the community at large with no particular geographic focus. "Hot spots" programs, on the other hand, are directed at specific places that are believed to be the centers of high levels of criminal activity.

Specific Offenders Some anticrime activities are directed at particular offenders. The best examples are the repeat offender programs that target people suspected of currently committing high rates of serious crime.

Specific Victims Some anticrime programs are directed at victims rather than offenders. The most important of these are the domestic violence programs and policies adopted by many police departments. Mandatory arrest policies, for example, are designed to protect victims of domestic assault against future violence.

Crime Control Assumptions

Police and Citizens One of the basic issues with respect to the police and crime involves the underlying assumptions about the role of the police in relation to other social control mechanisms. Many people see the police, and the entire criminal justice system, as society's primary mechanism for controlling crime. As part of the professionalization movement, the police emphasized their crime-fighting role and staked out crime as their professional domain.[2] Many experts today believe that this definition of professionalism isolated the police and cut them off from the public. To correct this problem, advocates of community policing emphasize the development of close working relationships with neighborhood residents.[3] This approach is based on the assumption that citizens are coproducers of police services, including crime-fighting activities.[4]

Police and Other Social Institutions A 1997 report on crime prevention programs by the University of Maryland places police activities in the context of other social institutions. The report argues that the traditional distinction between law enforcement and crime prevention is not valid. Law enforcement tactics such as arrest are designed to prevent crime, through either deterrence or incapacitation. Thus, it is appropriate to place all programs and institutions on a single crime prevention continuum.[5]

The report identified seven institutions that play a role in preventing crime. They include communities, families, schools, labor markets, places (in the sense of specific locales), the police, and other criminal justice programs. This innovative approach makes two important points about crime prevention. First, it indicates that the police are only one of several institutions with some impact on crime and cannot be expected to bear the primary responsibility. Second, the report emphasizes the interdependence of the different institutions. Thus, effective school-based crime prevention programs depend upon strong families, which in turn depend on healthy communities and good labor markets. Just as school programs are dependent upon this larger social network, so is the effectiveness of police crime control programs.[6]

Measuring Effectiveness

Measuring the effectiveness of police crime control programs requires both meaningful definitions of what is to be measured as well as valid and reliable data on the expected outcomes. As is discussed below, there are serious problems with the traditional measures of police effectiveness. Moreover, the move toward community policing and problem-oriented policing involves different assumptions about what the police do and, consequently, different measures of effectiveness.[7]

Summary

The different police activities covered in this chapter can be classified according to strategy, the underlying assumptions, and performance measures.

PREVENTING CRIME

The primary crime prevention activity of the police is routine patrol. As Chapter 4 explained, the visible presence of police officers in the community is designed to deter individuals from committing a crime.

Patrol has only limited deterrent effect on crime, however. For example, the Kansas City Preventive Patrol Experiment (1972–1973) found that an increased level of preventative patrol officers does not reduce crime. Conversely, reducing the level of patrol does not lead to an increase in criminal activity.[8] Similarly, the Newark Foot Patrol Experiment found that increased levels of foot patrol do not reduce crime.[9]

The Kansas City and Newark experiments did not prove that patrol has no effect on crime. A certain amount of patrol does have some deterrent effect. The experiments proved only that adding more patrol does not reduce crime any further. Some new problem-oriented policing strategies that focus on specific crimes and places, however, may be more effective in reducing crime. These issues are discussed in greater detail in Chapters 4 and 7.

Traditionally, many police departments maintained formal crime prevention programs. In his classic text on police administration, O. W. Wilson described these programs as including "security improvement, target hardening, and public education to prevent vulnerability to crime."[10] Crime prevention officers, for example, meet with community groups to explain door locks and alarm systems, marking of valuable property, as well as behavior that can increase personal safety. Some of these programs are housed in police–community relations (PCR) units (see Chapter 9).[11]

Police crime prevention strategies have undergone a revolution since the early 1980s. Instead of a peripheral activity, separated from the basic functions of patrol and criminal investigation, crime prevention is now seen as a central police activity.[12] Crime prevention is a basic element of community policing and many problem-oriented policing programs.[13] The basic principle of community policing is that the police need to establish a better partnership with neighborhood residents. The underlying assumption is that citizens are coproducers of police services. This view of policing rejects the professional model of policing, which holds that the police and only the police have primary responsibility for crime control.[14] These issues are discussed in detail in Chapter 7.

Community-based crime prevention programs include efforts to build neighborhood organizations, to improve the physical appearance of the neighborhood, to eradicate centers of drug activity, to reduce truancy, and so on. In these programs, police officers act as planners, problem solvers, community organizers, and information exchange brokers. Their role is not to fight crime in the traditional manner (e.g., patrol, arrests) but to help citizens mobilize resources to prevent crime.[15]

Because community policing and problem-oriented policing crime prevention programs are so varied and are such an important part of contemporary policing, they are covered in detail in Chapter 7.

APPREHENDING CRIMINALS

The second major crime-fighting responsibility of the police is to apprehend criminals once a crime has been committed. This process involves a complex set of social and organizational factors. The police must first learn that a crime has been committed, officially record it as a crime, and then attempt to identify and arrest a suspect.

Citizen Reporting of Crime

Police learn about crimes through (1) citizen reports, (2) police officer on-view observations, and (3) police-initiated investigations. The first two are reactive responses; the third is a proactive response.

Most of the crimes that come to the attention of the police are the result of a citizen report. Reporting a crime is one of the most important discretionary decisions in the criminal process. In this sense, citizens are the real "gatekeepers" of the criminal justice

---

SIDEBAR 6-1   WHAT IF ALL CRIMES WERE REPORTED?

What would happen if victims reported all crimes to the police? Would it result in more arrests and fewer crimes? Probably not. First, the police workload would increase enormously. There would be many more calls for service and about 200 percent more reported crimes. Patrol officers and detectives would be swamped. Second, most of these additional crimes would be the less serious crimes. The National Crime Victimization Survey (NCVS) data indicate that victims report the more serious crimes at a relatively high rate. Third, there is no reason to assume that there would be that many more arrests. As we will see later (pp. 171–172), the police are able to solve crimes when there is a good lead at the outset. There is no reason to assume that they would solve many of the additional burglaries and larcenies where there are no good leads.

In short, are we better off because citizens use their discretion not to report most crimes?

system. Patrol officers rarely discover crimes in progress. For example, in Chicago patrol officers spend only 0.1 percent of their total patrol time handling on-view criminal incidents.[16]

Victims, however, do not report most crimes to the police. According to the National Crime Victimization Survey (NCVS), only 36.3 percent of victims of crimes report the crime to the police.[17] The nonreporting of crime has important implications for the police, since they cannot be held responsible for solving crimes they do not know about.

The reporting of crime varies according to the type of crime and situational factors related to individual crimes (Table 6–1). Generally, citizens are more likely to report serious crimes than minor crimes, violent crimes rather than property crimes, crimes where there is personal injury rather than those without injury, crimes involving a high dollar loss more than those with little loss, and so on. African Americans report crimes at about the same rate as whites. Women report property crimes at about the same rate as males but are about 10 percent more likely to report a violent crime to the police. Except for teenagers, who report crime at a significantly lower rate, age does not influence the reporting of crime. People at different income levels also report crimes at roughly the same rate.[18]

For the most part, victims do not report crimes primarily because they do not think the crime is that important or because the victim does not think anything can be done about it. Victims also regard certain crimes as private or personal matters. Perception of the police also affects the decision not to report a crime. According to the National Crime Victimization Survey (NCVS), about 3 percent of those not reporting a victimization indicated that they thought the police were "inefficient, ineffective, or biased."[19]

Reporting and Unfounding Crimes

After a citizen reports a crime, the police must make an official record of it in order to enter it in the Uniform Crime Reports (UCR) system. Police officers often do not complete a crime report, however. This is called "unfounding" a crime. Donald Black found that police completed official crime reports in 64 percent of all crimes where no suspect was present, even though the complainant alleged a crime had occurred.[20] In 1995, meanwhile, crime victims told the NCVS that the police made reports in only 39.3 percent of all violent crimes and 49.3 percent of all property crimes.[21]

There is no penalty—in the law, in FBI regulations, or in police department policy—for a police officer not completing a crime report. This is an area of unregulated police discretion.

A police officer's decision to complete a crime report is affected by the same factors that influence arrest decisions. Black found that the police were more likely to record serious crimes, crimes where the complainant clearly expressed a preference for a crime report, crimes committed by strangers, and crimes where the complainant was deferential to the officer.[22]

There are several reasons why a police officer might unfound a crime. First, citizens do not always understand the criminal law and may believe that something is a crime when in fact it is not. For example, in Chicago 58 percent of all calls to the police were

TABLE 6–1 REPORTING OF CRIME TO THE POLICE, 1999	
	Percent Reported to Police
All crimes	36.3%
Violent crime	43.9
Rape/sexual assault	28.3
Robbery	61.2
Aggravated assault	55.3
Simple assault	38.5
Personal theft	25.9
Property crime	33.8
Burglary	49.3
Motor vehicle theft	83.7
Theft	27.1

Source: Bureau of Justice Statistics, *Criminal Victimization 1999: Changes 1998–99 with Trends 1993–99* (Washington, DC: Government Printing Office, 2000).

defined as a crime by the citizen, but only 17 percent of all calls to the police were recorded as crime-related by the police.[23]

Second, there may be insufficient evidence to convince the officer that a crime was committed. For instance, a citizen may report an attempted break-in, but the officer finds no physical evidence to support this allegation. The resident may have heard a storm door banging in the wind. These examples represent the proper exercise of discretion.

Third, officers may also abuse their discretion in unfounding crimes. A police officer may unfound a report of assault, for example, because of bias against the victim. Police officers may not make an arrest in a suspected assault incident when they perceive non-conforming behavior on the part of the victim: drinking or using drugs, being in the "wrong place," or being involved in questionable activity.

On a few occasions, police departments have been caught systematically unfounding crimes to lower the crime rate. In the early 1970s the news media caught the Washington, DC, police systematically lowering the value of stolen property to take the crimes out of the Index crime category. (At the time, the UCR system recorded larceny/thefts only when the value of the property was $50 or more.)[24]

Crime reports can also be altered later. A crime can be either unfounded completely or changed to a lesser criminal offense. Thus, a rape can be changed to an assault, or a robbery to a larceny or an assault. If the change is based on new information about the crime, it is legitimate. If it is done simply to lower the crime rate, however, it is illegitimate. Recording a crime in a lower category can alter the public's perception of community safety. The news media and the public tend to focus their attention on a few "high fear" crimes: murder, robbery, rape, and burglary. Recording a robbery as a larceny makes the community appear safer than it really is.

CRIMINAL INVESTIGATION

Once a crime has come to the attention of the police, and it has been officially recorded, and no suspect has been immediately arrested, the criminal investigation process begins.

Myths about Detective Work

Criminal investigation, or detective work, is surrounded by myths. Movies and television police shows usually portray detective work as exciting and dangerous. Individual detectives are presented as heroic characters, possessing either great personal courage or extraordinary skill. The media often foster the idea that a good detective "can solve any crime," if he or she is only given the freedom and enough time to do it.[25]

There is no empirical basis for any of these myths. Moreover, they have several harmful effects on the public and the police. First, they create unreasonable public expectations about the ability of the police to control crime. This results in public dissatisfaction when the police fail to solve a crime. Second, the glamorous image of detective work leads many officers to regard it as *real* police work and devalue routine patrol work.[26] Some detectives, in fact, imitate the behavior they see in the movies. Herman Goldstein observes that "many of the techniques employed by detectives today are more heavily influenced by a desire to imitate stereotypes than by a rational plan for solving crimes."[27]

The Organization of Detective Work

Criminal investigation is located in a separate unit of the department (except in small departments). Nationally, only about 12 percent of all sworn officers are assigned to detective units.[28] Large departments have specialized units devoted to particular types of crime (e.g., homicide, crimes against property, etc.). Medium-sized departments usually have a separate but unspecialized unit in which detectives handle all types of crime. Very small departments often have no specialized detective unit.

Assignment as a detective is generally considered a high status assignment by most police officers. In most departments it is a discretionary assignment, and one of the greatest rewards that a police chief has to hand out. In some departments it is a separate rank, with higher pay than patrol officers, and must be obtained through a competitive examination.

Detective work appeals to officers for several reasons. It offers greater opportunity to control one's work and to exercise initiative. Patrol work, by contrast, is largely reactive, in response to citizen calls. (Community policing, meanwhile, is designed to give patrol officers more responsibility for initiating activity.) Detectives have considerable discretion over which cases to work on, how much time to spend on each case, and how to investigate it. Working in civilian clothes enhances the sense of individuality and frees detectives from stereotyped reactions from citizens based on the uniform.

Criminal investigation also offers a clearly defined measure of success: arrest of the suspect. The quality of work can be measured in terms of the number of arrests, the importance of a particular arrest (for example, an arrest related to a highly publicized crime), and the percentage of arrests resulting in conviction.[29] Patrol work, by contrast, involves mainly order maintenance and peacekeeping activities (see Chapter 4), for which there have never been any real performance measures.[30]

Not all detective assignments are the same, however. William B. Sanders points out that "the status of an individual detective is linked to the kinds of crimes he investigates."[31] Homicide traditionally occupies the highest status, followed by robbery and sexual assault. Investigating the more serious crimes carries greater moral significance because of the harm involved. Homicide units also have the smallest workload and the highest clearance rate. Property crime units (burglary and larceny), on the other hand, rank lowest in terms of moral significance, and also have the highest workloads and the lowest clearance rates.

Vice units (narcotics, gambling, prostitution) are a special case. Because they involve victimless crimes, they require proactive police work, asking officers to exercise initiative. Undercover work also requires special skill, involves the greatest dangers, and poses the greatest moral hazards. Traditionally, the worst police corruption has been found in vice units (see Chapter 10).[32] For these reasons, some police officers do not seek assignment in vice units (see below).[33]

THE INVESTIGATION PROCESS

The process of investigating a crime consists of two basic stages: the preliminary investigation and the follow-up investigation.

The Preliminary Investigation

The preliminary investigation consists of five basic steps: (1) identifying and arresting any suspects, (2) providing aid to any victims in need of medical attention, (3) securing the crime scene to prevent loss of evidence, (4) collecting all relevant physical evidence, and (5) preparing a preliminary report.[34]

In practice, patrol officers rather than detectives make about 80 percent of all arrests.[35] The explanation for this is simple. Most arrests occur because a suspect is on the scene or immediately identifiable and nearby. For those crimes where the suspect is not immediately arrested and there is no good information about him or her, arrests are relatively rare. Patrol officers, in short, handle the easy arrests, while detectives are assigned those that are inherently difficult to solve.

Arrest Discretion

Police officers exercise great discretion in making arrests. Black found that officers make arrests in only about half of the situations where there is sufficient legal basis for an arrest.[36] In a number of situations officers simply ask the person to stop the illegal behavior. For example, in Indianapolis, Indiana, and St. Petersburg, Florida, 80 percent of the citizens were compliant with the officer's request.[37]

The decision to arrest is influenced by a number of situational factors. Generally, the probability of arrest rises when the evidence is relatively strong, the crime is more serious in nature, the victim requests an arrest, the victim and suspect are strangers rather than acquaintances, and the suspect is hostile or disrespectful toward the officer.[38] Smith, Visher, and Davidson also found that arrest is more likely in lower income neighborhoods, regardless of the race of the suspect.[39] Arrest discretion with respect to domestic violence situations and juveniles is discussed in more detail in Chapter 5.

Follow-Up Investigations

A case is assigned to the detective bureau for follow-up investigation after an arrest has been made or if there has been no arrest. The Police Executive Research Forum (PERF) study divided follow-up investigations into three categories of activities: routine, secondary, and tertiary activities.[40]

Routine activities include interviewing victims and checking the crime scene. These steps are taken in about 90 percent of all burglaries and robberies. Secondary activities include canvassing for witnesses, interviewing other people, interviewing witnesses, discussing the case with supervisors, and collecting physical evidence. Tertiary activities include discussing the case with patrol officers, interviewing suspects, discussing the case with other detectives, checking department records, checking the National Crime Information Center (NCIC) computer files, checking other records, interviewing informants, and conducting stakeouts.

The Reality of Detective Work

Contrary to popular belief, detective work is neither glamorous nor exciting. The Rand Corporation conducted the first detailed evaluation of detective units in the early 1970s, surveying 153 police departments by mail and interviewing officials in 29 departments. The study found detective work to be superficial, routine, and nonproductive. Many crimes receive only "superficial" attention, and some are not investigated at all. For example, detectives worked only 30 percent of all residential burglaries and 18 percent of all larcenies. Moreover, most investigative work involves "reviewing reports, documenting files, and attempting to locate and interview victims."[41] Most cases receive one day or less of investigative work, and most of that work involves paperwork: transferring information from one set of reports to another.

A PERF study of burglary and robbery investigations, meanwhile, found that about 25 percent of all burglary cases receive slightly less than 2 hours of investigative work,

---

SIDEBAR 6–2   POLICE, DISCRETION, AND CRIME

Police response to crime is affected by a number of discretionary decisions. They include (1) the citizen's decision to report a crime, (2) a police officer's decision to officially record the crime, (3) the officer's decision to arrest the suspect, or (4) the decision of detectives to investigate the case. The issue of discretion is covered in more detail in Chapter 8.

and only 11.9 percent are investigated for 3 days or more (at an average of about 1 hour per day). Only 24.8 percent of the robberies, meanwhile, are investigated for 2 days or more.[42] Harold Pepinsky argues that "most detectives spend the bulk of their time at their desks, going through papers and using the telephone."[43]

Case Screening

In practice, detectives routinely screen cases, deciding how much effort to put into different cases. Screening decisions are based primarily on the seriousness of the crime and the existence of evidence that is likely to lead to an arrest. The PERF study found that a detective's caseload actually consists of three components. The *nominal* caseload includes all cases assigned to that officer. The *workable* caseload includes those cases "that have sufficient leads and therefore are worth attempting to solve." Finally, the *actual* caseload includes those cases "actually worked by detectives."[44]

MEASURING THE EFFECTIVENESS OF CRIMINAL INVESTIGATION

The Clearance Rate

The traditional measure of success in criminal investigation is the clearance rate.[45] The FBI defines a crime as cleared when the police have "identified the offender, have sufficient evidence to charge him, and actually take him into custody, or in exceptional instances, when some element beyond police control precludes taking the offender into custody."[46]

Nationally, only about 21 percent of all reported Index crimes are cleared. Table 6–2 indicates national clearance rates for the eight UCR Index crimes for 1999.

The clearance rate is not a reliable performance measure for several reasons.[47] First, it is based on reported crimes, and since only 36 percent of all crimes are reported, the *true* clearance rate is much lower than the *official* rate. Only 49 percent of all burglaries

---

TABLE 6–2   CRIMES CLEARED BY ARREST, 1999

All Index crimes	21%
Murder	69
Rape	49
Robbery	29
Aggravated assault	59
Burglary	14
Larceny	19
Auto theft	15

Source: Federal Bureau of Investigation, *Crime in the United States, 1999* (Washington, DC: Government Printing Office, 2000).

are reported, and therefore, the police actually clear only about 7 percent of all burglaries, rather than 14 percent.

Second, despite the UCR guidelines, police departments do not use the same criteria for clearing crimes. The PERF study, for example, found that in one city, only 58 percent of the burglary cases recorded as cleared were actually cleared by an arrest.[48]

Third, the data can be manipulated to produce an artificially higher official clearance rate.[49] If officials unfound a large number of crimes, for example, this will lower the denominator and produce a higher percentage of crimes cleared. Alternatively, officials can attribute additional crimes to a suspect in custody and record them as cleared. This also raises the official clearance rate. In some instances attributing additional crimes to a suspect is legitimate. There may be some evidence that the suspect did commit these other crimes, but not enough to present to the prosecutor. In this situation, there is no reason to look for another suspect. The procedure can also be abused, however. Detectives may clear additional crimes even though there is no evidence to connect them with a suspect.

Clearance rate data, along with the entire UCR system, are not audited by outsiders. A Police Foundation study, for example, found wide variation in the quality of arrest data,[50] and there is good reason for assuming that similar variations exist with respect to official clearance rate data.

Defining an Arrest

Official data on arrests are also extremely problematic. The event referred to as an arrest has four different dimensions: legal, behavioral, subjective, and official.[51]

Legally, an individual is under arrest or in custody when deprived of his or her liberty by legal authority. A police officer must have the intent to arrest, must communicate that intent to the person, and must actually take the person into custody.[52] Many people are detained on the street and then released. Others are taken to the police station and later released. During the time they were in the custody of the police and not free to leave, they were legally under arrest.[53]

Behaviorally, taking a suspect into custody can involve a number of different actions by the police officer: a stop (in which the officer tells the individual not to leave), a verbal statement that the person is "under arrest," or physically restraining a person.

Subjectively, someone is under arrest whenever he or she believes they are not free to go. A police officer may regard an encounter as only a stop, but the individual may believe he or she is under arrest.

Officially, an arrest occurs only when the police make an official arrest report of it. Arrest record-keeping practices vary greatly from department to department, however, and may even vary within individual departments. Departments do not make arrest reports at the same stage in the process of detaining and taking someone into custody. A Police Foundation study found that only 16 percent of police departments always record an arrest whenever any restraint has been imposed on the suspect; only 11 percent always record an arrest whenever a suspect is brought to the station house. All departments make a record whenever the suspect is booked.[54]

The result is that in many departments, a lot of people are legally arrested (in custody on the street or at the station house) but no official record is made of these arrests. The lack of standard procedures makes it difficult if not impossible to use arrest data to compare departments. A police department that records all arrests at an early stage, for example, will appear to be working harder and engaging in more aggressive crime fighting than one that records arrests only at the booking stage. In fact, however, the two departments might be taking people into custody at exactly the same rate. The official data are not a reliable indicator of their real levels of activity.

Law enforcement agencies compile arrest statistics for different purposes and different audiences. One officer said, "We keep one set of statistics for the City Council and another for the BCS (the California Bureau of Criminal Statistics) and the FBI."[55] As already mentioned, despite UCR guidelines, police arrest data are not independently audited.

SUCCESS AND FAILURE IN SOLVING CRIMES

The police solve only 21 percent of all Part I felonies each year. As Table 6–2 indicates, they are far more successful in solving some crimes than others. The single most important factor is whether the police immediately obtain the name or description of a suspect. For example, the data in Figure 6–1 represent a sample of 1,905 crimes investigated by the Los Angeles police department. The LAPD cleared 86.2 percent of the 349 crimes in which a suspect was named, but only 11.6 percent of those in which a suspect was not named.[56]

Reiss and Bordua argue that most cleared crimes "solve themselves in the sense that the violator is 'known' to the complainant or to the police at the time the crime initially comes to the attention of the police."[57] Clearance rates are highest for violent crime because they involve direct contact between offender and victim. Few property crimes involve the same kind of direct contact and, consequently, have low clearance rates. Robbery is a violent crime, but usually committed by a stranger, resulting in low rates of identification and low clearance rates.

Detective screening of cases (see above) is based primarily on whether or not there is a good lead at the outset. Sanders found that "robberies, rapes, and assaults were typified as having leads, since the victim serves as a witness."[58] Burglaries and thefts, on the other hand, were routinely considered not to have leads.

The presence or absence of a good lead is a *structural* factor, in the sense that it is related to the nature of the crime and independent of police effort. Studies of criminal investigation have found that changes in police effort—more detectives, more or different levels of training, different management practices—have little effect on clearance rates. The Rand study of criminal investigation concluded that clearance rates are not higher where there are more detectives or where they put more effort into cases, or where they receive more training.[59] Even though detectives complain about being overworked, and do in fact have very heavy caseloads, the lack of resources is not the primary factor that keeps clearance rates low.

Subsequent research by Eck, and also Brandl and Frank, reached less pessimistic conclusions than the Rand study of criminal investigation. They argue that investigative effort does make a difference. Their analyses involve a "triage" model that categorizes cases according to the strength of the evidence: weak, moderate, or strong. Brandl and Frank found that the probability of arrest in moderate evidence burglary and robbery cases increased as a result of more investigative effort.[60]

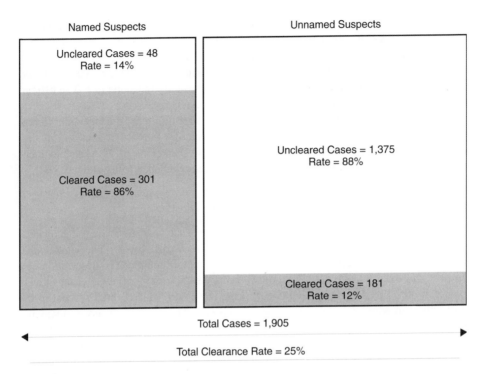

Named Suspects

Uncleared Cases = 48
Rate = 14%

Cleared Cases = 301
Rate = 86%

Unnamed Suspects

Uncleared Cases = 1,375
Rate = 88%

Cleared Cases = 181
Rate = 12%

Total Cases = 1,905

Total Clearance Rate = 25%

FIGURE 6–1
CRIMES CLEARED BY THE LOS ANGELES POLICE

Eyewitness Identification

Although victim and witness identification of suspects is extremely important in solving crimes, eyewitness identifications are also very problematic. The victim is often traumatized by the crime, frequently has only an incomplete description of the suspect, may exaggerate certain features (such as height or weight), or may resort to stereotyping in the sense of being unable to distinguish the individual features of a member of a certain racial or ethnic group. Psychologist Elizabeth Loftus, the leading expert on the subject, warns that despite the importance of eyewitness identifications, they are "not always reliable," for all the problems associated with human perception and memory.[61]

Criminalistics

Technical specialists from the crime lab may be used in some investigations. Large departments maintain their own criminalistics specialists, while the smaller departments utilize the services of either a neighboring large department or a state police agency. Virtually all police departments, including the smallest, have technical services available to them through cooperative arrangements with other agencies.[62]

Despite the great publicity they receive, fingerprints are rarely an important factor in solving crimes. A major part of the problem is that it is difficult to obtain useful prints. For example, New York City police are able to obtain a usable print in only 10 percent of all burglaries. Even when prints were obtained, only 3 percent led to an arrest. This meant that of the 126,028 burglaries occurring in New York City (in the year of the study), only 300 resulted in an arrest as a result of using fingerprints.[63] Similar findings have been found in other cities. For instance, in Long Beach, California, fingerprint technicians were requested in only 58 percent of all criminal cases. They successfully obtained a print in only half of those cases (or 29.4 percent of all cases), and fingerprints identified a suspect in only 1.5 percent of the total cases.[64]

Officer Productivity

There are significant differences in the productivity of detectives, as measured in terms of the number of arrests. Some make far more arrests than others. Productivity depends on a number of factors. Detectives assigned to high-solvability crimes such as robbery will have more chances to make arrests than those assigned to low-solvability crimes such as burglary. Nonetheless, it is also clear that, given the same assignment, some officers work harder and make more arrests than others. Riccio and Heaphy found that the number of arrests for Index crimes ranges from a low of 2.18 to a high of 12.06 per officer.[65]

More important than the total number of arrests is the *quality* of arrests—that is, whether the arrests lead to prosecution and conviction for a felony. For example, the Institute of Law and Society found that in one department 15 percent of the officers made over half of the arrests that resulted in a conviction.[66]

The Problem of Case Attrition

Only about half of all felony arrests result in conviction of the suspect.[67] These data raise serious questions about whether the attrition is the result of poor police work or some other factor. In California it was determined that 11 percent of persons arrested were released by the police; 15 percent of those arrested were declined for prosecution by prosecutors; and 18 percent of the cases resulted in dismissal or acquittal.[68] The total attrition rate was 44 percent. (And this analysis did not take into account persons who were legally arrested by the police but for whom no arrest report was made.)

Petersilia, Abrahamse, and Wilson attempted to identify those aspects of police work that were associated with high case attrition rates. They found that department practices explained little of the variation between the twenty-five departments studied. These practices included a case-screening process, a modus operandi (MO) file, a known offender file, a special victim/witness program, and other elements. Departments that used arrest statistics as a performance measure actually had lower clearance rates than departments that did not. The report did find that attrition rates were somewhat lower in cities that spent more money per arrest, a figure that seemed to indicate a connection between clearance rates and the availability of greater resources.[69]

An INSLAW study found that detectives expressed little interest in the performance measures associated with low attrition rates. None of the detectives interviewed knew what percentage of their cases were rejected by prosecutors. No supervisor reported evaluating detectives on the basis of the percentage of cases that resulted in convictions. None of the detectives expressed interest in feedback from prosecutors about the quality of their work.[70]

IMPROVING CRIMINAL INVESTIGATIONS

Several proposals have been made for improving criminal investigations. The most important is a PERF–Stanford Research Institute (SRI) recommendation for a formal case-screening system to determine which cases should receive the most investigative effort. Instead of the traditional method of relying on detectives' hunches and intuition about which cases are likely to be solved, the PERF–SRI model involves a point system based on factors (e.g., eyewitness identification) that contribute to success in clearing crimes.[71]

A second approach involves developing closer working relationships between patrol officers and detectives. Traditionally, officers in these two units have competed with one another instead of cooperating. Officers jealously guard information and sources in the hope of reaping the reward of an important arrest.[72]

However, since the advent of community policing, patrol officers and detectives have been facing increasing pressure to cooperate with one another. For example, in Glendale, Arizona, the police department moved detectives from central headquarters and placed them within each precinct so that they would develop a closer relationship with patrol officers and with the community that they served. Similarly, in Albuquerque, New Mexico, the police department abolished all of the specialized investigative units such as the homicide, robbery, and burglary units and created a general investigative unit within each precinct. Detectives were then responsible for investigating all crimes within the precinct to which they were assigned, rather than being responsible for investigating only one type of crime. This, the chief argued, would lead to greater cooperation between the patrol officers and the detectives and would result in commanders being geographically responsible for all crime in their precinct.[73]

A third approach focuses on increasing police–citizen cooperation. Citing the importance of victim or witness information about suspects in clearing crimes, Skogan and Antunes argue that citizens should be viewed as coproducers of information.[74] Community policing and problem-oriented policing programs (see Chapter 7) are based on this concept.

The Fear Reduction Experiment in Houston included a victim recontact program. Police officers recontacted crime victims by telephone to ask if they needed any assistance. The officers were prepared to offer advice on filing insurance claims and to answer any questions about the progress of the investigation or prosecution. The objective of the program was to provide the "information, recognition, advice, support, protection, and reassurance" that victims appeared to be seeking.[75] Contrary to expectations, however, the recontact program did not achieve its goals—and the most notable impact ran counter to the program's goals. Victims who were recontacted did not have more positive attitudes toward the police and were not less worried about crime.

Hispanic and Asian crime victims who were recontacted were more fearful of crime and less satisfied with their neighborhood than other victims. They were slightly more positive in their evaluation of the police, but not to a significant degree. Language appeared to be a factor. Victims whose command of English was rated as fair or poor were among those more fearful of crime (although this did not entirely explain the effect). The evaluators hypothesized that these people may not have understood why the recontact person was calling them. The experiment dramatized "the importance of sensitivity to cultural differences in the implementation of police programs."[76]

Targeting Career Criminals

In the 1980s several police departments experimented with programs to target career criminals, defined as people believed to be currently committing a high rate of offenses. This idea was based on the Wolfgang birth cohort study which estimated that a very small number of people (6 percent of any group of young men) commit an extremely high percentage of all serious crime.[77] Arresting, convicting, and imprisoning these career criminals, it was argued, would yield tremendous payoff in terms of crime reduction.[78]

Repeat offender programs consist of three different types: (1) targeting suspected high-rate offenders for surveillance and arrest, (2) special warrant service for suspected high-rate offenders who have outstanding warrants or are wanted for probation or parole violations, and (3) case-enhancement programs to provide prosecutors with full information about the criminal histories of high-rate offenders.[79]

The Repeat Offender Program (ROP) in Washington, DC, involved a team of eighty-eight officers (later reduced to sixty) assigned to locate and arrest persons believed to be committing five or more Index crimes per week. The suspects were selected on the basis of information provided by other police department units. Suspects remained on the list for 72 hours. Officers in the ROP team sought to locate the suspect through information in existing criminal records, supplemented by information available from the Department of Motor Vehicles, the phone company, and other sources. Many of the targeted individuals were already being sought on outstanding arrest warrants.[80]

An evaluation of ROP by the Police Foundation compared 212 suspects assigned to the ROP unit with a group of 212 comparable suspects. The arrest activity of ROP unit officers was also compared with the activity of a control group of officers. The evaluation found that ROP "increased the likelihood of arrest of targeted repeat offenders." Half of the suspects in the experimental group (106 out of 212) were arrested by ROP officers (another 17 were arrested by other officers), compared with only 4 percent (8 out of 212) in the control group.

Other data, however, raised some questions about the efficiency of the program. ROP officers made fewer arrests than comparison officers (although most of the additional arrests by the comparison officers were for nonserious crimes). The ROP program cost $60,000 in direct expenses and took officers away from other police responsibilities, raising serious questions about the cost-effectiveness of the program.[81]

SPECIAL INVESTIGATIVE TECHNIQUES

Undercover Police Work

Undercover police work presents a number of special problems for the police.[82] First, it involves deliberate deception by the officer: lying about who he or she is. The danger is that officers become socialized into the habit of lying and may be tempted to lie in other contexts as well, such as when testifying under oath.

Second, an officer working undercover associates with criminals and attempts to become their friend. This socialization can erode the values and standards of policing. Ties to peer officers and family are weakened. Some officers have "gone native," embraced the criminal subculture, and become criminals themselves.

Third, undercover officers are often subject to less direct supervision than other officers. This is particularly true of deep undercover operations where the officer must spend weeks or months attempting to penetrate a criminal enterprise. The Knapp Commission found that detectives in the New York City Special Investigative Unit (SIU), for example, did not see their supervisors for weeks, and this contributed to the corruption.[83]

Traditionally, police departments have had few if any meaningful controls over undercover work. Officers learned how to work undercover through informal training by veteran officers.[84]

To prevent possible abuses, police departments have instituted formal controls over undercover work. The Commission on Accreditation requires law enforcement agencies to have "written procedures for conducting vice, drug, and organized crime surveillance, undercover, decoy, and raid operations." These procedures should cover such activities as "supplying officers with false identity, disguises, and necessary credentials," "designating a single person as supervisor and coordinator," and "providing close supervision."[85] The city of Seattle, meanwhile, passed an ordinance limiting police investigations into political, religious, and private sexual activity. The ordinance included restrictions on the use of undercover officers in these areas.[86]

Informants

Informants are an important source of information about criminal activity. They are especially useful in victimless crimes and other covert criminal activity. Informants have special knowledge because they are often criminals themselves or are associated with criminals. Developing a group of informants is part of the art of police work. Jonathan Rubinstein observes that "vice information is a commodity, and the patrolman learns that he must buy it on a restricted market."[87]

The use of informants creates a number of potential problems. First, the police are involved in an exchange relationship with someone who is usually a known criminal offender. The police must give something in order to obtain the information they want. The most valuable commodity is a promise of leniency: an agreement not to arrest, or to recommend leniency to the prosecutor or judge. With respect to not arresting an offender, there are serious moral questions about the police knowingly overlooking criminal activity. Critics argue that the relationship compromises the integrity of the police and sets the stage for corruption. New York City police officers in the 1970s provided their informants with drugs, thereby turning the officers into drug dealers.[88] The information provided by informants may be questionable. Informants may invent information simply to please their handlers, or provide information only against their enemies. Jerome Skolnick found that in "Westville" narcotics detectives allowed their informants to steal, while burglary detectives allowed their informants to engage in drug dealing.[89] The danger, as Gary Marx points out, is that the informer begins "to control the sworn agent rather than the reverse."[90]

To control the potential problems involved in the use of informants, the CALEA (Commission on Accreditation for Law Enforcement Agencies) accreditation standards require that police departments maintain a set of "policies and procedures" covering the master file of informants, the "security of the informant file," "criteria for paying informants," and other "precautions to be taken with informants."[91] A joint Bureau of Justice Assistance–Police Executive Research Forum report recommended that "all understandings with a criminal informant should be put in the form of a written agreement."[92]

POLICING DRUGS

By the end of the 1980s, drugs represented the most serious problem facing the police, the criminal justice system, and American society as a whole. An epidemic of crack cocaine usage led to unstable drug markets in many large urban cities across the United States. The competition for control of drug markets produced a dramatic increase in homicides. While the subculture of crack use has declined over the past 5 years, and along with it general levels of violence, the nation still expends a substantial amount of resources toward combating the drug problem.[93] According to the Office of National Drug Control Policy the United States spends about $12.9 billion on domestic enforcement, interdiction, and international drug control efforts; $3.8 billion on drug treatment; and $2.5 billion on drug prevention.[94] Nonetheless, U.S. residents still spent an estimated $62.4 billion on illicit drugs in the same year.[95]

Drug Enforcement Strategies

Local police employ two basic strategies to combat illegal drug trafficking and use. The traditional supply reduction strategy includes four different tactics. The first is the simple buy-and-bust strategy: Undercover officers purchase drugs and then arrest the dealers. A second and related strategy is to attempt to disrupt the drug syndicate by "trading up": arresting low-level dealers and offering them leniency in return for information about higher-level dealers.[96] A third strategy involves penetrating the drug syndicate through long-term undercover work. The fourth is the drug crackdown, an intensive enforcement effort concentrated in a specific area over a limited period of time.[97]

The demand reduction strategy involves attempting to reduce the demand for drugs on the part of potential users. This strategy includes drug education programs such as D.A.R.E.

The traditional supply reduction strategies have never proved to be effective. Illegal drug use continues to remain at high levels, and in the poorest neighborhoods drug trafficking is open and rampant. Several reasons explain this failure.

First, there is no persuasive evidence that the threat of arrest, per se, deters drug use or sale (or deters any other form of criminal activity, for that matter). Second, through what is known as the "replacement effect," new drug dealers quickly replace those who are arrested. Particularly in poor neighborhoods where legitimate career opportunities are limited, the incapacitation of dealers does not affect the behavior of other new potential dealers. Third, the strategy of arresting low-level dealers and trading up to get key individuals in drug trafficking organizations has never proved to be effective in disrupting these organizations.[98]

An important question is, "Why do the police continue to engage in these activities despite their apparent ineffectiveness?" Peter Manning argues that drug arrests are made for their "dramaturgical effect": They generate publicity and create the appearance of doing something about the drug problem.[99] As Crank and Langworthy argue, police organizations exist in a larger social and political environment and need to create at least the impression that they are handling the problems that are within their professional domain.[100]

Retail Drug Enforcement

Retail drug enforcement deserves special attention because of the strategic shift in police tactics in the last decade. Prior to the introduction of crack cocaine, street-level drug enforcement was left to plainclothes detectives in vice or narcotics units. However, with the escalation of street-level drug dealing police agencies had to develop alternative strategies to cope with the problem—such as using patrol officers to assist in drug enforcement.[101]

Eck and Maguire point out that while most researchers agree that street-level drug dealing and drug use have declined, and that police antidrug efforts have contributed to the decline, researchers are unclear as to how the police impacted the decline.[102] For example, police crackdowns on drug markets have been found to have only a modest impact, and research examining police raids on drug houses has found that these tactics have only a small and limited impact. However, they argue that there might be two other explanations for how the change in police tactics has resulted in the decline of drug dealing and drug use.

First, Eck and Maguire argue that while the short-term impact of crackdowns and raids might be modest, the long-term impact of these strategies might be substantial. They claim that such strategies could be wearing down those who participate in drug markets. By "pinching" offenders regularly, offenders may become tired of being hassled and find something else to do. However, the authors are quick to point out that there is no evidence to support this claim. Second, Eck and Maguire maintain that the shift in police strategy toward the "management of places" may have contributed toward the decline in drug markets. They argue that for drug markets to be successful, dealers must find places where property owners and community members will not interfere with their business. With the implementation of community policing and problem-oriented policing, the authors argue that the police have begun to target these places—using tactics that reinvigorate neighborhoods to the point that such behavior is no longer acceptable. This will be discussed further in Chapter 7.

Minorities and the War on Drugs

There is a significant disparity in the arrest of racial and ethnic minorities for drug offenses. The National Household Survey has found that African Americans are only somewhat more likely than whites to be using illegal drugs in any given month.[103] Yet, as Figure 6–2 indicates, African Americans are significantly more likely to be arrested for drug offenses. Jerome Miller argues that the entire criminal justice system's policy toward young African American men represents a "search and destroy" mission.[104]

Many critics argue that the racial disparity in drug arrests is the result of department policies that deliberately target minority neighborhoods. As Castellano and Uchida point out, "Drug arrests are largely police-initiated (proactive) rather than citizen-initiated (reactive)." As a result, "Local drug arrest rates and patterns are largely dependent upon the arrest policies and enforcement priorities in police departments."[105] That is to say, it is not the result of discriminatory decisions by individual officers on the street, but of policy decisions made by commanders.

Demand Reduction: The D.A.R.E. Program

The most popular demand reduction strategy is the drug education program known as D.A.R.E. (Drug Abuse Resistance Education). D.A.R.E. originated with the Los Angeles police department (LAPD) in cooperation with the Los Angeles public schools in 1983. The program consists of seventeen 1-hour classroom sessions conducted by a sworn police officer. The content of the program involves both information about illegal drugs and their consequences and training in social skills to help resist illegal drug use.[106]

The D.A.R.E. program is extremely popular. By 1997 it was operating in an estimated 70 percent of all public school systems at an annual cost of $750 million per year. The program has also been adopted in forty-four foreign countries.[107] Several factors explain the program's popularity. First, it addresses parent concerns about juvenile drug abuse. Second, there is a widespread belief that education is an effective approach. Third, both police and public school officials want to appear to be doing something about the drug problem.

Most of the evaluations of D.A.R.E. have not found any significant reduction in actual drug use as a result of the program. Critics have claimed, however, that most of these evaluations have been limited to 1-year follow-up periods.[108] Recently, however, two major studies have been published that examine the long-term impact of the D.A.R.E. program: One of them examined the effects of the D.A.R.E. program 6 years after it had been administered, and the other, 10 years after it was administered. Both studies randomly assigned students to either a group that received the D.A.R.E. program or a group that did not receive the program. Both studies also measured the effects of D.A.R.E. on students' attitudes, beliefs, social skills, and drug use behaviors. They both found that the program had no measurable impact on those who participated compared with those who did not participate in the program.[109]

New Approaches to Drug Enforcement

A number of new approaches to drug enforcement are incorporated into community policing or problem-oriented policing programs.

One example is the Oakland SMART program. Under SMART, the Oakland police worked closely with other city agencies and emphasized non–law enforcement strategies.

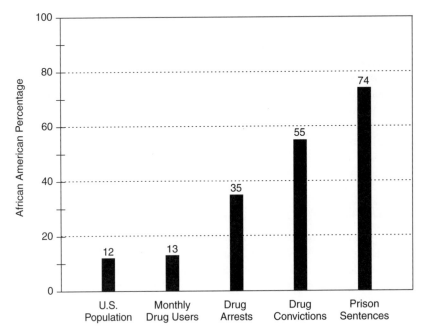

FIGURE 6–2
AFRICAN AMERICANS AND DRUG POSSESSION

Source: Marc Mauer and Tracy Huling. *Young Black Americans and the Criminal Justice System: Five Years Later* (Washington, DC: The Sentencing Project, 1995), p. 12.

These included attacking drug houses through vigorous enforcement of city building codes, using a state nuisance law, and educating landlords on how to identify drug dealers. An evaluation of SMART found that it not only reduced signs of illegal behavior in the target sites but did not displace crime or disorder to the surrounding areas, and in fact produced a diffusion of reduced crime and disorder to the immediately surrounding areas.[110]

POLICING GANGS AND GANG-RELATED CRIME

In 1982 Walter Miller reported that only 27 percent of cities with populations of 100,000 or more had a gang problem, noting that the gang problem was largely isolated in America's largest cities.[111] Today, however, the street gang can be found in every state and in almost every major city throughout the United States. The 1999 National Youth Gang Survey, a survey of police departments across the country, reported that youth gangs are active in 66 percent of large cities, 47 percent of suburban counties, 27 percent of small cities, and 18 percent of rural counties. Additionally, the survey reported that 26,000 gangs and 840,500 gang members were active in the United States in 1999.[112]

As a result, public officials and researchers have claimed that the increase in gangs is responsible for much of the rise in youth violence and drug use among youth, and has led to predictions that the current trend of rising juvenile violence will continue over the next 10 years.[113] These claims have been substantiated in that studies of official records have consistently found that gang members are disproportionately involved in criminal activity. For example, in Mesa, Arizona, the police department discovered that when comparing the arrest records of documented gang members with a similar group of non-documented delinquent youth, gang members were about twice as likely to have ever been arrested for a violent, weapon, drug, or status offense. Additionally, gang members were arrested for these offenses about four times as often as nondocumented delinquent youth.[114]

Recent evidence also suggests that gang members are heavily involved in drug use and drug sales. An examination of official records from the Pasadena and Pomona police departments found that gang members represented over 27 percent of those arrested for cocaine sales.[115] Evidence of this trend has also been found in self-report surveys among the general population. For example, self-report surveys administered to Denver youths found that gang members were 3 to 5 times more likely to use drugs and were 100 times more likely to self-report drug sales when compared with nongang members.[116]

Local police rely on two strategies to combat gang problems. One strategy is suppression, while the other relies on prevention.

Gang Suppression

The growth of gangs during the last two decades has been accompanied by the development and growth of specialized law enforcement responses to gangs. Traditionally, the police response to gangs and gang-related problems was to assign responsibility for gang control to existing units such as patrol, juvenile bureaus, community relations, investigations, and crime prevention.[117] However, in the 1980s many police departments established specialized units for gang control, including what is commonly referred to as the police gang unit. A police gang unit is a secondary or tertiary functional division within a police organization. It has at least one sworn officer whose sole function is to engage in gang control efforts.[118] Therefore, by its very nature, police gang units are specialized, have their own unique administrative policies and procedures, which are often distinct from the rest of the department, and have a front line of experts who are uniquely trained and dedicated to perform specific and focused duties.

In 1999, the Law Enforcement and Management Administrative Statistics (LEMAS) survey reported that among large agencies with 100 or more sworn officers, special gang units existed in 56 percent of all municipal police departments, 50 percent of all sheriff's departments, 43 percent of all county police agencies, and 20 percent of all state law enforcement agencies.[119] These findings led to an estimate of approximately 360 police gang units in the country. The recency of this phenomenon can be further seen by the fact that over 85 percent of specialized gang units have been established in the past 10 years.[120] (See Figure 6–3.)

While specialized police gang units represent a new feature in American policing, they are part of an overall trend among many police departments to create specialized units to address unique law enforcement problems such as repeat offenders, domestic violence, and hate crimes. Such units are created to focus departmental resources, energy, and skill

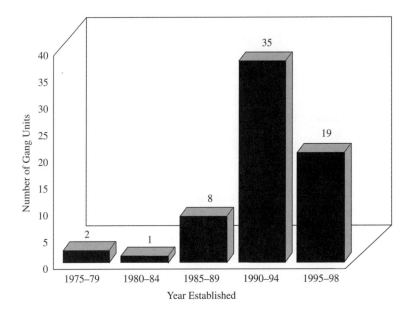

FIGURE 6–3
ESTABLISHMENT OF SPECIALIZED GANG UNITS BY FIVE-YEAR INTERVALS SINCE 1975

Source: Charles M. Katz, Edward Maguire, & Dennis Roncek, "A Macro-Level Analysis of the Creation of Specialized Police Gang Units: An Examination of Rational, Social Threat, and Resource Dependency Perspectives" (Unpublished manuscript: Arizona State University West, 2000).

on the reduction of gangs and gang-related activity. Additionally, such an approach is intended to be a symbolic act, signifying to the community, gang members, and police officers that the police department is taking the gang problem seriously.[121]

Not only do gang units symbolize the commitment the police have toward the gang problem, but they are also symbolic of a moral crusade in which the police are battling against gangs. This is often conveyed to the public through the unit's name. For example, San Bernardino County interagency task force uses SMASH (San Bernardino County Movement Against Street Hoodlums), and the Los Angeles sheriff's department uses GET (Gang Enforcement Team). Such acronyms express a Hollywood-like image that the police are at war with gangs, and that the gang problem can be solved as long as we intensify our efforts against them.

One of the few studies to examine the effectiveness of police gang units was conducted by Klein and his colleagues in Los Angeles. The authors compared gang-designated homicide cases to non-gang-designated homicide cases in both the Los Angeles police department and the Los Angeles sheriff's department. The authors reported that gang-designated cases were significantly more likely to have a greater number of (1) pages of investigation, (2) interviews conducted, (3) witness addresses, and (4) suspects charged than non-gang-designated cases. Klein and his colleagues also reported that in both departments, homicide cases that were investigated by the special gang unit were significantly more likely to be cleared compared with those that were not investigated by the special gang unit. As a result, it appears, at least initially, that gang units may contribute special knowledge that aids in the investigation of gang crimes.[122]

Gang Prevention: The G.R.E.A.T. Program

The most popular police-led gang prevention program is called the Gang Resistance Education and Training (G.R.E.A.T.) program. The Phoenix police department established the program in 1991, modeling it after the D.A.R.E. program. G.R.E.A.T. is a 9-week class, led by a uniformed police officer, offered once a week to middle school students. The program introduces students to conflict resolution skills, cultural sensitivity, and the problems that are associated with gangs and gang-related behavior. Today G.R.E.A.T. operates in all fifty states and several foreign countries.[123]

As of yet, there have been few evaluations of the G.R.E.A.T. program. One of the most thorough studies used a multisite methodological design to evaluate the effectiveness of the program. The researchers compared 2,626 eighth grade students who had completed the G.R.E.A.T. program with a comparable group of 3,207 students who had not participated in the program. The students who participated in G.R.E.A.T. self-reported lower rates of delinquency, lower rates of gang affiliation, more positive attitudes toward the police, more negative attitudes about gangs, more friends involved in prosocial activities, higher attachment to their parents, and more commitment to school. However, this study was limited in that it only collected the data from the youths 1 year after they participated in the program. The effects of the program may have worn off. The researchers are currently collecting additional data to determine the long-term effects of the program on students.[124]

POLICING GUNS AND GUN CRIMES

The Kansas City Gun Experiment

The Kansas City Gun Experiment was designed to reduce gun-related crimes by removing guns from the streets. The experiment represented a combination of both problem-oriented policing, by focusing on a particular problem, and hot spots, by concentrating on particular areas of high criminal activity.[125]

The experiment targeted a high-crime precinct in Kansas City where the murder rate in 1991 was 177 per 100,000, compared with a national rate of about 10 per 100,000. For a period of 29 weeks in 1992 and 1993 an extra pair of two-officer patrol cars patrolled the area for 6 hours at night between 7 P.M. and 1 A.M. The officers were directed to stop vehicles with people they believed to be carrying illegal handguns. The officers were directed to make only legally justified stops (e.g., traffic law violations) and then make legally justified searches for weapons (e.g., search incident to an arrest). The underlying assumption was that this program would reduce crime both by removing guns from the streets and by sending a deterrent message about aggressive enforcement in the area.

During the course of the experiment, the special unit officers seized twenty-nine guns, and another forty-seven guns were seized in the target beat by other officers. Gun crimes fell by 49 percent in the target beat, compared with a 4 percent increase in a control beat. Changes in gun crimes in other beats across the city were mixed. There was no evidence of either displacement of gun crimes or the diffusion of benefits. The experiment suggested the potential positive effect of hot spots oriented anticrime programs. A replication of the gun experiment in Indianapolis, however, was surrounded by controversy over the data on guns seized.[126]

POLICING HATE CRIME

Hate crimes, or bias motivated crimes, represent a new problem for the police. This is because hate crimes are not separate and distinct crimes per se but are offenses that are *motivated* by the offender's bias. The Hate Crimes Statistics Act of 1990 defined a hate crime as "a criminal offense against a person or property motivated in whole or in part by the offender's bias against a race, religion, disability, ethnic/national origin, or sexual orientation."[127] Because motivation is subjective, it is often difficult for police officers to determine if an offense was motivated by bias.

The Scope and Nature of Hate Crime

In 1999, 12,122 law enforcement agencies in forty-eight states and the District of Columbia reported 7,876 bias crimes to the Federal Bureau of Investigation. Most of these crimes were motivated by racial bias (55 percent), religious bias (18 percent), sexual orientation bias (17 percent), and ethnic/national origin bias (11 percent). Roughly 70 percent of the racial bias crimes were committed against blacks, 80 percent of the religious bias crimes were committed against Jews, and about 70 percent of the sexual orientation bias crimes were committed against male homosexuals.

The Federal Bureau of Investigation notes that there are five characteristics of hate crimes: (1) Hate crimes involve a higher level of assaults against persons than crimes generally; (2) hate crimes are generally more violent crimes—about two-thirds of bias crime incidents are crimes against persons and the remaining one-third are crimes against property; (3) attacks are often preceded by a series of confrontations and incidents that escalate in severity; (4) hate crimes are more likely than other criminal activity to be committed by groups of perpetrators; and (5) most crimes against persons are committed by someone the victim knows, whereas hate crimes are more likely to be committed by strangers.

The Police Response to Hate Crime

In response to the rising concern about bias crimes, a number of police departments have created specialized bias crime units. These units, like gang units, are intended to focus departmental resources and energy in an effort to increase the effectiveness of the department in combating hate crimes and to signify to the community that the police department is taking hate crimes seriously. Susan Martin argues that there are three other reasons for singling out hate crimes for special attention.

> First, because these offenses are based on who the victims are, they tend to cause victims greater difficulty in coming to terms with their victimization. Second, hate crimes appear to have particularly deleterious effects on communities, raising levels of mistrust, fear, and inter-

group tensions. Third, because many of these crimes are not very serious in terms of penal law, they would otherwise receive very little or no police attention.[128]

A number of alternative organizational structures have been established by police departments to combat hate crimes. For example, the New York City Bias Crime Incident Investigation Unit (BIIU) is a centralized unit with a number of bureaucratic features. Officers who encounter what they believe to be a bias crime are required to notify their supervisors, who are in turn required to notify their commander. The commander then performs a preliminary investigation, and if the offense is verified, the Operations unit is notified, which in turn notifies the Bias Crimes Unit.[129]

Conversely, the Baltimore County police department uses a decentralized strategy. The department did not establish a specialized bias crime unit, but rather delegates patrol officers, as part of their community policing duties, to address such problems. If the precinct commander believes that an incident requires additional attention, the commander may request assistance from the Investigations, Community Relations, or Intelligence Divisions.[130]

External evaluations have been conducted in both departments to determine the effectiveness of their strategies. In New York City, it was found that investigators in the special bias crime unit investigated more allegations of bias crimes and cleared more bias crimes than investigators assigned to a comparable group of nonbias crimes. Additionally, the victims of bias crimes expressed higher rates of satisfaction with the police response than victims in the comparison group. The higher clearance rate was particularly surprising since bias crimes are usually committed by strangers, whereas nonbias crimes are often committed by someone the victim knows. The fact that the investigators were able to clear offenses with less evidence suggests that the intensive investigative efforts by the special unit resulted in the higher clearance rate.[131]

Similarly in Baltimore, verified bias crimes received more extensive and intensive investigation and were more likely to be cleared when compared with similar nonbias crimes. The researchers found that the administration had communicated to patrol officers that bias crimes were to be taken seriously and that the patrol officers took the problem seriously.[132]

CURRENT PROBLEMS FACING LAW ENFORCEMENT

School Crime

Recent school shootings in Jonesboro, Arkansas; Littleton, Colorado; West Paducah, Kentucky; and Santee, California, have drawn heightened public attention to school crime and safety. While these events remind us that crime in schools affects the lives of many children, most schools have been found to be safe. The 1999 Annual Report on School Safety indicated that children are much more likely to be a victim of a serious violent crime when they are *away* from school compared with when they are *in* school. For example, in 1997 about 24 of every 1,000 students were victims of a serious violent crime away from school compared with 8 of every 1,000 students who were victims of a serious violent crime while in school.[133]

Contrary to popular opinion, school crime has declined substantially over past years. In 1997, 10 percent of students were victims of a school-related crime compared with 15.5 percent of students in 1992. Most crime within schools is theft, which accounts for over 60 percent of all crime against students in school. With this said, violence within schools is still a major concern among parents and students.[134] A recent Gallup Poll found that 47 percent of parents felt that a school shooting was very likely or somewhat likely to happen in their community.[135] Such fears, however, are not well founded. In the 1997–1998 school year there were fifty-eight school-associated violent deaths (eleven of which were suicides) in the 109,000 public and private schools across the country.[136]

What differentiates violent school crime from other types of crime is that it often results in multiple victims. For example, among the forty-three school-related homicides in the 1997–1998 school year 33 percent involved multiple victims. Since the 1992–1993 school year there has been at least one multiple victim homicide event each year (with the exception of the 1993–1994 school year). Such events, albeit isolated, capture the public's attention and bring to light the fears of parents and community members.[137] (See Figure 6–4.)

In response to the rising concern about school crime the federal government has established a program to encourage local police departments to hire additional police officers to be deployed in schools. From 1998 through 2001 the Community Oriented Policing Services (COPS) Office has provided $420 million to local police agencies to hire more than 3,800 school resource officers (SROs).[138] SROs are police officers who are permanently assigned to middle schools and high schools. These officers perform four major duties: first, they teach students about criminal laws and how they benefit society; second, they provide a visible and positive image of the police to students; third, they counsel students about personal problems; and fourth, they are responsible for providing a safe learning environment for students.[139]

Terrorism

On January 29, 1998, the New Woman All Women Health Care Clinic in Birmingham, Alabama, exploded. The explosion killed a Birmingham police officer who was working

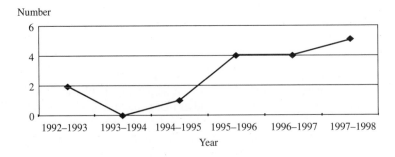

FIGURE 6–4
MULTIPLE VICTIM HOMICIDE EVENTS AT SCHOOL

Source: U.S. Departments of Education and Justice, *1999 Annual Report on School Safety* (Washington, DC: Department of Education and Department of Justice, 1999).

part-time at the clinic and severely injured a clinic employee. It was quickly learned that the explosion was a bombing—a terrorist act because of the clinic's involvement with abortions. The suspect, Eric Rudolph, was a member of the "Army of God." In letters to the media, the Army of God claimed responsibility for the bombing in Birmingham, and also claimed responsibility for bombing an abortion clinic and a gay nightclub in Atlanta in January and February 1997. In October 1998 Rudolph was charged with these incidents along with the Centennial Park bombing during the Summer Olympics in Atlanta.[140]

These incidents have not been the only acts of terrorism in the United States. Between 1990 and 1998 there was at least one act of domestic terrorism (with the exception of 1994) a year. Some of these included attacks by the Unabomber, now known as Ted Kaczynski; Timothy McVeigh, who bombed the Oklahoma City Federal Court Building; and Ramzi Ahmed Yousef and Eyad Mahmoud Ismail Najim, who bombed the World Trade Center. In total, between 1990 and 1998, there were thirty-nine acts of terrorism, with roughly two-thirds of them occurring within the contiguous forty-eight states and one-third of them taking place in Puerto Rico.[141]

In 1998 there were five acts of domestic terrorism. Three of these incidents took place in Puerto Rico, none of which resulted in a death. One of the incidents in Puerto Rico involved the bombing of a superaqueduct construction project, and the other two involved the bombing of banks. Of the other two acts of terrorism that took place in the states, one was the bombing of an abortion clinic, as discussed above, that resulted in the death of one person and serious injury to another. The other incident was an arson fire set at a ski resort in Vail, Colorado, by the Earth Liberation Front, which resulted in $12 million in damage.[142] (See Figure 6–5.)

The Federal Bureau of Investigation (FBI) has primary responsibility for investigating acts of domestic terrorism. However, it should be noted that there is no uniform

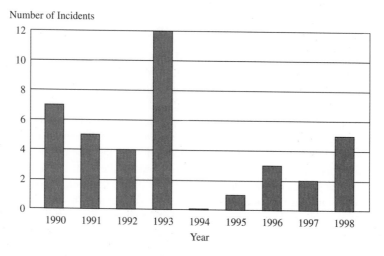

Number of Incidents

FIGURE 6–5
TERRORISM IN THE UNITED STATES: 1990–1998

Source: Federal Bureau of Investigation, *Terrorism in the United States: 1998* (Washington, DC: Federal Bureau of Investigation, 1999).

definition of domestic terrorism and there is no federal law that specifically makes terrorism a crime. The FBI defines domestic terrorism as "the unlawful use, or threatened use, of force or violence by a group or individual based and operating entirely within the United States or Puerto Rico without foreign direction committed against persons or property to intimidate or coerce a government, the civilian population, or any segment thereof in furtherance of political or social objectives." In responding to acts of terrorism, the FBI, along with other law enforcement agencies, uses existing criminal statutes to arrest and convict individuals involved in terrorist activity.[143]

Computer Crime

Computers have become a part of life for many Americans today. It is estimated that about 50 percent of households in the United States have access to the Internet, and over $230 billion a year is spent on Internet electronic commerce.[144] The increased use of computers and the Internet, however, has resulted in new opportunities for criminal activity.

David Carter and Andra Katz point out that three factors make computer-related crime difficult to address. First, computers have permitted criminals to use highly technical and innovative methods to engage in "old style" crimes, making it more difficult for the police to identify perpetrators. Second, computers are used to cross jurisdictional boundaries electronically, making it more difficult for detectives to investigate crimes. Third, "The evidence of these crimes is neither physical nor human, but if it exists, is little more than electronic impulses and programming codes."[145]

Because it is difficult to detect, investigate, and prosecute computer-related crimes, the harms resulting from them are difficult to estimate. However, a recent study by the Computer Security Institute suggests that 74 percent of major corporations have been victimized in the past year. Furthermore, over 19 percent of them have been victimized more than ten times in the past year. The institute also estimated that information theft and financial fraud alone cost these corporations at least $125 million a year.[146]

The Federal Bureau of Investigation (FBI) has categorized "cyber criminals" into four major groups: (1) insiders, (2) hackers, (3) virus writers, and (4) criminal groups. The *insider,* the most common type of cyber criminal, is a current or former employee of a company. The insider often has knowledge about the company's computer infrastructure, which allows him or her to steal proprietary data such as intellectual property, marketing strategies, client lists, and the like. The *hacker,* on the other hand, cracks into networks either for the thrill of the experience or for the purpose of making an illegal financial transaction. While hacking was infrequent in the past, it has become more popular with the sale of hacker software programs on the Internet. *Virus writers* differ from the others in that they are not motivated by financial gain, but rather typically behave maliciously, creating computer viruses that have the potential to destroy data within computers. These viruses are typically spread through the sending of electronic mail. The potential harm that viruses can cause to computer users and their data was seen with the Melissa Macro Virus created by David Smith, who pled guilty to infecting 1 million computers and causing $80 million worth of damage. *Criminal groups* are typically involved in stealing large amounts of information (or data) that can be sold for monetary profit. For example, "The Phonemasters," an international computer organized crime syndicate, were able to hack into the computer systems of MCI, Sprint, and AT&T and download calling card numbers, which they later sold to an organized crime group in Italy, who in turn sold them to the public.[147]

Law enforcement agencies have generally been slow to respond to computer-related crime. It was not until 1998, when the FBI founded the National Infrastructure Protection and Computer Intrusion Program (NIPCIP), that the United States began to develop a comprehensive national strategy to respond to computer crime. NIPCIP's mission is to continually assess the threat of computer crime in the United States; warn communities, corporations, and individuals when they might be vulnerable to a computer-related crime; and investigate incidents involving computer-related crimes that fall within the federal government's jurisdiction—such as hacking, which often involves the use of the nation's telecommunications system.

Much computer crime, however, is believed to fall within the jurisdiction of local police departments. For example, an insider could steal a client list, a marketing plan, or an architectural blueprint by gaining unauthorized electronic access to a corporate computer. If the perpetrator does not use the nation's telecommunications system, does not steal information that could be considered a threat to the nation's security, or does not cross state lines to commit the crime, it would fall to local authorities to investigate the incident. A national survey, however, found that most police departments are not prepared to respond to computer-related crimes. Police agencies were found not to have the personnel, equipment, or expertise to be able to investigate such crimes. This is probably because most police departments (69 percent) view computer-related crime as a low priority, and thus do not invest the needed resources.[148]

SUMMARY

Crime control is one of the major responsibilities of the police. Crime-related programs involve a number of different strategies and assumptions. There is mixed evidence about the effectiveness of these strategies in reducing crime, however. Patrol has only limited deterrent effect on crime. The police clear or solve only about 21 percent of all crimes that come to their attention. They are able to solve a high percentage of those crimes where a suspect is immediately known. Many experts today argue that the most promising programs are crime prevention efforts embodied in community policing and problem-oriented policing programs.

CASE STUDY: RECENT INNOVATIONS IN GANG VIOLENCE REDUCTION

The Office of Juvenile Justice and Delinquency Prevention's (OJJDP's) National Youth Gang Center recently completed the first nationwide survey of youth gang problems. In the 1995 survey, 2,007 law enforcement agencies reported gang activity in their jurisdictions, a total of 23,388 gangs, and 664,906 gang members. Forty-nine percent of their agencies described their gang activity as getting worse. Gang activity has extended beyond the inner cities into smaller communities and suburbs. Today's gangs are best characterized by their diversity in ethnic composition, geographical location, organization, and the nature and extent of members' involvement in delinquent or criminal activities.

Gang Violence Reduction Strategies

Communities are implementing a combination of prevention, intervention, and suppression strategies to address the gang problem. An effective gang program must be based on sound theory and work closely with the juvenile justice system. According to Dr. Irving Spergel, George Herbert Jones Professor at the School of Social Service Administration and the Department of Sociology, University of Chicago, "Policy and program must be based on appropriate targeting of both institutions and youth and also their relation to each other at a specific time and place, e.g., when the youth is entering the gang or ready to leave it and/or at the stage the gang problem is developing in the particular institution or community."*

In the late 1980s and early 1990s, OJJDP supported the completion of phases one and two of the National Youth Gang Suppression and Intervention Program. This program assessed youth gang research, including definitions, the nature and causes of the youth gang phenomenon, and the effectiveness of program strategies used by various agencies and organizations in the community. Conclusive evaluations of these strategies are still needed, but the following common elements appear to be associated with sustained reduction of gang problems:

1 Community leaders must recognize the presence of gangs and seek to understand the nature and extent of the local gang problem through a comprehensive and systematic assessment.
2 The combined leadership of the justice system and the community must focus on the mobilization of institutional and community resources to address gang problems.
3 Those in principal roles must develop a consensus on definitions (e.g., gang, gang incident); specific targets of agency and interagency efforts; and interrelated strategies based on problem assessment, not assumptions. Coordinated strategies should include the following:

- Community mobilization (including citizens, youth community groups, and agencies).
- Social and economic opportunities, including special school, training, and job programs. These are especially critical for older gang members who are not in school but may be ready to leave the gang or decrease participation in criminal gang activity for many reasons, including maturation and the need to provide for family.
- Social intervention (especially youth outreach and work with street gangs directed toward mainstreaming youth).
- Gang suppression (formal and informal social control procedures of the justice systems and community agencies and groups). Community-based agencies and local groups must collaborate with juvenile and criminal justice agencies

*Irving Spergel, *The Youth Gang Problem* (New York: Oxford University Press, 1995), p. 186.

in surveillance and sharing of information under conditions that protect the community and the civil liberties of youth.
- Organizational change and development (the appropriate organization and integration of the above strategies and potential reallocation of resources among involved agencies).†

4 Any approach must be guided by concern not only for safeguarding the community against youth gang activities but for providing support and supervision to present and potential gang members in a way that contributes to their prosocial development.‡

OJJDP's Response to the Gang Problem

OJJDP's Comprehensive Community-wide Approach to Gang Prevention, Intervention, and Suppression Program is testing the above comprehensive model. Five jurisdictions (Mesa, Arizona; Tucson, Arizona; Riverside, California; Bloomington, Illinois; and San Antonio, Texas) were awarded funding in 1995 to begin a 3-year effort to implement the comprehensive model developed by Dr. Spergel.

In the first year, the demonstration sites began the process of community mobilization, identifying or assessing the nature and extent of the gang problem, and exploring ways to address these problems. In the second year, based on previous and ongoing community assessment, the sites are implementing appropriate strategies to target gang violence. Training and technical assistance are being made available to the sites, and an independent evaluation of the programs and strategies is under way.

The Boys & Girls Clubs of America's Gang Prevention Through Targeted Outreach program is another key OJJDP gang initiative. Through a referral network that links the local clubs with courts, police, schools, social service, and other agencies and organizations, as well as through direct outreach efforts, at-risk youth are recruited into local club programs in a nonstigmatizing way. Once in the club, youth are provided with case-managed recreational and educational activities focusing on personal development to enhance communication skills, problem solving, and decision making. The most important aspect of this program is the alternative youth are being given to gang life.

Another component of OJJDP's broad-based response to the gang problem is the National Youth Gang Center, which was funded in 1995. The center will implement a national statistical data collection and analysis effort, the ultimate goal being creation of a national uniform gang reporting system. The center will also disseminate current information on gang-related legislation, compile and review current gang literature, identify promising gang program strategies across the country that merit replication, and support the National Youth Gang Consortium. Established in December 1995, the Consortium is composed of federal agencies with program or enforcement responsibility for youth gangs and related problems, gang demonstration program directors, and researchers. The Consortium's role is to formalize multidisciplinary and cross-department responses to the gang problem and create a line with state and local community efforts.

---

†Spergel, 1995.
‡Spergel et al., *Gang Suppression and Intervention: Problem and Response,* Research Summary (Washington, DC: Office of Juvenile Justice and Delinquency Prevention, U.S. Department of Justice, 1995, reprinted 1996).

OJJDP is also supporting field-initiated gang research on five major topics. Two studies are examining gangs in Indian (Navaho Nation) country and among Southeast Asian youth. A study jointly funded with the National Institute of Justice, Socialization to Gangs in an Emerging Gang City, is developing systematic baseline data on at-risk youth in St. Louis, Missouri. A fourth is determining the proportion of serious and violent juvenile crime committed by gang-involved youth. A fifth, longitudinal study is examining the relationship between gang membership and juvenile crime and delinquency.

These efforts constitute a comprehensive, coordinated federal campaign to prevent, intervene in, and suppress youth gang violence and help communities identify effective programs and strategies to address the youth gang problem.

Source: James Burch and Betty Chemers, A Comprehensive Response to America's Youth Gang Problem (Fact Sheet #40, Office of Juvenile Justice and Delinquency Prevention, 1997).

FOR DISCUSSION

1 Get into groups and discuss what a hate crime is and whether you believe that police agencies should police "hate."
2 As discussed in the text there are two primary strategies used by the police to reduce drug use: supply reduction and demand reduction. As a class, discuss which strategy you think works best, and how you, if you were a chief of police, would handle your community's drug problem.
3 As a class, discuss why you believe that D.A.R.E. has continued to be used in classrooms across the country.
4 Check with your campus police department and find out how much (school) crime occurs on your campus. Discuss the types of crimes that occur most frequently and what you think the university should do to address these problems (if anything).
5 Discuss the recent trends in multiple victim school shootings in the United States.

INTERNET EXERCISES

Exercise 1 Check out recent clearance rate data on the Web. Check the most recent FBI UCR data. Have national clearance rates changed for any crimes? Check out the websites for some local police departments. Do they provide their clearance rates? If so, how do different departments compare with the national clearance rates for particular crimes?

Exercise 2 Go to **http://www.fbi.gov/contact/fo/louisville/infraweb.htm** to learn more about the National Infrastructure Protection and Computer Intrusion program.

Exercise 3 Check out the website **http://nces.ed.gov** or **www.ed.gov/pubs.html** to learn more about trends in school crime.

Exercise 4 To learn more about trends in gang-related crime go to the websites of the Chicago police department and the Los Angeles police department. Also check out the site **http://www.streetgangs.com** to learn about gangs in Los Angeles and to access other websites on gangs.

Exercise 5 Go to the FBI's website, **www.fbi.gov,** and look up information related to school crime. If you are interested in learning about how the FBI suggests that school officials profile potential "school shooters," find the title *The School Shooter: A Threat Assessment Perspective* on their website.

REFERENCES

1 Lawrence W. Sherman, "Attacking Crime: Police and Crime Control," in Michael Tonry and Norval Morris, eds., *Modern Policing* (Chicago: University of Chicago Press, 1992), pp. 159–230.

2 Peter Manning, *Police Work* (Cambridge, MA: MIT Press, 1977).

3 George L. Kelling and Mark H. Moore, "From Political Reform to Community: The Evolving Strategy of Policing," in Jack R. Greene and Stephen D. Mastrofski, eds., *Community Policing: Rhetoric or Reality* (New York: Praeger, 1991), pp. 3–25.

4 Wesley G. Skogan and George E. Antunes, "Information, Apprehension, and Deterrence: Exploring the Limits of Police Productivity," *Journal of Criminal Justice,* 7 (Fall 1979): 232.

5 Lawrence W. Sherman et al., *Preventing Crime* (Washington, DC: Government Printing Office, 1997).

6 Ibid.

7 Geoffrey Alpert and Mark H. Moore, "Measuring Police Performance in the New Paradigm of Policing," in Bureau of Justice Statistics, *Performance Measures for the Criminal Justice System* (Washington, DC: Government Printing Office, 1993), pp. 109–140.

8 George L. Kelling et al., *The Kansas City Preventive Patrol Experiment* (Washington, DC: The Police Foundation, 1974).

9 The Police Foundation, *The Newark Foot Patrol Experiment* (Washington, DC: The Police Foundation, 1981).

10 O. W. Wilson and Roy C. McLaren, *Police Administration,* 4th ed. (New York: McGraw-Hill, 1977), p. 410.

11 Fred A. Klyman and Joanna Kruckenberg, "A National Survey of Police–Community Relations Units," *Journal of Police Science and Administration,* 7 (March 1979): 72–79.

12 David Bayley, *Police for the Future* (New York: Oxford University Press, 1994).

13 Dennis P. Rosenbaum, Eusevio "Ike" Hernandez, and Sylvester Daughtry, Jr., "Crime Prevention, Fear Reduction, and the Community," in William A. Geller, ed., *Local Government Police Management,* 3rd ed. (Washington, DC: International City Management Association, 1991), pp. 96–130.

14 Kelling and Moore, "From Political Reform to Community: The Evolving Strategy of Policing."

15 Jerome E. McElroy, Colleen A. Cosgrove, and Susan Sadd, *Community Policing: The CPOP in New York City* (Newbury Park, CA: Sage, 1993), pp. 9–11.

16 Albert Reiss, *The Police and the Public* (New Haven, CT: Yale University Press, 1971), p. 95.

17 Bureau of Justice Statistics, *Criminal Victimization 1999: Changes 1989–99 with Trends 1993–99* (Washington, DC: Government Printing Office, 2000).

18 Bureau of Justice Statistics, *Criminal Victimization in the United States, 1995* (Washington, DC, Government Printing Office, 2000).

19 Ibid., pp. 108–109.

20 Donald Black, "Production of Crime Rates," in Donald Black, *The Manners and Customs of the Police* (New York: Academic Press, 1980), p. 69.

21 Bureau of Justice Statistics, *Criminal Victimization in the United States, 1995,* p. 115.

22 Black, "Production of Crime Rates."

23 Reiss, *The Police and the Public,* p. 73.

24 David Seidman and Michael Couzens, "Getting the Crime Rate Down: Political Pressure and Crime Reporting," *Law and Society Review,* 8 (Spring 1974): 457–493.

25 Herman Goldstein, *Policing a Free Society* (Cambridge, MA: Ballinger, 1977), pp. 55–57.

26 William A. Westley, *Violence and the Police* (Cambridge, MA: MIT Press, 1970), p. 36.

27 Goldstein, *Policing a Free Society,* p. 55.

28 Police Executive Research Forum, *Survey of Police Operational and Administrative Practices—1981* (Washington, DC: PERF, 1981), pp. 22–23.

29 William B. Sanders, *Detective Work* (New York: The Free Press, 1977), pp. 39–47.

30 Alpert and Moore, "Measuring Police Performance in the New Paradigm of Policing."

31 Ibid., 43.

32 Westley, *Violence and the Police,* pp. 36–42.

33 David Giacapassi and Jerry Sparger, "Cognitive Dissonance in Vice Enforcement," *American Journal of Police,* 10 (No. 2, 1991): 39–51.

34 John E. Eck, *Solving Crimes: The Investigation of Burglary and Robbery* (Washington, DC: Police Executive Research Forum, 1983), pp. 69–93.

35 Reiss, *The Police and the Public,* p. 104.

36 Donald Black, *Manners and Customs of the Police* (San Diego, CA: Academic Press, 1980).

37 John McCluskey, Stephen Mastrofski, and Rodger Parks, "To Acquiesce or Rebel: Predicting Citizen Compliance with Police Requests," *Police Quarterly,* 2 (1999): 389–416.

38 Black, "The Social Organization of Arrest."

39 Douglas A. Smith, Christy A. Visher, and Laura A. Davidson, "Equity and Discretionary Justice: The Influence of Race on Police Arrest Decisions," *Journal of Criminal Law and Criminology,* 75 (Spring 1984): 234–249.

40 Eck, *Solving Crimes,* pp. 124–127.

41 Peter W. Greenwood et al., *The Criminal Investigation Process,* V. 1 *Summary and Policy Implications* (Santa Monica, CA: Rand, 1975), p. 35.

42 Eck, *Solving Crimes,* pp. 106–110.

43 Harold E. Pepinsky, "Police Decision Making," in Don Gottfredson, ed., *Decision Making in the Criminal Justice System* (Washington, DC: Government Printing Office, 1975), p. 27.

44 Eck, *Solving Crimes,* p. 250.

45 Alpert and Moore, "Measuring Police Performance in the New Paradigm of Policing."

46 Federal Bureau of Investigation, *Crime in the United States, 1999* (Washington, DC: Government Printing Office, 2000).

47 Greenwood et al., *The Criminal Investigation Process,* p. 32.

48 Eck, *Solving Crimes,* p. 203.

49 Black, "The Production of Crime Rates."

50 Lawrence W. Sherman and Barry D. Glick, *The Quality of Police Arrest Statistics* (Washington, DC: The Police Foundation, 1984).

51 Edna Erez, "On the 'Dark Figure' of Arrest," *Journal of Police Science and Administration,* 12 (December 1984): 431–440.

52 Steven H. Gifis, *Law Dictionary,* 2nd ed. (New York: Barron's, 1984), pp. 28–29.

53 Floyd Feeney, *Arrests without Conviction* (Washington, DC: Government Printing Office, 1983).

54 Sherman and Glick, *The Quality of Police Arrest Statistics.*

55 Malcolm W. Klein, Susan Labrin Rosensweig, and Ronald Bates, "The Ambiguous Juvenile Arrest," *Criminology,* 13 (May 1975): 82.

56 President's Commission on Law Enforcement and Administration of Justice, *Task Force Report: The Police* (Washington, DC: Government Printing Office, 1967), p. 8.

57 Albert Reiss and David J. Bordua, "Environment and Organization: A Perspective on the Police," in D. J. Bordua, ed., *The Police: Six Sociological Essays* (New York: John Wiley, 1967), p. 43.

58 William B. Sanders, *Detective Work: A Study of Criminal Investigations* (New York: The Free Press, 1977), p. 96.

59 Greenwood et al., *The Criminal Investigation Process,* vol. 1, Summary and Policy Implications (Santa Monica, CA: Rand, 1975).

60 Steven G. Brandl and James Frank, "The Relationship between Evidence, Detective Effort, and the Disposition of Burglary and Robbery Investigations," *American Journal of Police,* XIII, no. 3 (1994): 149–168.

61 Elizabeth Loftus, *Eyewitness Testimony* (Cambridge, MA: Harvard University Press, 1979), p. 7.

62 Elinor Ostrom et al., *Patterns of Metropolitan Policing* (Cambridge, MA: Ballinger, 1977), Ch. 7.

63 *The New York Times,* August 17, 1986.

64 Joan Petersilia, "Processing Latent Fingerprints—What Are the Payoffs?" *Journal of Police Science and Administration,* 6 (June 1978): 157–167.

65 Lucius J. Riccio and John F. Heaphy, "Apprehension Productivity of Police in Large U.S. Cities," *Journal of Criminal Justice,* 5 (Winter 1977): 271–278.

66 Brian Forst, *Arrest Convictability as a Measure of Police Performance* (Washington, DC: Government Printing Office, 1982).

67 Bureau of Justice Statistics, *The Prosecution of Felony Arrests, 1986* (Washington, DC: Government Printing Office, 1989).

68 Joan Petersilia, *Racial Disparities in the Criminal Justice System* (Santa Monica, CA: Rand, 1983), p. 21.

69 Joan Petersilia, Allan Abrahamse, and James Q. Wilson, *Police Performance and Case Attrition* (Santa Monica, CA: Rand, 1987).

70 Brian Forst, Judith Lucianovic, and Sarah J. Cox, *What Happens after Arrest?* (Washington, DC: INSLAW, 1977).

71 Eck, *Solving Crimes,* pp. 278–282.

72 Jonathan Rubenstein, *City Police* (New York: Ballantine Books, 1974), pp. 121–122.

73 Personal communication with Chief Galvin of the Albuquerque police department and Captain Krystek of the Glendale police department, 1999.

74 Skogan and Antunes, "Information, Apprehension, and Deterrence."

75 Wesley G. Skogan and Mary Ann Wycoff, "Some Unexpected Effects of a Police Service for Victims," *Crime and Delinquency,* 33 (October 1987): 490–501.

76 Ibid.

77 Marvin E. Wolfgang, Robert Figlio, and Thorsten Sellin, *Delinquency in a Birth Cohort* (Chicago: University of Chicago Press, 1972).

78 William Spelman, *Repeat Offender Programs for Law Enforcement* (Washington, DC: PERF, 1990).

79 Ibid., pp. 25–26.

80 Susan E. Martin and Lawrence W. Sherman, *Catching Career Criminals: The Washington, DC Repeat Offender Project* (Washington, DC: The Police Foundation, 1986).

81 Ibid.

82 Gary T. Marx, *Undercover: Police Surveillance in America* (Berkeley: University of California Press, 1988).

83 Knapp Commission, *Report on Police Corruption* (New York: Braziller, 1973).

84 Marx, *Undercover,* pp. 188–190.

85 Commission on Accreditation for Law Enforcement Agencies, *Standards for Law Enforcement Agencies,* 4th ed. (Fairfax, VA: CALEA, 1999), Standard 43.1.6.

86 Samuel Walker, "The Politics of Police Accountability: The Seattle Police Spying Ordinance as a Case Study," in E. S. Fairchild and V. Webb, eds., *The Politics of Crime and Criminal Justice* (Beverly Hills, CA: Sage, 1985), pp. 144–157.

87 Jonathan Rubenstein, *City Police* (New York: Ballantine, 1973), p. 381.

88 Robert Daley, *Prince of the City* (Boston: Houghton Mifflin, 1978).

89 Jerome Skolnick, *Justice without Trial* (New York: Macmillan, 1994), p. 129.

90 Gary Marx, *Undercover: Police Surveillance in America* (Berkeley, CA: University of California Press, 1988).

91 Commission on Law Enforcement Accreditation, *Standards for Law Enforcement Agencies,* 4th ed., Standard 42.2.9.

92 Bureau of Justice Assistance, *Informants and Undercover Investigations* (Washington, DC: Government Printing Office, 1990), p. 16.

93 Elliot Currie, *Reckoning: Drugs, the Cities, and the American Future* (New York: Hill and Wang, 1993); Bruce Johnson, Andrew Golub, and Eloise Dunlap, "The Rise and Decline of Hard Drugs, Drug Markets, and Violence in Inner-City New York," in Alfred Blumstein and Joel Wallman, eds., *The Crime Drop in America* (Cambridge, United Kingdom: Cambridge Press, 2000).

94 Cesar Fax, "Two-Thirds of National Drug Control Budget Dedicated to Domestic Enforcement, Interdiction, and International Efforts," 9 (College Park, University of Maryland: May 1, 2000).

95 Cesar Fax, "U.S. Illicit Drug Expenditures Stable at about $65 Billion," 10 (College Park, University of Maryland: March 5, 2001).

96 Mark H. Moore, *Buy and Bust* (Lexington, MA: Lexington Books, 1977).

97 Lawrence W. Sherman, "Police Crackdowns: Initial and Residual Deterrence," in Michael Tonry and Norval Morris, eds., *Crime and Justice: A Review of Research,* V. 12 (Chicago: University of Chicago Press, 1990), pp. 1–48.

98 Currie, *Reckoning;* Arnold S. Trebach, *The Great Drug War* (New York: Macmillan, 1987).

99 Peter K. Manning, *The Narcs' Game* (Cambridge, MA: MIT Press, 1978).

100 John Crank and Robert Langworthy, "An Institutional Perspective of Policy," *Journal of Criminal Law and Criminology,* vol. 83, no. 2 (1992), 338–363.

101 John Eck and Edward Maguire, "Have Changes in Policing Reduced Violent Crime?" in *The Crime Drop in America,* Alfred Blumstein and Joel Wallman, eds., (Cambridge, United Kingdom, Cambridge Press: 2000).

102 Ibid.

103 Department of Health and Human Services, *National Household Survey on Drug Abuse: Main Findings 1995* (Washington, DC: Government Printing Office, 1997).

104 Jerome G. Miller, *Search and Destroy: African-American Males in the Criminal Justice System* (New York: Cambridge University Press, 1996).

105 Thomas C. Castellano and Craig G. Uchida, "Local Drug Enforcement, Prosecutors and Case Attrition: Theoretical Perspectives for the Drug War," *American Journal of Police,* IX, no. 1 (1990): 147.

106 Bureau of Justice Assistance, *An Introduction to DARE,* 2nd ed. (Washington, DC: Government Printing Office, 1991).

107 Law Enforcement News. "When It Comes to the Young, Anti-Drug Efforts Are Going to Pot," *Law Enforcement News,* 22: 441–447.

108 Susan T. Emmett et al., "How Effective Is Drug Abuse Resistance Education?: A Meta-Analysis of Project DARE Outcome Evaluations," *American Journal of Public Health,* 84 (September 1994): 1394–1401.

109 Dennis Rosenbaum and Gordon Hanson, "Assessing the Effects of School-Based Drug Education: A Six-Year Multi-Level Analysis of Project D.A.R.E" (Unpublished manuscript: University of Illinois at Chicago, 1998); Donald Lynam et al., "Project DARE: No Effects at 10-Year Follow-Up," *Journal of Consulting and Clinical Psychology,* 67 (1999): 590–593.

110 Lorraine Green, "Cleaning Up Drug Hot Spots in Oakland: The Displacement and Diffusion Effects," *Justice Quarterly,* 12 (December 1995): 737–754.

111 Walter Miller, *Crime by Youth Gangs and Groups in the United States* (Washington, DC: Government Printing Office, 1982).

112 Arlen Egley, *Highlights of the 1999 National Youth Gang Survey* (Washington, DC: Office of Juvenile Justice Delinquency Prevention, 2000).

113 James Fox, *Trends in Juvenile Violence* (Washington, DC: Bureau of Justice Statistics, 1996).

114 Charles M. Katz, Vincent J. Webb, and David R. Schaefer, "The Validity of Police Gang Intelligence Lists: Examining the Differences in Delinquency between Documented Gang Members and Non-documented Delinquent Youth," *Police Quarterly,* 3 (2000): 413–437.

115 Cheryl Maxson, *Street Gangs and Drug Sales in Two Suburban Cities* (Washington, DC: National Institute of Justice, 1995).

116 Finn Esbensen and David Huizinga, "Gangs, Drugs, and Delinquency in a Survey of Urban Youth, *Criminology,* 31 (1993): 565–590.

117 C. Ronald Huff, *Gangs in America* (Newbury Park, CA: Sage, 1993); Jerome Needle and William Stapleton, *Police Handling of Youth Gangs. Reports of the National Juvenile Justice Assessment Centers* (Washington, DC: Government Printing Office, 1983).

118 Charles M. Katz, Edward R. Maguire, and Dennis Roncek, "A Macro-Level Analysis of the Creation of Specialized Police Gang Units: An Examination of Rational, Social Threat, and Resource Dependency Perspectives" (Unpublished manuscript: Arizona State University West, 2000), p. 14.

119 Bureau of Justice Statistics, *Law Enforcement Management and Administrative Statistics, 1997: Data for Individual State and Local Agencies with 100 or More Officers* (Washington, DC: Government Printing Office, 1999).

120 Katz, Maguire, and Roncek, "A Macro-Level Analysis of the Creation of Specialized Police Gang Units."

121 Charles M. Katz, "The Establishment of a Police Gang Unit: An Examination of Organizational and Environmental Factors," *Criminology,* 39, no. 1 (2001): 37–73.

122 Malcolm Klein, Margaret Gordon, and Cheryl Maxson, "The Impact of Police Investigations on Police Reported Rates of Gang and Nongang Homicides, *Criminology,* 24 (1986): 489–511.

123 Finn-Aage Esbensen, *Preventing Adolescent Gang Involvement* (Washington, DC: Office of Juvenile Justice and Delinquency Prevention, 2000).

124 Finn-Aage Esbensen and D. Wayne Osgood, *National Evaluation of G.R.E.A.T.* (Washington, DC: National Institute of Justice, 1997).

125 Lawrence W. Sherman, James W. Shaw, and Dennis P. Rogan, *The Kansas City Gun Experiment* (Washington, DC: Government Printing Office, 1995).

126 "Indy Gun-Interdiction Drive Proves an Inviting Target," *Law Enforcement News* (July 20, 1995).

127 http://www.fbi.gov/majcases/lovewolf/loneworlf2.htm

128 Susan Martin, "Police and the Production of Hate Crimes: Continuity and Change in One Jurisdiction," *Police Quarterly,* 2 (1999): 417–437.

129 James Garofalo and Susan Martin, *Bias-Motivated Crimes: Their Characteristics and the Law Enforcement Response* (Carbondale: Southern Illinois University, 1993).

130 Ibid.

131 Ibid.

132 Ibid.

133 U.S. Departments of Education and Justice, *1999 Annual Report on School Safety* (Washington, DC: Department of Education and Department of Justice, 1999).

134 Ibid.

135 Judi Villa, "Zero Tolerance Being Questioned," *The Arizona Republic* (May 19, 2001), p. 1.

136 U.S. Departments of Education and Justice, *1999 Annual Report on School Safety.*

137 Ibid.

138 http://www.usdoj.gov/cops/news_info/press_releases/pr_2_12_01.htm

139 http://www.nasro.org

140 Federal Bureau of Investigation, *Terrorism in the United States, 1998* (Washington, DC: Federal Bureau of Investigation, 1999).

141 Ibid.

142 Ibid.

143 Ibid.

144 http://www.decisiondrivers.com/static/aboutgg/pressrel/pr20001002a.html; http://www.findarticles.com/m3311/n20_v32/20365835/p1/article.jhtml

145 David Carter and Andra Katz, "Computer Crime: An Emerging Challenge for Law Enforcement," *Law Enforcement Bulletin* (December 1996).

146 Guadalupe Gonzalez, "Cybercrime," Congressional Statement to the Senate Committee on Judiciary on April 21, 2000. Available: http://fbi.gov/congress/congress00/gonza042100.htm

147 Ibid.

148 Mark Correia and Craig Bowling, "Veering toward Digital Disorder: Computer-Related Crime and Law Enforcement Preparedness," *Police Quarterly*, 2, no. 2 (1999): 225–244.

CHAPTER SEVEN

Innovations in Policing

CHAPTER OUTLINE

INTRODUCTION

For almost 20 years community policing and its many variations have become the new orthodoxy of policing.[1] Community policing, its advocates argue, represents a new philosophy of policing aimed at increasing the quality of police efforts.[2] This chapter examines community policing, along with its variations—problem-oriented policing and zero-tolerance policing—and discusses its assumptions, characteristics, and impacts.

KEY TERMS AND CONCEPTS

IMPETUS FOR CHANGE IN POLICING

Both community policing and problem-oriented policing originated in the late 1970s and early 1980s as a result of a series of crises in policing. First, the police–community relations problems of the 1960s had created a crisis of legitimacy. Local police departments were isolated and alienated from important segments of the community, particularly racial and ethnic minority populations.[3]

Second, recent research had undermined the assumptions of traditional police management and police reform. The Kansas City Patrol Experiment found that there were limits to the ability of traditional police patrol to deter crime (Chapter 4). Studies of the criminal investigation process raised doubts about the ability of the police to significantly increase the number of arrests (Chapter 5). Furthermore, research showed that faster response time does not usually increase the likelihood of arrests. In short, the traditional reforms of more police, more patrol, more detectives, and faster response time were seen as not likely to improve policing. At the same time, the traditional police goal of providing an immediate response to all citizen calls for service, regardless of the nature of the call, burdened the police with an enormous workload (Chapter 4).

Third, experts recognized that the police role is extremely complex, involving many different tasks and responsibilities (Chapter 1). It was discovered that only a small part of police work was related to criminal law enforcement and that most police work involves order maintenance and service activities (Chapter 4). As a consequence, experts recognized that if the police were to become more effective, they were going to have to broaden their characterization of police work from one that exclusively focused on crime control to one that also focuses on such issues as community quality of life, order maintenance, and fear of crime.

Fourth, experts began to recognize the importance of citizens as coproducers of police services.[4] The police depend on citizens to report crime and to request help in dealing with disorder. The decision to arrest is heavily influenced by the expressed preference for arrest on the part of a citizen. Successful prosecution of offenders depends heavily on the cooperation of victims and witnesses. Even more important, informal social control at the neighborhood level was increasingly recognized as the key to limiting crime and disorder. In short, there was growing recognition that the police cannot control crime by themselves.

THE ROOTS OF COMMUNITY POLICING: THE BROKEN WINDOWS HYPOTHESIS

James Q. Wilson and George L. Kelling influenced the history of policing forever when they teamed together and wrote an essay entitled "Broken Windows" for *Atlantic Monthly* magazine. They argued that the police should focus their resources on disorder problems affecting the quality of neighborhood life.[5] In particular, they emphasized that the police should address those problems that creates fear of crime and lead to neighborhood decay.

The image of broken windows symbolizes the relationship between disorder, neighborhood decay, and crime. A broken window, Wilson and Kelling argue, is a sign that nobody cares about the appearance of the property. Left unrepaired, it encourages other neighborhood residents to neglect their property. This sets in motion a downward spiral of deterioration. Houses deteriorate, homeowners move out, residential buildings are converted to rental properties, houses are converted from single-family to multifamily dwellings, and some houses are abandoned. As the income level of the neighborhood declines, neighborhood stores close and property values decline. Gradually, crime in the neighborhood increases.[6] (See Figure 7–1.)

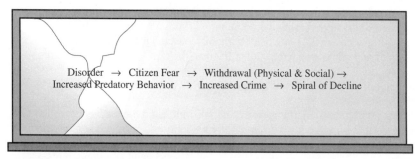

Disorder → Citizen Fear → Withdrawal (Physical & Social) → Increased Predatory Behavior → Increased Crime → Spiral of Decline

FIGURE 7–1
BROKEN WINDOWS HYPOTHESIS

Source: George Kelling and William Bratton, "Declining Crime Rates: Insiders' Views of the New York City Story," *The Journal of Criminal Law & Criminology,* 88, no. 4 (1998): 1217–1231.

These initial signs of disorder include drunks hanging out on the street or groups of teenagers on street corners. Such events create fear for personal safety in the minds of law-abiding residents in the neighborhood. Out of fear, they stay at home and withdraw from active participation in the neighborhood. In extreme cases they move out of the neighborhood altogether. The withdrawal of law-abiding citizens undermines the fabric of neighborhood life. The disorderly elements gain control of public areas, street corners, and parks; and the process of deterioration accelerates. The ultimate end of this process is serious predatory crime, such as burglary and robbery.

Wilson and Kelling maintain that traditional policing focuses on the end result of this process: serious crime. Yet the evidence indicates that the police officer's ability to fight crime is very limited. They argue that the police should intervene at the beginning of the process of neighborhood deterioration—at the first signs of neglect and disorder.

Types of Disorder

Wilson and Kelling emphasize the importance of disorder rather than serious crime. Disorder is an extremely broad category. Wesley Skogan has distinguished between two major subcategories of disorder: (1) human and (2) physical. Human disorder includes such issues as public drinking, streetcorner gangs, street harassment, street-level drug sale and use, noisy neighbors, and commercial sex. Physical disorder meanwhile includes such problems as vandalism, dilapidation and abandonment of buildings, and rubbish.[7]

SIDEBAR 7–1   BROKEN WINDOWS OR BROKEN THEORY?

While there has been a great deal of discussion surrounding the broken windows hypothesis, little research has actually examined the relationship between disorder, fear, and serious crime. One of the few studies to examine this theory is Wesley Skogan's research that examined disorder and crime in forty neighborhoods in six major cities. He found that perceptions of crime, fear of crime, and victimization are all related to physical and social disorder.[8]

However, Harcourt reexamined Skogan's data and found that his findings were largely driven by a few neighborhoods in which the relationship between disorder and crime was strong.[9] In particular, he found that if Skogan had excluded the neighborhoods of Newark, New Jersey, from his analyses, he would not have found a relationship between disorder and crime. Harcourt referred to this as the "Newark effect."

Eck and Maguire, addressing this debate, analyzed the data once again. They reported that had Skogan removed other neighborhoods from his analysis, outliers in which there was no relationship between disorder and crime, Skogan's finding of a relationship between disorder and crime would have been even stronger. They concluded that "Skogan's results are extremely sensitive to outliers and therefore do not provide a sound basis for policy. Rather, they suggest possible relationships that deserve further inquiry."[10]

CHARACTERISTICS OF COMMUNITY POLICING

While community policing is being ushered into police departments across the nation, studies have illustrated that few understand the underlying concept. For example, one national survey of law enforcement agencies found that only about 50 percent of the police chiefs and sheriffs queried had a clear understanding of what community policing means.[11] Therefore, it should not be surprising that community policing has come to mean different things to different people. Popular strategies include instituting foot or bicycle patrols, establishing neighborhood police substations, identifying neighborhood problems, dealing with disorder, organizing community meetings, or conducting community surveys.[12] In fact, because the label of community policing has been attached to such a variety of activities and programs, some reformers express concern that community policing has come to mean anything that is new and innovative in American policing.[13]

Despite this confusion, there does appear to be a consensus about some of the basic elements of community policing, and how it differs from previous policing strategies. The most important difference is that community policing represents a *major change in the role of the police.* While the police have traditionally defined their primary mission in terms of crime control, community policing seeks to broaden the police role to include such issues as fear of crime, order maintenance, conflict resolution, neighborhood decay, and social and physical disorder as basic functions of the police.

Mastrofski argues that this shift in mission of the police from being primarily concerned with serious crime to order maintenance is justified in two ways. First, reducing minor disorder may lead to a decrease in serious crime. The broken windows hypothesis, as discussed above, asserts that an increase in community decay produces an increase in serious crime, and only by redirecting police services toward neighborhood deterioration and disorder can a community prevent crime. Second, he asserts that order maintenance is "justifiable in its own right in that it contributes to the establishment of a civil, livable environment in which citizens may, without fear, exercise their right to pursue their livelihood."[14]

In an ideal sense, then, community policing seeks to change the basic tenets for which most Americans, including the police, view the police functions and priorities.

Because the implementation of community policing involves a number of philosophical, organizational, strategic, and tactical changes,[15] it is helpful to focus on the three most commonly discussed targets of community policing reform: (1) community partnerships, (2) organizational change, and (3) problem solving.

Community Partnerships

Community-policing advocates assert that the most effective way of reducing community decay and disorder is through a collaborative relationship between the police and the community. This broadened view recognizes that cooperation between the police and the public will give police greater access to information provided by the community, which in turn will lead the police to be more responsive to the community's needs.[16] Accordingly, the community-policing model stresses greater interaction between the police and the public, so that both entities act as coproducers of crime prevention and control.[17] Such a model, in an ideal sense, seeks to create a two-way working relationship between the community and the police, in which the police become more integrated into the local community and citizens assume an active role in crime control and prevention.[18]

Bayley, in his seminal book *The Police for the Future,* maintains that two elements are needed to successfully implement partnerships between the police and the public: consultation and mobilization.

Consultation   Under community policing, agencies have sought to improve the quality of their crime control and prevention efforts by consulting with citizens in their community. This strategy is intended to help the community and police define and prioritize problems. Consultation between the police and the public, usually done in the form of community meetings, serves four functions: (1) It provides a forum for citizens to express their problems and needs, (2) it allows the police to educate citizens about crime and disorder in their community, (3) it allows citizens to express complaints involving the police, and (4) it provides a forum for the police to inform the community about their successes and failures.[19]

For example, the Miami-Dade police department created the Marine Advisory Support Team (MAST) project in the late 1990s, which was "an effort to facilitate community participation . . . and to bring together concerned parties to provide input and identify ways to improve service to the boating public and related interests." Representatives on the team included residents and businesses that lived and operated in and around the Biscayne Bay as well as federal, state, and local law enforcement agencies that had jurisdiction over the bay. Once a month MAST team members meet to discuss crime and disorder. Aside from making agencies aware of problems, the meetings have also led to the prioritization of community problems and to the sharing of resources to address the problems.[20]

While ideally all four of the functions are fulfilled, research has found that partnerships between the police and the public vary in terms of the level of involvement of each partner and the expectations that each has of the other. In some agencies community members are simply encouraged to act as the eyes and ears of the police. In other agencies police officers speak at community meetings or work alongside citizen volunteers. In still other agencies, formal relationships are established between the police and citizens in which the community works alongside the police to identify problems, develop possible solutions, and actively participate in responding to problems.[21]

Regardless, a distinctive characteristic of the police under community policing is that the police seek to reposition themselves so that they become an integral part of community life rather than remain distant and alienated from the community as in years past. By embedding themselves within the community "it is asserted that the police and public actually co-produce public safety."[22]

Mobilization   Because the police have recognized their own limitations in preventing crime and disorder, police agencies that have embraced community policing have mobilized the community for assistance. Mobilization comes in the form of such programs as Neighborhood Watch, Operation ID, and Crime Stoppers. These community organization strategies not only are a deterrent mechanism but also increase neighborhood cohesion and provide a forum for the police to inform the community of crime prevention techniques.[23] Bayley adds that while the majority of mobilization efforts have dealt with the general public, other municipal agencies can play a critical role in the prevention of crime: "Sanitation departments can haul away abandoned cars, parks and recreation agencies [can] open facilities at night or develop programs for young people, [and] fire and building inspectors [can] condemn abandoned buildings."[24]

Accordingly, under community policing the police expand the number of tools available to them, taking them beyond a reliance on arrest to solve problems. For example, they also use civil and administrative law to broaden their capacity to address quality-of-life concerns in neighborhoods. Many police agencies today work closely with zoning inspectors and other city officials to deal with problems related to local businesses that detract from a neighborhood's quality of life (e.g., commercial sex shops, bars) as well as landlords and homeowners who fail to properly maintain their property.[25] In many communities today it is not unusual for the police to partner with another agency within the city to address city code violations such as weeds, debris, inoperable vehicles, and graffiti to ensure the quality of life in neighborhoods.

For instance, in Portland, Oregon, the police department saw the number of drug houses increase from just a few to over 200 in a single year. The police department did not have the time, or the resources, to address the problem using traditional methods such as undercover work. As an alternative strategy they decided to mobilize landlords, the individuals who would be able to evict drug-dealing renters. In particular, the police department embarked on a program that educated and trained landlords about their rights and responsibilities. They taught landlords how to screen applicants, identify drug activity, evict tenants, and work with neighbors and the police. Over a 2-year period more than 5,750 landlords, who oversaw 100,000 rental units, had received training.[26]

As such, community policing is largely focused on establishing and maintaining relationships between the police and the community—whether it be with citizens, community groups, other public or private agencies—to address neighborhood crime and disorder problems. The police seek to broaden their role to one that is "seen as shifting from first government responder to social diagnostician and community mobilizer." Building linkages and relationships with others in the community allows the police to bring together a variety of services to address a specific issue or problem that may affect community safety.[27]

The Effectiveness of Community Partnerships

Foot Patrol   One of the most common ways police agencies have attempted to bring the police and citizenry together while at the same time attempting to reduce crime has been through the use of foot patrol. A number of evaluations that examined foot patrol in the 1980s reported that while additional foot patrol did not reduce crime, it did increase feelings of safety. Moreover, citizens generalized these positive feelings to the police department—and not just to the foot patrol officers but to the department as a whole.[28] This finding has led some researchers to speculate that while the police might not be able to reduce crime, perhaps they can reduce fear of crime. And if people are less fearful, they might not withdraw from the communities, and the process of neighborhood deterioration might not begin.[29]

Other studies examining police efforts at increasing police–citizen interaction, however, have found that such strategies can be effective in reducing crime. For example, in Oakland and Birmingham researchers found that both fear of crime and violent crime substantially decreased in beats where police officers made door-to-door contacts with residents.[30] In Houston researchers examining community policing found that home visits by the police led to a decrease in violent crime and disorder in the city.[31]

Neighborhood Watch Neighborhood Crime Watch programs are another popular community partnership strategy. Neighborhood Watch programs, however, have repeatedly been found to have little impact on crime.[32] Research conducted in Britain, where some of the most comprehensive studies have taken place, has shown that "there is no strong evidence that Neighborhood Watch has prevented a single crime in Britain since its inception in the early 1980s."[33] These studies have found that Neighborhood Watch programs are typically more active, and have a closer working relationship with the police, in affluent suburban areas with little crime. Residents who live in areas with more crime, and who live in inner-city minority neighborhoods, have been less willing to participate in Neighborhood Watch programs, or any other activities that involve partnership with the police.[34]

Policing Where "Community" Has Collapsed One of the major questions surrounding community policing is whether it is a realistic strategy for the poorest and most crime-ravaged neighborhoods. Community organizing assumes that there is a viable community to help organize. The worst neighborhoods of many big cities—what some commentators call the "underclass"—are so devastated by unemployment, crime, and all the related social problems that no meaningful community remains. Most of the natural community leaders have left: those with stable employment, with families, and with a commitment to their neighborhood. In the absence of positive influences, gangs often become a focal point for young men's lives.

In their contribution to the *Perspectives on Policing* series, Hubert Williams and Patrick V. Murphy warned that "community-oriented approaches that are effective in most neighborhoods work less well, or not at all, in areas inhabited by low-income blacks and other minority groups."[35] Their point was confirmed by the University of Maryland report, *Preventing Crime*. Sherman and his colleagues found that programs directed at families, schools, and communities tend to be most effective where they are needed least. They are least effective in the families, schools, and communities that need the most help. The Maryland report made a very significant contribution to our understanding of crime prevention by emphasizing the interrelationship between families, schools, neighborhoods, and economic opportunities (what it called "labor markets").[36]

At the same time, communities in the traditional sense often do not exist in some newer and rapidly expanding cities. The Houston fear reduction experiment found that the city had an "almost nonexistent neighborhood life."[37]

It may be that community-organizing efforts may help organize only the middle class. The fear reduction experiment in Houston and the community-organizing programs in Minneapolis encountered the same phenomenon: They were more successful among middle-income people, homeowners, and whites than among the really poor, renters, and racial minorities.[38] Successful community organizing among white homeowners may be motivated by racism: their fear of blacks and Hispanics moving into the neighborhood. If this is the case, police-sponsored community-organizing activities may heighten racial conflict. A review of community-organizing efforts, in fact, reached the disturbing conclusion that the strongest community organizations it could identify "arose in response to impending or actual racial change." It would be tragic if community-policing efforts assisted resistance to equal housing opportunity.[39]

Community partnership efforts in Chicago have begun to challenge this often-cited criticism of community policing. New research conducted by Wesley Skogan suggests that after 4 years of intensive efforts by the police to partner with the community, residents in crime-blighted areas in Chicago are beginning to participate in neighborhood crime programs. They found that attendance at community meetings was highest among blacks who lived in high-crime areas and made less than $15,000 a year.[40] However, it has yet to be determined whether these findings are unique to Chicago and the Chicago community-policing experience or whether they signal a shift in citizen patterns of community partnership with the police.

Organizational Change

Community policing also calls for organizational change. Eck and Maguire argue that organizational change in agencies moving toward community policing is necessary for two reasons: "First, to stimulate and encourage officers to perform community policing functions; [and] second, to make the organization more flexible and amenable to developing community partnerships and creative problem solving strategies."[41] The authors maintain that there are three organizational changes that agencies need to make if they are to successfully implement community policing: (1) organizational structure, (2) organizational culture, and (3) management.

Organizational Structure   While traditionally police departments have been characterized by a highly centralized organizational design, community-policing organizations are decentralized. This means that they have fewer levels of management, have less specialization, and allow for more discretion on the part of the line officer.[42] A key assumption of community policing is that police agencies must remain flexible so that they can handle a variety of problems in different communities. Therefore, to accomplish this, line officers are given a great deal of discretion in diagnosing local problems.[43]

The community-policing organization is also characterized by consistently assigning officers to a particular neighborhood or geographic area. This strategy not only is intended to foster a sense of geographic responsibility but also is a means of holding officers accountable for what takes place in their beat. Community-policing advocates also argue that this tactic "is necessary in order to take advantage of the particular knowledge that can come through greater police involvement in the community and feedback from it."[44]

Organizational Culture   Traditional police organizational culture stressed the importance of crime fighting. As a consequence, the transition to community policing has largely been a battle for the hearts and minds of police officers.[45] Many advocates of community policing articulate that with the implementation of community policing will come a "new breed" of police officers who will be much more knowledgeable about, and experienced in, problem solving and community interaction, and who will be much more productive and satisfied with their work.[46]

A number of police departments have attempted to change their agency's organizational culture by implementing organizational reforms such as using participative management styles that embrace police officer input in departmental decision making (see Chapter 14); providing formal training to officers on community partnerships, problem solving, and other community-policing tactics; changing promotional standards so that officers who embrace community policing are advanced within the organization; and changing departmental evaluation standards so that evaluations reinforce the value of community-policing activities.[47]

Management   The adoption of community policing also affects police management. In the past police managers primarily focused on issues of control through discipline by emphasizing departmental rules and regulations.[48] In community policing managers are expected to assist neighborhood officers in developing community contacts, counsel the neighborhood officer on political issues, assist the neighborhood officer in acquiring resources, and facilitate training opportunities for the neighborhood officer. Therefore, community-policing organizations are characterized by having more managers and fewer supervisors.[49]

For example, in St. Petersburg Chief Goliath David made a number of management-oriented changes in an effort to enhance the department's community-policing efforts. Prior to the changes sergeants were responsible for supervising officers responding to calls for service, which coincidently conflicted with the sergeants' responsibility for supervising community-policing officers. As such, the supervisors had little time to assist the officers with projects or train new community-policing officers on community policing. After a police and community retreat Chief David made a number of organizational changes, including the addition of a shift community-police sergeant. This sergeant reported directly to the district major, instead of the lieutenant and captain as regular patrol sergeants were required to do, and was solely responsible for managing community-policing officers. This strategy, the chief argued, allowed the sergeants much more free time to work alongside officers and allowed them greater access to resources that were required to address neighborhood crime and disorder.[50]

Evidence of Organizational Change

There has been very little evidence suggesting that police organizations have changed their organizational structure as a consequence of implementing community policing. A 1997 study of police organizations found that police organizational structures had not changed significantly since 1987. In particular, they found that police organizations were no more likely to have fewer rules or policies or fewer supervisory levels since the inception of community policing.[51]

On the other hand, altering the structure of the organization so that officers are permanently assigned to a beat has been found to have some beneficial effects. For example, permanent beat assignment in Chicago neighborhoods resulted in residents reporting increased levels of police visibility, which was attributed to increased officer activity taking place as a consequence of the officers becoming more knowledgeable about the areas they were policing.[52] Similar findings were reported in Philadelphia where police officers were permanently assigned to public housing areas. In particular, officers who were permanently assigned to a public housing site were significantly more likely to initiate investigations, indicating an increased sense of officer ownership and responsibility, than officers who were not permanently assigned to a site.[53]

Research has shown that police occupational culture in many police agencies has changed significantly because of the implementation of community policing. Zhao and associates surveyed officers in one Northwestern police department that was well known for practicing community policing. He found that the officers' occupational values changed significantly from 1993 to 1996. The researchers reported an increase in the values reflecting personal happiness, comfort, and security.[54] Other studies have similarly found that after community policing has been implemented in an agency, police officers' attitudes toward community policing gradually improve along with knowledge about community policing.[55]

Many police agencies have incorporated community-policing-related principles in their academy training curricula to help facilitate cultural change. Haarr's research examining training in Arizona found that while training on community-policing principles has the desired effect, its impact quickly dissipates after the officer leaves the academy and is exposed to the work environment. The research also found that community-policing principles were not reinforced during the recruits' field training experience.[56]

Generally, these findings suggest that training alone may not have an impact on fostering a police culture that is supportive of community policing, but that police culture can change with the implementation of community policing, although the change will take a great deal of time.

Studies examining the changing role of management in community-policing organizations have generally been positive. Mastrofski's examination of community policing in Indianapolis found that community policing may have changed the role of supervisors. Sergeants in Indianapolis were found to believe that performing supportive activities, such as helping officers work through problems in their neighborhoods, was much more important than performing constraining activities, such as enforcing departmental policies or monitoring officers.[57]

Wycoff and Skogan likewise found that the implementation of participatory management in the Madison, Wisconsin, police department led to a number of positive outcomes. In particular, they found that officers were more satisfied with their work, thought that their work was more important, and believed that they had much more autonomy in the workplace.[58]

Problem Solving

The last element of community policing is problem solving. Here, the police and the community engage in a cooperative effort to solve neighborhood problems. The defining feature of problem solving is that it requires the participants to identify the underlying causes of problems rather than simply responding to the problem itself. Problem solving can be enacted in a number of ways: It can involve the police mobilizing and consulting with neighborhood residents; it can involve neighborhood residents, typically through neighborhood associations, identifying the root cause of a problem and mobilizing the police or another governmental service to address the problem; or it can be done by a neighborhood police officer who regularly confers with neighborhood residents as part of his or her regular duties.

Cordner notes that problem solving, as performed in the course of community policing, is often confused with problem-oriented policing (discussed in the next section). Problem solving, he articulates, was adopted as part of community policing as a neighborhood-level strategy to address chronic problems. As such, he argues that problem-solving activities tend to be small in nature.[59] With this said, problem-oriented policing has become an important part of community policing in many police departments across the country. In practice, problem-oriented policing can be implemented alone or as part of community policing.

Because problem solving and problem-oriented policing are often intertwined and examined together, we discuss their differences, characteristics, and impacts in greater detail in the section below.

PULLING IT ALL TOGETHER: IMPLEMENTING COMMUNITY POLICING AT THE DEPARTMENTAL LEVEL

While community policing has been said to be implemented in police agencies across the country, there has been little consensus about the extent to which community policing has been implemented on a departmentwide basis. Maguire and Katz, using data supplied by the Police Foundation, examined community policing in 1,600 police agencies. They found that agencies that claimed to have implemented community policing were more likely to embrace some elements of community policing more than others. In particular, they found that police departments that had implemented community policing were more likely to perform patrol-level and organizational activities associated with community policing than they were to perform citizen and management activities associated with community policing. The authors conclude that "changes in the role of mid-management and citizens in community policing may be particularly difficult to implement because they require that police agencies make real and substantial changes in the way that they do business."[60]

Chicago Alternative Policing Strategy (CAPS) Program

Chicago Alternative Policing Strategy (CAPS) represents one of the most ambitious community-policing efforts in the nation. With over 12,000 sworn officers, the Chicago police department is the second largest in the country. An ongoing evaluation by Wesley Skogan provides valuable insights into both the possibilities and the problems of implementing a new policing philosophy throughout a big-city department.[61]

The CAPS Plan   CAPS began with extensive planning, involving a number of experts from outside the police department. After much discussion and revision, CAPS was designed around six basic points:

1 Involvement of the entire police department and the entire city. Some community-policing programs, by contrast, involve specialized units separate from the basic operations of the department and/or particular neighborhoods.

2 Permanent beat assignments for officers. To enhance officer knowledge of and involvement in neighborhood problems, officers would be given permanent beat assignments.

3 A serious commitment to training. If community policing truly represents a different philosophy, it is necessary to train officers regarding the new expectations about their job.

4 Significant community involvement. One of the basic principles of community policing is that it involves a high level of citizen input and partnership with the police.

5 A close link between policing and the delivery of other city services. CAPS was intended to address neighborhood problems by helping citizens mobilize other city agencies to improve the delivery of services.

6 Emphasis on crime analysis. A heavy emphasis was placed on geographic analysis of crime patterns, using sophisticated computer analysis, to identify problems.

CAPS leaders assumed at the outset that the program would take between 3 and 5 years to implement. Although CAPS was implemented citywide, five districts were selected as prototype districts and subject to extensive evaluation. Each of these districts had a population of approximately 500,000 people, or about the size of many big cities.

Obstacles to Change   Implementation of CAPS encountered a number of major obstacles. The first was the problem of resources. Strong public opposition killed a proposed tax increase. Consultants, however, identified 1,600 officers in the department who could be reassigned to provide more efficient police services. Finally, the city obtained federal and state grants to hire more officers and support CAPS.

A second and related problem was strong public opposition to the planned closing of precinct station houses. Although designed as an efficiency measure, many residents felt that they were losing "their" police presence and the proposal was killed.

A third and major problem involved getting the rank-and-file officers committed to CAPS. Unlike some other community-policing programs, CAPS did not rely on volunteers. The police culture is highly resistant to change. Surveys of Chicago officers, however, found significant differences in attitudes within the rank and file. Generally, older officers, racial and ethnic minority officers, and female officers were more open to change than younger, white, and male officers. A majority of all officers were extremely pessimistic at the outset, believing that community policing would blur the lines of authority between police and citizens, and put unreasonable demands on the police to solve all community problems.

The attitudes of the rank and file were related to another serious problem: supervision and performance evaluations. Since CAPS represented a new philosophy and a new role for the police, it required new forms of supervision and performance evaluation. Rank-and-file officers understandably asked what they were expected to do under CAPS and how they would be evaluated. This proved to be a major controversy and was never fully resolved.

Another major problem was the 911 system. The traditional approach to calls for service would pull officers away from problem-solving activities and dispatch officers outside their beats (thereby violating the beat integrity principle of the program). CAPS attempted to address this extremely difficult problem in several ways. First, it capped the number of times officers could be dispatched out of their beats. Second, it created special rapid-response teams to handle critical incidents. Third, it attempted to limit the number of calls by developing new dispatching priorities.[62]

CAPS in Action   The heart of CAPS was citizen interaction with the police. This was attempted through a regular series of beat meetings, where citizens and beat officers would be able to discuss neighborhood problems and possible solutions.

As Skogan and Hartnett point out, "Making beat meetings work was hard."[63] Officers thought meetings took time away from "real" police work. The typical meeting involved about twenty-five citizens and five officers, and took about an hour and a half. The agenda for each meeting was "just frank talk."[64] Attendance tended to be higher in African American neighborhoods, primarily because of concern about crime.

Figure 7–2 indicates the problems identified at beat meetings in five districts evaluated by Skogan. Drugs were clearly the problem of greatest concern. Other crime-related issues were also frequently mentioned. Many of the problems fell into the disorder category: youth problems, loud music, and the like. Significantly, police disregard for citizens was the fourth most frequently mentioned problem, indicating that CAPS faced a significant problem in public distrust.

Observations of beat meetings found that the goal of police–citizen partnerships was not met. Police officers generally dominated meetings and controlled the agenda. The goals were met at a higher rate in some neighborhoods (Rogers Park) than in others (Morgan Park).

Getting other city agencies involved in problem solving was a major problem in Chicago. This has also been found to be a common problem in other cities that have attempted to implement community policing. An evaluation of community policing in eight cities, for example, had found that this effort failed in seven of them.[65] In Chicago, a special Mayor's Office of Inquiry and Information (MOII) was responsible to seeing that other agencies cooperated with CAPS. The key instrument was a one-page service request form, which indicated a problem and the agency responsible for it. Specific requests involved replacement of missing street signs, closing or demolition of abandoned buildings, removal of graffiti, and towing of abandoned vehicles. These involved the physical decay category of disorder.

CAPS produced a number of different problem-solving activities. Under Operation Beat Feet, sixty residents in Rogers Park marched through part of the neighborhood at night in a form of "positive loitering" to deter potential criminals. Members of the Englewood community also conducted a march against drugs. Rogers Park residents initiated court action against the owner of a building that was the center of criminal activity. Morgan Park developed a Beatlink program that allowed business owners to contact patrol officers directly through beepers.

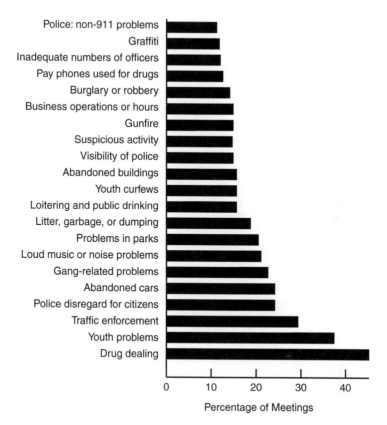

FIGURE 7–2
TOP PROBLEMS AT BEAT MEETINGS

Source: Wesley G. Skogan and Susan M. Hartnett, *Community Policing: Chicago Style* (New York: Oxford University Press), p. 121, fig. 5–1.

Evaluation of CAPS   A wide-ranging evaluation of CAPS found mixed results. Telephone surveys found a relatively high level of awareness of the program, but that awareness did not increase as time went on. Citizens in most of the evaluation districts also reported seeing police officers more often than before. In most of the evaluation districts there was also an increase in the visibility of informal contacts between police and citizens. There were significant increases as well in public perceptions that the police were responding to their concerns and dealing with crime, along with reduced fear of crime. Especially important, over 80 percent of the respondents indicated that police stopping too many people and being too tough was not a problem in their area. Consistent with previous surveys, African Americans (13 percent) were far more likely than whites (3 percent) to say that police use of excessive force was a problem.

In the end, CAPS met some but not all of its goals. Most important, officers did change the way they went about their jobs, spending more time on problem solving. There were significant perceived changes in the quality of life in the prototype districts: less crime, less fear, fewer gangs, and a greater sense of police responsiveness. The police department did not, however, succeed in fully implementing its crime-mapping program. There were also problems in achieving the desired level of citizen involvement.

The major achievement in Chicago is that some small but notable changes were accomplished in a citywide reorientation of policing. Most community-policing projects in other cities have been small pilot projects, focusing on limited areas or problems, and usually involving volunteers. The CAPS experience suggested that a reorientation of a major police department was possible.

The one major failure of CAPS was the inability to include some segments of the community. Latino renters, low-income households, and high school nongraduates in Chicago were the least aware of and least involved in CAPS. This is partially consistent with other community-oriented projects, which are generally more effective with whites and homeowners than racial and ethnic minorities and renters. (See Table 7–1.)

COMMUNITY POLICING: PROBLEMS AND PROSPECTS

Although community policing is an important development, many unanswered questions about it remain.[66] Some advocates maintain that the era of community policing has already arrived.[67] Critics argue, however, that it is premature to claim that community policing either dominates contemporary policing or has proved to be a long-term success. There are a number of key questions about community policing that need to be addressed.

Rhetoric or Reality?

The basic question, according to Greene and Mastrofski, is whether the concept is "rhetoric or reality."[68] Do particular community-policing programs represent something genuinely new, or is it simply new rhetoric being used to describe traditional policing?[69] Hunter and Barker warn that for many people community policing "seeks to be all things to all people," with little meaningful content. At the same time, some police executives use the rhetoric of community policing as a way of appearing to be progressive and innovative without actually abandoning traditional policing.[70]

David Bayley explains that it is simply too difficult to say whether or not "community policing" is being implemented in police departments across the country because the concept itself is too hard to describe. He argues that many of the strategies and tactics used by the police to implement community policing are diverse and varied, and that coupling the ambiguous concept (community policing) with such varied responses makes it too difficult to say how widespread changes have been.[71]

Too Rapid Expansion

Closely related to the problem of rhetoric rather than substantive programming is the danger of too rapid expansion. Because of its great popularity, some cities have adopted community policing without careful planning. The Chicago CAPS program illustrates the problems of reorienting police officers, securing compliance with other city agencies, and ensuring genuine community participation.[72]

TABLE 7-1   PERSONAL BACKGROUND AND AWARENESS OF CAPS, 1996–1999

	1996	1997	1998	1999
Total %	53	68	79	80
Whites	52	7	78	80
Blacks	58	74	84	84
Latinos	51	62	73	73
Spanish	47	51	65	68
English	54	71	80	81
Age 18–29	46	66	76	76
Age 30–49	61	74	83	84
Age 50–64	53	74	80	82
Age 65+	46	53	65	73
No. of Cases	1,868	3,066	2,937	2,871
Renters	50	67	75	76
Homeowners	58	74	83	84
Low income	48	59	69	73
Moderate income	59	76	84	84
Nongraduates	41	54	62	69
High school graduates	56	73	82	82
Females	50	66	76	76
Males	59	75	87	84

Note: All subgroup percentages are based on data weighted to standardize the racial composition of the samples across the years.
Source: Wesley Skogan, Susan Hartnett, Jill Dubois, Jennifer Comey, Karla Twedt-Ball, and J. Erik Gudell, *Public Involvement: Community Policing in Chicago* (Washington DC: National Institute of Justice, 2000).

A Legitimate Police Role?

One key issue in the community-policing debate involves the question of the proper police role. Should police officers function as community organizers and work on housing
problems and cleaning up vacant lots? Is this the proper role for a police officer with arrest power? Or should police officers spend their time and energy on serious crime?

There is no right or wrong answer to this question. It is a matter of policy choice. A
community may define the police role in those terms, if it wishes to do so. Another community may prefer the more traditional police role. The fact that the police role has been
defined one way for many years does not mean that it cannot be defined in a different
way. Change is not impossible. As historians of the police point out, the crime-attack
role that dominates today is not as traditional as many people think. In fact, it developed
only over the last 50 years (see Chapter 2).

A Political Police?

David Bayley warns that one aspect of changing the police role is the danger of involving the police in politics. One of the basic principles of Anglo-American law is the idea
of clearly defined limits on all government power, and on the police in particular.
Bayley refers to this as the "minimalist" tradition of policing.[73] These limits are embodied in the Bill of Rights. Community policing, however, expands the police role and
erodes the traditional limits. Bayley refers to this as "maximalist" policing. Should police officers, for example, be going door to door, calling on law-abiding citizens when
those people have not called the police? If the police organize community groups, there
is the danger that they will turn into political advocacy groups that will lobby for candidates or issues that the police support.[74]

Furthermore, Bayley adds, the deeper the police delve into social structural issues to
uncover the root causes of neighborhood problems, the greater the probability that they
will place limitations on individual liberties. For example, after police officers in
Portland, Oregon, researched the nature of increased citizen complaints about disorderly
conduct around neighborhood mini-marts, they found that the sale of malt liquor and
cheap wine was attracting gang members and transients. To remedy the problem the officers asked the shop owners to voluntarily stop selling the malt liquor and cheap wine.
However, the shop owners, who were all members of a single ethnic group, believed
that the police had discriminatorily singled them out. While the issue was eventually resolved, the police officers learned that while encouraging social responsibility is part of
their role within the community, it can have negative side effects.[75]

Decentralization and Accountability

One of the basic principles of community policing is decentralized decision making: giving rank-and-file officers more authority to decide what problems to work on and how to
use their time. Decentralization, however, creates the problem of potential loss of control
over police behavior, resulting in abuse of authority. As Herman Goldstein puts it, "How
free should community officers be to select alternatives for solving problems?"[76]

Most of the gains in controlling police misconduct, including corruption (Chapter 10)
and use of force (Chapter 11), have been achieved through centralized command and

control. One major device has been administrative rulemaking: providing officers with written rules about what kinds of conduct are not permitted (Chapter 8).

An evaluation of the New York City CPOP program found that the traditional methods of supervising patrol officers were inappropriate for community policing. These methods are bureaucratic in nature, asking officers to account for the use of their time and their contacts with the public, and designed primarily to control misbehavior. In New York City there was special concern that giving officers too much leeway would lead to corruption—a recurring problem in the department. The CPOP program required sergeants to play more of a manager role than a strictly disciplinarian role. Sergeants had to assist officers in problem solving, represent the CPOP unit to the rest of the department (where there was some hostility), and represent it to the community.[77]

George Kelling and James Stewart warn of the dangers inherent in encouraging police officers to be responsive to community residents. A majority of the residents may demand things that are illegal or improper. Kelling and Stewart point out that "a neighborhood anti-crime group that consists exclusively of home owning whites in a racially mixed neighborhood" may only increase the level of racial conflict in the area.[78] Critics of community policing point to the "kick ass" policing style described in Wilson and Kelling's "Broken Windows." In that article, a Chicago police officer explains how the police remove gang members from a public housing project: "We kick ass." Wilson and Kelling note that this approach is not consistent "with any conception of due process and fair treatment."[79] The issue here is the tension between community demands for order and the requirements of due process and equal protection.

Conflicting Community Interests

Working with the community sounds wonderful in theory, but Michael Buerger's study of the Minneapolis RECAP program found that in some instances community interests conflicted with the objectives of an innovative police program. One program targeted shoplifting at convenience stores. It turned out, however, that corporate officials were more worried about potential lawsuits from customers than shoplifting, which they tended to regard as a normal business expense. Some store owners, meanwhile, were afraid that a strong police presence would alienate and scare off their good customers. A proposal to exclude juveniles from stores after curfews conflicted with a larger corporate program to provide safe havens to children. The police also tried to discourage landlords from renting to suspected drug dealers. But many landlords preferred some drug dealers because they paid their rent on time, in cash, and generally tried to avoid attracting attention. In short, conflicting interests—especially financial interests—of some community residents can obstruct creative programs to solve community problems.[80]

THE ROOTS OF PROBLEM-ORIENTED POLICING

Herman Goldstein pioneered a new approach to the police role in 1979 with his concept of problem-oriented policing.[81] Goldstein had played a pivotal role in recognizing the complexity of the police role through his work with the American Bar Foundation Survey of Criminal Justice in the 1950s.[82] He then helped draft the American Bar Association (ABA) standards that emphasized the many different responsibilities of the police.[83] In his 1977 book, *Policing a Free Society,* Goldstein argues that we should think of the police as a government agency providing a wide range of miscellaneous services.[84]

The central idea in Goldstein's initial article on problem-oriented policing was that the police had traditionally defined their role in terms of vague and general categories: crime, order maintenance, and service. In practice, however, each of these general categories includes many different kinds of problems. The category of crime, for example, includes murder, burglary, and drunk driving, each of which is a very different kind of social event. The category of disorder includes domestic disputes, mental health problems, public drunkenness, and many other problems. Goldstein argues that the police should take these categories and break them down into discrete problems and then develop specific responses to each one—in short, problem-oriented policing.[85]

Goldstein also points out that the traditional measures of police effectiveness are not useful. Not only are the data in the official Uniform Crime Reports (UCR) system extremely problematic, but the UCR system collapses all crimes into one global category. A problem-oriented approach would require specific measures of effectiveness for specific problems.[86]

Along with a growing number of experts, Goldstein argues that the police are the prisoners of their communications system. The 911 system forces them into a reactive role: devoting most of their resources to responding to calls for service.[87] This reactive role means that the police think in terms of isolated incidents (calls). Goldstein argues that this prevents any serious planning with respect to underlying problems.

Figure 7–3 illustrates the differences between traditional, 911-driven, incident-based policing and problem-oriented policing. Under the traditional approach, each incident is handled as an isolated event. Police officers are concerned only with responding to each and every incident. Problem-oriented policing, on the other hand, emphasizes the analysis of problems and developing appropriate solutions to respond to the problems. Such a model necessitates the decentralization of power within the police department so that line-level officers not only have the ability to identify problems but also are empowered to do something about them.[88]

Problem-oriented policing is often confused with community-oriented policing or is implemented as part of a departmentwide community-policing strategy. However, as seen in Table 7–2 on page 233, what differentiates problem-oriented policing from community policing is its emphasis on the end product of policing rather than the means by which policing is done.[89] Eck and Maguire note that "simply put, in community policing building a strong positive relationship between the public and the police is the goal. Addressing problems is secondary. Whereas in problem-oriented policing the goal is to reduce problems of concern to the public. Close community partnerships are often important elements in addressing problems, but they are not the final objective."[90]

THE PROBLEM-SOLVING PROCESS

Eck and Spelman point out that problem-oriented policing is typically implemented through a four-stage process known as SARA: (1) scanning, (2) analysis, (3) response, and (4) assessment.

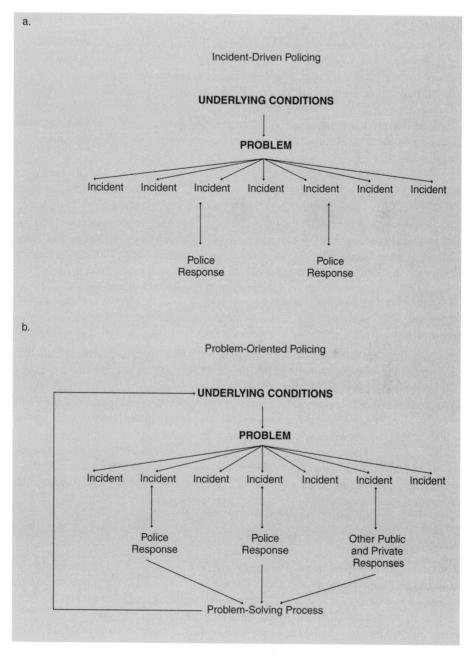

FIGURE 7–3
TRADITIONAL VERSUS PROBLEM-ORIENTED POLICING

Source: John Eck and William Spellman, *Problem Solving: Problem Oriented Policy in Newport News* (Washington, DC: PERF, 1987), Fig. 1, p. 4.

Scanning

The first stage of the SARA model is scanning. Scanning can be done in a number of ways. For example, over the course of their shift, the officers can look for and identify possible problems in their beat. Another strategy is for the officers to review calls for service and complaints to identify potential problems. Still another scanning strategy is to consult with residents who live or work in the officers' assigned area. However, the problems that are to be identified under the SARA model are not individual incidents with no association with one another, but rather problems that have some underlying cause.

Analysis

The second stage of the SARA model is analysis. This stage requires the police to collect information about the problem in an attempt to identify its scope, nature, and cause. This often leads to the police focusing on "three categories of problem characteristics: actors (victims, offenders, third parties); incidents (physical setting, social context, sequence of events); and past responses (by the community and its institutions)."[91]

Response

The third stage of the SARA model is response. The data collected during the analysis stage are used to develop a strategy to address the problem and implement a response. The response typically includes the use of alternative solutions that often incorporate the assistance of residents, other units within the police department, other governmental agencies, local businesses, private organizations, or any other person or group that might be able to help with the needed response. Problem-oriented policing emphasizes that the response should go beyond traditional crime control strategies and use strategies and tactics that will have an impact on the conditions that generate crime and disorder— rather than just treat the symptom itself (i.e., crime and disorder). Such a strategy then attempts to include a greater number of tools on the tool belt of the police.

Assessment

The last stage of the SARA model is assessment. The assessment involves an evaluation of the effectiveness of the response. It is intended to go beyond impressionistic or anecdotal evidence of success and incorporate rigorous feedback that allows the police to revise their response if it is not successful. The feedback also allows the police the opportunity to reexamine whether or not they identified the problem correctly. Because the police use a wide variety of responses, due to the wide variety of problems that they are required to address, no single type of assessment is possible. As such, the police are sometimes required to go beyond using existing data sources, such as calls for service, to measure, for example, changes in crime, and have to collect and analyze nontraditional data, such as photographs, to measure, for example, changes in physical disorder. (See Figure 7–4.)

FIGURE 7–4 SARA PROBLEM-SOLVING MODEL

SUMMARY OF SCANNING STEPS

Step 1
- Laundry list of potential problems.

Step 2
- Problems identified.

Step 3
- Problems prioritized.

Step 4
- State the specific problem.
- List examples of where the problem occurs.
- Which setting is causing the most difficulty?

Review and Preparation for Analysis

Hypothesis
- From what you already know, what do you think is causing the problem?
- General goal statement.
- How will data be gathered and reported?
- When will data collection begin?

SUMMARY OF ANALYSIS STEPS

Step 1
- What conditions or events precede the problem?
- What conditions or events accompany the problem?
- What are the problem's consequences?
- What harms result from the problem?

Step 2
- How often does the problem occur?
- How long has this been a problem?
- What is the duration of each occurrence of the problem?

Now that the data have been collected, should you continue with analysis or return to scanning and restate the problem?

Step 3
- Define a tentative goal.
- Identify resources that may be of assistance in solving the problem.
- What procedures, policies, or rules have been established to address the problem?

SUMMARY OF RESPONSE STEPS

Step 1
- Brainstorm possible interventions.

Step 2
- Consider feasibility and choose among alternatives.
- What needs to be done before the plan is implemented?
- Who will be responsible for preliminary actions?

Step 3
- Outline the plan and who might be responsible for each part.
- Will this plan accomplish all or part of the goal?
- State the specific goals this plan will accomplish.
- What are some ways data might be collected?

FIGURE 7-4 CONTINUED

Step 4
- Realistically, what are the most likely problems with implementing the plan?
- What are some possible procedures to follow when the plan is not working or when it is not being implemented correctly?

Implement the Plan
SUMMARY OF ASSESSMENT STEPS

Step 1
- Was the plan implemented?
- What was the goal as specified in the response?
- Was the goal attained?
- How do you know if the goal was attained?

Step 2
- What is likely to happen if the plan is removed?
- What is likely to happen if the plan remains in place?
- Identify new strategies to increase the effectiveness of the plan.
- How can the plan be monitored in the future?

Step 3
- Post-implementation planning
- Plan modification
- Follow-up assessment

Source: Police Executive Research Forum, *SARA Problem Solving Model,* **http://www.policeforum.org/sara.html**

EFFECTIVENESS OF PROBLEM-ORIENTED POLICING

Evaluations of problem-oriented policing have generally been more positive than evaluations of community policing. This section reviews those projects that have used the strongest research designs or that have received a significant amount of national attention.

Problem-Oriented Policing in Newport News

The first significant problem-oriented policing experiment occurred in Newport News, Virginia. For several years the police had faced a problem of a high rate of burglaries in the New Briarfield apartment complex. Increased police presence in the area reduced reported burglaries by 60 percent, but when the officers were transferred to other areas, the burglary rate increased again. By 1984 the apartment complex was generating more calls for service than any other residential area in the city. At this point, the police department decided to abandon traditional methods and to experiment with problem-oriented policing.[92]

The project utilized the SARA model. The scanning phase began with an analysis of crime patterns in the area and an opinion survey of apartment residents. The survey helped reveal the extent to which the physical deterioration in the buildings contributed to burglaries. The police department task force assigned to New Briarfield responded

FIGURE 7–5   PUBLIC AGENCIES CONTACTED FOR INFORMATION
ON THE NEW BRIARFIELD BURGLARY PROBLEM

Newport News city agencies
  Office of Business Licenses—business license records
  Clerk of Courts—deed records
  Department of Codes Compliance—building safety information
  Fire Department—fire and arson data
  Planning Department—land use and census data
  Department of Public Works—street cleaning and sanitation information
  Redevelopment and Housing Authority—data on housing subsidy programs
  Tax Assessor's Office—property values and tax payments

State agencies
  Virginia Corporation Commission—corporate records
  California Corporation Commission—corporate records

Federal agencies
  Federal Bureau of Investigation (local office)—fraud investigation issues
  Internal Revenue Service—ownership patterns
  Department of Housing and Urban Development (Washington, D.C., central office)—
    housing standards and loan default data
  Office of Management and Budget—multifamily housing problems and HUD
    assistance programs

Source: John E. Eck and William Spelman, *Problems-Solving: Problem-Oriented Policing in Newport News* (Washington, DC: Police Executive Research Forum, 1987), table 9, p. 70.

with tactics that addressed the physical condition of the buildings. The police also organized a meeting of the various government agencies that had some responsibility for the housing project. Figure 7–5 lists the public agencies contacted. The purpose of the meeting was to develop a coordinated strategy to improve conditions in the complex. A police officer assigned to the project helped organize a tenants' group, which put pressure on city officials to make improvements in the apartments before demolition began. Ultimately, however, a decision was made to demolish the apartments and relocate the residents.

Official statistics did indicate a drop in reported crime because of problem-oriented policing. More important, the activities of the officers represented a new role for the police in problem-oriented and community policing: conducting surveys of public opinion to identify neighborhood problems. By initiating the meetings about the apartment complex, police officers were acting as community organizers or brokers of government services.

SMART in Oakland

The SMART (Specialized Multi-Agency Response Team) program in Oakland[93] incorporated the concept of "hot spots": particular locations with high levels of reported crime, disorder, and/or high rates of calls for service.[94] The Oakland program concentrated on drug hot spots, particularly houses or apartment buildings where there were believed to be high rates of drug activity. The most important element of the program involved site visits by representatives of many different government agencies: housing code enforcement, fire department, utilities, and so on (see the section on Newport News, pp. 224–225). Special emphasis was placed on aggressive enforcement of housing code violations to force landlords to fix up their properties (the broken windows hypothesis). The California Health and Safety Code makes it a violation to maintain a dwelling where controlled substances are manufactured, sold, or used. In addition, there was a landlord-training program to help apartment owners screen tenants and keep out potential drug dealers.

Lorraine Green's evaluation of SMART found reductions in crime and disorder in most of the properties targeted by the program. Moreover, crime and disorder were not displaced to the surrounding areas, and in fact there appeared to be a "diffusion" of benefits to those areas. In short, targeting specific hot spots led to a general improvement in the quality of life in the immediately surrounding area.

SMART, in sum, combined many of the basic elements of problem-oriented policing: identifying specific problems (in this case, problem locations), coordinating the efforts of many different government agencies, and relying on measures outside the criminal justice system.

The Boston Gun Project: Operation Cease Fire

The Boston Gun Project was a problem-solving project that involved the Boston police department; the Bureau of Alcohol, Tobacco, and Firearms; federal and county prosecutors; county probation and patrol; City of Boston outreach workers; the Boston school

---

SIDEBAR 7–2   SAN DIEGO: CIVIL REMEDIES AS A PROBLEM-SOLVING TOOL

One of Herman Goldstein's main arguments is that the police should look beyond the criminal justice system for tools and resources to deal with problems of crime and disorder. The Oakland SMART program, for example, used aggressive housing code enforcement to attack drug hot spots.

The San Diego police department attacked the problem of street prostitution through restraining orders. Streetwalkers who would flag down cars and solicit pedestrians particularly affected one neighborhood. This activity degraded the quality of life for neighborhood residents and harmed local businesses by scaring away customers. Instead of the traditional approach of arresting the prostitutes, which rarely eliminates the problem, the San Diego police obtained restraining orders against individually named prostitutes, barring them from loitering and flagging down motorists. Violation of the restraining order would result in a 5-day jail term and a $1,000 fine. The restraining order approach appeared to work, as prostitutes disappeared from the area.

Sources: Office of Community Oriented Policing Services, *COPS Office Report* (Washington, DC: Government Printing Office, 1997), p. 32; Peter Finn and Maria O'Brien Hylton, *Using Civil Remedies for Criminal Behavior* (Washington, DC: Government Printing Office, 1994).

police; and youth corrections. In the early 1990s Boston was overwhelmed with an increase in youth homicides. Crime analysis revealed that there was an average of forty-three youth homicides per year in Boston between 1991 and 1995. After a thorough analysis facilitated by researchers at Harvard University, project participants found a strong illicit gun market providing firearms to youths. They also found that about 60 percent of the youths involved in the homicides were also associated with gangs that lived in three Boston neighborhoods.

The analyses led the project participants to believe that a successful response would have to include an attack on both the supply and demand for guns. A message was sent out to gang members that unless the shooting stopped gang members would be closely scrutinized by law enforcement officials and there would be serious repercussions. "Gang members were told that drug markets would be shut down, warrants would be served, the street would swarm with law enforcement officials (including federal presence), bed checks would be performed on probationers, rooms would be searched by parole officers, unregistered cars would be taken away, and disorder offenses such as drinking in public would be pursued." In one case a gang member who had been arrested on numerous other occasions for violent gang activity was found with a single bullet in his pocket. Because of his prior felony convictions he was prosecuted as a career criminal and received 20 years in prison.[95]

The assessment found that the project had an impact on crime, fear of crime, and resident satisfaction with the police. Two years after the operation had been in effect youth gang homicides dropped by 70 percent. Fear of crime among residents who lived in the impacted areas decreased by 21 percent and the number of residents having faith in the police to prevent crime increased by about 33 percent.[96]

The federal government has funded twenty-seven city Youth Crime Gun Interdiction initiatives based on the results of the Boston Gun Project. Minneapolis, Minnesota, and Lowell, Massachusetts, are beginning to see some positive results. Projects are currently under way in Chicago, Los Angeles, Rochester, New York City, Baltimore, Stockton, and other cities.[97]

Problem-Oriented Policing in Jersey City, New Jersey

In 1994, the National Institute of Justice funded a partnership between the University of Cincinnati, the Jersey City police department, and the Jersey City Housing Authority to implement and evaluate problem-oriented policing.[98] In one of the projects they used computerized mapping and database technologies to scan for areas with high levels of violence and drug trafficking. Twenty-four violent crime areas were identified, each of which was matched with another area based on the identified problem, the dynamics of the place, and the physical characteristics of the area.[99] The researchers then examined the twelve paired areas with one of the pair receiving problem-oriented policing and the other receiving the normal amount of traditional policing. After the analysis was completed, the officers responded to the root cause of the identified problem. Both official and observational data indicated that crime and disorder had decreased in the areas in which the police had used problem-oriented policing. Furthermore, they found that crime and disorder were not displaced to the surrounding areas.

A similar strategy was used to combat serious crime in six public housing sites in Jersey City.[100] Each public housing site was staffed with seven team members, including a police lieutenant, two community service officers, one site police officer, one civilian site manager, one social service agent, and one resident representative. Each site team used official and observational data as well as data gathered at community meetings to identify and analyze problems. In the end, the analysis at each site resulted in a variety of responses being used: situational crime prevention strategies (removing pay telephones), civil remedies (evictions and special leaseholder conditions), traditional policing (sweeps, arrests), treatment (alcohol and drug treatment), and crime prevention through environmental design tactics (increased lighting). They found that problem-oriented policing had a significant impact on serious crime in all six of the sites, regardless of the social structure of the site (i.e., age of residents, income level, percent single headed household, level of unemployment). They also found that the more problem-oriented policing activities used, the greater the impact that problem-oriented policing had on serious crime.

CHARACTERISTICS OF ZERO-TOLERANCE POLICING

Zero-tolerance policing is theoretically based on broken windows theory. It calls for the police to primarily focus on disorder, minor crime, and the appearance of crime.[101] It is characterized by interventions that aggressively enforce criminal and civil laws and that are conducted for the purpose of restoring order to communities. It is believed that through aggressive enforcement of disorder, residents will be more inclined to care for their community, which will increase order, which in turn will lead to a reduction in the fear of crime and ultimately signal to potential criminals that law breaking will not be tolerated.[102]

As shown in Table 7–2 (on page 233) zero-tolerance policing differs from other policing strategies in a number of important ways. First, community policing and problem-oriented policing are based on the notion that the police should focus on crime prevention, whereas zero-tolerance policing focuses on a crime attack model.[103] As such, Green notes that "zero tolerance policing has its roots in the suppressive aspect of policing. In some

FIGURE 7–6	THE SOCIAL INFLUENCE OF ZERO-TOLERANCE POLICING		
Police Conduct→	Social Meaning→	Social Norm→	Impact on Community
Police remove visible signs of disorder	Community cares and criminals are no longer in control	Orderliness	Law-abiders feel safe and criminals stop committing crimes

Source: Dorothy Roberts, "Forward: Race, Vagueness, and the Social Meaning of Order-Maintenance Policing," *The Journal of Criminal Law & Criminology,* 89, no. 3 (1992): 811.

respects it returns the police to a more traditional stance vis-à-vis law enforcement, a direction that is actively supported within many American police departments."[104]

Second, the strategy differentiates itself from community policing in that it is based on the presumption that the communities that need the police the most are also the least likely to have strong community social institutions. Therefore, while community policing is based on the idea that the community is a primary coproducer of crime control, zero-tolerance policing is based on the idea that the community may not be able to provide support for crime control strategies and that the police must take primary responsibility for crime control.[105]

Third, zero-tolerance policing differs from problem-oriented policing in that it does not attempt to carefully identify problems or thoroughly analyze the cause of problems.[106] Rather, zero-tolerance policing focuses on specific types of behavior. Minor crimes and disorder such as urinating in public, fare-beating (not paying the fare on the subway by jumping the turnstiles), prostitution, loitering, aggressive panhandling, graffiti, and "squeegeeing" (boys and young men who wash the windows of cars stopped at traffic lights) are a major focus.[107]

Fourth, zero-tolerance policing is characterized by its focus on place-specific interventions. Prior studies examining hot spots have found that a small proportion of addresses account for a disproportionate amount of crime and disorder (Chapter 4). Accordingly, a number of police departments across the country have begun to map crime, which allows them to direct zero-tolerance policing to hot spots.[108]

Fifth, zero-tolerance policing differentiates itself from other police innovations because it culturally and organizationally represents a back-to-the-basics strategy. Its crime-fighting emphasis lends itself to a more militaristic organizational design that is both centralized and internally focused (information flowing from the administration to the line officer)—a mission and organizational structure that many police are more comfortable and familiar with. Additionally, because of the emphasis on proactive law enforcement it does not require the police to make a fundamental change in police culture as do community policing and problem-oriented policing.[109]

The Effectiveness of Zero-Tolerance Policing

Perhaps the most well known implementation of zero-tolerance policing has taken place in New York City. On the basis of the broken windows theory, Police Commissioner William Bratton and Mayor Rudolph Giuliani instituted a zero-tolerance policing strategy in 1993. Prior to this time New York City was characterized by social disorder (unlicensed peddlers, homelessness, street-level drug use), physical disorder (graffiti), and crime. There was an overall sense that the city was out of control.[110] Chief Bratton commented that, "I can recall coming in from the airport, flying in to LaGuardia, and coming down that highway. It looked like something out of a futuristic movie in terms of graffiti on every highway wall, dirt on rubber tires that look like they have not been cleaned in years, burned out cars, litter everywhere."[111]

To address these problems the New York City police department instituted a zero-tolerance strategy that focused enforcement efforts on order maintenance offenses such as aggressive panhandling, vandalism, public drunkenness, public urination, and prostitution.[112] The strategy was, once again, based on the notion that by focusing police resources on disorder and minor crime, the police department could restore order, which would eventually lead to a reduction in crime. An analysis of crime data suggests that the department's shift in philosophy had a significant impact on the behavior of the officers. The number of misdemeanor arrests in New York City jumped dramatically from 1993 through 1996, increasing from 133,446 to 205,277.[113]

Many observers credit the new policing strategy with the drop in serious crime in New York City in the mid- to late 1990s. Since 1993, the overall crime rate has dropped by 27 percent, homicides have dropped by 40 percent (to their lowest level in 30 years), robbery has dropped by 30 percent, and burglary has dropped by 25 percent. These drops in crime are twice that of the national average.[114] These finding have led a number of experts to conclude that order maintenance policing is more effective than other police strategies.[115]

However, there is much controversy over whether zero-tolerance policing deserves credit for this accomplishment. While William Bratton, the police commissioner who instituted the policy, and criminologist George Kelling claimed that zero tolerance was directly responsible,[116] former New York City Mayor David Dinkins and former Police Commissioner Lee P. Brown claimed that the community policing program (CPOP) they initiated in the 1980s set in motion the reduction in crime. A number of criminologists have also pointed out that serious crime was declining in other cities, and that the reduction in New York City was part of a general trend. Serious crime fell in Washington, DC, for example, where the police department was marked by scandals and inefficiency. It also fell in Los Angeles, where officers were making fewer arrests in the aftermath of the 1991 Rodney King incident.[117]

A more systematic examination of the effects of zero-tolerance policing was conducted in Chandler, Arizona.[118] In 1995, it became clear to the Chandler City Council that the innermost part of the city had experienced an increase in physical and social disorder. The area was characterized by homes with broken and missing windows, doors falling off hinges, and trash and debris cluttering properties. The area was also well known for having high crime rates, street-level drug dealing, and prostitution.

The city responded by moving the zoning enforcement responsibilities from the planning and development department to the police department. This unit became responsible for the reduction of physical disorder by enforcing city code violations. The police department also established a specialized unit to aggressively enforce order maintenance laws. The two units worked in tandem, focusing their resources on four zones that were each approximately one square mile in size. This project became known as Operation Restoration and was theoretically based on the broken windows hypothesis.

Findings from the study suggested that the project had a significant impact on public morals crimes (e.g., prostitution), disorderly conduct, and physical disorder. Similar trends were also observed in the areas adjacent to the targeted area, suggesting that the project also had an impact on the surrounding area. These findings led the authors to conclude that cracking down on disorder and minor crime may not have a substantial impact on serious crime, but the benefits of such an approach may be limited to those problems that the project specifically focuses on—namely, physical and social disorder. It also led the researchers to question the theoretical foundations of zero-tolerance policing.

Potential Problems with Zero-Tolerance Policing

While zero-tolerance policing is quickly becoming a popular policing strategy across the country, a number of important questions remain. A number of critics have argued that there is no clear evidence that the strategy is effective in reducing crime. Others have questioned the negative impact that the strategy might have on communities.

Conflict between the Police and the Public   Zero-tolerance policing has been heavily criticized for encouraging officers to be overly aggressive. Some have gone as far as to refer to the policing strategy as "harassment policing."[119] Harcourt reports that since the inception of zero-tolerance policing in New York City the police department has seen a dramatic rise in the number of citizen complaints. From 1994 to 1996 the city received 8,316 abuse complaints, representing a 39 percent increase over the previous 3 years. Furthermore, these complaints have led to a 46 percent increase in settlements or judgments, with the city paying out about $70 million from 1994 to 1996 for police misconduct compared with $48 million in the previous 3 years.[120]

Amnesty International has reported similar findings: Citizens filing police misconduct charges against New York City police officers increased from 977 in 1987 to more than 2,000 in 1994. They further reported that the monetary awards granted to citizens in cases of police brutality increased from $13.5 million in 1992 to over $24 million in 1994.[121] In 2001 New York City agreed to pay $50 million to 58,000 people who were arrested in 1996 and 1997 as part of the department's zero tolerance practices. During the case, several men and women who had never been arrested before complained that instead of being issued a ticket for the minor offense (which was the policy in the past) they were booked and detained in a police detention center where they were required to disrobe, to lift their breasts or genitals, and to squat and cough.[122]

Some have alleged that the rise in complaints is largely a consequence of increases in arrests due to the zero-tolerance strategy. However, New York City's Civilian Complaint Review Board has reported that individuals who were not arrested by the officers made most of the complaints, and further reported that many of those who complained had never been arrested before.[123]

Increase in Crime in the Long Run   Sherman points out that while zero-tolerance policing might have a short-term impact on the reduction of crime, it may also result in an increase in serious crime in the long term. He argues that an arrest record can have a significant impact on a person's immediate and future employment. Additionally, he points out that arrests for minor offenses can lead to further, more serious crime by making a person more angry and defiant.[124]

Impact on Poor and Minority Communities   Harcourt argues that because zero-tolerance policing is focused on minor offenses such as loitering, panhandling, and public drinking, it will primarily be directed toward poorer communities, which, in turn, means minority communities. An examination of misdemeanor arrests shows that minorities are disproportionately arrested for misdemeanor offenses when compared with the percentage of minorities in the population. This trend is particularly strong for offenses that call for a great deal of discretion on the part of police officers such as arrests for suspicion. Accordingly, zero-tolerance policing may lead the police back down the path of losing legitimacy in the eyes of minorities, and minorities again seeing the police as a punitive occupying force.[125]

Harcourt emphasizes that the ultra-poor, minorities, and other "cultural outsiders" may be the most impacted. He states that "by handing over the informal power to define deviance to police officers and some community members, we may be enabling the repression of political, cultural, or sexual outsiders in a way that is antithetical to our conceptions of democratic theory or constitutional principles."[126]

An example of this can be found in Chandler, Arizona, where local businesses wanted day laborers—many of whom were illegal immigrants—removed from the streets for pandering because of their disruption to local business. In response, thirty Chandler police officers and six INS officers performed a crackdown for 5 days on illegal immigrants. The response team searched houses, stopped drivers, detained pedestrians, and interrogated children on their way to school to inquire about citizenship. In all, 432 immigrants and 2 United States citizens were deported. After the roundup several of the searches were found to be conducted illegally by the state's attorney general, and a number of residents came forward and complained about being harassed and beaten by the police because of their nationality. Official arrest records detailed the extent of the discrimination. One INS agent justifying an arrest in his report stated that he "immediately noticed a lack of personal hygiene displayed by the subject, and a strong odor common to illegal immigrants." The crackdown led to a $35 million lawsuit that was later settled out of court (see the section on the effectiveness of zero-tolerance policing in Chandler, Arizona, p. 230).[127]

The verdict is still out on the impact of zero-tolerance policing. There have been few studies examining its effectiveness. Future research is needed to assess whether or not this policing style is promising and whether or not there may be long-term negative consequences to its use.

SUMMARY: A NEW ERA IN POLICING?

For many police officials, community policing, problem-oriented policing, and zero-tolerance policing are simply buzzwords that mask traditional policing, or policing that many police officers believe they have been practicing for decades.[128]

Nonetheless, it is clear that the ideas of community policing, problem-oriented policing, and zero-tolerance policing have inspired a remarkable level of innovation in American policing. Bayley concludes that the last decade of the twentieth century may be the most creative period in policing since the modern police officer was put onto the streets of London in 1829."[129]

As a final note, Goldstein and Skolnick and Bayley all point out that we should not be too quick to argue that the innovations under these strategies have not proved to be effective. Neither have most of the activities labeled "traditional" policing. As we have

TABLE 7–2   COMPARISONS OF SOCIAL INTERACTIONS AND STRUCTURAL COMPONENTS OF VARIOUS FORMS OF POLICING

Social Interaction or Structural Dimension	Traditional Policing	Community Policing	Problem-Oriented Policing	Zero-Tolerance Policing
Focus of policing	Law enforcement	Community building through crime prevention	Law, order, and fear problems	Order problems
Forms of intervention	Reactive, based on criminal law	Proactive, on criminal, civil, and administrative law	Mixed, on criminal, civil, and administrative law	Proactive, uses criminal, civil, and administrative law
Range of police activity	Narrow, crime focused	Broad crime, order, fear, and quality-of-life focused	Narrow to broad—problem focused	Narrow, location and behavior focused
Level of discretion at line level	High and unaccountable	High and accountable to the community and local commanders	High and primarily accountable to the police administration	Low, but primarily accountable to the police administration
Focus of police culture	Inward, rejecting community	Outward, building partnerships	Mixed depending on problem, but analysis focused	Inward focused on attacking the target problem
Locus of decision making	Police directed, minimizes the involvement of others	Community-police coproduction, joint responsibility and assessment	Varied, police identify problems but with community involvement/action	Police directed, some linkage to others agencies where necessary
Communication flow	Downward from police to community	Horizontal between police and community	Horizontal between police and community	Downward from police to community
Range of community involvement	Low and passive	High and active	Mixed depending on problem set	Low and passive
Linkage with other agencies	Poor and intermittent	Participative and integrative in the overarching process	Participative and integrative depending on the problem set	'Moderate and intermittent
Type of organization and command focus	Centralized command and control	Decentralized with community linkage	Decentralized with local command accountability to central administration	Centralized or decentralized but internal focus
Implications for organizational change/development	Few, static organization fending off the environment	Many, dynamic organization focused on the environment and environmental interactions	Varied, focused on problem resolution but with import for organization intelligence and structure	Few, limited interventions focused on target problems, using many traditional methods
Measurement of success	Arrest and crime rates, particularly serious Part 1 crimes	Varied, crime, calls for service, fear reduction, use of public places, community linkages and contacts, safer neighborhoods	Varied, problems solved, minimized, displaced	Arrests, field stops, activity, location-specific reductions in targeted activity

Source: Jack R. Green, "Community Policing in America: Changing the Nature, Structure, and Function of the Police," in Julie Horney, ed., *Policies, Processes, and Decisions of the Criminal Justice System, Criminal Justice 2000, vol. 3* (Washington, DC: Government Printing Office, 2000), p. 311.

already learned, patrol (Chapter 4), criminal investigation (Chapter 5), and other activities are rarely subjected to rigorous evaluations; and even fewer evaluations have proved them to be effective.[130]

CASE STUDY: ADDRESSING REPEAT CALLS FOR SERVICE IN SAN DIEGO, CALIFORNIA: PROBLEM-ORIENTED POLICING IN ACTION

The intersection of First and Third Avenues was considered one of the busiest in southeastern San Diego. The only gas station and convenience store in the area occupied two corners of the intersection. Radio calls concerning belligerent panhandlers and drug-related activity at this corner increased dramatically over a 1-year period.

The gas station was the site of heavy pedestrian and vehicular traffic, and the liquor store across the street attracted gang members and panhandlers. Initially, patrol officers believed that the numerous police radio calls resulted from traffic in and around the gas station. Officer Abraham, a veteran of the area, had responded to many calls for service from the gas station, but had seldom observed evidence of illegal activity. Other officers responding to identical calls at the station confirmed her observations.

Officer Abraham called the crime analysis unit for a breakdown of the area's calls for service. She found that more than 100 radio calls had been dispatched to the gas station in the previous month, yet no arrests had been made. Officer Abraham became suspicious and decided to investigate more closely.

While on patrol a short time later, Officer Abraham responded to a radio call that reported panhandlers harassing customers at the gas station. When she arrived, however, the station clerk told her the panhandlers had just left the parking lot. The officer then drove across the street to observe the store while writing her report. While Officer Abraham observed the activity around the gas station, a second radio call was dispatched that again reported panhandlers harassing customers. When she saw no panhandlers, however, she drove across the street to speak with the manager. She learned from their discussion that the station's clerks were afraid of its clientele and thought that if the police were called on a regular basis (whether needed or not), the station's owner might be compelled to hire full-time security guards.

Officer Abraham explained that initiating false calls was illegal and that police would not participate in any scheme to manipulate the station's owner. She encouraged the clerks to discuss their fears with the owner, and she stressed that they must not call for police assistance unless it was really needed.

The radio calls to the property decreased to only a few per week. When she was in the vicinity, Officer Abraham occasionally stopped by the store to check on the clerks.

Source: Adapted from the Bureau of Justice Assistance, "Problem-Oriented Drug Enforcement: A Community-Based Approach for Effective Policing" (Washington, DC: 1993).

FOR DISCUSSION

Are the law enforcement agencies in your community doing community policing, problem-oriented policing, or zero-tolerance policing? Discuss the activities of your local agency:

1 What label is used to describe the program (COP, POP)?
2 What is the content of the program (community meetings, intensive drug enforcement, coordinated activities with noncriminal justice programs)?
3 Is the program departmentwide or operated by a special unit?
4 Has it been evaluated, and if so, what were the results of that evaluation?
5 Did the agency receive funds for additional officers from the COPS office?
6 What did the agency do with those officers?
7 If your agency is not engaged in community policing, problem-oriented policing, or zero-tolerance policing, find out why.

INTERNET EXERCISES

Exercise 1 The Chicago police department maintains a website with information about CAPS. Check out the site. What can you learn about the program? Are there any new developments since this book was written?

Exercise 2 Many police agencies describe their community policing, problem-oriented policing, and zero-tolerance policing programs on the Web. Check out the websites for several departments in your region of the country. What can you learn? Do they describe their programs in detail that is useful to you?

Exercise 3 The Police Executive Research Forum provides police departments across the country with technical assistance to implement community policing and problem-oriented policing. See the Internet site **http://www.policeforum.org.** What would you, as a student, like to see on the Internet site that is not already there? What would you, if you were a police administrator, want to see on the website that is not already there? Why would the inclusion of the missing content be helpful to others?

REFERENCES

1 John Eck and Dennis Rosenbaum, "The New Police Order: Effectiveness, Equity, and Efficiency in Community Policing," in Dennis Rosenbaum, ed., *The Challenge of Community Policing: Testing the Promise* (Thousand Oaks, CA: Sage Publications, 1994).
2 Jack R. Greene and Stephen D. Mastrofski, *Community Policing: Rhetoric or Reality* (New York: Praeger, 1988).
3 George L. Kelling and Mark H. Moore, "The Evolving Strategy of Policing," *Perspectives on Policing,* no. 4 (Washington, DC: Government Printing Office, 1988), p. 8; John P. Crank, "Watchman and Community: Myth and Institutionalization in Policing," *Law and Society Review,* 28, no. 2 (1994): 325–351.
4 Wesley G. Skogan and George E. Antunes, "Information, Apprehension, and Deterrence: Exploring the Limits of Police Productivity," *Journal of Criminal Justice,* 7 (Fall 1979): 232; James Frank, Steven G. Brandl, Robert E. Worden, and

Timothy S. Bynum, "Citizen Involvement in the Coproduction of Police Outputs," *Journal of Crime and Justice,* XIX, no. 2 (1996): 1–30.

5 James Q. Wilson and George L. Kelling, "Broken Windows: The Police and Neighborhood Safety," *Atlantic Monthly,* 249 (March 1982): 29–38.

6 Wesley G. Skogan, *Disorder and Decline: Crime and the Spiral of Decay in American Neighborhoods* (New York: Free Press, 1990), pp. 21–50.

7 Ibid.

8 Ibid.

9 Bernard Harcourt, "Reflecting on the Subject: A Critique of the Social Influence Conception of Deterrence, the Broken Windows Theory, and Order-Maintenance Policing New York Style," *Michigan Law Review,* 97 (1998): 1–51.

10 John Eck and Edward Maguire, "Have Changes in Policing Reduced Violent Crime? An Assessment of the Evidence," in Alfred Blumstein and Joel Wallman, eds., *The Crime Drop in America* (Cambridge: Cambridge University Press, 2000), pp. 207–265.

11 Mary Ann Wycoff, *Community Policing Strategies* (Washington DC: National Institute of Justice, 1995).

12 Dennis Rosenbaum, ed., *The Challenge of Community Policing: Testing the Promises* (Thousand Oaks, CA: Sage, 1994).

13 David Bayley, *Policing in America: Assessment and Prospects* (Washington, DC: Police Foundation, 1998); Jerome Skolnick and David Bayley, "Theme and Variation in Community Policing," in Michael Tonry and Norval Morris, eds., *Crime and Justice: A Review of the Research* (Chicago: University of Chicago Press, 1988).

14 Stephen Mastrofski, "Community Policing as Reform: A Cautionary Tale," in Stephen Mastrofski and Jack Greene, eds., *Community Policing: Rhetoric or Reality* (New York: Praeger, 1988); the above section was taken from a paper presented by Edward Maguire and Charles Katz entitled *The Validity and Reliability of Police Agencies' Community Policing Claims,* presented on November 22, 1997, at the annual meetings of the American Society of Criminology in San Diego, California.

15 Gary Cordner, "Community Policing: Elements and Effects" in Roger Dunham and Geoffrey Alpert, eds., *Critical Issues in Policing* (Prospect Heights, IL: Waveland, 1997).

16 Community Policing Consortium, *Understanding Community Policing: A Framework for Action* (Washington, DC: Bureau of Justice Assistance, 1994).

17 Jerome Skolnick and David Bayley, *The New Blue Line: Police Innovation in Six American Cities* (New York: The Free Press, 1986).

18 The above paragraph was taken from a paper presented by Edward Maguire and Charles Katz entitled *The Validity and Reliability of Police Agencies' Community Policing Claims.*

19 David Bayley, *Police for the Future* (New York: Oxford Press, 1994).

20 Daniel W. Flynn, *Defining the "Community" in Community Policing* (Washington, DC: PERF, 1998).

21 Community Policing Consortium, *Understanding Community Policing: A Framework for Action.*

22 Jack Green, "Community Policing in America: Changing the Nature, Structure, and Function of the Police," in Julie Horney, ed., *Policies, Processes, and Decisions of the Criminal Justice System* (Washington, DC: National Institute of Justice, 2000).

23 David Carter, "Community Alliance," in Larry Hoover, ed., *Police Management: Issues and Perspectives* (Washington, DC: PERF, 1992).

24 David Bayley, *Police for the Future;* the above paragraph was taken from a paper presented by Edward Maguire and Charles Katz entitled *The Validity and Reliability of Police Agencies' Community Policing Claims.*

25 Green, "Community Policing in America: Changing the Nature, Structure, and Function of the Police."

26 E. J. Williams, "Enforcing Social Responsibility and the Expanding Domain of the Police: Notes from the Portland Experience," *Crime & Delinquency,* 42, no. 2 (1996): 309–323.

27 Green, "Community Policing in America: Changing the Nature, Structure, and Function of the Police." p. 314.

28 The Police Foundation, *The Newark Foot Patrol Experiment* (Washington, DC: The Police Foundation, 1981).

29 James Q. Wilson and George L. Kelling, *"Making Neighborhoods Safe,"* The *Atlantic Monthly,* 263 (2) 46–52 (1989).

30 Craig Uchida, Brian Forst, and Sampson Annon, *Modern Policing and the Control of Illegal Drugs: Testing New Strategies in Two American Cities,* Final Report (Washington, DC: Police Foundation, 1992).

31 Wesley Skogan, "The Impact of Community Policing on Neighborhood Residents: A Cross-Site Analysis," pp. 167–181 in Dennis Rosenbaum, ed., *The Challenge of Community Policing* (Thousand Oaks, CA: Sage, 1994).

32 David Kessler and Sheila Duncan, "The Impact of Community Policing in Four Houston Neighborhoods," *Evaluation Review,* 20 (1996): 627–669.

33 Trevor Bennett, "Community Policing on the Ground: Developments in Britain," in Dennis Rosenbaum, ed., *The Challenge of Community Policing* (Thousand Oaks, CA: Sage, 1994) p. 240.

34 Ibid.

35 Hubert Williams and Patrick V. Murphy, "The Evolving Strategy of Police: A Minority View," *Perspectives on Policing,* no. 13 (Washington, DC: Government Printing Office, 1990), p. 12.

36 University of Maryland, *Preventing Crime: What Works, What Doesn't, What's Promising—A Report to the Attorney General of the United States* (Washington, DC: U.S. Department of Justice, Office of Justice Programs, 1997), pp. 8–1 to 8–58.

37 Skogan, *Disorder and Decline,* p. 95.

38 Ibid., p. 148.

39 Wesley G. Skogan, "Fear of Crime and Neighborhood Change," in Albert Reiss and Michael Tonry, eds., *Communities and Crime* (Chicago: University of Chicago Press, 1986), p. 222.

40 Wesley Skogan, Susan Hartnett, Jill DuBois, Jennifer Comey, Karla Twedt-Ball, and Erik Gudell, *Public Involvement: Community Policing in Chicago* (Washington, DC: National Institute of Justice, 2000).

41 Eck and Maguire, "Have Changes in Policing Reduced Violent Crime? An Assessment of the Evidence."

42 Green, "Community Policing in America: Changing the Nature, Structure, and Function of the Police."

43 Jerome Skolnick and David Bayley, *Community Policing: Issues and Practices around the World* (Washington, DC: National Institute of Justice, 1988); Bayley, *Police for the Future.*

44 Skolnick and Bayley, *Community Policing: Issues and Practices Around the World,* p. 14.

45 Arthur Lurigio and Wesley Skogen, "Winning the Hearts and Minds of Police Officers," in Ronald Glensor, Mark Correia, and Kenneth Peak, *Policing Communities* (Los Angeles: Roxbury Publishing, 2000).

46 Ibid.

47 Deb Weisel and John Eck, "Toward a Practical Approach to Organizational Change," in Ronald Glensor, Mark Correia, and Kenneth Peak, *Policing Communities* (Los Angeles: Roxbury Publishing, 2000).

48 Stephen Mastrofski, Roger Parks, and Robert Worden, *Community Policing in Action: Lessons from an Observational Study* (Washington, DC: National Institute of Justice, 1998).

49 R. Trojanowicz and B. Bucqueroux, *Toward Development of Meaningful and Effective Performance Evaluations* (East Lansing, MI: National Center for Community Policing, 1992); Bayley, *Police for the Future.*

50 Dennis J. Stevens, *Case Studies in Community Policing* (Upper Saddle River, NJ: Prentice Hall, 2000–2001).

51 Edward Maguire, "Structural Change in Large Municipal Police Organizations During the Community Policing Era," *Justice Quarterly,* 14, no. 3 (1997): 547–576.

52 Wesley G. Skogan and Susan M. Hartnett, *Community Policing, Chicago Style* (New York: Oxford University Press, 1997).

53 Robert Kane, "Permanent Beat Assignment in Association with Community Policing: Assessing the Impact on Police Officers' Field Activity," *Justice Quarterly,* 17, no. 2 (2000): 259–280.

54 Jihong Zhao, Ni He, and Nicholas Lovrich, "Value Change among Police Officers at a Time of Organizational Change: A Follow-Up Study Using Rokeach Values," forthcoming in *Policing: An International Journal of Police Strategies and Management.*

55 Dennis Rosenbaum, Sandy Yeh, and Deanna Wilkinson, "Impact of Community Policing on Police Personnel: A Quasi-Experimental Test," *Crime and Delinquency,* 40, no. 3 (1994): 331–353.

56 Robin Haarr, *The Impact of Community Policing Training and Program Implementation on Police Personnel: A Final Report,* presented to the National Institute of Justice, 2000.

57 Mastrofski, Parks, and Worden, *Community Policing in Action: Lessons from an Observational Study.*

58 Mary Ann Wycoff and Wesley G. Skogan, "The Effect of a Community Policing Management Style of Officers' Attitudes," *Crime and Delinquency,* 40, no. 3 (1994): 371–383.

59 Gary Cordner, "Problem-Oriented Policing vs. Zero Tolerance," in Tara O'Connor Shelly and Anne Grant, eds., *Problem Oriented Policing* (Washington, DC: Police Executive Research Forum, 1998).

60 Edward R. Maguire and Charles M. Katz, *Community Policing, Loose Coupling and Sensemaking in American Police Agencies,* presented at the annual meeting of the American Society of Criminology in San Diego, California, 1997.

61 Skogan and Hartnett, *Community Policing: Chicago Style.*

62 Ibid., pp. 67–68.

63 Ibid., p. 113.

64 Ibid., p. 114.

65 Susan Sadd and Randolph Grinc, "Innovative Neighborhood Policing: An Evaluation of Community Policing Programs in Eight Cities," in Dennis P. Rosenbaum, ed., *The Challenge of Community Policing: Testing the Promises* (Newbury Park, CA: Sage, 1994), pp. 27–52.

66 David Bayley, "Community Policing: A Report from the Devil's Advocate," in Greene and Mastrofski, eds., *Community Policing: Rhetoric or Reality,* pp. 225–237.

67 George L. Kelling and Mark H. Moore, "The Evolving Strategy of Policing," *Perspective on Policing,* no. 4 (Washington, DC: Government Printing Office, 1988).

68 Greene and Mastrofski, eds., *Community Policing: Rhetoric or Reality.*

69 Ibid.

70 Ronald D. Hunter and Thomas Barker, "BS and Buzzwords: The New Police Operational Style," *American Journal of Police,* 12, no. 3 (1993): 157–158.

71 David Bayley, *Policing in America: Assessment and Prospectus* (Washington, DC: Police Foundation, February 1998).

72 Skogan and Hartnett, *Community Policing: Chicago Style.*

73 Bayley, *Police for the Future,* pp. 126–128.

74 Bayley, "Community Policing: A Report from the Devil's Advocate."

75 Williams, "Enforcing Social Responsibility and the Expanding Domain of the Police: Notes from the Portland Experience."

76 Herman Goldstein, "Toward Community-Oriented Policing," *Crime and Delinquency,* 33 (January 1987): 12.

77 Jerome McElroy, Colleen Cosgrove, and Susan Sadd, *Community Policing: The CPOP in New York* (Newbury Park, CA: Sage, 1993).

78 George L. Kelling and James K. Stewart, "Neighborhoods and Police: The Maintenance of Civil Authority," *Perspectives on Policing,* no. 10 (Washington, DC: Government Printing Office, 1989), p. 4.

79 Wilson and Kelling, "Broken Windows."

80 Michael E. Buerger, "The Problems of Problem-Solving: Resistance, Interdependencies, and Conflicting Interests," *American Journal of Police,* XIII, no. 3 (1994): 1–36.

81 Herman Goldstein, "Improving Policing: A Problem-Oriented Approach," *Crime and Delinquency,* 25 (1979): 236–258; Herman Goldstein, *Problem-Oriented Policing* (New York: McGraw-Hill, 1990).

82 Samuel Walker, "Origins of the Contemporary Criminal Justice Paradigm: The American Bar Foundation Survey, 1953–1969," *Justice Quarterly,* 9 (March 1992): 47–76.

83 American Bar Association, *Standards Relating to the Urban Police Function,* 2nd ed. (Boston: Little, Brown, 1980), Standard 1–2.2.

84 Herman Goldstein, *Policing a Free Society* (Cambridge, MA: Ballinger, 1977).

85 Goldstein, "Improving Policing."

86 See the discussion in Geoffrey Alpert and Mark H. Moore, "Measuring Police Performance in the New Paradigm of Policing," in Department of Justice, *Performance Measures for the Criminal Justice System* (Washington, DC: Government Printing Office, 1993), pp. 109–140.

87 Malcolm K. Sparrow, Mark H. Moore, and David M. Kennedy, *Beyond 911* (New York: Basic Books, 1990).

88 Green, "Community Policing in America."

89 John Eck and William Spelman, "Who Ya Gonna Call: The Police as Problem Busters," *Crime and Delinquency,* 33 (1987): 31–52.

90 Eck and Maguire, "Have Changes in Policing Reduced Violent Crime? An Assessment of the Evidence," pp. 47–48.

91 John Eck and William Spelman, *Problem Solving: Problem Oriented Policing in Newport News* (Washington, DC: Police Executive Research Forum, 1987), p. 47.

92 Ibid.

93 Lorraine Green, "Cleaning Up Drug Hot Spots in Oakland, California: The Displacement and Diffusion Effects," *Justice Quarterly,* 12 (December 1995): 737–754.

94 Lawrence W. Sherman, Patrick R. Gartin, and Michael Buerger, "Hot Spots of Predatory Crime: Routine Activity and the Criminology of Place," *Criminology,* 27 (1989): 27–55.

95 David Kennedy, *Juvenile Gun Violence and Gun Markets in Boston* (Washington, DC: National Institute of Justice, 1997).

96 *Operation Cease Fire* (Boston: Boston Police Department, 1998).

97 Ibid.

98 Lorrain Green Mazerolle, Justine Ready, William Terrill, and Elin Waring, "Problem-Oriented Policing in Public Housing: The Jersey City Evaluation," *Justice Quarterly,* no. 1 (2000): 129–159.

99 Anthony Braga, David Weisburd, Elin Waring, Lorraine Green Mazerolle, William Spelman, and Francis Gajewski, "Problem-Oriented Policing in Violent Crime Places: A Randomized Controlled Experiment," *Criminology,* no. 3 (1999): 541–580.

100 Mazerolle, Ready, Terrill, and Waring, "Problem-Oriented Policing in Public Housing: The Jersey City Evaluation."

101 Cordner, "Problem-Oriented Policing vs. Zero Tolerance."

102 Dorothy Roberts, "Forward: Race, Vagueness, and the Social Meaning of Order-Maintenance Policing," *The Journal of Criminal Law & Criminology,* 89, no. 3 (1992) p. 811.

103 Green, "Community Policing in America: Changing the Nature, Structure, and Function of the Police."

104 Ibid., p. 318.

105 Ibid.

106 Cordner, "Problem-Oriented Policing vs. Zero Tolerance."

107 George Kelling and Catherine Coles, *Fixing Broken Windows* (New York: The Free Press, 1996).

108 Green, "Community Policing in America: Changing the Nature, Structure, and Function of the Police."

109 Ibid.

110 William Bratton, "Remark: New Strategies for Combating Crime in New York City," *Fordham Urban Journal,* 23 (1996): 781–785.

111 Ibid.

112 Dan Kahn, "Social Influence, Social Meaning, and Deterrence," *Virginia Law Review,* 83, (1997): 349–395.

113 Bernard Harcourt, "Reflecting on the Subject: A Critique of the Social Influence Conception of Deterrence, the Broken Windows Theory, and Order Maintenance Policing New York Style," *Michigan Law Review,* 97 (1998): 291–389.

114 Dan Kahn, "Social Influence, Social Meaning, and Deterrence."

115 Ibid.

116 William Bratton, *Turnaround: How America's Top Cop Reversed the Crime Epidemic* (New York: Random House, 1998).

117 Kelling and Coles, *Fixing Broken Windows;* Samuel Walker, *Sense and Nonsense about Crime,* 4th ed. (Belmont, CA: Wadsworth, 1998), pp. 273–279.

118 Charles Katz, Vincent Webb, David Schaefer, *An Assessment of the Impact of Quality of Life Policing on Crime and Disorder: A Final Report* (Phoenix: Arizona State University West, 2000).

119 Robert Panzarella, "Bratton Reinvents 'Harassment Model' of Policing," *Law Enforcement News,* June 15/30, 1998: 13–15.

120 Harcourt, "Reflecting on the Subject: A Critique of the Social Influence Conception of Deterrence, the Broken Windows Theory, and Order Maintenance Policing New York Style."

121 Amnesty International, *United States of America: Police Brutality and Excessive Use of Force in the New York City Police Department* (New York: Amnesty International, 1996).

122 Benjamin Weiser, "N.Y. Agrees to Pay $50 Million over Strip Searches in Minor Offenses," *International Herald Tribune,* January 11, 2001, p. 3.

123 Harcourt, "Reflecting on the Subject: A Critique of the Social Influence Conception of Deterrence, the Broken Windows Theory, and Order Maintenance Policing New York Style."

124 Lawrence Sherman, "Policing for Crime Prevention," *Preventing Crime: What Works, What Doesn't, What's Promising—A Report to the Attorney General of the United States,* pp. 8–1 to 8–58.

125 Green, "Community Policing in America: Changing the Nature, Structure, and Function of the Police."

126 Harcourt, "Reflecting on the Subject: A Critique of the Social Influence Conception of Deterrence, the Broken Windows Theory, and Order Maintenance Policing New York Style," p. 48.

127 Christian Parenti, *Lockdown America: Police and Prisons in the Age of Crisis* (New York: Verso, 2000).

128 Hunter and Barker, "BS and Buzzwords."

129 Bayley, *Police for the Future,* p. 101.

130 Goldstein, "Toward Community-Oriented Policing," p. 27; Skolnick and Bayley, *The New Blue Line.*

PART **THREE**

POLICE PROBLEMS

CHAPTER EIGHT

Police Discretion

CHAPTER OUTLINE

INTRODUCTION

Police officers routinely exercise discretion while doing their jobs. They make important decisions that affect citizens' lives: whether or not to stop a car, whether or not to make an arrest, and so on. This chapter examines the phenomenon of police discretion. It gives special attention to the underlying reasons for discretion, how discretion is used, the problems that result from its misuse, and different strategies for controlling discretion.

KEY TERMS AND CONCEPTS

DISCRETION IN POLICE WORK

A police officer patrolling a city park sees three young men hanging out together. He stops, investigates, and finds that they are drinking beer in violation of the local ordinance. At least one and possibly two of the guys may be underage. The officer confiscates the beer, pours it out, and tells the three guys to get out of the park. He could have issued citations but exercised his discretion not to do so.

Police officers routinely make critical decisions involving the life and liberty of citizens. These decisions call for *discretion*, or judgment on the part of the officer. Previous chapters have already covered many examples of police discretion. They include:

- **Domestic Violence Arrests.** Donald Black found that only 58 percent of people suspected of felonies were arrested.[1]
- **Mental Health Commitments.** Linda Teplin reported that only 11.8 percent of persons judged mentally disordered were referred to a medical facility.[2]
- **Traffic Tickets.** John Gardiner found that Dallas police officers wrote traffic tickets at a rate twenty times higher than that of Boston police.[3]
- **Juvenile Court Referrals.** Nathan Goldman found that in one city 8.6 percent of arrested juveniles were referred to juvenile court, compared with 71.2 percent in another city.[4]
- **Deadly Force.** The decision to use deadly force is the ultimate life and death decision made by police officers.[5]

A DEFINITION OF DISCRETION

Discretion may be defined as (1) an official action (2) by a criminal justice official (3) based on that individual's judgment about

FIGURE 8-1 DISCRETION AND THE LAW

Law and policy	xxxxxxxxxxxxxxxxxxxxxxxxxxx
Exercise of discretion	yyyyyyyyyyyyyyyyyyyyyyyyyyyyyyyyyyyyyyyyyyyyy
Abuse of discretion	zzzzzzzzzzzzzzzzzzzzzzz

| Strict compliance with the law and policy | Exercise of discretion within law and policy | Abuse of discretion outside of law and policy |

the best course of action.[6] The power to exercise discretion is not unlimited. Most important, it is limited by the law and administrative policy. The law defines the crime of arrest. A police officer uses his or her judgment about whether the facts of a particular situation fit the definition of a crime. Any decision that falls outside the parameters of the law is illegal. A decision within those parameters may not be the best decision, but it nonetheless represents a lawful exercise of discretion. Figure 8-1 illustrates the range of police officer actions, from full compliance with the law, to the lawful exercise of discretion, to the abuse of discretion.

Discretion is not confined to the police. It pervades the criminal justice system. Wayne LaFave argues that "it is helpful to look at the total criminal justice system as a series of interrelated discretionary choices."[7] The administration of justice is essentially the sum total of a series of discretionary decisions, from arrest through prosecution, trial, sentencing, and parole release. Judges, for example, sentence convicted offenders within the limits prescribed by law: prison versus probation; 1 year versus 3 years in prison.

ASPECTS OF POLICE DISCRETION

Street-Level Bureaucrats

The 911 center receives a call about a disturbance in an apartment, and two patrol officers are dispatched to the scene. They arrive to find clear evidence of a physical assault; the woman is bruised and the man may also have been hit. The department has a mandatory arrest policy directing officers to make an arrest where there is evidence of a felonious assault. It is about 40 minutes until shift change, the officers are tired from a busy night of calls, and they just give the two people a verbal warning and leave. In effect, the officers have undermined the department's mandatory arrest policy.

The example above illustrates the point that one of the special features of policing is that the lowest-ranking employees—patrol officers—exercise the greatest amount of discretion. James Q. Wilson comments that, in policing, "discretion increases as one move down the organizational hierarchy."[8] For this reason, patrol officers have been described as "street-level bureaucrats." They make the decisions that produce actual police policy as it affects citizens.[9] Through their discretion to arrest or not arrest, police officers are the gatekeepers of the criminal justice system. They determine the system's workload. If they do not arrest, there is no case for the rest of the system to handle. Police discretion also determines public policy. If police officers systematically do not make arrests for possession of small amounts of marijuana, for example, they effectively decriminalize that offense.

Potential Abuse of Discretion

Controlling discretion is important for many reasons.[10] The misuse of discretion by police officers can result in abuses of citizens or ineffective management of a police department. The major problems include:

• **Discrimination.** Abuse of discretion can involve discrimination based on race or ethnicity, in violation of the Fourteenth Amendment guarantee of equal protection of the law. The disparities in traffic stops of African Americans by the Maryland State Police, documented in the lawsuit against the department, indicate abuse of discretion in the decision to stop drivers on Interstate 95.[11]

• **Denial of Due Process.** In his study of police discretion in Chicago, Davis found that many discretionary police actions were illegal. He found officers deliberately harassing suspected drug dealers, prostitutes, and pimps, using illegal tactics rather than making arrests.[12]

• **Police–Community Relations Problems.** Uncontrolled discretion in arrest, stops and frisks, and use of deadly force that results in discriminatory treatment of racial and ethnic minorities creates serious police–community relations problems.[13]

• **Poor Personnel Management.** Effective supervision requires clear performance standards. Officers need to be provided clear guidelines regarding how they are to handle different situations. If there are no guidelines and discretion is completely unregulated, it is impossible to fairly evaluate their performance.[14]

• **Poor Planning and Policy Development.** To implement a law enforcement policy (e.g., community policing), it is necessary for officers on the street to make decisions consistent with that policy. If their discretion is not guided, there is no guarantee that the policy will be carried out.

Positive Uses of Discretion

A patrol officer is dispatched to an attempted burglary call at 1 A.M. The residents were sleeping and heard the sound of a break-in. When the officer arrives and investigates, he can find no physical evidence of an attempted break-in: no marks on any door or window. He tells the people it must have been some noise in the neighborhood. They were already very upset and now become angry, tell him that there really was a burglar, and demand that he make out a crime report and call more officers to look for the suspect. The officer politely disagrees and leaves. The people yell at him, saying, "The police never do anything in this city." He has "unfounded" what citizens are convinced was a real crime but for which there was no evidence.

Most experts agree that discretion can be used in good ways, including:

• **Proper Exercise of Professional Judgment.** In the example given above, the police officer exercised his professional judgment in determining that no crime had been committed and that he should not fill out a crime report. In this case, there was no objective evidence of a crime and therefore no basis for a crime report.

• **Effective Use of Scarce Resources.** The police cannot possibly enforce all of the criminal laws that exist. They do not have enough officers to arrest everyone who violates the law, and the courts could not handle all of the cases.[15] The careful exercise of discretion allows the police to concentrate on important crimes and to disregard unimportant ones. According to Davis, "The common sense of the officers very often prevails over the legislative excesses in criminal legislation."[16] Legislators may pass laws, but police officers decide whether a law is enforced.

• **Individualized Justice.** The proper use of discretion can allow officers to individualize justice and choose the best course of action for particular events. A juvenile may have in fact violated the law, but in the case of a relatively minor offense and/or a first offense, arrest might not be the best response for that individual.

• **Sound Public Policy.** The proper use of discretion can allow police departments to make sound judgments about public policy. Many homeless people, for example, do things that could justify an arrest (e.g., lying down in the street, where they might be technically obstructing the sidewalk). Arresting them, however, might not be the best public policy with regard to homeless people.

Given the fact that discretion can be used for good purposes, most experts argue that the best approach is not to try to eliminate it but to control it and prevent it from being abused.[17]

DECISION POINTS AND DECISION MAKERS

Police discretion is not limited to arrest. Officers at different ranks make discretionary decisions covering a wide range of actions.[18] As James Q. Wilson observes, police organizations are unique in that discretion increases as one moves down the organization.[19] The following is a list of some of the major discretionary decisions made by officers in different assignments.[20]

Patrol Officer Decisions

Discretionary decisions by patrol officers related to crime include:

- To patrol an area more intensively than normal.
- To conduct a high-speed pursuit.
- To stop, question, or frisk a suspect.
- To write a crime report.
- To make an arrest.
- To use physical or deadly force.

Order Maintenance Decisions

Decisions by patrol officers in order maintenance situations include:

- To mediate a domestic dispute rather than make an arrest.
- To suggest that one party to a dispute leave the premises.

- To refer a person to a social service agency (e.g., alcohol abuse treatment).
- To commit a mentally disturbed person to a mental health facility.

Criminal Investigation Decisions

Decisions by detectives related to criminal investigations include:

- To stop investigating a crime because of a lack of leads.
- To seek a warrant for a search.
- To conduct a stakeout.

Law Enforcement Policy Decisions

Police managers make discretionary decisions about law enforcement policy and priorities. These include:

- To adopt community policing or problem-oriented policing.
- To give high priority to traffic law violations.
- To ignore minor drug offenses such as possession of small amounts of marijuana.
- To crack down on prostitution.
- To give social gambling low priority.

UNDERLYING SOURCES OF POLICE DISCRETION

Discretion is the result of several sources that underlie the nature of policing itself.

The Nature of the Criminal Law

Two officers are dispatched to a bar on the basis of a reported disorder. They arrive and calm things down. It is clear that hostile words were exchanged between two people in particular. One of them probably said something about "getting" the other guy. Did these words constitute a threat to do bodily harm? The guy who made the remark had a pool cue in his hand and may have moved it in a way that could be interpreted as threatening. Did this constitute threat with a dangerous weapon?

The criminal law is one of the basic causes of police discretion. First, definitions of crimes are inherently vague. The law defines the crime of assault, but the police officer on the street has to determine whether an incident fits the definition and, if so, whether it is a simple or aggravated assault. LaFave argues that "no legislature has succeeded in formulating a substantive criminal code which clearly encompasses all conduct intended to be made criminal and which clearly excludes all other conduct."[21]

Second, the criminal law in the United States reflects conflicting public expectations about what behavior should be illegal. The law criminalizes much behavior that some people regard as acceptable forms of recreation: gambling, drinking, certain forms of sexual behavior. Officers are often caught between these conflicting expectations and use their discretion about the best course of action.[22]

Third, the criminal law is often used to deal with social and medical problems such as homelessness or chronic alcohol abuse.[23] Police officers on the street have to use their discretion about whether arrest or referral to a social service program is the appropriate response to the situation.

The Work Environment of Policing

The work environment of policing contributes to the exercise of discretion. Skolnick observes that "police work constitutes the most secluded part of an already secluded system of criminal justice and therefore offers the greatest opportunity for arbitrary behavior."[24] Patrol officers often work alone or in pairs.[25] The Project on Policing Neighborhoods observations of patrol work found that only one officer was present in about half of all encounters with citizens.[26]In many critical situations there is no direct supervision. Also, the majority of police–citizen encounters occur in private places, with no other observers present—observers who might be able to testify about the officer's behavior.[27] For this reason, policing has been described as low-visibility work.[28] Hidden from public view, police officers have tremendous opportunity to choose whatever course of action they prefer, and this work environment creates the opportunity for using and potentially abusing discretion.

Limited Police Resources

It is Saturday night, and the 911 communications center is flooded with calls for service. Patrol officers are running from one call to another, and for about 2 hours there are always several calls waiting for dispatch. On one call, the patrol officer could make an arrest for disorderly conduct in a parking lot outside of a bar. But there are other calls waiting, some of which are probably more serious, so the officer gives the person a stern warning and moves on to another call.

Police departments are caught between the broad scope of the criminal law and their own limited resources. Full enforcement of the law is not possible.[29] An arrest is a time-consuming event. Arresting, transporting, and booking a suspect may take between 1 and 3 hours. And in some cases an arrest may involve more than one officer. Police discretion allows officers to make decisions about how best to use their time and energy and, in particular, to concentrate on important crimes or problems.[30]

FACTORS INFLUENCING DISCRETIONARY DECISIONS

The exercise of discretion in particular situations is the result of several different possible influences.

Situational Factors

Police discretion is influenced by the circumstances of each situation. Studies of the decision to arrest, for example, have found that it is affected by the following situational factors.

• **Seriousness of the Crime.** The more serious the crime, the more likely the officer is to make an arrest. Black found that officers made arrests in 58 percent of suspected

felonies but only 44 percent of suspected misdemeanors. He concluded that "the probability of arrest is higher in legally serious crime situations than those of a relatively minor nature."[31] Seriousness of the situation also affects the handling of mental illness
incidents. The more serious the disorder, or the more likely it is to offend other people,
the higher the probability of arrest or commitment to a medical facility.[32]

• **Strength of the Evidence.** The police are more likely to arrest in situations where
the evidence of the crime is strong. In crimes against persons, and in many property
crimes, the primary evidence is the testimony of a victim or witness. When that kind of
evidence or testimony does not exist, arrest is much less likely.[33]

• **Preference of the Victim.** Two officers respond to a domestic disturbance call.
The boyfriend is there in violation of a civil protection order. State law in this case permits but does not mandate an arrest in this kind of situation. One of the officers asks the
woman, "Do you want us to take him in?" She says no. The other officer asks, "Are you
sure? We can, you know." She says no again. The officers warn the boyfriend and leave.

A number of studies have found that an arrest is more likely when the victim or complaining party asks for an arrest. Conversely, police are unlikely to arrest when the victim clearly indicates that he or she does not want an arrest. Black found that "arrest
practices sharply reflect the preferences of citizen complainant."[34]

• **Relationship between Victim and Suspect.** Arrests are more likely when the victim and offender are strangers, and are least likely when the two parties are married.
Police officers traditionally regarded these incidents as private matters.[35] There has been
much controversy and some litigation over the failure of the police to arrest in domestic
violence situations involving married couples (Chapter 5). Recent mandatory arrest
policies are designed to ensure arrest in all felonious assault cases regardless of the relationship of the two parties.

• **Demeanor of the Suspect.** Black and others found that the demeanor of the suspect is a very important factor in arrest decisions: "The probability of arrest increases
when a suspect is disrespectful toward the police."[36] Along the same lines, Reiss found
that the police used physical force most often against people who were disrespectful.[37]
Worden, meanwhile, found that police are more likely to use force, including both reasonable and unjustified force, against citizens who are antagonistic or who actively resist the police.[38] Klinger, however, has challenged the early research on the relationship
between demeanor and arrest. He argues that in many instances the disrespect occurred
after the arrest and, therefore, was a consequence and not a cause of the arrest.[39] In short,
the impact of demeanor on arrest decisions is very complex, and more research is
needed on this important subject.

• **Characteristics of the Victim.** Some decisions are based on characteristics of the
victim. Decisions reflect a moral judgment about the victim by the police officer. LaFree
found substantial evidence that police officers discounted the allegations of rape victims
whose life style was nonconformist.[40]

The Influence of Race and Gender   There is also some evidence that arrest decisions are based on race. Smith, Visher, and Davidson found that police officers were more
responsive to white victims who complained about black suspects, particularly in property crimes.[41] Donald Black, however, did not find any direct evidence of race discrimi-

nation in arrests, but did find some indication that black officers were more responsive to complaints by black victims and, thus, more likely to arrest in those situations.[42]

The "driving while black" controversy suggests that in some traffic enforcement situations, decisions to stop drivers are heavily influenced by race and ethnicity. In Maryland and New Jersey, data indicate that state troopers were stopping a disproportionate number of African American drivers on interstate highways.[43]

Visher found some evidence that the gender of the suspect influences arrest decisions, although this depended on the perceived behavior of the woman. Women who conform to traditional gender role stereotypes are more likely to be treated more leniently than men who are suspected of the same offense. Women who violate gender role expectations, however, do not receive preferential treatment.[44]

Police–Citizen Interactions

A police officer observes a drug sale and moves in to arrest the seller. The suspect first calls the officer a name. The officer ignores it and starts to handcuff him pursuant to department policy. The suspect resists and the officer uses a little more physical force. The suspect then frees one of his arms and hits the officer. The officer uses mace and subdues the suspect. In this scenario, the officer encountered verbal disrespect and then two levels of physical resistance. Later, the suspect files a citizen complaint alleging use of excessive force. The officer argues that he used appropriate force for each level of citizen action.

Police officer actions need to be understood in relationship to citizen behavior. Officer actions are heavily influenced by what citizens do, or at least how officers perceive their attitudes and actions. Alpert's concept of the *force factor* provides a framework for examining police use of force in relation to the actions of the citizen. In a force-related situation, a citizen's behavior can fall into one of four categories: no resistance, slight resistance, moderate or high resistance, or violent or explosive resistance. The important question is whether the officer's actions were reasonably related to that behavior. In a study of one department, Alpert found that officer actions exceeded the resistance level of citizens in 19 percent of all situations and were less than the level of citizen resistance in 31 percent of all situations.[45]

Most police–citizen interactions are routine and uneventful, with neither side exhibiting disrespect to the other or using force. Mastrofski, Snipes, and Supina investigated the extent to which citizens comply with requests from police officers by observing 346 interactions where officers asked or told a citizen (or citizens) to do something. Police officer actions involved asking or telling someone to either (1) leave another person or persons alone, (2) calm down or cease being disorderly, or (3) cease illegal behavior. Citizens complied with officer requests in 78 percent of the observed cases. Failure to comply increased the chances of arrest. In 28 percent of the failure to comply cases an arrest resulted.[46]

The Neighborhood Environment

The immediate work environment also influences police discretion. Fyfe found that officers working in high-crime neighborhoods fired their weapons more than twice as often as officers working in low-crime areas.[47] Higher-crime areas have more incidents (especially robberies) in which an officer is likely to confront an armed criminal and use deadly force in response.

Smith, Visher, and Davidson, meanwhile, found that police officers were more likely to make arrests in low-income neighborhoods than in higher-income areas, with the result that poor whites and poor blacks were both more likely to be arrested than people in higher-income areas.[48] Arrests for vagrancy are rare on skid row but more common when a homeless person wanders into the central business district.[49]

Characteristics of the Individual Officer

The characteristics of individual officers do not appear to have a major influence on police behavior. The behavior of white, African American, and Hispanic officers is remarkably similar. White and African American officers, for example, respond to the seriousness of the crime and the preference of the victim in roughly the same way. Fyfe found that when assignment and location are controlled, officers fire their weapons at the same rate, regardless of race and ethnicity.[50] Reiss found that African American officers are slightly more likely to use physical force than white officers, but that all officers are more likely to use force against members of their own race.[51] In San Jose and New York City, the distribution of citizen complaints by race and ethnicity matches the racial and ethnic composition of those departments (Table 8–1).[52]

Studies comparing male and female officers have found similar patterns of behavior in most but not all situations. Male and female officers in New York City use the various control techniques—arrest, orders, reasoning, display of weapon, and so on—at similar rates.[53] Alissa Worden found that female officers do not differ significantly from male officers with respect to their attitudes toward the job, citizens, and their departments.[54]

There is evidence, however, that female officers do engage in fewer actions that either result in citizen complaints or generate some kind of disciplinary action. They generally receive citizen complaints at half the rate of male officers and are less likely to be identified as potential problem officers by early warning systems (see Chapter 11) than male officers.[55]

Studies of the effect of higher education on the police have failed to identify any significant differences in the behavior of officers with different levels of education.[56] One study, however, found that officers with more education are less likely to receive citizen complaints than officers with less education.[57]

Official Department Policy

Official department policies have a powerful influence over police discretion. Fyfe found that a restrictive shooting policy adopted by the New York City police department in 1972 reduced firearms discharges 30 percent over the next 3½ years.[58] Shootings of fleeing felons in Memphis disappeared following the adoption of a restrictive shooting policy.[59] Restrictive policies on high-speed pursuits reduce the number of pursuits. Alpert found that pursuits in the Miami-Dade police department declined 82 percent after the introduction of a restrictive policy. In Omaha, meanwhile, pursuits increased 600 percent after a permissive policy was reintroduced.[60] Mandatory arrest policies on

TABLE 8–1 CITIZEN COMPLAINTS AGAINST OFFICERS, SAN JOSE, CALIFORNIA, BY RACE AND ETHNICITY, COMPARED WITH COMPOSITION OF THE DEPARTMENT

Ethnicity	Number of Complaints	%	Number of Officers in the Police Department	%
African American	21	8%	73	5%
Asian American	41	11%	101	7%
Hispanic Latino	82	23%	314	23%
Native American	2	1%	7	1%
Filipino American	2	1%	24	2%
European American	210	59%	860	62%
Total	358	100%	1,379	100%

Source: San Jose Independent Police Auditor, *1999 Year End Report* (San Jose: Independent Police Auditor, 2000), p. 54.

domestic violence have contributed to a relative increase in arrests for aggravated assaults since the 1970s.[61]

The impact of written department policies on police discretion is discussed in more detail in the section on control of discretion and in Chapter 11 on police accountability.

Informal Organizational Culture

Police departments also have their own informal organizational culture that influences officer discretion. In his classic study the *Varieties of Police Behavior,* Wilson identifies three different organizational styles of policing: watchman, legalistic, and service.[62] Historically, the Los Angeles police department had a reputation for a legalistic style that involved aggressive crime-fighting tactics (e.g., high rates of field interrogations and arrests).[63] The organizational culture of a police department is not necessarily established by written policy. It is more the impact of values and traditions that are communicated informally. In a comparison of six police departments, the Project on Policing Neighborhoods found that the percentage of contacts with citizens that were officer-initiated ranged from a low of about 20 percent to a high of 50 percent. These different patterns of work activity obviously reflect different informal norms about patrol activity.[64]

Local Political Culture

In almost every state there are small towns where, according to local folklore, you want to be sure to drive five miles an hour under the speed limit. These towns have reputations for making a lot of arrests for speeding.

Police officer discretion is also influenced by the local political culture. One community might place a high priority on, for example, traffic enforcement, with the result that the police department engages in aggressive enforcement.[65] Another small community might place a very high priority on order maintenance, with the result that the police aggressively enforce laws on disturbing the peace, loitering, and so on. Local political culture influences police departments informally (e.g., through communication from elected officials or other community leaders), and not necessarily through written policy. Although experts believe that local political culture is an important influence on the police, it has not been studied in detail.[66]

THE CONTROL OF DISCRETION

The Need for Control

Virtually all experts agree on the need to control police discretion in order to prevent abuse of police authority. Davis and Goldstein argue that the first step toward controlling police discretion is admitting that it exists, that it can create problems, and that control is necessary.[67] Historically, the police denied that they exercise discretion, claiming, instead, that they fully enforce all laws. The so-called myth of full enforcement exists for several reasons.[68] First, the police want to maintain a public image of authority. Admitting that they sometimes do not enforce the law would undermine their authority in encounters with citizens. It would give suspects a basis for challenging an arrest, with comments like "Why me?" and "You don't arrest everyone."

Second, if the police admitted that they do not arrest everyone, it would raise serious questions about equal protection of the law. Third, to admit that the police exercise discretion in enforcing certain laws would raise questions about all police policies and how departments determine what their enforcement policies are. Fourth, most states have laws requiring the police to enforce all laws fully. Some states have criminal penalties for police and other officials who do not enforce the law. For this reason, some legal scholars have questioned whether police discretion is legal.[69]

Finally, denying that discretion exists allows supervisors to avoid closely reviewing officer behavior and developing performance expectations. Commanders can justify this neglect on the ground that they trust the professional judgment of officers on the street. Uviller's study of New York City officers found that supervisors approve of the exercise of discretion far more than the officers under their command believe.[70]

Experts on the subject of police discretion argue that the myth of full enforcement creates a number of serious problems. Most important, it represents a denial of the basic reality of police work. As mentioned earlier, it creates potential due process and equal protection problems, increases the likelihood of police–community relations problems, makes it difficult to manage personnel effectively, and makes meaningful planning impossible.[71]

There are three basic strategies for controlling discretion: abolishing it, enhancing the professional judgment of police officers, and regulating it through written policies.

Abolishing Discretion

In one of the first studies of police discretion, Joseph Goldstein concluded that it was illegal and should be abolished.[72] He and others have argued that the police do not have the legal authority to nullify the criminal law by not arresting a criminal offender. Virtually all other experts have rejected the idea of abolishing discretion. They argue that discretion is both inevitable and, as was pointed out earlier in this chapter, can often be used for positive purposes.

The debate over abolishing police discretion parallels similar debates over the control of discretion in other parts of the criminal justice system.[73] The National Advisory Commission on Criminal Justice Standards and Goals, for example, recommended abolishing plea bargaining.[74] Despite some attempts to do so, most experts argue that plea bargaining serves some useful purposes and cannot be completely abolished in any event. Instead, it has been regulated by administrative rules issued by prosecutors.[75] Along the same lines, mandatory sentencing systems represent an attempt to abolish the discretion of sentencing judges. Research on sentencing reform indicates that mandatory sentencing provisions are often evaded. Experts on sentencing reform argue in favor of controlling (but not eliminating) discretion by narrowing the range of sentences available to judges.[76]

Enhancing Professional Judgment

When you go to a doctor because of some symptoms that worry you, the doctor asks a series of questions and decides what tests to give you. He or she decides whether to refer you to a specialist for further tests and decides what medication to prescribe. The doctor does not follow some rigid set of rules in making these decisions, but uses professional judgment.

A second means of controlling discretion is to enhance the professional judgment of police officers. This represents the professional model employed by the professions of medicine, law, and education. In these occupations, practitioners are granted broad discretion to make judgments about how to handle specific incidents. Control is exercised through the process of screening, training, and socializing members of the profession. Admission standards to medical schools, for example, are very high; medical school training is long and rigorous; and the training process serves to socialize prospective doctors into high standards of professionalism. Once a doctor is licensed, he or she is expected to make professional judgments without direct supervision.[77]

Many critics argue that the traditional professional model does not apply to policing. First, recruitment standards are low compared with law and medicine. Preservice training is very short (six months even in the best departments) compared with these other professions (three years for law school). Second, the peer culture of policing has often tolerated and even covered up improper behavior.[78] Third, policing has been described as a craft rather than a profession. That is to say, it involves a set of skills that are learned through practice. There is no body of specialized professional knowledge equivalent to the body of knowledge that the tax lawyer or the heart specialist possesses. Police officers are generalists rather than specialists. For all these reasons, James Q. Wilson argues that "the police are not in any of these senses professionals."[79] Consequently, the traditional professional model of controlling discretion is not applicable to policing.

Bureaucracy and the Control of Discretion

To a certain extent, police discretion is controlled by the bureaucratic setting of the criminal justice system. An arrest, for example, raises the "visibility" of a police officer's behavior. The arrest is reviewed by a supervisor, a prosecutor, defense attorney, and one or more judges. A competent defense attorney will challenge improper or illegal behavior and may succeed in persuading the judge to dismiss the case. In short, a police officer is not totally free to act out his or her prejudices. Reiss, for example, found that about 75 percent of the officers in his field study made verbal expressions of racial prejudice in the presence of the observers. Yet the data on arrests did not indicate any direct pattern of race discrimination.[80] In short, police officer attitudes do not automatically translate into behavior. Bureaucratic procedures, involving routine review by other persons, constrain officers' behavior. (The relationship between police officer attitudes and behavior is discussed in more detail in Chapter 13.)

Written Policies

The method of control that has evolved is through the use of written policies that guide the police officer's exercise of discretion. This approach is called administrative rulemaking. Because it is currently the dominant approach in American police management, it is discussed at length below

ADMINISTRATIVE RULEMAKING

Administrative rulemaking seeks to guide the exercise of police discretion through written departmental rules and the requirement that officers complete written reports on how they handled situations. Rules typically specify (1) what an officer must do in certain situations, (2) what he or she may not do in those situations, and (3) where an officer may properly exercise discretion. Virtually all experts on policing endorse this approach. The Commission on Accreditation for Law Enforcement Agencies (CALEA) accreditation *Standards for Law Enforcement Agencies* requires that "a written directive governs procedures for assuring compliance with all applicable constitutional requirements."[81] The American Bar Association *Standards* for police include a similar recommendation (Figure 8–2).[82]

Examples of Administrative Rulemaking

• **Deadly Force.** The defense-of-life standard for the use of deadly force clearly spells out when deadly force may be used (threat to the life of the officer or another person) and when it may not be used (an unarmed fleeing felon).[83] Many department

FIGURE 8–2   STANDARD 1–4.3   ADMINISTRATIVE RULEMAKING

Police discretion can best be structured and controlled through the process of administrative rulemaking by police agencies. Police administrators should, therefore, give the highest priority to the formulation of administrative rules governing the exercise of discretion, particularly in the areas of selective enforcement, investigative techniques, and enforcement methods.

policies also include specific prohibitions on the use of warning shots, shots to wound, or shots at moving vehicles. (See Figure 8–3.)

• **Domestic Violence.** Mandatory arrest policies related to domestic violence instruct police officers that they may not exercise their discretion and must make an arrest when a felonious assault has occurred. Arrest-preferred policies state that arrest is the expected action, but allow the officers a range of discretion depending on various circumstances.

• **High-Speed Pursuits.** Department policies on high-speed pursuits instruct officers to consider road conditions, the presence of pedestrians, and other potential risks before initiating a pursuit.[84]

FIGURE 8–3   INTERNATIONAL ASSOCIATION OF CHIEFS OF POLICE: MODEL POLICY, USE OF DEADLY FORCE (EXCERPTS)

I. PURPOSE

The purpose of this policy is to provide law enforcement officers of this agency with guidelines for the use of deadly and non-deadly force.

II. POLICY

It is the policy of this law enforcement agency that officers use only the force that reasonably appears necessary to effectively bring an incident under control, while protecting the lives of the officer and others.

III. DEFINITIONS

Deadly Force: Any use of force that is reasonably likely to cause death.

Non-Deadly Force: Any use of force other than that which is considered deadly force. This includes any physical effort used to control or restrain another, or to overcome the resistance of another.

Objectively Reasonable: This term means that, in determining the necessity for force and the appropriate level of force, officers shall evaluate each situation in light of the known circumstances, including, but not limited to, the seriousness of the crime, the level of threat or resistance presented by the subject and the danger to the community.

IV. PROCEDURES

A. Use of Deadly Force

1. Law enforcement officers are authorized to use deadly force to:

a. Protect the officer or others from what is reasonably believed to be a threat of death or serious bodily harm; and/or

b. To prevent the escape of a fleeing violent felon whom the officer has probable cause to believe will pose a significant threat of death or serious physical injury to the officer or others. Where practicable prior to discharge of the firearm, officers shall identify themselves as law enforcement officers and state their intent to shoot.

B. Deadly Force Restrictions

1. Officers may use deadly force to destroy an animal that represents a threat to public safety, or as a humanitarian measure where the animal is seriously injured when the officer reasonably believes that deadly force can be used without harm to the officer or others.

2. Warning shots may be fired if an officer is authorized to use deadly force and only if the officer reasonably believes a warning shot can be fired safely in light of all circumstances of the encounter.

3. Decisions to discharge a firearm at or from a moving vehicle shall be governed by this use-of-force policy and are prohibited if they present an unreasonable risk to the officer or others.

Principles of Administrative Rulemaking

Kenneth Culp Davis, a leading authority on administrative law, describes the principles of administrative rulemaking in terms of a strategy to fill the gap between law and practice.[85] Laws are written in very broad language. The criminal law, for example, describes categories of criminal behavior in general terms ("threat to do serious bodily harm"). In practice, someone has to use his or her discretion to apply these general definitions to a specific situation. Administrative rulemaking is designed to fill in the gap by providing additional detail on how to handle specific situations.

The specific objectives of administrative rulemaking, according to Davis, are to confine, structure, and check discretion.[86]

- **Confining Discretion.** Rules confine discretion by "fixing the boundaries." The defense-of-life standard on the use of deadly force, for example, fixes the boundaries by clearly indicating situations where an officer may not shoot. A mandatory arrest policy on domestic violence fixes the boundaries by instructing officers that an arrest is required if there is a felonious assault.
- **Structuring Discretion.** Discretion is structured, according to Davis, when there is a rational system for developing policies. Such a system calls for open policy statements and open rules. This approach is designed to eliminate the secrecy surrounding discretion. With respect to policing, it informs the public about what official policy is. It also offers an opportunity to object to an existing policy. Both Davis and Herman Goldstein argue that a system of open rulemaking would create an atmosphere of openness that would have a positive effect on police–community relations.[87]
- **Checking Discretion.** Discretion is checked when decisions are reviewed by another person. The use of deadly force is checked by the requirement that officers fill out reports after each firearms discharge and by having those reports automatically reviewed by supervisors. New York City policy on deadly force specifies such a report-and-review mechanism.[88] It puts officers on notice that their decisions will be set in writing and examined by other people, including the chief of police.

The Advantages of Written Rules

A patrol officer sees a car he believes is stolen and starts to make a traffic stop by turning on his flashing lights. Suddenly, the suspect car accelerates in an obvious attempt to flee. The officer has to make a quick decision: pursue or not pursue? He knows the roads are wet and dangerously slick and sees that the fleeing vehicle is headed for an area with a lot of traffic. The officer immediately remembers that the department's high-speed pursuit policy advises against pursuits where road conditions and traffic levels might pose a danger to innocent bystanders. He does not pursue, but calls in the identity of the fleeing vehicle to the 911 dispatcher.

Written rules offer obvious advantages. They provide direction for officers on how to handle critical incidents. In a Justice Department report, *"Broken Windows" and Police Discretion,* George L. Kelling argues that in order for the police to effectively address quality-of-life issues in neighborhoods, officers need clear guidance in the form of rules that tell them both what they should do and what they should not do.[89]

Since policies are in writing, there can be no dispute about official policy. Because policy directives are circulated to all sworn officers and collected in a standard operation procedure (SOP) manual, they promote consistent performance throughout the department. This, in turn, helps ensure equal protection of the law. Written policies provide the basis for effective supervision. Officers can be rewarded for following policy and can be disciplined for violations.[90]

One of the main arguments in favor of administrative rulemaking is that it is more effective than other means. Abolishing discretion is not realistic. Allowing unlimited discretion opens the door to potential abuse. And rules that are written by outsiders are less likely to be respected and followed by police officers than internally developed rules.[91]

The Impact of Administrative Rulemaking

There is persuasive evidence that administrative rulemaking has produced some significant improvements in policing.

- Fyfe found that a restrictive policy on deadly force adopted by the New York City police department in 1972 reduced the weekly average number of firearms discharges by about one-third (29.1 percent).[92]
- Alpert's study of high-speed pursuit policies found that where restrictive policies were adopted, there was a reduction in the number of pursuits, accidents, and injuries to both officers and citizens.[93]

Ensuring Compliance with Rules

A major issue in the control of discretion is whether officers comply with departmental policies. The principal strategy for ensuring compliance is to require officers to file written reports after each incident and to have those reports automatically reviewed by supervisors. The CALEA accreditation *Standards,* for example, require a police officer to file a written report whenever he or she "discharges a firearm," causes "injury or death of another person," uses "lethal or less-than-lethal weapons," or "applies physical force as defined by the agency."[94]

Another factor influencing compliance is the immediate work setting. Firearms discharges are, by definition, highly public events: They occur in public areas and are accompanied by a loud noise and the presence of at least one citizen, along with other potential witnesses. All of these factors put pressure on the officer to comply with the reporting requirement. There is always the chance that a citizen might report the incident and/or contradict the officer's report. High-speed pursuits are public events in the same way. Domestic violence incidents, however, are very private events. They occur indoors, usually with no witnesses other than the immediate parties. Thus, it is easier for the officer to ignore both the policy and the reporting requirement.[95]

Codifying Rules: The Standard Operation Procedure (SOP) Manual

Written rules and policies are collected and codified in department standard operation procedure (SOP) manuals. The SOP manual is the central tool of modern police management. The typical SOP manual in a big-city department is several hundred pages long.

SOP manuals have certain limits. First, they have traditionally overemphasized relatively trivial issues (such as proper uniforms) and ignored critical issues in the use of law enforcement power (such as arrest and deadly force). In recent years some departments have adopted written policies on deadly force, pursuits, and other important matters. Yet many important issues remain uncovered. Many departments still do not have policies on the use of informants or on arrest discretion in situations other than domestic violence.

A second problem is the "crisis management" process by which manuals develop. New policies are typically adopted in response to an immediate crisis: a lawsuit, a community protest. Peter Manning quotes a British police sergeant as saying that his department's procedures manual represented "140 years of screw-ups. Every time something goes wrong, they make a rule about it."[96] The result of crisis management is that SOP manuals are generally unsystematic. Some areas of police discretion are covered, but many are not. Manuals are often not revised for many years, and, as a result, important subjects are not reviewed or updated.

Systematic Rulemaking

Leading experts on police discretion have urged the police to engage in systematic rulemaking. Davis and Goldstein argue that a systematic approach allows the police to anticipate problems before they become crises and represents a professional approach to planning. Despite these recommendations, police departments have not engaged in systematic planning. Davis points out that the "research and planning" units in most police departments are usually occupied with trivial matters.[97] A model policymaking process is presented in Figure 8–4.

Several attempts have been made to encourage systematic rulemaking. The CALEA accreditation *Standards for Law Enforcement Agencies* require accredited departments to have a system of written directives governing police policy.[98] Accreditation, however, is a voluntary system, and by 2000 only about 500 of the nearly 18,000 law enforcement agencies in the United States were accredited. In 1987 the International Association of Chiefs of Police (IACP) established the National Law Enforcement Policy Center, which began publishing model policies on specific discretionary decision points.[99] The Police Executive Research Forum (PERF) also adopts model policies on various aspects of police work. Finally, a number of citizen review agencies engage in policy review, recommending new policies in areas that have generated citizen complaints.[100]

Wayne Schmidt proposes that, to make administrative rulemaking systematic, each state create an administrative council on law enforcement. This agency would have the authority to develop policies for all local police departments in the state.[101] Walker recommends that states enact laws requiring police departments to develop rules on a specific set of critical decision points.[102] To a certain extent, this approach already exists for some decisions. Police use of deadly force, for example, is covered by state statute. The

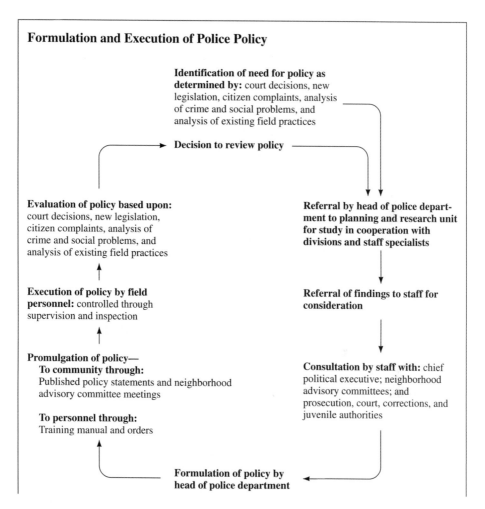

FIGURE 8–4
FORMULATION AND EXECUTION OF POLICE POLICY

Source: President's Commission on Law Enforcement and Administration of Justice, *The Challenge of Crime in a Free Society: A Report by the President's Commission on Law Enforcement and Administration of Justice* (Washington, DC: U.S. Government Printing Office, 1967), p. 105.

1985 Supreme Court decision in *Tennessee v. Garner* ruled as unconstitutional state laws embodying the "fleeing felon" standard. Some states have enacted laws governing police pursuits. Walker's proposal would require the police to adopt rules on a broader range of police decision points.

Citizen Oversight and Policymaking   Some citizen oversight agencies also contribute to rulemaking through a process known as *policy review.* Individual citizen complaints are analyzed to determine whether the underlying cause was a lack of policy (or a bad policy) on the part of the police department, and then recommendations for new policy are sent to the department. The San Francisco Office of Citizen Complaints and the San Diego County Citizens Law Enforcement Review Board develop several policy recommendations each year. Walker argues that policy review is one of the most important functions of citizen oversight of the police.[103]

The Limits of Administrative Rulemaking

Administrative rulemaking also has some important limitations. First, it is impossible to write a rule that covers every possible situation. Although a policy can confine discretion, in the end there will always be ambiguous situations where an officer will have to exercise some discretion.

Second, formal rules may encourage evasion or lying. The exclusionary rule, for example, may encourage officers to lie about how they obtain evidence. With respect to narcotics, observers cited the "dropsy" phenomenon: Officers lied, claiming that the suspect dropped the narcotics on the ground (thus making the seizure legal).[104] Fyfe found that in New York City the number of reported "accidental" firearms discharges increased after the restrictive shooting policy was implemented, suggesting that officers were using this category to cover improper shootings. But accidents as a percentage of all shootings increased only from 3 to 9 percent of all discharges, suggesting that if this did represent an attempt to evade policy, it was still rather limited.[105]

Third, as Michael K. Brown argues in *Working the Street,* complex written rules may only make the situation worse, creating more uncertainty for the police officer rather than less. He observes that "simply enveloping policemen in a maze of institutional controls without grappling with the grimy realities of police work does not necessarily promote accountability and may only exacerbate matters."[106] Harold Pepinsky agrees, citing the example of the *Miranda* decision. He argues that the decision created more uncertainty: When is the suspect "in custody"? What is an "interrogation"? Advocates of written rules reply that a police officer's job is easier when clear, written guidelines are provided on how to handle critical incidents. Although some incidents still leave room for discretion, the range of situations is greatly limited. Davis sees this as the major contribution of confining discretion.[107]

Finally, elaborate rules may only create a negative atmosphere in the department where officers believe that the rules only exist to "get" them and as a result do as little work as possible. As Kelling argues, in this kind of organizational environment officers are unlikely to engage in any creative, proactive police work.[108] Police organizations have been characterized as punishment-centered bureaucracies, with many rules that tell officers what not to do and few rewards for positive police work. Part of the reason for this is that, historically, police managers have been concerned with control, in the sense of keeping officers from inappropriate behavior, with too little attention to guiding officers on the proper courses of action.

Walker replies to these criticisms by arguing that uncertainty is inherent in the nature of policing; that some rules are better than no rules at all; and that if officers evade rules, the task is to ensure greater compliance and not to throw out the rules altogether.[109]

SUMMARY

Discretion is a pervasive part of policing. Officers routinely make critical decisions affecting the life and liberty of citizens. Uncontrolled discretion results in serious problems, including denial of due process and equal protection of the law.

Discretion can be controlled through formal written policies adopted by police departments. Written policies do not completely eliminate discretion; they guide it by providing directions on what the officer should or should not do in certain situations. There is evidence that written policies have reduced the number of persons shot and killed by police. Some controversy remains, however, over whether written policies can effectively control all discretionary decisions.[110]

CASE STUDY: "BROKEN WINDOWS" AND POLICE DISCRETION
IV. Philosophy of Order Maintenance Practices

The New Haven Police Department will always use the least forceful means possible to achieve its purposes. While we will not hesitate to cite or arrest offenders, our approach, at all levels of organization, will be to attempt to get citizens to obey laws and ordinances as unintrusively as possible.

The first level of intervention, whether by managers, supervisors, or by police officers, will be to educate the public about civility, the consequences of incivility, and the laws that oblige citizens to behave in particular ways. This can be done in neighborhood meetings, in schools, or in interactions with citizens. Some citizens do not fully understand their obligations, and if those obligations—for example, regarding a noisy car or public drinking in parks—are patiently explained, they will adhere to the law.

The second level of intervention will be to remind citizens of their responsibilities if they are disorderly—that is, that they are breaking the law and subject to penalties if they persist. This too can be done in a variety of ways. It could be done by visiting a problem location and warning people that if their behavior continues they will be subject to penalties. Similarly, owners of locations that are chronic problems could be so warned by individual officers.

The final level of intervention will be law enforcement—the use of citation and arrest.

Having said that the least intrusive means of intervention will always be used should not be read to mean that in every incident police must start with education. Since police deal with incidents that have histories (for example, with problems), it may well be that in a particular incident the offenders might have a history of outrageous behavior which warrants forceful action at the outset of the encounter (for example, warning or citation).

Source: Excerpt from George Kelling, *"Broken Windows" and Police Discretion*, p. 50.

FOR DISCUSSION

The New Haven police department policy calls for police officers to use a three-stage process in exercising discretion: (1) educate, (2) remind, and finally (3) enforce the law. As an in-class project, discuss experiences and perceptions regarding police discretion, following these steps:

1 As an in-class discussion, identify several different order maintenance situations where the police intervened (e.g., party with loud noise).

2 Survey the experiences of students in the class by having each student complete an anonymous report of (a) their experience with one or more of these situations and (b) their experience/observation with the police response (e.g., warning, arrest, lecture, etc.).

3 With the instructor reading the anonymous reports, discuss the responses in class.

INTERNET EXERCISES

Exercise 1 In response to allegations of racial profiling (an abuse of discretion) a number of law enforcement agencies have adopted new policies and procedures to control traffic enforcement activities by their officers.

What departments have taken these steps? Exactly what do these policies and procedures involve? Some policies involve only the collection of data on traffic stops. What other kinds of controls have been adopted?

Search the Web for reports on racial profiling. Try key words "racial profiling" or "driving while black." Also, go to **www.officer.com** and look for some agency reports.

In class discuss what policies and procedures you found. Do you think they will be effective in controlling discretion? Will data collection control discretion? That is, will officers avoid questionable actions if they know they have to report them? Or will data collection deter them from taking any kind of law enforcement action?

Exercise 2 In January 2001 the U.S. Department of Justice issued a report, *Principles for Promoting Police Integrity,* which included a number of recommended practices for police departments. Find that report on the Justice Department's website.

Do any of the recommended policies and practices relate to controlling discretion? Which ones in particular? How are they designed to work? In your opinion will they work effectively? Or will they actually interfere with good police work? Discuss this in class.

Exercise 3 One important area of police discretion involves the handling of domestic violence situations. A number of states have addressed this issue by enacting laws attempting to control police discretion. Some of these are "mandatory arrest" laws; some others are "arrest preferred" laws.

Research the law in your state. Is there a state statute related to domestic violence? Does it cover police discretion? Is it a mandatory arrest law? If not, how would you characterize it? Does the law provide guidelines for police officer handling of domestic violence? What do those guidelines say? In your opinion, do you think this law provides clear and effective guidance for police officers?

If your state does not have such a law, find one that does and study it with regard to the questions above.

State statutes can be found through some of the legal resource sites on the Web. One starting point would be the Reference Desk site (**www.refdesk.com**). Another way to find states that have domestic violence laws would be to do a Web search under the subject of domestic violence. See if any of those sites have reference material on state statutes.

REFERENCES

1 Donald Black, "The Social Organization of Arrest," in D. Black, *The Manners and Customs of the Police* (New York: Academic Press, 1980), p. 90.
2 Linda Teplin, *Keeping the Peace: Parameters of Police Discretion in Relation to the Mentally Disordered* (Washington, DC: Government Printing Office, 1986).
3 John A. Gardiner, *Traffic and the Police: Variations in Law Enforcement Policy* (Cambridge, MA: Harvard University Press, 1969).
4 Nathan Goldman, *The Differential Selection of Juvenile Offenders for Court Appearance* (New York: National Council on Crime and Delinquency, 1963).
5 William A. Geller and Michael Scott, *Deadly Force: What We Know* (Washington, DC: Police Executive Research Forum, 1992).
6 Kenneth Culp Davis, *Discretionary Justice: A Preliminary Inquiry* (Urbana: University of Illinois, 1971), p. 4.
7 Wayne R. LaFave, *Arrest* (Boston: Little, Brown, 1965), p. 9.
8 James Q. Wilson, *Varieties of Police Behavior* (New York: Atheneum, 1973), p. 21.
9 Michael Lipsky, *Street-Level Bureaucracy* (New York: Russell Sage, 1968).
10 Samuel Walker, *Taming the System: The Control of Discretion in Criminal Justice, 1950–1990* (New York: Oxford University Press, 1993).
11 ACLU, *Driving While Black* (New York: ACLU, 1999).
12 Kenneth C. Davis, *Police Discretion* (St. Paul, MN: West, 1975).
13 Samuel Walker, Cassia Spohn, and Miriam DeLone, *The Color of Justice,* 2nd ed. (Belmont, CA: Wadsworth, 2000).
14 Frank J. Landy *Performance Appraisal in Police Departments* (Washington, DC: The Police Foundation, 1977); Timothy N. Oettmeier and Mary Ann Wycoff, *Personnel Performance Evaluations in the Community Policing Context* (Washington, DC: PERF, 1997).
15 Herman Goldstein, *Policing a Free Society* (Cambridge, MA: Ballinger, 1977), p. 9.
16 Davis, *Police Discretion,* pp. 62–66.
17 Walker, *Taming the System;* Davis, *Police Discretion.*
18 Albert J. Reiss, Jr., "Consequences of Compliance and Deterrence Models of Law Enforcement for the Exercise of Discretion," *Law and Contemporary Problems,* 47 (Autumn 1984): 88–89.
19 Wilson, *Varieties of Police Behavior,* p. 7.
20 Goldstein, *Policing a Free Society,* pp. 94–101.
21 LaFave, *Arrest,* pp. 70, 84–87.
22 Ibid., pp. 83–101.
23 Raymond T. Nimmer, *Two Million Unnecessary Arrests* (Chicago: American Bar Foundation, 1971).
24 Jerome Skolnick, *Justice without Trial,* 3rd. ed. (New York: Macmillan, 1994), p. 13.

25 Albert Reiss, *The Police and the Public* (New Haven, CT: Yale University Press, 1971).

26 Stephen D. Mastrofski, Roger B. Parks, Albert J. Reiss, Jr., Robert E. Worden, Christina DeJong, Jeffrey B. Snipes, and William Terrill, *Systematic Observation of Public Police: Applying Field Research Methods to Policy Issues* (Washington, DC: Government Printing Office, 1998), p. 25.

27 Herman Goldstein, "Administrative Problems in Controlling the Exercise of Police Authority," *Journal of Criminal Law, Criminology, and Police Science,* 58, no. 2 (1967): 165.

28 Joseph Goldstein, "Police Discretion Not to Invoke the Criminal Process: Low Visibility Decisions in the Administration of Justice," *Yale Law Journal,* 69, no. 4 (1960): 543–588.

29 Goldstein, *Policing a Free Society,* p. 9.

30 Davis, *Police Discretion,* pp. 62–66.

31 Black, "The Social Organization of Arrest."

32 Teplin, *Keeping the Peace.*

33 Black, "The Social Organization of Arrest."

34 Ibid., p. 101.

35 Ibid., p. 104.

36 Ibid., pp. 107–108.

37 Albert Reiss, "Police Brutality—Answers to Key Questions," *Transaction,* 5 (July–August 1968): 10–19.

38 Robert E. Worden, "The 'Causes' of Police Brutality: Theory and Evidence on Police Use of Force," in W. A. Geller and H. Toch, eds., *And Justice for All* (Washington, DC: Police Executive Research Forum, 1995), pp. 31–60.

39 David A. Klinger, "Demeanor or Crime? Why 'Hostile' Citizens Are More Likely to Be Arrested," *Criminology,* 32, no. 3 (1994): 475–493.

40 Gary LaFree, *Rape and Criminal Justice* (Belmont, CA: Wadsworth, 1989), p. 76.

41 Douglas A. Smith, Christy A. Visher, and Laura A. Davidson "Equity and Discretionary Justice: The Influence of Race on Police Arrest Decisions," *Journal of Criminal Law and Criminology,* 75 (Spring 1984): 234–249.

42 Black, "The Social Organization of Arrest," pp. 107–108.

43 ACLU, *Driving While Black.*

44 Christy A. Visher, "Gender, Police Arrest Decisions, and Notions of Chivalry," *Criminology,* 21 (February 1983): 5–28.

45 Geoffrey P. Alpert, "The Force Factor: Measuring and Assessing Police Use of Force and Suspect Resistance," in Bureau of Justice Statistics, *Use of Force by Police: Overview of National and Local Data* (Washington, DC: Government Printing Office, 1999), pp. 45–60.

46 Stephen D. Mastrofski, Jeffrey B. Snipes, and Anne E. Supina, "Compliance on Demand: The Public's Response to Specific Police Requests," *Journal of Research in Crime and Delinquency,* 33 (August 1996): 269–305.

47 James J. Fyfe, "Who Shoots?: A Look at Officer Race and Police Shooting," *Journal of Police Science and Administration,* 9 (December 1981): 367–382.

48 Smith, Visher, and Davidson, "Equity and Discretionary Justice."

49 Egon Bittner, "The Police on Skid Row: A Study in Peacekeeping," *American Sociological Review,* 32 (October 1967): 694–715.

50 Fyfe, "Who Shoots? A Look at Officer Race and Police Shooting."

51 Reiss, "Police Brutality—Answers to Key Questions."

52 San Jose Independent Police Auditor, *1999 Year End Report* (San Jose, CA: Independent Police Auditor, 2000), p. 54; New York City, Civilian Complaint Review Board, *Annual Report.*

53 Joyce Sichel et al., *Women on Patrol: A Pilot Study of Police Performance in New York City* (Washington, DC: Government Printing Office, 1978).

54 Alissa Pollitz Worden, "The Attitudes of Women and Men in Policing: Testing Conventional and Contemporary Wisdom," *Criminology,* 31, no. 2 (1993): 203–241.

55 San Jose Independent Police Auditor, *1999 Annual Report,* p. 54; New York City, Civilian Complaint Review Board, *Annual Report;* Samuel Walker and Geoffrey P. Alpert, "Early Warning Systems for Police: Concept, History, and Issues," *Police Quarterly,* 3 (June 2000): 132–152.

56 Lawrence W. Sherman, *The Quality of Police Education* (San Francisco: Jossey-Bass, 1978), pp. 238–239.

57 Victor E. Kappeler, David Carter, and Allen Sapp, "Police Officer Higher Education, Citizen Complaints and Departmental Rule Violations," *American Journal of Police,* 11, no. 2 (1992): 37–54.

58 James J. Fyfe, "Administrative Interventions on Police Shooting Discretion: An Empirical Examination," *Journal of Criminal Justice,* 7 (Winter 1979): 309–323.

59 Jerry R. Sparger and David J. Giacopassi, "Memphis Revisited: A Reexamination of Police Shootings after the Garner Decision," *Justice Quarterly,* 9 (June 1992): 211–225.

60 Geoffrey P. Alpert, *Police Pursuit: Policies and Training* (Washington, DC: Government Printing Office, 1997).

61 Lawrence W. Sherman, *Policing Domestic Violence* (New York: Free Press, 1992), pp. 109–111.

62 Wilson, *Varieties of Police Behavior.*

63 Lou Cannon, *Official Negligence* (New York: Times Books, 1997), Ch. 3.

64 Mastroski et al., *Systematic Observation of Public Police,* p. 25.

65 Gardiner, *Traffic and the Police.*

66 Wilson, *Varieties of Police Behavior.*

67 Herman Goldstein, *Policing a Free Society* (Cambridge, MA: Ballinger, 1977), pp. 93–130; Davis, *Police Discretion,* pp. 70–78.

68 Davis, *Police Discretion,* pp. 52–78.

69 Ibid.; Ronald Allen, "The Police and Substantive Rulemaking: Reconciling Principle and Expediency," *University of Pennsylvania Law Review,* 125 (Spring 1976): 62–118.

70 H. Richard Uviller, "The Unworthy Victim: Police Discretion in the Credibility Call," *Law and Contemporary Problems,* 47 (Autumn 1984): 28.

71 Davis, *Police Discretion,* pp. 70–78; Goldstein, "Police Discretion Not to Invoke the Criminal Process," 146–147.

72 Goldstein, "Police Discretion Not to Invoke the Criminal Process."

73 Walker, *Taming the System.*
74 National Advisory Commission on Criminal Justice Standards and Goals, *Courts* (Washington, DC: Government Printing Office, 1973), p. 46.
75 William F. McDonald, *Plea Bargaining: Critical Issues and Common Practices* (Washington, DC: Government Printing Office, 1985).
76 Walker, *Taming the System.*
77 Wilbert E. Moore, *The Professions: Roles and Rules* (New York: Russell Sage, 1970).
78 Westley, *Violence and the Police* (Cambridge, MA: MIT Press, 1970).
79 Wilson, *Varieties of Police Behavior,* p. 30. See the discussion, pp. 29–31.
80 Reiss, *The Police and the Public,* p. 147.
81 Commission on Accreditation for Law Enforcement, *Standards for Law Enforcement Agencies,* 4th ed. (Fairfax, VA: CALEA, 1999), Standard 1.2.2.
82 American Bar Association, *Standards Relating to the Urban Function,* 2nd. ed. (Boston: Little, Brown, 1980), Standard 1-4.3.
83 Fyfe, "Administrative Interventions on Police Shooting Discretion."
84 Geoffrey P. Alpert and Roger D. Dunham, *Police Pursuit Driving: Controlling Responses to Emergency Situations* (New York: Greenwood, 1990).
85 Davis, *Discretionary Justice.*
86 Ibid.
87 Davis, *Police Discretion;* Goldstein, *Policing a Free Society,* pp. 119–120.
88 Fyfe, "Administrative Interventions on Police Shooting Discretion."
89 George L. Kelling, *"Broken Windows" and Police Discretion* (Washington, DC: Government Printing Office, 1999).
90 Walker, *Taming the System.*
91 Goldstein, "Administrative Problems in Controlling the Exercise of Police Authority."
92 Fyfe, "Administrative Interventions on Police Shooting Discretion."
93 Geoffrey P. Alpert, *Pursuit Policies and Training* (Washington, DC: Government Printing Office, 1997).
94 CALEA, *Standards for Law Enforcement Agencies,* Standard 1.3.6.
95 Walker, *Taming the System.*
96 Peter K. Manning, *Police Work* (Cambridge, MA: MIT Press, 1977), p. 165.
97 Davis, *Police Discretion,* pp. 32–33.
98 CALEA, *Standards for Law Enforcement Agencies,* Ch. 1.
99 National Law Enforcement Policy Center, *Policy Review* (Washington, DC: IACP, 1987).
100 Samuel Walker and Betsy Wright Kreisel, "Varieties of Citizen Review: The Implications of Organizational Features of Complaint Review Procedures for Accountability of the Police," *American Journal of Police,* XV, no. 3 (1996): 65–88.
101 Wayne Schmidt, "A Proposal for a Statewide Law Enforcement Administrative Law Council," *Journal of Police Science and Administration,* 2, no. 2, (1974): 330–338.
102 Samuel Walker, "Controlling the Cops: A Legislative Approach to Police Rule-making," *University of Detroit Law Review,* 63 (Spring 1986): 361–391.

103 Samuel Walker, *Police Accountability: The Role of Citizen Oversight* (Belmont, CA: Wadsworth, 2001).

104 Dallin H. Oaks, "Studying the Exclusionary Rule in Search and Seizure," *University of Chicago Law Review,* 37 (1970): 665–757.

105 Fyfe, "Administrative Interventions on Police Shooting Discretion."

106 Michael K. Brown, *Working the Street: Police Discretion and the Dilemmas of Reform* (New York: Russell Sage, 1981).

107 Davis, *Discretionary Justice,* pp. 52–96.

108 Kelling, *"Broken Windows" and Police Discretion,* pp. 1–2.

109 Walker, *Taming the System.*

110 New Haven Police Division, Order Maintenance Training Bulletin 96-1, in Kelling, *"Broken Windows" and Police Discretion,* pp. 49–50.

CHAPTER NINE

Police–Community Relations

CHAPTER OUTLINE

INTRODUCTION

Conflict between the police and racial and ethnic minority communities is one of the most serious problems in American policing. The focus of the problem in recent years has been the controversy over "driving while black" (DWB)—the allegation that the police single out African American or Hispanic drivers for traffic stops on the basis of their

273

KEY TERMS AND CONCEPTS

race or ethnicity rather than suspected criminal conduct.[1] A 1998 Gallup Poll found that 77 percent of African Americans and 56 percent of whites believe that racial profiling is widespread.[2] Moreover, 42 percent of African Americans believe that they were stopped just because of their race compared with only 6 percent of whites.

The DWB controversy symbolizes the larger problem of police–community relations in America. There are persistent allegations that racial and ethnic minorities are the victims of unwarranted stops and frisks, discriminatory arrest patterns, and excessive use of both physical and deadly force. In addition, minorities are underrepresented among sworn officers in most police departments.[3]

This chapter examines the police–community relations (PCR) problem. It reviews the history of the problem, public attitudes toward the police, the different aspects of policing that affect racial and ethnic minorities, and programs designed to solve the problem.

A DEFINITION OF POLICE–COMMUNITY RELATIONS

A 1999 *New York Times Magazine* article declared that "the way cops perceive blacks—and how those perceptions shape and misshape crime fighting—is now the most charged racial issue in America." "Neither side understands the other," it continued. "The innocent black man, jacked-up and humiliated during a stop and frisk or a pretext stop, asks: whatever happened to the Fourth Amendment?" The police officer responds by asking, "Why shouldn't I look at race when I'm looking for crime? It's no state secret that blacks commit a disproportionate amount of crime, so 'racial profiling' is simply good police work."[4] Conflicting perceptions based on race or what constitutes fair treatment of people and/or good police work are at the heart of the police–community relations problem.

Police–community relations (PCR) refers primarily to *relations between the police and racial and ethnic minority communities.* The American police have never had the same kinds of conflicts with the white majority community as they have with minorities.

The PCR problem is one aspect of the larger problem of racial and ethnic inequality in America. The National Academy of Sciences concluded that "black crime and the position of blacks within the nation's system of criminal justice administration are related to past and present social opportunities and disadvantages and can be best understood through consideration of blacks' overall social status."[5]

Disparities based on race and ethnicity are found in all parts of the criminal justice system.[6] African Americans represent 13 percent of the population, but 31 percent of all persons arrested and 49 percent of all persons in prison.[7] Walker, Spohn, and DeLone conclude that "the criminal justice system is characterized by obvious disparities based on race and ethnicity."[8] Jerome Miller believes the problem is even more serious, arguing that the criminal justice system has been conducting a "search and destroy" mission against African American males.[9] A 2000 report by the Leadership Conference on Civil Rights, a coalition of civil rights groups that lobbies Congress, concluded that "police departments disproportionately target minorities as criminal suspects, skewing at the outset the racial composition of the population ultimately charged, convicted and incarcerated."[10]

Different Racial and Ethnic Groups

While the most serious PCR problems have historically involved the African American community, similar problems also exist with respect to other racial and ethnic groups.

The Hispanic Community   PCR problems exist with respect to the Hispanic American community.[11] A report by the National Council of La Raza declared that "relations between the Hispanic community and local police across the country have grown tense as the Latino population has increased both in number and as a proportion of those reporting civil rights abuses."[12] A Bureau of Justice Statistics report on police–citizen contacts found that Hispanics are far more likely to experience police-initiated contact than either whites or African Americans.[13] The Hispanic community experiences particular problems related to the enforcement of immigration laws. In addition to abuses by federal agents along the U.S.–Mexican border, Hispanics have been subject to workplace raids at places of employment across the country. In some of these incidents, local police officers have worked in cooperation with federal Immigration and Naturalization Service (INS) agents.

The Changing Hispanic/Latino Community in America   The Hispanic or Latino community in America is heterogeneous, complex, and rapidly growing. Demographers expect that it will become the largest racial or ethnic minority group by the year 2010.[14] It is also extremely heterogeneous. The Hispanic or Latino community actually consists of a number of different nationality groups: people whose original country of origin is Mexico, Puerto Rico, Cuba, Haiti, and other Central American and South American countries. The experiences of different nationality groups with the police vary considerably, depending on such factors as immigration status, length of residence in the United States, and social and economic status.[15] Diaz-Cotto explains that the experiences of different groups with public agencies, including the police, "tend to differ from one another according to how each group came into the country." Many people are indigenous to the United States and have been here for many generations. Others have arrived from Mexico, the Caribbean, or Central or South America. Some immigrants are undocumented workers. Cubans have entered the United States since the 1960s primarily as refugees. Puerto Ricans, meanwhile, enter the United States as citizens.[16]

One of the most complex issues involves the proper term to be used for people classified as "Hispanic" by the U.S. Bureau of the Census and other government agencies. Labels are not neutral. The choice of a label or name can be the expression of power, depending on who chooses the terminology. Certain labels, meanwhile, can convey stereotypical images or badges of inferiority or pride. The problem of the proper terminology is especially complex for Hispanics because that label encompasses many different nationality groups. DeJesus-Torres characterizes the process of imposing a label based on color, race, or ethnicity as a "microaggression" by the dominant society. Labels are often adopted because they are convenient, particularly to government agencies, and not on the basis of how groups identify themselves.[17]

Native Americans Problems also exist between the police and Native Americans, both in urban areas and in communities near Indian reservations.[18] Special problems exist with respect to Native American reservations that are served by tribal police departments. A Justice Department report found that crime rates are much higher on reservations than in the general American population. Many tribal police departments are understaffed and lack sufficient equipment and resources to provide adequate police protection on reservations that encompass large geographic areas. Police services are highly fragmented, and there are often jurisdictional problems between tribal police and local police and sheriff's departments regarding who has authority over offenses committed on reservations by Anglo Americans.[19]

Asian Americans In areas with large Asian American communities—which include recent immigrants from Vietnam, Laos, Cambodia, and other countries—as is the case with the Hispanic community, there are great differences among Asian nationality groups according to immigration status, length of residency in the United States, and social class.

A Changing Multicultural Society

On April 17, 1998, federal immigration officers and a Passaic County sheriff's deputy raided three outdoor recreation areas in a sweep to pick up "Mexican gang members." They arrested nineteen Hispanics, but twelve turned out to be American citizens and very few had any gang affiliations."[20] This case is one of many in which police officers act on the basis of stereotypes about illegal immigrants and gang members.

The face of America is changing dramatically and rapidly. These changes are the result of both immigration and natural population growth, as some groups have much higher birthrates than others. The Census Bureau estimates that by the year 2010 Hispanics will be the largest racial or ethnic group in the country. The changing demographic face of America creates new challenges for all social institutions, including the police. A report on *Policing a Multicultural Community* by the Police Executive Research Forum concludes that "preventing, mitigating and negotiating intergroup conflict in the community must become an integral part of police practice. . . . To remain effective, indeed to increase effectiveness, police must become skilled intercultural craftspeople."[21]

Immigration and the increasing number of people whose primary language is not English pose special challenges for the police and the rest of the criminal justice system. A National Institute of Justice survey found that immigrants report crimes at lower rates than other Americans. As a result, many offenders remain unpunished and many victims are vulnerable to repeat victimization. Language and cultural barriers make it difficult for many immigrants to contact and communicate with officials, in addition to understanding the criminal justice system.[22]

Police departments are responding to the changing demographics of their communities in different ways. One of the most important is ensuring that they can communicate with residents who do not speak English. Some police departments, for example, offer incentive pay to bilingual officers. The National Crime Prevention Council, meanwhile, urges police departments to hire officers from recently arrived immigrant groups who can serve as liaisons between the police and newly arrived ethnic communities.[23] Some departments offer training in "street Spanish" to equip their officers with the basic words and phrases necessary for police work. As mentioned in Chapter 4, departments have the option of subscribing to 911 translation services to handle calls from people who speak different languages. Citizen oversight agencies publish informational material and complaint forms in various languages for people who want to file a complaint against a police officer. The Minneapolis Civilian Review Authority publishes brochures on how to file a complaint against a police officer in eight languages other than English, including Spanish, Lakota, and Somali.[24]

Definitions of Race and Ethnicity

Race has traditionally been defined as referring to the major biological divisions of the people of the world. The traditional categories are Caucasian, Negroid, and Mongoloid. Anthropologists today, however, do not believe that differences in skin color, hair texture, and body proportions represent fundamental differences between people. There are substantial differences in physical features between people within each traditional racial category. *Ethnicity*, on the other hand, refers to cultural differences, such as language, religion, family patterns, and foodways. A person in the United States may be ethnically Hispanic, for example, but either white, black, or Native American in terms of race.[25] In the U.S. census, individuals self-identify their race and ethnicity. Figure 9–1 presents the official racial and ethnic categories used by the U.S. government.

FIGURE 9-1   OFFICIAL U.S. CENSUS CATEGORIES, RACE AND ETHNICITY, 2000

Race

One race
  White
  Black or African American
  American Indian and Alaska Native
  Asian
  Native Hawaiian and other Pacific Islander
  Some other race
Two or more races

Ethnicity

  Hispanic or Latino (of any race)
  Not Hispanic or Latino

Gender and Sexual Preference

Police–community relations problems also exist with regard to other groups in society, particularly women, gay men, lesbians, and transgendered persons. With regard to women, there is a specific problem of some police officers targeting young women for traffic stops as a form of harassment. With regard to gay men, lesbians, and transgendered persons, the problem is one of disrespect and physical abuse.

DISCRIMINATION VERSUS DISPARITY

The PCR problem involves allegations of discrimination against minorities. *Discrimination* is defined as the differential treatment based on some extralegal category such as race, ethnicity, or gender. If an employer refuses to hire members of a certain ethnic group, for example, that represents discrimination. *Disparity,* on the other hand, refers to different outcomes that are not necessarily caused by differential treatment. Most college students, for example, are in their twenties. This is not the result of discrimination, but because of the normal life course: Younger people have not completed high school, and middle-aged people have either finished college or do not plan to attend.

There are different forms and degrees of discrimination. Figure 9–2 represents the discrimination–disparity continuum developed by Walker, Spohn, and DeLone.

A CONTEXTUAL APPROACH TO POLICE–CITIZEN INTERACTIONS

The most serious examples of racial profiling that have been documented involve traffic stops by state police officers on interstate highways in Maryland and New Jersey. Additionally, the pattern of stops in these cases appears directly related to drug enforcement. This evidence lends support to the contextual approach to police–citizen

FIGURE 9–2   DISCRIMINATION–DISPARITY CONTINUUM

Systematic Discrimination	Institutionalized Discrimination	Contextual Discrimination	Individual Acts of Discrimination	Pure Justice

Definitions

Systematic discrimination—Discrimination at all stages of the criminal justice system, at all times, and all places.

Institutionalized discrimination—Racial and ethnic disparities in outcomes that are the result of the application of racially neutral factors such as prior criminal record, employment status, demeanor, etc.

Contextual discrimination—Discrimination found in particular contexts or circumstances

(e.g., certain regions, particular crimes, special victim–offender relationships).

Individual acts of discrimination—Discrimination that results from the acts of particular individuals but is not characteristic of entire agencies or the criminal justice system as a whole.

Pure justice—No racial or ethnic discrimination at all.

Source: Samuel Walker, Cassia Spohn, and Miriam DeLone, *The Color of Justice* (Belmont, CA: Wadsworth, 2000), p. 16.

interactions: the argument that interactions are different according to location, police unit, enforcement activity, and so on. This approach holds that police–community relations problems will also be concentrated in certain contexts.

Police–community relations in America represent an apparent contradiction. On the one hand, there are disparities in arrest and incarceration based on race. As already mentioned, African Americans are arrested and imprisoned at far higher rates than their presence in the general population. At the same time, however, public opinion surveys consistently find that the majority of both African Americans and Hispanic Americans give the police very favorable ratings. A 1998 Justice Department survey found that 85 percent of all Americans were satisfied with their local police, including 76 percent of African Americans.[26]

How do we explain this contradiction? Walker offers a contextual interpretation: Experiences and attitudes toward the police vary according to different contexts—different departments, different types of police actions, different departmental units, and so on.[27] For example, some departments have better relations with minority communities than others; in some cities, regular patrol officers have relatively good relations with the communities they serve, while special crime or drug units have very bad relations because of their aggressive tactics. To understand this interpretation, it is necessary to look at the evidence on PCR in detail. The next section examines public opinion poll data regarding the police. Sections after that look at the evidence on police operations.

PUBLIC OPINION AND THE POLICE

Many national and local opinion surveys of attitudes toward the police have been conducted since the 1960s. (See Table 9–1.) Tuch and Weitzer found that attitudes are remarkably stable over time, although local incidents do affect local attitudes.[28] Polls consistently find that most Americans are satisfied with the police in their communities.

TABLE 9–1   ATTITUDES TOWARD FAIR TREATMENT OF PERSONS OF DIFFERENT RACES BY POLICE IN OWN COMMUNITY, BY DEMOGRAPHIC CHARACTERISTICS, UNITED STATES, 2000

Question: Do you think the police in your community treat all races fairly, or do they tend to treat one or more of these groups unfairly?

	Treat all races fairly	Treat one or more groups unfairly	Don't know
National	64%	26%	10%
Sex			
Male	65	27	8
Female	84	24	11
Race ethnicity			
White	69	20	10
Black	36	58	6
Hispanic	63	27	10
Age			
18 to 24 years	55	41	4
25 to 29 years	62	28	10
30 to 39 years	67	24	9
40 to 49 years	68	23	9
50 to 64 years	64	23	12
65 years and older	69	17	14
Education			
College postgraduate	59	31	9
College graduate	65	23	11
Some college	68	24	7
High school graduate or less	62	27	10
Income			
Over $75,000	64	24	12
$50,001 to $75,000	70	23	7
$35,001 to $50,000	69	25	6
$25,001 to $35,000	60	30	10
$15,001 to $25,000	65	30	5
$15,000 or less	62	31	7
Region			
East	65	24	10
Midwest	68	24	8
South	61	27	11
West	64	26	10
Politics			
Republican	75	17	8
Democrat	58	32	10
Independent	63	26	10

Source: Bureau of Justice Statistics, *Sourcebook of Criminal Justice Statistics, 1999* (Washington, DC: Government Printing Office, 2000), p. 110.

A 1998 survey of twelve major cities found that 85 percent were either satisfied or very satisfied with their local police.[29] A 1997 national survey, meanwhile, found that almost 90 percent of all Americans have a great deal or some confidence in the police. Only 11 percent have very little or none.[30]

Racial and Ethnic Differences

There are significant differences in the attitudes of different racial and ethnic groups toward the police. The 1998 survey found that 76 percent of African Americans are satisfied with their police, compared with 90 percent of whites. Meanwhile, 24 percent of African Americans are dissatisfied, compared with only 10 percent of whites. Polls consistently find that the attitudes of Hispanics fall somewhere between those of whites and African Americans. Unfortunately, most polls have failed to survey Hispanics as a separate group.[31]

It is important to note that a majority of African Americans and Hispanics have a favorable attitude toward the police. In the 1997 national survey, a combined total of 76 percent of African Americans had either a great deal or some confidence in the police. There are important differences within racial and ethnic communities, however. In a study of five different neighborhoods in Miami, Dunham and Alpert found that attitudes about the police role vary according to social class as well as by race and ethnicity. Thus, middle-class and lower-class African Americans do not share identical attitudes.[32]

Attitudes about Police Use of Force

The gap between white and minority group attitudes widens when people are asked specifically about police use of force or respectful treatment by the police. The 1997 survey found that 60 percent of whites had a favorable attitude toward the police with respect to the use of force, compared with only 33 percent of blacks and 42 percent of Hispanics.[33] A survey of 3,000 people in Boston found that while 72 percent of whites rated the Boston police department as good or excellent in being fair and respectful to all people, only 58 percent of Hispanics and 51 percent of African Americans rated them as high.[34]

In a survey of Cincinnati residents, 46.6 percent of African Americans indicated they had been personally hassled by the police, compared with only 9.6 percent of whites. Hassled was defined as being "stopped or watched closely by a police officer, even when you had done nothing wrong." Additionally, 66 percent of African Americans reported that someone they knew had been hassled, compared with only 12.55 of whites.[35] Among many African American families there is much fear of the police. A *New York Times* article in 1997 described how some African American and Hispanic parents made a special effort to teach their children to be very respectful of police officers, primarily because they were afraid their children might be arrested, beaten, or even shot if they displayed any disrespect to an officer.[36]

Race and Class

To a great extent race and social class interact to affect perceptions and experience with the police. Weitzer interviewed 169 residents of Washington, DC, representing one middle-class white, one middle-class African American, and one lower-income African American neighborhood. The residents of the lower-income African American neighborhood were seven times more likely to believe that the police stop people on the street in their neighborhood without good reason than residents of the black middle-class neighborhood and three times more likely than residents of the white middle-class neighborhood. Also, half (49 percent) of the residents of the lower-income African American neighborhood reported having seen the police use excessive force in their neighborhood, while none of the residents of the white middle-class neighborhood reported seeing excessive force incidents.[37]

Age

"They judge people by how old they are," argued one Chicago high school student. "They think all teenagers are bad." Another charged that "they judge people by the way they look." A white female student added, "Just because you have a different color skin, or hair, or wear bizarre clothes doesn't mean you are a criminal." These responses were obtained in a survey of 1,000 Chicago high school students.[38]

Age ranks second to race and ethnicity as a factor in public attitudes toward the police. Young people consistently express more dissatisfaction with the police than older people, and attitudes steadily become more favorable with age.[39] A survey of 1,000 Chicago high school students by the Chicago Alliance for Neighborhood Safety (CANS) found that 71 percent had been stopped by the police, including 80 percent of African Americans, 72 percent of whites, and 60 percent of Latinos. Moreover, about 60 percent of those who had been stopped believed the police treated them with disrespect, including 63 percent of Latinos, 62 percent of African Americans, and 59 percent of whites.[40]

A survey of over 800 high school students in Cincinnati found that African American students generally rated the police less favorably than white students, but when other variables were controlled, the difference was not statistically significant. Seeing or hearing about police misconduct had a significant negative impact on attitudes. One particularly interesting finding of this study was that among those students who had been stopped or arrested by the police, whites were about as likely to believe they were mistreated as African Americans.[41]

Other Variables

People with more education consistently rate the police more favorably than people with less education. Education, however, is significantly correlated with social class. Gender has little effect on attitudes toward the police. Most surveys have found little significant difference in the attitudes of men and women toward the police. Crime victims rate police performance less favorably than nonvictims. The 1998 survey of twelve cities found that 31 percent of the victims of a violent crime were dissatisfied with the police, compared with only 14 percent of nonvictims of violent crime.[42]

Intercity Variations

There are significant variations in how the residents of different cities rate their police. The 1998 Bureau of Justice Statistics survey found that 93 percent of San Diego residents were satisfied with their police, compared with only 80 percent of Chicago residents and 78 percent of Washington, DC, residents. The survey also found that the attitudes of whites and African Americans parallel each other. Both groups rated the San Diego police very high, and both groups rated the Chicago and Washington, DC, police relatively low.[43] In short, there are important differences in public attitudes among cities that apparently reflect differences in the activities and reputations of these departments.

The Impact of Controversial Incidents

George Holliday never imagined that he would make the most famous videotape in the history of the police. A little after midnight on March 3, 1991, he was awakened by the noise of a police siren and screeching tires. Looking out the window, he saw an incredible scene of a white Hyundai surrounded by six police cars, all illuminated by the light from a police helicopter. Holliday got his brand new video camera and taped police officers subduing Rodney King by force. The tape was soon shown on television around the world, setting off a chain of events that included two criminal trials, a major riot (1992), and an independent investigation of the Los Angeles police department. This one event had a significant impact on public attitudes about the police, in Los Angeles, the United States, and the rest of the world.[44]

Public attitudes are affected by controversial incidents, particularly questionable shootings or use of physical force. Tuch and Weitzer found that the 1991 Rodney King beating had a dramatic short-term effect on attitudes toward the Los Angeles police department. Prior to the incident about 70 percent of whites consistently indicated that they approve of the way the LAPD does its job. From March 1991 through May 1992, responses fell into the 40 percent range. By 1993, however, responses of whites had returned to the 70 percent range. The percentage of African Americans indicating that they approve of the LAPD fell even more dramatically (to only 14 percent in late March 1991). Approval ratings of African Americans returned to previous levels but at a slower rate than for whites.[45] In New York City, meanwhile, approval of the police department dropped from 61 to 48 percent following the highly publicized police assault on Abner Louima in 1997.[46]

The Detroit Exception

The major exception to the general patterns of attitudes toward the police by race is found in a survey of Detroit residents. Contrary to all prior research, more African Americans (71.8 percent) indicated they were satisfied with the police than whites (52.8 percent). The study explained this result in terms of African American domination of the local political establishment. An African American has been mayor of Detroit since 1973, and a majority of the police force is African American. Thus, African Americans are more likely than whites to identify positively with the police and other parts of the political system.[47]

Expectations about Police Performance

Another factor influencing attitudes toward the police is the expectation that citizens bring to specific encounters. Dissatisfaction is likely to be greater where people have high expectations about what officers should do and where those expectations are not fulfilled. In his study of Hispanics and the police, Carter argues that racial and ethnic minority crime victims have lower expectations than white victims.[48] Chandek, however, found that minorities have greater expectations of police performance. They expect police officers to take more steps reflecting investigative effort (e.g., take notes, make out a report, provide information about available services, etc.). Minorities in this study were not less satisfied with the service they received, however, and the race of the officer also did not appear to affect levels of satisfaction.[49]

The Police and the Larger Society

Attitudes toward the police do not necessarily reflect personal experience with or even perceptions of a local police department. Albrecht and Green argue that attitudes toward the police reflect a broader set of attitudes toward society, government, and the criminal justice system. People who express the greatest dissatisfaction with the police also have the most negative attitudes toward courts and judges. They are more alienated from society and participate less in politics than people with more favorable attitudes toward the police.[50]

Public attitudes about the police reflect the symbolic role of the police as the agents of authority who represent the coercive power of the state. The badge, baton, and gun are the visible reminders of the police officer's power to use force, which Bittner argues is the defining aspect of the police role.[51] Blumberg argues that the police are a "social lightning rod" for public attitudes about other social and political issues.[52] Niederhoffer calls the police officer a "Rorschach in uniform"—someone onto whom people project their fears and fantasies.[53] Thus, people who are the victims of discrimination, or who feel powerless or alienated from society, are likely to have more negative attitudes toward the police than people who feel powerful and integrated.

Police and Other Occupations

If you do a Web search for "lawyer jokes," you will quickly find a number of websites that specialize in that subject. In addition, you will find several general humor sites that have a lawyer jokes category. Lawyer jokes are very popular. Most of them characterize lawyers as unethical, amoral, and greedy. Lawyer jokes may be even more common than jokes about police officers sitting in donut shops.

Despite the fact that many police officers believe they do not get adequate respect from the public, the police compare very favorably with other occupations in terms of public attitudes. A 1997 survey found that they ranked sixth out of twenty-six occupations in terms of perceived honesty and ethical standards (Table 9–2). Almost half (49 percent) rated the police very high or high, compared with only 15 percent for lawyers. Additionally, public estimates of police honesty have been rising. The percentage of people rating the police as very high and high rose from 37 percent in 1977 to 49 percent in 1996.[54]

Summary

The available data allow us to draw several conclusions about public attitudes toward the police: (1) The vast majority of Americans have a positive attitude toward the police;

TABLE 9–2 RATINGS OF HONESTY AND ETHICAL STANDARDS OF VARIOUS OCCUPATIONS, 1999

Occupation	Percentage of Public Rating Occupation "Very High" or "High"
Nurses	73%
Druggists, pharmacists	69
Clergy	56
Elementary and high school teachers	57
Medical doctors	58
Judges	53
College teachers	52
Dentists	52
Police	52
TV reporters, commentators	20
Business executives	23
Newspaper reporters	20
Senators	17
Lawyers	13
Gun salespeople	12
Congress members	11

Source: The Gallup Poll, as reported in Bureau of Justice Statistics, *Sourcebook of Criminal Justice Statistics, 1999* (Washington, DC: Government Printing Office, 2000), p. 106.

(2) racial and ethnic minorities consistently rate the police less favorably than whites; (3) a majority of African Americans and Hispanics, however, give the police a generally favorable rating; (4) young people rate the police less favorably than older people; (5) poor people, less educated people, and crime victims tend to rate the police lower than other Americans rate them; and (6) there are significant differences in opinions about the police among different cities. These findings support the contextual interpretation of police–community relations.[55] That is, while the police get favorable ratings from the general population, certain segments of the population rate them much less favorably: racial and ethnic minorities, low-income minorities in particular, and poor young male minorities especially.

POLICE PERCEPTIONS OF CITIZENS

The former commander of a high-crime racial minority neighborhood in St. Louis made several racial references to "those people" and "that group." The department adopted community policing, and he was transferred to another assignment and replaced by a new captain. Several rank-and-file officers assigned to that neighborhood, meanwhile, talked about the need for "kick ass" policing, where officers were free to "take down" the "shit heads" who are criminals and troublemakers.[56] These views reflect the hostile attitudes some police officers develop toward the neighborhoods where they work.

Police officers generally do not have an accurate perception of public attitudes toward them. James Q. Wilson argues that police officers "probably exaggerate the extent of citizen hostility."[57] In his pioneering work on the police subculture, William A. Westley found that 73 percent of the officers thought that the public was "against the police, or hates the police." Only 12 percent thought that the public "likes the police."[58] Jerome Skolnick also found that suspicion of and hostility toward the public were among the key ingredients of the police officer's "working personality."[59]

In the 1960s a study sponsored by the Kerner Commission found that 31 percent of police officers in thirteen large cities believed that most African Americans regard the police as enemies, while only 31 percent thought that most African Americans were on their side. The study concluded that white police officers were more likely "to project their own prejudices and fears upon blacks, ascribing to them a level of hostility that more adequately reflects the hostility of the perceiver."[60] Bayley and Mendelsohn's study of police–community relations in Denver is the only one to find that police officers had a "rosier" view of public attitudes toward the police than actually existed.[61]

Sources of Police Attitudes

Police officer misperception of public attitudes is the result of several factors. Most important is the pattern of *selective contact* between police and public. Officers do not have regular contact with a cross section of the community. An analysis of police emergency (911) calls in Minneapolis found that 5 percent of the addresses in the city generated 64 percent of all the calls.[62] A Bureau of Justice Services survey estimated that in 1999 only 21 percent of all Americans had a face-to-face encounter with a police officer.[63] Low-income people and racial minorities, moreover, have a disproportionate level of contact with the police. Police departments deploy more patrol officers in their neighborhoods because of higher crime levels, and they are more likely than other Americans to call the police. Finally, the police have relatively more contact with low-income young males who use public places as their recreation spots.[64]

In addition to selective contact, police officer attitudes are shaped by the phenomenon of *selective perception*. Most contacts between citizens and the police are civil; only between 2 and 5 percent involve hostility or conflict.[65] Like most people, however, police officers are more likely to remember unpleasant or traumatic incidents than routine uneventful ones.[66] Observations of police work by Piliavin and Briar and also by Black found that young African American men were more likely than young white men to express hostility to the police.[67] Consequently, officers tend to stereotype young African American males in terms of what Skolnick called the "symbolic assailant" and a potential source of conflict.[68]

SOURCES OF POLICE–COMMUNITY RELATIONS PROBLEMS

The public opinion poll data raise a number of important questions. How do we explain the apparent contradiction between the generally favorable ratings given the police by racial and ethnic minority communities and the persistence of conflict between the police and these groups? Is it simply because the media exaggerate a small number of bad incidents? Or are there systematic problems affecting racial and ethnic minorities? One way to answer these questions is to examine specific aspects of policing: (1) the level of police protection received by different neighborhoods, (2) police officer field practices, (3) administrative practices, and (4) employment practices.

LEVEL OF POLICE PROTECTION

Inadequate Police Protection

When the U.S. Civil Rights Commission held hearings about police–community relations in Milwaukee in the early 1990s, an African American attorney explained why he did not call the police after being robbed: "I didn't call . . . because I didn't really feel that there was any use. I felt like I was already a victim and I would now be a victim of the police . . . I am saying I think people [in the African American community] have these feelings of frustration."[69]

Some minority community leaders accuse the police of not providing adequate police protection for their neighborhoods: not assigning enough patrol officers to their communities and not aggressively fighting crime. In a 1975 National Crime Survey African Americans expressed greater concern about more police protection than about better quality of police service.[70]

Historically, African Americans have been the victims of underenforcement of the law. Gunnar Myrdal's classic study of race relations in America found that during the period of institutionalized segregation in the South, the police disregarded many crimes in the African American community.[71] The result was four different systems of justice, depending on the racial components of the offender/victim relationship:[72] (1) Crimes by whites against whites were handled as "normal" crimes; (2) crimes by whites against African Americans were rarely prosecuted, if at all; (3) crimes by African Americans against whites received the harshest response; and (4) crimes by African Americans against African Americans were often ignored.

Failure to enforce the law in minority neighborhoods has often involved crimes of vice. Historically, gambling, after-hours drinking, prostitution, and narcotics trafficking were allowed to exist in low-income and racial minority neighborhoods. A 1986 survey of attitudes in Philadelphia found that 65 percent of Hispanic residents believed that the police underenforced gambling laws, compared with 55 percent of African American and 46 percent of white Philadelphians.[73]

Tolerating vice crimes harms low-income and racial-minority communities in several ways. First, it breeds disrespect for the law and the police, in large part because of the corruption that usually accompanies it. The Knapp Commission investigation of police corruption in New York City found that the monthly vice payoffs to police in the predominantly African American areas of Harlem averaged $1,500, compared with $300 in predominantly white downtown precincts.[74]

Additionally, the new form of police corruption that emerged in the 1980s involved both corruption and physical brutality. The Mollen Commission report on corruption in

New York City was the first to document this problem.[75] The Rampart scandal that was exposed in Los Angeles in 1999 involved corruption, physical brutality, and framing citizens on false charges.[76] The new form of corruption has been confined to racial and ethnic minority communities.

Second, underenforcement of the law exposes law-abiding citizens in minority communities to criminal activity: prostitution and drug dealing, and the secondary crimes such as shootings and robberies that often accompany them. These crimes expose individuals and their families to personal risk and lower the quality of life in the neighborhood. Exposure to criminal activity increases the risk that juveniles will engage in crime themselves.

There is an important distinction between enforcement activities and patrol staffing levels. In the 1970s African Americans in Washington, DC, sued the police department charging inadequate police protection (*Burner v. Washington, DC*). Peter Bloch compared two areas, one about 90 percent African American and another about 90 percent white. He measured the level of police protection in terms of calls per officer, police per 100 reported robberies, and officers per 100 Index crimes. He concluded that "police units are distributed equally and that both neighborhoods were receiving levels of police service equal to their apparent needs."[77]

Underprotection versus Overenforcement

While some minority community residents allege that they receive inadequate police protection, other minority citizens argue that they are the victims of overenforcement: that the police are an oppressive force in their neighborhoods and that citizens are stopped, questioned, frisked (e.g., harassed, or hassled), and arrested at very high rates. Where does the truth lie between these two contradictory allegations?

Generally, police departments assign more patrol officers to low-income and racial-minority neighborhoods than to other parts of the community. This is because of higher rates of reported crimes and more calls for service in those neighborhoods. As Chapter 4 explains, professional standards in police management dictate that departments should adjust their assignment of officers according to workload, primarily reported crime and calls for service. The result is that the police are a more visible presence in minority neighborhoods than in other neighborhoods. Bayley and Mendelsohn argue that "the police seem to play a role in the life of minority people out of all proportion to the role they play in the lives of the dominant white majority."[78]

A police department that uses the standard workload formula for assigning patrol officers (see Chapter 4) will probably assign more officers to minority neighborhoods. This formula, however, addresses only the assignment of officers. The crucial question is what the police *do* and whether they treat minorities differently with regard to stops and frisks, arrest, and other police actions.

The apparent contradiction can be explained in part in terms of actual police activities, as opposed to patrol staffing levels. First, it is important to recognize the diversity within racial and ethnic minority communities. Complaints about police harassment generally come from young males who have a high level of contact with the police. Most members of a racial-minority community, however, are law-abiding adults with

SIDEBAR 9–1   AN INTERNATIONAL PERSPECTIVE:
PCR IN ENGLAND

Conflict between the police and racial and ethnic minority communities is not confined to the United States. Similar problems exist in England. Serious riots erupted in London and other cities in April 1981 as a result of incidents involving the police. The Scarman Report on the disorders concluded that the police "were partly to blame for the breakdown in community relations," because of "instances of harassment and racial prejudice among junior officers" and a "failure to adjust policies and methods to meet the needs of policing a multiracial society."

Source: Lawrence W. Sherman, "After the Riots: Police and Minorities in the United States, 1970–1980," in Nathan Glazer and Ken Young, eds., *Ethnic Pluralism and Public Policy* (Lexington, MA: Lexington Books, 1983), pp. 232–233; Lord Scarman, *The Scarman Report* (London: Penguin Books, 1982), pp. 118–119.

jobs and families. Like their white counterparts, they want more, not less, police protection.[79] As noted earlier, Weitzer found significant differences in perceptions of the police between a low-income and a middle-income African American neighborhood in Washington, DC.[80] Dunham and Alpert found differences in public attitudes about such issues as police responsibility for crime control *within* different racial and ethnic groups on the basis of social class. They concluded that the police "need to approach crime control in each of these areas in a different manner."[81]

Second, it is necessary to examine particular police field practices. Certain activities, such as field interrogations, have particularly negative impact on certain segments of minority communities, notably young men. Different police practices are examined in the next section.

POLICE FIELD PRACTICES

Police field practices are the greatest source of tensions between the police and racial minorities. This category includes actions by individual police officers such as use of deadly force, physical force, stops and frisks, verbal abuse, and slow response to calls for service.

Deadly Force

Edward Garner was a slightly built, 110-pound 15-year-old African American on October 3, 1974, but his name is now one of the most famous in criminal justice history. Garner was shot and killed by two Memphis, Tennessee, police officers while fleeing a suspected burglary. It turned out that he did have a stolen purse containing $10 in his possession. A lawsuit brought by his family eventually reached the U.S. Supreme Court and addressed the issue of when and under what circumstances police officers can use deadly force. The Court decided, in *Tennessee v. Garner* (1985), that the fleeing-felon rule under which the Memphis officers acted (both of whom were also African

American) was unconstitutional. The decision accelerated the trend toward adoption of the defense-of-life standard, which greatly restricts the use of deadly force by police officers.[82]

The use of deadly force has been the source of major conflict between minorities and the police. James Fyfe concluded that "blacks and Hispanics are everywhere overrepresented among those on the other side of police guns."[83] One of the most controversial incidents in recent years was the fatal shooting of Amadou Diallo by New York City police officers in 1999 (and the subsequent acquittal of officers on criminal charges). Diallo was unarmed, apparently reaching for his wallet when shot. This shooting, together with other incidents of police misconduct, created a strong feeling among many minorities in the city that they are the target of systematic police abuse.[84]

Police use of deadly force has changed significantly over the past 40 years. In the 1960s and 1970s, the ratio of African Americans to whites shot and killed by the police was as high as 6 to 1, or even 8 to 1. Gerald Robin found that between 1950 and 1960, Chicago police shot and killed African Americans at a rate of 16.1 per 100,000, compared with 2.1 whites per 100,000.[85] The disparity between whites and African Americans, moreover, has been greatest among unarmed people—usually defined as fleeing felons. Between 1969 and 1974 Memphis police officers shot and killed thirteen unarmed and nonassaultive African Americans but only one white.[86] Many of the riots of the 1960s were sparked by the shooting of an African American male by a white police officer (see Chapter 2).

Since the 1960s and early 1970s, the number of police shootings has declined. The major reason is that the old fleeing-felon rule, which allowed the police to shoot unarmed suspects, has been replaced by the more restrictive defense-of-life rule as a result of the U.S. Supreme Court ruling in the 1985 *Tennessee v. Garner* case.[87] Meanwhile, many departments had previously adopted the defense-of-life rule on their own.

Fyfe found that adoption of the defense-of-life standard by the New York City police in 1972 reduced the average number of shots fired by 30 percent. The greatest reduction occurred in fleeing-felon situations.[88] In Memphis, a restrictive shooting policy eliminated all shootings in the unarmed and nonassaultive category, greatly reducing the racial disparity in persons shot and killed in the process.[89] The total number of persons shot and killed per year fell by 50 percent between 1970 and 1984, and the ratio of African Americans to whites shot and killed fell from about 6 to 1, to 3 to 1.[90] The data suggest that permissive shooting policies permit racially prejudiced attitudes to affect shootings, while restrictive policies, by controlling discretion, curb the impact of personal attitudes.[91]

The important question is whether the current disparity between African Americans and whites shot and killed represents *systematic* discrimination as defined by Walker, Spohn, and DeLone (Figure 9–2), or whether it is *contextual* discrimination (e.g., certain departments), or *individual* discrimination (e.g., particular officers). Some analysts argue that the proper standard involves the number of persons in each racial and ethnic group who are at risk of a shooting incident. "At risk" may be defined in terms of involvement in serious crime. Geller and Karales examined shootings by Chicago police between 1974 and 1978. They found that African Americans were shot and killed six times as often as whites in terms of their presence in the total population. When they controlled for participation in violent crimes, however, the disparity disappeared. Whites were shot and killed at a rate of 5.6 per 1,000 arrests for forcible felonies, compared with 4.5 blacks shot per 1,000 arrests for the same category of crime.[92]

Use of Physical Force

Allegations of police brutality, defined as the use of excessive physical force by the police, represent the most common complaint voiced by minorities about the police. The videotaped beating of Rodney King in 1991 by Los Angeles police officers provided dramatic visual evidence of excessive force by police officers.[93]

The issue of excessive physical force is particularly complex. Police officers are authorized by law to use force in certain situations: to protect themselves, to effect an arrest, to overcome resistance, and to bring a dangerous situation under control. The relevant question is, "When is the use of force excessive?" The CALEA accreditation standards state that officers "will use only the force necessary to accomplish lawful objectives." Excessive force is any level of force more than is necessary.[94] A police officer is not justified in using physical force in response to mere disrespect, for example.

Whether or not a certain level of force is necessary in a particular situation is frequently a matter of opinion. It often involves conflicting perceptions of whether a person was resisting arrest, or whether he or she posed a threat to the safety of the officer.[95] Police departments have generally adopted a *use of force continuum*, indicating the different levels of force (Figure 9–3) appropriate for particular situations.

FIGURE 9–3   USE OF FORCE CONTINUUM, SELECTED POLICE DEPARTMENTS

Charlotte-Mecklenburg	Colorado Springs	Dallas
Officer Presence	Officer Presence	Officer Presence
Verbal Direction	Verbal Control	Verbal Control
Soft Empty Hand	Soft Control Techniques	Empty Hand Control
Oleoresin Capsicum	Control and Compliance	Intermediate Weapons
Hard Empty Hand	Hard Control Techniques	Lethal Force
Intermediate Weapons	Impact Weapons	
Lethal Force	Lethal Force	

St. Petersburg	San Diego Police	San Diego Sheriff
Officer Presence	Officer Presence	Deputy Presence
Verbal Direction	Verbal Commands	Verbal Direction
Restraint Devices	Control/Compliance	Soft Hand Control
Transporter	Soft Impact	Chemical Agents
Takedown	Lethal Force	Hard Hand Control
Pain Compliance		Intermediate Weapons
Countermoves		Lethal Force
Intermediate Weapons		
Lethal Force		

Source: National Institute of Justice, *Use of Force by Police* (Washington, DC: Government Printing Office, 1999), p. 37.

Police use of force is a statistically infrequent event. The Bureau of Justice Statistics surveyed 80,453 people in 1999 and found that police officers used some kind of force in less than 1 percent of all encounters with citizens.[96] The questions in this survey will eventually be added to the National Crime Victimization Survey (NCVS). Other studies of policing have also found that officers use force in about 1 percent of all interactions. About two-thirds of all uses of force are justified, given the circumstances, and about one-third are unjustified or excessive. Thus, police use excessive force in an estimated one-third of 1 percent (0.3 percent) of all encounters with citizens.[97]

Many people regard the estimate that police use force in only 1 percent of all encounters as extremely low and believe that the real incidence is much higher. The 1 percent figure acquires a different meaning when examined more closely. The Bureau of Justice Statistics estimate of 421,000 force incidents per year translates into 1,100 per day. If we accept the conservative estimate that one-third involve excessive or unjustified use of force, the result is about 360 excessive force incidents every day of the year. If we further assume that most of these incidents occur in the cities, the result is a large number of annual incidents in every city. Moreover, as Reiss points out, use of force incidents accumulate over time with the result that "a sizeable minority of citizens experience police misconduct at one time or another."[98] And since most force incidents involve young, low-income men, with a disproportionate representation of racial and ethnic minorities, this group of people will have a very strong perception of police harassment. (See Figure 9–4.)

Police use of force is associated with certain situational factors. Officers are more likely to use force against criminal suspects (about 4 to 6 percent of all encounters with suspects). Worden's analysis of the Police Services Study (PSS) data from the 1970s found that officers were more likely to use force against male suspects, African American males, and citizens who were drunk and antagonistic to the police. Physical resistance to a police officer significantly increased the likelihood of use of force.[99]

Citizen resistance or discourtesy is highly associated with police use of force. Since officers are legally authorized to use force in certain circumstances, it is important to determine whether the officer used more force than was necessary. To facilitate this analysis, Alpert developed the *force factor* framework, which examines police officer behavior in relationship to the citizen's actions. If an officer used force where there was no resistance or threat on the part of the citizen, then the force would be considered excessive. Analyzing data from one police department, Alpert found that officers used more force than was indicated by citizen behavior in 19 percent of all cases and less force than was indicated in 32 percent of all cases.[100]

A number of police officers concede that other officers sometimes use excessive force. A national survey of police officers by the Police Foundation found that 21.7 percent agree that officers in their departments sometimes, often, or always use more force than is necessary to make an arrest. There were significant differences in the attitudes of white and African American officers in how they treat minority group citizens. Over half of the African American officers (57.1 percent) agree that officers are more likely to use physical force against blacks and other minorities than against whites in similar situations. Only 5.1 percent of the white officers agreed with that statement. African American officers also agreed more than white officers that the police are more likely to use force against poor people than middle-class citizens (54.4 percent versus 8.8 percent).[101]

FIGURE 9–4   CITIZEN CONTACTS WITH POLICE, AND POLICE USE OF FORCE, 1999

Total U.S. population (age 16 and over)	209,350,600	
Contact with police	43,827,400	(21% of population)
Motor vehicle stop	19,300,000	
Other contact	24,527,400	
Use of force by police	421,700	(1% of all contacts)

Source: Bureau of Justice Statistics, *Contacts between Police and the Public: Findings from the 1999 National Survey* (Washington, DC: Government Printing Office, 2001).

Many critics of the police assume that use of excessive force primarily involves white officer interactions with minority citizens. Reiss, however, found that white and African American officers were about equally likely to use force and were most likely to use force against members of their own race.[102] This finding is supported by citizen complaint data from San Jose and New York City, which indicate that white, African American, and Hispanic officers receive citizen complaints at rates equal to their presence on the police force.[103] In short, the use of force is primarily a function of the police role and situational factors rather than the race or ethnicity of officers.

Arrests

African Americans are arrested more often than whites relative to their numbers in the population. In 1998 they represented 30 percent of all arrests, 34.2 percent of all Part I felony arrests, and 40 percent of all arrests for violent crimes, despite the fact that they constitute only 12 percent of the U.S. population. Arrest is an extremely common experience for young African American men in the inner city. Tillman estimates that 65.5 percent of all African American males are arrested before the age of 30, compared with 33.9 percent of white males. Meanwhile, 29.6 percent of all African American females are arrested before the age of 30 compared with only 10.1 percent of white females.[104]

Donald Black's study of arrest found that police decisions to arrest are influenced by a number of situational factors (see Chapter 8). These include (1) the strength of the evidence, (2) the seriousness of the crime, (3) the preference of the victim, (4) the relationship between victim and suspect, and (5) the demeanor of the suspect.[105] Race was not a direct factor in arrest decisions. African Americans were more likely to be disrespectful of the police, however, and arrested for that reason.

Although the evidence is not strong, it appears that the characteristics of crime victims have some impact on the racial pattern of arrests. African American complainants request arrests more often than whites, and since most crimes are *intra*racial (with victim or complainant the same race as the suspect), this results in more arrests of African Americans.[106] Lundman and his colleagues also found that "the preference of black citizens explained the higher arrest rate for black juveniles."[107] At the same time, the Police Services Study data indicate that the police are more likely to comply with the wishes of white victims when they seek the arrest of African American suspects than in other situations, particularly in property crimes.[108]

The effect of the demeanor of the suspect on arrests is extremely complex. Black found that African Americans were more likely to be antagonistic to the police, and more likely to be arrested for that reason.[109] Piliavin and Briar found a similar pattern among juveniles.[110] David Klinger, however, argues that these earlier studies did not control for when the antagonistic demeanor occurred. He concludes that much of it occurs after the arrest and in those instances, therefore, is a consequence and not a cause of arrest.[111]

There have been no studies, however, to determine the extent to which the demeanor of suspects is provoked by police officers. Bayley and also Mastrofski and Parks argue that police officers approach encounters with citizens with a "script" representing their preliminary perception of the situation.[112] Thus, an officer may approach an encounter with an expectation of conflict and, as a consequence, provoke a hostile response through informal cues or unconscious behavior. To the extent that officers stereotype young African American males as potential suspects,[113] they may provoke high rates of antagonistic behavior that in turn results in higher rates of arrest.

Several studies have found that African Americans are arrested on the basis of less stringent legal criteria than whites. Hepburn found that arrests of blacks were more likely to be declined for prosecution than arrests of whites, suggesting that the arrests were made for reasons other than law enforcement.[114] A Rand study of the criminal process in California found that African Americans were more likely to have arrest charges dropped by the police or prosecutor. Although these data might suggest greater leniency at the prosecution stage, they could also mean that African Americans were arrested on weaker evidence.[115]

The greatest racial disparities in arrest involve drug offenses. About 37 percent of all drug arrests in 1998 involved African Americans. The National Household Survey of Drug Use, however, estimates that the rates of illegal drug use among different racial and ethnic groups are not that different, with African Americans only slightly more likely to use illegal drugs than whites.[116] These data suggest that the police target African Americans for drug enforcement. The National Criminal Justice Commission concludes that *"police enforcement of new drug laws . . . focus almost exclusively on low-level dealers in minority neighborhoods."*[117] This is an example of what Walker calls contextual discrimination. In this instance, drug enforcement is a particular context in which police activities are significantly different than law enforcement patterns related to other crimes.[118]

Traffic Stops: "Driving While Black" and "Driving While Brown"

The most serious allegations of discrimination in recent years have involved traffic enforcement. Civil rights groups allege that minority group drivers are stopped solely on the basis of their race or ethnicity and not because of any criminal activity. This practice has been labeled *racial profiling* and is characterized by the term "driving while black (or brown)." An ACLU lawsuit against the Maryland State police produced evidence that while African Americans represented 17 percent of all drivers on Interstate 95 and 18 percent of observed traffic law violators, 73 percent of the drivers stopped were African American. Additionally, of those drivers who were stopped, 81 percent of those subsequently searched were African American.

Many critics argue that the racial disparities in traffic stops and subsequent searches are a consequence of the "war on drugs."[119] They believe that the police are profiling or stereotyping African Americans as drug dealers. The police generally respond by citing arrest data indicating that African Americans and Hispanics are more heavily involved in drug-related offenses. Critics of the police reply by pointing out that this argument is circular and represents a self-fulfilling prophecy: The police originally target minorities for drug arrests, and then the arrest data are used to justify stops, searches, and more arrests.[120]

Professor William Chambliss of George Washington University spent more than 100 hours riding with the Rapid Deployment Unit (RDU) of the Washington, DC, Metropolitan police. The RDU had been created in the 1960s in response to the riots of that period. At the time of his study, it consisted of three two-officer cars engaged in aggressive anticrime tactics. Chambliss found that "it . . . became commonplace for the RDU officers to stop any car with young black men in it."[121]

To eliminate racial profiling, civil rights groups have demanded that police departments collect data on traffic stops by race. A bill to require data collection was introduced in Congress, and by mid-2001 several states had passed data collection legislation of their own. Meanwhile, a large and growing number of police departments began their own voluntary traffic stop data collection programs.

Sex Discrimination: "Driving While Female"

In early 2001 a Long Island, NY police officer was placed on suspension after three women alleged that he had stopped them while driving and threatened them with arrest if they did not take off their clothes and stand naked. Immediately after these cases became public, another Long Island officer was charged with forcing a woman to perform oral sex or be arrested.[122]

These cases are examples of the problem of "driving while female," a gender-based variation on "driving while black." The full extent of this problem is not known, but there is evidence that some male officers target young female drivers and stop them as a form of sexual harassment.

Field Interrogations and Searches

An African American resident of Washington, DC, explained how he and his friends perceive police practices: "If they [the police] stop a white guy at three in the morning, they'll figure he was working late and he's on his way home to see his wife. [They] stop a black person at three in the morning and figure he was up to no good . . . always assuming the worst when it's someone of color."[123] The perception of harassment by the police is very strong, especially with regard to police-initiated stops on the street. These actions are referred to as pedestrian stops or field interrogations. Stops are sometimes accompanied by searches.

Field interrogations are a police crime control strategy designed to both apprehend offenders and at the same time send a message of deterrence to people on the street. Young racial and ethnic minority males in particular regard this practice as harassment.

The President's Crime Commission found that field interrogations and "aggressive preventive patrol were a major cause of tensions between the police and minority communities."[124] A 1990 report by the Massachusetts attorney general concluded that the Boston police "engaged in improper, and unconstitutional, conduct . . . with respect to stops and searches of minority individuals."[125] A Cincinnati survey found that 46.6 percent of African Americans reported being hassled by the police, compared with only 9.6 percent of whites.[126] Finally, a survey of 1,000 Chicago high school students found that 71 percent had been stopped by the police, and two-thirds of those who were stopped thought they had been treated with disrespect. Significantly, white students were almost as likely to think they were treated with disrespect as African Americans.[127]

The most sophisticated investigation of stop and frisk practices is a study of the New York City police department by the attorney general of the State of New York. The study found, first, that African Americans were more likely to be stopped than their presence in the population would indicate. Second, to control for participation in crime, the study compared the percentage of African Americans stopped with the percentage of African Americans arrested in eight selected precincts. This analysis was based on the assumption that arrest data are a valid substitute for participation in crime, an assumption that not all criminologists agree with. The study found that African Americans were stopped at a higher rate than the arrest data would predict. Third, analyzing a sample of stop and frisk reports, the study found that the police frequently lacked adequate cause for a stop. And in fact, few stops of African Americans resulted in an arrest.[128]

Being "Out of Place" and Getting Stopped

A white resident of Washington, DC, explained that "if a black person were in this neighborhood and they were walking around, the police might stop them just because of their skin color and because they look like they don't belong in the neighborhood."[129]

Many field interrogations involve people who police officers believe are "out of place." Typically, this means an African American or Hispanic in a white neighborhood or a white person in an African American or Hispanic neighborhood. The officer or officers make an assumption that the person does not live there and consequently must be there for some criminal purpose. In fact, the New York attorney general's study of stops and frisks in New York City found a pattern of disproportionate stops of whites in minority neighborhoods along with stops of minorities in white neighborhoods.[130]

Conflicting Evidence

There is conflicting evidence regarding the extent to which the police systematically target racial and ethnic minorities for traffic stops and field interrogations. The Bureau of Justice Statistics (BJS) study of police–citizen contacts found that in some instances minorities have less contact with police than whites. Overall, an estimated 21 percent of Americans had face-to-face contact with a police officer in 1999. Whites had a slightly higher overall rate of contact (16 percent) with the police, but African Americans were more likely to be contacted by the police as suspects in a crime.[131]

The data from the Bureau of Justice Statistics survey do not support the allegations of systematic racial profiling by the police, at least with respect to African Americans.

They do indicate that Hispanics are stopped by the police at a higher rate than other racial or ethnic groups. There are several possible explanations for the apparent contradiction between the Bureau of Justice Statistics data and the widespread belief that racial profiling exists. First, as Walker argues, police interactions with minorities are highly contextual. It is possible that the worst forms of profiling exist in special contexts such as interstate highways, and in a national survey these incidents are simply drowned out by the larger patterns of police–citizen interactions. Second, the psychological impact of a few racial profiling incidents may well be far greater than their statistics would predict. These incidents become surrogates for the larger patterns of racism and discrimination in American society.[132]

The Heart of the Problem: Crime Fighting, Stereotyping, Race, and Ethnicity

Traffic stops and field interrogations illustrate one of the major conflicts over goals in policing. The police regard these practices as a legitimate and effective crime-fighting tactic. These practices, however, tend to encourage stereotyping of citizens. This problem is deeply rooted in policing. As Skolnick points out, police officers are trained to be suspicious and from experience develop a visual "shorthand" for suspects, based on visual cues. Inevitably, this involves a certain amount of stereotyping, by gender, age, and race. Skolnick concludes that "a disposition to stereotype is an integral part of the policeman's world."[133]

Stereotyping minorities as criminal suspects can be reinforced by department policy. The Christopher Commission concluded that the aggressive war-on-crime style of the Los Angeles police department "in some cases seems to become an attack on [minority] communities at large. The communities, and all within them, become painted with the brush of latent criminality."[134] Serious questions exist about the crime control effectiveness of aggressive law enforcement. Following the Rodney King incident in 1991, arrests by LAPD officers dropped from 312,870 in 1990 to 189,191 in 1995 (or 39 percent). Yet, the crime rate in Los Angeles also dropped during those years.[135]

The basic question is whether race or ethnicity can *ever* be used by police or other criminal justice officials in making a decision.[136] It is clearly wrong if race is the *only* factor used to make a decision. And it is wrong if race is included in a list of factors that are used as a profile of criminal suspects. Given the pervasiveness of racial stereotyping in American society, and the inherent tendency of police to use shorthand in making decisions, the task of completely eliminating all race-based decision making is extremely difficult.

Verbal Abuse and Racial and Ethnic Slurs

The Christopher Commission, created to investigate the Los Angeles police department after the 1991 Rodney King beating, reviewed 180 days of computer-based communications between LAPD police officers. These communications were sent over the LAPD's sophisticated MDT (mobile digital transmission) system. A large number of these messages contained offensive racial stereotypes for African Americans and Hispanics, while others openly referred to use of physical force. While these messages were internal communications between officers, and not addressed directly to citizens, they indicate that the culture of the LAPD tolerated the use of offensive language.[137]

Verbal abuse, particularly racial and ethnic slurs, are also a source of tension between the police and minority communities. Allegations of inappropriate language represent about 17 percent of all complaints against officers received by the Minneapolis Civilian Review Authority.[138] In 2001 Washington, DC officers were found to be sending offensive racist, sexist, and homophobic email messages within the department.[139] Reiss found that 75 percent of all police officers in his study were heard using offensive racial terms (although in conversation with other officers and not to citizens). In that study, officers "openly ridiculed and belittled" citizens in only 5 percent of all encounters.[140]

Most departments have official policies forbidding the use of offensive language toward citizens. See, for example, the policy of the Chicago police department on human rights presented in Sidebar 9–2.

Canine Units

Police Canine Units have also been a police–community relations problem in some cities. Minorities believe that police dogs are used more often against them, and that they are bitten far more often than whites. The special counsel to the Los Angeles sheriff's department (LASD) found that in 1991 African Americans and Latinos were 81 percent of those bitten by the department's dogs. By 1999 the total number of bites had been reduced by 90 percent (from 58 to 5), but all of those bitten were minorities.[141]

Delay in Responding to Calls

Several studies of police work found that patrol officers often deliberately delayed responding to calls for service, especially in the case of family disturbances.[142] Furstenburg and Wellford's interviews with citizens in Baltimore who had called the police found that black citizens perceived greater delays than whites. A higher percentage of whites reported the police responding in less than 5 minutes, while nearly twice as many blacks as whites reported that the police took more than 15 minutes to respond.[143] A recent study of a high-crime, predominantly African American neighborhood in St. Louis

---

SIDEBAR 9–2   CHICAGO POLICE DEPARTMENT HUMAN RIGHTS AND RESOURCES POLICY

"Members [of the Chicago police department] will not exhibit any bias or prejudice against any individual or group because of race, color, gender, age, religion, disability, national origin, ancestry, sexual orientation, marital status, parental status, military discharge status or source of income. Members will not direct any derogatory terms toward any person in any manner."

Source: Chicago Police Department, General Order 92-1, "Human Rights and Human Resources," July 4, 1992.

found that "most complaints about policing . . . centered around poor police response." This included delayed response time and complete failure to respond to a 911 call.[144]

Abuse of Gay Men, Lesbians, and Transgendered Persons

Surveys of gay and lesbian people have found a pattern of police abuse directed toward them. Reports of police abuse range from a high of 30 percent of respondents to a low of 8 percent. In addition to abuse, gay and lesbian people also experience ordinary disrespect from some police officers. Where it occurs, mistreatment of gay and lesbian people reflects, in part, prejudice against people who do not have conventional lifestyles. Abuse also reflects a sense that in many instances gay and lesbian people are vulnerable and powerless because filing a complaint or a suit would identify them as gay or lesbian.[145]

Some police departments have responded to this problem in several different ways. Some departments actively recruit gay and lesbian officers. Some have established active outreach or liaison programs with the gay and lesbian community. Many departments incorporate material on equal treatment of gay and lesbian people in their regular human relations training.

Summary

In conclusion, there is considerable evidence that racial-minority citizens, especially young African American males, are subject to differential treatment by police officers because of their race. These incidents, moreover, accumulate over time and create the perception of systematic police harassment.

ADMINISTRATIVE PRACTICES

Handling Citizen Complaints

An African American resident of Milwaukee told the U.S. Civil Rights Commission that "people who have police complaints are literally afraid to go down to the fire and police commission and fill out these complaints."[146] A 1978 U.S. Civil Rights Commission report on Memphis found that "the single most aggravating factor . . . is the failure of the existing internal and external mechanisms which purportedly exist to prevent and combat" police misconduct. The commission cited the case of two officers who shot and killed a 16-year-old boy fleeing from the scene of a burglary. The officers were temporarily suspended for 2 days and then reinstated. Later, two other officers were fired for killing a dog.[147]

Certain police administrative practices generate distrust among racial and ethnic minority community members. The most serious problem is the belief that police departments fail to investigate citizen complaints and to discipline officers who are guilty of misconduct.

In the first national study of police use of force, Pate and Fridell found that for the municipal police departments surveyed, African Americans represented 21.4 percent of the population but 42.3 percent of all complaints filed against the police. Additionally, these city police departments were less likely to sustain complaints filed by African Americans than by whites.[148] These data lend support to the long-standing allegations by civil rights leaders that internal police complaint procedures "whitewash" officer misconduct.

Hispanic Americans represent a somewhat different situation with regard to citizen complaints. Hispanics are less likely to file complaints against the police than African Americans.[149] One reason is the language barrier. Persons who do not speak English are not able to access the complaint process. To overcome this barrier, a number of citizen oversight agencies publish brochures in Spanish explaining the complaint process. The Minneapolis Civilian Review Authority publishes brochures in eight different languages other than English. Cultural factors also inhibit the filing of citizen complaints for many ethnic groups, particularly recent immigrants. A study of citizen perceptions of the complaint process in Omaha found that Spanish-speaking Hispanic residents were extremely fearful of the police and the possible consequences of filing a complaint. Much of this fear was the result of concern about being arrested for not having proper immigration documents.[150]

Because of distrust of police complaint procedures, civil rights leaders have demanded the creation of external or citizen oversight agencies to handle citizen complaints. Many of these agencies engage in active outreach programs to reach different racial and ethnic groups. Citizen oversight is discussed in detail in Chapter 11, along with other mechanisms of police accountability.

POLICE EMPLOYMENT PRACTICES

Employment Discrimination

Discrimination in employment by police departments is another important cause of police–community relations tensions. Racial and ethnic minority officers are underrepresented in most police departments. Underrepresentation exists when the percentage of a minority group as sworn officers does not equal the percentage of that group in the local community served by that department. Virtually every national commission that has studied the police over the past 40 years has recommended that police departments hire more minority officers: the President's Crime Commission (1967), the Kerner Commission (1968), the National Advisory Commission on Criminal Justice Standards and Goals (1973), and the American Bar Association (1980).[151]

Most police experts argue that the police should represent the communities they serve. The CALEA accreditation standards recommend that each law enforcement agency have "minority group and female employees in the sworn law enforcement ranks in approximate proportion to the makeup of the available work force in the agency's law enforcement service community."[152]

In 1968 the Kerner Commission concluded that the underrepresentation of African Americans in big-city police departments was a contributing factor to the riots of the 1960s. At that time, African Americans represented 34 percent of the population in Cleveland but only 7 percent of the sworn officers in the Cleveland police department. In Detroit, meanwhile, African Americans were 39 percent of the population but only 5 percent of the sworn officers.[153]

The 1964 Civil Rights Act outlawed employment discrimination on the basis of race, color, or national origins. Amendments to the law in 1972 strengthened the enforcement powers of the federal Equal Employment Opportunity Commission (EEOC) with respect to employment practices by public agencies. At the same time, Executive Order #11246 requires all organizations receiving federal funds to develop affirmative action plans.

The Goals of Equal Employment Opportunity

As a strategy for improving police–community relations, increased employment of racial and ethnic police officers has three separate objectives.[154] First, it is intended to end unlawful employment discrimination. Among police leaders there is little dispute about the goal of having police forces represent the communities they serve. There is, however, considerable dispute over affirmative action as the proper *means* to that end.[155]

Second, many civil rights leaders argue that increased employment of minority officers will improve the quality of police services. This argument is based on the assumption that minority officers will be better able to relate to minority citizens and will not engage in discriminatory behavior.

There is little evidence, however, that white, African American, or Hispanic police officers behave differently because of their race or ethnicity. Fyfe found that white and black officers assigned to comparable precincts used deadly force at about the same rate.[156] Reiss found that white and black officers used excessive physical force at about the same rate (9.8 per 100 black officers, compared with 8.7 per 100 white officers).[157] No study has found a clear pattern of differences in arrest activity by the race or ethnicity of the officer. Citizen complaint data from San Jose and New York City indicate that officers receive complaints in proportion to their presence in those departments.[158] One study, however, found that African American officers were more likely to be knowledgeable about African American neighborhoods and more aware of local citizen organizations than white officers.[159]

Third, some observers argue that adding minority officers will alter the police subculture and, through peer pressure, affect the attitudes and behavior of other officers. There is some evidence to support this argument. In Los Angeles and other cities, African American officer groups have spoken out against brutality, challenging the view of the predominantly white police union.[160] The National Black Police Officers Association (NBPOA) published a pamphlet on how to stop police brutality, encouraging officers to report misconduct by fellow officers.[161]

Fourth, the presence of more minority-group officers may improve the perception of the department in the community. A survey of Chicago residents found a small but significant number of people who thought that the police department had improved in recent years as a result of having more minority officers. Significantly, no white respondents thought that the department had gotten worse because of increased minority employment.[162] Finally, a recent survey of attitudes in Detroit found it to be the only city where African Americans expressed more positive attitudes toward the police than whites. The authors suggest that this may be the result of greater African American representation in both city government as a whole and the police department in particular.[163]

Signs of Progress

The employment of African Americans and Hispanics in municipal police departments has increased significantly since the early 1970s. The percentage of all sworn officers who were African American rose from an estimated 6.5 percent in 1973 to about 10 percent in 1997. Hispanics represented about 7 percent of all sworn officers in municipal departments in 1997.[164]

Certain cities have made particularly significant progress in minority employment. African Americans represented 58 percent of all sworn officers in the Detroit police department and 69 percent of the Washington, DC, metropolitan police department by 1997. Hispanic officers represented 66 percent of the El Paso police and 40 percent of the San Antonio police by 1993. New York City, on the other hand, made almost no progress in the employment of African American officers between the mid-1980s and the mid-1990s, despite a massive hiring program.[165] A report on the Los Angeles police department 5 years after the Rodney King incident found that, in terms of total sworn officers, the LAPD had a good record with respect to African Americans (14 percent of the population; 14 percent of all officers) but lagged with respect to Hispanic Americans (40 percent of the population versus 30 percent of the officers).[166] Ethnic and racial minorities were even more seriously underrepresented in supervisory positions. By 1996 the Los Angeles police department had made some progress in the promotion of African American officers to higher ranks but much less progress with respect to Hispanic officers.[167]

Discrimination also exists with respect to assignment. In the past, police departments deliberately assigned incompetent officers to racial minority neighborhoods. The President's Crime Commission reported in 1967 that Philadelphia officers known as "goof-offs" were assigned to the ghetto areas of the city as a form of punishment.[168] Albert Reiss commented that "slum police precinct stations, not unlike slum schools, collect the 'rejects' of the system."[169]

There are no data on whether this practice continues today. In most departments, however, union contracts require assignments to be made on the basis of seniority, thereby limiting the opportunity of the department to engage in blatant race discrimination in assignments. A report on the Los Angeles police department, however, found that minorities were underrepresented in recognized "coveted positions—ones that are generally perceived as more desirable, attractive, and prestigious or that provide career-enhancing promotional opportunities."[170]

Employing Newly Arrived Ethnic Groups

The National Crime Prevention Council makes a strong argument in favor of police departments hiring members of newly arrived ethnic groups. The council itself uses several different terms to describe members of these groups, many of whom are recent immigrants: "newcomer," "foreign-born," and "non-native."[171]

First, there are enforcement benefits to police departments. Sworn officers from newly arrived groups can alleviate the reluctance of crime victims to cooperate with the police and testify in court, can expedite case processing by facilitating communication, and on patrol duty can educate newcomers in the community about police practices.

Second, newcomer officers can help to increase public safety. In particular they can overcome misunderstandings that create dangerous situations. The council pointed out that some recent immigrants, following their own cultural traditions, leave their cars when stopped for a traffic violation and bow to show their respect. Since many police departments ask drivers to remain in their cars, some officers might interpret the driver leaving the car as a potentially threatening gesture and unnecessarily use force.

Third, there are intangible benefits. Native-born officers benefit from an enriched multicultural understanding by virtue of working with and getting to know colleagues from newcomer groups. Greater cultural understanding enhances the professionalism of the department and improves public perception of it.

Does the Color of the Officer Make a Difference?

The traditional assumption among some reformers has been that assigning racial and ethnic minority-group officers to minority neighborhoods will improve police–community relations. The first empirical test of this proposition did not find support for it, however. Ron Weitzer interviewed 169 residents of three neighborhoods in Washington, DC (one middle-class African American, one middle-class white, and one lower-income African American neighborhood). Two-thirds of the middle-class residents, white and African American, reported that they could see no difference between white and African American officers. Residents in the lower-income African American neighborhood were more likely to see differences, but the differences they perceived were very mixed. Some residents saw white officers being more courteous and African American officers being less courteous than their counterparts. Only 13 percent of the residents of the lower-income African American neighborhood expressed a preference for having mostly African American officers in their neighborhood. Generally, the overwhelming number of respondents in all neighborhoods either expressed a preference for racially mixed teams of officers or said that the race of officers doesn't matter.[172]

IMPROVING POLICE–COMMUNITY RELATIONS

Police departments have adopted several specific programs for improving police–community relations. The two most important are (1) creating special police–community relations units and (2) providing officers with training in race relations and human relations.

The first step is for police departments to acknowledge that the problem exists. In 1999 the Police Executive Research Forum (PERF) held an unprecedented meeting in which a group of police chiefs were asked to bring a community spokesperson to Washington, DC, for a day-long dialogue. For half the meeting, the chiefs listened to the community representatives' views about the police, and for the other half, the chiefs spoke while the community people listened.[173] Also in 1999, the U.S. Justice Department held a 2-day conference on improving police–community relations. At the Justice Department conference, President Bill Clinton ordered federal law enforcement agencies to collect data on the race and ethnicity of persons they stop, and a series of task forces began developing a list of best practices designed to improve race relations.[174]

Special Police–Community Relations Units

In response to the urban riots of the 1960s most big-city police departments created special police–community relations (PCR) units, which operated programs designed to improve relations with minority communities. PCR units spent most of their time speaking in schools and to community groups.[175] About half also operated "ride-along" programs that allowed citizens to spend a few hours riding in a patrol car.[176] Ride-along police cars were generally driven by a PCR unit officer. They followed patrol cars to calls for service but, in the interests of safety and privacy, did not allow citizens to observe actual encounters too closely.

Some departments also created neighborhood storefront offices, staffed by PCR unit officers, in an effort to overcome the isolation of the police and provide a more convenient access for community residents.[177] Police headquarters buildings are often forbidding places for many citizens and can be difficult to reach. The Detroit police department established fifty-two "ministations" throughout the city beginning in 1975. Each precinct had at least three, and some had four. Crime prevention officers (CPOs) assigned to the ministations did not engage in regular patrol and did not answer calls for service. Their activities included organizing teenage summer employment programs, encouraging trash pickup in neglected areas, and maintaining a volunteer escort service for the elderly.[178] The Houston Fear Reduction Experiment (Chapter 7) also included neighborhood offices.[179]

Critics questioned the effectiveness of PCR units. The President's Crime Commission found that minorities regarded most PCR programs as "public relations puff" and a "deliberate con game."[180] Most police officers did not regard PCR units as an essential part of police operations. A Justice Department report found that PCR units "tended to be marginal to the operations of the police department," with little or no relationship to patrol or criminal investigation activities.[181] Using 1968 public opinion data, Decker, Smith, and Uhlman found that in cities with special PCR units public attitudes toward the police were only slightly more positive than in those cities where no PCR unit existed. The existence of a program had no effect on the attitudes of whites, but did have a positive effect among those respondents who expressed the least trust in government.[182]

Ride-along programs, meanwhile, tend to attract only those people who already have a favorable attitude toward the police and, consequently, do not reach those people who have serious complaints about the police. Many departments have abandoned their ride-along programs because of budget constraints. Some have been replaced by Citizen–Police Academies, which attempt to provide interested citizens with a more comprehensive understanding of policing.[183]

Special PCR programs encounter the same problems as community-policing programs (Chapter 7). Generally, they tend to be more successful with those groups of people who already have favorable attitudes toward the police: whites, homeowners, and older people. In the Houston fear reduction program, as well as many other experiments, innovations designed to improve relations with the public were less successful with racial minorities than whites.[184] Overcoming deeply rooted racial and ethnic barriers in policing represents an extremely difficult challenge.

Race Relations and Human Relations Training

Police training programs have improved dramatically over the past thirty years. Not only has the average length of preservice training more than doubled, but most police academies have either added or greatly expanded the coverage of race relations and human relations. In 1952, police academy training programs devoted an average of 4 hours to human relations; by 1982, the average was 25.3 hours.[185]

No research has established a direct connection between race relations training and either improved police officer behavior or improved public attitudes, however. A study of a police–community relations program in San Francisco found a significant change in police officer attitudes as a result of structured meetings with community residents. Officers reported more positive attitudes toward African American residents and perceived less community hostility toward them as a result of the training sessions. There was no evaluation of police officer behavior, however.[186] The Los Angeles police department (LAPD) instituted a program of cultural awareness training after the 1991 Rodney King incident. Five years later, however, only 2,700 of the more than 9,000 officers had undergone the training program.[187]

Speaking at a 1999 national conference on police–community relations, Billy Johnston, retired commander with the Boston police department, described his personal transformation. He joined the department in 1966 and was assigned to the riot squad. "I was trained to go to war," he recalled, "and to do so you must have an enemy." The "enemy," in this case, became the people in the community. Johnston's views underwent a dramatic change after he worked undercover as a decoy. "It was the first time I understood being different, a victim of crime, and scared." Leaving a bar known to serve gay people, he was attacked and threatened. "I realized what it meant to be hated." Johnston's views changed not because of a classroom lecture, but through a real-life experience that gave him a new perspective on crime.[188]

A number of experts question the value of classroom training. A review of cultural diversity training programs for police found that the content of these programs had not changed much since the 1960s, that they tended to perpetuate negative stereotypes of racial minorities, and that they focused on individual officers and ignored problems related to the organization as a whole.[189] Alpert, Smith, and Watters argue that "mere classroom training" on issues of race relations "is insufficient." They stress the importance of on-the-street police behavior and recommend that both new recruits and veteran officers "experiment with methods of communicating with members of racial and cultural groups other than their own."[190] A Detroit crime-victims training program found that recruits' attitudes toward citizens changed dramatically after only 4 months on the job, suggesting that street experience is a far more powerful influence over officer attitudes than classroom training.[191]

Language Training for Non-English Speakers

A police officer in a Midwestern city, assigned to patrol the part of town that is the center of the growing Hispanic community, explained, "The way I figure, we're here to provide a service and if you can't provide a service to a certain group of people, then you're not doing your job." The officer was referring specifically to being able to communicate with community residents who do not speak English.[192]

Because so much of police work involves communication between people, language barriers create potentially serious barriers to the delivery of high-quality police services. Barriers are likely to arise when the citizen speaks a language other than English that the responding officer does not speak. If the officer is bilingual—for example, able to speak both English and Spanish—these barriers can be overcome.[193]

A study of potential Spanish-language barriers in one Midwestern city found some minor problems and delays but no serious problems. Potential language barriers represented only 15 percent of all police–citizen contacts in the precinct that is the center of that city's Hispanic community. Delays occurred in 87 percent of those contacts, and frustration on the part of either the citizen or the officer occurred in 73 percent. Some conflict occurred in 27 percent of the calls because of language barriers, but none of those situations involved serious conflict (e.g., violence). Generally officers who did not have a command of Spanish "muddled through" their interactions with Spanish-speaking citizens. They either utilized "street Spanish" (a few basic phrases they had learned on the job), used command Spanish (which they had learned through formal training), or found a bystander who could translate.[194]

"Best Practices" in Policing

In his introduction to the department's first traffic stop data report, San Jose (California) Police Chief William Lansdowne explained that the department "prides itself upon being responsive to the needs and concerns of everyone" and, therefore, "has an obligation to members of the community concerned about racial profiling to look into the matter to see if there is any indication that it occurs in San Jose."[195] Along with San Diego, San Jose was one of the first police departments to undertake traffic stop data collection and release the data. The first San Jose report included some indications of racial and ethnic disparities in traffic stops, but it was not clear if they represented discrimination as explained earlier in this chapter.

With traffic stop data collection, the San Jose police department adopted one of the major "best practices" in policing. A Justice Department report issued in January 2001 listed the best practices as (1) a comprehensive policy requiring officers to report all uses of force; (2) an open and accessible citizen complaint procedure; (3) an early warning system to identify potential "problem" officers (see Chapter 11); (4) improved police training; (5) traffic stop data collection; and (6) improved recruitment, hiring, and retention of officers.[196]

The recommended best practices are particularly important for improving police–community relations because the victims of police abuse of authority are disproportionately racial and ethnic minority citizens. A comprehensive program to control officer use of force, for example, is likely to reduce abuse of African Americans and Hispanic people.

Community Policing and Improving PCR

Community policing represents a different approach to improving police–community relations in several respects. First, as Alpert, Smith, and Watters point out, it represents a comprehensive philosophy of policing. It may better address on-the-street police behavior than most of the traditional PCR programs that emerged after the riots of the 1960s and were essentially add-ons to basic police operations.[197] Second, community policing is directed toward the community as a whole, and not just racial and ethnic minority communities. A survey of large police departments found that over 87 percent claimed that community policing had led to improved relations with minority communities.[198] These claims have not been independently confirmed, however.

SUMMARY

Conflict between the police and racial and ethnic communities remains a serious problem in American policing. This problem persists despite general improvements in policing. There is evidence of racial discrimination in police field practices, such as the use of force, the handling of citizen complaints about police behavior, and police employment practices. Many of these problems are the responsibility of the police themselves. At the same time, conflict between police and minorities is a product of the larger structure of racism and racial discrimination in American society.

CASE STUDY: RESPONDING TO COMMUNITY CRISES: THE U.S. COMMUNITY RELATIONS SERVICE

The Community Relations Service (CRS) of the U.S. Department of Justice provides direct services to local communities experiencing racial or ethnic crises. These services include:

1 Professional mediation and conciliation to help resolve tensions. The CRS offers services on a 2-hour notice in crisis situations and within 3 weeks for noncrisis situations.
2 Technical assistance to local officials in implementing new policies and practices.
3 Training for police, other government officials, and community leaders.
4 Event contingency planning when a community faces an event (e.g., a demonstration or march) that might generate racial or ethnic conflict.

The CRS has been involved in an experimental program with the New Haven, Connecticut, police department, the Board of Young Adult Police Commissioners (described on p. 308).

What, exactly, does this program consist of? Based on what you have learned in this chapter, do you think this is likely to be an effective program? If so, why? If not, why not?

BOARD OF YOUNG ADULT POLICE COMMISSIONERS
NEW HAVEN, CONNECTICUT

Contact:

Sergeant Patrick Redding
New Haven Police Department
Department of Police Services
One Union Avenue
New Haven, CT 06519
(203) 946-6946

Background:

As the New Haven, Connecticut, Police Department began shifting toward a community-based policing style, the chief visited city high schools to speak with students about his department's changing role. Through these visits, he discovered there was a lot of distrust among many students who felt police were an adversarial presence. Realizing the need to improve police–youth relations, the chief formed the Board of Young Adult Police Commissioners (BYAPC), which is composed of 22 high-school students selected from New Haven school districts.

Efforts:

BYAPC meets monthly in the chief's conference room at the police department. A police sergeant acts as the adult advisor, but four elected members lead the meetings. These sessions provide opportunities for the youth to discuss such local issues as curfews, metal detectors in schools, and the lack of teen residential drug treatment programs. Each year, the group also schedules sessions for the chief at each of the city high schools, which allow the student body to voice concerns and share opinions. BYAPC members have also had the opportunity to interview each police recruit that has joined the force since their group was formed.

The Role of CRS:

The BYAPC police advisor confers with the regional CRS representative on a monthly basis. CRS has also used the student group as a model for promoting positive police–urban youth relations—inviting members to share their success stories at conferences and meetings—and the BYAPC is recognized as a model program in the CRS publication, "Police-Urban Youth Relations: An Antidote to Racial Violence."

Lessons Learned:

The program has succeeded as a result of two key elements: first, the police department had a real desire to find a creative, collaborative solution to the problem of youth distrust. Second, BYAPC gave New Haven youth a voice that is actually heard in the community. According to the group's current advisor, Sergeant Patrick Redding, "Other youth programs fail because they aren't taken seriously or aren't given access." In contrast, the BYAPC is empowered by the City and given access to government and law enforcement executives. As a result, it is making a difference in New Haven.

Source: U.S. Community Relations Service, *Police Use of Force—Addressing Community Racial Tensions* (Washington, DC: Government Printing Office, nd).

FOR DISCUSSION

1 What exactly does the New Haven Young Adult Police Commissioners program consist of? What does it do? Who selects the commissioners? Does it have any power?
2 Discuss whether you think this program is likely to make a real difference in police–community relations. If you do, explain why. If not, explain why not.
3 Check the websites for the New Haven police department and the City of New Haven. Is there any evidence that this program is still functioning? If so, are any activities described? If so, are they different from the original description of the program?

INTERNET EXERCISES

Exercise 1 A number of police departments have active programs designed to improve police–community relations. Select ten departments and search their websites (**www.officer.com**) to see how many describe PCR programs.

Select your ten departments on the basis of some rational formula: geographic distribution, size (measured by number of sworn officers). For example, you might choose the ten largest in the entire country, or the two largest in each of five different regions, or ten departments from your immediate three- or four-state region.

Report your findings in class. How many departments report having any program? What do those programs consist of (citizen attitude surveys, ride-along programs, citizen police academies)?

Exercise 2 In the spring of 2001 the City of Cincinnati experienced riots as a result of a fatal shooting of an African American man by a white police officer. This was the fifteenth such fatal shooting in 6 years.

This riot was very similar to the riots of the 1960s. Has nothing changed in Cincinnati? Have there been no improvements in police–community relations in that city? Using the Web, locate news stories and reports on the situation in Cincinnati. Some can be found through the "Archives" section of local or national newspapers.

What do these stories and reports conclude about the situation in Cincinnati? Were police–community relations significantly worse than in other cities? What factors explain the riot in the spring of 2001?

Exercise 3 Many observers believe that, unlike Cincinnati, police–community relations have significantly improved in Boston in recent years. Go to the Boston police department website. What programs do they claim to have related to police–community relations? Check other Boston-related websites for related material. Does the mayor's office website describe any community relations programs? In the end, can you identify any significant differences between Cincinnati and Boston?

REFERENCES

1 ACLU, *Driving While Black* (New York: ACLU, 1999).
2 The Gallup Organization, "Racial Profiling Is Seen as Widespread" (Princeton, NJ, December 9, 1999).
3 Samuel Walker, Cassia Spohn, and Miriam DeLone, *The Color of Justice: Race, Ethnicity, and Crime in America,* 2nd ed. (Belmont, CA: Wadsworth, 2000).
4 Jeffrey Goldberg, "The Color of Suspicion," *New York Times Magazine* (June 20, 1999), p. 52.
5 National Research Council, *A Common Destiny: Blacks and American Society* (Washington, DC: National Academy Press, 1989), p. 453.
6 Walker, Spohn, and DeLone, *The Color of Justice: Race, Ethnicity, and Crime in America,* 2nd ed.
7 Bureau of Justice Statistics, *Sourcebook of Criminal Justice Statistics, 2000* (On-line Edition: www.albany.edu/sourcebook), Table 4–10, 6–20.
8 Walker, Spohn, and DeLone, *The Color of Justice: Race, Ethnicity, and Crime in America,* 2nd ed., p. 287.
9 Jerome G. Miller, *Search and Destroy: African-American Males in the Criminal Justice System* (New York: Cambridge University Press, 1996).
10 Leadership Conference on Civil Rights, *Justice on Trial* (Washington, DC: LCCR, 2000), p. 1.
11 Alfredo Mirande, *Gringo Justice* (Notre Dame, IN: University of Notre Dame Press, 1987).
12 National Council of La Raza, *The Mainstreaming of Hate: A Report on Latinos and Harassment, Hate Violence, and Law Enforcement Abuse in the '90s* (Washington, DC: National Council of La Raza, 1999), p. 15.
13 Bureau of Justice Statistics, *Police Use of Force: Collection of National Data* (Washington, DC: Government Printing Office, 1997).
14 U.S. Census Bureau, *Statistical Abstract of the United States, 1999* (Washington, DC: Government Printing Office, 1999), p. 14.
15 Geoffrey P. Alpert and Roger Dunham, *Policing Multi-Ethnic Neighborhoods* (New York: Greenwood Press, 1988).
16 Juanita Diaz-Cotto, "The Criminal Justice System and Its Impact on Latinas(os) in the United States," *The Justice Professional,* 13, no. 1 (2000): 49–50.
17 Migdalia DeJesus-Torres, "Microaggressions in the Criminal Justice System at Discretionary Stages and Its Impact on Latino(a) Hispanics," *The Justice Professional,* 13, no. 1 (2000): 69–89.
18 Marianne O. Nielsen and Robert A. Silverman, eds., *Native Americans, Crime, and Justice* (Boulder, CO: Westview, 1996).
19 Executive Committee for Indian Country Law Enforcement Improvements, *Final Report to the Attorney General and the Secretary of the Interior* (Washington, DC:

October 1997); Eileen Luna, "The Growth and Development of Tribal Police," *Journal of Contemporary Criminal Justice,* 14 (February 1998): 75–86.

20 Carmen T. Joge and Sonia Perez, *The Mainstreaming of Hate: A Report on Latinos and Harassment, Hate Violence, and Law Enforcement Abuse in the '90s* (Washington, DC: National Council of La Raza, 1999), p. 17,

21 Ibid., p. 20.

22 Robert C. Davis and Edna Erez, *Immigrant Populations as Victims: Toward a Multicultural Criminal Justice System* (Washington, DC: Government Printing Office, 1998).

23 National Crime Prevention Council, *Building and Crossing Bridges: Refugees and Law Enforcement Working Together* (Washington, DC: National Crime Prevention Council, 1994).

24 *If You Have a Complaint against the Minneapolis Police Department* (Minneapolis, MN: Minneapolis Civilian Review Authority, nd). Brochures in English and other languages.

25 Definitions of race and ethnicity are discussed in Walker, Spohn, and DeLone, *The Color of Justice,* pp. 5–15.

26 Bureau of Justice Statistics, *Criminal Victimization and Perceptions of Community Safety in 12 Cities, 1998* (Washington, DC: Government Printing Office, 1999), p. 25.

27 Samuel Walker, *Police and Minority Group Interactions* (Washington, DC: Police Executive Research Forum, 2000).

28 Steven A. Tuch and Ronald Weitzer, "Racial Differences in Attitudes toward the Police," *Public Opinion Quarterly,* 61 (1997): 642–663.

29 Bureau of Justice Statistics, *Criminal Victimization and Perceptions of Community Safety in 12 Cities, 1998,* Table 33.

30 W. S. Wilson Huang and Michael S. Vaughn, "Support and Confidence: Public Attitudes toward the Police," in T. J. Flanagan and D. R. Longmire, eds., *Americans View Crime and Justice: A National Public Opinion Survey* (Newbury Park, CA: Sage, 1996), pp. 31–45.

31 Bureau of Justice Statistics, *Criminal Victimization and Perceptions of Community Safety in 12 Cities, 1998,* p. 25.

32 Roger G. Dunham and Geoffrey P. Alpert, "Neighborhood Differences in Attitudes toward Policing: Evidence for a Mixed-Strategy Model of Policing in a Multi-Ethnic Setting," *Journal of Criminal Law and Criminology,* 79, no. 2 (1988): 504–523.

33 Huang and Vaughn, "Support and Confidence," pp. 40–41.

34 Louis Garcia, *Police and Minority Citizen Interactions: An Overview of Issues and Initiatives within the City of Boston* (Boston: Boston Police Department, 1998), p. 5.

35 Sandra Lee Browning, Francis T. Cullen, Liqun Cao, Renee Kopache, and Thomas J. Stevenson, "Race and Getting Hassled by the Police: A Research Note," *Police Studies,* 17, no. 1 (1994): 1–11.

36 "From Some Parents, Warnings about Police," *The New York Times* (October 23, 1997), p. A18.

37 Ronald Weitzer, "Citizens' Perceptions of Police Misconduct: Race and Neighborhood Context," *Justice Quarterly,* 16 (December 1999): 1101–1128.

38 Warren Friedman and Marsha Hott, *Young People and the Police: Respect, Fear and the Future of Community Policing in Chicago* (Chicago: Chicago Alliance for Neighborhood Safety, 1995).

39 Huang and Vaughn, "Support and Confidence."

40 Friedman and Hott, *Young People and the Police,* p. 7.

41 Yolander G. Hurst, James Frank, and Sandra Lee Browning, "The Attitudes of Juveniles toward the Police: A Comparison of Black and White Youth," *Policing,* 23, no. 1 (2000): 37–53.

42 Bureau of Justice Statistics, *Criminal Victimization and Perceptions of Community Safety in 12 Cities, 1998.*

43 Bureau of Justice Statistics, *Criminal Victimization and Perceptions of Community Safety in 12 Cities, 1998.*

44 The events of March 3, 1991, are described in detail in Jerome H. Skolnick and James J. Fyfe, *Above the Law* (New York: Free Press, 1993), pp. 1–3.

45 Tuch and Weitzer, "Racial Differences in Attitudes toward the Police," 647–649.

46 "Poll: NYPD's Image Took a Beating in Louima Case," *New York Post* (October 24, 1998).

47 James Frank, Steven G. Brandl, Francis T. Cullen, and Amy Stichman, "Reassessing the Impact of Race on Citizens' Attitudes toward the Police: A Research Note," *Justice Quarterly,* 13 (June 1996): 321–334.

48 David Carter, "Hispanic Perception of Police Performance: An Empirical Assessment," *Journal of Criminal Justice,* 13, no. 2 (1985): 487–500.

49 Meghan Stroshine Chandek, "Race, Expectations and Evaluations of Police Performance: An Empirical Assessment," *Policing,* 22, no. 4 (1999): 675–695.

50 Stan L. Albrecht and Miles Green, "Attitudes toward the Police and the Larger Attitude Complex," *Criminology,* 15 (May 1977): 67–86.

51 Egon Bittner, "The Functions of the Police in Urban Society," in Bittner, *Aspects of Police Work* (Boston: Northeastern University Press, 1990), pp. 89–232.

52 Abraham Blumberg, *Criminal Justice,* 2d ed. (New York: New Viewpoints, 1979), p. 58.

53 Arthur Niederhoffer, *Behind the Shield: The Police in Urban Society* (Garden City, NY: Anchor Books, 1967), p. 1.

54 Department of Justice, *Sourcebook of Criminal Justice Statistics, 1998,* p. 108.

55 Walker, *Police Interactions with Racial and Ethnic Minorities.*

56 Carolyn M. Ward, "Policing in the Hyde Park Neighborhood, St. Louis: Racial Bias, Political Pressure, and Community Policing," *Crime, Law and Social Change,* 26 (1997): 172–173, 181.

57 James Q. Wilson, *Varieties of Police Behavior* (New York: Atheneum, 1973), p. 28.

58 William A. Westley, *Violence and the Police* (Cambridge, MA: MIT Press, 1970), p. 93.

59 Jerome H. Skolnick, *Justice without Trial,* 3rd ed. (New York: Macmillan, 1994), pp. 41–68.

60 W. Eugene Groves and Peter H. Rossi, "Police Perceptions of a Hostile Ghetto: Realism or Projection?" in Harlan H. Hahn, ed., *Police in Urban Society* (Beverly Hills, CA: Sage Publications, 1971), pp. 175–191.

61 David H. Bayley and Harold Mendelsohn, *Minorities and the Police* (New York: Free Press, 1969), p. 40.

62 Lawrence W. Sherman, Patrick R. Gartin, and Michael E. Buerger, "Hot Spots of Predatory Crime: Routine Activities and the Criminology of Place," *Criminology,* 27, no. 1 (1989): 27–55.

63 Bureau of Justice Services, *Contacts between Police and the Public* (Washington, DC: Government Printing Office, 2001).

64 Albert Reiss, *The Police and the Public* (New Haven, CT: Yale University Press, 1971).

65 Ibid., pp. 50–54; Robert E. Worden, "The 'Causes' of Police Brutality: Theory and Evidence," in W. A. Geller and H. Toch, eds., *And Justice for All* (Washington, DC: Police Executive Research Forum, 1995), p. 44.

66 John A. Groeger, *Memory and Remembering: Everyday Memory in Context* (New York: Addison Wesley, 1997), pp. 189–196.

67 Irving Piliavin and Scott Briar, "Police Encounters with Juveniles," *American Journal of Sociology,* 70 (September 1964): 206–214; Donald Black, "The Social Organization of Arrest," in Black, *The Manners and Customs of the Police* (New York: Academic Press, 1980), pp. 85–108.

68 Skolnick, *Justice without Trial.*

69 U.S. Commission on Civil Rights, *Police Protection of the African American Community in Milwaukee* (Washington, DC: Government Printing Office, 1994), p. 41.

70 Department of Justice, *Public Opinion about Crime* (Washington, DC: Government Printing Office, 1977).

71 Gunnar Myrdal, *An American Dilemma: The Negro Problem and Modern Democracy* (New York: Harper and Brothers, 1944); Samuel Walker, "'A Strange Atmosphere of Consistent Illegality': Myrdal on 'The Police and Other Public Contacts,'" in O. Clayton, ed., *An American Dilemma Revisited* (New York: Russell Sage, 1996), pp. 226–246.

72 Guy B. Johnson, "The Negro and Crime," *Annals of the American Academy of Political and Social Science,* 217 (September 1941): 93–104.

73 Philadelphia Police Study Task Force, *Philadelphia and Its Police* (Philadelphia: The City, 1987), p. 169.

74 The Knapp Commission, *Report on Police Corruption* (New York: Braziller, 1973), p. 75.

75 Mollen Commission, *Report of the Commission* (New York: The Mollen Commission, 1994).

76 Los Angeles Police Department, *Board of Inquiry Report on the Rampart Scandal* (Los Angeles: LAPD, 2000).

77 Peter B. Bloch, *Equality of Distribution of Police Services—A Case Study of Washington, DC* (Washington, DC: Urban Institute, 1974).

78 David H. Bayley and Harold Mendelsohn, *Minorities and the Police* (New York: The Free Press, 1969), p. 109.

79 Department of Justice, *The Police and Public Opinion* (Washington, DC: Government Printing Office, 1977), pp. 39, 40.

80 Weitzer, "Citizens' Perceptions of Police Misconduct: Race and Neighborhood Context," 1101–1128.

81 Dunham and Alpert, "Neighborhood Differences in Attitudes toward Policing: Evidence for a Mixed-Strategy Model of Policing in a Multi-Ethnic Setting."

82 The facts of the case are in *Tennessee v. Garner,* 471 U.S. 1 (1985).

83 James J. Fyfe, "Reducing the Use of Deadly Force: The New York Experience," in Department of Justice, *Police Use of Deadly Force* (Washington, DC: Government Printing Office, 1978), p. 29.

84 U.S. Commission on Civil Rights, *Revisiting* Who Is Guarding the Guardians: *A Report on Police Practices and Civil Rights in America* (Washington, DC: U.S. Commission on Civil Rights, 2000).

85 Gerald Robin, "Justifiable Homicide by Police Officers," *Journal of Criminal Law and Criminology, and Police Science,* 54 (1963): 225–231.

86 James J. Fyfe, "Blind Justice: Police Shootings in Memphis," *Journal of Criminal Law and Criminology,* 73, no. 2 (1982): 707–722.

87 *Tennessee v. Garner,* 471 U.S. 1 (1985); William A. Geller and Michael S. Scott, *Deadly Force: What We Know* (Washington, DC: Police Executive Research Forum, 1992).

88 James J. Fyfe, "Administrative Interventions on Police Shooting Discretion: An Empirical Assessment," *Journal of Criminal Justice,* 7 (Winter 1979): 309–323.

89 Jerry R. Sparger and David J. Giacopassi, "Memphis Revisited: A Reexamination of Police Shootings after the Garner Decision," *Justice Quarterly,* 9 (June 1992): 211–225.

90 Lawrence W. Sherman and Ellen G. Cohn, *Citizens Killed by Big City Police* (Washington, DC: Crime Control Institute, 1986); Geller and Scott, *Deadly Force: What We Know.*

91 Samuel Walker, *Taming the System: The Control of Discretion in Criminal Justice, 1950–1990* (New York: Oxford University Press, 1993), pp. 21–53.

92 William A. Geller and Kevin J. Karales, *Split Second Decisions* (Chicago: Chicago Law Enforcement Study Group, 1981).

93 Lou Cannon, *Official Negligence* (New York: Times Books, 1997).

94 Commission on Accreditation for Law Enforcement Agencies, *Standards for Law Enforcement Agencies,* 4th ed. (Fairfax, VA: CALEA, 1999), Standard 1.3.1.

95 Carl B. Klockars, "A Theory of Excessive Force and Its Control," in W. A. Geller and H. Toch, eds., *And Justice for All,* pp. 11–29.

96 Bureau of Justice Statistics, *Contacts between Police and the Public* (Washington, DC: Government Printing Office, 2001).

97 Kenneth Adams, "Measuring the Prevalence of Police Abuse of Force," in Geller and Toch, eds., *And Justice for All,* pp. 61–97; Albert Reiss, *The Police and the Public* (New Haven, CT: Yale University Press, 1971), p. 142.

98 Reiss, *The Police and the Public,* p. 151.

99 Robert Worden, "The 'Causes' of Police Brutality: Theory and Evidence on Police Use of Force," in Geller and Toch, eds., *And Justice for All,* p. 52.

100 Geoffrey P. Alpert, "The Force Factor: Measuring and Assessing Police Use of Force and Suspect Resistance," in Bureau of Justice Statistics, *Use of Force by Police: Overview of National and Local Data* (Washington, DC: Government Printing Office, 1999), pp. 45–60.

101 David Weisburd and Rosann Greenspan, *Police Attitudes toward Abuse of Authority: Findings from a National Study* (Washington, DC: Government Printing Office, 2000).

102 Albert Reiss, "Police Brutality—Answers to Key Questions," *Transaction,* 5 (July–August 1968): 10–19.

103 San Jose, Independent Police Auditor, *2000 Year End Report* (San Jose: IPA, 2001), p. 51; New York City, Civilian Complaint Review Board, *Status Report, January–December 2000* (New York: CCRB, 2001), p. 38.

104 Robert Tillman, "The Size of the 'Criminal Population,' The Prevalence and Incidence of Adult Arrest," *Criminology,* 25 (August 1987): 561–579.

105 Donald Black, "The Social Organization of Arrest," in Black, *The Manners and Customs of the Police.*

106 Robert Friedrich, "Racial Prejudice and Police Treatment of Blacks," in R. Baker and F. Meyer, eds., *Evaluating Alternative Law Enforcement Policies* (Lexington, MA: Lexington Books, 1979), pp. 160–161.

107 Richard Lundman et al., "Police Control of Juveniles: A Replication," *Journal of Research in Crime and Delinquency,* 15 (January 1978): 74–91.

108 Douglas A. Smith, Christy A. Visher, and Laura A. Davidson, "Equity and Discretionary Justice: The Influence of Race on Police Discretion," *Journal of Criminal Law and Criminology,* 75 (Spring 1984): 234–249.

109 Black, "The Social Organization of Arrest."

110 Irving Piliavin and Scott Briar, "Police Encounters with Juveniles," *American Journal of Sociology,* 70 (September 1964): 206–214.

111 David A. Klinger, "Demeanor or Crime? Why 'Hostile' Citizens Are More Likely to Be Arrested," *Criminology,* 32, no. 3 (1994): 475–493.

112 David H. Bayley, "The Tactical Choices of Police Patrol Officers," *Journal of Criminal Justice,* 14, no. 1 (1986): 329–348; Stephen Mastrofski and Roger B. Parks, "Improving Observational Studies of Police," *Criminology,* 28, no. 3 (1990): 475–496.

113 Skolnick, *Justice without Trial,* pp. 44–47.

114 John R. Hepburn, "Race and the Decision to Arrest: An Analysis of Warrants Issued," *Journal of Research in Crime and Delinquency,* 15, no. 3 (1978): 54–73.

115 Joan Petersilia, *Racial Disparities in the Criminal Justice System* (Santa Monica, CA: Rand, 1983), pp. 20–33.

116 U.S. Department of Health and Human Services, *National Household Survey on Drug Abuse: Main Findings, 1997* (Washington, DC: Government Printing Office, 1999).

117 Steven R. Donziger, ed., *The Real War on Crime: The Report of The National Criminal Justice Commission* (New York: Harper, 1996), p. 115.

118 Walker, *Police Interactions with Racial and Ethnic Minority Groups.*

119 ACLU, *Driving While Black.*

120 David Harris, "The Stories, the Statistics, and the Law: Why 'Driving While Black' Matters," *Minnesota Law Review,* 84 (December 1999): 265–326; ACLU, *Driving While Black.*

121 William J. Chambliss, "Policing the Ghetto Underclass: The Politics of Law and Law Enforcement," *Social Problems,* 41 (May 1994): 179.

122 Oscar Corral, "Woman Says Cop Assaulted Her," Newsday (January 23, 2001); the concept of "driving while female" is explained in Samuel Walker, "Searching for the Denominator," unpublished paper.

123 Quoted in Ronald Weitzer, "Racialized Policing: Residents' Perceptions in Three Neighborhoods," *Law and Society Review,* 34, no. 1 (2000): 138.

124 President's Commission on Law Enforcement and Administration of Justice, *Task Force Report: The Police* (Washington, DC: Government Printing Office, 1967), pp. 183–186.

125 *Report of the Attorney General's Civil Rights Division on Boston Police Department Practices* (Boston: Attorney General's Office, 1990), p. 60.

126 Browning et al., "Race and Getting Hassled by the Police: A Research Note."

127 Warren Friedman and Marsha Hott, *Young People and the Police* (Chicago: Chicago Alliance for Neighborhood Safety, 1995).

128 Eliot Spitzer, *The New York City Police Department's "Stop and Frisk" Practices* (New York: Attorney General of New York, 1999).

129 Quoted in Weitzer, "Racialized Policing," 137.

130 Spitzer, *The New York Police Department's "Stop and Frisk" Practices.*

131 Bureau of Justice Statistics, *Contacts between Police and the Public.*

132 Walker, *Police Interactions with Racial and Ethnic Minorities.*

133 Skolnick, *The Police and the Urban Ghetto* (Chicago: American Bar Foundation, 1968).

134 Christopher Commission, *Report of the Independent Commission on the Los Angeles Police Department* (Los Angeles: The Commission, 1991), p. 74.

135 Merrick Bobb, Special Counsel, *Five Years Later: A Report to the Los Angeles Police Commission* (Los Angeles: The Police Commission, 1996), p. 5.

136 Randall Kennedy, *Race, Crime, and the Law* (New York: Vintage Books, 1998).

137 Christopher Commission, *Report of the Independent Commission on the Los Angeles Police Department,* pp. 48–55.

138 Minneapolis Civilian Review Authority, *1999 Annual Report* (Minneapolis, MN: Civilian Review Authority, 2000).

139 Petula Dvorak, "Federal Probe Begins on Police E-mails," *Washington Post* (April 5, 2001), B2.

140 Reiss, *The Police and the Public,* p. 142.

141 Special Counsel to the Los Angeles Sheriff's Department, *11th Semiannual Report* (Los Angeles, October 1999), p. 78.

142 Black, *Manners and Customs of the Police,* p. 117; Richard J. Lundman, "Domestic Police–Citizen Encounters, *Journal of Police Science and Administration,* 2 (March 1974): 25.

143 Frank Furstenburg and Charles Wellford, "Calling the Police: the Evaluation of Police Service," *Law and Society Review,* 7 (Spring 1973): 402.

144 Carolyn M. Ward, "Policing in the Hyde Park Neighborhood, St. Louis: Racial Bias, Political Pressure, and Community Policing," 169.

145 Gregory M. Herek and Kevin T. Berrill, eds., *Hate Crimes: Confronting Violence against Lesbians and Gay Men* (Newbury Park, CA: Sage, 1992).

146 U.S. Civil Rights Commission, *Police Protection of the African American Community in Milwaukee,* p. 45.

147 U.S. Civil Rights Commission, Tennessee Advisory Committee, *Civic Crisis— Civic Challenge: Police Community Relations in Memphis* (Washington, DC: Government Printing Office, 1978), pp. 1. 88.

148 Anthony M. Pate and Lorie A. Fridell, *Police Use of Force,* Vol. 1 (Washington, DC: The Police Foundation, 1993), p. 95.

149 Ibid.

150 Samuel Walker, "Complaints against the Police: A Focus Group Study of Citizen Perceptions, Goals, and Expectations," *Criminal Justice Review,* 22 (Autumn 1997): 207–226.

151 Walker, Spohn, and DeLone, *The Color of Justice,* pp. 110–116.

152 Commission on Accreditation for Law Enforcement Agencies, *Standards for Law Enforcement Agencies,* 4th ed. (Fairfax, VA: CALEA, 1994), Standard 31.2.1.

153 National Advisory Commission on Civil Disorders, *Report* (New York: Bantam Books, 1968), Ch. 11.

154 National Advisory Commission on Civil Disorders, *Report,* p. 315.

155 Walker, "Declaration."

156 James J. Fyfe, "Who Shoots: A Look at Officer Race and Police Shooting," *Journal of Police Science and Administration,* 9, no. 4 (1981): 367–382.

157 Reiss, "Police Brutality—Answers to Key Questions."

158 San Jose Independent Police Auditor, *2000 Year End Report;* New York Civilian Complaint Review Board, *Status Report 2000.*

159 Stephen Mastrofski, "Police Knowledge of the Patrol Beat as a Performance Measure," in Gordon Whitaker, ed., *Understanding Police Agency Performance* (Washington, DC: Government Printing Office, 1984), pp. 68–70.

160 "Black Officers Take on the LAPD and Protective League: An Interview with Sgt. Leonard Ross," *Policing by Consent* (October 1995): 8–9.

161 National Black Police Officers Association, *Police Brutality: How to Stop the Violence* (Washington, DC: NBPOA, nd).

162 Walker and Webb, Paper, ASC, 1997.

163 Frank, Brandl, Cullen, and Stichman, "Reassessing the Impact of Race on Citizens' Attitudes toward the Police: A Research Note."

164 Bureau of Justice Statistics, *Law Enforcement Management and Administrative Statistics, 1997* (Washington, DC: Government Printing Office, 1999), p. ix.

165 Samuel Walker and K. B. Turner, *A Decade of Modest Progress* (Omaha: University of Nebraska at Omaha, 1992).

166 Merrick J. Bobb, *Five Years Later: A Report to the Los Angeles Police Commission* (Los Angeles: Police Commission, 1996), p. 21.

167 Ibid.

168 President's Commission on Law Enforcement and Administration of Justice, *Task Force Report: The Police,* p. 165.

169 Reiss, *The Police and the Public,* p. 168.

170 Bobb, *Five Years Later,* pp. 23–24.

171 National Crime Prevention Council, *Lengthening the Stride: Employing Peace Officers from Newly Arrived Ethnic Groups* (Washington, DC: National Crime Prevention Council, 1995).

172 Ronald Weitzer, "White, Black, or Blue Cops?: Race and Citizen Assessment of Police Officers," *Journal of Criminal Justice,* 28 (2000): 313–324.

173 "Police Chiefs Say Criticism Is Founded, and Vow to Regain the Public Trust," *The New York Times* (April 10, 1999).

174 U.S. Department of Justice, Attorney General's Conference, *Strengthening Police Community Relationships; Summary Report* (Washington, DC, June 1999).

175 Fred A. Klyman and Joanna Kruckenberg, "A National Survey of Police–Community Relations Units," *Journal of Police Science and Administration,* 7 (March 1979): 74.

176 Charles E. Reasons and Bernard A. Wirth, "Police–Community Relations Units: A National Survey," *Journal of Social Issues,* 31 (Winter 1975): 27–34.

177 Ibid.

178 Jerome Skolnick and David Bayley, *The New Blue Line: Police Innovation in Six American Cities* (New York: Free Press, 1986), pp. 54–70.

179 Lee P. Brown and Mary Ann Wycoff, "Policing Houston: Reducing Fear and Improving Service," *Crime and Delinquency,* 33 (January 1986): 71–89.

180 President's Commission on Law Enforcement and Administration of Justice, *Field Studies,* IV, Vol. 1, (Washington, DC: Government Printing Office, 1967), p. 58.

181 U.S. Department of Justice, *Improving Police/Community Relations* (Washington, DC: Government Printing Office, 1973), pp. 3–4.

182 Scott H. Decker, Russell L. Smith, and Thomas M. Uhlman, "Does Anything Work? An Evaluation of Police Innovations," in Baker and Meyer, eds., *Evaluating Alternative Law Enforcement Policies,* pp. 43–54.

183 Ellen G. Cohn, "The Citizen Police Academy: A Recipe for Improving Police–Community Relations," *Journal of Criminal Justice* 24, no. 3 (1996): 265–271.

184 Brown and Wycoff, "Policing Houston"; University of Maryland, *Preventing Crime* (Washington, DC: Government Printing Office, 1997).

185 Thomas M. Frost and Magnus J. Seng, "Police Entry Level Curriculum: A Thirty-Year Perspective," *Journal of Police Science and Administration,* 12 (September 1984): 27.

186 John E. Boydstun and Michael E. Sherry, *San Diego Community Profile: Final Report* (Washington, DC: The Police Foundation, 1975).

187 Bobb, *Five Years Later,* p. 27.

188 Quoted in U.S. Department of Justice, *Attorney General's Conference: Strengthening Police–Community Relationships: Summary Report* (Washington, DC: U.S. Department of Justice, 1999), pp. 9–10.

189 Jerome L. Blakemore, David Barlow, and Deborah L. Padgett, "From the Classroom to the Community: Introducing Process in Police Diversity Training," *Police Studies,* XVIII, no. 1 (1995): 71–83.

190 Geffrey P. Alpert, William C. Smith, and Daniel Watters, "Implications of the Rodney King Beating," *Criminal Law Bulletin,* 28 (September–October 1992): 477.

191 Arthur J. Lurigio and Dennis P. Rosenbaum, "The Travails of the Detroit Police–Victims Experiment: Assumptions and Important Lessons," *American Journal of Police,* XI, no. 3 (1992): 22–23.

192 Leigh Herbst and Samuel Walker, "Language Barriers in the Delivery of Police Services," *Journal of Criminal Justice,* 29, no. 4 (2001: 329–340).

193 Robert C. Davis and Edna Erez, *Immigrant Populations as Victims: Toward a Multicultural Criminal Justice System* (Washington, DC: Government Printing Office, 1998).

194 Herbst and Walker, "Language Barriers in the Delivery of Police Services."

195 San Jose Police Department, *Vehicle Stop Demographic Study: First Report* (San Jose, CA: San Jose Police Department, December 1999).

196 U.S. Department of Justice, *Principles for Promoting Police Integrity: Examples of Promising Police Practices and Policies* (Washington, DC: U.S. Justice Department, 2001).

197 Alpert, Smith, and Watters, "Implications of the Rodney King Beating," 477.

198 Robert Trojanowicz and Cynthia J. Lent, eds., *Community Policing: A Survey of Police Departments in the United States* (Washington, DC: National Center for Community Policing, 1994).

CHAPTER TEN

Police Corruption

CHAPTER OUTLINE

INTRODUCTION

"For as long as there have been police," Lawrence Sherman observes, "there has been police corruption."[1] Corruption is one of the oldest and most persistent problems in American policing. Historians have found evidence of bribery in the earliest years of colonial America (Chapter 2). Although a number of police departments have success-fully reduced it in recent years, corruption persists as a major problem in some depart-ments today. Recently, an investigation into the Los Angeles police department found serious corruption in the organization. Officers in the Rampart Division of the Los An-geles police department were found to be involved in the theft of drugs, bank robbery, false imprisonment, planting evidence, and the beating of arrestees.[2] In the 1990s, the Mollen Commission found serious corruption in the New York City police department. Officers were found on the payroll of drug dealers, earning up to $4,000 a week.[3] Similarly, in 1998, in Cleveland forty-nine police officers and jail guards were convicted of accepting money to protect drug shipments.[4]

This chapter examines the nature of police corruption, the factors that cause it, and strategies for controlling it.

A DEFINITION OF POLICE CORRUPTION

Herman Goldstein defines police corruption as "acts involving the misuse of authority by a police officer in a manner designed to produce personal gain for himself or for others."[5] The two key elements are (1) misuse of authority and (2) personal gain.

Corruption is only one form of misconduct or deviant behavior by police officers. Barker and Carter's typology of police deviance distinguishes between occupational deviance and abuse of authority. Occupational deviance includes criminal and noncriminal behavior "committed during the course of normal work activities or committed under the guise of the police officer's authority." This includes improper behavior that is not illegal, such as sleeping on the job. Abuse of authority includes an action by a police officer "that tends to injure, insult, trespass upon human dignity . . . and/or violate an inherent legal right" of a citizen.[6] An illegal arrest or use of excessive force is wrong but does not involve any personal gain. Some illegal activity by a police officer, meanwhile, is not occupational deviance. A criminal assault on a friend or family member by an off-duty police officer is a private act. Finally, some actions are unwise but not necessarily illegal. Some police departments, for example, do not allow their officers to receive free meals at restaurants. Taking a free meal is a violation of department policy but not a crime.

Figure 10–1 represents an excerpt from the personnel standards of the Omaha police department, indicating behavior that is prohibited.

THE COSTS OF POLICE CORRUPTION

Corruption imposes high costs on the police, the criminal justice system, and society. First, a corrupt act by a police officer is a criminal act. Criminal activity by a police officer undermines the basic integrity of law enforcement.

Second, corruption usually protects other criminal activity. Much corruption involves bribes to protect illegal gambling or narcotics trafficking. Historically, corruption protected gambling syndicates, which were the major source of income for organized crime. However, today corruption is often related to drug trafficking. A 1998 Government Accounting Office (GAO) report revealed that about half of all police officers convicted as a consequence of FBI-led corruption cases between 1993 and 1997 were convicted for drug-related offenses.[7]

Third, police corruption undermines the effectiveness of the criminal justice system. The New York City Commission to Combat Police Corruption argues that "The honesty and integrity of police officers is . . . critical to the workings of the criminal justice system."[8] Officers routinely testify in court, and if they have a reputation for dishonesty, their credibility in criminal cases is damaged. In 2000, as a consequence of the Rampart

FIGURE 10–1   PERSONNEL STANDARDS, OMAHA POLICE DIVISION

CHAPTER 1: SECTION 18

Receiving or accepting any fee, reward or gift, of any kind for services rendered, or pretending to be rendered:
No officer or employee of the Police Department shall expect or accept extra compensation in any form from any person, outside the Police Department, for services rendered as part of his official duties, unless same is approved by the Chief of Police.

No officer or employee shall solicit or accept any form of compensation or gift for the performance of, or failure to perform, an act or service which is part of his official duties. This includes, but is not limited to, accepting or soliciting free or reduced rate meals at restaurants/food establishments, or free or reduced admission into theaters/sporting events.

Any person offering anything of value to an officer or employee as an incentive to influence the action of said employee, shall be brought immediately before a Command Officer for investigation of attempted bribery.

The assurance that any law enforcement officer or employee can carry out his lawfully assigned duties in a fair and impartial manner is based completely on the premise that he is not under obligation to anyone.

Source: Omaha Police Department, *Standard Operating Procedure Manual,* p. 77.

scandal hundreds of drug convictions were threatened because of revelations that police officers in Los Angles framed individuals by planting drugs on them and then lying about it.[9]

Fourth, corruption undermines the professionalism of a police department. Effective discipline becomes impossible if supervisors are corrupt and threatened with exposure by officers under their command. Corruption encourages police lying, as officers protect one another. Lying to protect oneself or other officers can then spread to other areas of policing, such as covering up excessive use of force.[10]

Fifth, as former *New York Times* reporter David Burnham argues, corruption is "a secret tax totaling millions of dollars a year" on individual citizens of New York City.[11] In some instances, it is a direct tax, as when corrupt police extract bribes from businesses.

Sixth, corruption undermines public confidence in the police. The belief that a department is corrupt undermines respect for officers and public support for the department as a whole. This has a special impact on police–community relations (see Chapter 9). Illegal vice activities have generally been relegated to low-income and racial-minority neighborhoods. The President's Crime Commission found that minorities were ten times more likely than whites to believe that police officers are "almost all corrupt."[12]

The Mollen Commission's report on police corruption in New York City addressed this issue only indirectly. It noted that the worst examples of corruption and brutality existed "particularly in crime-ridden, drug-infested precincts, often with large minority populations."[13] It did not, however, specifically discuss the point that the officers in these areas probably felt free to engage in rampant corruption and brutality because they perceived the residents to be politically powerless.

On the positive side, public opinion polls consistently indicate that the police rank relatively high compared with other occupations in terms of perceived honesty and integrity. In a 1997 Gallup Poll, for example, the police ranked seventh out of twenty-six occupations, just ahead of bankers and much higher than lawyers (see Chapter 9, Table 9–2).[14]

The percentage of white Americans rating the honesty and ethical standards of the police as "high" or "very high" rose somewhat between the late 1970s and the early 1990s, but then declined slightly. The ratings by nonwhites remained consistently lower than those of whites, rising and falling over the same period.[15]

TYPES OF CORRUPTION

Corruption takes many different forms. Some are far more serious than others. For some activities, such as receiving free meals, there is debate over whether they should be defined as corruption. Different corrupt acts have different causes and call for different control strategies.[16]

Gratuities

The most common form of police corruption involves gratuities: free meals, free dry cleaning, or discounts on other purchases. Some departments prohibit gratuities, while others do not. One survey found that only half of all police departments had written policies mentioning free meals—and not all of those policies clearly prohibited the practice.[17]

Gratuities involve mixed motives on the part of businesspeople. In some cases they represent a sincere effort to thank police officers for doing a dangerous job to protect the community. In other cases, they reflect self-interest: the belief that the presence of police cars near their stores will deter robbers and burglars, or the expectation that the police will return the favor by providing extra patrol coverage in the area.

People who believe that the police should never be allowed to receive gratuities argue that they open the door to more serious forms of corruption.[18] Gratuities encourage officers to believe they are entitled to special privileges and may lead them to demand such privileges. The Knapp Commission, which investigated New York City corruption in the early 1970s, made a distinction between "grass eaters," who passively accept what is offered to them, and "meat eaters," who aggressively demand favors.[19]

A survey of North Carolina residents found very mixed opinions about police accepting gratuities (Table 10–1). Only 36 percent did not believe it was appropriate for a police officer to accept an occasional free coffee, nonalcoholic drink, or discounted meal when on duty. At the same time, however, only 23 percent thought accepting a meal when off duty was appropriate.[20]

Bribes

Accepting bribes not to enforce the law is a far more serious form of corruption. Some bribes are isolated acts, such as when an officer takes money not to write a traffic ticket. Other bribes are more systematic, particularly regular payoffs to protect a gambling operation. Historically, the most serious police corruption has involved regular payoffs to protect an ongoing illegal activity—gambling, prostitution, after-hours drinking, or narcotics. In New York City, regular payoffs were referred to as "the pad." New York City police officers "on the pad" were found to receive up to $850 a month to protect a single dealer.[21] In New Orleans eleven officers were convicted of accepting $100,000 for protecting a warehouse that was being used to store 286 pounds of cocaine.[22]

Corrupt officers can also be bribed to sell information about criminal investigations, either before or after arrests are made. A tip about an investigation may help gamblers or drug dealers avoid arrest. In the 1950s New York City police officers reportedly took bribes to remove people's cards from the "known gambler" file.[23] Robert Daley reported in 1978 that New York City detectives regularly sold information to defense attorneys about pending cases. Officers took money in exchange for altering their testimony, "forgetting" important points on the witness stand, destroying evidence, or revealing important points about the prosecution's case.[24] A person engaged in a civil lawsuit against someone else may bribe a police officer for damaging information about that person contained in police files. In the past, before bail reform, police officers frequently took kickbacks for referring arrested persons to certain bail bondsmen or defense attorneys.

Some bribes protect illegal activities, while others support legitimate businesses. David Burnham found that New York City building contractors regularly paid the police

TABLE 10–1   SURVEY STATEMENTS, QUESTIONS, AND RESPONSES

Statements	Strongly Agree	Agree	Disagree	Strongly Disagree
It is appropriate for a police officer to accept an occasional free coffee, nonalcoholic drink, or discounted meal when on duty.	51 (5%)	549 (59%)	265 (28%)	69 (8%)
It is appropriate for a police officer to accept free meals in restaurants when off duty.	10 (1%)	201 (22%)	589 (64%)	122 (13%)
It is appropriate for a police officer to accept repairs at no cost to privately owned vehicles.	1 (0%)	70 (8%)	668 (71%)	191 (21%)
It is appropriate for a police officer to show special consideration toward someone who has given him/her one of these favors in the past.	4 (0%)	79 (8%)	608 (66%)	246 (26%)

Questions	Yes	No
If you ran a small business such as a coffee shop, restaurant, movie theater, or automotive repair shop, would you offer police officers free gifts or discounts on items like coffee, meals, movie tickets, or vehicle repairs?	334 (37%)	558 (63%)
If offered these gifts or discounts, and they were accepted, would you expect special consideration by the police in return, such as extra patrol or a warning on a traffic stop instead of a citation?	242 (26%)	689 (74%)

	Prohibited by the Department	Left to the Officer's Discretion
Do you think gratuities and favors to police officers should be prohibited by the department or left to the discretion of the officer?	569 (64%)	319 (36%)

Source: Mark Jones, "Police Officer Gratuities and Public Opinion," *Police Forum,* 4 (October 1997): 9.

$50 a week to avoid being ticketed for such violations as double-parking, blocking streets and sidewalks.[25]

Theft and Burglary

Theft or burglary by officers on duty is a particularly serious form of corruption. One example involves officers taking money from people arrested for drunkenness. The victim often has a hard time remembering how much money he or she actually had, much less convincing anyone that the officer stole any money. Another example involves officers who steal property, money, or drugs from the police department's property room. Between 1992 and 1996, forty police officers in New Orleans were arrested for bank robbery, auto theft, and other illegal acts. An additional 200 officers were later reprimanded, fired, or retired as a consequence of criminal activity.[26]

Narcotics arrests offer special temptations for theft. Officers making a drug raid usually find large amounts of both money and drugs. For example, the "River Cops" case in Miami, Florida, revealed that a large number of police officers were involved in the stealing and selling of cocaine. Upon further scrutiny of police activities, nineteen officers were arrested, convicted, and sentenced to prison and seventy officers were fired.[27]

Similarly, the Mollen Commission found that corrupt officers in New York City stole drugs, money, and guns from drug dealers. One officer took $32,000 in money and goods in one theft. In some instances, officers arranged for phony 911 calls that allowed them to enter business premises and steal goods.[28]

Internal Corruption

In very corrupt departments, promotions or favored assignments must be purchased with bribes. During the nineteenth century, payment for promotion was so systematic in the New York City police department that there was a printed schedule of the "price list" for each rank.[29] The Knapp Commission found a "widespread" pattern of police officers bribing other officers "to gain favorable assignments." It was rumored that a bribe of between $500 and $2,000 could gain assignment as a detective.[30]

Corruption and Brutality

The Mollen Commission argues that a new form of corruption emerged in the 1980s and 1990s, characterized by a convergence of corruption and brutality. Officers brutally beat drug dealers, stole their drugs and money, and then sold the drugs to other dealers or other officers. Not all corruption involved brutality, and not all brutality in the department was associated with corruption. Nonetheless, the two were closely related. Particularly disturbing was the extent to which officers testified that brutality was their "rite of initiation" into other forms of misconduct: "Once the line was crossed without consequences, it was easier to abuse their authority in other ways, including corruption."[31]

The most notorious case to date may involve officers from the Los Angeles police department's Rampart Division in which officers in 1998 and 1999 were found to be engaging in "hard core" criminal activity. Officers in the Rampart CRASH unit, which was considered an elite antigang squad, were found to be actively attacking known gang members and falsely accusing individuals of crimes that they did not commit. Investigation into the scandal uncovered that officers routinely choked and punched individuals for the sole purpose of intimidating them. In one case, officers used a suspect as a "human battering ram" and thrust his face continuously into a wall. In several other instances officers planted drugs on suspects to make arrests. Corrupt sergeants in the division promoted these activities by giving out awards for misdeeds. One officer was given an award for shooting an unarmed innocent person.[32]

LEVELS OF CORRUPTION

The level of corruption varies from department to department. In some, corrupt acts involve only an occasional deviant officer. In others, the corruption is systemic through the department. Sherman argues that the relevant question is, "Why are there different kinds and extents of police corruption in different communities, and in the same communities at different points in their history?"[33]

Measuring the level of corruption is extremely difficult. By definition, it is a covert crime. Normally, there is no victim to complain, since the person who offers a bribe is also guilty of a crime. Consequently, no reliable data exist on the extent of police corruption. The available data consist of the revelations of corruption scandals and the reports of investigations that usually follow major scandals. The exposure of corruption, however, is contingent on a variety of often arbitrary factors (e.g., an especially aggressive news reporter), and the resulting information cannot be regarded as systematic evidence of the problem.[34]

Sherman identified different levels of corruption, using a three-part typology based on "the pervasiveness of corruption, its organization, and the sources of bribes."[35]

Type I: Rotten Apples and Rotten Pockets

The least serious form of corruption exists when it involves only a few police officers acting on their own. The "rotten apple" theory describes a situation where only a few officers are independently engaged in corrupt acts. A "rotten pocket" exists when several corrupt officers cooperate with one another. An example of a rotten pocket is a group of narcotics officers stealing money or drugs during a narcotics raid. The Mollen Commission found corruption centered in crews. In the Thirtieth Precinct, for example, groups of three to five officers worked semi-independently, protecting and assisting each other.[36]

Type II: Pervasive Unorganized Corruption

Corruption reaches a higher degree of intensity when it has "a majority of personnel who are corrupt, but who have little relationship to each other."[37] Many officers may be taking bribes for not issuing traffic tickets, but the officers are not actively cooperating with one another. Here the corruption is pervasive, but unorganized.

Type III: Pervasive Organized Corruption

The most serious form of corruption exists at an organized level that penetrates the higher levels of the department. An example is a systematic payoff to protect illegal activities, with the payoff shared among all members of a unit and their supervisors. In his study of one West Coast city, William Chambliss describes how one restaurant owner had to pay $200 a month to the beat officers (the sum was divided equally among them) and $250 a month to the higher-ranking officers (also divided among several officers). Failure to pay meant that the owner faced frequent citations for building code violations.[38] The Knapp Commission found that in New York City a newly assigned plain-clothes detective was not entitled to a share of the payoffs for about 2 months until he was checked out for reliability. The earnings lost by this delay were made up in the form of 2 months' "severance pay" when the officer left the division.[39]

THEORIES OF POLICE CORRUPTION

Theories of police corruption fall into four different categories, depending upon whether they focus on the individual officer, the social structure, the nature of police work, or the police organization.

Individual Officer Explanations

The most popular explanation of police corruption is the so-called rotten-apple theory. It is appealing because it emphasizes the moral failings of one or more individuals, provides convenient scapegoats, and avoids dealing with more difficult issues. It also points in the direction of a simple remedy.

Police officials prefer the rotten-apple theory because it allows them to blame a few individuals without having to investigate larger problems in the department. The department can appear to solve the problem by firing the guilty officers. The rotten-apple theory also appeals to private citizens, because they can understand personal guilt more easily than complex legal or organizational issues. Further, the theory allows citizens to avoid considering the extent to which police corruption may be rooted in their own preferences for gambling or other illegal activities.

Most experts, however, believe that the rotten-apple theory fails to adequately explain most police corruption. It does not account for the long history of corruption or its pervasiveness in certain departments. How could so many "bad" people be concentrated in one organization? Nor does it explain why some honest people become corrupt. Studies of police recruitment indicate that most people attracted to policing are not morally inferior; they are rather average people, attracted to policing for the same reasons that people choose other careers.[40] Finally, the rotten-apple theory does not explain why some police departments have long histories of corruption while others are relatively free of corruption. The Knapp Commission concluded that "the rotten-apple doctrine has in many ways been a basic obstacle to meaningful reform."[41]

Social Structural Explanations

Most experts explain police corruption in terms of the American social structure. In their view, closely related aspects of the criminal law, cultural conflict, and politics encourage and sustain corruption.[42]

The Criminal Law   The criminal law is a major cause of much police corruption. State and federal laws prohibit or seek to regulate many activities that people regard as legitimate recreation or matters of private choice. These include gambling, alcohol and drug consumption, and various sexual practices. The basic problem is a conflict of cultures and lifestyles. Some people believe these activities are immoral and harmful, while others believe they are acceptable and not harmful to others.[43]

Prohibition in the 1920s is an excellent example of the extent to which an industry will arise to provide products or services that have been outlawed. The providers of illegal goods and services have a self-interest in maintaining their enterprise. The profits from these nontaxed enterprises provide sufficient revenue to corrupt the administration of justice—to bribe police, prosecutors, and judges as needed. Police corruption, then, is a routine business expense—an "insurance policy" designed to guarantee continuation of the enterprise. In 1982 James Cook found that organized crime had become a major part of the American economy, estimating revenues greater than $150 billion per year. He estimated that narcotics ($63 billion), gambling ($22 billion), and loan-sharking ($20 billion) activities produced the majority of the revenues.[44]

Criminal syndicates have sufficient financial resources to support candidates for political office who, in turn, may use their power to influence the administration of justice, including, for example, blocking the investigation of certain criminal activities. In 1935 V. O. Key noted a change in the nature of police corruption as the delivery of vice services became more centralized and criminal syndicates took on the characteristics of legitimate big business enterprises.[45]

The law also includes many regulatory ordinances that contribute to police corruption. Laws prohibiting double-parking, for example, are designed to facilitate the smooth flow of traffic, but some business owners are afraid the tough enforcement will deny them some customers. Particularly in cities with congested central business districts, there have been payoffs to the police to ignore certain traffic law violations.

The example of regulatory ordinances illustrates an important distinction between different types of corruption. Some forms of corruption involve the use of deviant means to further deviant goals. An example is bribery to protect illegal gambling. Other forms of corruption involve deviant means to achieve legitimate goals. An example is a bribe to sustain a profitable business.

William Chambliss emphasizes the intimate connection between the law, the political structure, the police, and criminal activity. "Organized crime," he argues, "becomes not something that exists outside law and government but is instead a creation of them." Chambliss adds that "the people who run the organizations which supply the vices in American cities are members of the business, political, and law enforcement communities—not simply members of a criminal society."[46]

Cultural Conflict   The criminal law is a reflection of the cultural diversity of American society. Different groups have used the law to prohibit behavior that offends their values. Other groups, however, regard the same behavior as legitimate. McMullen argues that conflict over the goals of the legal system is a basic precondition for corruption: "A high level of corruption is the result of a wide divergence among the attitudes, aims, and methods of the government of a country and those of the society in which they operate."[47]

Local Political Culture   The level of corruption in a police department is heavily influenced by the local political culture. Sherman argues that there will be less corruption in "communities with a more public-regarding ethos." Some communities develop traditions of efficient and honest public service, while others develop self-serving, or "private-regarding," traditions that encourage corruption.[48] Police corruption persists in New York City and New Orleans because corruption pervades other parts of government. But police corruption has been largely eliminated in cities such as Charlotte, North Carolina, and Portland, Oregon, where the local political culture emphasizes good government.

Although an important factor, the concept of political culture has not been clearly defined or investigated. It is not clear why some cities and counties have a different political culture, or exactly how it affects law enforcement.

The Nature of Police Work

Barker argues that the "occupational setting" of police work "provides the police officer with more than ample opportunity for a wide range of deviant activities."[49] Three aspects of police work contribute to police corruption. First, police work exposes officers to many opportunities to be corrupt. The police enforce the law, and inevitably, some people seek to avoid arrest by offering a bribe. Thus, officers face constant temptations from people seeking to corrupt them. Organized crime syndicates, in particular, have enormous financial resources at their disposal. This helps to explain why corruption has generally been worst among vice officers. The increase in drug activity in the 1980s, particularly with the advent of crack cocaine, exposed officers to greater temptations than in the past.

Second, policing is low-visibility work.[50] Officers generally work alone or in pairs, with no direct supervision. The risk of being caught is often very low. Detectives work with even less direct supervision than patrol officers. Thus, they face the greatest temptations and have the lowest risk of being caught.

Third, the impact of police work on officer attitudes also contributes indirectly to corruption. Herman Goldstein argues that "the average officer—especially in large cities—sees the worst side of humanity. He is exposed to a steady diet of wrongdoing. He becomes intimately familiar with the ways people prey on one another." As a result, officers easily develop a cynical attitude toward people. Constant exposure to wrongdoing can lead to the belief that "everyone does it."[51]

The Police Organization

Some departments have more corruption than others, while others have succeeded in reducing it. The most important organizational variable is leadership: the quality of management and supervision. Corruption flourishes in departments that tolerate it. Assuming that temptations or "invitations" to corruption are prevalent in all communities, individual officers are more likely to succumb if they believe they won't be caught or the punishment, if caught, will not be severe.

Carl Klockars examined the impact of organizational culture on corruption in thirty police departments across the country. He found that officers, regardless of the police organization that they worked for, ranked the seriousness of various types of corruption similarly. However, he found that officers in departments that scored high on organizational integrity were more likely to expect to be severely disciplined if caught committing a corrupt act than officers in departments that scored low on organizational integrity. He also found that officers in departments that scored high on organizational integrity were more likely to believe that officers should be severely disciplined for engaging in corrupt acts.[52] Such findings suggest that while police officers view the seriousness of various forms of corruption similarly, officers in organizations that do not tolerate corruption may be less tempted to engage in corruption.

Robin Haarr emphasizes the importance of organizational commitment and its relationship with police deviance. In her examination of patrol officers in one Midwestern police department she found that officers with a low level of organizational commitment were more likely to engage in work avoidance and police misconduct such as sex with prostitutes and unnecessary use of force. On the other hand, she found that officers with a high level of organizational commitment were more likely to engage in deviance *for* the organization such as falsifying arrest reports and lying in court to increase work productivity.[53]

The Police Subculture

The occupational subculture of policing is a major factor in both creating police corruption, by initiating officers into corrupt activities, and sustaining it, by covering up corrupt activities by other officers.

In his classic study of the police subculture Westley, in 1970, reported that officers were willing to lie to cover up an illegal act by another officer.[54] Recent studies suggest that little has changed in the last 30 years. In a survey of 925 officers from 121 police departments, Weisburd and colleagues reported in 2000 that 52.4 percent of officers thought that it is not unusual for a police officer to turn a blind eye to improper conduct by other officers; and only 39 percent of officers agreed that police officers would report serious criminal violations involving abuse of authority of fellow officers.[55]

This is in large part a consequence of peer pressure, which is particularly strong among police officers. The police subculture puts a high value on loyalty and group solidarity (Chapter 13). Officers defend one another in the face of criticism because they expect their colleagues to come to their aid as well. This kind of group solidarity, however, tends to foster lying and cover-ups.[56] Officers who are not loyal to other officers are often ostracized in the police department. One national survey of police officers reported that 67 percent of police officers believed that an officer who reports another officer's misconduct is likely to be given the cold shoulder by his or her fellow officers.

BECOMING CORRUPT

The Moral Careers of Individual Officers

With very few exceptions, police officers are honest at the outset of their careers. (The exceptions are those individuals who have prior histories of criminal activity and who are not rejected during recruitment.) The Mollen Commission found that "most corrupt officers start off as honest and idealistic." In fact, "some of the most notoriously corrupt cops in the [New York City] Department were ideal recruits on paper."[57] Officers who do become corrupt typically go through a process involving a series of stages that move from lesser to greater tolerance and/or involvement in corrupt activities. Sherman describes this process as the "moral career" of an officer.[58]

The moral career of a corrupt officer begins with relatively minor gratuities. The officer begins to regard free meals as a normal part of the job. Peer pressure is extremely important in this first stage. The new officer is introduced to corrupt acts by veteran officers. Sherman writes that the "moral experience about accepting these perks usually occurs in the recruit's first days on duty, and the peer pressure to accept them is great."[59] The Mollen Commission found that in New York the unpunished use of excessive force initiated many officers into patterns of misconduct, including corruption.[60]

At the same time, the officer is under pressure from citizens offering bribes. There are many stories of free meals being forced on police officers even though they are willing to pay.

The second and third stages of becoming corrupt, according to Sherman, involve regulatory offenses: An officer accepts a free drink from a bar owner and allows the bar to remain open after the legal closing hour, or the officer takes a bribe from a driver who has exceeded the speed limit. Peer pressure is important if the officer knows that other officers routinely do the same thing. At this point, the individual officer is still passively accepting such offers.

At some point, the officer becoming corrupt changes from one who only passively accepts gratuities (the "grass eater") into one who aggressively solicits bribes (the "meat eater").[61] Corrupt acts begin to involve more serious violations of the law, become more systematic, and involve larger amounts of money; the officer begins to initiate corrupt acts. The fourth, fifth, and sixth stages in Sherman's hypothetical model involve regular payoffs for the protection of gambling, prostitution, and narcotics trafficking. Sherman points out that "accepting narcotics graft . . . is the most difficult moral experience of all." Officers must adjust their self-image to accept the fact that they are actively assisting the sale and distribution of what they know to be an illegal and destructive drug. At this point the moral career of the officer is complete. The officer has reached the final point of not just accepting but actively furthering illegal and harmful activities.

Corrupting Organizations

Entire organizations become corrupt as they move through similar stages from less serious to more serious corruption. The "moral career" of a department can be viewed as moving through the various stages identified by Sherman. Initially, corruption involves isolated individuals or a few isolated groups. When virtually all officers are engaged in corrupt acts, the second and third stages have been reached. The final stages involve "pervasive organized corruption," in which virtually all officers are engaged in systematic arrangements with criminal elements. A police department becomes progressively corrupt because the department's leadership does not actively combat corruption.

CONTROLLING CORRUPTION

Controlling police corruption is extremely difficult. The history of the police indicates that many apparently successful reform efforts have been only temporary. Herman

Goldstein observes that "the history of reform provides many illustrations of elaborate attempts to eliminate dishonesty followed by rapid reversion to prior practices."[62] In New York City, for example, there have been corruption scandals followed by special investigations every 20 years since the 1890s (see Sidebar 10–1). Each investigation made recommendations for reform, and yet corruption continued to flourish.

At the same time, however, there are examples of police departments that have successfully reduced or eliminated corruption: Los Angeles and Oakland in the 1950s. Sherman calls the reform of the Oakland police department during the same period "one of the most lasting of any American police agency."[63]

The control of corruption involves two different tasks. The first is to prevent it from occurring in the first place. The second is to reduce and eliminate it once it exists. There are two basic approaches to the control of corruption. One involves *internal* approaches, including activities undertaken by a police department itself. The other involves *external* approaches, including agencies outside of the department.

INTERNAL CORRUPTION CONTROL STRATEGIES

There are several components of an effective internal corruption control program.

The Attitude of the Chief

Experts agree that successful control of corruption begins with the attitude of the chief administrator. The head of the department must make it clear that corruption will not be tolerated. The Mollen Commission argued that "commitment to integrity cannot be just an abstract value. It must be reflected not only in the words, but in the deeds, of the Police Commissioner, the Department's top commanders, and the field supervisors who shape the attitudes of the rank and file."[64] The known examples of successful corruption control all involved strong action by chiefs: William Parker in Los Angeles, Wyman Vernon in Oakland, Clarence Kelley in Kansas City, and Patrick V. Murphy in New York City.

SIDEBAR 10–1   INVESTIGATIONS OF POLICE CORRUPTION, NEW YORK CITY

1885—Lexow Commission

1913—Curran Commission

1932—Seabury Commission

1954—Gross Commission

1973—Knapp Commission

1994—Mollen Commission

Source: Frank Anechiarico and James B. Jacobs, *The Pursuit of Absolute Integrity* (Chicago: University of Chicago Press, 1996), p. 157.

SIDEBAR 10–2   LAW ENFORCEMENT CODE OF ETHICS
(EXCERPT)

I recognize the badge of my office as a symbol of public faith, and I accept it as a public trust to be held so long as I am true to the ethics of police service. I will never engage in acts of corruption or bribery, nor will I condone such acts by other police officers. I will cooperate with all legally authorized agencies and their representatives in the pursuit of justice.

Source: O. W. Wilson and Roy C. McLaren, *Police Administration,* 4th ed. (New York: McGraw-Hill, 1977), p. 8.

A police chief faces certain risks in taking a strong public stand against corruption. Open discussion of the subject is an admission of existing or possible wrongdoing. The Mollen Commission found that anticorruption mechanisms in New York City failed in part because department officials did not want any bad publicity. As a result, allegations of corruption were not investigated.[65]

Rules and Regulations

The second step in a corruption control process involves clearly defining what actions will not be tolerated. One way to draw the line clearly is to develop written policies that specify forbidden acts. The use of written policies, or what is known as administrative rulemaking, is also used to control police discretion (see Chapter 8) and to achieve police accountability (Chapter 11). Carter and Barker argue that administrative rules on corruption serve six basic purposes. They (1) "inform officers of expected standards of behavior; (2) inform the community about those standards; (3) establish the basis for consistency in police operations; (4) provide grounds for discipline and counseling of errant officers; (5) provide standards for officer supervision; and (6) give direction for officer training."[66]

There is much disagreement over where to draw the line on some issues.[67] Not all law enforcement officials believe that it is necessary or possible to prohibit free meals or other discounts, for example. A Police Foundation survey of Oregon State police officers found that 62 percent did not think it was proper for officers to accept discounts even if they were offered to other customers, while 20 percent thought it was acceptable.[68]

Other leaders, however, argue that the line must be drawn prohibiting all gratuities. Patrick V. Murphy told his officers, "Except for your paycheck there is no such thing as a clean buck."[69] William Parker in Los Angeles and O. W. Wilson in Chicago believed that even a free cup of coffee compromised the integrity of the police. The argument against all gratuities is premised on the belief that this one small step creates a climate in which successively larger steps become possible. Other experts, however, argue that anticorruption efforts should focus on serious acts of corruption.

One survey of police agencies found an inconsistent pattern among departments with respect to written policies. Only half (49 percent) of the departments surveyed had policies that even mentioned free meals. Only 52 percent had policies that mentioned accepting money from lawyers ("kickbacks") for referring clients to them. A total of 61 percent had policies mentioning shaking down criminals for money, and 74 percent had policies that covered accepting money from traffic law violators.[70]

Managing Anticorruption Investigations

The effective control of corruption requires meaningful investigation of suspected corruption by the department itself. Typically, this is the responsibility of the internal affairs unit (IAU) or office of professional standards (OPS). (See Figure 10–2.)

A successful anticorruption effort requires several elements. First, as already noted, it needs the strong backing of the chief executive. The International Association of Chiefs of Police (IACP) recommends that the unit commander "should report directly to or have regular access to the chief," since that person is ultimately responsible for discipline.[71] The Mollen Commission, however, found that in New York City command officers sent clear messages to corruption investigators that they should not aggressively pursue reports of corruption. The most notorious officer in that scandal, Michael Dowd,

---

FIGURE 10–2   INTERNAL AFFAIRS UNIT, ST. PETERSBURG POLICE DEPARTMENT

IV Internal Affairs Unit Procedures
    A. Purpose of the Internal Affairs Unit
        1. To conduct complete investigations and to make fair and impartial evaluations of complaints which are made against employees of the department in the following instances:
           a. Upon receipt of an allegation or complaint of misconduct against the department or its employees.
           b. Any matter as directed by the Chief of Police.
        2. To make random inspections to ensure proper conduct and integrity in the following areas:
           a. Property and evidence
           b. Cellular phones
           c. Bail bond procedures
           d. Wrecker service
    B. Organizing and Staffing
        1. The Internal Affairs Unit shall report directly to the Major of Staff Inspections, who shall report directly to the Chief of Police. The unit will be staffed by such personnel and assigned to such duty hours as directed by the Major of Staff Inspections and approved by the Chief of Police.
        2. The Chief of Police will be familiar with the basis for each formal complaint investigated by the Internal Affairs Unit and may become personally involved in an investigation when its severity so warrants, or when, in his judgement, it is appropriate to do so.

Source: St. Petersburg Police Department, *Annual Report 1994* (St. Petersburg, FL: City of St. Petersburg, 1994), p. 3.

was in fact arrested on drug charges by suburban Suffolk County police, and not by New York City police.[72]

Second, an IAU needs a sufficient number of personnel to handle the investigative workload. Patrick V. Murphy increased the size of the Internal Affairs Division (IAD) in the New York City police department, bringing the ratio of investigators to officers from 1 to 533 line officers, to 1 to 64. Sherman found investigator-to-officer ratios of 1 to 110 and 1 to 216 in two other departments he studied.[73] Murphy also decentralized anticorruption by creating a network of field internal affairs units (FIAUs). Twenty years later, however, the Mollen Commission found that IAD investigated few corruption allegations, while most cases were delegated to the FIAUs, which were then too overloaded to conduct effective investigations.[74] The problem was not necessarily the structure of the anticorruption effort but the lack of administrative commitment to make it work effectively.

There is disagreement over whether anticorruption efforts should be centralized or decentralized within the department. Most police departments have centralized the management of investigations, with the commander of the IAU reporting directly to the chief. However, some agencies, such as New York City, take a different approach by decentralizing their anticorruption efforts.[75]

Staffing IAUs is a problem in many departments. Police officers generally do not like IAUs, regarding them as "snitches," and do not want the assignment themselves. Interviews with current and former internal affairs officers in one Southwestern metropolitan area found many examples of the stigma attached to internal affairs assignments. One officer was told by a friend, "You're crazy, what the hell do you want to work there for?" Another was told "I thought you were better than that."[76]

From the perspective of many officers, internal affairs violates the norms of group solidarity. Also, many officers regard internal affairs investigations as more intrusive than criminal investigations. Under the *Garrity* ruling, an officer can be disciplined and even dismissed for refusing to answer questions by internal affairs (although anything the officer discloses cannot then be used against him or her in a criminal prosecution). Finally, many officers believe that internal affairs is biased and out to "get" certain officers.[77]

In some departments, because of union contracts, the chief has no choice over who is assigned to the IAU. Common sense suggests that someone who does not want the assignment, or who may have a problematic performance record, is not likely to be an aggressive anticorruption investigator. In other departments the chief has full control over assignment to the IAU, and it is a preferred assignment that is considered a key to promotion.

Investigative Tactics

The major obstacle facing anticorruption investigations is the same one that all detectives face: obtaining credible evidence. Corruption is often a victimless crime with no complaining party. Investigators usually have to initiate investigations on their own. In corrupt departments, the major problem has always been the "blue curtain," the refusal of officers to testify against corrupt officers. Even honest officers are reluctant to inform on their colleagues.

Successful investigations have often relied on a few corrupt officers who decided to cooperate with investigators. In the New York City scandal of the 1970s, officers David Durk, Frank Serpico, and Robert Leuci provided the most important evidence for investigators. These officers did so, however, only at a tremendous personal cost: ostracism within the department and even potential threats against their lives. Similarly, in the Los Angeles Rampart scandal it was not until after officer Rafael Perez was arrested for auto theft, forgery, and the sale of cocaine, and was offered a reduced prison sentence, that he provided departmental investigators with information that broke the case open.[78]

Cracking the "Blue Curtain"

The so-called blue curtain of silence—the refusal of officers to testify against other officers—is one of the major factors protecting police corruption. In Los Angeles and New York City new initiatives have been developed to catch and punish officers who give false testimony. In Los Angeles, the inspector general for the Police Commission launched a new effort in 1997 to identify officers who give "false and misleading testimony" in investigations.[79] The Commission to Combat Police Corruption, established in the wake of the Mollen Commission investigation, reviewed the police department's handling of perjury cases and concluded that "the penalties imposed for lying are insufficient." It recommended that officers be automatically terminated for lying unless there were special circumstances.[80]

On the other hand, some police agencies have found that such policies actually serve to reinforce the code of silence. For example, in Los Angeles, the Rampart Independent Review Panel reported that there are a variety of reasons that officers do not immediately come forward to report an incident, including friendship, loyalty, and fear of retaliation. However, the panel found that officers often reconsider their decision, especially if they witness repeated misconduct by the same officer. It argued that policies that punish officers for failing to report misconduct *immediately* discourage officers from reporting misconduct later, and further serve to reinforce the need for secrecy.[81]

Proactive Integrity Tests

In response to a series of corruption scandals the New Orleans police department created a new Public Integrity Division in the mid-1990s. The division began conducting integrity tests of police officers to identify corruption. Figure 10–3 represents excerpts of a report by the division on the conduct of integrity tests.

Effective Supervision

Standards of integrity also require effective supervision of routine officer behavior. Herman Goldstein comments that "corruption thrives best in poorly run organizations where lines of authority are vague and supervision is minimal."[82] If officers learn from experience that their day-to-day behavior is not being monitored, or that they are not being disciplined for minor neglect of duty, they will conclude that corrupt acts will not be

FIGURE 10–3   NEW ORLEANS POLICE DEPARTMENT PUBLIC INTEGRITY DIVISION, INTEGRITY TESTS

The Public Integrity Division (PID) implemented a process to ensure that employees of the New Orleans Police Department abide by the rules and procedures established to provide the highest level of protection to the citizens and visitors of New Orleans. The Integrity Test program is a process by which investigators observe employees performing routine law enforcement duties. Two types of tests are utilized: *Directed*, where the test is focused on a specific individual or unit; and *random*, which is not directed toward a specific individual or unit.

     Scenarios are set up mimicking situations common to everyday law enforcement duties and officers are summoned to the scene to conduct an investigation. The officer(s) under observation are unaware that they are being tested. Scenarios such as staged auto accidents, found personal property, and information on search warrants have been used.

Integrity test results, January through June 1997

- Number of tests conducted: 15
- Number of individual employees tested: 15
- Number of employees passed: 14
- Number of employees failed: 1
- *Attempts: 2

*Attempts are scenarios enacted, but officers were unable to respond to the scene before the operatives secured from the location.
Source: New Orleans Police Department, Public Integrity Division, *Report, 1997* (New Orleans: City of New Orleans, 1997), np.

caught. Historically, departments with reputations for pervasive corruption have also had reputations for general inefficiency. A review of the Rampart scandal in Los Angeles found that CRASH unit sergeants and watch commanders were not involved in the day-to-day operations of the unit and failed to consult, participate, or oversee routine officer activity.[83]

Officers themselves argue that good first-line supervision is perhaps the best way to control police deviance. For example, in one national survey "almost 90 percent of officers believed that good first-line supervisors are effective in preventing police officers from abusing their authority." In focus group sessions, supervisors agreed, articulating that supervisors, through good role modeling and mentoring, can prevent police deviance.[84]

As a means of enhancing supervision, the IACP and the Justice Department's Police Integrity conference both recommend early warning (EW) systems to identify officers with chronic problems. EW systems are designed not just to punish officers but also to "address, and hopefully resolve, problems early in their development."[85] (See Chapter 11 for further discussion.)

Rewarding the Good Officers

Experts on police corruption argue that corruption flourishes because police departments fail to reward the honest officers. As Herman Goldstein points out: "Many competent officers have found that to have reported corruption even once had the effect of permanently impairing their careers."[86] The Mollen Commission argued that "Reforms must focus on making honest officers feel responsible for keeping their fellow officers honest, and ridding themselves of corrupt ones." Unfortunately, it found that honest officers "were often discouraged from doing so." Officers were told not to report corruption, and when they did report corrupt officers, the information was ignored.[87]

Personnel Recruitment

Effective screening of recruits is an important element in controlling corruption. Unfortunately, however, it is not always possible to spot potentially corrupt officers at this stage. The Mollen Commission found that some of the most corrupt officers were ideal recruits in terms of their backgrounds.[88]

The Miami, Florida, Washington, DC, and Los Angeles, California, police departments have had major corruption scandals as a result of hiring officers with crime and drug-related histories. The problem, however, was that these departments were under political pressure to hire more officers and did not conduct the normal background checks.[89] For example, officers involved in the Rampart scandal in Los Angeles were found to have criminal records, financial problems, histories of violent behavior, and drug problems. Upon further investigation the department found that these officers were all hired in the late 1980s and early 1990s, a time when the department compromised its hiring protocol in an effort to quickly fill empty positions within the police department.[90]

Background investigations of job applicants are regarded as an essential part of an effective anticorruption effort. Experience indicates that persons with prior arrest records (even without convictions) and particularly people with prior involvement with drugs are extremely high risk in terms of becoming corrupt if employed as police officers.

There is considerable disagreement among police departments over whether applicants should be automatically eliminated on the basis of any prior criminal activity and/or drug involvement. Virtually all agencies refuse to hire anyone with a felony conviction. Only half, however, automatically reject someone with a misdemeanor conviction. About a third reject applicants with a misdemeanor arrest but no conviction.[91]

With respect to drugs, the IACP argues that the ideal standard should be "no prior drug abuse of any kind."[92] However, given the extent of drug usage in contemporary society, maintaining an absolute standard would screen out a very large percentage of applicants. Generally, most departments are willing to hire individuals with some prior drug history, making distinctions between experimentation, use, and abuse. Most departments are willing to accept individuals with some minor usage or experimentation, but not recent and/or heavy use.

Many departments have initiated drug-testing programs to identify both applicants and currently employed officers who are involved with drugs. One survey of police agencies found that 73 percent of all departments gave drug-screening tests to applicants; 21 percent indicated that they were considering mandatory drug testing for all employees. Of those departments that had some kind of drug-testing program, several tested officers currently in or seeking transfer to "sensitive" assignments (internal affairs, vice, or narcotics units). Officers found to be using drugs were not necessarily dismissed automatically. Many departments indicated that they preferred offering counseling to the officers.[93]

EXTERNAL CORRUPTION CONTROL APPROACHES

Once corruption exists in a department, it is extremely difficult to eliminate. Often, the internal mechanisms of control have broken down or, in the case of pervasive corruption, are inadequate to the task. In those situations, external corruption control strategies may be necessary.

Special Investigations

Because of the difficulties in investigating corruption, special investigating commissions have sometimes been used. The Knapp Commission investigated the New York City police in the early 1970s, and the Mollen Commission conducted another investigation in the 1990s.

Special commissions have the advantage of being independent of the police department. On the other hand, commissioners may lack intimate knowledge of the inner, day-to-day workings of the department. Also, external investigations arouse the hostility of the rank and file, aggravating the existing tendency of the police to close ranks and refuse to cooperate.

Criminal Prosecution

Because police corruption involves violations of the criminal law, prosecution under federal or state law is one potential remedy. Criminal offenses include specific corruption-related offenses, theft, possession and sale of narcotics, and perjury. Prosecution on federal charges offers certain advantages over prosecution on state charges. The U.S. attorney's office usually has fewer ties with local criminal justice officials who also may be implicated in corrupt activities.[94]

Since 1996 the number of officers convicted in Justice Department cases has increased significantly as a consequence of increased focus by the attorney general's office. In 1996, 83 officers were convicted compared with 246 officers in 1998. This has led to an increase of over 500 percent in the number of police officers serving time in federal prison, from 107 in 1994 to 655 in 1999.[95]

Criminal prosecution of alleged corruption is in many respects easier than prosecution of excessive force complaints. It is usually easier to prove that, for example, an officer received a bribe, and had criminal intent to receive it, than that an officer had criminal intent in beating someone. Nonetheless, there are reasons to question the effectiveness of criminal prosecution, by itself, as a long-term remedy for police corruption. In almost all of the investigations of corruption in the New York City police department, officers have been prosecuted and convicted. And yet, corruption persists.

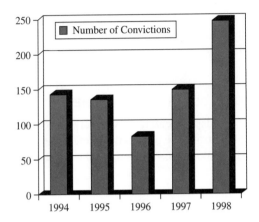

FIGURE 10–4
THE NUMBER OF POLICE OFFICERS CONVICTED FROM 1994 TO 1998 IN JUSTICE
DEPARTMENT CASES.

Source: Richard Willing and Kevin Johnson, "More Law Enforcers Becoming Lawbreakers," *USA Today* (July 29, 1999): p. 4a.

The lesson appears to be that criminal prosecution can remove individual officers but cannot eliminate the factors that cause corruption.

Mobilizing Public Opinion

Many experts argue that police corruption flourishes in certain departments because of a local political culture that tolerates it. Controlling corruption, therefore, requires mobilizing public opinion. The media play a major role in shaping public opinion about corruption. The media often expose the existence of corruption and set in motion the reform process. *New York Times* reporter David Burnham, for example, was instrumental in exposing corruption in the New York City police department in the 1970s. His front-page article on corruption on April 25, 1970, led to the Knapp Commission investigation.[96] It is worth noting that the *Times* took up the issue only after both the mayor and high-ranking officials in the police department had refused to follow up on the allegations brought to them by officers Frank Serpico and David Durk.

Relying on the media has certain limitations, however. Media-generated scandals tend to be short-lived. Both the media and the public have very short attention spans, and they quickly turn to other crises. The media also tend to cover the most dramatic aspects of a scandal, usually focusing on individuals who become scapegoats. The underlying causes of corruption are complex and do not offer a dramatic newsworthy event. Finally, scandals tend to produce dramatic responses, such as the removal or transfer of certain officers, which does not necessarily address the underlying problem. Departments often reassign personnel in response to a scandal. Kornblum found that mass transfers in New York City affected honest officers as well as corrupt ones and failed to address the underlying causes of corruption.[97]

Altering the External Environment

Sherman argues that police departments are not completely at the mercy of the external political environment. He cites Oakland in the 1950s where a reform-minded police chief influenced that environment by threatening to arrest politicians who were involved in gambling and other illegal activities. The threat helped to reduce corruption both in the police department and in the city as a whole. The result was a new political environment that was less supportive of corruption.[98]

The Limits of Anticorruption Efforts

In a provocative book, Frank Anechiarico and James B. Jacobs argue that anticorruption efforts not only have been ineffective but have made government itself ineffective. In their view, rules and regulations designed to prevent corruption limit the capacity of government agencies to be creative and flexible in carrying out their basic missions.[99]

The Anechiarico–Jacobs argument is a provocative one. As they point out, corruption persists in the New York City police department despite special investigations every 20 years since the 1890s. Nonetheless, their argument suffers from two flaws. Most important, it is almost entirely New York–specific. Other cities do not have the same level of corruption as New York, and police departments in other cities have successfully reduced corruption.[100]

SUMMARY

Police corruption remains one of the most serious problems in policing. Not only does it have a long history, but the current drug problem threatens to make it even worse. Controlling corruption is extremely difficult. Corruption is not simply the result of a few bad apples but is deeply rooted in the nature of American society and the criminal law. Despite these problems, there are some hopeful signs. A few departments have succeeded in reducing or eliminating corruption through effective control techniques.

CASE STUDY: POLICE INTEGRITY—NEW ORLEANS STYLE

Since taking over the helm of the New Orleans police department (NOPD) in October 1994, Superintendent Richard J. Pennington has instituted many reforms that have brought the department national attention. The results have led to a 38 percent reduction in the city's murder rate since 1994 and a decrease in violent crime for 1997 that was four times lower than the national average. Contributing to the department's renaissance is a Public Integrity Division that Pennington formed in 1995 to eradicate police corruption and raise the agency's ethical standard.

The Public Integrity Division (PID) is a partnership between the Federal Bureau of Investigation (FBI) and Louisiana law enforcement officials. The NOPD has the privilege of being the nation's only police agency to have FBI agents assigned to it full-time. Through PID initiatives, and with the help of its federal partners, the NOPD has once again gained citizen confidence and support. Contributing to this effort was locating the PID office outside of the department's central administration building. The off-site location has made citizens much more comfortable about registering complaints against the rank and file. Having access to a toll-free 24-hour hotline where they can report police misconduct or offer feedback has also won the NOPD favor with the public.

"The New Orleans Police Department is on the cusp of progressive policing," says Major Felix Loicano, commander of the Public Integrity Division. "You are going to see that the procedures Superintendent Pennington has implemented here become the norm throughout the country."

The PID's three-pronged approach is implemented through aggressive criminal and administrative investigations using undercover personnel to detect wrongdoing, a Professional Performance Enhancement Program, and staged integrity checks. The first of the PID's three strategies is a complete and thorough investigation of all complaints received, whether criminal or administrative. Undercover personnel are used in some cases to prove or disprove allegations.

The PID's early warning system marks the beginning of the second strategy to address integrity issues. When an officer receives a third complaint, a red flag appears in the NOPD's computer system. These officers are enrolled in the PID's Professional Performance Enhancement Program, better known as PPEP.

The Professional Performance Enhancement Program is offered as in-service training to all officers; however, those officers who have been "flagged" must repeat the course, joining their colleagues in the 40-hour sensitivity training session. The full-week course teaches verbal Judo (using communication skills instead of physical confrontation), conflict resolution training, and complaint avoidance. During the week, every officer meets one-on-one with the department psychologist. Together they create strategies, personalized to the officer, that can be used to manage anger, tension, and other stressors.

The officers attending PPEP for disciplinary reasons are there for a refresher course; they complete their week knowing the behavior expected of them and are closely monitored for the next 6 months to ensure they are doing their jobs according to department regulations. The follow-up training and monitoring has resulted in a significant decline in officer infractions.

Finally, the PID coordinates a routine series of integrity checks to ensure officers are complying with the department's policies and procedures as well as state and federal laws. The PID stages scenarios where randomly selected officers, or in some instances targeted officers, are called on to investigate cases. The NOPD, for example, will set up a "found property" scenario involving money, jewelry, or narcotics, and dispatch an officer to the scene. The PID monitors the officer's activity, checking to see that he or she collects and logs the items according to department procedure. Other officers are observed in staged traffic accidents where undercover police pose as citizen drivers while the entire scene is monitored through surveillance equipment.

"We want the entire department to know we're going to check and see if everyone is complying with our policies and procedures," says Superintendent Pennington. "We just want to make sure our officers are out there doing their job properly and not violating the law."

Source: Written by Lieutenant Marlon A. Defillo. Adapted from
http://www.communitypolicing.org/publications/exchange/e19%5F98/e19defillo.htm

FOR DISCUSSION

1 What are the costs of corruption? How could corruption cost your community?

2 What are the five types of corruption? Give an example of each.

3 What are grass eaters and meat eaters? Which type of officer causes the greatest amount of harm to a community?

4 Explain the three levels of corruption and give an example of each.

5 Identify the four different theories of police corruption. Explain which theory you believe best explains why police corruption occurs.

INTERNET EXERCISES

Exercise 1 Go to the website **http://www.policeabuse.com/**. Select one of the many telephone and video recordings in which investigators attempt to assess the quality of police departmental complaint procedures. After viewing the recording discuss how the officer conducted him/herself. What did the officer do well? How could the officer have better handled the situation?

Exercise 2 Do some research on corruption in your local police department by going to the city newspaper's website. How often has there been a corruption scandal? Have there been any patterns (e.g., involvement in drugs, prostitution, gambling)? How has the department typically handled the problems? Has the department typically blamed the problems on a few "bad apples" or have they tried to address the root cause of the problems?

REFERENCES

1 Lawrence W. Sherman, ed., *Police Corruption: A Sociological Perspective* (Garden City, NY: Anchor Books, 1974), p. 1.

2 Bernard Parks, *Rampart Area Corruption Incident: Public Report* (Los Angeles: Los Angeles Police Department, 2000).

3 Mollen Commission to Investigate Allegations of Police Corruption, *Commission Report* (New York: The Mollen Commission, 1994).

4 Richard Willing and Kevin Johnson, "More Law Enforcers Becoming Lawbreakers," *USA Today* (July 29, 1999): 4a.

5 Herman Goldstein, *Police Corruption: A Perspective on Its Nature and Control* (Washington, DC: The Police Foundation, 1975), p. 3.

6 Thomas Barker and David L. Carter, "A Typology of Police Deviance," in T. Baker and D. L. Carter, eds., *Police Deviance,* 2nd ed. (Cincinnati, OH: Anderson, 1991), pp. 3–12.

7 Government Accounting Office, *Report to the Honorable Charles B. Rangel, House of Representatives, Law Enforcement: Information on Drug-Related Police Corruption* (Washington, DC: Government Printing Office, 1998), p. 35.

8 New York City Commission to Combat Police Corruption, *The New York City Police Department's Disciplinary System* (New York: The Commission, 1996), p. 10.

9 Parks, *Rampart Area Corruption Incident: Public Report.*

10 William A. Westley, *Violence and the Police* (Cambridge, MA: MIT Press, 1970), pp. 109–152.

11 David Burnham, "How Police Corruption Is Built into the System—And a Few Ideas for What to Do about It," in Sherman, ed., *Police Corruption,* p. 305.

12 President's Commission on Law Enforcement and Administration of Justice, *The Challenge of Crime in a Free Society* (Washington, DC: Government Printing Office, 1967), p. 99.

13 Mollen Commission, *Commission Report,* p. 45.

14 The Gallup Poll, as reported in Bureau of Justice Statistics, *Sourcebook of Criminal Justice Statistics, 1999* (Washington, DC: Government Printing Office, 2000), p. 106.

15 Steven A. Tuch and Ronald Weitzer, "Racial Differences in Attitudes toward the Police," *Public Opinion Quarterly,* 61 (1997): 642–663.

16 Goldstein, *Police Corruption,* pp. 16–22.

17 Tom Barker and Robert O. Wells, "Police Administrators' Attitudes toward the Definition and Control of Police Deviance," *Law Enforcement Bulletin* (March 1982): 11.

18 Richard Kania, "Should We Tell the Police to Say 'Yes' to Gratuities?" *Criminal Justice Ethics,* 7, no. 2 (1982): 37–49.

19 Knapp Commission, *Report on Police Corruption* (New York: George Braziller, 1973), p. 4.

20 Mark Jones, "Police Gratuities and Public Opinion," *Police Forum* (October 1997), pp. 6–11.

21 Victor Kappeler, Richard Sluder, and Geoffery Alpert, *Forces of Deviance: Understanding the Dark Side of Policing* (Prospect Heights, IL: Waveland, 1994).

22 Government Accounting Office, *Report to the Honorable Charles B. Rangel.*

23 Allan Kornblum, *The Moral Hazards* (Lexington, MA: Lexington Books, 1976), p. 54.

24 Robert Daley, *Prince of the City* (Boston: Houghton Mifflin, 1978).

25 David Burnham, "How Police Corruption Is Built into the System—And a Few Ideas for What to Do About It," in Sherman, ed., *Police Corruption,* p. 305.

26 Kappeler, Sluder, and Alpert, *Forces of Deviance: Understanding the Dark Side of Policing.*

27 Ibid.

28 Mollen Commission, *Commission Report,* pp. 22–31.

29 Jay Stuart Berman, *Police Administration and Progressive Reform: Theodore Roosevelt as Police Commissioner of New York* (New York: Greenwood Press, 1987).

30 Knapp Commission, *Report on Police Corruption,* pp. 3, 167–168.

31 Mollen Commission, *Commission Report,* p. 47.

32 CNN.COM, "Testimony: Alleged 'Corrupt LAPD Cops Gave Each Other Awards," **http://www.cnn.com/2000/us/02/10/lapd.scandal/** (February 10, 2000); CNN.COM, "Outside Probe of LAPD Corruption Scandal Demanded," **http://www.cnn.com/2000/us/02/16/lapd.scandal/** (February 16, 2000).

33 Sherman, ed., *Police Corruption,* p. 3.

34 See the attempt to resolve this problem in Sherman, *Scandal and Reform* (Berkeley: University of California Press, 1978).

35 Sherman, *Police Corruption,* p. 7.

36 Mollen Commission, *Commission Report,* p. 17.

37 Sherman, ed., *Police Corruption,* p. 9.

38 William Chambliss, "The Police and Organized Vice in a Western City," in Sherman, ed., *Police Corruption,* pp. 153–170.

39 Knapp Commission, *Report on Police Corruption,* p. 74.

40 David H. Bayley and Harold Mendelsohn, *Minorities and the Police* (New York: The Free Press, 1969), pp. 1–33.

41 Knapp Commission, *Report on Police Corruption,* p. 7.

42 Goldstein, *Police Corruption,* pp. 32–38.

43 Robert F. Meier and Gilbert Geis, *Victimless Crime?* (Los Angeles: Roxbury, 1997).

44 James Cook, "Fish Story," *Forbes* (April 26, 1982): 61–67.

45 V. O. Key, "Police Graft," *American Journal of Sociology,* 40 (March 1935): 624–636.

46 Chambliss, "The Police and Organized Vice," p. 154.

47 M. McMullen, "A Theory of Corruption," *Sociological Review,* 9 (June 1961): 184–185.

48 Sherman, ed., *Police Corruption,* pp. 16–17.

49 Thomas Barker, "Peer Group Support for Police Occupational Deviance," *Criminology,* 15 (November 1977): 353–366.

50 Joseph Goldstein, "Police Discretion Not to Invoke the Criminal Process: Low-Visibility Decisions in the Administration of Justice," *Yale Law Journal,* 69, no. 4 (1960): 543–588.

51 Goldstein, *Police Corruption,* p. 25.

52 Carl Klockars, Sanja Ivkovich, William Harver, and Maria Haberfeld, *The Measurement of Police Integrity* (National Institute of Justice: Washington DC, 2000).

53 Robin Haarr, "They're Making a Bad Name for the Department: Exploring the Link between Organizational Commitment and Police Occupational Deviance in a Police Patrol Bureau," *Policing: An International Journal of Police Strategy and Management,* 20, no. 4 (1997): 786–817.

54 Westley, *Violence and the Police.*

55 David Weisburd and Rosann Greenspan, *Police Attitudes toward Abuse of Authority: Findings from a National Study* (Washington, DC: National Institute of Justice, 2000).

56 Westley, *Violence and the Police.*

57 Mollen Commission, *Commission Report,* pp. 5, 20.

58 Lawrence W. Sherman, "Becoming Bent: Moral Careers of Corrupt Policemen," in Sherman, ed., *Police Corruption,* pp. 191–208.

59 Ibid., p. 199.

60 Mollen Commission, *Commission Report,* p. 47.

61 Knapp Commission, *Report on Police Corruption,* p. 4.

62 Goldstein, *Police Corruption,* p. 37.

63 Sherman, *Scandal and Reform,* p. xxxiv.

64 Mollen Commission, *Commission Report,* p. 112.

65 Ibid., pp. 70–109.

66 David L. Carter and Thomas Barker, "Administrative Guidance and Control of Police Officer Behavior: Policies, Procedures, and Rules," in Barker and Carter, eds., *Police Deviance,* 2nd ed., pp. 22–23.

67 Kania, "Should We Tell the Police to Say 'Yes' to Gratuities?"

68 Karen Amendola, *Assessing Law Enforcement Ethics: A Summary Report Based on the Study Conducted with the Oregon Department of State Police* (Washington, DC: The Police Foundation, 1996), p. 12.

69 Goldstein, *Police Corruption,* p. 29.

70 *Law Enforcement Bulletin* (March 1982): 11.

71 IACP, *Building Integrity and Reducing Drug Corruption in Police Departments,* p. 68.

72 Mollen Commission, *Commission Report.*

73 Sherman, *Police Corruption,* p. 10.

74 Mollen Commission, *Commission Report,* pp. 85–90.

75 Sherman, *Police Corruption,* p. 8.

76 Aogan Mulcahy, "'Headhunter' or 'Real Cop': Identity in the World of Internal Affairs Officers," *Journal of Contemporary Ethnography,* 24 (April 1995): 99–130.

77 Ibid; *Garrity v. New Jersey.* 385 U.S. 493 (1967).

78 Parks, *Rampart Area Corruption Incident.*

79 Inspector General, *First Annual Report* (Los Angeles: Los Angeles Police Commission, 1997).

80 New York Commission to Combat Police Corruption, *The New York City Police Department's Disciplinary System: How the Department Disciplines Members Who Make False Statements,* pp. 32, 39.

81 Richard Drooyan, *Report of the Rampart Independent Review Panel* (Los Angeles: November 16, 2000).

82 Goldstein, *Police Corruption,* p. 42.

83 Parks, *Rampart Area Corruption Incident.*

84 David Weisburd et al., *Police Attitudes toward Abuse of Authority: Findings from a National Study,* p. 6.

85 Department of Justice, *Police Integrity* (Washington, DC: Government Printing Office, 1997).

86 Goldstein, *Police Corruption,* pp. 50–51.

87 Mollen Commission, *Commission Report,* p. 5.

88 Ibid., p. 20.

89 "D.C. Police Force Still Paying for Two-Year Hiring Spree," *Washington Post* (August 28, 1994), p. 1; Parks, *Rampart Area Corruption Incident.*

90 Parks, *Rampart Area Corruption Incident.*

91 Terry Eisenberg et al., *Police Personnel Practices* (Washington, DC: The Police Foundation, 1973).

92 IACP, *Building Integrity and Reducing Drug Corruption in Police Departments,* p. 26.

93 J. Thomas McEwen, Barbara Manili, and Edward Connors, *Employee Drug-Testing Policies in Police Departments* (Washington, DC: Government Printing Office, 1986).

94 Herbert Biegel, "The Investigation and Prosecution of Police Corruption," *Journal of Criminal Law and Criminology,* 135 (1974): 135–156.

95 Willing and Johnson, "More Law Enforcers Becoming Lawbreakers."

96 David Burnham, *The Role of the Media in Controlling Corruption* (New York: John Jay College, 1977).

97 Kornblum, *Moral Hazards,* pp. 58–59.

98 Sherman, *Scandal and Reform,* pp. 140–145.

99 Frank Anechiarico and James B. Jacobs, *The Pursuit of Absolute Integrity* (Chicago: University of Chicago Press, 1996).

100 Comments, Samuel Walker, "Author Meets Critics," American Society of Criminology, Annual Meeting, 1997.

CHAPTER ELEVEN

Accountability of the Police

CHAPTER OUTLINE

INTRODUCTION

In a democratic society it is essential that the police be held accountable for their actions. Accountability is an extremely complex subject, however. This chapter examines the issues of what accountability is, what the police should be accountable for, to whom they should be accountable, and specific mechanisms or procedures for ensuring accountability.

A DEFINITION OF ACCOUNTABILITY

Accountability is defined as having to answer for your conduct.[1] This basic definition leaves a number of important questions unanswered, however. First, there is an important distinction between accountability for police departments and accountability for individual police officers. Organizations and individuals should be held accountable for different things. Second, there are important questions about to whom police organizations and officers should be accountable. A police department should be held accountable to elected officials, but it is a bad idea for politicians to question individual officers about specific actions. That approach would represent political interference in policing. Third, there are major issues related to the best means of achieving accountability for both organizations and individual officers.

BASIC ISSUES IN POLICE ACCOUNTABILITY

What, How, and to Whom?

When we ask the question, "Is that police department doing a good job," what do we mean? Do we mean that it keeps the crime rate low? Or do we mean that it does its job without wasting a lot of money? Or do we mean that it treats everyone fairly?

Accountability in policing has three dimensions. First, the police should be accountable for *what* they do. In practice, this means that they should be accountable for how well they control crime, maintain order, and provide services to the public.

Second, the police should be accountable for *how* they do their job. This includes performing their tasks in an efficient manner, complying with the law, and treating all citizens with equal respect.

The third dimension involves the process of *to whom* the police are accountable. In general, the police are accountable to the public. In practice, this means that the police are accountable to the elected officials who are responsible for particular law enforcement agencies: for example, mayors who appoint police chiefs, city councils that appropriate police department budgets, governors who appoint directors of state police agencies. In our legal system, the police are also accountable to the courts. A court, for example, may rule that a police officer violated a suspect's *Miranda* rights and throw out a confession.

The "Three E's"

It is also useful to think of accountability in terms of the "three E's": effectiveness, efficiency, and equity (or what David Bayley refers to as rectitude).[2] Effectiveness refers to whether the police actually accomplish what they are supposed to do. Do they effectively control crime? Are they successful in arresting offenders? Do they successfully maintain order? Efficiency involves the question of whether they accomplish their assigned tasks in a cost-effective manner. If a police department tripled the number of sworn officers, for example, it might control crime more effectively, but this would not necessarily be an efficient or cost-effective way of accomplishing this. Equity refers to whether they accomplish their tasks in a fair manner. Do they treat all citizens equally? If the police rounded up all young men, for example, it might effectively reduce gang violence. But this would involve violating the rights of many innocent people and, therefore, would not be equitable.

The Dilemmas of Policing in a Democracy

When Jerry Brown was elected mayor of Oakland, California, in 1999, one of the first things he did was to fire the police chief. A controversy arose because that chief was popular with many people and groups in the community. Yet, as the elected representative of the people, Mayor Brown had a right to appoint a police chief he believed was best for the community. Many people thought that Brown did the wrong thing in firing a popular chief. But by appointing his own chief, Brown was seeking to make the police department accountable to him.

A basic principle of a democratic society is that government agencies are accountable to the public. Accountability distinguishes democratic from totalitarian societies. In totalitarian regimes, the police do not have to answer to either the public or the law. They are, in a sense, "lawless." With the collapse of communism, Russia began the transition to democratic principles of policing. Louise Shelley observes that "in the late 1980s, for the first time in seventy years of Soviet history, the regular police (*militsiia*) were expected to abide by the rule of law."[3] In a democratic society the police must answer to the public and to legal principles. As the title of Herman Goldstein's book indicates, the challenge for America is policing a *free* society.[4] This chapter examines the issue of police accountability, covering the questions of what the police should be accountable for and how accountability should be achieved.

One of the most serious problems in policing is that the "three E's" often conflict. In his classic work *Justice without Trial*,[5] Jerome Skolnick argues that the demand for effective crime control often conflicts with the requirements of the law and considerations of equity. If police officers beat confessions out of people, they would probably solve a lot more crimes. But that would buy effectiveness only at the price of equity. The police might also be more effective if they had two or three times as many sworn officers as they currently have. But this would purchase effectiveness at the price of efficiency. Conflicts between the different goals of policing are inherent in the nature of the police role, and police departments deal with them on a regular basis.

A Historical Perspective on Accountability

Until 1965, a Los Angeles police officer faced an automatic internal investigation if he damaged a patrol car but no similar investigation if he shot and wounded a citizen.[6]

The above example from Los Angeles illustrates the point that meaningful accountability of the police is a relatively recent development. Through most of their history, the American police were not accountable at all (see Chapter 2). Police departments were corrupt and inefficient, and individual officers evaded duty and assaulted citizens without fear of being disciplined.[7] Elected officials who were responsible for the police were mainly interested in graft, protection of illegal enterprises, and getting jobs for their friends. They took almost no interest in standards of on-the-street police behavior. Finally, there were no standards of professionalism among police chiefs in the nineteenth century. There were no textbooks on police administration, and chiefs were selected on the basis of their political connections rather than any qualifications.

Procedures for accountability began to develop in the late 1950s.[8] Most important, the Supreme Court began to impose constitutional standards on routine police work. By the 1970s police departments began to develop elaborate standard operating procedure (SOP) manuals to control police officer behavior. And by the 1980s the community-policing movement represented new demands on the part of the public regarding what the police do and how they do it.[9]

ACCOUNTABILITY FOR *WHAT* THE POLICE DO

The Traditional Approach

The police role involves law enforcement, order maintenance, and service (see Chapter 1). Traditionally, however, the police were held accountable primarily for their law enforcement or crime control role. The measures used in this regard include the crime rate, the clearance rate, and response times.[10] As discussed in Chapter 6, these data are not reliable measures of police performance. The official UCR crime rate is limited to eight Index crimes and provides no data on several major categories of crime, including white collar crime, organized crime, and narcotics offenses. For the eight Index crimes, the UCR includes only reported crime, omitting the two-thirds of all crimes that are not reported.[11] Police officers unfound, or refuse to record, an unknown number of crimes reported by citizens.[12] Also, an unknown number of crimes are lost through inefficiency. Because of extreme variations in department practices about recording crimes and maintaining records, the UCR is not a reliable performance measure for comparing different departments.

Official arrest data are also not a completely reliable measure for accountability because there are wide variations in how police departments record arrests.[13] Some departments complete an official arrest report only when a suspect is booked. Others complete an arrest report whenever a suspect is detained and questioned. Because report practices are not comparable, arrest data are not reliable as indicators of comparative performance.

The clearance rate, or the percentage of reported crimes solved or cleared by the police, is also not a reliable performance measure. The data are not independently audited, and there are many opportunities for manipulating the data to produce high clearance rates. Officers can unfound reported crimes or improperly count certain crimes as cleared.

Finally, the traditional crime rate and clearance rate data ignore the order maintenance and service-related activities of the police. They also do not address the *quality* of police services—for example, citizen perceptions of how they are treated. And it is inappropriate to hold the police entirely responsible for crime control when, as many criminologists argue, crime is a product of social factors that are beyond the control of the police.

New Measures of Police Service

The city auditor's office in Portland, Oregon, surveyed city residents in 1996 and found that in one neighborhood 20 percent of the people knew who their police officer was; but in another area, only 11 percent said they knew who their neighborhood officer was. The auditor's officer regularly surveys citizens about their perceptions of the quality of the police department.[14] Surveys of this sort are a new alternative to the traditional crime-related performance measures.

The community-policing movement has dramatized the need for new and more relevant measures of what the police do. One of the principal goals of community policing is to improve the quality of life in neighborhoods. In a Justice Department report, *"Broken Windows" and Police Discretion,* George L. Kelling offers a proposal for developing accountability measures related to order maintenance policing. Through written guidelines, he argues, police departments can specify the objectives of order maintenance and provide guidelines for use of arrest, force, or other forms of intervention in handling different kinds of situations.[15]

The quality of life in neighborhoods can be measured in several ways. Citizen surveys can assess citizen fear of crime and disorder, as well as perceptions of the police department.[16] Police departments can also survey citizens who have had contact with the police and ask them to evaluate police officer performance. Evaluations of the Chicago Alternative Policing Strategies (CAPS) program have also measured the extent of citizen participation in neighborhood beat meetings, which is an indicator of citizen trust in and involvement with the police department.[17]

COMPSTAT: A New Approach

Every other Thursday afternoon, the command staff of the Minneapolis police department meets in the conference room. Up-to-date crime data for each district are projected onto a screen, and commanders from each district have to explain what has happened in their area and what they are doing about any crime trends that appear—for example, a series of household burglaries. These meetings are a part of the CODEFOR program, modeled after COMPSTAT, which was developed by the New York City police department (NYCPD).[18]

CODEFOR and COMPSTAT represent a new system for holding middle-level police managers accountable for crime in their areas. They are computer-based systems that generate timely and detailed data about criminal activity. Both systems are capable of producing data on criminal activity within 24 hours of the reported events. Thus, the police chief and other top commanders can obtain an almost instant picture of crime trends in particular precincts. At regular command staff meetings precinct commanders are expected to explain the data and what they are doing in response to particular problems.

ACCOUNTABILITY FOR *HOW* THE POLICE DO THEIR JOB

There are a number of different ways in which the police are held accountable for *how* they do their job. It is useful to discuss these different ways in terms of whom the police are accountable to. From this perspective, there are two basic approaches to accountability: Internal mechanisms, meaning accountability procedures within the police department, and external mechanisms, meaning procedures that are outside the department.

INTERNAL MECHANISMS OF ACCOUNTABILITY

Primary responsibility for holding police officers accountable for their actions lies with the police department itself. Herman Goldstein argues that "the nature of the police function is such that primary dependence for the control of police conduct must continue to be placed upon internal systems of control."[19] This function is carried out in several different ways: routine supervision, officers' reports on critical incidents, periodic performance evaluations, and investigation of alleged misconduct by the internal affairs unit (IAU) or the office of professional standards (OPS).

SUPERVISION

Routine Supervision

A newspaper report described the midnight shift in the Suffolk County police department as the "lost battalion." It found that officers "can go for hours without speaking to a supervisor, or weeks without having contact with their precinct's top managers."[20] In other words, the department was failing to provide routine supervision—the kind recommended in police management textbooks since the 1940s—to officers working between midnight and 8 A.M. The newspaper investigation was prompted by a series of allegations that male officers in the department had stopped, harassed, and even abused young, single female drivers.

Routine supervision is one of the central tasks of police management, and this responsibility primarily falls on sergeants. A Police Foundation survey of police officers found that almost 90 percent agree that "good first-line supervisors can help prevent police officers from abusing their authority."[21] Supervision by sergeants involves a number of different activities. First, they are expected to monitor officers under their command on a regular basis, either through face-to-face meetings or over the police radio. In the case of potentially serious incidents, sergeants are expected to appear at the scene, provide advice if needed, and if necessary take command of the situation. Sergeants also supervise by reviewing and approving the written reports completed by rank-and-file officers. Typically, sergeants review and sign off on arrest reports. Based on these contacts, sergeants are expected to advise officers under their command whenever their performance is less than satisfactory and to instruct them on proper procedure. If a sergeant becomes aware that an officer has violated a department policy or committed some act of misconduct, he or she is expected to file a report with the internal affairs unit or the office of professional standards, which would then investigate the allegation.[22]

In the mid-1990s the Los Angeles County sheriff's department experienced a number of officer-involved shooting incidents by officers assigned to the Century Station. An investigation by Special Counsel Merrick Bobb—the department's form of citizen oversight—found that the source of the problem was not a few "bad apples" but bad management practices. Most seriously, Bobb found that at times each sergeant was supervising twenty to twenty-five officers, a ratio that far exceeded the department's own standard of 8 to 1.[23]

The ratio of sergeants to officers is referred to as the span of control. The theory of span of control assumes that any supervisor can effectively supervise a limited number of people.[24] In policing, the recommended span of control is between eight and twelve patrol officers for each sergeant. When the recommended span of control is exceeded, performance may deteriorate.

One problem that affects supervision by sergeants is that they often develop close personal ties with the officers under their command. In some cases they become unwilling to criticize those officers and exercise the proper level of control and discipline. These relationships represent an important part of the police subculture (see Chapter 13). Departments that allow personal ties to affect supervision and discipline do not have high standards of accountability.

The Impact of Organizational Culture

The Los Angeles police department delivered a devastating criticism of its own personnel evaluation system: "Our personnel evaluations have little or no credibility at any level in the organization." This criticism was delivered by the LAPD's internal Board of Inquiry report on the Rampart scandal in 2000. The report's chapter on the department's integrity systems, meanwhile, identified over thirty policies and procedures designed to ensure integrity and accountability. Yet, it concluded that all these systems had not prevented the Rampart scandal from occurring.[25]

The findings of the Board of Inquiry report raised serious questions about the effectiveness of personnel evaluations and other internal accountability mechanisms. There is an important distinction between meaningful accountability, where actions have consequences, and superficial accountability, where an organization has elaborate policies and forms but does not use them in any meaningful way.

Whether or not meaningful discipline occurs depends on the organizational culture of a police department. The Chemerinsky report on the LAPD's Board of Inquiry report argued that "every police department has a culture—the unwritten rules, mores, customs, codes, values, and outlooks—that creates the policing environment and style." The culture of the LAPD, it concluded, involves the enforcement of "voluminous rules and regulations, some of them very petty." While petty rules are enforced, serious misconduct is covered up. First, the code of silence results in officers being reluctant to report misconduct by other officers. Second, when they do report misconduct, officers are not only not rewarded for doing so but often punished by the department.[26] And in fact, ninety current and former LAPD officers filed suit against the department for having been demoted or otherwise punished for reporting misconduct by other officers.

Close Supervision

The commanders in the Forty-Second and Forty-Fourth precincts in the New York City police department took a hands-on approach to supervision. They personally spoke to officers who received a high number of citizen complaints, communicating a message that improper behavior toward citizens would not be tolerated. And when some of those officers received more complaints, they were reassigned from patrol to desk duty. A Vera Institute study found that this approach to close supervision helped reduce complaints and improve relations with the community.

Close supervision goes beyond routine performance appraisal. It involves focusing on specific problems and taking extra steps to correct them. Both of the precinct commanders in the Vera study communicated to their officers that reducing citizen complaints was a high priority, both personally spoke at roll call sessions, and both paired younger officers with more experienced veterans. Most important, they spoke personally to officers who received citizen complaints in an effort to both help them correct their behavior and warn them about the consequences if there were more complaints or other problems. Both reassigned or passed over for promotion officers who continued to receive citizen complaints. These actions communicated to all officers in each precinct that they would be held accountable for unacceptable performance. The Vera Institute study found that citizen complaints fell in both precincts while complaints rose for the department as a whole.[27]

Written Policies and Reporting Requirements

Any police officer who uses any kind of force against a citizen "shall make an immediate verbal report" to his or her supervisor and then file a written use of force report. Moreover "any officer who witnesses a use of force [incident] shall advise a supervisor and shall submit a use-of-force report." These steps are recommended by the International Association of Chiefs of Police (IACP) Model Policy on "Reporting Use of Force" adopted in 1997. This recommendation goes even further than most department policies with the requirement that officers *witnessing* other officers use force notify their supervisors.[28]

To hold officers accountable for their actions, contemporary police management relies heavily on written reports. As explained in Chapter 8 on police discretion, this approach is known as administrative rulemaking. The basic strategy is to guide and control officer behavior by specifying proper conduct in writing, requiring officers to complete written reports on specific incidents, and then investigating to determine whether officers complied with departmental policy.

To be effective, the system of reports needs to be comprehensive. The Justice Department's *Principles for Promoting Police Integrity* recommends that "agencies should define 'force' broadly." This should include "any use of a weapon, electronic restraint device, or chemical agent such as pepper spray; and any use of punches, hits, kicks, or other physical efforts to seize, control, or repel a civilian." Although some departments regard the routine use of handcuffs as a use of force, the Justice Department report does not take that approach.[29]

In many departments, reports on use of deadly force are automatically investigated by the internal affairs unit or the office of professional standards. The mandatory report and review process is credited with reducing police use of deadly force between the 1970s and the 1990s and also for controlling high-speed pursuits.[30]

Performance Evaluations

Regular performance evaluations are a standard technique for holding employees accountable. Annual (or more frequent) evaluations by an immediate supervisor are designed to provide feedback to employees by identifying areas of outstanding, acceptable, or inadequate performance. Identifying areas of inadequate performance is intended to provide feedback to the officer so that he or she has an opportunity to improve. Performance evaluations can also be used when considering employees for promotion.[31]

Officer Michael Dowd of the New York City police department's Seventy-Fifth Precinct received excellent performance evaluations. His supervisor wrote that he "has excellent street knowledge; relates well with his peers and is empathetic to the community, [and could] easily become a role model for others to emulate." Unfortunately, Dowd was one of the most corrupt and brutal officers in the entire NYPD, and he was eventually convicted on criminal charges.[32] Dowd's case dramatizes the fact that standard performance evaluations sometimes completely fail to accurately assess an officer's real performance.

Standard performance evaluations in police departments have a number of serious problems. A 1997 report found that "most performance evaluations currently used by police do not reflect the work officers do."[33] They also suffer from a number of technical problems. Evaluation categories and criteria often lack clarity. Many reports, for example, ask supervisors to rate officers' "quality of work," without specifying either the nature of the work or how quality should be measured. Reports also suffer from the "halo" effect, meaning that a high rating in one particular area of performance tends to affect the ratings in other areas. Evaluations are also affected by the central tendency phenomenon. That is, the ratings of all officers tend to cluster around one evaluation level (e.g., everyone receives a rating of 4 on a scale of 1 to 5). Finally, there is a problem of leniency or grade inflation: virtually everyone is rated "above average," and even a rating of "average" is considered to be highly negative.[34]

The Christopher Commission, for example, identified forty-four Los Angeles police officers with extremely high rates of citizen complaints. Yet, many of them received excellent performance evaluations. One officer who had been accused of striking a handcuffed suspect with the butt of a shotgun for no apparent reason was evaluated as having an "easy going manner which he used to his best advantage in the field."[35]

Another failure is that performance evaluations are often not used effectively for purposes of promotion or selection for important assignments. In short, once the evaluations are completed, they sit in a file without being used to make decisions about the quality of different officers and whether they merit an important promotion or assignment.

INTERNAL AFFAIRS UNITS

An internal affairs unit (IAU) or office of professional standards (OPS) is responsible for investigating alleged misconduct by police officers. Investigations are either reactive, in response to a citizen complaint or official report, or proactive, in the sense that the department has some unverified evidence of possible misconduct by an officer. Some police departments conduct "stings" designed to detect potential officer corruption.[36]

An internal affairs unit or office of professional standards is considered an essential element of modern police management. Standard 52.1.2 of the CALEA accreditation standards states that "a written directive specifies that the position responsible for the internal affairs functions has the authority to report directly to the agency's chief executive officer."[37] CALEA explains that "the sensitivity and impact of internal affairs matters on the direction and control of an agency require that the agency's chief executive officer receive all pertinent information directly."

Internal affairs units occupy a difficult position with police departments. Because their responsibility is to investigate other officers, they face hostility from the rank and file. Officers assigned to IAUs are often regarded as "snitches" for the chief. A study of IAUs in a metropolitan area in the Southwest quoted an IAU lieutenant as saying, "It's always been the perception of any internal affairs function . . . that they are a bunch of headhunters, and they're headhunters for the police chief."[38] Officers traditionally do not like to serve in internal affairs units. One officer who requested the assignment said that his friends "thought I was nuts."[39] Because of the reluctance of officers to work in IAUs, many departments assign them against their will.

Officers in many departments believe that IAU investigations are biased, favoring some officers and targeting others. A survey of Baltimore police department officers found that 80 percent believe that discipline within the department is "unfair and not uniform." The perception of inconsistent discipline has led some departments to adopt a formal discipline matrix, specifying the punishment for each offense and taking into consideration the officer's disciplinary record.[40] These discipline matrices are designed to control discretion and are similar to the sentencing guidelines used by the criminal courts in many states. The Baltimore police department has a disciplinary matrix, but the survey of officers found that 63 percent believe that it "does not ensure fair and uniform disciplinary treatment."[41]

The effectiveness of IAUs depends on several factors. Most important is the attitude and the actions of the chief. Virtually all experts on the subject agree that the chief must communicate to all officers that misconduct will not be tolerated, and follow up with meaningful discipline against officers who are in fact found guilty.[42] Internal affairs units also need sufficient resources. This is measured in terms of the number of IAU investigators per sworn officer. Following the Knapp Commission investigation of corruption in the New York City police department in the 1970s, Police Commissioner Patrick V. Murphy increased the ratio of IAU investigators to officers from 1 to 533, to 1 to 64.[43]

Training for internal affairs investigators is an important issue. Many departments provide no special training related to investigating citizen complaints or corruption allegations. The PERF evaluation of the Omaha police department found that "no formal training is provided, [and] all training is on the job."[44] Most IAU officers had prior experience in criminal investigation, however.

The "Code of Silence"

A corrupt New York City police officer explained the "code of silence" in blunt terms. Asked by the Mollen Commission investigating corruption if he was ever afraid that one of his fellow officers might turn him in, he answered, "Never." "Why not?" commission investigators asked. "Because it was the Blue Wall of Silence. Cops don't tell on cops." Anyone who might report his corrupt activities would "be labeled as a rat."[45]

The code of silence is a major part of the organizational culture of policing. Many experts regard the code as the major obstacle to police accountability. The code of silence (also known as the "blue curtain") is defined as the unwillingness of police officers to report misconduct by other officers. Westley identified the code of silence in his pioneering study of the police subculture.[46] The Christopher Commission found that the code of silence was a major factor in protecting abuse of force by Los Angeles police officers.[47] A national survey of police officers by the Police Foundation in the 1990s found that slightly more than half (52.4 percent) agreed that "it is not unusual for a police officer to turn a blind eye to improper police conduct by other officers."[48]

The informal organizational culture of a police department has a major impact on accountability. A report on the Baltimore police department defined organizational culture as "the collection of embraced values, activities, rules, and standards that enable it to achieve its core identity." Focus groups with 250 officers found that the positive "cultural assets" of the department included professionalism, bravery, and commitment. However, the culture also included bitterness and cynicism on the part of officers, distrust of others in the organization, and low morale. As a result, the "operating culture" of the department included "individual survival, group loyalty, frustration and resentment."[49]

There have been few efforts to break the code of silence and to punish officers for giving false testimony in investigations of officer misconduct. The New York City Civilian

Complaint Review Board reported instances of officers lying to the New York City police department, but the department declined to act on these reports.[50]

Early Warning Systems

Two officers in the Boston police department accumulated twenty-four citizen complaints each between 1981 and 1990. For one of the officers, three of the complaints were sustained; none of the twenty-four complaints were sustained against the other officer. An investigation by the *Boston Globe* found that a very small number of officers accounted for a large percentage of all citizen complaints: 11 percent of the officers received 62 percent of all the complaints.[51]

The pattern of complaints found in the Boston police department appears to exist in almost every department. In response to this phenomenon, departments have developed early warning (EW) systems as a new mechanism of police accountability. EW systems are management information systems that systematically compile and analyze data on problematic police officer behavior: citizen complaints, police officer use of force reports, officers being named in suits against the department, along with other indicators. The data are then analyzed to identify those officers who seem to have recurring performance problems. Officers who are identified are then given counseling or training designed to improve their performance. (See Figure 11–1.) The U.S. Civil Rights Commission recommended EW systems in 1981, as did a 2001 Justice Department report on *Principles for Promoting Police Integrity.*[52]

The empirical basis of EW systems is the evidence that in nearly every police department a small group of officers receive a disproportionate share of all citizen complaints. They are referred to as "problem prone" officers. The Christopher Commission identified forty-four problem officers in the Los Angeles police department. They averaged 7.6 complaints for excessive force or improper tactics, compared with only 0.6 for all other officers; while in Kansas City, 2 percent of the officers were responsible for 50 percent of all citizen complaints.[53]

FIGURE 11–1   EARLY WARNING SYSTEM COMPONENTS

Selection Criteria
  Citizen complaints
  Use of force reports
  Involvement in civil litigation
  Other indicators of performance problems
Intervention
  Counseling
  Training
  Reassignment
Postintervention Monitoring
  Informal performance monitoring
  Formal performance monitoring

EW systems vary in terms of their program components. In terms of selection criteria, some systems use only citizen complaints to identify potential problem officers. Others, however, use a broad range of indicators: citizen complaints, use of force reports, resisting arrest charges filed by officers, officer involvement in civil litigation, and so on. The intervention also varies. In most departments, officers are given informal counseling by their immediate supervisor, usually a sergeant. In New Orleans, however, the intervention consists of a 4-day training class. With respect to postintervention monitoring, New Orleans requires supervisors to observe EW officers under their command and to file biweekly performance evaluations for a period of 6 months. Other EW systems rely on informal postintervention monitoring by supervisors.[54]

A national evaluation of EW systems found that they are effective in reducing citizen complaints, use of force, and other problematic behavior. Officers subject to intervention by the EW systems in three police departments generally received an average of only one-third as many complaints per year after intervention compared with beforehand. The evaluation also found that EW systems are extremely complex to administrate and require a considerable amount of continuing management attention if they are to be effective.[55]

ACCREDITATION

Accreditation is a process of professional self-regulation, and it is used in virtually all professions: law, medicine, education, and others. An accreditation process for law enforcement was created in 1979. A coalition of the leading professional associations created the Commission on Accreditation for Law Enforcement Agencies (CALEA). The group originally included representatives from the International Association of Chiefs of Police (IACP), the National Sheriffs' Association (NSA), the National Organization of Black Law Enforcement Executives (NOBLE), and the Police Executive Research Forum (PERF). CALEA published its first set of *Standards for Law Enforcement Agencies* in 1983 and accredited the first police departments in 1984. By mid-2000, over 500 agencies had been accredited.[56]

CALEA establishes minimum standards for all law enforcement agencies. Some standards are mandatory; others are recommended but optional. Some standards are mandatory for large agencies, but not for small ones. The third edition of the *Standards,* published in 1994, includes 436 specific standards. Accredited departments are required, for example, to have a written policy on the use of force and the use of deadly force, a system of written directives for all rules and regulations, an affirmative action plan, a system for handling citizen complaints, and so on.[57]

Advocates of accreditation argue that it is an essential aspect of any occupation that aspires to professional status. Self-governance is preferable to regulation and control by external groups because members of the profession know the field best.[58]

Accreditation has serious limits, however. First, it is a voluntary process. Police departments suffer no penalty for not being accredited. This is unlike the field of education, where lack of accreditation means that students' credentials may not be accepted by other institutions, as well as possible ineligibility for federal education funds. Second, some critics argue that accreditation standards set minimum conditions but do not define the optimum standards of excellence. That is, they define the "floor" but not the "ceiling." Third, some critics argue that the accreditation standards address purely formal aspects of administration, without addressing specific content, or what is called the "standard of care" in the medical field.[59] Fourth, a number of law enforcement officials believe that the accreditation process is too expensive and time-consuming.

EXTERNAL MECHANISMS OF ACCOUNTABILITY

The Political Process

As explained at the beginning of this chapter, mayors have the right to choose their police chiefs. On the one hand, this represents a direct way of making the police accountable to the public. On the other hand, when mayors fire police chiefs, it often represents political interference. To limit political interference, some jurisdictions limit the ability of the mayor to fire the police chief. The chief in Minneapolis serves under a 3-year contract. The chief of the Los Angeles police department has a 5-year contract.

Citizens control the police and other government agencies through the political process.[60] The executive branch of government—elected mayors, appointed city managers, governors, presidents—exercises control primarily by appointing police chiefs, directors of state police, and the U.S. attorney general. The legislative branch—city

---

SIDEBAR 11–1   ACCOUNTABILITY AND POLICE USE OF FORCE: THE NEED FOR BETTER DATA

One of the major obstacles to greater accountability regarding police use of force is the lack of reliable, systematic data. The major research needs include:

- **Establishing Clear Definitions of Both Force and Excessive Force.** What actions by a police officer constitute the use of force? Some departments include a "control of person" action, including the use of handcuffs in a routine arrest. What constitutes *excessive* force?
- **Improving the Measurement of the Use of Force.** The basic source of data on police use of force is official departmental records. How reliable are those records? Are we confident that officers complete reports in every instance where they are required to? And are we confident that the reports accurately reflect what really happened?
- **Identifying Variations and Correlates in the Use of Force.** In what kinds of situations are police officers most likely to use force? Are there any officer characteristics that correlate with frequent uses of force?
- **Evaluating Use of Force Control Strategies.** Are there any management strategies that have proved to be effective in controlling officer use of force? Are some strategies more effective than others?

Source: Kenneth Adams, "A Research Agenda on Police Use of Force," in Bureau of Justice Statistics, *Use of Force by Police: Overview of National and Local Data* (Washington, DC: Government Printing Office, 1999), pp. 61–73.

councils, county boards of commissioners, state legislators, the Congress—exercises control through budgets. The judicial branch serves as a check and balance on both the executive and legislative branches, ensuring compliance with the law.

A few cities have special commissions to govern their police departments. In the nineteenth century this approach was very common (see Chapter 2).[61] Only a few police commissions survive today, however. The Los Angeles Police Commission, for example, consists of five members, appointed by the mayor, and has full responsibility for running the Los Angeles police department.[62] Detroit and San Francisco also have police commissions.[63]

THE COURTS

The Supreme Court and the Police

In one of the most famous cases ever decided by the Supreme Court, Cleveland police officers barged into Dolree Mapp's house in 1957 waving what they said was a search warrant. They had previously been to the house looking for a suspect they thought was hiding there. When they could not find the suspect, they arrested Ms. Mapp for possessing some obscene literature she had in the house. Mapp was convicted, but appealed and eventually took her case to the Supreme Court. No copy of the alleged search warrant was ever found, either in police files or in any court, and there was strong suspicion that the police did not actually have a warrant. The U.S. Supreme Court overturned Mapp's conviction.

The *Mapp v. Ohio* (1961) decision is still one of the most controversial in the history of the Supreme Court.[64] The Court ruled that the evidence against Dolree Mapp had been obtained illegally, violating her Fourth Amendment right to protection against "unreasonable searches and seizures." The Court imposed the exclusionary rule, which holds that "all evidence obtained by searches and seizures in violation of the Constitution is, by that same authority, inadmissible in a state court." The Court had previously applied the exclusionary rule to federal criminal proceedings in 1914 (*Weeks v. United States*), while a number of state supreme courts had applied it to state proceedings, including California in 1955 (*People v. Cahan*). The significant aspect of *Mapp* was that the Supreme Court applied the exclusionary rule to state and local police through the Fourteenth Amendment, which holds that no state may deprive one of its citizens due process of law. Thus, the Court set national standards for all police agencies and assumed the role of policing local police.[65]

The judicial branch of government is an important but indirect part of the political process. Although federal judges are appointed by the president and confirmed by the Senate, thereby ensuring some political control, judicial independence protects them against direct political influence once they are appointed. Courts at all levels of government play some role in holding the police accountable. At bail settings, preliminary hearings, and trials, local court judges rule on the admissibility of evidence and other issues that impact on police work.[66] The most important court with respect to police accountability is the U.S. Supreme Court. In the 1960s the Supreme Court issued a series of rulings that imposed new standards for police conduct.

In another extremely controversial case, *Miranda v. Arizona* (1966),[67] the Supreme Court ruled that to guarantee the Fifth Amendment right to protection against self-incrimination, the police must advise a suspect of his or her rights. The resulting *Miranda* warning includes the right to remain silent, the right to have an attorney, and the right to have a court-appointed attorney if the suspect cannot afford one. After reviewing police investigation manuals, the Court found that the police used techniques that were coercive and likely to induce people to waive their protection against self-incrimination. It concluded that the atmosphere inside the police station was inherently coercive. Chief Justice Earl Warren ruled that "when an individual is taken into custody or otherwise deprived of his freedom by the authorities in any significant way and is subjected to questioning, the privilege against self-incrimination is jeopardized." The *Miranda* decision incorporated both the Fifth Amendment protection against self-incrimination and the Sixth Amendment right to an attorney with the due process clause of the Fourteenth Amendment.

The Impact of Supreme Court Decisions

Law professor Paul Cassell was almost single-handedly responsible for bringing a case before the Supreme Court in 2000, asking it to overturn the original *Miranda* decision. Cassell's research estimated that *Miranda* has produced serious costs to society's ability to fight crime. Cassell did not succeed, however. In the *U.S. v. Dickerson* (2000) decision the Supreme Court rejected his argument and reaffirmed the *Miranda* warning in a 7 to 2 decision.[68]

Cassell's efforts were the latest in a long debate over the impact of the *Miranda* decision. One reason why he did not succeed may have been his own data. He estimated that *Miranda* results in a net loss of convictions in only 3.8 percent of all criminal cases. Many observers did not find this to be a significant impact. And, in fact, 84 percent of the suspects in his study voluntarily waived their *Miranda* rights.[69] Richard Leo, meanwhile, observed interrogations in one West Coast police department (and observed videotapes of interrogations in others) and found that 78 percent of the suspects waived their *Miranda* rights and talked to the police. He also found that in 30 percent of the cases the police lied to the suspect by falsely claiming they had a confession from a partner or some other incriminating evidence.[70] In short, the specific intent of *Miranda* is frequently undermined by both police and suspects.

Milner studied four Wisconsin police departments and found considerable variation in the impact of the *Miranda* decision. Officers in the most professional of the four departments he studied were less hostile to the decision than in the other three less professional departments. The officers in all four departments indicated a high degree of knowledge of the *Miranda* requirements, and all indicated that changes had been made as a result of the decision. These changes included using new methods to gather evidence and improved education and training. The majority of officers in all departments indicated that their jobs had been changed by the *Miranda* requirements.[71]

Miranda and other Supreme Court decisions on police practices touched off a major political and legal controversy. The police argued that they were being "handcuffed" in their effort to control crime.[72] This argument stimulated much research on the impact of Supreme Court decisions on the police.

Studies have found that the exclusionary rule does not limit the crime-fighting capacity of the police.[73] The rule is largely confined to drug, gambling, and weapons cases that raise issues of how the police obtained the evidence. The rule has little impact on murder, robbery, rape, or burglary cases. Reviewing criminal cases in Boston, Sheldon Krantz found that "very few motions to suppress evidence are raised, and very few of these are granted."[74] Motions to suppress evidence were raised in only 48 of 512 district court cases (or 9.4 percent), and only 10 of those 48 motions were granted. Thus, the defendant was successful in only 20.8 percent of the motions and 1.9 percent of all cases. A General Accounting Office (GAO) study found that defense attorneys filed motions to suppress evidence in only 11 percent of 2,804 cases. Less than 20 percent of those motions were successful, producing an overall success rate of 2.2 percent.[75]

Supporters of the Supreme Court's decisions on the police argue that they had three positive effects. First, the Court defined basic principles of due process. Second, decisions such as *Mapp* and *Miranda* created penalties for police misconduct (excluding the evidence or the confession). This served as a basic mechanism of accountability. Third, the decisions stimulated police reform, including improvements in recruitment, training, and supervision.[76]

Orfield's interviews with Chicago narcotics officers found several positive effects of the exclusionary rule. The *Mapp* decision led to better training of officers, including closer supervision of warrants by prosecutors. Detectives were also more likely to use warrants than to conduct impulsive warrantless searches. Many officers indicated that the exclusionary rule was a good thing that helped to maintain high standards of professionalism.[77]

The Supreme Court decisions also increased public awareness about the details of police procedures. This knowledge, and the consequent tendency to demand one's rights, serves as a constraint on the police, preventing many abuses. Increased awareness of individual rights has also led to higher public expectations about police performance. The Court decisions defined an ideal against which actual performance is measured. By raising public expectations, the decisions generated pressure for continued police reform.

At the same time, there are significant limitations on the role of the Court as a mechanism of accountability. First, the Court cannot supervise day-to-day police operations. It cannot ensure that individual police officers are in fact complying with its decisions.[78] An individual has a remedy only if he or she is arrested and convicted. Second, most police work does not involve an arrest and, therefore, never comes before a court.[79] Third, the police may or may not be informed about current court decisions. Wasby found that small-town police in Massachusetts and Illinois did not receive information of Court decisions in a systematic fashion in the 1970s.[80] Fourth, some critics argue that Court-imposed rules only encourage evasion or lying by police officers. Finally, the exercise of rights may become an empty formality, with little real meaning. Both Cassell and Leo, for example, found that most suspects waive their right to silence and agree to be interrogated by the police.

Civil Suits against the Police

The City of Detroit paid out more than $124 million in lawsuits involving police misconduct in the 1990s, an average of almost $10 million a year. Despite these huge costs, almost nothing was done to reduce misconduct and reduce the huge cost to taxpayers. Finally, in late 2000, the U.S. Justice Department stepped in and announced that it was beginning an investigation of civil rights violations by the Detroit police.[81]

People who are the victims of police abuse can sue for civil damages. A person may sue in federal court under state or federal law. An 1871 federal law (now 42 U.S.C. 1983) provides that a person can sue for damages if he or she has been deprived of any rights by an official acting "under color of law" (that is, in an official capacity). Lawsuits under this law are often referred to as "1983 actions."[82]

The number of successful damage suits against the police has risen dramatically in recent years. The total damages paid by the City of Los Angeles for police-related cases increased from $7,000 in 1965 to $1.5 million in 1975 and to $8 million in 1990.[83] The City of Albuquerque paid an average of $1 to $2 million a year in police-related damage suits in the mid-1990s, despite having a department of only about 900 sworn officers.[84]

The primary purpose of a damage suit is to compensate the victim or victims of police misconduct for the harm done. Lawsuits, however, are expensive, time-consuming, difficult to win, and offer a potential remedy only in cases of extreme harm. The potential damage awards in cases of minor misconduct do not make litigation worthwhile. A report on civil litigation on police misconduct found that, even among those cases where the plaintiff won, the average award was only 10 percent of the initial claim. The median award, in fact, was only $8,000.[85]

Some research suggests that the strategy of suing police departments to achieve general reforms was not successful. Edward Littlejohn's study of police misconduct litigation in Detroit through the 1970s found that suits produced few reforms.[86] A study of 149 police misconduct suits filed in Connecticut between 1970 and 1977 found that they had little apparent effect on the police. The plaintiffs rarely won, because juries tended to be sympathetic to the police, and neither the individual officers nor the department directly bore the financial cost of losing.[87]

McCoy argues that rising damage awards involving police abuse provoked an insurance crisis in many cities by the late 1970s and forced them to take steps to curb misconduct.[88] McCoy suggests that city attorneys need to provide feedback to the police department not just in the few cases where large damages are awarded but in all cases that are filed.[89] The director of the Institute for Liability Management argues that an effective risk management program must include training for all officers, ensuring that officers have copies of department policies, regular training for supervisors, an atmosphere of accountability in the department, constant monitoring of changes in relevant laws, and good legal advice.[90]

The rising cost of civil suits over officer misconduct has prompted some cities and counties to take proactive steps to reduce misconduct. The Los Angeles County Board of Supervisors hired an attorney as special counsel to the Los Angeles sheriff's department for the specific purpose of investigating problems in the department, recommending reforms, and reducing the costs of misconduct litigation.[91] The special counsel represents one form of citizen oversight (see pp. 371–374). Special Counsel Merrick

Bobb has investigated virtually every aspect of the department: recruitment, training, and assignment of officers; the use of deadly force and canines; sexual harassment in the workplace; and other issues. The result has been improvements in several areas. The current docket of excessive force lawsuits against the LASD fell from an average of 300 in fiscal years 1992–1993 and 1993–1994 to about 77 in fiscal years 1997–1998 and 1998–1999. The number of "bites" by LASD canines fell from an average of more than 50 in 1991 and 1992 to an average of only 11 in 1998 and 1999.[92]

"Pattern or Practice" Suits

A 1997 consent decree against the Pittsburgh police department ordered sweeping changes in the management and accountability procedures in the department. The Pittsburgh police were ordered to begin keeping systematic data on all officer uses of force,

SIDEBAR 11–2 CONTROLLING THE CANINE UNIT IN THE LOS ANGELES SHERIFF'S DEPARTMENT

The Los Angeles sheriff's department had a serious problem with its canine unit (the Canine Services Detail) in the early 1990s. The unit's dogs were biting a large number of people, and even worse, a very high percentage of the people bitten were African American or Latino. In 1991, the LASD deployed canines 1,228 times. Citizens were encountered 213 times, and 58 people were bitten. This represented a "bite ratio" of 27 percent. Of the 58 people bitten, 23 were African American and 24 were Latino. In short, 81 percent of those bitten were people of color.

Merrick Bobb, the special counsel to the LASD, investigated the problem and made recommendations for better training for the unit's officers and control of the dogs. The results were dramatic. In 1999 only 15 people were bitten (a reduction of almost 75 percent!), and the "bite ratio" was down to 17 percent. In short, the LASD was using the Canine Services Detail less frequently and controlling the dogs better. And, it should be noted, crime fell dramatically in the Los Angeles area during this time period, as it did in most of the country. So, the less frequent use of the canine unit did not mean less effective crime control.

The situation was not entirely free of problems by 1999, however. Of the 15 people bitten that year, all were people of color: 7 African American and 8 Latino. Nonetheless, the total number of people of color bitten was down by 68 percent (15 versus 47).

The special counsel is the form of citizen oversight for the Los Angeles County sheriff's department. Merrick Bobb has the authority to investigate any problem and to make recommendations for change. His twice-a-year reports, moreover, inform the public about the LASD, its problems, and what is being done about them. The special counsel represents one of the most effective forms of external accountability in the country.

Sources: Special Counsel to the Los Angeles Sheriff's Department, 12th Semiannual Report (Los Angeles: The Special Counsel, June 2000), pp. 39–43; Samuel Walker, *Police Accountability: The Role of Citizen Oversight* (Belmont, CA: Wadsworth, 2001).

to create an early warning system, and to require officers to record the race and ethnicity of all persons they stopped for questioning, including pedestrians and motor vehicle drivers.[93] The consent decree was a result of a suit brought by the Civil Rights Division of the U.S. Department of Justice. Three years later, the Justice Department negotiated a similar consent decree with the City of Los Angeles as a result of the Rampart scandal in the Los Angeles police department.

The Justice Department suits were brought under a section of the 1994 Violent Crime Control Act that authorizes the Justice Department to bring civil suits against police departments where there is a "pattern or practice" of abuse of citizens' rights. In addition to Pittsburgh and Los Angeles, the Justice Department has sued and reached consent decrees with the New Jersey State Police over racial profiling and the Steubenville, Ohio, police over excessive force. In each of these cases, the federal courts have appointed a monitor to ensure compliance with the consent decree.[94]

The "pattern or practice" section of the 1994 law became a powerful tool for achieving police accountability. Instead of the traditional pattern of private lawsuits that focus on individual acts of misconduct, the federal law addresses general patterns. And instead of monetary damages for individual plaintiffs, successful suits result in court-ordered reforms of police management practices. In this respect, they look to the future and seek to prevent misconduct in the years ahead.[95]

Injunctions

In the case of police practices that systematically violate citizen rights, civil rights groups have sought injunctions against the police to stop the alleged practice.[96] If, for example, police officers are systematically stopping, questioning, and frisking all black males in a community—without regard for individualized suspicion—members of that group can seek an injunction ordering the practice stopped. For the most part, however, injunctions have not been an effective remedy for police misconduct.[97] In an important case involving the Philadelphia police department (*Rizzo v. Goode,* 1976), the U.S. Supreme Court held that the plaintiffs had failed to prove that the police chief and other city officials were directly responsible for the alleged police misconduct and that the plaintiffs themselves were likely to be the targets of this misconduct in the future.[98]

Criminal Prosecution

Four New York City police officers were prosecuted for the fatal shooting of Amadou Diallo in early 1999. The shooting and the trial that followed were among the most controversial events in the city, sharply dividing people along racial and ethnic lines. Diallo, a Haitian immigrant, was unarmed and shot while standing in the doorway of his apartment. Many civil rights activists saw the shooting as an example of the police targeting racial minorities, and they demanded that the officers be convicted. At the end of the trial, however, the four officers were acquitted. The Diallo case dramatizes the role of criminal prosecution as a mechanism of police accountability.[99]

Police officers who violate the law can be prosecuted as criminals. Successful criminal prosecution of a police officer is extremely difficult, however. First, local prosecutors routinely work closely with the police and are reluctant to bring criminal charges against them. The Criminal Division of the U.S. Justice Department is extremely small and has responsibility for many other types of criminal activity.[100] Second, in the case of allegations of police use of excessive force, it is often difficult to prove that the force was in fact excessive and that the officer had criminal intent. The officer can always claim that his or her actions were a legitimate exercise of police powers under the circumstances. In such cases, it is important to distinguish between *improper* police action, which can be subject to internal departmental discipline, and *illegal* action, where the prosecution must prove criminal intent.[101] The successful conviction on federal charges of three Los Angeles police officers involved in the Rodney King beating was a relatively rare exception.[102] Convictions are much easier to obtain in corruption cases where there is less ambiguity about the facts than in use of force cases. Third, convictions are difficult to obtain because, as a Vera Institute study found, juries are often sympathetic to police officers and "suspicious of victims" [of police abuse].[103]

Criminal prosecution by itself appears to have limited deterrent effect in departments where other effective controls do not exist. A number of New York City police officers were prosecuted and convicted in the scandals of the 1970s and 1980s, and yet the Mollen Commission found serious criminal law violations in the 1990s. Evidently, the officers were not deterred by the prosecutions and convictions in the previous years.

Summary

In a review of criminal prosecution and civil litigation as remedies for police misconduct, Mary M. Cheh concludes that the problems of excessive force "cannot be solved by criminal and civil remedies." They have *some* role to play, and the federal government can help state and local leaders deal with problems, but they cannot be the principal mechanisms of accountability.[104] Federal suits against a "pattern or practice" of abuse are a potential remedy for the worst police departments, where accountability measures have clearly failed. But for police departments in general, such litigation is not likely to be a primary accountability measure. In short, accountability requires a "mix" of internal and external measures as depicted in Figure 11–3.

CITIZEN OVERSIGHT OF THE POLICE

In 1998 the Los Angeles police department reported ten times as many complaints as in 1997: 8,000 as opposed to 800. The performance of LAPD officers did not suddenly deteriorate tenfold in 1 year. The increase in the number of complaints was the result of changes in how the LAPD receives and reports citizen complaints. Prior to 1998, most complaints were not forwarded from precinct stations to a centralized internal affairs unit. Some complaints were not even officially recorded at the precinct level. As a result, the department did not know exactly how many citizen complaints it received every year.[105]

The problems with the LAPD citizen complaint data are only one example of the criticism by civil rights groups that police departments fail to investigate citizen complaints thoroughly or fairly. As an alternative, civil rights groups have demanded citizen oversight (also called external review or civilian review) of the police. Citizen oversight has grown tremendously in the last 20 years. In almost all big cities there is now some form of oversight agency. Citizen oversight takes many different forms, and agencies engage in a number of different activities.

Forms of Citizen Oversight

Citizen oversight is designed to provide some independent citizen input into the complaint process. Citizen oversight takes many different forms, and almost no two agencies are alike. There are four basic models of citizen oversight, defined according to the nature and extent of the citizen input into the complaint process.[106] (See Figure 11–2.)

In Class I systems, a separate agency investigates citizen complaints and makes a recommendation about disposition to the police chief. Members of these boards are appointed community representatives. The board employs full-time professional staff to investigate complaints. The Minneapolis Civilian Review Authority (CRA) and the San Francisco Office of Citizen Complaints (OCC) are examples of Class I systems.

In Class II systems, complaints are investigated by internal affairs, but the civilian review agency examines the complaint files and makes recommendations regarding discipline. The Kansas City Office of Citizen Complaints (OCC) is an example of a Class II system.

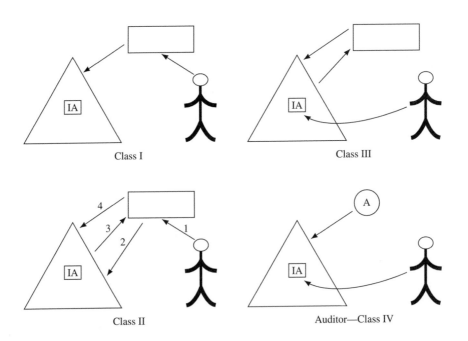

FIGURE 11–2
FOUR MODELS OF CITIZEN OVERSIGHT

Source: Samuel Walker, *Police Accountability: The Role of Citizen Oversight* (Belmont, CA: Wadsworth, 2001), p. 61.

In Class III systems, the police department is responsible for investigating and disposing of citizen complaints. If a complainant is not satisfied with the result, he or she may appeal to the citizen review procedure.

Class IV systems are referred to as auditor systems. The police department retains full responsibility for handling citizen complaints. An independent agency, however, has the authority to audit or monitor the performance of the department's internal affairs unit. The old Portland Police Internal Investigations Auditing Committee (PIIAC) and the San Jose Independent Police Auditor (IPA) are examples of Class IV systems.

The Roles of Citizen Oversight

Citizen oversight agencies play, or potentially can play, several different roles. One role is to provide an *independent review of citizen complaints.* The underlying assumption is that investigators who are not sworn officers will be independent of the police subculture and therefore conduct investigations that are more fair, independent, and unbiased than investigations conducted by internal affairs units. In addition, advocates of citizen review argue that an independent complaint procedure will be perceived as independent and therefore create greater public confidence in the complaint process.

Citizen oversight agencies also play a *monitoring role:* monitoring both the complaint process and general police department policies and practices. Many oversight agencies, for example, engage in active community outreach programs, holding meetings with community groups to explain the complaint process and hear citizen concerns about police problems. Outreach is particularly important with regard to recent immigrant groups who do not understand American policing or the complaint process, as well as for groups for whom English is not the primary language. The Minneapolis Civilian Review Authority, for example, publishes brochures explaining the complaint process in seven languages other than English.

Citizen review agencies also engage in policy review: using individual citizen complaints to identify underlying police problems and then recommend changes in police department policies. The San Francisco OCC, for example, developed a new police department policy for handling crowds and demonstrations and, in 1999 alone, made fourteen separate policy recommendations. One involved providing translators for people who do not speak English, and another involved access to necessary medication for suspects being booked or detained.[107] Monitoring is the primary function of Class IV auditor forms of citizen oversight. The San Jose Independent Police Auditor made forty separate policy recommendations between 1993 and 1999, and had thirty-eight of them adopted by the police department.

Another monitoring activity involves auditing the quality of complaint investigations. In many police departments, interviews with citizen complainants and police officers are tape-recorded. Auditors then review these recordings for the purpose of identifying potential bias (either against the complainant or in favor of the officer) or inadequate investigations.

Merrick Bobb, special counsel to the Los Angeles County sheriff's department, operates one of the most active and successful forms of citizen oversight of the police. Bobb was originally hired to reduce the cost of lawsuits against the sheriff's department. But he takes a very broad view of his monitoring role and examines almost every aspect of the department's operations. His semiannual reports include investigations of the use of force by deputies, the canine unit, sexual harassment within the department, the quality of training, and assignment and promotion patterns, along with many other issues. The reports provide a revealing "window" into the department, ending the secrecy that has traditionally surrounded law enforcement agencies. Bobb's successes include reducing the cost of lawsuits, the use of deadly force, and bites of citizens by the canine unit.

Citizen Review: Pro and Con

Opponents of citizen review argue that (1) it intrudes on the professional independence of the police, (2) people who are not police officers are not qualified to review police operations, (3) it is expensive and unnecessarily duplicates the work of internal affairs, and (4) internal affairs units sustain more complaints against police officers.[108]

Advocates of citizen review, on the other hand, argue that it serves to open up police departments, ending the historic isolation from the public. They cite evidence that the number of citizen complaints is higher in cities with some form of external review, suggesting that it enhances public confidence in the complaint process.[109] Hudson's research on Philadelphia found that internal affairs sustained a higher percentage of complaints primarily because it generally handled violations of departmental rules, which are inherently easier to sustain than citizen complaints about use of force.[110]

There have been few evaluations of citizen review procedures. Kerstetter found that public confidence in the complaint process did improve with the existence of a citizen review procedure.[111] A Vera Institute study of the New York City Civilian Review Board (CCRB) found that both complainants and police officers thought it was biased against them.[112] The New York CCRB is regularly criticized by the New York Civil Liberties Union, the leading advocate of citizen review.[113] An evaluation of the citizen review procedure in Albuquerque, New Mexico, found that it failed to use all of the powers that it possessed.[114]

In short, some forms of citizen review appear to be relatively more effective than others. Effectiveness depends upon several factors, including the agency's definition of its role, its resources, the quality of its staff, and the degree of political support it receives from the community.

Blue-Ribbon Commissions

In a forceful statement, the 1931 Wickersham Commission concluded that "the third degree—the inflicting of pain, physical or mental, to extract confessions or statements—is widespread throughout the country."[115] The Wickersham report on illegal use of force by police was unprecedented, and it sparked the first serious national effort to control police misconduct. Exactly 60 years later, the Christopher Commission report on use of force in the Los Angeles police department following the Rodney King incident received almost as much national attention.[116]

The Wickersham Commission and the Christopher Commission are two of the most famous examples of special blue-ribbon commissions in police history (see Chapter 2).[117] Blue-ribbon commissions are a form of external accountability and serve several important functions. First, national commissions bring together the leading experts in the field and define minimum standards that can then be used to seek improvements in local departments. Second, as the President's Crime Commission (1965–1967) did, commissions can sponsor original research and generate new knowledge about policing. Third, blue-ribbon commissions are usually comprehensive in scope, addressing the full range of police issues, and not just a single problem. The major weakness of blue-ribbon commissions is that their recommendations are only advisory and are often ignored by local officials if they choose to do so.[118]

The News Media

New York Times reporter David Burnham is almost single-handedly responsible for exposing one of the biggest corruption scandals in the New York City police department. The scandal that is closely identified with officer Frank Serpico, who testified against corrupt officers, was first exposed by Burnham in a front-page *Times* story on April 25, 1970. Many people in the department and city government had known about the pattern of corruption, but no one did anything. Following Burnham's revelations they were forced to act. The mayor appointed the Knapp Commission to investigate, a number of officers were convicted of corrupt acts, and Patrick V. Murphy was brought in as police commissioner to clean up the department.[119]

The news media play an important role in police accountability.[120] On a day-to-day basis, the media report on what the police are doing. This informs the public and, hopefully, helps them to make intelligent political choices related to policing. The media have also been important in exposing serious police problems, as they did with the New York City police scandal in 1970.

At the same time, the news media often contribute to police problems. First, they tend to emphasize sensational stories, especially violent crimes or major police misconduct. They do not provide good coverage of routine police activities because these events are not dramatic. Second, the media present a distorted picture of police work by focusing on crime and ignoring the non-crime-related aspects of police work. Third, the media tend to emphasize the negative aspects of policing. They will give considerable coverage to a questionable shooting by a police officer, for example, but not cover the fact that there are long periods with no shootings. One of the unwritten rules of the news media is that good news is not news.

Public Interest Groups

The local chapter of the American Civil Liberties Union (ACLU) in Oakland, California, had volunteers systematically call different units of the Oakland police department in 1996 and ask about how to file a citizen complaint. The callers found that few Oakland officers handling their calls gave out correct information. Many, apparently, were simply uninformed about the department's complaint process. Some others may have deliberately not given out the right information.[121] The ACLU report blasting the Oakland police department for this failure was only one in a long series of investigations and reports on police misconduct by that organization.

The ACLU is a private, nonprofit public interest organization. Private groups play an important role in police accountability. For the most part, they have been involved in attacking police misconduct. The National Association for the Advancement of Colored People (NAACP) has a long record of fighting police use of excessive force against African Americans.[122] The ACLU was responsible for some of the most important Supreme Court cases involving the police. ACLU briefs were the basis for the Court's decisions in the landmark *Mapp* and *Miranda* cases, for example.[123] The ACLU has been the leading advocate of citizen review of the police in New York City, Los Angeles, and many other cities. At the same time, the ACLU has defended the rights of police officers in cases involving, for example, grooming standards and department investigations of alleged police misconduct. The ACLU published a handbook on *The Rights of Police Officers.*[124]

A MIXED APPROACH TO POLICE ACCOUNTABILITY

No single mechanism is the key to achieving police accountability. Each of the different mechanisms has its strengths and weaknesses. Internal mechanisms are both strong, because they are internal and the officials involved are close to the situation, and weak, because these same officials are too close to the officers they have to monitor. By the same token, external mechanisms are strong, because they are independent of the police, but weak, because they are remote from the activities they attempt to monitor.

The current approach represents a mix of internal and external mechanisms. (See Figure 11–3.) In important respects, this reflects the concept of checks and balances, which is one of the fundamental principles of American democracy. Elected officials have significant control over police departments, but not total control. Police administrators have a great deal of autonomy, but not complete autonomy. The courts have some influence over policing, but only in limited areas. Citizens have some input, but not total control over the police.

Viewed from a historical perspective, there has been a shift in the mix of internal and external forms of accountability. Direct political interference in policing declined as a result of the professionalization movement (see Chapter 2). Some other forms of external accountability—particularly the courts and citizen review — have grown in recent decades. At the same time, some forms of internal accountability have also grown, with the development of better mechanisms for the control of misconduct and the supervision of routine police work.

SUMMARY

Holding the police accountable to the public for what they do and how they do it is an essential feature of a democratic society. In the past, few meaningful accountability mechanisms existed. The result was widespread inefficiency, abuse of citizens, and

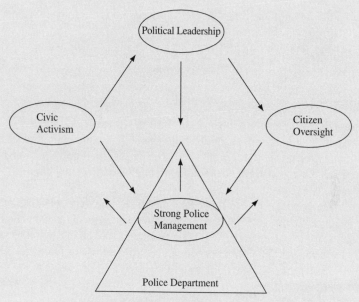

FIGURE 11–3
A MIXED APPROACH TO POLICE ACCOUNTABILITY

Source: Samuel Walker

corruption. A variety of accountability mechanisms have developed in recent years. They represent a mix of internal and external approaches.

CASE STUDY: MIAMI–DADE POLICE DEPARTMENT, EARLY IDENTIFICATION SYSTEM (EXCERPT)

III. EMPLOYEE PROFILE SYSTEM: Instituted and operated by PCB, the system establishes a data collection source profiling departmental employees to identify patterns of stress-induced or performance problems.

   A. Profile Criteria: Profiles will document specified criteria for assessment:
   1. Complaints.
   2. Use of force incidents.
   3. Commendations.
   4. Correctional action.
   5. Promotional status change.

   B. Report Assessment: Profile reports will be reviewed by immediate supervisors as deemed necessary. The concerned commander or designee will review profile reports annually, in conjunction with other criteria, to identify problems.

   C. Action Alternatives: Based on profile reports and relevant data, the following will result:
   1. Referral to the Psychological Services Program for counseling or referral assistance.

2. Participation in the Stress Abatement Program for training assistance.

3. Correctional action.

4. Assessment that no problem exists, terminating further action.

Source: Miami–Dade Police Department, *Early Identification System* (1992).

FOR DISCUSSION

The Miami–Dade Employee Identification System represents its version of an early warning system. As the materials supplied indicate, officers are identified on the basis of citizen complaints, use of force incidents (using officer reports), commendations they have received, any correctional action already taken, and any change in promotional status.

Discuss these criteria. Do you think they are likely to reduce misconduct and improve the quality of police performance? Or do you think they are likely to deter officers from doing important police work? Will police officers avoid taking action because they are afraid of getting a complaint or becoming involved in a use of force incident?

INTERNET EXERCISES

Exercise 1 Several law enforcement agencies have been sued for a "pattern or practice" of abusing the rights of citizens. Some of these suits have resulted in consent decrees where the department agrees to make a series of reforms related to accountability.

Locate one of these consent decrees. *Hint:* Some of the first agencies involved are the Pittsburgh police, the New Jersey State police, and the Los Angeles police department. You can also check the website of the Civil Rights Division of the U.S. Department of Justice for other departments.

Study the consent decree you have found. What changes must the department make? Do you think they will improve accountability? What does this consent decree say about the department before the suit? What was the department not doing to ensure accountability?

Exercise 2 The San Jose Independent Police Auditor (IPA) is one important citizen oversight agency. Find the IPA's website and review its annual reports from 1993 to the present. What has the San Jose IPA done over the years? What does it claim as its most important achievements? Do you believe these are valuable contributions to police accountability? Do you believe any of the activities of the IPA interfere with the management of the San Jose police department? If so, which activities? Discuss in class why you think they interfere with professional management.

Exercise 3 Do any police departments describe their COMPSTAT programs on their websites? Check New York City, New Orleans, and Minneapolis for a start. Some departments use different names to describe them (in Minneapolis, for example, it is CODEFOR). Can you find any other departments that say they have similar systems?

Do these departments describe their systems in detail? Do they make any claims about their effectiveness? How much do you really learn about these systems from the websites?

REFERENCES

1 Harold E. Pepinsky, "Better Living through Police Discretion," *Law and Contemporary Problems,* 47 (Autumn 1984): 250.

2 Bayley uses *rectitude* instead of *equity.* David H. Bayley, *Police for the Future* (New York: Oxford University Press, 1994), pp. 79–101.

3 Louise Shelley, "The Soviet Police and the Rule of Law," in David Weisburd and Craig Uchida, eds., *Police Innovation and Control of the Police* (New York: Springer Verlag, 1993), p. 127.

4 Herman Goldstein, *Policing a Free Society* (Cambridge, MA: Ballinger, 1977).

5 Jerome H. Skolnick, *Justice without Trial,* 3rd ed. (New York: Macmillan, 1994).

6 Paul Jacobs, *Prelude to Riot* (New York: Vintage Books, 1968), p. 38.

7 Samuel Walker, *Popular Justice: A History of American Criminal Justice,* 2nd ed. (New York: Oxford University Press, 1998).

8 George L. Kelling, *"Broken Windows" and Police Discretion* (Washington, DC: Government Printing Office, 1999), "A Short History of Police Accountability," pp. 5–7.

9 Samuel Walker, "Historical Roots of the Legal Control of Police Behavior," in David Weisburd and Craig Uchida, eds., *Police Innovation and the Rule of Law* (New York: Springer, 1991), pp. 32–55.

10 Geoffrey P. Alpert and Mark H. Moore, "Measuring Police Performance in the New Paradigm of Policing," in Bureau of Justice Statistics, *Performance Measures for the Criminal Justice System* (Washington, DC: Government Printing Office, 1993), pp. 109–142.

11 Bureau of Justice Statistics, *Criminal Victimization in the United States, 1994* (Washington, DC: Government Printing Office, 1997).

12 Donald Black, "Production of Crime Rates," in D. Black, *The Manners and Customs of the Police* (New York: Academic Press, 1980), pp. 65–84.

13 Lawrence W. Sherman and Barry D. Glick, *The Quality of Police Arrest Statistics* (Washington, DC: The Police Foundation, 1984).

14 Office of the City Auditor, *Service Efforts and Accomplishments: 1995–96* (Portland, OR: City of Portland, 1996).

15 Kelling, *"Broken Windows" and Police Discretion.*

16 Bureau of Justice Assistance, *A Police Guide to Surveying Citizens and Their Environment* (Washington, DC: Government Printing Office, 1993).

17 Wesley G. Skogan and Susan M. Hartnett, *Community Policing, Chicago Style* (New York: Oxford, 1997).

18 Jack Maple, *The Crime Fighter* (New York: Doubleday, 1999).

19 Herman Goldstein, "Administrative Problems in Controlling the Exercise of Police Authority," *Journal of Criminal Law, Criminology, and Police Science,* 58, no. 2 (1967): 171.

20 "The Lost Battalion," *Newsday* (February 2, 2001), p. 1.

21 David Weisburd and Rosann Greenspan, with Edwin E. Hamilton, Hubert Williams, and Kellie A. Bryant, *Police Attitudes toward Abuse of Authority: Findings from a National Study* (Washington, DC: Government Printing Office, 2000), p. 7.

22 John Van Maanen, "The Boss: First-Line Supervision in an American Police Agency," in Maurice Punch, ed., *Control in the Police Organization* (Cambridge, MA: MIT Press, 1983), pp. 275–317.

23 Special Counsel Merrick Bobb, *9th Semiannual Report* (Los Angeles: The Special Counsel, 1998), pp. 22–23.

24 James J. Fyfe, Jack R. Greene, William F. Walsh, O. W. Wilson, Roy Clinton McLaren, *Police Administration,* 5th ed. (New York: McGraw-Hill, 1997), p. 139.

25 Los Angeles Police Department, *Board of Inquiry into the Rampart Area Corruption Incident* (Los Angeles: LAPD, March 2000), Executive Summary, p. 7; Chapter 10, "Police Integrity Systems."

26 Erwin Chemerinsky, *An Independent Analysis of the Los Angeles Police Department's Board of Inquiry Report on the Rampart Scandal* (Los Angeles: September 11, 2000).

27 Robert C. Davis and Pedro Mateu-Gelabert, *Respectful and Effective Policing: Two Examples in the South Bronx* (New York: Vera Institute of Justice, 1999).

28 International Association of Chiefs of Police, Model Policy, "Reporting Use of Force," Effective Date, February 1, 1997.

29 U.S. Department of Justice, *Principles for Promoting Police Integrity* (Washington, DC: U.S. Department of Justice, 2001), pp. 5–6.

30 Samuel Walker, *Taming the System* (New York: Oxford University Press, 1993); Geoffrey P. Alpert and Roger G. Dunham, *Police Pursuit Driving: Controlling Responses to Emergency Situations* (New York: Greenwood Press, 1990).

31 Fyfe et al., *Police Administration,* 5th ed., Ch. 10, "Personnel Management II: Human Resource Management," pp. 318–363.

32 Commission to Investigate Allegations of Police Corruption (Mollen Commission), *Commission Report* (New York: City of New York, 1994), p. 81.

33 Timothy N. Oettmeier and Mary Ann Wycoff, *Personnel Performance Evaluations in the Community Policing Context* (Washington, DC: Police Executive Research Forum, 1997), p. 5.

34 Frank J. Landy, *Performance Appraisal in Police Departments* (Washington, DC: The Police Foundation, 1977), pp. 11–13.

35 Christopher Commission, *Report of the Independent Commission on the Los Angeles Police Department* (Los Angeles: Christopher Commission, 1991), p. 43.

36 Fyfe et al., *Police Administration,* "The Internal Affairs Unit," pp. 467–475.

37 Commission on Accreditation for Law Enforcement Agencies, *Standards for Law Enforcement Agencies,* 4th ed. (Fairfax, VA: CALEA, 1999), Standard 52.1.2.

38 Aogan Mulcahy, "'Headhunter' or 'Real Cop'? Identity in the World of Internal Affairs Officers," *Journal of Contemporary Ethnography,* 24 (April 1995): 106.

39 Ibid., 108.

40 Samuel Walker and Eileen Luna, *An Evaluation of the Oversight Mechanisms of the Albuquerque Police Department* (Albuquerque, NM: City Council, 1997).

41 Baltimore Maryland, *The Mayor's Plan to Dramatically Reduce Crime in Baltimore,* "Current Practices of the Baltimore Police Department: The Internal Reality" (Baltimore, MD: City of Baltimore, 2000).

42 Herman Goldstein, *Police Corruption* (Washington, DC: The Police Foundation, 1975), pp. 40–41.

43 Lawrence W. Sherman, *Controlling Police Corruption* (Washington, DC: Government Printing Office, 1978), p. 10.
44 Police Executive Research Forum, *Organizational Evaluation of the Omaha Police Division* (Washington, DC: PERF, 1992), p. 75.
45 Mollen Commission, *Commission Report,* p. 53.
46 William Westley, *Violence and the Police* (Cambridge, MA: MIT Press, 1970).
47 Christopher Commission, *Report of the Independent Commission,* pp. 168–171.
48 Weisburd and Greenspan, with Hamilton, Williams, and Bryant, *Police Attitudes toward Abuse of Authority: Findings from a National Study.*
49 Baltimore Maryland, *The Mayor's Plan to Dramatically Reduce Crime in Baltimore,* "The Cultural Diagnostic" (Baltimore, MD: The City of Baltimore, 2000).
50 Public Advocate for the City of New York, *Disciplining Police: Solving the Problem of Police Misconduct* (New York: The Public Advocate, 2000), pp. 31–36.
51 "Wave of Abuse Claims Laid to a Few Officers," *Boston Sunday Globe* (October 4, 1992), p. 1.
52 U.S. Civil Rights Commission, *Who Is Guarding the Guardians?* (Washington, DC: Government Printing Office, 1981), p. 159; Department of Justice, *Principles for Promoting Police Integrity* (Washington, DC: Government Printing Office, 2001).
53 Christopher Commission, *Report of the Independent Commission on the Los Angeles Police Department,* pp. 39–48; "Kansas City Police Go After Their 'Bad Boys,'" *The New York Times* (September 10, 1991).
54 Samuel Walker and Geoffrey P. Alpert, "Police Accountability: Establishing an Early Warning System," International City Management Association, *IQ Service Report,* 32, no. 8 (August 2000).
55 Samuel Walker, Geoffrey P. Alpert, and Dennis J. Kenney, *Responding to the Problem Police Officer: A National Evaluation of Early Warning Systems,* Final Report to the National Institute of Justice, 2000
56 Current information is available on the CALEA website: **www.calea.org**.
57 CALEA, *Standards for Law Enforcement,* 4th ed.
58 Jack Pearson, "National Accreditation: A Valuable Management Tool," in James J. Fyfe, ed., *Police Management Today* (Washington, DC: ICMA, 1985).
59 James J. Fyfe, comments to author.
60 Goldstein, "Directing Police Agencies through the Political Process," in *Policing a Free Society,* pp. 131–156.
61 Samuel Walker, *A Critical History of Police Reform* (Lexington, MA: Lexington Books, 1977).
62 C. A. Novak, *The Years of Controversy: The Los Angeles Police Commission, 1991–1993* (Washington, DC: The Police Foundation, 1995).
63 Edward Littlejohn, "The Civilian Police Commission: A Deterrent of Police Misconduct," *University of Detroit Journal of Urban Law,* 59 (Fall 1981): 5–62.
64 *Mapp v. Ohio,* 367 U.S. 643 (1961).
65 Walker, "Historical Roots of the Legal Control of Police Behavior."
66 Herman Goldstein, "Trial Judges and the Police," *Crime and Delinquency,* 14 (January 1968): 14–25.
67 *Miranda v. Arizona,* 384 U.S. 436 (1966).

68 *Dickerson v. U.S.* No. 99-5525 (June 26, 2000).

69 Paul G. Cassell and Bret S. Hayman, "Police Interrogation in the 1990s: An Empirical Study of the Effects of Miranda," *UCLA Law Review,* 43 (February 1996): 860.

70 Richard A. Leo, "Inside the Interrogation Room," *Journal of Criminal Law and Criminology,* 86, no. 2 (1996): 266–303; Richard A. Leo and George C. Thomas III, eds., *The Miranda Debate: Law, Justice, and Policing* (Boston: Northeastern University Press, 1998).

71 Neal Milner, *The Court and Local Law Enforcement* (Beverly Hills, CA: Sage Publications, 1971).

72 Fred Graham, *The Self-Inflicted Wound* (New York: Macmillan, 1970).

73 Samuel Walker, *Sense and Nonsense about Crime,* 5th ed. (Belmont, CA: Wadsworth, 2001), pp. 87–95.

74 Sheldon Krantz et al., *Police Policymaking* (Lexington, MA: Lexington Books, 1979).

75 Controller General of the United States, *Impact of the Exclusionary Rule on Federal Criminal Prosecutions,* Report #GGD-79-45 (April 19, 1979).

76 Walker, "Historical Roots of Legal Control of Police Behavior."

77 Myron W. Orfield, Jr., "The Exclusionary Rule and Deterrence: An Empirical Study of Chicago Narcotics Officers," *University of Chicago Law Review,* 54 (Summer 1987): 1016–1055.

78 Carl McGowan, "Rulemaking and the Police," *Michigan Law Review,* 70 (March 1972): 659–694.

79 Goldstein, "Administrative Problems in Controlling the Exercise of Police Authority," 168.

80 Stephen Wasby, *Small-Town Police and the Supreme Court* (Lexington, MA: Lexington Books, 1976).

81 "City Had Bad-Cop Warning," *Detroit Free Press* (December 29, 2000), p. 1.

82 Michael Avery, David Rudovsky, and Karen Blum, *Police Misconduct: Law and Litigation,* 3rd ed. (St. Paul, MN: West, 1997).

83 *The New York Times* (March 15, 1991).

84 Samuel Walker and Eileen Luna, *An Evaluation of the Oversight Mechanisms of the Albuquerque Police Department* (Albuquerque, NM: City Council, 1997), pp. 105–112.

85 Charldean Newell, Janay Pollock, and Jerry Tweedy, "Financial Aspects of Police Liability," *ICMA Baseline Data Report,* 24 (March–April 1992): 1–8.

86 Edward J. Littlejohn, "Civil Liability and the Police Officer: The Need for New Deterrents to Police Misconduct," *University of Detroit Journal of Urban Law,* 58 (1981): 365–431.

87 "Project: Suing the Police in Federal Court," *Yale Law Journal,* 88 (1979): 781–824.

88 Candace McCoy, "Lawsuits against Police: What Impact Do They Really Have?" *Criminal Law Bulletin,* 20 (January–February 1984): 53.

89 Ibid.

90 Cited in Newell, Pollock, and Tweedy, "Financial Aspects of Police Liability," p. 8.

91 Special Counsel, Los Angeles County Sheriff's Department, *6th Semiannual Report* (Los Angeles: Los Angeles County, 1996), pp. 33–39.

92 Special Counsel to the Los Angeles County Sheriff's Department, *11th Semiannual Report* (Los Angeles: October 1999); Special Counsel to the Los Angeles County Sheriff's Department, *12th Semiannual Report* (Los Angeles: June 2000), p. 40.

93 *United States v. City of Pittsburgh* (W. D. Pa., 1997).

94 Ibid.

95 *United States v. State of New Jersey* (2000).

96 Avery, Rudovsky, and Blum, *Police Misconduct: Law and Litigation,* Ch. 15.

97 Monrad G. Paulson, "Securing Police Compliance with Constitutional Limitations," National Commission on the Causes and Prevention of Violence, *Law and Order Reconsidered* (New York: Bantam Books, 1970), pp. 402–405.

98 *Rizzo v. Goode,* 423 U.S. 362 (1976).

99 U.S. Commission on Civil Rights, *Revisiting* Who Is Guarding the Guardians? (Washington, DC: Government Printing Office, 2000).

100 Vera Institute of Justice, *Prosecuting Police Misconduct* (New York: Vera Institute, 1998).

101 Goldstein, "Administrative Problems in Controlling the Exercise of Police Authority," 162.

102 Jerome Skolnick and James J. Fyfe, *Above the Law* (New York: The Free Press, 1993).

103 Vera Institute of Justice, *Prosecuting Police Misconduct,* 1998, p. 8.

104 Mary M. Cheh, "Are Law Suits an Answer to Police Brutality?" in W. A. Geller and H. Toch, eds., *And Justice for All* (Washington, DC: Government Printing Office, 1997), p. 259.

105 Samuel Walker, *Police Accountability: The Role of Citizen Oversight* (Belmont, CA: Wadsworth, 2001).

106 Ibid., p. 129.

107 San Francisco Office of Citizen Complaints, *1999 Annual Report* (San Francisco: OCC, 2000), pp. 72–85.

108 Americans for Effective Law Enforcement, *Police Civilian Review Boards AELE Defense Manual,* Brief 82–3 (San Francisco: AELE, 1982); Douglas Perez, *Common Sense about Police Review* (Philadelphia: Temple University Press, 1994).

109 The arguments on both sides are reviewed in Walker, *Police Accountability: The Role of Citizen Oversight,* pp. 54–60.

110 James R. Hudson, "Organizational Aspects of Internal and External Review of the Police," *Journal of Criminal Law, Criminology, and Police Science,* 63 (September 1972): 427–432.

111 Wayne A. Kerstetter and Kenneth A. Rasinski, "Opening a Window into Police Internal Affairs: Impact of Procedural Justice Reform on Third-Party Attitudes," *Social Justice Research,* 7, no. 2 (1994): 107–127.

112 Michele Sviridoff and James E. McElroy, *Processing Complaints against Police in New York City* (New York: Vera Institute of Justice, 1989).

113 New York Civil Liberties Union, *A Third Anniversary Overview of the Civilian Complaint Review Board, July 5, 1993–July 5, 1996* (New York: NYCLU, 1996).

114 Walker and Luna, *An Evaluation of the Oversight Mechanisms of the Albuquerque Police Department.*

115 National Commission on Law Observance and Enforcement, *The Third Degree* (Washington, DC: Government Printing Office, 1931), p. 153.

116 Christopher Commission, *Report of the Independent Commission on the Los Angeles Police Department.*

117 Walker, *Popular Justice.*

118 Samuel Walker, "Setting the Standards: The Efforts and Impacts of Blue-Ribbon Commissions on the Police," in W. A. Geller, ed., *Police Leadership in America: Crisis and Opportunity* (New York: Praeger, 1985), pp. 354–370.

119 David Burnham, *The Role of the Media in Controlling Corruption* (New York; John Jay College, 1977).

120 See the contributions in "The Chief and the Media," in W. A. Geller, ed., *Police Leadership in America: Crisis and Opportunity,* pp. 99–146.

121 Walker, "Police Accountability," p. 128.

122 NAACP, *Beyond the Rodney King Story: An Investigation of Police Misconduct in Minority Communities* (Boston: Northeastern University Press, 1995).

123 Samuel Walker, *In Defense of American Liberties: A History of the ACLU* (New York: Oxford University Press, 1990).

124 Gilda Brancato and Eliot E. Polebaum, *The Rights of Police Officers* (New York: Avon Books, 1981).

PART FOUR

FOUR

OFFICERS AND ORGANIZATIONS

CHAPTER TWELVE

Police Officers I:
Entering Police Work

CHAPTER OUTLINE

INTRODUCTION

The Changing American Police Officer

The profile of the American police officer has changed dramatically over the past 30 years. The typical officer today is better educated, better trained, and more likely to be female, African American, or Hispanic than ever before. Figure 12-1 indicates the major changes in the profile of the American police officer.

This chapter approaches policing from the perspective of occupational sociology. It examines policing in terms of the kinds of people who are recruited into police work, how different factors influence that selection process, and what happens to officers once they are hired. It attempts to explain how these different factors influence the attitudes and behavior of police officers on the job.

ASPECTS OF THE PERSONNEL PROCESS

A Career Perspective

Who enters policing, and why do they choose this occupation? Why do they behave as they do? Why do some officers leave their jobs before retirement? To answer these questions it is useful to look at police personnel from a career perspective, examining officers' progress from recruitment to retirement. Discussions of police personnel too often focus on recruitment alone, ignoring other important aspects of the personnel process that affect the quality of policing. Good personnel practices at one stage can be undermined by poor practices at another. A police department might recruit outstanding individuals, for example, but then fail to train them adequately. Or it might do an excellent job of recruiting and training but lose the best officers because of poor management practices. Failure to adequately reward officers for good performance may lead to cynicism, burnout, and reduced levels of effort by senior officers.

Beyond Stereotypes of Cops

How many times have you heard someone make a statement such as "All cops are ____"? How many jokes have you heard about police officers spending all their time at donut shops? How often have you heard someone say that people become cops because they like to use force? Statements and jokes of this sort reflect negative stereotypes about police officers. At the same time, how many times have you heard someone say that

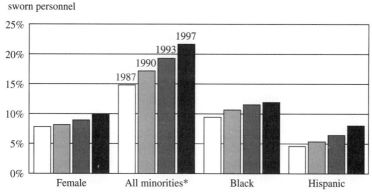

Percent of full-time
sworn personnel

*Includes blacks, Hispanics, Asians, Pacific Islanders,
American Indians, and Alaska Natives.

FIGURE 12–1
FEMALE AND MINORITY LOCAL POLICE OFFICERS, 1987, 1990, 1993, AND 1997
Source: Bureau of Justice Statistics, *Local Police Departments, 1997* (Washington, DC: Government Printing Office, 2000), p. 4.

police officers do no wrong, or more likely that they have such dangerous and stressful jobs that we should never criticize them for maybe using a little too much force in some situation? This point of view reflects a positive stereotype about police officers.

The public image of policing is heavily influenced by stereotypes about police officers: about who they are, what they believe, and how they act. These stereotypes fall into two categories. On the one side, a negative stereotype views officers as uneducated, untrained, prejudiced, brutal, and corrupt. On the other side, a positive stereotype views them as heroic saints, risking their lives in the face of hostility from the public, the media, and the courts. Arthur Niederhoffer characterizes the police officer as "a 'Rorschach' in uniform. . . . To people in trouble the police officer is a savior," but to others he is "a fierce ogre."[1]

Neither stereotype is accurate. As Bayley and Mendelsohn conclude in their study of police–community relations in Denver, the average police officer is a rather average person in terms of values and political beliefs, although a little more conservative than the population as a whole.[2] The special nature of police work does, however, encourage certain attitudes and behavior, and there is a distinct police subculture among officers. No studies, however, have concluded that police officers are fundamentally different from other people in any important respect. The issues surrounding police officer attitudes and behavior are examined in detail in Chapter 13.

The Personnel Process: A Shared Responsibility

Personnel decisions in policing are a shared responsibility. Police departments control some of the decisions, but other government agencies, such as the civil service system or the city personnel department, control the others. A police chief, for example, cannot unilaterally change recruitment standards (such as the minimum educational requirement).

The lack of complete control over personnel decisions is often an emotional issue among police chiefs. At a national chiefs' meeting a few years ago, a police chief from Texas described how he fired an officer for using excessive force only to have the officer reinstated on appeal. The chief received a burst of applause from his fellow chiefs when he declared that this particular officer never belonged in law enforcement in the first place but there was nothing he could do about it.

Typically, the civil service agency has the responsibility for (1) developing job descriptions; (2) establishing the minimum standards required for each position; (3) developing tests for each position; (4) announcing job openings; (5) conducting some, but not all, of the tests; and (6) certifying a list of persons to be hired or promoted. Police departments generally (1) advise the civil service agency on job descriptions, requirements, and tests; (2) conduct some of the recruiting; and (3) administer some of the tests.[3] Civil service systems are discussed in more detail in Chapter 14.

RECRUITMENT

Recruitment is the process of attracting a pool of applicants. It includes three separate elements: (1) the minimum qualifications, (2) the recruitment effort, and (3) the applicant's decision to apply for a position.

Minimum Qualifications

Age Is a person 21 years old mature enough to be a police officer? Does a 21-year-old have sufficient work experience and emotional maturity to be able to handle the stress and complex demands of police work? An increasing number of experts believe that police departments should raise the minimum age level for recruits. Most law enforcement agencies require all applicants to be at least 21 years old. Some departments have recently raised the minimum age level on the grounds that many 21-year-olds are not mature enough for the difficult decisions that police work requires.

In years past, most police departments had maximum age limits for recruits. Typically you could not be older than 35 to be eligible for employment. This limit was primarily designed to reduce financial strains on pension systems by officers who would retire after fewer years on the job than younger officers. Federal law banning age discrimination has forced most departments to eliminate these limits, however. In 1994 only 12 percent of all big-city departments had a maximum age limit for new officers.[4]

Height and Weight Height and weight requirements have changed dramatically. Thirty years ago, nearly all police departments (85 percent) required officers to be at least 5 foot 8 inches tall.[5] This requirement reflected the old stereotype that police work frequently involves physical confrontations with suspects, and the assumption that officers need to be physically imposing in order to gain the respect of citizens. As discussed in Chapters 4 and 6, however, police work rarely involves physical confrontations, citizens generally comply with officers' requests, and communication skills and good judgment are considered more important for police work than physical strength.[6]

The old height requirements were challenged in lawsuits arguing that they discriminated against women, Hispanic Americans, and Asian Americans. Only a handful of big-city departments still had minimum height requirements by 1994.[7] Departments today require that weight be proportional to height.

But as everyone can see, many police officers are overweight. In some cases they are seriously overweight relative to their height. Why are they still on the force? If police departments have strict entry-level weight requirements, why not have the same standards for veteran officers? Traditionally, law enforcement agencies have not enforced fitness standards throughout officers' careers. This practice has begun to change. The Ohio State Highway Patrol began a fitness program in 1992, with penalties for veteran officers who did not meet the standards.[8]

Education   The vast majority (75 percent) of police departments in 1997 required only a high school education or the equivalent. Only 2 percent require a four-year college degree, and a total of 25 percent require at least some college (twice the figure in 1993).[9] Minimum requirements, however, do not reflect actual hiring practices. Many departments select applicants with more than the minimum level of education. The average recruit in the San Diego police department in the late 1980s had 2 years of college, despite the fact that there was no formal college education requirement.[10] Susan Martin found that both male and female recruits in Birmingham and Detroit averaged about 2 years of college.[11] By 1988, 65.2 percent of all sworn officers had some college education, and 22.6 percent had undergraduate or graduate degrees.[12]

Some people argue that all police officers should have a college degree.[13] In 1967 the President's Crime Commission recommended that "the ultimate aim of all police departments should be that all personnel with general enforcement powers have baccalaureate degrees."[14] According to Worden, advocates of the college education requirement argue that it is likely to contribute to improved policing in three ways. First, higher education will shape the values of students and make them better appreciate the role of the police in a democratic society. Second, it will improve on-the-street performance directly by giving them the resources to make better judgments. Third, education itself may not have any direct effect, but the requirement will select out people who differ in better ways from those who do not go to college.[15] Others point out that police officers need to be able to deal with the complex and constantly changing law of criminal procedure, and that the police need to raise their requirements to keep pace with rising levels of education in society. Between 1960 and 1998 the percentage of adults completing high school doubled, from 41 to 83.8 percent, and the percentage graduating from college tripled, from 7.7 to 24.4 percent.[16] Finally, community policing and problem-oriented policing place new responsibilities on rank-and-file officers, asking them to be planners and problem solvers. Some experts argue that college educated officers are better prepared to perform these tasks.[17]

Requiring all applicants to have a college degree is opposed primarily because it would limit the pool of applicants and, in particular, have a disparate impact on racial minorities who have been the victims of inferior schooling. In 1998, 25 percent of all

white Americans had completed 4 years of college or more, compared with 14.7 percent
of African Americans, 11.9 percent of Hispanic Americans of Puerto Rican origin, and
7.5 percent of Hispanics of Mexican origin.[18] There is no conclusive evidence that officers with college degrees perform more effectively than those without degrees.[19] In
1985, however, federal courts upheld a requirement by the Dallas police department that
recruits have at least 45 hours of college education with a minimum average of C.[20] A
1991 Police Executive Research Forum (PERF) discussion paper concluded that "there
appears to be an adequate pool of both minority and majority college-educated men and
women interested in police employment" to justify a college requirement.[21]

Some evidence, however, suggests that officers with relatively more education are
more likely to become dissatisfied with their jobs than officers with less education, primarily because of a lack of rewards and opportunities for career advancement. Dantzker
found relatively higher levels of job stress among officers with only a high school education and with college degrees, and lower levels among those with some college education. He suggested that college-educated officers may become "more easily frustrated
with how the police system actually works, and with how their police agencies failed to
accept and utilize their knowledge and skills."[22] In some departments where the average
educational levels are low, officers with more education are informally punished by being denied certain career opportunities.[23]

Almost three-quarters (72 percent) of all municipal police departments have educational incentive pay programs to encourage their officers to continue their education.[24]
These programs include tuition assistance or incentive pay to officers with a college education, or both. Nearly half (42.6 percent) of all departments allow officers to adjust
their assignments in order to accommodate their course schedules.[25]

Can you be too smart to be a police officer? In a case that resulted in a federal lawsuit and received national publicity, the New London, Connecticut, police department
rejected an applicant because his score on an intelligence test was *too high.* He scored
33 on a test, but the department only interviewed applicants who scored between 20 and
27, on the theory that people who scored too high would get bored with police work and
soon quit their jobs. A federal court upheld the department's practice, ruling that it had
a rational basis for the policy and treated all applicants the same. The court ruled that the
department's policy was legal, though it did not address the question of whether the policy was good.[26]

Criminal Record   There is much controversy over whether anyone with a criminal
record should be eligible for police employment. Some experts argue that a criminal
record of any sort should automatically disqualify an applicant, on the grounds that it indicates a lack of ethical standards. Others argue in favor of a variable standard, depending on the nature of the offense (felony or misdemeanor, adult or juvenile), the number
of offenses, and how recently the last offense was committed.

A Justice Department survey found that 95 percent of all departments refuse to hire
anyone with an adult felony conviction, while 75 percent reject those with a juvenile
felony conviction. Only 30 percent, however, reject applicants with either an adult or a
juvenile misdemeanor conviction. Twenty percent reject those with an adult felony arrest
but no conviction, and 25 percent reject those with a juvenile arrest but no conviction.[27]

SIDEBAR 12–1   ISSUE FOR DISCUSSION: SHOULD DEPARTMENTS
HIRE SOMEONE WITH A JUVENILE DRUG
CONVICTION?

Should police departments hire someone who has a juvenile drug conviction?
What if it is for possession of a small amount of marijuana, when the individual
was 16 years old, and he or she has no arrests or convictions in the past 5 years?

Is this person acceptable as a police officer? What if the arrest occurred 2
years ago? What if the arrest was for cocaine possession at age 16? Would it
make a difference if the person was convicted as a juvenile for possession with
intent to sell?

What standards of integrity would you maintain? What kinds of behavior are
you willing to amnesty? What offenses? How far in the past?

What if the applicant had a drunk driving conviction at age 16? What about a
conviction at age 19?

What if the applicant lied about the drunk driving conviction at age 16, and the
conviction was discovered through the background investigation?

Drug offenses pose the most difficult problem with respect to recruitment standards.
On the one hand, there is evidence that officers with any kind of drug involvement history are far more likely to become corrupt. On the other hand, drug use is extremely
prevalent. According to the National Household Survey, 31.1 percent of all Americans
reported "ever" having used marijuana. Among persons 18 to 25 (the age of potential
police recruits) the figure was 41 percent.[28] Rejecting every applicant who used drugs as
a juvenile would severely limit the applicant pool. Some experts suggest that applicants
should be considered as long as the drug involvement was limited to "experimentation"
rather than heavy use, to "soft" drugs (marijuana) rather than "hard" drugs (heroin), and
as long as there had been no use for several years.

Residency Requirements   Do police officers who live in the city they police make
better officers than officers who live outside the city? Are they less knowledgeable and
less committed to serving people in the city if they do not themselves live there? The
American Civil Liberties Union believes it does make a difference. In a 1994 report it
found that 83 percent of all Los Angeles police officers lived outside the city of Los Angeles. It argued that police officers must be "a true part of the community they patrol"
and not appear to be "an outside hired force."[29]

The subject of residency requirements is a major controversy across the country.
About one-quarter of all city police departments require their officers to live within the
city or county. Another 40 percent have some other residency requirement (e.g., within
the state).[30] Residency requirements are intended to heighten the familiarity of officers
with the city and their commitment to the well-being of the community. Opponents of
residency requirements argue that it infringes on the freedom of officers to choose where
they live. Others argue that where a person chooses to live does not predict his or her behavior as a police officer. In New York City, for example, officers who live outside the

city receive fewer citizen complaints than officers who live inside the city.[31] Residency requirements may not produce the expected improvements in police–community relations, however. A national survey of public attitudes about the police found that contrary to expectations, officers who are required to live within the city or county are likely to be viewed *less* favorably than officers who are not.[32]

A second and related issue is whether officers should be encouraged to live not just in the city but within the specific neighborhood where they work. Are police officers who live in the neighborhood they police better police officers? Advocates of residency-assistance programs argue that officers who live where they work will both understand the problems of the neighborhood better and feel a greater commitment to helping others who live there. The intended result would be better policing.

Opponents of this idea argue that officers would quickly "burn out." They believe that all employees need to get away from the pressures and stress of the job and be able to return fresh each day. Living within the neighborhood might also mean that residents would feel free to call on the officer when off duty for help with their problems. The result could be that an officer would never have any real time away from the job. Another problem is, what should the officer do when the opportunity for a good transfer or promotion arises? Should the officer pass up a good career opportunity just to stay working in the neighborhood?

The federal government created a program, Homes for Peace Officers and Firefighters, to assist people in these occupations to purchase homes in the city where they work. The program offers loans with no down payment, debt counseling, and other forms of assistance. This program is based on the assumption that officers will take a greater interest in policing neighborhoods if they live there themselves, and that other residents will have more positive feelings about the police department if they know an officer lives in the area. The program got off to a very slow start in Los Angeles. In the first year, only 12 of the city's 9,600 police officers and firefighters who had lived outside the city used the program to buy a house within the city.[33]

Recruitment Effort

The number and quality of persons in the applicant pool depend in part on a department's recruitment effort. An active effort will produce a larger applicant pool, more of whom are likely to be highly qualified. If a department wants to increase the representation of college-educated, African American, Hispanic, or female officers, it needs to direct recruitment efforts toward those groups. To recruit more Hispanic applicants, for example, it needs to meet with Hispanic community groups.

The Cleveland police department made a significant improvement in the employment of African American officers between the 1980s and 1990s, despite the fact that the overall number of officers in the department was shrinking. The key to this achievement was an active recruitment effort that involved fourteen sworn officers assigned to recruitment and targeting recruitment efforts toward minority neighborhoods.[34]

Historically, police departments did not engage in active, publicized recruitment efforts. This approach gave an advantage to persons with political or family ties to the police department, since they were most likely to hear about hiring opportunities. Open recruitment efforts, including public advertising of opportunities, are required by law today. The U.S. Equal Employment Opportunity Commission recommends that employers "contact media, agencies, organizations, schools, colleges, community groups and others who have special contacts with women and minority groups."[35] The 1994 Academy of Criminal Justice Sciences (ACJS) survey of recruitment, selection, and training standards found that 90 percent of all departments had a special recruitment strategy for minorities, slightly more than half (52.5 percent) had a special strategy for recruiting women, 37.3 percent actively sought veterans and college graduates, while 20 percent had a special program for recruiting people with prior police experience.[36]

CHOOSING LAW ENFORCEMENT AS A CAREER

Motivations

Why do people want to become police officers? There are many stereotypes related to the question of why people choose law enforcement as a career. Some people think that many applicants are motivated by reasons that make them unsuited for police work: a desire to use force, for example.

These stereotypes have not been confirmed by research, however. Surveys of recruits and new police officers consistently indicate that they choose law enforcement as a career for two main reasons: the nature of police work and the material benefits of the job.

The nature of the job includes the opportunity to help people, to help the community, and the fact that the work is nonroutine, with different situations constantly arising. The President's Crime Commission found that 14 percent of officers said that they were attracted by the prospect of working with people or by the variety of the work.[37] Among the female recruits in New York City, 14 percent cited "opportunity to help others" and 12 percent said it was "interesting work."[38] Contrary to the negative stereotypes about police, recruits appear to be relatively idealistic, perhaps even slightly more than the average person.

A survey of male and female officers in two Midwestern police departments found that they listed the top five reasons for choosing policing as a career in the following rank order: (1) "help people," (2) "job security," (3) "fight crime," (4) "excitement of the job," and (5) "prestige of the job." There were no significant differences between the male and female officers. Interestingly, the women ranked "excitement of the job" third, while the men ranked it fourth.[39]

Significantly, both male and female officers ranked "authority/power" ninth out of a total of eleven items. Contrary to the negative stereotype about police, officers are not primarily motivated by a desire to enforce the law or to use force against other people. Only 7 percent of the female officers in Ermer's study of New York policewomen, for example, listed "law enforcement orientation" as their motivation.[40]

For many applicants, a law enforcement career offers better pay, higher benefits, and greater job security than their parents' occupations. Traditionally, most officers were white males who came from blue collar backgrounds (70 percent of those in Westley's study of Gary, Indiana, and 69.7 percent in McNamara's study of New York City officers).[41] Bayley and Mendelsohn found that many Denver police officers were "upwardly mobile"; policing represented an advance over their parents' occupational status, and most had tried other jobs before settling on the police department.[42]

The appeal of jobs with a police department often depends on the state of the economy, as well as how the pay and benefits of a police job compare with those of other jobs available to the applicant. In 1999 and 2000 police departments in New York City, Los Angeles, and many other cities had difficulty attracting recruits because of the strong economy and the availability of other good jobs. In the mid-1970s, by contrast, police salaries and benefits were relatively attractive in the context of a stagnant economy.

Police officers enjoy a high degree of job security because of civil service rules and police union contract provisions that make it very difficult to fire officers.[43] After the probationary period, officers can be fired only for specific cause, and any officer who is terminated has the right to appeal. Job security is a particularly appealing factor for individuals whose family experience included periodic unemployment.

Given the long history of conflict between the police and the African American community (see Chapter 9), why would an African American want to become a police officer? Research has consistently found that racial-minority and female applicants are motivated by the same factors as white recruits: the nature of the work and the material benefits of the job. In a study of African American officers in New York City, Nicholas Alex concludes that "the motives of the white policeman for choosing police work seem little different from those of the black policeman."[44] Some studies, however, have found that economic factors are a little more important for African Americans than for whites.[45]

Another factor that does seem to have some impact on choosing law enforcement as a career is a family connection. Some applicants are motivated by the fact that they have a parent, a brother or sister, or some other relative who is a police officer. In the 1960s over half of all sergeants in the Chicago police department had a relative on the force.[46] In Ermer's study, 7 percent of the women cited family influence.[47] Because of past discrimination, African Americans, Hispanics, and women are less likely to have a family member to provide a role model or encouragement for choosing law enforcement as a career.

Not all police recruits have clearly defined goals when they initially apply for jobs with a police department. Several studies found that individuals "drifted" into police work, often after trying several other jobs.[48] Among those with clear goals, meanwhile, career expectations are often not fulfilled. Persons expecting an exciting job discover that patrol work is often very boring. Others expecting good opportunities for advancement are also disappointed by the limited opportunities in police organizations.

Most of the studies of officers' motivations for choosing police work are based on surveys of recruits regarding their perceptions and expectations. In some important respects, their expectations are not fulfilled. Police work is not as exciting as many applicants expect. Many officers believe that they do not receive enough support from the public. As a result, officer attitudes change significantly after they are on the job. These changes, and the concept of a police subculture, are discussed in detail in Chapter 13.

People Who Do Not Apply

An important aspect of the recruitment process involves those people who are potentially eligible but choose not to apply for jobs. Some potential African American recruits may not apply because of the negative image of the police in their community. In a survey of high school seniors, Kaminski found that African Americans were significantly less likely to accept a job with the Albany police department if it were offered to them.[49] Young African American men consistently express more negative attitudes toward the police than do any other group.[50] Nicholas Alex found that African American police officers experience conflict between their identification with their community, on the one hand, and with the police department, on the other.[51]

Susan Martin titled her 1980 book *Breaking and Entering* for a reason. The first thorough study of women as patrol officers, Martin's book makes the point that policing was traditionally a male occupation, with women not assigned to patrol duty and confined to a few special assignments (especially juvenile units). The culture of policing had a heavy masculine tone, emphasizing aggressiveness, psychological toughness, and physical strength. Undoubtedly, many women do not apply for jobs as police officers because they perceive this culture and do not want to have to "break and enter" to fit in. In a second 1986 study, Martin found that patterns of resistance to women persisted. Although women represented over 40 percent of the adult workforce at that time, they represented only 20 percent of all police job applicants in the 319 departments she surveyed.[52]

SELECTION

Selection Tests

Once a pool of applicants has been recruited, various tests are used to select a group of new officers from it. Virtually all big-city police departments conduct a background check, give written and medical exams, and interview finalists. About 18 percent use a polygraph or lie detector (see Table 12–1).[53]

TABLE 12–1	SCREENING METHODS USED BY LOCAL POLICE DEPARTMENTS, 1997
Method	**Percentage of Departments Using Method**
Personal interview	97%
Criminal record check	95
Background investigation	94
Driving record check	90
Medical exam	82
Psychological screen	64
Drug test	54
Written aptitude test	46
Physical agility test	45
Polygraph exam	18
Voice stress analyzer	2

Source: Bureau of Justice Statistics, *Local Police Departments, 1997,* (Washington, DC: Government Printing Office, 2000), p. 4

The recruitment and selection process often takes many months and is delayed by various administrative or economic factors. In 1994, the average elapsed time of the recruitment and selection process was 8.1 months in big-city departments, an increase from about 6 months in 1990.[54] Long delays cause many applicants to drop out, because they either find other jobs or lose interest. Cohen found that delay accounted for a significant degree of attrition among minority applicants in New York City. Nearly 60 percent of black applicants who passed the initial written and physical examinations dropped out before the background investigation phase. This compared with an overall dropout rate of 18 percent.[55]

Ninety percent of all the largest police departments (populations 100,000 or more) test job applicants for drug use. Many departments (61 percent of all departments and over 80 percent of the largest) also require drug tests of all officers. Some administer mandatory drug tests to both sworn and civilian employees, some use random tests, and others test employees when drug use is suspected.[56]

Oral Interviews

Oral interviews of applicant finalists are used by almost all big-city police departments. Interviews typically last about 45 minutes and involve two or three interviewers. On the positive side, interviews are a good opportunity to detect attitudes that might be incompatible with good police work (e.g., arrogance, inability to listen, extreme passivity, racial bias). The ACJS survey found that interviews explore such areas as common sense, verbal communication skills, motivation, appearance, quick thinking, racism, compassion, sexism, and patience. On the negative side, interviews are time-consuming and expensive, and open the door to possible bias on the part of the interviewers. Several strategies have been devised to ensure consistency and eliminate potential bias. The ACJS survey found that almost all departments utilize an identical interview format, about three-quarters have a structured marking sheet, and a similar percentage train their interviewers.[57]

Can a 45-minute interview really determine who will be a good police officer? Can an applicant successfully hide attitudes he or she thinks the interviewers will not like? And can an interview determine how a person will behave in a real-world situation? William G. Doerner attempted to answer these questions by correlating oral interview scores in the Florida state law enforcement training academy with subsequent performance records. He found a "persistent inability of this selection technique to isolate suitable candidates" for law enforcement.[58]

Background Investigations

Background investigation of applicants is perhaps the most important part of the selection process. A thorough investigation can identify factors such as a good work record in previous jobs, the ability to get along with people, and the absence of disciplinary problems that indicate potential success on the job. It can also identify a criminal record, prior involvement with drugs, or behavior problems in school or on jobs that indicate potential problems as a police officer. The ACJS survey found that virtually all big-city departments conduct background investigations. These investigations cover previous employment, possible criminal records, interviews with neighbors, a check of educational attainment, a review of the applicant's financial status, and a home visit.[59]

Improperly conducted background investigations, however, open the door to subjective judgments and discrimination. In 1972 Anthony Bouza, deputy chief inspector of the New York City police department, argued that character investigations traditionally reflected the "biases of the investigating sergeant." The problem was greatest with respect to African American and Hispanic applicants, whose character backgrounds were being assessed by white sergeants unfamiliar with the culture and lifestyle of racial-minority communities. In the early 1970s, the NYPD adopted standardized procedures in an effort to eliminate bias.[60]

The Washington, DC, police department proved in the early 1990s what disaster can result when good background investigations are not conducted. Congress had directed the department to quickly hire an additional 2,000 officers. In its haste to comply with this directive, the department abandoned its standard background investigations. A large number of applicants submitted false references and work histories that were never checked. Some of these officers even had serious criminal histories. As a result of this failure, many of the officers hired in this cohort became corrupt and involved in drug activity after they became police officers. The department paid a terrible price in terms of negative publicity, loss of public respect, serious damage to department morale and ethical standards, and tremendous costs in terms of the effort necessary to fire the corrupt officers.[61]

PREDICTING WHO WILL BE GOOD POLICE OFFICERS

Who will become a good police officer? Are there any specific factors that help to predict which applicants are likely to be the best possible officers and which ones should not be hired at all? Considerable effort has gone into answering these questions. Many people are convinced that the key to improving policing is largely a matter of developing the right set of tests and selection criteria. The research in this area is not promising, however.

Some studies have attempted to correlate background characteristics with subsequent performance records. Cohen and Chaiken studied 1,608 New York City police officers hired in 1957. Thirty-three background characteristics were examined, including race, age, IQ, father's occupation, previous occupational history (last job, number of jobs, and so on), military record, marital status, education, and criminal record. The only factor that correlated with good on-the-job performance (as indicated by their official records), however, was the recruit training score.[62] The study concluded that it is not possible to predict which individuals will become good officers on the basis of background characteristics.

In a review of selection procedures commonly used by police departments, J. Douglas and Joan Grant conclude that "efforts to improve the quality of police officer performance by screening out those recruits who will not make good police officers have generally been unsuccessful." They argue that existing preemployment psychological tests, such as the widely used MMPI, are not successful in accurately predicting future behavior as a police officer. Standard psychological tests may screen out applicants with very serious mental health problems but fail to predict the behavior of those who pass such tests. A major flaw with using psychological tests to predict behavior is "the assumption that good police performance can be explained solely by pre-existing personality traits."[63]

Similar problems affect widely used selection criteria. Many applicants, for example, have 2 years of college education. Some of them are likely to be excellent police officers, but others are not. At best, written tests screen out the illiterate and very poorly educated. The applicant who has superior academic skills and who might, for example, make an excellent researcher might not be able to work with people under conditions of stress. Psychological tests screen out only those candidates with serious problems and do not identify people who have good judgment. A study of Tallahassee, Florida, police recruits found that neither preemployment psychological test scores (the MMPI and CPI tests were used) nor a clinical assessment by a psychologist correlated with recruits' performance ratings during field training.[64]

The Christopher Commission, reviewing psychological evaluations given to LAPD applicants, concluded that "this initial screening can identify obvious social misfits in the grossest sense, but cannot test for more subtle abnormalities which may make an individual ill-suited to be a police officer, such as poor impulse control and the proclivity toward violence."[65]

A major part of the problem in selecting the best potential officers is that the measures of police performance are themselves very weak. Performance evaluations by supervisors are generally very subjective (e.g., "works well with people") and may reflect the values and/or biases of the supervisors. Supervisors who value aggressive policing and frequent use of force, for example, will give high ratings to officers who perform in that manner. Performance standards tend to "reflect the internal standards of police departments rather than the requirements of the community being served."[66]

The difficulty of predicting good police performance was noted by the Fifth Circuit Court of Appeals in a suit over the Dallas police department's requirement of 45 hours of college credits. The court ruled that the desirable characteristics in a police officer include "individual judgment, ability to intervene in volatile situations (i.e., domestic quarrels), ability to make important decisions, [and] presence and performance as a witness in Court." It concluded that these characteristics "are not easily measured in terms of statistical analyses."[67] None of the recruitment and selection procedures currently used adequately measure judgment or the ability to make decisions under conditions of stress. In his study of the oral interview process in Florida, Doerner concluded that "a holistic scheme for identifying or pinpointing the qualities that make one a suitable police officer still eludes administrators."[68]

Some experts believe that the best predictor of officer performance is actual performance on the job. There are two ways of evaluating performance. First, the performance of new recruits during the probationary period can be carefully evaluated, and those recruits who appear to be deficient in some way can be dismissed. The probationary period is discussed in more detail below. A second performance-based approach involves early warning (EW) systems (see Chapter 11). EW systems do not attempt to predict behavior but only review actual on-the-job performance.

EQUAL EMPLOYMENT OPPORTUNITY

The Law of Equal Employment Opportunity

Employment discrimination on the basis of race, ethnicity, and sex is illegal in the United States. The underemployment of minorities and women in policing continues to be a major controversy. Title VII of the 1964 Civil Rights Act provides that it is unlawful for an employer "to fail or refuse to hire or to discharge any individual, or otherwise to discriminate against any individual with respect to his compensation, terms, conditions, or privileges of employment, because of such individual's race, color, religion, sex, or national origin." The 1972 Equal Employment Opportunity Act extended the coverage of the 1964 law to state and local governments, which includes most police and sheriff's departments, and strengthened the enforcement powers of the federal Equal Employment Opportunity Commission (EEOC).[69]

As Figure 12–2 indicates, federal laws prohibit other forms of employment discrimination. The term *protected class* refers to any category specifically identified by an employment discrimination law (e.g., race, sex, religion).

State and local civil rights laws also prohibit employment discrimination. Virtually all cover discrimination on the basis of race, religion, age, and national origin. Some state laws cover other categories not covered by federal law. Several states and over sixty cities, for example, prohibit discrimination on the basis of sexual orientation, meaning that employers may not discriminate against homosexuals.

Job-Related Qualifications

Is a handicapped person qualified for a job as a police officer? It is easy to answer this question about a paraplegic person who cannot walk a patrol beat, chase a suspect, or subdue a person who is physically resisting arrest. But what about a person who only suffers from some limited use of one hand? What about the person with a moderate speech impediment?

Equal employment opportunity laws and affirmative action programs do not guarantee a job to every person in a protected class. Employers may establish bona fide occupational qualifications (BFOQ) and refuse to hire people who do not possess those qualifications. A BFOQ is any requirement that is "reasonably necessary to the normal operation of that particular business."[70]

A few examples illustrate how the concept of BFOQ applies to policing. Since driving a patrol car is one of the basic tasks of a police officer, a department can legitimately refuse to hire someone who cannot drive a car because of a certain handicap. On the other hand, the old height requirements are not job-related because it has not been demonstrated that people shorter than 5 feet 8 inches cannot effectively perform police work. In *Davis v. City of Dallas*, the Fifth Circuit Court of Appeals ruled that a requirement of 45 hours of college credits was reasonably related to the job of a police officer, on the grounds that officers are expected to exercise judgment in complex and difficult situations.[71]

The 1990 Americans With Disabilities Act (ADA) has added a new element to police employment practices. There are a number of issues that have not been resolved by the

FIGURE 12–2   FEDERAL EMPLOYMENT DISCRIMINATION LAWS

The ADA is just one of many Federal laws governing employment discrimination. The key Federal provisions are:

- *The Equal Pay Act of 1963,* which extends the prohibition against sex discrimination and requires equal pay for equal work by forbidding pay differentials predicated on gender.
- *The Civil Rights Act of 1964* (Title VII), which prohibits employment discrimination on the basis of race, color, religion, sex, age, or national origin by employers who employ 15 or more persons and are engaged in an industry affecting commerce.
- *The Age Discrimination in Employment Act of 1967,* which prohibits employment discrimination against persons over the age of 40.
- *Rehabilitation Act of 1973,* which prohibits discrimination on the basis of disability by programs receiving Federal funds or by Federal agencies. This law, the precursor to the ADA, was created to help persons with disabilities receive rehabilitation, obtain access to public buildings, and enjoy equal employment opportunity.
- *The Americans with Disabilities Act of 1990 (ADA),* which makes it illegal to discriminate against qualified individuals with disabilities. The purpose of the law is to provide the estimated 43 million persons with disabilities equal access to employment opportunities; the programs, services, and activities provided by government entities; and public accommodations, such as restaurants, hotels, shopping centers, and businesses, open to the general public.
- *The Civil Rights Act of 1991,* which reverses a series of cases decided by the United States Supreme Court in 1989 that had revised long-standing interpretations (previously favorable to employees) of several Federal employment discrimination laws. The Act reinstates the earlier interpretations. In large part, the Act changes technical court rules that affect employment discrimination litigation. Highlights of the Act include permitting full-jury trials and, in certain cases, allowing for recovery of emotional suffering and punitive damages.
- *The Family and Medical Leave Act of 1993,* which requires employers with 50 or more employees to provide eligible employees with up to 12 weeks of unpaid, job-protected leave for family and medical reasons such as birth, adoption, or foster care of a child or care of a spouse, child, or parent with a serious health condition.
- *The Pregnancy Discrimination Act,* which extends the prohibition against sex discrimination and amends the Civil Rights Act of 1964 to add pregnancy, childbirth, and pregnancy-related medical conditions as protected against employment discrimination.
- *Vietnam Era Veterans Readjustment Assistance Act,* which requires Federal contractors with contracts of $10,000 or more to actively endeavor to hire qualified veterans of any war who have disabilities and, specifically, qualified Vietnam War veterans who may or may not have disabilities.

Source: Paula N. Rubin, *Civil Rights and Criminal Justice: Employment Discrimination Overview* (Washington, DC: Government Printing Office, 1995), p. 4.

courts as to what conditions represent a disability and which disabilities legitimately disqualify a person from employment as a police officer.[72]

Employment of Racial and Ethnic Minorities

The employment of racial- and ethnic-minority police officers has increased significantly in recent years. In the mid-1960s, African Americans represented only 3.6 percent

FIGURE 12–3 ACCREDITATION STANDARDS ON DIVERSITY

Standard 31.5.1. "The agency has a ratio of minority group employees in approximate proportion to the makeup of the agency's law enforcement service community. . . ."

of all sworn police officers. The figure rose to 6 percent in 1973, 7.6 percent in 1982, and 10 percent by 1997. Hispanics represented 7 percent of all officers in 1997 (up from 6.2 percent in 1993, and 4.8 percent in 1988).[73] It is important to note, however, that these trend data are not strictly comparable because national surveys over the years used different samples: Some used all police departments, while others used only large departments. Obtaining long-term data on Hispanic employment is difficult if not impossible because early surveys did not ask for data on Hispanic employment.

The aggregate data on racial- and ethnic-minority employment are somewhat misleading, however. Racial and ethnic minorities are not evenly distributed throughout the United States. African Americans are concentrated in the South and the big cities across the country. Hispanic Americans are concentrated in particular cities in the Southwest, East, and South.

The most useful measure of employment practices is the extent to which a police department *reflects the composition of the community it serves.* Federal courts have used the percentage of minorities in the local adult workforce as the standard in settling employment discrimination suits. The CALEA *Standards for Law Enforcement Agencies* recommend that the composition of police departments reflect the composition of the community (Figure 12–3).

Lewis and Walker each independently developed an equal employment opportunity (EEO) index to measure the extent to which a police department reflects the community it serves. The EEO index is computed by dividing the percentage of a particular minority group on the police force by the percentage in the population of the local community. Thus, if a community is 30 percent Hispanic and the police department is 15 percent Hispanic, the EEO index is .50.

The index is useful for measuring the employment performance of individual cities, for measuring change over time, and for taking into account the changing racial and ethnic composition of cities. A police department, for example, might hire more Hispanic officers, but if the Hispanic population of the city also increases, it may still be unrepresentative of the community. In the mid-1960s, African Americans were significantly underrepresented in cities with large minority populations. In 1966 they represented 23 percent of the population of Oakland, California, but only 2.3 percent of the police officers (resulting in an index of .10). African Americans were 30 percent of the population of Detroit in 1966, but only 3.9 percent of the police officers (for an index of .13). Similar disparities were found in Chicago, Cleveland, and other cities.[74]

Racial- and ethnic-minority employment has increased significantly in many departments in recent years, although some still lag behind. And in some departments people of color now represent a majority of all sworn officers. The Law Enforcement Management and Administrative Statistics (LEMAS) data indicate that in 1997 the Miami,

Florida, police department was 53 percent Hispanic, 26 percent African American, and 20 percent white. The Atlanta, Georgia, police department was 58 percent African American, 40 percent white, and 1 percent Hispanic. The San Antonio, Texas, police department was 57 percent Hispanic, 34 percent white, and 9 percent African American.[75]

Hispanic and Latino Officers

Special considerations relate to the employment of Hispanic and Latino officers. The 2000 Census found that the American population is changing rapidly, and the Hispanic population is growing even faster than most experts had expected. As a result, police departments increasingly serve communities where large numbers of people speak Spanish. Since the ability to communicate with people is the most important aspect of police work, it is important that police departments take active steps to ensure that they are able to communicate with Spanish-speaking people.[76] As explained in Chapter 4 some departments subscribe to translation services that allow them to handle 911 calls in languages other than English. Having an adequate number of Spanish-speaking officers on the force is also extremely important.

With respect to employment, there are a number of steps that police departments can take to increase the number of Hispanic officers. The first, and most important, is to actively recruit applicants in the Hispanic community. This involves contacting community groups and leaders and arranging for personal contact with potential applicants. A second approach might be offering incentive pay for officers who are bilingual. Higher pay for bilingual officers is justified on the grounds that officers should receive additional compensation if they have special skills that help the department fulfill its mission. The National Latino Police Officers Association (LPOA) helped to initiate a bilingual pay program with the California Highway Patrol in the 1970s. Since then, many other California agencies and others across the country have adopted similar programs.[77]

Another barrier to the employment of Hispanics in policing was the old minimum height requirement. In 1976 the LPOA testified before the California State Personnel Board, along with a group representing Japanese Americans, and succeeded in ending the height requirement for the California Highway Patrol. Since then, minimum height requirements have been eliminated across the country.

Women in Policing

Lucy Duvall, one of the first female officers in Cleveland, Ohio, had a difficult and often humiliating experience as a rookie officer. The department's precinct stations did not have separate locker rooms or rest rooms for women. Some of the male officers who resented their presence on the force deliberately changed clothes in front of them, as a form of subtle harassment.[78] As more women entered policing, other department policies had to be changed.[79] Old rules on hair falling below the collar were not consistent with common women's hairstyles. Police departments had to develop policies for pregnant officers. The federal Pregnancy Discrimination Act prohibits employment discrimination on the basis of pregnancy, childbirth, or any pregnancy-related medical condition.

Prior to the late 1960s, police departments did not hire women on an equal basis with men. Only a few were hired; and they were restricted to a separate job category of "policewoman," excluded from many assignments, including patrol, and in some departments not eligible for promotion above a certain rank. The major change occurred in the late 1960s with the assignment of women to patrol duty on an equal basis with men. Official discrimination against women was outlawed by the 1964 Civil Rights Act. Nonetheless, many forms of covert discrimination continue to exist. As a result, women are even more seriously underrepresented in police departments than racial and ethnic minorities. The percentage of all sworn officers who are women increased from 2 percent in 1972 to 4.2 percent in 1978 and 9 percent in 1997. The National Center for Women in Policing found that women represented 13.8 percent of all sworn officers in 1998 in large departments, up from 10.6 percent in 1990. The percentage of female officers is generally higher in large police departments, but reaches 20 percent in only a handful of departments. Yet, in 1993, women made up over 40 percent of the adult labor force.[80]

Female officers are concentrated in the lower ranks. They represent only 7.5 percent of top command positions and 9.6 percent of supervisory positions. Of the ten city departments with the largest percentage of female officers, eight were, or at some point had been, under a consent decree to hire more women. Among big-city police departments, Pittsburgh had the highest percentage of female officers, with 24.8 percent. Washington, DC, was a close second with 24.6 percent.[81]

Barriers to Women in Policing

The 1998 report by the National Center for Women in Policing found a number of barriers to the employment of women. Entrance examinations that emphasize upper body physical strength favor men. There is no evidence, however, that great physical strength (as opposed to good health) affects an officer's ability to perform well. On-the-job discrimination, particularly sexual harassment and discriminatory assignments, either discourages women from applying or encourages them to resign their jobs. Many police departments, meanwhile, recruit heavily from the military, which is a male-dominated occupation. Finally, some police departments embrace an old-fashioned model of policing, emphasizing aggressiveness and authoritarianism that is unappealing to many potential women applicants.[82]

Gay and Lesbian Officers

Sergeant Charles Cochrane, Jr., of the New York City police department took a bold step in 1982, announcing that he was gay and planned to form an organization of gay officers in the NYPD. As a staff psychologist with the NYPD later explained, the words *gay* and *police* "did not fit together comfortably in American society [at that time] let alone in the NYPD." Four years earlier, the mayor of New York City had banned employment discrimination against homosexuals in all city agencies. The head of the police union angrily denounced the policy, arguing that it would "do more harm than good." In his view, police officers form very close working relationships with their colleagues and the employment of homosexual officers would undermine cohesion among the rank and file.[83]

In the past 20 years, gay and lesbian people have become increasingly open as working police officers. Some departments actively recruit gay and lesbian officers. In some jurisdictions, state and local law prohibits discrimination on the basis of sexual orientation. And in jurisdictions with large gay and lesbian populations, serving the community requires serving that segment of the population. Having officers who are gay and lesbian who can serve as liaisons helps to advance a police department's mission.

Employment Discrimination Litigation

Employment discrimination suits under Title VII of the 1964 Civil Rights Act have been a major factor in increasing the number of minorities and women in policing. Successful suits produce a number of different results. First, they can result in direct benefit to the plaintiffs, including financial damages. Second, they often result in a court order eliminating tests or procedures that were discriminatory (e.g., height requirements that discriminated against women and Hispanics). Third, there may be a court-ordered affirmative action plan with specific goals and timetables for future recruiting.

In 1980 the Los Angeles police department signed a consent decree with the U.S. Justice Department awarding $2 million in back pay and agreeing that 45 percent of all new recruits would be African American or Hispanic, and 20 percent of all new recruits would be women. By 1990, the department had met its target of having 10.9 percent African American officers, but was still short of its goal on Hispanic officers (20 versus 24.6 percent target) and women (12 versus 20 percent target).[84]

Increasing the number of racial- and ethnic-minority officers has three objectives.[85] First, it is designed to end discrimination and ensure compliance with equal employment opportunity laws. Second, some reformers believe that minority officers will be better able to relate to minority citizens, and thereby reduce discrimination and reduce police–community relations tensions. This argument is examined in detail in Chapter 9. Third, many people believe that having a police department representative of the community it serves will improve public opinion about the department. A survey of Chicago residents found that a significant minority of residents did believe that the increase in minority police officers had contributed to the improvement of the department. Significantly, no residents indicated that the increase in minority officers had made the department worse than before.[86]

THE AFFIRMATIVE ACTION CONTROVERSY

The Law of Affirmative Action

The most controversial issue in police employment is affirmative action. The concept of affirmative action means that an employer must take positive steps (hence, "affirmative action") to remedy past discrimination. Affirmative action originated in 1965, with presidential Executive Order 11246 requiring all federal contractors to develop written affirmative action programs. Today, all private employers and government agencies receiving federal funds are required to have affirmative action plans. The basic premise of affirmative action is that simply ending discrimination (as required by the 1964 Civil Rights Act) does not automatically correct for the legacy of past discrimination.

An affirmative action plan consists of several elements. The employer must (1) conduct a census of current employees, (2) identify underutilization or concentration of minorities and women, and (3) develop a recruiting plan to correct any underutilization. The U.S. Equal Employment Opportunity Commission defines underutilization as "having fewer minorities or women in a particular job category than would reasonably be expected by their presence in the relevant labor market."[87] The EEO index (see p. 403) is a useful tool for identifying underutilization. Concentration is defined as the overrepresentation of minorities or women in the lowest-level job categories.

A 1991 report by the International City Management Association (ICMA) found that 67 percent of all cities and 70 percent of all counties had affirmative action policies. Only about one-fourth, however, used numeric goals as part of their policy.[88]

The Issue of Quotas

Affirmative action plans generally include goals and timetables for correcting underutilization. An employer establishes a goal of having a certain percentage of female employees by a certain date. Goals and timetables do not necessarily include rigid hiring quotas, however.

Some hiring quota plans are adopted voluntarily by employers. The Detroit police department, for example, substantially increased its employment of African American officers through a voluntary affirmative action plan adopted in 1974. In addition to a new recruitment plan, it adopted a policy of promoting one black officer to sergeant for every white officer promoted.[89]

Most affirmative action plans with quotas, however, are court-ordered. Employment discrimination suits are frequently settled through a consent decree, with the employer agreeing to a recruitment plan to increase either minorities or women. In 1980, for example, the Omaha police department settled a discrimination suit with a consent decree requiring that 40 percent of all new recruits be African Americans until the department's total officer population was 9.5 percent African American. The target was based on the percentage of blacks in the Omaha labor force.[90]

Supporters of affirmative action argue that it is necessary to correct past employment discrimination. Susan Martin found that affirmative action plans succeeded in increasing the number of women in applicant pools. Women represented 20.5 percent of all applicants in those departments with a court-ordered plan, but only 16.7 percent in those with a voluntary plan, and 12.9 percent in those with no plan.[91] In other words, affirmative action worked primarily at the recruitment stage, increasing the number of applicants. Ellen Hochstedler also found that the use of a specific hiring quota was one of the most important correlates of increased minority employment.[92]

Opponents of affirmative action and quotas argue that they involve reverse discrimination against whites and/or males, in violation of the 1964 Civil Rights Act and the

---

SIDEBAR 12–2 HIRING QUOTAS: FAIR OR UNFAIR?

Many police departments have been sued for employment discrimination under Title VII of the 1964 Civil Rights Act because of alleged discrimination against women, African Americans, or Latinos. A number of these suits have been settled through consent decrees that include affirmative action hiring plans with specific quotas. A consent decree, we should remember, is a judicially enforceable settlement that both sides must obey.

A typical example of a consent decree quota system would be the requirement that 40 percent of all new recruits hired by a police department must be women, until a specified target is reached.

Are quotas fair? Consider the following example.

Assume that a department is operating under a 40 percent quota for women. It plans to hire fifty new officers, and therefore, twenty must be women and thirty will be men. When all the test scores are compiled, the twentieth highest scoring female applicant has a combined score of 82 out of 100. She is hired. A male applicant who has a combined score of 83 ranked thirty-first on the men's list. He is not hired.

Is this system fair? Consider the following questions. Is it fair to the male applicant who had a higher score but was not hired? Is it fair to women as a group, who have historically been denied employment with the police?

How significant is the difference between a score of 83 and a score of 82? Do those numbers really predict who will be the better police officer? How reliable are the tests that went into that composite score? If they used a general intelligence test, does it really identify who will be an effective police officer? Does a difference of a few points on a standard psychological test indicate that the person with the slightly higher score will be the better police officer? (Point of fact: The department set a combined score of 70 as the minimum for employment. Anyone with a score of 69 or lower could not be hired.)

The courts have upheld quota systems as a remedy for past discrimination. If you feel this system is unfair, what strategy would you recommend for remedying past discrimination?

---

equal protection clause of the Fourteenth Amendment to the U.S. Constitution. White officers, for example, challenged the Detroit one-for-one promotion plan. In 1996, California voters approved Proposition 209 outlawing affirmative action in the state.

The U.S. Supreme Court has issued a confusing and often contradictory series of decisions on affirmative action. In 1987 it upheld the constitutionality of a voluntary affirmative action plan in Santa Clara, California. Quotas for increasing the number of female employees were acceptable as long as the program was short-run and would end as soon as past discrimination was corrected.[93] Since 1987, however, the Supreme Court has become increasingly opposed to any form of preference based on race. The state of California banned all racial preferences with Proposition 209 in 1996, and the ban was upheld by the U.S. Supreme Court.

Opponents of affirmative action also argue that it lowers personnel standards by forcing the employer to hire people with lower qualifications. Law professor John Lott argues that affirmative action not only lowered police personnel standards but led to higher crime rates as a result.[94] His study, however, included no data on actual recruitment standards and studied crime trends from 1987 to 1990. Including crime data from 1990 to 1997 might find that affirmative action lowers the crime rate.[95]

A PERF study, however, found a steady rise in the levels of education among police officers from the 1960s through the late 1980s, a period that included affirmative action programs. The educational levels of white, African American, and Hispanic officers in 1988, moreover, were nearly comparable. It found that 62.2 percent of whites had some college credits, compared with 67.5 percent of Hispanics and 63.2 percent of African Americans.[96]

The question of whether affirmative action results in lower personnel standards depends on how a police department implements its affirmative action plan. If, for example, an agency hires people who do not meet the normal minimum standards, then it is lowering its standards. The intent of affirmative action is to prod employers to recruit more aggressively in order to find qualified employees. If an agency cannot meet a quota, the proper course of action is to suspend the hiring process and conduct a more vigorous recruitment effort in order to increase the size of the applicant pool.

Some critics of affirmative action cite the example of the Washington, DC, police department, which conducted a major hiring campaign in the early 1990s and in the process failed to conduct the standard background investigations of applicants. As a result, many unqualified officers were hired, some of whom had criminal records and eventually became corrupt officers.[97] Two comments on the Washington, DC, experience are relevant, however. First, the speeded-up hiring was directed by Congress not as a minority employment effort but as a "get tough on crime" program. Second, whatever the goals of speeded-up hiring, the department was irresponsible in failing to conduct standard background checks.[98]

Even assuming that affirmative action is a valid approach, the empirical question is whether or not it achieves its goals. There is conflicting evidence on this question. Susan Martin's research on women in policing found that departments with affirmative action plans did, in fact, have a higher percentage of women in their applicant pools. And partly as a result, they hired more women as police recruits.[99] With respect to the employment of African American officers, however, a national survey of 281 police departments found that the presence of an affirmative action plan had only modest impact. The most important explanation of the employment of African American officers was the size of the African American population in the local community.[100]

TRAINING

Over the past 30 years, significant changes have been made in preservice training for police officers. The typical training period is much longer than before, covers more subjects, and is required by state law.

Police Academy Training

About three-quarters of all big-city police departments operate their own academies (departments in smaller cities tend to use state-run academies).[101] The status of police academies has risen over the years. In the 1950s training occupied "a minor position within the [police] organization." By the 1980s, most big-city academies had been elevated to the level of a division within the organization. Academy staff tend to be much larger and are provided access to greater classroom and gymnasium space.[102]

The average length of preservice training programs tripled between the 1950s and 1997, increasing from about 300 to over 1,000 hours, including both classroom and field training. In 1997, departments in cities with populations over 100,000 provided an average of about 1,200 hours of training, divided between about 800 hours of classroom training and 400 hours of field training. Departments in very small cities (population of 10,000 or less), meanwhile, required an average of only about 600 hours of training.[103] (See Table 12–2).

The police academy experience serves several functions. First, it provides formal training. Second, it is a process for weeding out recruits who prove to be unqualified. An average of about 10 percent of all recruits fail the police academy training program according to the ACJS survey.[104] Third, it is a rite of passage that socializes recruits into the police subculture. This subculture includes a strong ethos of identification with the profession, the department, and fellow officers.[105]

The content of police academy curricula has changed significantly, with less emphasis on the purely technical aspects of policing (e.g., effecting an arrest, booking a suspect, firing a weapon) and more on the legal and behavioral aspects. One survey found that in the 1950s, 93 percent of all firearms-related training time involved skill development

TABLE 12–2   TRAINING REQUIREMENTS FOR NEW OFFICER RECRUITS IN LOCAL POLICE DEPARTMENTS, BY SIZE OF POPULATION SERVED, 1997

Population Served	Average Number of Hours Required		
	Total	Class-room	Field
All sizes	599	395	204
1,000,000 or more	1,252	878	374
500,000–999,999	1,357	822	535
250,000–499,999	1,356	782	574
100,000–249,999	1,145	649	496
50,000–99,999	938	537	501
25,000–49,999	919	518	401
10,000–24,999	780	470	310
2,500–9,999	602	399	203
Under 2,500	422	321	101

Note: Average number of training hours excludes departments not requiring training.
Source: Bureau of Justice Statistics, *Local Police Departments, 1997* (Washington, DC: Government Printing Office, 2000), p. 5.

in shooting; almost no time was devoted to the legal aspects of when an officer could fire a weapon and to the general issue of discretion in shooting.[106] As the law of police work changed in the 1960s, largely as a result of Supreme Court rulings, the amount of pre-service training devoted to criminal procedure increased. Subjects such as race relations, human relations, domestic violence, and ethics were also added to curricula.

Police academy instructors vary according to background, expertise, and orientation toward education. In an observational study of three police academies, Berg developed a typology of five different categories of instructors. "Police academics" were sworn police officers who had obtained college credentials and used college-style teaching techniques. "Police careerists" were sworn officers who relied primarily on "war stories" of the lessons of their experience. "Maladaptive generalists" were officers who were not prepared to teach, who offered personal advice, and sometimes contradicted departmental policy. "Legalists" were instructors who confined their teaching to legal issues. Finally, "civilians" were people who were not sworn officers but were specialists in some particular area.[107]

Field Training

To supplement classroom academy training, most departments also operate field training programs. These involve practical experience in police work under the supervision of an experienced field training officer (FTO). A 1986 survey found that nearly two-thirds (64 percent) of the departments had a field training program. More than half (57 percent) indicated that their program was directly modeled after the innovative San Jose program created in 1972.[108]

The original San Jose FTO program consisted of 16 weeks of classroom training, followed by 14 weeks of field training. During field training, the recruit is assigned to three different FTOs for 4-week periods each, followed by a final 2 weeks with the original FTO. Each FTO makes daily reports on the recruit's performance, and supervisors complete weekly evaluation reports.[109]

FTO programs also vary in quality. A sex discrimination suit by female officers in one department exposed serious problems with the existing informal postacademy field training program. The officers alleged that the field training officers were biased against them. The suit found that the FTO program had no curriculum, no performance evaluation system based on actual tasks, and no training for the field training officers. The suit resulted in a new and improved FTO program.[110] This particular case illustrates the way in which employment discrimination suits often result in general reforms of police department policies and practices.

State Training and Certification

One of the most important changes in police training in the past 30 years has been the development of state laws requiring preservice training for all officers. California and New York were the first states to adopt this requirement in 1959. By the early 1980s, every state had some form of mandated training.[111] The impact of state-mandated training has been greatest among small police departments, which cannot afford to operate their own training academies. Historically, these departments put officers on duty with no formal training whatsoever. A 1965 International Association of Chiefs of Police (IACP) survey of 4,000 police departments found that 85 percent of all officers had received no preservice training.[112]

In most states, small departments send their new officers to a state training academy or program certified by the state. Some programs are operated through community colleges. The separate police academies run by the large police departments are similarly certified by the state. The minimum state training requirements are usually lower, in terms of the number of hours of training, than the programs operated by big-city police academies. Officers who complete state training are then certified or licensed as peace officers in the state.

If a police officer has been fired by one department, should he or she be hired by another law enforcement agency? Many people worry about the problem of the "gypsy cops" who move from one department to another despite bad performance histories. There has never been any national registry of officers and their career patterns. An applicant may simply lie and not tell a police department that he or she was fired by another department. Many small agencies may not have the resources to do a thorough background investigation. Some, in fact, may not care. One partial solution to this problem is state certification of officers with procedures for decertification.

A majority (thirty-nine) of states now have procedures for decertifying officers by revoking their license to work as police officers in the state. Decertification addresses the problem of officers who are fired from one department for misconduct but are then hired by another. If they are decertified, this is not possible. The process does not, however, prevent the fired officer from being hired in another state (assuming the individual meets the requirements, and the hiring department does not check the person's work history).[113]

Florida was one of the first states to adopt a comprehensive decertification process. Between 1976 and 1983 the Florida Criminal Justice Standards and Training Commission took action against 148 officers. It decertified 132, suspended 14, and placed 2 on probation. Most cases involved private or departmental misconduct; only 22 of the 148 involved official misconduct.[114]

Shortcomings of Current Police Training

Do police training programs cover the really important aspects of police work? So far in this book we have learned that officers routinely exercise tremendous discretion (Chapter 8). They also deal with a lot of difficult social problems such as domestic disputes and mental health problems (Chapter 5). Only some of these incidents involve an arrest. Use of deadly force, moreover, is a very rare event. Do police training programs adequately cover the kinds of situations that occur most frequently, or are they too heavily weighted toward criminal law enforcement and infrequent critical incidents?

Despite the recent improvements, police training programs suffer from a number of limitations. Many programs still do not cover important subjects such as discretion, the use of informants, and ethics. Also, preservice training by itself may not adequately prepare officers for the tasks they face. A 1-hour police academy lecture on spouse abuse, for example, may have no effect on how officers handle a domestic violence incident months or years later. A short session on mental illness may not prepare officers to recognize serious mental illness or provide adequate guidance on how to handle mentally ill people.

The Detroit police department conducted an experimental training program for recruits on dealing with crime victims. An evaluation found that crime victims did not rate officers who had received the training any better than officers who had not been through the program. (Both groups of officers, in fact, received very high ratings.) Even more serious, all recruits experienced a significant change in attitudes after being out on the street, developing significantly less positive attitudes toward the public.[115] McNamara found a similar shift in attitudes after 1 year on the street in a study of New York City recruits.[116] These findings lend support to the argument that the working environment of policing—rather than background characteristics or training—is the principal factor in shaping police officer attitudes and behavior.[117] The police subculture is discussed in more detail in Chapter 13.

Because of persistent police–community relations problems (Chapter 9), most departments have introduced race relations, human relations, or cultural diversity training into the curriculum. A review of cultural diversity training programs, however, found that the content has not changed much since the 1960s, that they tend to perpetuate negative stereotypes about racial and ethnic minorities, and that they focus on the attitudes of individual officers and ignore the policies of the department as a whole.[118] Alpert, Smith, and Watters argue that "mere classroom training" on issues such as race relations "is insufficient." In particular, they recommend experimenting with training officers in communication skills with racial and ethnic groups "other than their own."[119]

THE PROBATIONARY PERIOD

Upon completing preservice training, a recruit is sworn in and assigned to regular duty. The officer is on probationary status for a period that may range from 6 months to 2 years, depending upon the department (some departments count the time in training as part of this period). In 1994 the average length was about 1 year.[120] During the probationary period an officer can be dismissed without cause. After the probationary period is completed, dismissal must be based on cause under rules established by the local civil service regulations and/or police union contract.[121]

About 7 percent of the recruits either resign or are dismissed during this period.[122] Susan Martin found significant differences in how departments used the probationary period, however. In Phoenix, 47 percent of all officers who left the department were on probation at the time. This included 26 percent of all female recruits and 14 percent of all males. In Washington, DC, however, only 15 percent of those leaving the department were in the probationary phase (representing 5 percent of both males and females).[123] Many experts argue that a longer probationary period permits more time for observing performance and an opportunity to dismiss those whose performance is unsatisfactory. In Philadelphia the 6-month probationary period includes 19 weeks of academy training, leaving only a 7-week period of on-the-street experience. A report found this "insufficient to allow supervisors to determine whether a particular candidate is qualified to be a police officer" and recommended at least a 6-month probationary period following completion of academy training.[124]

SUMMARY

The profile of the American police officer has changed significantly over the past 25 years. There are now more racial-minority, female, and college-educated officers than ever before. Many old personnel practices have been eliminated because they discriminated against particular groups. Meanwhile, the training of officers has improved substantially during the same period. In short, the police recruit of today is a very different kind of person from the recruit of 25 years ago.

CASE STUDY: EXCERPT FROM THE PRESIDENT'S COMMISSION ON LAW ENFORCEMENT AND ADMINISTRATION OF JUSTICE, *THE CHALLENGE OF CRIME IN A FREE SOCIETY*

The Commission recommends:

Police departments should take immediate steps to establish a minimum requirement of a baccalaureate degree for all supervisory and executive positions.

The long-range objective for high-ranking officers should be advanced degrees in the law, sociology, criminology, police or public administration, business management, or some other appropriate specialty.

Of equal importance with his education is a police candidate's aptitude for the job: His intelligence, his moral character, his emotional stability, his social attitudes. The consequences of putting on the street officers who, however highly educated, are prejudiced, or slow witted, or hot tempered, or timid, or dishonest are too obvious to require detailed discussion. Thorough personal screening of police candidates is a clear necessity. The amount of thoroughness with which local departments screen candidates varies enormously. Some departments screen quite sketchily; others, including those in many of the biggest cities, make in-depth background investigations, administer intelligence tests and interview candidates exhaustively. However, it is fair to say that even the most thorough departments do not evaluate reliably the personal traits and characteristics that contribute to good police work, not because they lack the desire to do so but because a technique for doing so does not exist. Clearly this is a field in which intensive research is needed.

Source: President's Commission on Law Enforcement and Administration of Justice, *The Challenge of Crime in a Free Society* (Washington, DC: Government Printing Office, 1967), p. 110.

FOR DISCUSSION

Over 30 years ago, the President's Crime Commission recommended that all police officers have an undergraduate baccalaureate degree. When the commission made this recommendation, there was very little research on policing (either on police work or on police officers). We have learned much more about policing since then.

In light of this research, discuss the commission's recommendation.

1 Is it a good strategy for improving policing?
2 What are the underlying assumptions of this approach?
3 What evidence do we have that it improves policing?

INTERNET EXERCISES

Exercise 1   How do the recruitment standards for the law enforcement agencies in your area compare with those in other parts of the country? First, select a list of agencies in your area. Choose either the agencies in your immediate metropolitan area (which would include the major city police department and suburban departments) or the state, or, for example, a multistate region if applicable (say, for example, the Kansas City area, which would include two states and a combination of city and suburban departments).

Second, use the Web to identify the minimum qualifications for each agency. Most (but not all) agencies post employment opportunities on their website.

Third, compile the data in a table that is easily readable. Are there any significant differences in employment standards by size of agency or other factor? Does any particular agency appear to have relatively low standards?

Exercise 2   Some police departments have special hiring provisions for applicants who are bilingual. This represents an effort to increase the number of officers who can speak Spanish, or Vietnamese, or some other language. Often, the special provision involves granting extra points in the application process.

First, identify cities with large Hispanic/Latino and/or Asian populations. Data from the 2000 Census are available on the Web. One place to start looking would be **www.refdesk.com.** Then, search the websites of the police departments in those cities (**www.officer.com**). Identify any cities that are making special efforts to hire bilingual officers. How prevalent are such efforts? What special provisions do these efforts involve?

REFERENCES

1 Arthur Niederhoffer, *Behind the Shield: The Police in Urban Society* (Garden City, NY: Anchor Books, 1967), p. 1.

2 David H. Bayley and Harold Mendelsohn, *Minorities and the Police: Confrontation in America* (New York: The Free Press, 1969).

3 George W. Griesinger, Jeffrey S. Slovak, and Joseph J. Molkup, *Civil Service Systems: Their Impact on Police Administration* (Washington, DC: Government Printing Office, 1979).

4 Robert Langworthy, Thomas Hughes, and Beth Sanders, *Law Enforcement Recruitment, Selection and Training: A Survey of Major Police Departments in the U.S.* (Highland Heights, KY: ACJS, 1995), p. 24.

5 President's Commission on Law Enforcement and Administration of Justice, *Task Force Report: The Police* (Washington, DC: Government Printing Office, 1967), p. 130.

6 Stephen D. Mastrofski, Jeffrey B. Snipes, and Anne E. Supina, "Compliance on Demand: The Public's Response to Specific Police Requests," *Journal of Research in Crime and Delinquency*, 33 (August 1996): 269–305.

7 Langworthy, Hughes, and Sanders, *Law Enforcement Recruitment, Selection and Training*, p. 24.

8 "Weighty Matters: Court Rules against Ohio Troopers in Fitness-Standards Suit," *Law Enforcement News* (February 2, 1997), p. 1.

9 Bureau of Justice Statistics, *Local Police Departments, 1997* (Washington, DC: Government Printing Office, 1999).

10 David L. Carter, Allen D. Sapp, and Darrell W. Stephens, *The State of Police Education* (Washington, DC: Police Executive Research Forum, 1989), p. 84.

11 Susan E. Martin, *On the Move: The Status of Women in Policing* (Washington, DC: The Police Foundation, 1990), p. 78.

12 Carter, Sapp, and Stephens, *The State of Police Education*, p. 38.

13 Michael Heidingsfield, "Six Reasons to Require College Education for Police Officers," *Subject to Debate*, 9 (December 1995): 5–7.

14 President's Commission on Law Enforcement and Administration of Justice, *The Challenge of Crime in a Free Society* (Washington, DC: Government Printing Office, 1967), p. 109.

15 Robert E. Worden, "A Badge and a Baccalaureate: Policies, Hypotheses, and Further Evidence," *Justice Quarterly*, 7 (September 1990): 566–567.

16 Bureau of the Census, *Statistical Abstract of the United States, 1999* (Washington, DC: Government Printing Office, 1999), Table 263.

17 Wesley G. Skogan and Susan M. Hartnett, *Community Policing, Chicago Style* (New York: Oxford University Press, 1997), pp. 70–109.

18 Bureau of the Census, *Statistical Abstract of the United States, 1997* (Washington, DC: Government Printing Office, 1997), Table 263.

19 Lawrence W. Sherman, *The Quality of Police Education* (San Francisco: Jossey-Bass, 1978), Ch. 7.

20 David L. Carter, Allen D. Sapp, and Darrel W. Stephens, "Higher Education as a Bona Fide Occupational Qualification (BFOQ) for Police: A Blueprint," *American Journal of Police*, 7 (Fall 1988): 1–27; *Davis v. City of Dallas*, 777 F.2d. 205 (5th Cir. 1985).

21 David L. Carter and Allen D. Sapp, *Police Education and Minority Recruitment: The Impact of a College Requirement* (Washington, DC: PERF, 1991), p. 27.

22 M. L. Dantzker, "Do College Education Requirements for Police Create an Over-education Problem?" *Subject to Debate*, 9 (December 1995): 4.

23 Sherman, *The Quality of Police Education,* pp. 185–188.

24 Bureau of Justice Statistics, *Law Enforcement Management and Administrative Statistics, 1997* (Washington, DC: Government Printing Office, 2000).

25 Carter, Sapp, and Stephens, *The State of Police Education*, p. 61.

26 "Man Who Scored Too High on Police Test Loses Federal Appeal," Associated Press, September 8, 2000.

27 Griesinger et al., *Civil Service Systems*, p. 102.

28 Department of Health and Human Services, *National Household Survey on Drug Use: Population Estimates, 1995* (Washington, DC: Government Printing Office, 1996), pp. 23–27.

29 American Civil Liberties Union of Southern California, *From the Outside In: Residency Patterns within the Los Angeles Police Department* (Los Angeles: ACLU-Southern California, 1994), p. i.

30 Bureau of Justice Statistics, *Law Enforcement Management and Administrative Statistics, 1997;* Langworthy, Hughes, and Sanders, *Law Enforcement Recruitment, Selection and Training*, p. 24.

31 New York City Civilian Complaint Review Board, *Annual Report 1993* (New York: CCRB, 1993), p. 28.

32 David W. Murphy and John L. Worrall, "Residency Requirements and Public Perceptions of the Police in Large Municipalities," *Policing*, 22, no. 3 (1999): 327–342.

33 "Incentives Draw Few L.A. Officers into City," *The Los Angeles Times* (September 18, 1999).

34 "Gains Despite Downsizing," *Law Enforcement News* (October 31, 1992).

35 U.S. Equal Employment Opportunity Commission, *Affirmative Action and Equal Employment*, Vol. 1 (Washington, DC: Government Printing Office, 1974), p. 23.

36 Langworthy, Hughes, and Sanders, *Law Enforcement Recruitment, Selection and Training*, p. 23.

37 President's Commission on Law Enforcement and Administration of Justice, Field Surveys III, v. 2, *Studies in Crime and Law Enforcement* (Washington, DC: Government Printing Office, 1967), p. 18.

38 Virginia B. Ermer, "Recruitment of Female Police Officers in New York City," *Journal of Criminal Justice*, 6 (Fall 1978): 233–246.

39 M. Steven Meagher and Nancy Yentes, "Choosing a Career in Policing: A Comparison of Male and Female Perceptions," *Journal of Police Science and Administration*, 14, no. 4 (1986): 320–327.

40 Ermer, "The Recruitment of Female Police Officers in New York City," 233–246.

41 William A. Westley, *Violence and the Police* (Cambridge, MA: MIT Press, 1970), p. 205; John H. McNamara, "Uncertainties in Police Work: The Relevance of Police Recruits' Backgrounds and Training," in David J. Bordua, ed., *The Police: Six Sociological Essays* (New York: Wiley, 1967), pp. 163–252.

42 Bayley and Mendelsohn, *Minorities and the Police*, p. 6.

43 Griesinger et al. , *Civil Service Systems*.

44 Nicholas Alex, *New York Cops Talk Back* (New York: John Wiley, 1976), p. 9.

45 Ermer, "Recruitment of Female Police Officers."

46 James Q. Wilson, "Generational and Ethnic Differences Among Career Police Officers," *American Journal of Sociology,* 69 (March 1964): 526.

47 Ermer, "Recruitment of Female Police Officers."

48 Bayley and Mendelsohn, *Minorities and the Police*, p. 30.

49 Robert J. Kaminski, "Police Minority Recruitment: Predicting Who Will Say Yes to an Offer for a Job as a Cop," *Journal of Criminal Justice*, 21 (1993): 395–409.

50 W. S. Wilson Huang and Michael S. Vaughan, "Support and Confidence: Public Attitudes toward the Police," in T. J. Flanagan and D. R. Longmire, eds., *Americans View Crime and Justice: A National Public Opinion Survey* (Newbury Park, CA: Sage, 1996), pp. 31–45.

51 Nicholas Alex, *Black in Blue: A Study of the Negro Policeman* (Englewood Cliffs, NJ: Prentice-Hall, 1969).

52 Martin, *On the Move.*

53 Langworthy, Hughes, and Sanders, *Law Enforcement Recruitment, Training and Selection*, p. 26.

54 Ibid., p. 24.

55 Bernard Cohen, "Minority Retention in the New York City Police Department: A Policy Study," *Criminology*, 11 (November 1973): 287–306.

56 Bureau of Justice Statistics, *Local Police Departments, 1997*, pp. 4, 11.

57 Langworthy, Hughes, and Sanders, *Law Enforcement Recruitment, Selection and Training*, p. 27.

58 William G. Doerner, "The Utility of the Oral Interview Board in Selecting Police Academy Admissions," *Policing*, 20, no. 4 (1997): 784.

59 Langworthy, Hughes, and Sanders, *Law Enforcement Recruitment, Selection and Training*, p. 29.

60 Anthony V. Bouza, "The Policeman's Character Investigation: Lowered Standards or Changing Times?" *Journal of Criminal Law, Criminology, and Police Science*, 63 (March 1972): 120–124.

61 "D.C. Police Force Still Paying for Two-Year Hiring Spree," *The Washington Post* (August 28, 1994).

62 Bernard Cohen and Jan M. Chaiken, *Police Background Characteristics and Performance* (Lexington, MA: Lexington Books, 1973), pp. 87, 90–91.

63 J. Douglas Grant and Joan Grant, "Officer Selection and the Prevention of Abuse of Force," in W. A. Geller and H. Toch, eds., *And Justice for All* (Washington, DC: PERF, 1995), pp. 161–162.

64 Benjamin S. Wright, William G. Doerner, and John C. Speir, "Pre-employment Psychological Testing as a Predictor of Police Performance during an FTO Program," *American Journal of Police*, IX, no. 4 (1990): 65–84.

65 Christopher Commission, *Report of the Independent Commission on the Los Angeles Police Department* (Los Angeles: City of Los Angeles, 1991), p. 110.

66 Cohen and Chaiken, *Police Background Characteristics and Performance*, p. 4.

67 *Davis v. City of Dallas*, 777 F.2d 205, 216.

68 Doerner, "The Utility of the Oral Interview Board in Selecting Police Academy Admissions," 784.

69 Paula Rubin, *Civil Rights and Criminal Justice: Employment Discrimination Overview* (Washington, DC: Government Printing Office, 1995).

70 Ibid., p. 102.

71 *Davis v. City of Dallas*, 777 F.2d 205.

72 Paula N. Rubin, *The Americans With Disabilities Act and Criminal Justice: An Overview* (Washington, DC: Government Printing Office, 1993).

73 Bureau of Justice Statistics, *Law Enforcement Management and Administrative Statistics, 1997*, p. xiii.

74 President's Commission, *Task Force Report: The Police*, pp. 167–174; (Kerner Commission) *Report of the National Advisory Commission on Civil Disorders* (New York: Bantam Books, 1968), pp. 315–316, 321–322.

75 Bureau of Justice Statistics, *Law Enforcement Management and Administrative Statistics, 1997*, Table 3a.

76 Leigh Herbst and Samuel Walker, *Journal of Criminal Justice,* 29 (July 2001).

77 National Latino Peace Officers Association, "History" (**www.nlpoa.com/history**), p. 4.

78 Tamar Husansky and Pat Sparling, *Working Vice: The True Story of Lt. Lucy Duvall—America's First Woman Vice Squad Chief* (New York: Harper Paperbacks, 1993).

79 Martin, *On the Move.*

80 Bureau of Justice Statistics, *Local Police Departments, 1997;* National Center for Women and Policing, *Equality Denied: The Status of Women in Policing* (Los Angeles: National Center for Women and Policing, 1998).

81 National Center for Women and Policing, *Equality Denied*, pp. 2, 10.

82 Ibid., p. 4.

83 Patrick Suraci, Ph.D., "The Beginning of GOAL" (**www.goalny.org**).

84 George Felkenes and Peter Charles Unsinger, *Diversity, Affirmative Action, and Law Enforcement* (Springfield, IL: Charles C. Thomas, 1992).

85 Samuel Walker, Cassia Spohn, and Miriam DeLone, *The Color of Justice,* 2nd ed. (Belmont, CA: Wadsworth, 2000).

86 Samuel Walker and Vincent J. Webb, "Public Perceptions of Racial and Minority Employment and Its Perceived Impact on Police Service," Paper, Annual Meeting, American Society of Criminology, 1997.

87 U.S. Equal Employment Opportunity Commission, *Affirmative Action and Equal Employment*, Vol. 1 (Washington, DC: Government Printing Office, 1974), p. 23.

88 Evelina R. Moulder, "Affirmative Action in Local Government," *Municipal Yearbook, 1991* (Washington, DC: ICMA, 1991), Appendix 6.

89 Lawrence W. Sherman, "Minority Quotas for Police Promotions (A Comment on *Detroit Police Officers Association v. Young*)," *Criminal Law Bulletin*, 15 (January–February 1979): 79–84.

90 Consent Decree, *Midwest Guardians v. Omaha* (1980).

91 Martin, *On the Move*, p. 39.

92 Ellen Hochstedler, "Impediments to Hiring Minorities," *Journal of Police Science and Administration,* 12 (June 1984): 233.

93 *Johnson v. Transportation Agency*, 480 U.S. 616 (1987); Melvin I. Urofsky, *A Conflict of Rights: The Supreme Court and Affirmative Action* (New York: Scribner's, 1991).

94 John Lott, "Does a Helping Hand Put Others at Risk? Affirmative Action, Police Departments, and Crime," *Subject to Debate*, 12 (May 1998).

95 Samuel Walker, "Ideology as an Intervening Variable in Affirmative Action," *Subject to Debate*, 12 (May 1998).

96 David L. Carter, Allen D. Sapp, and Darrel W. Stephens, *The State of Police Education* (Washington, DC: Police Executive Research Forum, 1988).

97 "D.C. Police Force Still Paying for Two-Year Hiring Spree."

98 Ibid.

99 Martin, *On the Move*, p. 39.

100 Jihong Zhao and Nicholas Lovrich, "Determinants of Minority Employment in American Municipal Police Agencies: The Representation of African American Officers," *Journal of Criminal Justice*, 26, no. 4 (1998).

101 Langworthy, Hughes, and Sanders, *Law Enforcement Recruitment, Selection and Training*, p. 32.

102 Thomas M. Frost and Magnus J. Seng, "The Administration of Police Training: A Thirty Year Perspective," *Journal of Police Science and Administration*, 12 (March 1984): 66–73.

103 Bureau of Justice Statistics, *Local Police Departments, 1997* (Washington, DC: Government Printing Office, 2000), p. 5.

104 Langworthy, Hughes, and Sanders, *Law Enforcement Recruitment, Selection and Training*, p. 32.

105 Westley, *Violence and the Police*, pp. 153–159; Richard N. Harris, *Police Academy: An Inside View* (New York: John Wiley, 1973).

106 Thomas M. Frost and Magnus J. Seng, "Police Entry-Level Curriculum: A Thirty-Year Perspective," *Journal of Police Science and Administration*, 12 (September 1984): 254.

107 Bruce L. Berg, "Who Should Teach Police: A Typology and Assessment of Police Academy Instructors," *American Journal of Police*, IX, no. 2 (1990): 79–100.

108 Michael S. Campbell, *Field Training for Police Officers: State of the Art* (Washington, DC: Government Printing Office, 1986).

109 Ibid.

110 William G. Doerner and E. Britt Patterson, "The Influence of Race and Gender upon Rookie Evaluations of their Field Training Officers," *American Journal of Police*, XI, no. 2 (1992): 23–36.

111 Richard C. Lumb, ed., *Sourcebook of Standards and Training Information in the United States* (Charlotte: University of North Carolina at Charlotte, 1993).

112 President's Commission on Law Enforcement and Administration of Justice, *Task Force Report: The Police*, p. 138.

113 Steven Puro, Roger Goldman, and William C. Smith, "Police Decertification: Changing Patterns among the States, 1985–1995," *Policing*, 20, no. 3 (1997): 481–496.

114 Roger Goldman and Steven Puro, "Decertification of Police: An Alternative to Traditional Remedies for Police Misconduct," *Hastings Constitutional Law Quarterly*, 15 (Fall 1987): 45–80.

115 Arthur J. Lurigio and Dennis P. Rosenbaum, "The Travails of the Detroit Police–Victims Experiment: Assumptions and Important Lessons," *American Journal of Police*, XI, no. 3 (1992): 1–34.

116 McNamara, "Uncertainties in Police Work."

117 Jerome H. Skolnick, *Justice without Trial*, 3rd ed. (New York: Macmillan, 1994).

118 Jerome L. Blakemore, David Barlow, and Deborah L. Padgett, "From the Classroom to the Community: Introducing Process in Police Diversity Training," *Police Studies*, XVIII, no. 1 (1995): 71–83.

119 Geoffrey P. Alpert, William C. Smith, and Daniel Watters, "Implications of the Rodney King Beating," *Criminal Law Bulletin*, 28 (September–October 1992): 477.

120 Langworthy, Hughes, and Sanders, *Law Enforcement Recruitment, Selection, and Training*, p. 39.

121 Griesinger et al., *Civil Service Systems*.

122 James J. Fyfe, "Police Personnel Practices, 1986," *Municipal Yearbook 1987* (Washington, DC: International City Management Association, 1987).

123 Martin, *On the Move*, pp. 131–132.

124 Philadelphia Police Study Task Force, *Philadelphia and Its Police: Toward a New Partnership* (Philadelphia: City of Philadelphia, 1986), p. 94.

CHAPTER THIRTEEN

Police Officers II: On the Job

CHAPTER OUTLINE

INTRODUCTION

After completing the probationary period a police officer enters into a law enforcement career. Many factors influence the course of an individual career. Some officers achieve promotion and advancement, while others remain at the rank of police officer for their entire careers. Some officers leave their jobs, either by choice or because they are terminated. Officers' attitudes about the job, the profession, and citizens often change over the course of a career. This chapter examines the experience of being on the job as a police officer. Particular attention is given to those factors that influence officers' attitudes and behavior.

KEY TERMS
AND CONCEPTS

REALITY SHOCK: BEGINNING POLICE WORK

The first weeks and months on the job for a new police officer are often a rude awakening. In his classic study of the police subculture, Westley describes the experience as "reality shock."[1] The new officer quickly encounters the unpleasant aspects of dealing with the public, the criminal justice system, and the department itself.

Encountering Citizens

Police officer attitudes toward the public change significantly during the first weeks and months on the job. McNamara found that the percentage of officers agreeing with the statement "patrolmen almost never receive the cooperation from the public that is needed to handle police work properly" rose from 35 percent at the beginning of academy training to 50 percent after 2 years on the job. Meanwhile, at the start of academy training, 31 percent agreed that it was necessary to use force to gain respect in "tough" neighborhoods, while 2 years later 55 percent agreed.[2] A similar change in attitudes toward the public occurred among new Detroit police officers who participated in a special victims' services training program. After 4 months on the job, officers gave substantially lower ranking to the importance of "listening attentively when the victim expresses feelings or emotions."[3]

Changes in officers' attitudes are the result of several different aspects of police work. Officers encounter some hostility from citizens. This is a shock because officers tend to choose law enforcement as a career because they want to work with people and help the community (see Chapter 12). Although citizen hostility is statistically infrequent (about 10 percent of all encounters),[4] officers are likely to remember such experiences. Recalling unpleasant or traumatic experiences is a phenomenon common to all people.[5]

Officers also experience being stereotyped, with citizens reacting to the uniform, the badge, and the gun. As is the case with racial stereotyping, it is an unpleasant experience to have people react to you as a category rather than as an individual. In still other instances, citizens feel discomfort at being around a person with arrest powers. Sometimes citizens openly make jokes about breaking the law. To avoid the discomfort of these incidents, police officers tend to socialize primarily with other officers, thereby increasing their isolation from the public.[6]

Police officer attitudes also change because they perform society's "dirty work," handling unpleasant tasks that no one else wants to perform or is able to handle. The police see humanity at its worst.[7] They are the first people to find the murder victim, for example. Officers encounter the victims of serious domestic abuse, child abuse, and rape firsthand. These kinds of situations accumulate over time, affecting their attitudes about people in general. In one study, for example, officers ranked dealing with an abused child as the most stressful kind of situation they encounter.[8]

Encountering the Criminal Justice System

A second shock involves learning about the criminal justice system. Police officers are "insiders" in the sense that they have firsthand knowledge about how the system works. They see what happens to arrests, how cases are plea-bargained, and how judges work. They observe incompetent prosecutors, defense attorneys, and judges every day. As a result, many become cynical about the ability of the system to be fair and effective in dealing with offenders. Generally, police officers believe that the courts are too lenient.[9] Only 27 percent of police officers in Washington, DC, expressed trust in the courts, compared with 63 percent who expressed trust in their commanders and 87 percent expressing trust in their fellow officers.[10] Officers also react negatively to the fact that they are not respected by lawyers, judges, and other actors in the criminal justice system.[11]

Encountering the Department

When researchers asked New York City police officers what they disliked about being a cop, most cited aspects of their own department, not hostility from citizens. The most frequently mentioned problem was that the leadership of their department "doesn't care" about them. The second most frequently cited problem was "precinct-level supervisors." "Lack of respect from the public" ranked a distant third in this survey.[12]

The survey of NYPD officers illustrates the point that new officers' experience with their own department is often disillusioning. They discover the "politics" of the organization and learn that it does not always act in a rational and efficient manner. They discover that some of their supervisors are incompetent, that promotions are not necessarily based on ability, and that personal favoritism governs some decisions. Many officers quickly conclude that hard work will not be rewarded and that the best approach is to do as little as possible and avoid situations that might create trouble for them.[13]

As in other large organizations, there is conflict between the rank and file and the top command. A study of Washington, DC, police officers found that while 82 percent were satisfied with their jobs, and 87 percent expressed trust in their fellow officers, 63 percent trusted their commanders, and only 51 percent expressed trust in the chief of police.[14] Conflict between the rank and file and management is now channeled through police unions and the process of collective bargaining (see Chapter 14). Finally, as discussed below, many police departments are characterized by internal conflicts along racial, ethnic, and gender lines.

THE SENIORITY SYSTEM

New officers are generally assigned to patrol duty, usually in high-crime areas and on the evening shift. Assignments in most police departments are governed by civil service procedures or union contracts that embody the principle of seniority.[15] Officers with more experience have first priority in requesting assignments. This leaves the least desirable assignments to the new officers.[16]

The seniority principle has both good and bad points. On the positive side, it eliminates favoritism and discrimination. In the 1960s, the President's Crime Commission found that some departments assigned their worst officers to black neighborhoods.[17] On the negative side, it means that the least experienced officers get the most difficult assignments: patrolling the highest-crime neighborhoods on the busiest shift with the most crime and calls for service. On the other hand, in departments that have significantly improved their personnel standards, the younger officers are likely to be better qualified and better trained for such work than the older officers.

Because many departments have hired significant numbers of racial and ethnic minority and female officers in recent years, these officers tend to be disproportionately represented in the least desirable assignments, such as assignment to high-crime precincts.[18]

POLICE OFFICER ATTITUDES AND BEHAVIOR

Police officer attitudes, and the relationship between attitudes and behavior, are complex. Public stereotypes about police officers are generally inaccurate. Much of the

---

SIDEBAR 13–1   ISSUE FOR DISCUSSION: THE IMPACT OF THE SENIORITY SYSTEM

The seniority system means that rookie officers will generally be assigned to patrol in the highest-crime neighborhoods during the busiest shift (usually 4 P.M. to midnight) when most of the serious crime occurs.

Is this a good system for assigning officers? Does it result in the best police service in those times and places that demand the most skill?

Discuss the major drawbacks to this system. What are the advantages? Can you devise an alternative system?

scholarly research on police officer attitudes has arisen from an attempt to explain bad police officer behavior: the use of force and police–community relations tensions. With the exception of Muir's study, *Streetcorner Politicians,* little attention has been given to understanding good officers and good police performance.[19] It is significant, for example, that the title of William Westley's pioneering study of the police subculture is *Violence and the Police.*[20]

Explanations of attitudes and behavior fall into two general categories. One focuses on the sociological aspects of police work: the special characteristics of police work, the nature of police organizations, and the situational factors associated with police–citizen encounters. The other approach focuses on the background characteristics of individual officers: social and economic status, race, ethnicity, gender, and education. The bulk of the research tends to support the sociological interpretation of police work as an explanation of officer attitudes and behavior.[21]

The Concept of a Police Subculture

William Westley tells a poignant and revealing story about his pioneering research on the police subculture. For his dissertation he chose to study the Gary, Indiana, police department. When his interviews began to touch on a particularly sensitive subject the officers stopped talking to him. Eventually, he explained to a sergeant that his career would be ruined if he could not complete his research. The sergeant then "gave the officers hell" for not helping him, and immediately afterward all of them were extremely cooperative. Westley's experience illuminates two aspects of the police subculture: on the one hand, an attitude of secrecy toward outsiders seeking to investigate the realities of police work; and on the other hand, a genuine eagerness to help someone who was having difficulty and needed assistance. The basic point is that the so-called police subculture is an extremely complex phenomenon.[22]

Westley's 1950 study of the Gary police approached the subject from the standpoint of occupational sociology. He sought "to isolate and identify the major social norms governing police conduct, and to describe the way in which they influence police action in specific situations."[23] He found a distinct subculture among police officers that emphasizes secrecy, solidarity, and violence. Police officers view the public as the "enemy" and believe that they are justified in lying to protect other officers from criticism by citizens. Of the officers interviewed by Westley, 73 percent thought citizens were hostile to the police.[24]

Westley argues that police attitudes are a product of selective contact with the public. Officers rarely meet the average person but, instead, meet people with problems who often resent police presence. Officers also resent the fact that the other professionals they routinely deal with—lawyers, news reporters, social workers, and so on—have negative attitudes about the police.[25] In the face of perceived public hostility, Westley continues, officers believe they can rely only on their fellow officers in times of crisis.

An officer in Washington, DC, explains that "I've been working with my partner now for two and one-half years. I think I know more about him than his wife does. . . . He knows everything about me. . . . I think you get a certain relationship when you work together with a partner."[26] The very nature of police work—working closely together, often spending long hours together in a patrol car, facing the same uncertainties and danger—fosters a very strong sense of solidarity among officers. To outsiders, group solidarity is the defining characteristic of the police subculture.

One important consequence of group solidarity is secrecy, which serves "as a shield against the attacks of the outside world." Secrecy justifies lying. Westley asked officers if they would report a fellow officer who took money from a citizen (a person arrested for drunkenness). A total of 73 percent said they would not. Westley concluded that most officers believed that "illegal action is preferable to breaking the secrecy of the group."[27] A recent national study by the Police Foundation found that over half (52.4 percent) of all officers agree with the statement that "it is not unusual for a police officer to turn a blind eye to improper conduct by other officers."[28]

Westley also found that group solidarity justifies violence against citizens. Officers feel a need to maintain respect in encounters with citizens. More than a third of the officers (39 percent) surveyed by Westley thought that they were justified in using force when faced with citizen disrespect. Two-thirds of the officers (66 percent) gave some rationalization for the illegal use of force.[29] The Police Foundation survey found that about one-quarter (24.5 percent) of all officers agree that "it is sometimes acceptable to use more force than is legally allowable to control someone who physically assaults an officer."[30]

Secrecy and the "code of silence" mean that officers refuse to testify against other officers who are accused of misconduct, for example, in a citizen complaint. The Christopher Commission reported a Los Angeles police officer saying, "It is basically a non-written rule that you do not roll over, tell on your partner, your companion."[31] In the Police Foundation study, almost 17 percent believed that the "code of silence is an essential part" of good policing.[32] The code of silence is widely recognized as perhaps the most serious obstacle to police accountability and the reduction of both corruption and police use of excessive force.

Jerome Skolnick developed Westley's concept of a police subculture further in a study of "Westville" (Oakland, California). He found that police officers develop a "working personality" shaped by two aspects of the police role: danger and authority. Because the potential for danger is an ever-present feature of police work, officers become routinely suspicious of all people. Officers develop a "perceptual shorthand" of visual cues associated with criminals and other people they believe to be potentially dangerous. This shorthand is a form of stereotyping, applied with particular intensity to males: young men, low-income young men, and low-income racial-minority men.[33] This aspect of the police subculture is a major contributor to police–community relations problems (Chapter 9).

The Capacity to Use Force   The capacity to exercise authority further isolates the officer from the public. Bittner argues that the capacity to use force is the defining feature of the police, distinguishing them from other occupations.[34] Bittner's point is that the police have powers that no other occupation has: the power to deprive people of their liberty (arrest) and, most important, the legal authority to take human life. These powers are inherent in the police role and apply to all police officers regardless of race, ethnicity, gender, or education. The authority to use force is symbolized by the uniform, the badge, and an officer's weapon. Citizens are very conscious of these symbols and the power they represent. An officer rarely has to explicitly remind someone that he or she could be arrested.

Danger: Potential versus Actual   Skolnick argues that the potential for danger, especially attacks by citizens, shapes the police subculture. It is important, however, to distinguish between potential and actual danger. First, police work is not the most dangerous occupation in the United States. Mining and construction consistently have higher rates of on-the-job deaths.[35] Measured in terms of felonious killings of police officers, police work has actually become much safer in the last 20 years. The felonious death rate per 100,000 officers fell by almost two-thirds between 1976 and 1998 (see Figure 13–1).[36]

Skolnick also found that the norms of police work often conflict with constitutional standards regarding the rights of suspects. Officers are under pressure to produce to get results, usually in the form of arrests, evidence, confessions, and convictions. The law, however, limits police powers in order to protect the rights of individual citizens. Officers feel pressured to evade or bend the rules: to conduct illegal searches or to obtain confessions through coercion.[37] The Police Foundation found that almost half (42.9 percent) of all officers agree that "always following the rules is not compatible with getting the job done."[38] Herbert Packer defines the tension between the demand for results and the rule of law as a conflict between "crime control" values and "due process" values.[39]

In another study, Arthur Niederhoffer argues that the police subculture is characterized by cynicism and authoritarianism. A former New York City police officer himself, he argues in *Behind the Shield* that police officers are cynical about both the outside world and the inside world of the police department. Cynicism contributes to authoritarianism.

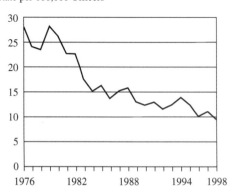

Police Officers Murdered by Felons,
Rate per 100,000 Officers

FIGURE 13–1
FELONIOUS DEATH RATE PER 100,000 POLICE OFFICERS

Drawing upon earlier research in social psychology, Niederhoffer maintains that the "police personality" fits the cluster of values associated with authoritarianism: conventional social values, cynicism, aggression, superstition, and a tendency to stereotype, to project personal values onto others (projectivity), and to define the world in terms of good versus bad people.[40]

Criticisms of the Police Subculture Concept

Is there really a distinctive police subculture? Are police officers really different from people in other occupations? The early research by Westley, Skolnick, and Niederhoffer on the police subculture paints a highly negative view of police officers, portraying them as isolated, hostile to the public and to the norms of a democratic society, prejudiced, and opposed to accountability. The major elements of this view have been heavily criticized, however. Reviewing the literature on the concept of a police personality, Joel Lefkowitz concludes that "a significant portion of the relevant literature is primarily mere opinion." Moreover, "almost all of the research studies reviewed are methodologically inadequate to the task of supporting reasonable inferences" about the existence or origins of a police personality. Much of the early research was impressionistic, based on small samples, or imprecise in the specification of key concepts. Particularly important, most of it is out of date and fails to take into account significant recent changes in police employment (see below).

Lefkowitz concludes that the personalities of police officers "do differ in systematic ways from the rest of the population, but differ in an evaluatively neutral sense." In short, police officers are somewhat different, but their personality traits are not pathological.[41] In their study of Denver police officers, Bayley and Mendelsohn found that "on all personality scales the data show that policemen are absolutely average people." Research on police officers' reasons for choosing law enforcement as a career has consistently found that most seek to help people and to serve the community (Chapter 12). In this respect, officers are rather idealistic, at least at the outset of their careers. The police officers surveyed by Bayley and Mendelsohn were somewhat more conservative than the population at large (regardless of whether they were Republicans or Democrats) but were not authoritarian.[42]

The most comprehensive critique of the police subculture concept is offered by Steve Herbert, who identifies six different factors that shape and help to explain police officer behavior. The first is the law. Even though officers have broad discretion (Chapter 8), they exercise that discretion within boundaries defined by the law. The second factor is bureaucratic control. Although police officers generally work with little direct supervision, the rules and regulations of their department do shape what they do and how they handle specific situations. The third factor, according to Herbert, is the element of "adventure/machismo." The subculture of the Los Angeles police department, which he observed, put high emphasis on active and aggressive police work. Concern for safety is a fourth factor. Herbert argues that concern for their own safety, and the safety of other officers, "shapes how officers define and respond to situations." A fifth factor, competence, refers to officers having a sense that they are good at their work and are respected by their colleagues for doing a good job. Having to call in officers from other divisions to help handle calls (referred to as "dropping calls") is a sign of a lack of competence. The final factor, according to Herbert, is morality. Officers make moral judgments about people: Some are good and some are bad; some people on the street are defined not merely as bad but as threats to the moral order of society. Officers develop slang terms to describe the people they regard as either bad or threats. Herbert's main point is that the traditional definition of the police subculture is too limited, and there are a number of different factors that enter into how officers think about and carry out their jobs.[43]

THE CHANGING RANK AND FILE

A major problem with the original concept of a police subculture is that it is ahistorical and fails to account for significant changes in the composition of the rank and file and other changes in policing over the past 30 years.[44] At the time the early research was conducted (1950s through 1960s), police officers were overwhelmingly male and white, with most coming from blue collar backgrounds with little college education. Changing employment patterns have brought significant numbers of African American, Hispanic, female, and college-educated officers. Robin Haarr argues that "the initial concept of a single, unified occupational culture is now being replaced by an alternative conceptualization of diversity, variation, and contrast within the police organization and occupation."[45]

Women Police Officers

Susan Martin found that the introduction of women into policing has broken up the traditional solidarity of the work group. Women officers, for example, do not share the same outside interests as male officers: hunting, fishing, and cars. Martin also argues that policewomen "alter the rules of the game" of how to act as a police officer. Traditional masculine characteristics of not expressing emotion publicly and of settling disputes physically are no longer appropriate. Expressions of friendship, which were acceptable between two male officers, are problematic between officers of different sexes.[46]

Martin also found significant differences among the male officers, especially in terms of their attitudes toward women officers. The *traditionals* are emotionally committed to the image of policing as dangerous physical work and put an emphasis on aggressive policing. Holding stereotyped views about women's physical strength and their role in society, the traditionals have the most difficulty accepting women officers. The *moderns,* on the other hand, accept policewomen relatively easily. They recognize that police work rarely calls for physical strength, accept the idea that job opportunities should be open to everyone on the basis of individual merit, and are not tied to traditional views of women's roles. The *moderates* have more complex attitudes. Many accept the idea of policewomen in principle but do not like the idea of women on patrol duty. Others support some policewomen but are highly critical of others. In short, Martin's research suggests that the traditional male police rank and file are more diverse than earlier studies had suggested.[47]

There is some evidence that with the passage of time, the differences in attitudes between male and female officers have been reduced. The Police Foundation study of officer attitudes toward abuse of authority finds no significant differences between male and female officers. The report explains that this could be due to either the adaptation of female officers to the male-dominated police subculture or a process of self-selection by which only women who are likely to adapt to the police subculture seek law enforcement jobs.[48]

Although the percentage of women in policing has increased since the early 1970s, there appears to be an invisible "glass ceiling" at both the entry level and in terms of promotion. The overall percentage of women among sworn officers remains at around 13 to 14 percent, and has not increased significantly in recent years. Also, in 1998 there were only twelve departments where women were more than 20 percent of all officers. Also, the number of women officers in supervisory and command positions remains small (Figure 13–2).

Female Officers and the Use of Force

The National Center for Women in Policing (NCWP) makes a bold claim: Police departments should hire more women officers because "female officers are less likely to use excessive force."[49] Is this true? Does the evidence support this view?

A report by the NCWP found that in the Los Angeles police department, male officers cost the city $63.4 million in damage awards between 1990 and 1999, compared with only $2.8 million for female officers. The study examined suits involving allegations of excessive force, sexual assault, and domestic violence that resulted in judgments of $100,000 or more. Females represent about 18 percent of the LAPD officers, but were responsible for only 4.2 percent of the total damage awards in this study. Kathy Spillar, head of the Feminist Majority, which cosponsored the study, argues that "the single most fundamental reform that the LAPD could make would be to gender balance its police force."[50]

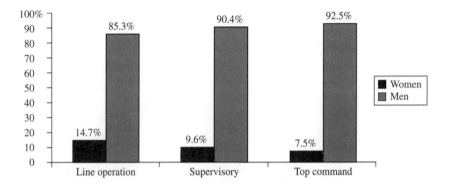

FIGURE 13–2
PERCENTAGE OF SWORN LAW ENFORCEMENT OFFICERS BY RANK AND GENDER, 1998

Comparisons of the performance of male and female officers have found only slight differences in their handling of routine police work.[51] Bloch and Anderson compared eighty-six new female recruits with eighty-six new male recruits in Washington, DC. They concluded that, in general, males and females performed patrol work in a similar manner. Both groups responded to similar types of calls for police service while on patrol and encountered similar proportions of citizens who were dangerous, angry, upset, drunk, or violent. The study found "no reported incidents which cast serious doubt on the ability of women to perform patrol work satisfactorily." Slight differences between men and women were found, but they were not significant. Female officers made slightly fewer arrests and issued fewer traffic citations. On the other hand, female officers were less likely to engage in conduct unbecoming to an officer.[52]

A study of patrol officers in New York City compared forty-one male and forty-one female officers over a 7-month period between 1975 and 1976. The researchers found that the style of police work used by the female officers was "almost indistinguishable" from that used by the male officers. Male and female officers used different verbal and nonverbal techniques to control situations at virtually identical rates. Although the female officers were "slightly less active" than the male officers, "civilians rated the female officers more competent, pleasant, and respectful."[53]

Data on citizen complaints in both New York City and San Jose indicate that female officers receive fewer complaints than male officers.[54] A national evaluation of police early warning systems (Chapter 11) also finds that women officers are less likely than male officers to be identified as potential "problem" officers as a result of citizen complaints and use of force incidents.[55]

African American Officers

In a remarkable break with the traditional police subculture, the National Black Police Officers Association published a pamphlet on police brutality urging officers to report misconduct by other officers. An officer who witnesses brutality should "report the incident to your supervisor, whether or not he/she is supportive." No other police officer organization had ever urged its officers to report misconduct. This position reflects some of the differences between African American and white rank-and-file officers.[56]

The addition of substantial numbers of African American and Hispanic officers has also affected the police subculture since the 1960s. White and African American officers have very different attitudes on a number of issues, particularly police use of force. A Police Foundation study found that African American officers are far more likely to believe that the police use excessive force against both racial and ethnic minorities and poor people. Nearly half of all African American officers (47.7 percent) agreed with the statement that police officers are more likely to use force against blacks, compared with only 4.5 percent of whites. By nearly the same margin, African American officers were more likely to agree that police officers are more likely to use force against poor people.[57] In several cities, African American officers have spoken out publicly on the issue of police use of force, criticizing their own departments and in some cases the police union, which is dominated by white officers.[58]

African American officers are also more likely to support innovation and change. They are more supportive of citizen oversight of the police than white officers.[59] And in their study of community policing in Chicago, Skogan and Hartnett found that African American officers were far more receptive to change and supportive of community policing.[60]

There are also differences among African American officers. Alex notes a generational difference between the older and younger officers. The newer officers are more likely to be assertive and willing to express their criticisms of the department than are the older officers.[61] Martin, meanwhile, found that African American female officers are multiple minorities, representing both race and gender, who have a unique and more critical perspective on policing.[62]

In a survey of 522 police officers assigned to minority-group neighborhoods in thirteen large cities, Peter Rossi found that African American officers have more positive attitudes toward their assigned districts. They are less likely than white officers to rate the assignment as more difficult than other assignments, three times more likely to live in the precinct where they work, and more likely to have friends there. The African American officers are also more likely to believe that the residents of the area where they are assigned are "honest" and "industrious."[63]

Hispanic/Latino Officers

There is very little research on Hispanic/Latino police officers. In one study, Carter found that Hispanic officers believed that the department discriminated against Hispanic citizens and that it discriminated against Hispanic officers in promotions.[64] A study of Hispanic officers in one Midwestern police department found that they negotiated between their identities as police officers and as members of the Hispanic community in different ways. A few identified themselves entirely as police officers, many had dual identities as both police officers and members of the Hispanic community, but none identified completely with the Hispanic community. Those who had dual identities used their identification with and knowledge about the Hispanic community as a guide and resource in their police work. This did not involve leniency toward Hispanic offenders, however.[65]

Civil rights leaders have urged police departments to hire more African American and Hispanic officers as a way to improve police–community relations. They argue that these officers will have more rapport with the African American community and will not discriminate in arrests or other police actions (see Chapter 9).[66] The relationship between race and ethnicity, attitudes, and actual job performance is extremely complex, however.

Race, Ethnicity, and Performance

There is no strong evidence, however, that African American or Hispanic officers perform differently from white officers. Reiss did not find significant differences in the use of force by white and African American officers.[67] Official data on citizen complaints in New York City and San Jose, meanwhile, indicate that white, African American, and Hispanic officers receive complaints in proportion to their presence in police departments.[68] Fyfe found that, after controlling for place of assignment, white and African American officers fired their weapons at the same rate; that is, the nature of the precinct was the primary variable influencing police shootings. Officers assigned to high-crime precincts in New York City used deadly force more frequently than those assigned to low-crime precincts. Within each type of precinct, white and black officers used deadly force at essentially the same rate. The characteristics of the neighborhood rather than race or personal attitudes influenced their behavior.[69] There are no studies that systematically compare the behavior of Hispanic police officers with white and African American officers.

Gay and Lesbian Officers

A number of police officers are lesbian or gay. In some departments they are open about their sexual orientation, and in some have formed their own organizations. The Gay Officer Action League (GAOL) in New York City began publishing a newsletter in 1982. By 1992 at least ten police departments openly recruited lesbian and gay officers. Some of these departments are in states where antidiscrimination laws cover sexual orientation. Others are in cities with large lesbian and gay communities, and they have officers designated as liaisons to them.[70]

Lesbian and gay officers represent a clear challenge to the traditional stereotype of policing as a tough, macho, male occupation. In New York City the police union, along with a coalition of twenty-five religious and social organizations, attempted to block the police department's program for recruiting lesbian and gay officers. There are, however, no studies of the performance of gay and lesbian officers.

The Intersection of Race, Gender, and Sexual Identity

A comment by an African American female supervisor interviewed by Susan Martin illustrates the complex conflicts that arise as a result of the increased diversity of police departments. This supervisor had problems with a white male officer under her command. After he transferred, however, he had similar problems with his new male supervisor. She concluded that "it wasn't a female thing . . . but at the time I couldn't be sure. . . . I felt he was rebelling against me because I was a female lieutenant and a black lieutenant."[71]

In a study of one Midwestern department, Robin Haarr found limited day-to-day interaction between officers of different race or gender. She measured interaction in terms of daily "meets" between officers, including handling calls together, backing each other up, eating meals together, and gossiping or joking. White male officers largely interacted with other white male officers. Most (75 percent) of the African American male officers indicated that other male officers (either African American or white) were the officers they interacted with on duty. The three African American female officers interacted primarily with other African American officers, either male or female. White female officers were the least likely to identify interactions and friendships with partners or former partners, and to interact with female officers in other units. Finally, at roll call, officers "separated themselves spatially by race and gender as to where they sat and whom they interacted with."[72]

In many departments a certain level of tension and conflict exists between racial, ethnic, and gender groups. Haarr found that officers believed that they were being discriminated against because promotions and preferred assignments were being given to African American officers who were less qualified.[73] In a study of a Texas police department, meanwhile, David Carter found that Hispanic officers believed that there was discrimination against them on the job. In Washington, DC, 66 percent of the white officers thought that the promotion system favored African Americans, while 49 percent of the African American officers thought that it favored whites.[74] Martin and Jurik report that "the resistance faced by the first women on patrol was blatant, malicious, widespread, organized, and sometimes life-threatening."[75] With the passage of time, the hostility has become less blatant and more subtle.[76]

Divisions along racial, ethnic, and gender lines are reflected in the fact that groups generally separate social and fraternal associations representing African American, Hispanic, and female officers. In many departments, the recognized police union (e.g., the official collective bargaining organization) reflects the views of the white officers. There are also national associations of African American, Hispanic, and female officers.

Education

The educational levels of police officers have also been rising steadily. In the 1960s, 80 percent of all sworn officers had only a high school education. By 1988 the figure had fallen to 34.8 percent. The percentage of officers with a 4-year college degree rose from 2.7 to 22.6 percent in the same period.[77] In many departments there is a generation gap between the younger, better-educated officers and the veteran officers with less education.

Does education make a difference? Is a police officer with a college education better and more effective than an officer with only a high school diploma? There is no strong evidence that officers with college education behave differently on the street than officers with less education.[78] One study, however, did find that college-educated officers tended to receive fewer complaints than officers with less education.[79]

Cohort Effects

Generally, in society, there are recurring generation gaps: conflicts between young people and old people, between children and their parents. These conflicts involve clothes, hairstyles, music, lifestyle, and issues of morality. In the 1960s there were deep conflicts between generations over the Vietnam War. Then and now there are conflicts over sexual morality, over what is acceptable behavior. Similar conflicts exist within police departments. Social scientists refer to these as *cohort effects.* That is, the officers hired in one decade will have different ideas and lifestyles than officers hired in later decades.

As new groups of officers enter policing, the dominant attitudes of rank-and-file officers also change over time. While officers at any one point in time might react negatively to a dramatic change in policing (e.g., a Supreme Court decision, the introduction of community policing), new cohorts of officers arrive to find these circumstances an established fact of life.

Skolnick's finding that officers were hostile to the Supreme Court and other limitations of their practices arose from research on officers who reacted to the most controversial Supreme Court decisions in the early 1960s.[80] With the passage of time, however, new cohorts of recruits continually enter the ranks of policing. These officers find constitutional requirements regarding search and seizure and interrogations an established fact of life, not something new imposed on them as was the case for officers in the 1960s. A study of narcotics officers in Chicago found a high degree of support for the exclusionary rule. On the whole, officers did not regard it as a barrier to effective police work, and many officers felt that it played an important role in deterring police misconduct.[81]

Along the same lines, Reuss-Ianni found two cultures among police officers in the department she studied. One group identified with the old street cop culture that values street experience and a tough, personalized way of dealing with people on the street. The other group identified with the new bureaucratic style of written rules and formal procedures for dealing with both police work on the street and departmental governance. This latter group is more accepting of, for example, Supreme Court rules on police practices, along with other formal procedures designed to control discretion (Chapter 8) and ensure police accountability (Chapter 11).[82] Milner found a higher degree of support for the *Miranda* decision in the more professionalized departments than in the less professionalized ones.[83] In short, the informal culture of a police organization affects officer attitudes toward certain important subjects.

With the retirement of officers who identify with the old street cop culture, and the recruitment of more officers with higher education, the dominant culture of particular police departments changes significantly over the course of 20 years.

Attitudes toward Community Policing

"Can we affect crime?" asked a Chicago police officer. "Not really," he said, answering his own question. "We can't control the social fabric. It can't be done." These comments reflect the negative attitude toward community policing on the part of many tradition-bound police officers. Other Chicago officers are more favorable toward community policing, agreeing with the idea that "police officers should work with citizens to try and solve problems in their beat."[84]

The attitude of police officers toward community policing is a particularly important issue. Community policing is a major effort to reorient police service to the public. Most experts agree that if the rank-and-file officers who will be carrying out community policing are strongly opposed to it, the effort will not succeed.

For this reason, the community-policing program in Chicago (Chicago Alternative Policing Strategy, or CAPS) devoted considerable effort to "winning the hearts and minds" of the rank and file. Skogan's evaluation of CAPS found significant differences of opinion among Chicago police officers regarding community policing. Older officers and African American officers were consistently more supportive of community policing. African American officers were "ready for change," while white officers were satisfied with the status quo and most pessimistic about the likely success of CAPS.[85]

In a review of evaluations of community policing in twelve different cities, Lurigio and Rosenbaum found that involvement in community policing had a somewhat positive effect on officer attitudes (and on citizen perceptions of the police). Officers were generally more likely to have increased job satisfaction and motivation, as well as improved relationships with both citizens and their coworkers. Because of methodological problems associated with most of these studies, however, Lurigio and Rosenbaum advise against being overly optimistic about the impact of community policing on officer attitudes. Nonetheless, there is some evidence that changes in the police organization, in this case community policing, can affect officer attitudes.[86]

Summary

In short, the composition of the rank and file of police departments has changed dramatically over the past 30 years. Earlier research suggesting the existence of a set of attitudes based on a homogeneous police subculture fails to take into account this new reality. Female, racial and ethnic minority, lesbian and gay, and college-educated officers bring different backgrounds and experiences to their jobs as police officers.

THE RELATIONSHIP BETWEEN ATTITUDES AND BEHAVIOR

The graduate students observing police work in Boston, Chicago, and Washington, DC, in the summer of 1966 for the President's Crime Commission noted one significant contradiction. More than 75 percent of the officers they observed made prejudiced statements about African Americans. (Remember, the research was conducted in the midst of the series of "long hot summers" of urban racial disorders in the mid-1960s.) And yet, the officers were not observed to treat African American citizens in a systematically uncivil or discriminatory fashion.[87] The observations by the research team in this study illustrate the complex relationship between the attitudes and behavior of members of any occupation.

Common sense might suggest a one-to-one relationship between attitudes and behavior: that people who express prejudicial *attitudes* about race or gender will automatically *behave* in a discriminatory manner. Research on policing, however, suggests that the relationship is extremely complex and that attitudes are mediated by a number of factors.

In their field studies for the President's Crime Commission, Black and Reiss found that verbal expressions of racial prejudice were common among white officers. Of the 510 white officers studied in Boston and Chicago, 38 percent were deemed highly prejudiced, and 35 percent prejudiced, against African Americans. And as noted above, three-quarters of the officers expressed some racial prejudice in the presence of field observers.[88] Yet, these attitudes did not translate directly into the observed behavior of these officers. Analyzing Reiss and Black's data, Friedrich found that the more prejudiced officers were somewhat more likely to make arrests, but the influence was meager. At the same time, the less prejudiced officers were more likely to treat citizens in a neutral manner—that is, neither punitively nor favorably. At the same time, however, white officers with positive racial attitudes were more likely to arrest African American suspects. Friedrich suggests that this may be the result of their "particularly dim view of black offenders."[89]

One reason why attitudes do not translate into behavior is that police officers are constrained by the bureaucratic aspects of the police department and the criminal justice system. An arrest is a highly visible action. (Joseph Goldstein characterizes police decisions not to arrest as low-visibility activity.)[90] It comes to the attention of other people—sergeant, prosecutor, judge (in many departments, sergeants review all arrests)—who have the opportunity to review an officer's performance. If those other officials are doing a professional job, they will reject arrests where there is no probable cause (and perhaps based on prejudice) and exclude evidence or confessions that were obtained improperly. Rejections of this sort embarrass the officer and are an incentive to improve performance. In short, the values and expectations of other criminal justice officials limit the ability of the officer to act solely on the basis of his or her personal prejudices.[91]

STYLES OF POLICE WORK

Conducting a series of ride-alongs with patrol sergeants in the Wilshire Division of the Los Angeles police department in 1993 and 1994, Steve Herbert identified different work styles among patrol officers. Or, to be more precise, he found that officers used different labels to describe their fellow officers. Some officers were "hardchargers": active, often aggressive officers, who would volunteer to handle potentially dangerous situations and enjoyed the excitement of high-speed pursuits. Some other officers, meanwhile, were labeled "station queens" because colleagues thought they avoided danger.[92]

Herbert's observations confirm the point that individual police officers have different work styles. The LAPD, which he observed, has its own unique organizational culture, but in all departments there are clear differences between active and passive officers. Active officers are those who (1) initiate more contacts with citizens (field interrogations, traffic stops, building checks); (2) assert control of situations with citizens; and (3) make more arrests. Passive officers respond only when calls are dispatched and make few arrests. Bayley and Garofalo's study of New York City police officers identified specific actions that distinguished active from passive officers in asserting control of situations. Passive officers were more likely simply to observe a situation and take notes. Active officers were more likely to ask probing questions and request that citizens explain themselves.[93]

Some studies of police work have found that officers generally initiate little activity. Reiss's study of patrol, for example, found that most police–citizen contacts are citizen-initiated rather than officer-initiated.[94] Mastrofski's more recent studies, however, have found great variation in the ratio of officer-initiated to citizen-initiated contacts. In one department 50 percent of all contacts were officer-initiated, compared with only 20 percent in another department.[95] Studies of arrest productivity have found that many officers make no arrests and that a small number of officers make a very high proportion of all arrests.[96] Van Maanen argues that new officers quickly learn that hard work will not be rewarded and, consequently, try to avoid situations that might create trouble. Officers who work harder than everyone else are disliked as "rate busters."[97]

Differences in work style are the result of both personal temperament and career expectations. James Leo Walsh identifies three distinct career styles. Street cops are attracted to policing by the prospects of a secure work environment (good pay, good job security, and so on). Action seekers are attracted to policing by the potential for exciting work, particularly crime-fighting tasks. Middle-class mobiles are attracted by the professional status of policing and the opportunities for career advancement and upward social mobility. Street cops are likely to be much less aggressive than the other two types. Action seekers initiate activity for the immediate excitement, while middle-class mobiles do so for the eventual reward.[98]

William K. Muir created a typology of police officers on the basis of how they use power. Muir's approach is somewhat unique in the literature because it seeks to identify the qualities that make a *good* police officer. Virtually all the other studies of the police subculture and officer attitudes focus on explaining police misconduct.[99]

The professional police officer, Muir argues, is one who develops two virtues: passion and perspective. The professional officer grasps the nature of human suffering intellectually (passion), but at the same time understands that unjust means cannot be used to deal with this problem (perspective). Officers who respond with passion to human problems but see no limits on their power are enforcers. Reciprocators have perspective but no passion; they are too objective, too detached from the human problems they encounter, and fail to act. Finally, the avoiders have neither passion nor perspective; they do not respond to the problems they face and take no action.[100]

CAREER DEVELOPMENT

Many experts on police administration argue that one of the most serious problems in American policing is a lack of adequate career opportunities. The problems include (1) limited opportunities for promotion, (2) inadequate rewards for good job performance, and (3) lack of opportunities for professional development and personal fulfillment. In a two-wave survey of Detroit police officers, over half in both 1978 (53 percent) and 1988 (54 percent) indicated low satisfaction with the opportunity for career advancement. Few (10 percent in 1978 and 16 percent in 1988) expressed high satisfaction with the advancement opportunities.[101]

Promotion

Opportunities for promotion are severely limited in American police departments. First, civil service regulations usually require that an officer serve a certain number of years in rank before being eligible to apply for promotion. Time-in-rank requirements range from 2 to 5 years.[102]

Second, promotional opportunities occur at irregular intervals. The decision to promote may depend on the city's financial condition rather than on the needs of the police department. Sometimes promotions are postponed for many years as a way of coping with a financial crisis. In 1986 about 25 percent of all departments reported that they had not filled vacancies in the previous 3 years because of budget cuts.[103]

Third, promotions are based on a formal testing process, involving a written examination and an oral interview. Interviews are generally conducted by the chief of police, a committee of high-ranking officers, and often members of the local civil service agency group.[104] Some departments use the assessment center technique, which attempts to evaluate the ability of the applicant to handle the job being sought.

SIDEBAR 13–2   STUDYING YOUR OWN COMMUNITY

What are the salary schedules for the major law enforcement agencies in your community? How does the major municipal police department compare with the county sheriff's department? How do starting salaries compare? What are the maximum salaries for the entry-level positions (e.g., police officer, deputy sheriff)?

There is considerable controversy over whether the commonly used tests select the best-qualified persons. Written examinations, for example, test for factual knowledge but may not indicate the applicant's potential for working as a supervisor. Oral interviews may be extremely subjective and reflect the biases of the interviewers.[105] In an unprofessional department, officers with high standards of integrity and college educations could receive low scores. If the command staff conducting the interviews are all white males, women and racial minorities may be at a disadvantage.[106]

Salaries and Benefits

The salaries and benefits offered police officers in most departments are generally very attractive.[107] Along with job security, they are one of the main reasons why people choose law enforcement as a career (see Chapter 12). Salaries are rigidly structured by civil service procedures and/or union contracts, however. Pay is tied to an officer's rank. Typically, there are several pay steps at the rank of police officer, which an officer gains through seniority. Other raises result from renegotiation of the entire department's pay scale.

The only way to achieve a significant pay increase is through promotion. Unlike employees in the private sector, a police chief cannot reward an outstanding officer through a bonus or discretionary pay increase. Thus, there are no immediate financial rewards for outstanding performance.

Most departments offer additional pay for certain assignments or qualifications. The 1997 LEMAS data indicate that 72 percent of all municipal departments offer incentive pay for college education, 27 percent offer hazardous duty pay for certain assignments, and 47 percent provide shift differential pay. Another 32 percent offer various forms of merit pay increases.[108]

The major source of additional pay is overtime. Certain assignments, particularly those that involve frequent court appearances such as criminal investigation and traffic, offer the greatest opportunities for overtime.

Assignment to Special Units

The principal reward available to a police officer is to be assigned to a special unit: criminal investigation, training, juvenile, and so on. These assignments are generally made at the discretion of the chief, subject to applicable seniority rules. Thus, for example, an officer may bid for assignment as a detective or to the training or gang unit. The choice is at the discretion of the chief. Traditionally, giving preferential assignments to friends and allies was one of the informal ways a chief maintained control over a department. These allies could be counted on to provide information about what was really going on in particular units.[109]

Assignments must be within the officer's rank. A sergeant, for example, cannot be assigned as commander of a unit if that position is designated as a lieutenant's position. The rigidity of these personnel classification systems limits both the career opportunities for individual officers and the management flexibility of the chief executive.[110]

Special assignments play an important role in promotional opportunities. Holding a number of different assignments allows an officer to become known to a wide range of other officers, to establish a reputation for ability, and to learn about different aspects of the department. Reputation and knowledge can lead to more favorable evaluations in promotion interviews.

Racial, ethnic, and gender conflicts within police departments affect personnel assignments and subsequent opportunities for promotion. Martin found that female officers were less likely to be given certain preferred special assignments.[111]

Lateral Entry

The opportunity to move to other police departments is extremely limited. Virtually all American police departments start new officers as rookies, discounting any experience with other departments. The officer who moves to another department loses all of his or her seniority. Thus, a sergeant in one department must start all over again at a new department at the rank of police officer. Police pension systems pose another obstacle to officer mobility. Most are local systems that cannot be transferred. Officers who move face the loss of some or all of their previous investment in the pension system. By contrast, college professors are able to participate in a national retirement system (TIAA/CREF) that is portable: The faculty member who changes jobs remains in the same system. The President's Crime Commission recommended developing a national police retirement system that would permit the transfer of personnel without the loss of benefits.[112] A few experiments with portable police pensions have been tried, but they are the exception rather than the rule.[113]

Lateral entry, or moving to another department at the same or higher rank, is very uncommon in American policing. The major exception is hiring at the rank of chief. A 1986 survey found no large police departments (cities with populations of 250,000 or more) that allowed lateral entry at lower ranks. Meanwhile, only 19 percent of all departments permitted hiring a police chief from "outside," and most of those were in smaller cities (populations of 50,000 or less).[114]

Some experts regard lateral entry as a potential means of enhancing police professionalism. They argue that it would create greater career opportunities for talented and ambitious officers and would allow departments to bring in fresh blood and new ideas.[115] Lateral entry is opposed because officers jealously guard the few promotional opportunities that do arise in a department and resent the idea of outsiders getting these jobs.

PERFORMANCE EVALUATION

Traditional Performance Evaluations

New York City police officer Michael Dowd received outstanding performance evaluations. His 1987 evaluation concluded that he had "excellent street knowledge" and could "easily become a role model for others to emulate."[116] Unfortunately, the Mollen Commission investigating corruption in the NYPD found that he was one of the most brutal and corrupt officers in the police department. One of the most serious problems in police departments is that official performance evaluations do not always reflect actual performance. The Christopher Commission, for example, found that some of the Los Angeles officers with the highest number of citizen complaints had received excellent performance evaluations.[117]

In the course of a career, a police officer's performance will be regularly evaluated by supervisors. The CALEA accreditation standards state that "a written directive requires that a performance evaluation of each employee be conducted and documented at least annually."[118] There are some departments where regular evaluations are not conducted. The Pittsburgh police bureau, for example, did not conduct regular performance evaluations prior to a 1997 consent decree with the U.S. Justice Department to settle a suit over officer use of excessive force.[119] These departments do not meet the accreditation standards and would generally be considered unprofessional and poorly managed.

Problems with Performance Evaluations

Traditional police performance evaluation systems have been heavily criticized, however. A 1977 Police Foundation report concluded that "the current status of performance appraisal systems is discouragingly low."[120] Changes over the next 20 years resulted in only marginal improvements. A 1997 report by the Community Policing Consortium concluded that "most performance evaluations currently used by police agencies do not reflect the work officers do."[121]

Performance evaluations suffer from a number of problems. First, the definitions are often not clear. They do not explain, for example, how effectiveness is to be measured. Second, because of the halo effect, officers who are rated high on one factor are likely to be rated high on all others. Third, because of the central tendency phenomenon, the ratings of all officers tend to cluster around one numerical level. Finally, there is a tendency to rate everyone highly.[122] Performance evaluations may also reflect patterns of racial, ethnic, or gender bias within a department. There is some indication that African American and Hispanic officers are more likely to be cited for departmental violations. Martin and Jurik argue that traditional performance criteria such as aggressiveness are male-oriented and inevitably biased against female officers.[123]

Even the traditional measure of arrest is not necessarily used systematically in performance evaluations. Only some departments evaluate officers on the basis of the number of arrests, and few of those departments keep systematic records on arrest outcomes. Thus, they do not reward officers who make quality arrests (defined as leading to a felony conviction) as opposed to a large number of arrests.[124]

Perhaps the most serious problem is that performance evaluation systems have few, if any, procedures for identifying and rewarding good behavior in the non–law enforcement situations that constitute the bulk of police work.

Another serious problem with police personnel systems is that they focus on punishing misconduct rather than rewarding good behavior. Police organizations have been characterized as punishment-centered bureaucracies.[125] There are elaborate rules that can be used, often selectively, to catch and punish officers, but few methods for positively rewarding officers.

The CALEA accreditation standards require that evaluations include explanatory comments to justify the rating, and that officers be counseled about the rating and have an opportunity to sign and make written comments about their ratings. Officers whose performance is deemed unsatisfactory should be advised in writing of that evaluation.[126]

The Rampart scandal that was exposed in the Los Angeles police department in 1999 brought to light a number of serious problems with personnel evaluations and discipline in the LAPD. First, a Los Angeles police department Board of Inquiry report on the Rampart scandal concluded that the LAPD's regular performance evaluations were widely regarded as worthless by members of the department.[127] Second, an independent report sponsored by the police union in Los Angeles following the Rampart scandal concluded that supervisors often harassed officers by citing them for minor violations of department policy while ignoring major forms of misconduct such as use of excessive force.[128] Third, a large number of officers, many of whom had quit or been fired by the LAPD, sued the department for having punished them for attempting to report misconduct by other officers. The problems exposed by the Rampart scandal are extremely serious. And it is important to remember that the LAPD always had a reputation for strict personnel standards.

A more positive view of police personnel evaluation emerged from Bayley and Garofalo's study of New York City police officers. Officers in three precincts were asked in confidence to identify three other officers they thought were "particularly skilled at handling conflict situations." The officers receiving the highest scores were then matched with comparison groups in the same precincts. An analysis of 467 police–citizen encounters involving potential violence found that officers rated highly by their peers handled situations differently than the members of the comparison groups. They were more likely to take charge of situations, less likely to simply stand by and observe, more likely to probe with questions and ask citizens to explain themselves, and more likely to verbally defuse situations. They were less likely to threaten the use of physical force, more likely to request people to disperse, and less likely to order people to do so.[129]

Bayley and Garofalo found that peer evaluations corresponded with observed differences in officer behavior. More important, the officers who were rated more highly by their peers and who performed better on the job also received higher ratings in official departmental evaluations. They received higher ratings in such categories as appearance, community relations skills, impartiality, decision making, ethics, and street knowledge.[130]

Experts on community policing argue that it requires a new approach to police officer performance evaluation. New procedures are necessary to take into account the new role of the police and the different tasks that officers are expected to perform.[131] Figure 13–3 represents portions of an experimental assessment report developed for the Houston police department's Neighborhood Oriented Policing program.

HOUSTON POLICE DEPARTMENT

Patrol Officer's Bi-Annual
Assessment Report

OFFICER INFORMATION		ACTIVITY PERIOD BASED ON DATE OF ENTRY
NAME: _____		
Last *First* *MI*		
EMP. # ____ SHIFT: ____ DIST/BEAT: _____ NEIGH.: _____		From:(m/d/y) _____
COMMAND/BUREAU/DIVISION: _____		To:(m/d/y) _____

SECTION 1

WORK ASSIGNMENT

List any changes in work assignment, responsibilities, or work environment which affect an officer's ability to complete assigned tasks.

PROGRESS

Describe status of and progress made toward attaining objectives set forth in previous monthly assessments.

ACCOMPLISHMENTS

List successful completion of specific projects, notable actions taken, and any other significant deed(s) initiated by the officer.

SPECIAL RECOGNITION

List any awards, letters of commendation, or recognition for activities performed by the officer.

FIGURE 13–3

SECTION II

DIRECTIONS: From the following scale, circle the response which most closely describes the quality of work demonstrated by the officer. Following each response, a written explanation of each choice is necessary. If the performance criterion is not observed by the supervisor or not verified through other means (i.e., survey questionnaires), circle the "Not Observed" (N.O.) response.

STATEMENTS and EXPLANATIONS	SCALE

PROFESSIONALISM	Not Observed	Strongly Disagree	Disagree	Average	Agree	Strongly Agree
1. Consistently exhibits a professional appearance.	N.O.	1	2	3	4	5
Explanation:_____						
2. Displays adaptability and flexibility.	N.O.	1	2	3	4	5
Explanation:_____						
3. Shows initiative in improving skills.	N.O.	1	2	3	4	5
Explanation:_____						

KNOWLEDGE						
4. Demonstrates working knowledge of laws.	N.O.	1	2	3	4	5
Explanation:_____						
5. Demonstrates working knowledge of General Orders/SOPs.	N.O.	1	2	3	4	5
Explanation:_____						

RELATIONSHIPS						
6. Effectively expresses oneself verbally.	N.O.	1	2	3	4	5
Explanation:_____						
7. Successfully interacts well with other officers.	N.O.	1	2	3	4	5
Explanation:_____						

FIGURE 13–3 (continued)

STATEMENTS and EXPLANATIONS	SCALE					

PATROL MANAGEMENT	Not Observed	Strongly Disagree	Disagree	Average	Agree	Strongly Agree
8. Efficiently manages uncommitted time.	N.O.	1	2	3	4	5
Explanation:_____						
_____						
9. Identifies problems and concerns in his/her area.	N.O.	1	2	3	4	5
Explanation:_____						
_____						
10. Formulates appropriate plan(s) of action.	N.O.	1	2	3	4	5
Explanation:_____						
_____						
11. Efficiently manages calls for service.	N.O.	1	2	3	4	5
Explanation:_____						
_____						
12. Maintains self-control in stressful situations.	N.O.	1	2	3	4	5
Explanation:_____						
_____						

SECTION III

OFFICER COMMENTS | This section is reserved for officer's comments relative to his/her interpretation of this assessment.

SECTION IV

This report is based on my observation and knowledge. It represents my best judgment of the officer's performance.

Rated by: _____   Date: _____
    (Signature of Immediate Superior Officer)   *Title*

Received by: _____   Date: _____
    (Signature of Higher Superior Officer)   *Title*

Approved by Department Head: _____   Date: _____

Report Furnished to Civil Service Commission: _____   Date: _____

I certify this report has been discussed with me.
My signature indicates that I   ☐ Agree   ☐ Disagree with this assessment.

Officer's Signature: _____   Date: _____

Source: Mary Ann Wycoff and Timothy N. Oettmeier, *Evaluating Patrol Officer Performance Under Community Policing: The Houston Experience* (Washington, DC: U.S. Government Printing Office, 1994), pp. 18–21.

JOB SATISFACTION AND JOB STRESS

Sources of Stress

What don't police officers like about their jobs? What factors cause them stress on the job? Several studies have found that, contrary to what many people think, officers are more stressed out by what their own department does than by what citizens on the street do. A survey of community policing officers in New York City found that, in response to the question "What do you dislike about being a cop?" the most frequently cited factor was "department/headquarters doesn't care" (mentioned by 58.2 percent of the officers). Another 22.4 percent mentioned "precinct level supervisors." Meanwhile, "lack of respect from the public" ranked third and was mentioned by only 16.4 percent of the officers.[132]

Police officer job satisfaction and job stress are often treated as separate subjects, despite the fact that they are closely related. The same factors cause satisfaction or stress, depending upon whether they are present or absent.

The factors that cause satisfaction or stress fall into five general categories: (1) the nature of police work; (2) organizational factors such as perceived support from leaders, relations with fellow officers, and opportunities for career advancement; (3) relations with the community; (4) relations with the media and the political establishment; and (5) personal or family factors that influence a person's job.[133]

A majority of police officers are generally satisfied with their jobs. In Washington, DC, 82 percent indicated that they were satisfied or very satisfied. A study of Detroit police officers found that in 1988 61 percent expressed medium satisfaction and 8 percent expressed high satisfaction. This represented lower levels of satisfaction than 10 years earlier, when 53 percent expressed medium and 28 percent expressed high satisfaction with their jobs. About three-quarters (78 percent) said they would choose law enforcement again as a career, but 64 percent also said that the work is stressful. Few of the Detroit officers indicated that they felt low satisfaction in terms of job fulfillment (3 percent in 1978 and 8 percent in 1988), defined in terms of freedom to make decisions and overall feelings of accomplishment.[134]

There is some disagreement over whether policing is more stressful than other demanding occupations. Some studies have reported higher rates of suicide, alcoholism, heart attack, and divorce among police officers than among the general population. A study of suicides in New York City between 1964 and 1973 found a rate of 17.2 per 100,000 among police officers compared with 8.3 for the city as a whole and 11 per 100,000 for males in the city. Niederhoffer found inconsistent evidence on divorce rates. Some studies claimed to find divorce rates as high as 30 percent in some police departments, but it was not clear that the rate for police officers was significantly higher than for the general population in the areas studied.[135]

The threat of danger is a basic element of police work that creates stress. Threatening incidents, such as physical assaults in the form of being attacked with a weapon, are statistically infrequent. The number of police officers feloniously killed in the line of duty, in fact, fell by 50 percent between the 1970s and 1990s, and averages less than 70 a year at present.[136] In fact, measured in terms of on-the-job deaths, mining, construction, and farming are considerably more dangerous. The fatality rate in coal mining was

38 per 100,000 employees in 1995, compared with 22 in agriculture and 15 in construction. The rate for law enforcement is about 20 per 100,000, including both accidental and felonious deaths.[137] Nonetheless, as Skolnick argues, the potential threat is a constant factor that affects officers' attitudes toward the public.[138]

Citizen disrespect and challenges to police authority are another source of on-the-job stress. Even though such incidents are statistically infrequent, they loom large in an officer's consciousness. Equally important is the problem of boredom. Routine patrol work often involves long periods of inactivity. Shifting suddenly from inactivity to a high state of readiness is another source of stress. Another major cause of stress in policing involves dealing with extreme human suffering. Officers regularly handle people who have been killed or seriously injured, or who are in a state of extreme psychological disorder.

The police department itself is a major source of stress. For many officers it is more serious than problems arising from dealing with the public. Officers often feel that command officers do not support them adequately, that incompetent officers are given preferred assignments because of personal friendships, and that the department changes policies in reaction to criticism from the media or politicians. As noted above, racial, ethnic, and gender conflicts exist in many police departments, causing stress among officers. Some police departments rotate shifts on a regular basis. This disrupts a person's family life and has adverse physiological effects, including loss of sleep.[139]

Female police officers experience special gender-related forms of stress. Some involves a lack of acceptance by male police officers and the absence of the supportive behavior (e.g., sharing of information, sponsorship for special assignments) that other officers receive. Sexual harassment creates additional stress.[140] Finally, female officers often have greater child care responsibilities than male officers and take more sick leave in order to handle them.

Coping with Stress

Until recently, few police departments tried to help officers cope with job stress. They either ignored the problem or assigned the officer with obvious difficulties to an easier job. For their part, troubled officers either relied on the support of their fellow officers or internalized their problems—a response that often led to alcohol abuse, mental illness, or even suicide.[141]

Today, many police departments maintain programs to help officers cope with the pressures of the job and/or other personal problems. These programs take several different forms. Some use mental health professionals, while others rely on peer support. Mental health professionals are employed either on a contract/referral basis or as full-time staff members of an employee assistance program (EAP). Many EAPs serve all city or county employees. Many experts regard peer counseling as particularly valuable, since the officer can relate well to the counselor as a fellow police officer. Also, some peer counselors can provide a role model of having dealt, for example, with an alcohol abuse problem.[142]

One of the key issues in employee assistance programs is confidentiality. Officers seek out assistance when they are assured that the information will not be used against them in a disciplinary action. Some EAPs have been damaged by unauthorized leaks of information, or the belief that such leaks occur.[143] Many officers refuse to seek professional help when they are having problems because of the traditional macho image of police officers as tough individuals who can handle any problem.

THE RIGHTS OF POLICE OFFICERS

Police officers enjoy the same civil and constitutional rights as other citizens, subject only to certain limitations related to the special circumstances of law enforcement. This was not always the case. In the past, the law held that all public employees, including police officers, gave up certain rights when they began their jobs. Public employment was considered to be a privilege, and the employee accepted it on the employer's terms. In a famous opinion over 100 years ago, involving an officer who had been fired for discussing politics on the job, Massachusetts judge (and later Supreme Court Justice) Oliver Wendell Holmes declared that the person "may have a constitutional right to talk politics, but he has no constitutional right to be a policeman."[144]

Over the past 20 years this view has been rejected, and police officers, along with other public employees, now enjoy basic constitutional rights of freedom of speech and association, due process of law, and privacy. The U. S. Supreme Court ruled in the 1966 *Garrity* case that "policemen [sic], like teachers and lawyers, are not relegated to a watered-down version of constitutional rights."[145] In 1981 the American Civil Liberties Union published a short handbook entitled *The Rights of Police Officers,* summarizing these rights.[146]

Under the First Amendment, police officers may not be barred from employment or be disciplined for private political or religious activities. Thus, a police officer has a constitutional right to belong to unpopular political or religious organizations. This right is not absolute, however, and departments may place restrictions on an officer's participation in partisan political activity, such as running for political office. Political or religious activity on the job is not permitted. The right of freedom of speech includes, to a limited extent, the right of an officer to criticize his or her own department publicly. Generally, a department may discipline an officer if the public criticism undermines the department's effectiveness.

Polygraph examinations are an exception to the rights enjoyed by other citizens. The federal Polygraph Protection Act prohibits employers from using lie detectors in recruitment. Law enforcement agencies, however, are exempted and may administer polygraph tests to job applicants.

Officers also enjoy procedural due process protections on the job. They may not be fired or disciplined without adequate cause. Due process in personnel decisions is guaranteed in part by existing civil service regulations, by union contract in some departments, and by a police officers' "bill of rights" in Maryland, Florida, and other states.

Officers' Rights versus Accountability

One important question is whether the rights of police officers interfere with efforts to hold officers accountable for their actions (Chapter 11). That is, do provisions of state police officers' bills of rights or union contracts prevent supervisors from collecting information necessary to investigate alleged officer misconduct?

There are two answers to this question. Most officers' rights are consistent with standards of fairness and due process. Any person has a right to be informed of the charges against him or her. A person facing charges that could result in significant punishment (in this case possible loss of job) has the right to be represented by an attorney. A police officer, meanwhile, should not be subject to extended or intimidating forms of interrogation. At the same time, however, some police union contracts have provisions that do in fact impede the legitimate investigation of misconduct. In Seattle, for example, the union contract included provisions that made it virtually impossible for a commander to conduct a face-to-face interview with an officer suspected of misconduct; additionally, all questions to a suspected officer had to be submitted in writing in advance. As a result of a police scandal, the city of Seattle committed itself to eliminating these provisions.[147]

OUTSIDE EMPLOYMENT

A significant number of police officers supplement their incomes with outside employment. In addition, many officers who are frustrated by the lack of career opportunities look for challenges and rewards outside the department. Many of those jobs are in private security, where the officer wears his or her police uniform. A 1988 Justice Department study found that half of all officers in some departments work off duty but in uniform.[148]

Outside employment creates a number of potential problems. First, it may diminish an officer's commitment to his or her job with the police department. A study of arrest productivity among New York City police officers found that those officers who held outside jobs made significantly fewer arrests than officers who did not. Apparently, officers were deterred from making arrests out of fear that the resulting court appearances would interfere with their outside work.[149]

Second, off-duty work in uniform creates potential conflicts of interest. An off-duty officer working in a bar, for example, may be caught between the duty to enforce the law and the interests of the bar owner. Finally, outside work in uniform may lower the dignity of the department.[150]

The San Jose independent police auditor exposed another conflict of interest by pointing out that some officers working off duty were hiring their supervisors as employees on those jobs. This practice potentially undermines discipline in the department, as a supervisor might be afraid to discipline an officer under his or her command out of fear of being fired from the off-duty job.[151]

TURNOVER: LEAVING POLICE WORK

Every year, about 5 percent of all police officers leave their jobs. This attrition rate appears to have been steady since the 1960s. Officers leave police work because of retirement, death, dismissal, voluntary resignation, or layoffs resulting from financial constraints.[152]

Martin found that women leave policing at a slightly higher rate than men, but for reasons other than retirement (6.3 percent annually compared with 4.6 percent). Women are more likely to resign voluntarily (4.3 versus 3.0 percent) and to be terminated involuntarily (1.2 versus 0.6 percent). Women officers experience a more hostile work environment. Women, especially single parents, have greater difficulty combining work with family responsibilities. Inadequate pregnancy leave policies make it difficult or impossible for women to have children and continue to work.[153]

Doerner found significantly higher attrition rates for female officers, both African American and white, compared with male officers in the Tallahassee police department. He suggests that this pattern raises an issue of concern for affirmative action programs, which focus almost exclusively on recruitment and ignore long-term employment patterns.[154]

Relatively little research has been done on the reasons for voluntary resignation. A Memphis study of police officers who resigned found that dissatisfaction with opportunities for promotion and with department policies was more important than inadequate pay and benefits or the feeling that their efforts were not being appreciated. Not all officers who are unhappy choose to resign, however. The Memphis study concludes that "dissatisfaction is a necessary but not a sufficient condition to cause resignation." As is the case with employees in all occupations, the decision is made in the context of many different personal, familial, and economic factors, including perceived career alternatives. The Memphis study identifies several key "turning points" leading to the decision to resign. These include, in order of importance, (1) the feeling that one's career had stagnated (e.g., "I just can't see any future in being a police officer"); (2) a particularly intense experience that brought accumulated frustrations to a head; (3) lack of a sense of fulfillment on the job; (4) family considerations; (5) the conduct of coworkers; (6) a particular department policy or policies; and (7) new employment opportunities.[155]

SUMMARY

Careers in law enforcement are subject to many different influences. Most popular stereotypes about police officer attitudes and behavior are not supported by the evidence. There is no evidence that a particular type of person is attracted to law enforcement, or that this explains police behavior. The evidence does suggest, however, that certain aspects of police work do have a powerful influence on both attitudes and behavior. At the same time, it is evident that recent changes in police employment patterns have brought a new diversity to the rank and file. Racial and ethnic minorities and women bring different expectations to policing. Law enforcement careers are heavily influenced by factors associated with police departments, particularly the opportunities for career advancement. The nature of police organizations is explored in more detail in Chapter 14.

CASE STUDY: NATIONAL CENTER FOR WOMEN AND POLICING (EXCERPT)

Underrepresentation of Women Hurts Law Enforcement

National and international research shows conclusively that increasing the numbers of women on police departments measurably reduces police violence and improves police effectiveness and service to communities. The studies also show that women officers respond more effectively than their male counterparts to violence against women, which accounts for up to 50% of all calls to police. Yet this record stands in stark contrast to women's dramatic under-representation in police departments where they make up 13.8% of sworn officers nationwide.

Escalating Cost of Police Brutality

Study after study shows that women officers are not as likely as their male counterparts to be involved in the use of excessive force. As a result, the under-representation of women in policing is contributing to and exacerbating law enforcement's excessive force problems. The actual and potential liability for cities and states is staggering, with lawsuits due to excessive force by male law enforcement personnel costing millions of dollars of taxpayer money every year.

Ineffective Response to Domestic Violence

Domestic violence is the single major cause of injury to women and yet the majority of these violent crimes against women go unreported and uninvestigated by law enforcement agencies. At the same time, law enforcement officers who commit domestic abuse are routinely ignored or exonerated, often leading to tragic results. With studies showing that as many as 40% of male law enforcement officers commit domestic abuse, more women law enforcement officers can serve as a strong force to promote a more effective response by agencies to domestic violence cases that occur both within police departments and community-wide.

Damaged Police–Community Relations

Women favor a community-oriented approach to policing which is rooted in strong interpersonal and communication skills and which emphasizes conflict resolution over force. Women tend to rely on their verbal skills over employing the use of force. With greater numbers of women, this highly effective model of policing will increasingly improve the public image of law enforcement agencies as well as have a positive impact on police–community relations nationwide.

Costly Sexual Harassment and Sexual Discrimination Lawsuits

Law enforcement agencies have tolerated workplace environments that are openly hostile and discriminatory towards female employees, forcing women to bring successful lawsuits against their agencies. The ongoing serious under-representation of women in policing leads to greater numbers of incidents of sexual harassment and discrimination. Increasing the number of women, treating women equally on the job, and holding women to fair hiring and promotion practices will reduce the enormous costs resulting from widespread lawsuits.

Source: National Center for Women and Policing, *Equality Denied* (1998), p. 5.

FOR DISCUSSION

The National Center for Women and Policing argues that adding more women officers to a police department will produce a number of benefits.

1 Is this argument sound?
2 What evidence does the center cite?
3 Is the evidence persuasive?
4 Is there any contrary evidence that is ignored?
5 What does the center's argument say about the culture of policing?

INTERNET EXERCISE: THE DIVERSE POLICE SUBCULTURE ON THE WEB

Many organizations representing different groups of police officers maintain their own websites. Check out the websites for such groups as the National Hispanic Police Association, the International Association of Women Police, the Emerald Society of Boston, the Federation of Lesbian and Gay Police Organizations, and others.

Whom do these organizations represent? Do they provide their membership figures? What do they do? What activities do they sponsor? Do they offer any reports or other literature?

REFERENCES:

1 William A. Westley, *Violence and the Police* (Cambridge, MA: MIT Press, 1970), pp. 159–160.
2 John H. McNamara, "Uncertainties in Police Work: The Relevance of Police Recruits' Backgrounds and Training," in David J. Bordua, ed., *The Police Six Sociological Essays* (New York: Wiley, 1967), pp. 163–252.
3 Arthur J. Luirgio and Dennis P. Rosenbaum, "The Travails of the Detroit Police–Victims Experiment: Assumptions and Important Lessons," *American Journal of Police,* XI, no. 3 (1992): 24.
4 Albert Reiss, *The Police and the Public* (New Haven, CT: Yale University Press, 1971), p. 51.
5 John A. Groger, *Memory and Remembering: Everyday Memory in Context* (New York: Longman, 1997), pp. 189–197.
6 John P. Clark, "Isolation of the Police: A Comparison of the British and American Situations," *Journal of Criminal Law, Criminology, and Police Science,* 56 (September 1965): 307–319.
7 Westley, *Violence and the Police,* pp. 18–19.
8 Stephen B. Perrott and Donald M. Taylor, "Crime Fighting, Law Enforcement and Service Provider Role Orientations in Community-Based Police Officers," *American Journal of Police,* XIV, no. 3/4 (1995): 182.
9 Ibid., p. 7.
10 Richard Seltzer, Sucre Aone, and Gwendolyn Howard, "Police Satisfaction with Their Jobs: Arresting Officers in the District of Columbia," *Police Studies,* 19, no. 4 (1996): 33.

11 Westley, *Violence and the Police,* pp. 76–82.

12 Jerome E. McElroy, Colleen A. Consgrove, and Susan Sadd, *Community Policing: The CPOP in New York* (Newbury Park, CA: Sage, 1993), p. 27.

13 John Van Maanen, "Police Socialization: A Longitudinal Examination of Job Attitudes in an Urban Police Department," *Administrative Science Quarterly,* 20 (June 1975): 222.

14 Seltzer, Aone, Howard, "Police Satisfaction with Their Jobs: Arresting Officers in the District of Columbia," 33.

15 George W. Griesinger, Jeffrey S. Slovak, and Joseph J. Molkup, *Civil Service Systems: Their Impact on Police Administration* (Washington, DC: Government Printing Office, 1979).

16 James L. O'Neill and Michael A. Cushing, *The Impact of Shift Work on Police Officers* (Washington, DC: PERF, 1991).

17 President's Commission on Law Enforcement and Administration of Justice, *Task Force Report: The Police* (Washington, DC: Government Printing Office, 1967), p. 165.

18 James J. Fyfe, "Who Shoots?: A Look at Officer Race and Police Shooting," *Journal of Police Science and Administration,* 9 (December 1981): 373.

19 William K. Muir, *Streetcorner Politicians* (Chicago: University of Chicago Press, 1977).

20 Westley, *Violence and the Police.*

21 Lawrence W. Sherman, "Causes of Police Behavior: The Current State of Quantitative Research," *Journal of Research in Crime and Delinquency,* 17 (January 1980): 69–100.

22 Westley, *Violence and the Police,* p. viii.

23 Ibid., p. 11.

24 Ibid.

25 Ibid., pp. 76–82.

26 Susan Martin, *Breaking and Entering: Police Women on Patrol* (Berkeley: University of California Press, 1980), p. 97.

27 Ibid., p. 113.

28 David Weisburd and Rosann Greenspan, with Edwin E. Hamilton, Hubert Williams, and Kellie Bryant, *Police Attitudes toward Abuse of Authority: Findings from a National Study* (Washington, DC: Government Printing Office, 2000).

29 Ibid., pp. 121–122.

30 Weisburd et al., *Police Attitudes toward Abuse of Authority.*

31 Christopher Commission, *Report of the Independent Commission to Investigate the Los Angeles Police Department* (Los Angeles: City of Los Angeles, 1991), pp. 168–171.

32 Weisburd et al., *Police Attitudes toward Abuse of Authority.*

33 Jerome H. Skolnick, *Justice without Trial,* 3rd ed. (New York: Macmillan, 1994), pp. 44–47.

34 Egon Bittner, "The Functions of the Police in Modern Society," in Bittner, *Aspects of Police Work* (Boston: Northeastern University Press, 1990), pp. 120–132.

35 Bureau of the Census, *Statistical Abstract of the United States, 1999* (Washington, DC: Government Printing Office, 1999), Table 712.

36 Bureau of Justice Statistics, *Policing and Homicide, 1976–98: Justifiable Homicide by Police, Police Officers Murdered by Felons* (Washington, DC: Government Printing Office, 2000).

37 Skolnick, *Justice without Trial,* pp. 1–21, 199–123.

38 Weisburd et al., *Police Attitudes toward Abuse of Authority.*

39 Herbert Packer, *The Limits of the Criminal Sanction* (Stanford: Stanford University Press, 1968), Ch. 8.

40 Arthur Niederhoffer, *Behind the Shield* (Garden City, NY: Anchor Books, 1967), pp. 100, 112–113.

41 Joel Lefkowitz, "Psychological Attributes of Policemen: A Review of Research and Opinion," *Journal of Social Issues,* 31, no. 1 (1975): 3–26.

42 David H. Bayley and Harold Mendelsohn, *Minorities and the Police* (New York: The Free Press, 1969), pp. 15–18.

43 Steve Herbert, "Police Subculture Reconsidered," *Criminology,* 36, no. 2 (1998): 343–368.

44 Samuel Walker, "Racial-Minority and Female Employment in Policing: The Implications of 'Glacial Change,'" *Crime and Delinquency,* 31 (October 1985): 555–572.

45 Robin N. Haarr, "Patterns of Interaction in a Police Patrol Bureau: Race and Gender Barriers to Integration," *Justice Quarterly,* 14 (March 1997): 53.

46 Martin, *Breaking and Entering,* pp. 79–108.

47 Ibid., pp. 102–107.

48 Weisburd et al., *Police Attitudes toward Abuse of Authority.*

49 Kimberly A. Lonsway, *Hiring and Retaining More Women: The Advantages to Law Enforcement Agencies* (Los Angeles: National Center for Women and Policing, 2000).

50 "A Look Ahead," *The Los Angeles Times* (September 18, 2000).

51 The various studies are summarized in Susan Ehrlich Martin and Nancy C. Jurik, *Doing Justice, Doing Gender: Women in Law and Criminal Justice Occupations,* Chs. 3, 4. For a critique of these studies, however, see Merry Morash and Jack R. Greene, "Evaluating Women on Patrol: A Critique of Contemporary Wisdom," *Evaluation Review,* 10 (April 1986): 230–255.

52 Peter B. Bloch and Deborah Anderson, *Policewomen on Patrol: Final Report* (Washington, DC: The Police Foundation, 1974).

53 Joyce L. Sichel, Lucy N. Friedman, Janice C. Quint, and Michael E. Smith, *Women on Patrol: A Pilot Study of Police Performance in New York City* (Washington, DC: Government Printing Office, 1978).

54 San Jose, Independent Police Auditor, *Annual Report 1996* (San Jose, CA: City of San Jose, 1997); New York City, Civilian Complaint Review Board, *Annual Report 1997* (New York: CCRB, 1997), pp. 62–63.

55 Samuel Walker and Geoffrey P. Alpert, "Police Accountability: Establishing an Early Warning System," International City Management Association, *IQ Service Report,* 32, no. 8 (August 2000); Samuel Walker, Geoffrey P. Alpert, and Dennis J.

Kenney, "Early Warning Systems for Police: Concept, History, and Issues," *Police Quarterly,* 3 (June 2000): 132–152.

56 National Black Police Officers Association, *Police Brutality: How to Stop the Violence* (Washington, DC: NBPOA, nd.).

57 Weisburd et al., *Police Officer Attitudes toward Abuse of Authority.*

58 "Black Officers Take on the LAPD and Protective League: An Interview with Sgt. Leonard Ross," *Policing by Consent* (October 1995): 8–9.

59 Weisburd et al., *Police Attitudes toward Abuse of Authority.*

60 Wesley G. Skogan and Susan M. Hartnett, *Community Policing, Chicago Style* (New York: Oxford University Press, 1997).

61 Nicholas Alex, *Black in Blue* (Englewood Cliffs, NJ: Prentice-Hall, 1969).

62 Susan E. Martin, "'Outsider Within' the Station House: The Impact of Race and Gender on Black Women Police," *Social Problems,* 41 (August 1994): 398.

63 Peter H. Rossi et al., *The Roots of Urban Discontent: Public Policy, Municipal Institutions, and the Ghetto* (New York: John Wiley, 1974).

64 David L. Carter, "Hispanic Police Officers' Perceptions of Discrimination," *Police Studies,* 9 (Winter 1986): 204–210.

65 Dawn M. Irlbeck, "Latino Police Officers: Negotiating the Police Role," Unpublished M.A. Thesis, University of Nebraska at Omaha, 2000.

66 President's Commission on Law Enforcement and Administration of Justice, *The Challenge of Crime in a Free Society* (Washington, DC: Government Printing Office, 1967), pp. 101–102.

67 Albert Reiss, "Police Brutality—Answers to Key Questions," *Transaction,* 5 (July–August, 1968): 10–19.

68 New York City, Civilian Complaint Review Board, *Annual Report, 1997,* pp. 60–61; San Jose, Independent Police Auditor, *Annual Report, 1996,* p. 26.

69 Fyfe, "Who Shoots?: A Look at Officer Race and Police Shooting," 367–382.

70 Stephen Leinen, *Gay Cops* (New Brunswick, NJ: Rutgers University Press, 1993).

71 Martin, "Outsider Within the Station House: The Impact of Race and Gender on Black Women Police," 393.

72 Haarr, "Patterns of Interaction in a Police Patrol Bureau," 65.

73 Ibid.

74 Seltzer, Aone, and Howard, "Police Satisfaction with Their Jobs," 33.

75 Susan Ehrlich Martin and Nancy C. Jurik, *Doing Justice, Doing Gender: Women in Law and Criminal Justice Occupations* (Thousand Oaks, CA: Sage, 1996), p. 68.

76 Susan E. Martin, *On the Move: The Status of Women in Policing* (Washington, DC: The Police Foundation, 1990).

77 David L. Carter, Allen D. Sapp, and Darrel W. Stephens, *The State of Police Education* (Washington, DC: Police Executive Research Forum, 1989), p. 38.

78 Lawrence W. Sherman, *The Quality of Police Education* (San Francisco: Jossey-Bass, 1978).

79 Victor E. Kappeler, David Carter, and Allen Sapp, "Police Officer Higher Education, Citizen Complaints, and Departmental Rule Violation," *American Journal of Police,* 11, no. 2 (1992): 37–54.

80 Skolnick, *Justice without Trial,* pp. 199–223.

81 Myron Orfield, "The Exclusionary Rule and Deterrence: An Empirical Study of Chicago Narcotics Officers," *University of Chicago Law Review,* 54 (Summer 1987): 1016–1055.

82 Elizabeth Reuss-Ianni, *The Two Cultures of Policing* (New Brunswick, NJ: Transaction Books, 1983).

83 Neal A. Milner, *The Court and Local Law Enforcement: The Impact of Miranda* (Beverly Hills, CA: Sage, 1971).

84 Skogan and Hartnett, *Community Policing, Chicago Style,* pp. 80, 83.

85 Ibid., pp. 85–86.

86 Arthur J. Lurigio and Dennis P. Rosenbaum, "The Impact of Community Policing on Police Personnel," in Dennis P. Rosenbaum, ed., *The Challenge of Community Policing* (Thousand Oaks, CA: Sage, 1994), pp. 147–163.

87 Reiss, *The Police and the Public,* p. 147.

88 Ibid.

89 Robert Friedrich, "Racial Prejudice and Police Treatment of Blacks," *Evaluating Alternative Law-Enforcement Policies,* eds. Ralph Baker and Fred A. Meyer (Lexington, MA: Lexington Books, 1979), pp. 149–167.

90 Joseph Goldstein, "Police Discretion Not to Invoke the Criminal Process: Low Visibility Decisions in the Administration of Justice," *Yale Law Journal,* 69, no. 4 (1960): 543–588.

91 Friedrich, "Racial Prejudice and Police Treatment of Blacks."

92 Steve Herbert, "Police Subculture Revisited," *Criminology,* 36, no. 2 (1998): 355–356.

93 David H. Bayley and James Garofalo, "The Management of Violence by Police Patrol Officers," *Criminology,* 27 (February 1989): 1–25.

94 Reiss, *The Police and the Public,* pp. 69–70.

95 Stephen D. Mastrofski et al., *Systematic Observation of Public Police* (Washington, DC: Government Printing Office, 1998).

96 Joan Petersilia et al., *Police Performance and Case Attrition* (Santa Monica, CA: Rand, 1987).

97 Van Maanen, "Police Socialization."

98 James Leo Walsh, "Career Styles and Police Behavior," in D. Bayley, ed., *Police and Society* (Beverly Hills, CA: Sage, 1977), pp. 149–167.

99 Muir, *Streetcorner Politicians.*

100 Ibid.

101 Eve Buzawa, Thomas Austin, and James Bannon, "The Role of Sociodemographic and Job-Specific Variables in Predicting Patrol Officer Job Satisfaction," *American Journal of Police,* 13, no. 2 (1994): 68.

102 Police Executive Research Forum, *Survey of Police Operational and Administrative Practices—1981* (Washington, DC: PERF, 1981), pp. 378–382.

103 James J. Fyfe, "Police Personnel Practices, 1986," *Municipal Yearbook 1987* (Washington, DC: International City Management Association, 1987), pp. 16–17.

104 Police Executive Research Forum, *Survey of Police Operational and Administrative Practices—1981,* pp. 342–346.

105 Anthony M. Bouza, "The Policeman's Character Investigation: Lowered Standards or Changing Times?" *Journal of Criminal Law and Criminology,* 63 (March 1972): 120–124.

106 Martin and Jurik, *Doing Justice, Doing Gender.*

107 Comparative salary data are available in Bureau of Justice Statistics, *Law Enforcement Management and Administrative Statistics, 1999* (Washington, DC: Government Printing Office, 2001).

108 Bureau of Justice Statistics, *Law Enforcement Management and Administrative Statistics, 1997,* p. xiv.

109 Westley, *Violence and the Police.*

110 Dorothy Guyot, "Bending Granite: Attempts to Change the Rank Structure of American Police Departments," *Journal of Police Science and Administration,* 7, no. 3 (1979): 253–284.

111 Martin, *On the Move.*

112 President's Commission on Law Enforcement and Administration of Justice, *The Challenge of Crime in a Free Society* (Washington, DC: Government Printing Office, 1967), p. 111.

113 Geoffrey N. Calvert, *Portable Police Pensions—Improving Interagency Transfers* (Washington, DC: Government Printing Office, 1971).

114 Fyfe, "Police Personnel Practices, 1986," p. 20.

115 Herman Goldstein, *Policing a Free Society* (Cambridge, MA: Ballinger, 1977), pp. 241–243.

116 Mollen Commission, *Commission Report* (New York: City of New York: 1994), p. 81.

117 Christopher Commission, *Report of the Independent Commission on the Los Angeles Police Department.*

118 Standard 35.1.2, Commission on Accreditation for Law Enforcement Agencies, *Standards for Law Enforcement Agencies,* 4th ed. (Fairfax, VA: CALEA, 1999), p. 35–1.

119 *United States v. City of Pittsburgh* (W.D. Pa., 1997).

120 Frank J. Landy, *Performance Appraisal in Police Departments* (Washington, DC: The Police Foundation, 1977), p. 1.

121 Timothy N. Oettmeier and Mary Ann Wycoff, *Personnel Performance Evaluations in the Community Policing Context* (Washington, DC: Community Policing Consortium, 1997), p. 5.

122 Landy, *Performance Appraisal in Police Departments.*

123 Martin and Jurik, *Doing Justice, Doing Gender,* pp. 86–87.

124 Petersilia, *Police Performance and Case Attrition.*

125 McNamara, "Uncertainties in Police Work," pp. 177–178.

126 CALEA, *Standards for Law Enforcement Agencies,* p. 35–2.

127 Los Angeles Police Department, *Board of Inquiry Report on the Rampart Scandal* (Los Angeles: LAPD, 2000).

128 Erwin Chemerinsky, *An Independent Analysis of the Los Angeles Police Department's Board of Inquiry Report on the Rampart Scandal* (Los Angeles: Police Federation, 2000).

129 Bayley and Garofalo, "The Management of Violence by Police Patrol Officers."

130 Ibid.

131 Oettmeier and Wycoff, *Personnel Performance Evaluations in the Community Policing Context.*

132 Jerome E. McElroy, Colleen A. Cosgrove, and Susan Sadd, *Community Policing: The CPOP in New York* (Newbury Park, CA: Sage, 1993), p. 27.

133 See the categories used in Jack R. Greene, "Police Officer Job Satisfaction and Community Perceptions: Implications for Community-Oriented Policing," *Journal of Research in Crime and Delinquency,* 26 (May 1984): 168–183.

134 Buzawa, Austin, and Bannon, "The Role of Selected Sociodemographic and Job-Specific Variables in Predicting Patrol Officer Job Satisfaction," 70.

135 Arthur Neiderhoffer, *The Police Family* (Lexington, MA: Lexington Books, 1978).

136 Bureau of Justice Statistics, *Policing and Homicide, 1976–98: Justifiable Homicide by Police, Police Officers Murdered by Felons;* Federal Bureau of Investigation, *Law Enforcement Officers Killed and Assaulted* (Washington, DC: Government Printing Office, annual).

137 Ibid.; Bureau of the Census, *Statistical Abstract of the United States, 1997* (Washington, DC: Government Printing Office, 1997), Table 686.

138 Skolnick, *Justice without Trial,* pp. 41–68.

139 O'Neill and Cushing, *The Impact of Shift Work.*

140 Martin and Jurik, *Doing Justice, Doing Gender,* p. 95.

141 Gail A. Goolkasian, *Coping with Police Stress* (Washington, DC: Government Printing Office, 1985), pp. 11–12.

142 Peter Finn and Julie Esselman Tomz, *Developing a Law Enforcement Stress Program for Officers and Their Families* (Washington, DC: Government Printing Office, 1997).

143 Ibid., pp. 79–88.

144 *McAuliffe v. New Bedford,* 155 Mass. 216, 29 N. E. 51.

145 *Garrity v. New Jersey,* 385 U.S. 493 (1966).

146 Gilda Brancato and Eliot E. Polebaum, *The Rights of Police Officers* (New York: Avon Books, 1981).

147 Seattle, Citizens Review Panel, *Final Report* (Seattle, WA: City of Seattle, 1999).

148 Albert J. Reiss, *Private Employment of Public Police* (Washington, DC: Government Printing Office, 1988).

149 William F. Walsh, "Patrol Officer Arrest Rates: A Study of the Social Organization of Police Work," *Justice Quarterly,* 3 (September 1986): 276.

150 Reiss, *Private Employment of Public Police.*

151 San Jose Independent Police Auditor, *Annual Report, 1995,* pp. 2–12.

152 President's Commission on Law Enforcement and Administration of Justice, *Task Force Report: The Police,* p. 9.

153 Martin, *On the Move.*

154 William G. Doerner, "Officer Retention Patterns: An Affirmative Action Concern for Police Agencies?" *American Journal of Police,* XIV, no. 3/4 (1995):197–210.

155 Terry Sparger and David Giacopassi, "Swearing In and Swearing Off: A Comparison of Cops' and Ex-Cops' Attitudes toward the Workplace," *Police and Law Enforcement,* eds. Daniel B. Kennedy and Robert J. Homer (New York: AMS, 1987), pp. 35–54.

CHAPTER FOURTEEN

Police Organizations

CHAPTER OUTLINE

INTRODUCTION

Police services are delivered to the public through organizations. The quality of policing depends on how well a department is organized and managed. Some critics argue that the nature of police organizations is a major problem in policing: that the departments are isolated from the public, resist change, and do not make good use of their personnel.

This chapter examines the dominant features of American law enforcement organizations. Some of those features are unique to police organizations, while others are common to all large bureaucracies. It identifies the major strengths and weaknesses of the prevailing style of organization and discusses alternative ways of organizing police work. It also discusses the impact of both civil service and police unions on police organizations.

THE QUASI-MILITARY STYLE OF POLICE ORGANIZATIONS

American law enforcement agencies are organized along quasi-military lines.[1] That is, they resemble the military in some but not all respects. This style of organization originated with Robert Peel's plan for the London Metropolitan Police in 1829 and was adopted by American police departments (see Chapter 2).

The police resemble the military in the following respects. First, police officers wear uniforms. Second, police departments use military-style rank designations, such as sergeant, lieutenant, and captain. Third, the command structure is hierarchical, with commands flowing from the top. Fourth, the organizational style is authoritarian, with penalties for failing to obey orders. Fifth, police officers carry weapons and have the legal authority to use deadly force, physical force, and to deprive people of their liberty through arrest.

At the same time, however, the police are different from the military in several important respects. First, the police serve a citizen population rather than fight a foreign enemy. Second, they provide services designed to help people, and these services are often requested by individual citizens. Third, they are constrained by laws protecting the rights of citizens. Fourth, they routinely exercise individual discretion (see Chapter 8), whereas military personnel are trained and expected to operate as members of military units.[2]

Criticisms of the Quasi-Military Style

Many experts believe that the quasi-military style is inappropriate for the police. They

SIDEBAR 14–1   THE MYTH OF THE MILITARY MODEL

For years the police organizational structure has been said to be modeled after the military. A recent essay by Thomas Cowper, a former Marine and 17-year veteran of the New York State police, argues that this perception is the result of several "wrong" assumptions. In particular, he states that the military and policing professions differ in terms of organizational characteristics and operational activities. With respect to organizational characteristics he argues that the military is founded on the idea of teamwork and leadership, while the police profession emphasizes individuality, monitoring (from a variety of distances), and supervision. Cowper believes that military leaders are schooled in the art of war to more effectively perform their job and innately have the ability to promote esprit and heighten morale; whereas police leaders, he argues, are not highly trained on matters of concern to their profession and only monitor the activities of their subordinates to ensure that they follow policies. Similarly, he adds that while police officers act as a "lone ranger" on patrol, rarely working with others in their department, soldiers work closely as a team, producing a more effective result. With regard to operational strategy Cowper points out that the military has one mission—to wage war—whereas the police have several missions: crime fighting, order maintenance, and service. Additionally, he argues that the military engages in proactive operations, while police work is primarily reactive in nature.

1 Discuss whether or not you think that Cowper is correct in his characterization of the military and police professions.
2 As a class, discuss other differences between the military and the police.
3 As a class, discuss similarities between the military and the police.

Source: Adapted from Thomas Cowper, "The Myth of the Military Model of Leadership in Law Enforcement," *Police Quarterly,* 3, no. 3 (2000): 228–246.

argue that, first, the military ethos cultivates an "us versus them" attitude that justifies mistreatment of citizens. Second, it encourages the idea of a "war on crime" that is inappropriate for serving a citizen population.[3] Third, the authoritarian command style is contrary to democratic principles of participation. Fourth, the authoritarian style produces low morale, and the rigid rank structure fails to provide sufficient job satisfaction for police officers. In other occupations, professionalism is based on participation and peer review of performance.[4]

In the 1960s and early 1970s, some critics argued that the police should deemphasize their military image, primarily in order to improve police–community relations. Specifically, they suggested using civilian-style blazers rather than military-style uniforms. A few small police departments experimented with using blazers. For example, the Menlo Park (California) police department found that they created no serious problems. The Lakewood (Colorado) police department adopted blazers and did not use the traditional rank designations when the department was first organized in the 1970s. After a few years, however, it returned to the traditional style. Problems arose because the public image of the police was so closely associated with military-style uniforms that it was difficult for the department to depart from the norm.[5]

POLICE DEPARTMENTS AS ORGANIZATIONS

The quasi-military aspect is only one feature of American police departments. To understand how police departments operate, and how they deliver services to the public, it is necessary to understand them as *organizations*. Many of the problems in policing are related to organizational features. It is important to also understand why these features exist and what positive contributions they make.

The Dominant Style of American Police Organizations

American police departments are remarkably similar in terms of organizational structure and administrative style. The typical police department is a complex bureaucracy, with a hierarchical structure and an authoritarian management style. The only exceptions to this rule are the very small departments, which have simple organizational structures and more informal management styles. At the same time, all but the very smallest agencies are governed by some form of civil service rules that regulate personnel policies. Finally, most of the large police departments are legally bound by collective bargaining contracts with unions representing rank-and-file officers.

Police Organizations as Bureaucracies

The modern police department is a bureaucratic organization, as are other large organizations in modern society: private corporations, universities, religious organizations, government agencies, and so on. Police departments share similar characteristics of bureaucracy with these other organizations.[6]

The bureaucratic form of organization exists because it is the most efficient means that has been developed for organizing and directing many different activities in the pursuit of a common goal. This does not mean that the bureaucratic form is completely efficient, but only that no other organizational form has been found that is better able to carry out multiple tasks simultaneously in the pursuit of a common goal.

The modern bureaucracy has the following characteristics:[7]

1 It is a complex organization performing many different tasks in pursuit of a common goal.

2 The different tasks are grouped into separate divisions, or "bureaus" (hence the term *bureaucracy*).

3 The organizational structure is hierarchical or pyramidal, with a clear division of labor between workers, first-line supervisors, and chief executives.

4 Responsibility for specific tasks is delegated to lower-ranking employees.

5 There is a clear chain of command, which indicates who is responsible for each task, and who is responsible for supervising each employee.

6 There is a clear unity of command, so that each employee answers to one and only one supervisor.

7 Written rules and regulations are designed to ensure uniformity and consistency.

8 Information flows up and down through the organization according to the chain of command.

9 There are clear career paths by which personnel move upward through the organization in an orderly fashion.

The modern police bureaucracy began to emerge in the early twentieth century, as a part of the professionalization movement.[8] With the creation of new specialized units (traffic, juvenile, vice, training, etc.), departments became more complex organizations. The new field of police management developed in order to help cope with this new complexity. Experts borrowed modern management principles from business administration and applied them to police administration. The leaders of this movement were August Vollmer, Bruce Smith, and O. W. Wilson. Wilson's textbook, *Police Administration*, became the unofficial bible on the subject by the 1950s.[9]

For example, see Figure 14–1, which is the organizational chart of the Milwaukee Police Department. It has been selected at random for this chapter, but it is representative of other big-city police departments and illustrates the main features of the modern police bureaucracy.

First, as is evident in the chart, the Milwaukee Police Department's organizational structure is pyramidal, reflecting a hierarchical management style. Second, the organization is structured to be able to perform many different tasks simultaneously: patrol, traffic, criminal investigation, records, training, research and development, and so on. Third, the Milwaukee Police Department has grouped together related tasks in a logical fashion: patrol and traffic are in the same bureau, criminal investigation is in another bureau, administrative services are in another.

Fourth, the lines of authority in the Milwaukee Police Department are clear, with responsibility for supervision flowing from the chief of police down through the organization. It is possible to identify who is responsible for particular tasks. This approach reflects the principle of unity of supervision: Each person reports to one supervisor. Under the principle of span of control, each supervisor is responsible for a limited number of people. In the patrol units, the ideal span of control involves a sergeant supervising between eight and twelve patrol officers.

The degree of specialization in a police department depends on the size of the community, the nature of its problems, and the size of the department itself.[10] The police department in a medium-sized city with relatively little serious crime does not need a separate homicide unit. The police department in a big city with many murders does need, and can afford to create, a homicide unit. Small and medium-sized departments cannot afford to maintain their own training academies. These tasks can be performed more efficiently for them by a state agency that serves many departments.[11]

What is not evident from the organizational chart is the set of rules governing employee behavior. As Chapters 8 and 11 explained, police departments rely on written rules and collect them in a standard operating procedure (SOP) manual or policy manual. Also, the career paths for officers will be indicated in its civil service procedures.

The Problems with Bureaucracy

There are several major criticisms of the bureaucratic form of organization, all of which apply to police organizations.[12] First, bureaucracies are often rigid, inflexible, and un-

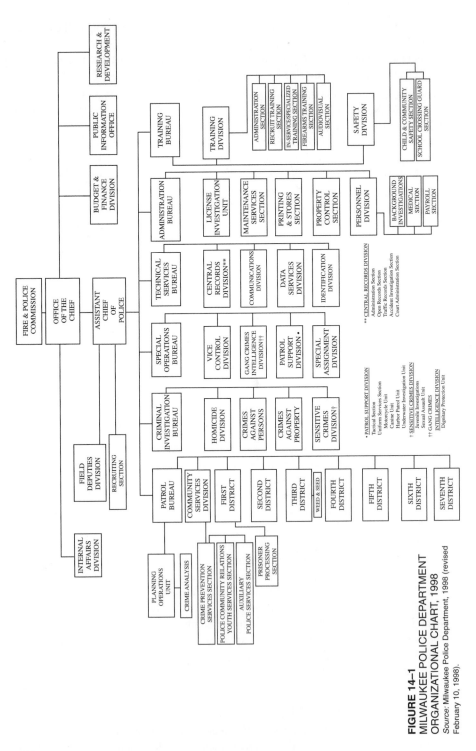

FIGURE 14-1
MILWAUKEE POLICE DEPARTMENT ORGANIZATIONAL CHART, 1998

Source: Milwaukee Police Department, 1998 (revised February 10, 1998).

able to adapt to external changes. Thus, for example, many business administration experts argue that American corporations have failed to adapt to changing markets and the new global economy. Police departments have often failed to respond to changes in patterns of crime and in the composition of the communities they serve.[13]

Second, communication within the organization often breaks down. Important information does not reach the people who need it. As a result, bad decisions are made, or the organization pursues conflicting goals.

Third, bureaucracies tend to become inward looking, self-serving, and isolated from the people they serve. Organizational self-protection and survival take precedence over the basic goals of the organization. Thus, businesses are accused of not catering to customer demands, universities are accused of not serving the needs of students, and police departments are accused of being isolated from the public. The problem of isolation is particularly acute with respect to police–community relations, as police departments have been accused of not listening to the concerns of racial- and ethnic-minority communities (see Chapter 9).

Fourth, bureaucracies are accused of not using the talents of their employees and even stifling creativity.[14] Many observers have found a serious morale problem among rank-and-file police officers and argue that departments need to provide greater opportunities for personal fulfillment and career advancement.[15]

PROBLEMS WITH POLICE ORGANIZATIONS

Police departments share all of the problems characteristic of other bureaucracies. First, they have been accused of failing to respond creatively to changing social conditions. This criticism was particularly prevalent during the police–community relations crisis of the 1960s (see Chapter 9). Second, they have been accused of being closed and unresponsive to the citizens they serve. New developments such as citizen review of complaints against the police are designed to make the police more responsive and accountable to the public (Chapter 11). Third, they have been accused of failing to utilize the talents of rank-and-file police officers, and of failing to offer sufficient opportunities for career advancement.[16]

A fourth criticism is that police organizations in practice are not true bureaucracies but are actually mock bureaucracies. That is to say, they have the appearance of a bureaucracy, and some of the form, but without the actual substance. For example, despite many written rules, police departments do not necessarily control the behavior of their officers on the street in making routine decisions. In practice, officers exercise a great deal of discretion (see Chapter 8).

Community policing (Chapter 7) is an attempt to respond to all of these criticisms of police organizations.

The Positive Contributions of Bureaucracy in Policing

Because of the widespread dissatisfaction with the state of police organization and management, the positive contributions of bureaucracy to policing are often overlooked. These contributions are best appreciated from a historical perspective (see Chapter 2).

A comparison of the typical police department in 1900 with the typical big-city department today illustrates the contributions of the modern bureaucracy. The police department of 1900 was very unspecialized, with only two units, patrol and detective. The development of many specialties—juvenile, traffic, community relations, training, and criminalistics—has required the growth of complex organizations that have the capacity to coordinate all of these activities.[17]

The control of police discretion and the reduction of misconduct have also been achieved through bureaucratic principles (Chapters 8 and 11). Written rules on the use of deadly force or the response to domestic violence (Chapter 5) represent the technique of administrative rulemaking. The paperwork involved in this approach is characteristic of bureaucracies.[18]

Informal Aspects of Police Organizations

The formal aspects of police organizations represent only one part of their actual operations. Every organization has important informal aspects, which are often referred to as office politics.[19] Dorothy Guyot argues that "within police departments, as in any formal organization, there are subdivisions, hierarchies, status groupings, and other formal arrangements. There are also informal relationships, cliques, friendship patterns, and temporary collaborations."[20]

Information does not always flow up and down the organization in the manner prescribed by the organizational chart. Sensitive and potentially embarrassing information is often withheld. Rank-and-file officers cover up each other's mistakes. Sergeants cover up mistakes by officers under their command because it would reflect poorly on their own performance. In some important respects, chief executives do not want to know about certain things. This allows them to publicly deny that such things exist when questioned by the news media or members of the public.

At the same time, however, information does flow to friends in the organization, outside of the prescribed channels. Such information is often referred to as gossip. Gossip falls into two general categories: true and false information. Gossip that is false is created and circulated to discredit someone. Gossip that is true is often useful. It may be important to know, for example, that someone is planning to retire or leave the organization, or that a person is in serious trouble because of mistakes on the job.

Important informal relationships in a police department are based on work groups. Officers who work together day in and day out, on patrol or as detectives, tend to develop close personal ties. They see things from the perspective of their unit and, when a conflict arises, defend their colleagues, even if they know their colleagues are wrong.

One dysfunctional result of this process is rivalry among different units. Patrol officers often resent the higher status that detectives enjoy. There are also rivalries between patrol officers assigned to different shifts. To a certain extent, the seniority system aggravates these tensions, as the evening shift gets the youngest officers while the day shift has the older officers.

At the same time, there are networks of relationships throughout the organization based on personal friendships. Often these relationships originated in shared experiences as members of the same recruit class or members of the same patrol crew. The folklore of policing includes the belief that some police officers develop closer relationships with their partners than with their spouses. A partner is someone who can understand the unpleasant aspects of policing that an officer would not want to discuss at home.

Friendship patterns become important in the management of a police department. Westley found that a police chief needs both information about what is going on in the organization and people to perform sensitive tasks. As a result the chief relies on "a group of favorites within the department whom he can depend on to handle delicate assignments."[21] A chief maintains this network of friends by handing out rewards in the form of favorable assignments and by punishing real or imagined enemies by giving them low-status assignments.

BUREAUCRACY AND POLICE PROFESSIONALISM

The bureaucratic aspects of policing conflict in many ways with the professionalism as understood in other occupations. In law, medicine, and education, a professional is someone with special expertise, resulting from extensive training and experience, who exercises independent judgment about critical events. The doctor, for example, makes critical decisions about diagnosis and treatment of patients. The professional is not expected to follow a rigid set of rules.[22]

The bureaucratic aspects of policing represent a different approach to the control of behavior. First, the quasi-military nature of police organizations has emphasized hierarchical command and control rather than collegial decision making. Second, police organizations attempt to control police officer behavior through formal, written rules (see Chapter 11).

Because of the history of the American police, police professionalism acquired a special meaning. Professionalism meant the same thing as bureaucratization. Thus, the professional departments were the ones that adopted O. W. Wilson's principles of police administration: specialization, hierarchy, clear lines of authority, written rules and policies, and so on.[23] Professional departments were the ones in which officers did their job "by the book," meaning that they followed written departmental rules.[24]

To a certain extent, however, the professional autonomy of the traditional professions is disappearing. Doctors increasingly work in large hospitals or medical facilities. Like other bureaucracies, these organizations impose formal controls over doctors' behavior. Lawyers increasingly work in large law firms or corporations, which also seek to control their behavior by monitoring the number of hours billed.

CHANGING POLICE ORGANIZATIONS

There is much dissatisfaction with the current state of police organizations. There are two schools of thought on how to improve them. The dominant school of thought accepts the basic principles of bureaucratic organization and seeks to apply them more effectively. Advocates of this approach, for example, support greater control of discretion through written rules, as described in Chapter 8.[25] The other school of thought seeks to use alternative decision-making procedures that operate within the existing formal structure.

Community Policing

Community policing represents an alternative to the traditional form of police organizations (Chapter 7). Traditional police organizations are extremely bureaucratic structures, which are said to necessarily limit the effectiveness and efficiency of the police because of the many impersonal rules, the lack of discretion officers are permitted to use, and the hierarchical nature of the organizational structure. Accordingly, community policing attempts to modify the police organization through debureaucratization. Specifically, it attempts to decentralize decision making both territorially and administratively. This requires the police to place greater responsibility on rank-and-file officers at the neighborhood level and to become more responsive to neighborhood residents. It also requires the police to *deformalize*, eliminating many of the rules and policies that often stifle creativity and do not encourage problem solving. Under community policing organizations are also encouraged to *despecialize* functions. This means replacing specialized units with neighborhood officers, who are more knowledgeable about the problems that face their neighborhood. Finally, community policing attempts to *delayerize*, decreasing the amount of social and administrative distance between the beat officer and the chief of police. This, reformers argue, will increase the speed at which decisions are made and will empower beat officers. In this respect, community policing responds to the standard criticisms of bureaucracies (see above).[26]

Whether or not organizations have been able to accomplish these goals is still a matter of debate. In 1997, Maguire surveyed 236 large municipal police organizations and examined structural change during the community-policing era. He found that between 1987 and 1993 police organizations had delayerized, but he also found that they had become more specialized.[27]

Total Quality Management

The implementation of total quality management (TQM) in police departments across the country has largely been a result of its increased use by organizations in private industry. TQM seeks to transform the police organization from one that is highly militaristic and bureaucratic to one that is democratic and emphasizes participative management, shared decision making, and problem solving. Zhao explains that there are four assumptions about TQM: (1) Organizations that produce quality products are more likely to survive; (2) employees "naturally" care about their work and, if given the opportunity, will take the initiative to improve the quality of their work; (3) problems are rarely restricted to one particular part of an organization, and to improve the quality of work, it is important to include all parties in decisions that seek to make improvements; and (4) top managers are ultimately responsible for the quality of services and should be held accountable.[28]

Little is known about the impact that TQM has had on police organizations. One of the first police departments to implement TQM was Madison, Wisconsin, where the chief experimented with the organizational style in one precinct. The chief found that TQM led to increased job satisfaction and greater organizational commitment among officers.[29] However, other police departments have not had as much success with TQM.

In Omaha, Nebraska, Chief Skinner attempted to implement TQM throughout the police department. He was interested in trying to transform the department from a traditional bureaucratic model—which emphasized chain of command, rules and regulations, and a hierarchical organizational structure—to a democratic model—which empowered officers and allowed for participatory management. The chief began the transformation in 1995 by training officers on the principles of TQM. A number of the officers spent over 40 hours in training covering such topics as TQM philosophy, principles, and intervention methods. He also created a Quality Council, which was empowered to take the lead in implementing TQM. The Quality Council focused on improving service delivery in certain neighborhoods. An independent evaluation of the TQM initiative, however, concluded that TQM had no impact on officer beliefs, attitudes, or performance.[30] As such, while TQM has been found to be a successful organizational strategy in private industry, its effectiveness in police organizations is still unclear.

Task Forces

An alternative to changing the structure of police organizations is to develop decision-making procedures that operate within the existing formal structure. One example is the use of task forces consisting of officers from different ranks within the same agency. A task force on drug enforcement, for example, might include a captain, a lieutenant, two sergeants, and three police officers. An interagency task force allows the police chief to select particular officers from different ranks, based on their talents rather than just their rank.[31]

The interagency task force approach addresses several problems related to the traditional police organizational structure. It recognizes the fact that many officers at the lowest rank are competent to make intelligent decisions about police policy. Involving them offers them greater job satisfaction, prepares them for supervisory responsibilities later in their careers, and increases the likelihood that innovations will be accepted within the organization.

The success of interagency task forces has led a number of law enforcement organizations to adopt multiagency task forces. Multiagency task forces operate as special law enforcement organizations, usually with multijurisdictional authority, created through formal agreements between several governmental agencies for the purpose of more effectively and efficiently combating specific crime problems.[32] It is estimated that there are between 900 and 1,100 multiagency task forces funded by the federal government alone.[33]

Multiagency task forces typically consist of two or more sworn officers from several participating agencies with each agency donating personnel and equipment. Often one of the participating agencies is selected as the lead agency to coordinate law enforcement efforts. Arizona's Anti-Gang Task Force, for example, consists of sworn officers from many of the state's larger cities as well as agents from a number of federal law enforcement agencies. The Anti-Gang Task Force is organizationally led and coordinated by the state's Department of Public Safety. This task force, while responsible for gang enforcement, is also responsible for managing gang intelligence for all law enforcement agencies in the state—a specialized function that is too expensive and time intensive for many of the police agencies in the state.

Phillips notes that there are five major advantages to using multiagency task forces: (1) They eliminate the duplication of services in surrounding communities, (2) they afford smaller agencies services that they otherwise might not be able to afford, (3) they result in the benefit of shared resource management, (4) they allow officers to work in jurisdictions where they might not otherwise have authority, and (5) they increase the amount of information that officers have at their disposal.[34]

Creating Learning Organizations

Since the 1960s, police executives and academic experts have wrestled with the challenge of revitalizing police organizations. Police departments are alleged to be highly resistant to change. Dorothy Guyot defines the problem as equivalent to "bending granite."[35] Many bold experiments have failed. A Police Foundation project designed to overhaul the Dallas, Texas Police Department ended in failure.[36]

William A. Geller defines the challenge in terms of creating learning organizations. It is not a matter of working harder, but of working *smarter*. Also, the challenge is to institutionalize the learning process so that departments develop the capacity to think about their own needs, plan and implement changes, and then learn from the achievements and failures.[37] To a great extent, change in policing has been initiated and then conducted by people and organizations outside of police departments.[38]

There are several obstacles to the development of learning organizations in policing. First, there is much cynicism among rank-and-file police officers. Many have seen innovative programs come and go, and consequently believe that the latest innovation is also just another temporary fad. This attitude affects departmental attempts to implement community policing, for example.[39] Another problem is that traditional research and planning units did not have the capacity to do any real research or planning. In many cases the officers assigned to those units did not have either the technical skills or the administrative support for this task.[40]

Geller lists six beliefs that prevent police departments from becoming learning organizations. First, many police officers believe that research is impractical and an "ivory tower" enterprise. Second, they are often reluctant to cooperate with outside researchers. Third, they fear evaluation research because of unfavorable results of previous evaluations. Fourth, many believe that findings from another jurisdiction do not apply to them. There is the widespread belief that "my city is *different*." Fifth, many command officers are afraid that encouraging critical thinking among rank-and-file officers will undermine discipline. Sixth, there is the widespread belief that "*thinking* inhibits *doing*."[41]

Geller describes thirteen steps a police department needs to take to become a genuine learning organization. First, it has to establish a research and planning unit with adequate resources and staff who understand research. Second, it needs to develop a process that spans all units in the department (patrol, criminal investigation, etc.). Third, it needs to develop a process for reducing turf battles between units in the department. Fourth, it needs to take a talent inventory of its own employees, to see what skills are available and perhaps not currently being used. Fifth, it needs to take a similar talent inventory of community groups to see what resources it can draw upon. Sixth, it needs to organize planning around particular problems, in the problem-oriented policing approach (see Chapter 7).

Seventh, departments might try to avoid the problem of "groupthink," where no one challenges the official policy, by designating certain people to serve as the devil's advocate and to question official assumptions and policies. Eighth, middle managers can be designated to facilitate critical thinking. Ninth, performance evaluations could assess how well officers engage in critical thinking. Tenth, departments need to develop meaningful procedures for soliciting suggestions from the rank and file. Eleventh, procedures need to be developed for convincing officers that research and innovation in other departments have led to real improvements (e.g., increased officer safety). Twelfth, departments need to expand their cooperative efforts with outside organizations. Thirteenth, and last, departments should contract with researchers they trust to serve as research brokers.[42]

It is not clear whether police departments will succeed in becoming true learning organizations. There is reason for some optimism, however. David Bayley argues that there is a tremendous amount of creative experimentation occurring in policing, and that the last years of the twentieth century may have been the most creative period in the history of modern policing.[43]

COMPSTAT

Over the past two decades police organizations have been increasing the amount of technology they employ to more effectively and efficiently make use of their resources. However, it was not until 1994 when the New York City Police Department, led by Commissioner William Bratton, implemented COMPSTAT (short for computer comparison statistics) that technology was used as an organizational tool to achieve crime control through accountability. In the New York City Police Department the COMPSTAT model attempts to blend timely intelligence, effective tactics, rapid deployment of personnel, and relentless follow-up and assessment.[44] Under COMPSTAT the police department continuously collects arrest, calls for service, and complaint data from each precinct or beat within the agency and analyzes them for reporting purposes at that level. This organizational model of management in New York City places the responsibility for crime control on precinct commanders. At weekly meetings crime trends are examined, and precinct commanders are "grilled" about the strategies that they have used to control crime in their precinct. Commanders who are not successful in reducing crime are reassigned to less prestigious and demanding positions.[45]

A number of policymakers and police officials claim that COMPSTAT is responsible for the dramatic drop in crime in New York City. From 1990 to 1997, Index crimes in New York City decreased by 55 percent compared with 24 percent in other large cities. Similarly, during the same period, homicides in New York City decreased by 66 percent compared with a decrease of 24 percent in other cities. Some have argued, though, that the drop in crime has come at the expense of precinct commanders having to use more aggressive policing strategies, which has led to more conflict between the police and the public they serve. For example, from 1994, the year that COMPSTAT was instituted, through 1998 there was a 40 percent increase in citizen complaints against the police.[46]

Regardless of the potential problems with COMPSTAT, the model has been implemented in a number of police departments across the country. For example, Boston, Baltimore, Los Angeles, Seattle, New Orleans, and Newark have all implemented, to varying degrees, the COMPSTAT model.[47]

CIVIL SERVICE

Civil service procedures are a major feature of American police organizations. Civil service represents a set of formal and legally binding procedures governing personnel decisions. Civil service is nearly universal. With the exception of some of the very smallest departments, almost every law enforcement agency in the United States operates under some form of civil service.[48] The purpose of civil service is to ensure that personnel decisions are based on objective criteria, and not on favoritism, bias, and political influence.

State law or local ordinance establishes civil service systems. In 80 percent of the cities ultimate authority over personnel procedures rests with a board or commission consisting of three to five persons. The mayor or a city manager government unit typically appoints board members for a specified term. The board sets basic policy and hires a personnel director to administer policy on a day-to-day basis.[49]

The civil service agency and the police department share responsibility for personnel policies. Civil service agencies are responsible for developing job descriptions and pay scales, developing recruitment procedures, developing and administering recruitment tests, certifying qualified applicants, developing promotional criteria, developing and administering promotional tests, developing disciplinary procedures, and hearing appeals of disciplinary actions. Police departments provide input on job descriptions, participate in recruiting, conduct some of the recruitment tests, and select recruits from certified lists.

Civil service systems reinforce the quasi-military rank structure of police departments. Dorothy Guyot points out that there are two different types of rank systems: rank in job and rank in person. Under a rank-in-person system an officer carries his or her rank permanently, until promoted (demotions are extremely rare under civil service).[50] For instance, an officer holding the rank of sergeant is restricted to those jobs designated for sergeants by civil service job descriptions. Under a rank-in-job system, an employee carries a title and responsibilities while assigned to a particular job; if demoted or reassigned, the employee loses both the title and the responsibilities. In private industry, for example, a person might be promoted to assistant vice president for marketing. That employee loses the title and the responsibilities if demoted or reassigned. Management has considerable flexibility in making these decisions.

Civil service creates a number of problems for police organizations. First, it limits the power of police chiefs in making personnel decisions. A chief cannot hire, fire, or promote those people at will. Nor can a chief change existing personnel standards at will (e.g., impose a college education requirement for all new recruits).

Second, it limits the opportunities and incentives for individual officers. Officers cannot earn financial bonuses or receive rapid promotions for exceptional performance.

Third, many critics argue that the provisions for discipline make it extremely difficult for chiefs to terminate bad officers, or even to discipline officers for poor performance.

POLICE UNIONS

Police unions are another structural feature of police organizations. A police union is an organization legally authorized to represent police officers in collective bargaining with the employer. Under American labor law, employers are required to recognize and negotiate with democratically chosen unions. Police unions are extremely powerful, and union contracts are an important feature of police organizations.

Aspects of Police Unions

The majority of sworn police officers in the United States today are members of police unions. According to the 1997 Law Enforcement Management and Administrative Statistics (LEMAS) survey, officers are represented by unions in 73 percent of all municipal police departments and 43 percent of all sheriff's departments.[51] Almost all of the big and medium-sized cities have police unions, while the small cities and county departments (ten sworn officers or fewer) do not. Although union membership has been declining in the private sector of the economy, it has been growing in the public sector. The police are not the most heavily unionized group of public employees. A higher percentage of firefighters and public school teachers are members of unions.[52]

Unlike other parts of the economy, there is no single national union that represents all police officers. The United Automobile Workers, for example, represents all employees in the automobile industry; the Teamsters union represents all truck drivers, and so on. Police unions are fragmented among several different national federations. The major union federations include the Fraternal Order of Police (FOP) and the International Union of Police Associations (IUPA).[53]

Police officers also belong to many other social and fraternal associations. These other organizations, however, do not represent officers in negotiating with their employers. The Fraternal Order of Police (FOP) is the oldest and largest police association. It currently represents several hundred thousand officers nationwide. Some, but not all, FOP lodges act as police unions. Most other associations are based on racial or ethnic groups. African American officers in many departments belong to chapters of the Guardians. The Latino Police Officers Association is a national group representing Latino and Hispanic officers. In New York City Irish American officers belong to the Emerald Society, Italian American officers to the Columbia Association, and German American officers to the Steuben Association.

Collective Bargaining

Collective bargaining is defined as "the method of determining conditions of employment through bilateral negotiations." The basic principles of collective bargaining are that (1) employees have a legal right to form unions of their own choosing, (2) employers must recognize employee unions, (3) employees have a right to participate in negotiations over working conditions, and (4) employers are required to negotiate with the union's designated representatives. The process is designed to provide a structured framework for settling differences between employers and employees.[54]

In some departments, the union represents all of the officers except the chief. In others, it represents all of the officers from the rank of captain on down; deputy chiefs are excluded on the grounds that they are part of management. In some large departments there are separate unions for different ranks: one for police officers, one for sergeants, and so on. In these cases, the chief must negotiate with two and, in some cases, three unions. There may also be a separate union for the civilian employees.

The 1935 National Labor Relations Act defined the scope of collective bargaining as "wages, hours, and other conditions of employment." The scope of conditions of employment is ambiguous and subject to negotiations. It generally excludes management rights issues, such as the right to recruit, assign, transfer, or promote employees. In some cities, however, the union has won the right to control such issues as patrol staffing.[55]

Grievance Procedures

One of the most important conditions of work involves disciplinary procedures. Almost all police unions have formal grievance procedures designed to protect officers against unfair discipline. Grievance procedures provide due process for employees.

The typical grievance procedure (see Figure 14–2) requires that an officer be notified (usually in writing) about a disciplinary action, that the officer has the right to a hearing, a right to an attorney, and a right to appeal any disciplinary action. In some instances, these procedures are referred to as the police officers' bill of rights. (See Figure 14–3.)

Unions and Shared Governance

Collective bargaining represents a form of shared management. Unions give officers a voice in some, but not all, decisions about the operation of the department. The major impact of police unions, therefore, has been to greatly reduce the power of police chiefs. Prior to the late 1960s, chiefs had an almost completely free hand in managing their departments.

The chief, for example, might announce a plan to add a fourth patrol shift. The union might argue that this represents a change in working conditions, because the officers involved will have to work different hours. The chief will reply that his power to create a fourth shift is a management right. The two sides will try to settle this disagreement informally. If they cannot, the union may file a grievance under the contract. Contracts normally contain a formal grievance procedure to settle these conflicts.

Impasse Settlement and Strikes

When the union and the city or county cannot agree on a contract, an impasse exists. In the private sector, the union often goes out on strike, or the employer conducts a lockout of the employees. Police strikes are illegal in many states, and other impasse settlement procedures exist, such as mandatory mediation, fact finding, or arbitration.

Strikes are the most controversial aspect of police unionism. Many people argue that the police have absolutely no right to strike: that it is unprofessional and that it creates a

FIGURE 14–2   ARTICLE 8: GRIEVANCE PROCEDURE

Step 1 An employee or Union who has a grievance shall present the same, in writing, to the Police Chief, or his designated representative, within ten (10) working days from the date on which the employee or Union became aware of the grievance. The written grievance must set forth the sections and articles of this Agreement upon which the matter of interpretation or application is involved. The Chief, or his designated representative, will respond to the grievant in writing within ten (10) working days from the date on which the written grievance was received.

Step 2 If satisfactory settlement is not reached under Step 1 hereof, then the aggrieved employee of Union may, within ten (10) working days of receipt of the Chief's response to Step 1 hereof appeal the Chief's decision to the Department Head, or his designated representative, shall have ten (10) working days in which to respond, in writing, to the employee.

Step 3 In the event the employee or Union is still dissatisfied with the response of the Department Head, or his designated representative, then the employee or Union may, within ten (10) working days from the date of the response given by the Department Head or his designated representative appeal said decision, in writing to the Labor Relations Director, or his designated representative. The Labor Relations Director or his designated representative shall respond to the grievant, in writing, within ten (10) working days from the date on which the grievance appeal was received. An extension on the time period may be granted when mutually agreed to by the Labor Relations Director and the Union.

Step 4 If satisfactory settlement is not reached under Step 3 hereof, either the aggrieved employee, the Union or the City of Omaha by and through the Labor Relations Director, or his representative shall, within twenty (20) working days from the expiration of the limits as set forth in Step 3 or any extension thereof as set forth in Section 3, by written notice to the other party, request arbitration. The City shall furnish the Union with a copy of any such notice sent or received requesting arbitration.

The arbitration proceeding shall be conducted by an arbitrator to be mutually selected by the parties within thirty (30) calendar days after the submission of written demand for arbitration. The UNION shall at its discretion become a party for the purpose of selecting an arbitrator. The UNION and the grievant shall together be considered one party. If the parties are unable to mutually agree as to the selection of an arbitrator within such time limit and either party continues to demand arbitration, the parties shall jointly request the Federal Mediation and Conciliation Service to provide a list of five (5) arbitrators. Each party shall have the right to strike two (2) names from the list of arbitrators as submitted. The party requesting arbitration shall have the right to strike the first name and the other party shall then strike one name with the same process being repeated so that the person remaining on the list shall be the arbitrator.

Source: Omaha Police Department, "Union Contract," *Standard Operating Procedure Manual,* pp. 12–13.

serious danger to the public. Police unions reply that they should have the same right to strike as other unions. Withholding one's labor is the ultimate weapon that working people have to force the employer to reach an agreement. Most union leaders, however, are opposed to strikes either because they are illegal in that state or because of the negative public reaction.[56]

Instead of actual strikes, police officers occasionally engage in job actions, defined as a deliberate disruption of normally assigned duties. One example is the "blue flu,"

FIGURE 14–3   FLORIDA POLICE OFFICERS' BILL OF RIGHTS

112.532   Law Enforcement Officers' and Correctional Officers' Rights

All law enforcement officers and correctional officers employed by or appointed to a law enforcement agency or a correctional agency shall have the following rights and privileges:

1 **Rights of Law Enforcement Officers and Correctional Officers While Under Investigation.** Whenever a law enforcement officer or correctional officer is under investigation and subject to interrogation by members of his agency for any reason which could lead to disciplinary action, demotion, or dismissal, such interrogation shall be conducted under the following conditions:

   a The interrogation shall be conducted at a reasonable hour, preferably at a time when the law enforcement officer or correctional officer is on duty, unless the seriousness of the investigation is of such a degree that immediate action is required.

   b The interrogation shall take place either at the office of the command of the investigating officer or at the office of the local precinct, police unit or correctional unit in which the incident allegedly occurred, as designated by the investigating officer or agency.

   c The law enforcement officer or correctional officer under investigation shall be informed of the rank, name, and command of the officer in charge of the investigation, the interrogating officer, and all persons present during the interrogation. All questions directed to the officer under interrogation shall be asked by and through one interrogator at any one time.

   d The law enforcement officer or correctional officer under investigation shall be informed of the nature of the investigation prior to any interrogation, and he shall be informed of the name of all complainants.

   e Interrogating sessions shall be for reasonable periods and shall be timed to allow for such personal necessities and rest periods as are reasonably necessary.

   f The law enforcement officer or correctional officer under interrogation shall not be subjected to offensive language or be threatened with transfer, dismissal, or disciplinary action. No promise or reward shall be made as an inducement to answer any questions.

   g The formal interrogation of a law enforcement officer or correctional officer, including all recess periods, shall be recorded, and there shall be no unrecorded questions or statements.

   h If the law enforcement officer or correctional officer under interrogation is under arrest, or is likely to be placed under arrest as a result of the interrogation, he shall be completely informed of all his rights prior to the commencement of the interrogation.

   i At the request of any law enforcement officer or correctional officer under investigation, he shall have the right to be represented by counsel or any other representative of his choice, who shall be present at all times during such interrogation whenever the interrogation relates to the officer's continued fitness for law enforcement or correctional service.

Source: Florida Statutes, Sec. 112.532.

where many officers do not go to work, claiming they are sick.[57] In some cases, such as San Francisco in 1975, police officers tried to exert pressure on the city by refusing to write any traffic tickets or writing massive numbers of tickets.[58] A police strike is a major crisis for the community. Police strikes in Baltimore (1974), San Francisco (1975), and New Orleans (1979) resulted in violence and disorder. In many strikes, some officers remain on duty, feeling a sense of obligation to the community.

Police strikes are actually very rare, and there have been very few since the 1970s. Public school teachers strike far more often than police officers. Even in the private sector, the number of strikes has declined substantially since the 1970s.[59]

The Impact of Police Unions

Police unions have had a powerful impact on American policing. First, they have produced significant improvements in police officer salaries and benefits. In the mid-1960s many police departments were having great difficulty recruiting and holding qualified officers. By the late 1980s the picture had changed dramatically. Police departments generally had many applicants for each opening and were able to recruit people with at least some college education. In other words, jobs with the police department were competitive with other jobs that a person with some college education might consider (see Chapter 12).

Second, police unions have radically altered the process of police management, reducing the power of chiefs and introducing a process of shared governance.

Third, unions have introduced due process into union discipline procedures, limiting the power of police chiefs to arbitrarily or unfairly discipline officers.

Fourth, critics argue that unions have had an important and negative impact on police–community relations. Generally, police unions have represented white police officers in opposition to civil rights leaders and, in some cases, racial-minority officers. In Boston, New York, and Cleveland police unions strongly opposed changes proposed by mayors designed to improve police–community relations. In recent years, police unions have often represented white police officers who have sued to block affirmative action plans designed to increase the number of racial-minority officers.[60]

Fifth, many critics argue that unions have hindered the development of police professionalism. Historically, reform relied on powerful and often charismatic police chiefs. Unions in some cities, for example, have opposed incentive pay for officers with college educations. Unions in several cities opposed the creation of a fourth patrol shift. And many unions fought programs designed to improve police–community relations.[61]

POLICE ORGANIZATIONS AND THEIR ENVIRONMENT

There are three primary theories that have been used by researchers to understand police organizational structures and operational strategies: contingency theory, institutional theory, and resource dependency theory. Each of these models emphasizes the importance of understanding the environment in which the police operate and how that environment impacts police organizations.

Contingency Theory

Contingency theory has emerged as the dominant theoretical framework for understanding the structures and practices of police organizations. The underlying premise of contingency theory is the belief that organizations are created and structured to achieve specific goals, such as crime control. According to contingency theory, organizations are rational entities, adopting organizational structures and operational activities that are most effective and efficient in achieving specific goals. It is argued that organizations which fail to make the appropriate adjustments to the environmental contingencies they face will not prosper and, in some cases, will not survive.[62]

Contingency theory has often been used by researchers and policymakers to understand police innovation. For example, Inglewood, California, faced a growing gang problem in the early 1970s. In response to the proliferation of gangs and gang-related problems the police department established a police gang unit to enhance the success of departmental crime control efforts. Similarly, many researchers and policymakers have argued that community-oriented policing has been adopted because past attempts by the police to control crime have failed.[63]

Institutional Theory

Institutional theory holds that police organizations are social institutions that operate in relation to their external social and political environment. John Crank and Robert Langworthy argue that understanding the relationship between police organizations and their external environment is important to understanding how police departments function. They point out that the police do not produce a product (as does a factory, for example). Instead, police organizations interact with other institutions and receive their legitimacy from them. In short, how well a department functions depends in large part on how well it meets the expectations of these other institutional actors.[64]

The institutional reality of police organizations is the product of myths and myth building. Much of the behavior of police organizations represents efforts to define their legitimacy in the eyes of other organizations and actors and to respond to challenges to their legitimacy. Traditionally, for example, the police have claimed crime control as their professional domain and sought to maintain their authority over this domain by creating and maintaining the appearance of effective crime control.[65] Some argue that the community-policing movement represents an attempt to redefine their professional domain and their central role over it.

Resource Dependency Theory

Resource dependency theory suggests that organizations must obtain resources to survive, and that to obtain these resources they must engage in exchanges with other organizations in their environment. This, resource dependency theorists argue, requires organizations to alter their organizational structure and/or operational strategy so that it accommodates others in their environment who have the capacity to provide much needed resources. However, proponents of resource dependency theory hold that organizations are not simply passive organisms at the mercy of others in their environment, but also have the capacity to influence their environment to ensure the flow of resources.[66]

Only a few studies to date have used resource dependency theory to understand police organizations. Katz, Maguire, and Roncek, who examined 285 police agencies across the country, found that even when controlling for the amount of gang-related crime, departments that received external funding for gang control functions were about

3.5 times more likely to have established a specialized gang unit than agencies that had not received funding. They argued that gang units might have been created because of the plentiful resources that were available for crime control efforts aimed at gangs rather than because there was a real and growing gang problem.[67] Similarly, Maguire, Zhao, and Lovrich argue that one of the reasons so many police agencies have implemented community-oriented policing is to obtain their share of the $8.8 billion to be distributed by the Department of Justice to facilitate community policing.[68]

SUMMARY

Police organizations are a critical element in policing. They are the instruments through which police services are organized and delivered to the public. Many police problems are associated with the problems of bureaucracy. Past attempts to restructure police departments, such as team policing, have not been successful. More recent attempts, such as community policing and problem-oriented policing, represent efforts to revitalize police organizations by making them more open and responsive to the communities they serve and to changing social conditions.

CASE STUDY: UNION INFLUENCE IN THE LOWELL, MASSACHUSETTS, POLICE DEPARTMENT

In the City of Lowell, Massachusetts, the one way in which patrol officers could influence department policy (primarily concerning contracts and discipline) was through their union. The most important decision the union became involved in, in recent years, occurred as Lowell's economic crisis mounted and the department had to absorb its share of budget cuts. The relevant decisions were made jointly by the chief and some members of the command staff, the unions, and city hall.

At the beginning of the 1990s, the department decided to freeze hiring and offer some two dozen officers early retirement. The number of sworn officers dropped from 195 to 159 from 1991 to 1993. The police department saved money in other ways as well, like making promotions without pay raises. But in 1993 the city (apparently "egged on" by press stories about the officers' "excessive" benefits) demanded further cuts from the police: The officers would have to give up their holiday pay—some $3,000 to $4,000 per officer—or the department would have to lay off staff to reduce the budget by the same amount (which worked out to be thirty-two officers).

The city gave the officers little time to consider its ultimatum, and when it came time to make the final decision, the union—whose approval was needed to suspend the holiday pay—had not voted on the issue. The city decided to suspend the officers, but Tom Meehan, the president of the patrol officers' union, wanted time to get a vote from his membership. Jerry Flynn, who was the union's treasurer at the time, remembers that Ed Davis was instrumental in the negotiation, and the episode earned the superintendent-to-be enormous credibility in the department:

> [Davis] is somebody who took a department that had 127 patrolmen at [the] time and we were in the midst of laying off 32 more. . . . I think he was a captain at the time, but it was him and I who sat at the table, and at the time everybody else got up from the negotiating table. And we

stood there and requested the addendum of city manager Dick Johnson to give us another seven days to post this [union rules demanded this much advance notice for a vote], and for the union to go as a body and say, "Look, we need to reduce this holiday pay in order to save these 32 police officers.

Meehan and Davis got their extension, and the union ultimately voted to suspend the benefits, thereby saving the patrol officers' jobs.

Source: Case study obtained from David Thacher, Organizational Change Case Study: Lowell, Massachusetts (Washington, DC, Urban Institute). As found at **http://www.ncjrs.org/nij/cops_casestudy/lowell4.html**

FOR DISCUSSION

1 If you were a police chief, how would you organize your department? For example, would it have many specialized units? Would it have more or fewer rules?
2 How has police professionalism been enhanced in the last 20 years?
3 Explain the difference between a centralized and decentralized organization. What are the advantages and disadvantages of each?
4 Explain how police unions affect police departments today.
5 What are some of the advantages and disadvantages of specialization?

INTERNET EXERCISES

Exercise 1 Many police departments have their organizational charts on their websites. Find the organizational charts for several very large (3,000 sworn officers), large (700 plus sworn officers), medium-sized (200 to 700 sworn officers), and small (under 100 sworn officers) departments. What are the obvious differences? How do they compare in terms of degree of specialization?

Exercise 2 Go to **http://www.cleat.org/ppp/0996.html** to learn about why there is no national police union. After reading the article discuss the benefits and limitations to police unions.

REFERENCES

1 Egon Bittner, *Aspects of Police Work* (Boston: Northeastern University Press, 1990), pp. 136–147.
2 Ibid.
3 Ibid., pp. 132–136.
4 W. E. Moore, *The Professions: Rules and Roles* (New York: Russell Sage Foundation, 1970).
5 James H. Tenzel, Lowell Storms, and Harvey Sweatwood, "Symbols and Behavior: An Experiment in Altering the Police Role," *Journal of Police Science and Administration*, 4, no. 1 (1976): 21–28.
6 Charles Perrow, *Complex Organizations: A Critical Essay* (Glenview, IL: Scott, Foresman, 1972).
7 Ibid.

8 Samuel Walker, *A Critical History of Police Reform* (Lexington, MA: Lexington Books, 1977).

9 O. W. Wilson and Roy C. McLaren, *Police Administration*, 4th ed. (New York: McGraw-Hill, 1977).

10 Ibid., pp. 77–79.

11 Elinor Ostrom, Roger Parks, and Gordon Whitaker, *Patterns of Metropolitan Policing* (Cambridge, MA: Ballinger, 1978).

12 James Q. Wilson, *Bureaucracy* (New York: Basic Books, 1989).

13 Henry I DeGeneste and John P. Sullivan, *Policing a Multicultural Community* (Washington, DC: PERF, 1997).

14 Perrow, *Complex Organizations*, pp. 6–7.

15 National Advisory Commission on Criminal Justice Standards and Goals, *Police* (Washington, DC: Government Printing Office, 1973), pp. 195–198.

16 National Advisory Commission, *Police*, pp. 195–198.

17 Walker, *A Critical History of Police Reform*.

18 Samuel Walker, "Legal Control of Police Behavior," in D. Weisburd and C. Uchida, *Police Innovation and Control of the Police* (New York: Springer-Verlag, 1993), pp. 32–55.

19 William A. Westley, *Violence and the Police* (Cambridge, MA: MIT Press, 1970), pp. 15–47.

20 Dorothy Guyot, "Police Departments under Social Science Scrutiny," *Journal of Criminal Justice*, 5 (Summer 1977): 109.

21 Westley, *Violence and the Police*, p. 23.

22 Moore, *The Professions: Rules and Roles*.

23 Walker, *A Critical History of Police Reform*.

24 James Q. Wilson, *Varieties of Police Behavior* (New York: Atheneum, 1973).

25 Samuel Walker, *Taming the System* (New York: Oxford University Press, 1994).

26 Edward Maguire, "Structural Change in Large Municipal Police Organizations during the Community Policing Era," *Justice Quarterly*, 14, no. 3 (1997): 547–576; Stephen Mastrofski and Richard Ritti, "Making Sense of Community Policing: A Theory Based Analysis," presented at the annual meeting of the American Society of Criminology, Boston (1995).

27 Maguire, "Structural Change in Large Municipal Police Organizations during the Community Policing Era."

28 Jihong (Solomon) Zhao, *Evaluation on the Implementation of Total Quality Management in the Omaha Police Department: An Interim Report* (Omaha: 1998).

29 Mary Anne Wycoff and Wesley Skogan, *Community Policing in Madison: Quality from the Inside Out* (Washington, DC: National Institute of Justice, 1993).

30 Zhao, *Evaluation on the Implementation of Total Quality Management in the Omaha Police Department*.

31 Marvin Weisbord, Howard Lamb, Allan Drexler, *Improving Police Department Management through Problem-Solving Task Forces* (Reading, MA: Addison-Wesley, 1974).

32 Peter W. Phillips, "De Facto Police Consolidation: The Multi-Jurisdictional Task Force," *Police Forum*, 9, no. 3 (1999): 1–5; G. Orvis, "The Evolution of the Crime

Task Force and Its Use in the Twenty-First Century," presented at the annual meeting of the Academy of Criminal Justice Sciences, Orlando (1999).

33 Terry Dunworth, P. Hayes, and A. Saiger, *National Assessment of the Byrne Formula Grant Program* (Washington, DC: National Institute of Justice, 1997).

34 Phillips, "De Facto Police Consolidation: The Multi-Jurisdictional Task Force."

35 Dorothy Guyot, "Bending Granite: Attempts to Change the Rank Structure of American Police Departments," *Journal of Police Science and Administration*, 7, no. 3 (1979): 253–284.

36 Mary Ann Wycoff and George L. Kelling, *The Dallas Experience: Organizational Reform* (Washington, DC: The Police Foundation, 1978).

37 William A. Geller, "Suppose We Were Really Serious about Police Departments Becoming Learning Organizations?" *National Institute of Justice Journal*, No. 234 (December 1997): 2–8.

38 Herman Goldstein, *Policing a Free Society* (Cambridge, MA: Ballinger, 1977), pp. 307–333.

39 Westley Skogan and Susan Hartnett, *Community Policing, Chicago Style* (New York: Oxford University Press, 1997).

40 Gary W. Cordner, Craig B. Fraser, and Chuck Wexler, "Research, Planning, and Implementation," in W. A. Geller, ed., *Local Government Police Management* (Washington, DC: ICMA, 1991), pp. 333–362.

41 Geller, "Suppose We Were Really Serious," p. 4.

42 Ibid.

43 David H. Bayley, *Police for the Future* (New York: Oxford University Press, 1994), p. 101.

44 U.S. Department of Justice, *Mapping Out Crime* (Washington, DC: National Partnership for Reinventing Government, 1999).

45 John Eck and Edward Maguire, "Have Changes in Policing Reduced Violent Crime? An Assessment of the Evidence" (pp. 207–265), in Alfred Blumstein and Joel Wallman, eds., *The Crime Drop in America* (Cambridge, UK: Cambridge University Press, 2000).

46 Robert Davis and Mateu-Gelabert, *Respectful and Effective Policing: Two Examples in the South Bronx* (New York: Vera Institute of Justice, March 1999).

47 Phyllis McDonald, "COP, COMPSTAT, and the New Professionalism," pp. 233–256, in Geoffrey Alpert and Alex Piquero, eds., *Community Policing: Contemporary Readings* (Prospect Heights, IL: Waveland Press, 2000).

48 George W. Griesinger, Jeffrey S. Slovak, Joseph J. Molkup, *Civil Service Systems: Their Impact on Police Administration* (Washington, DC: Government Printing Office, 1979).

49 Ibid.

50 Guyot, "Bending Granite."

51 Bureau of Justice Statistics, *Law Enforcement Management and Administrative Statistics, 1997* (Washington, DC: Government Printing Office, 1999), p. xiv.

52 Bureau of the Census, *Statistical Abstract of the United States, 1997* (Washington, DC: Government Printing Office, 1997), pp. 438–442.

53 Hervey A. Juris and Peter Feuille, *Police Unions* (Lexington, MA: Lexington Books, 1973).

54 International Association of Chiefs of Police, *Guidelines and Papers from the National Symposium on Police Labor Relations* (Washington, DC: IACP, 1974).

55 Michael T. Leibig and Robert B. Kliesmet, *Police Unions and the Law: A Handbook for Police Organizers* (Washington, DC: Institute for Police Research, 1988).

56 Jack Steiber, *Public Employee Unionism: Structure and Growth* (Washington, DC: The Brookings Institution, 1973), pp. 159–192.

57 Margaret Levi, *Bureaucratic Insurgency* (Lexington, MA: Lexington Books, 1977), pp. 91–130.

58 William J. Bopp, "The San Francisco Police Strike of 1975: A Case Study," *Journal of Police Science and Administration*, 5, no. 1 (1977): 32–42.

59 Bureau of the Census, *Statistical Abstract of the United States, 1997*, p. 439.

60 Stephen C. Halpern, *Police-Association and Department Leaders* (Lexington: Lexington Books, 1974).

61 Juris and Feuille, *Police Unions*, pp. 103–117.

62 Lex Donaldson, *American Anti-Management Theories of Organization* (Cambridge, UK: Cambridge University Press, 1995); Charles Katz, Ed Maguire, and Denn Roncek, "The Creation of Specialized Gang Units: Testing Contingency, Social Threat, and Resource Dependency Theories," presented at the annual meeting of the American Society of Criminology (1998); Stephen Mastrofski, "Community Policing and Police Organizational Structure," pp. 161–189, in Jean-Paul Brodeur, ed., *How to Recognize Good Policing* (Thousand Oaks, CA: Sage, 1998).

63 Charles Katz, Ed Maguire, and Denn Roncek, "The Creation of Specialized Gang Units: Testing Contingency, Social Threat, and Resource Dependency Theories," presented at the annual meeting of the American Society of Criminology (1998).

64 John P. Crank and Robert Langworthy, "An Institutional Perspective on Policing," *Journal of Criminal Law and Criminology*, 83, no. 2 (1992): 338–363.

65 Peter K. Manning, *Police Work* (Cambridge, MA: MIT Press, 1977).

66 Donaldson, *American Anti-Management Theories of Organization;* Katz, Maguire, and Roncek, "The Creation of Specialized Gang Units."

67 Katz, Maguire, and Roncek, "The Creation of Specialized Gang Units."

68 Ed Maguire, Jihong Zhao, and Nicholas Lovrich, "Dimensions of Community Policing," unpublished manuscript (Omaha, Nebraska).

GLOSSARY

abuse of authority   Actions by a police officer, under the guise of his or her authority, that tend to injure, insult, trespass on human dignity, and/or violate a citizen's inherent civil rights.

accountability   Having to answer for one's conduct. Both police organizations and individual officers are distinctly accountable to the public, elected officials, and the courts for how well they control crime, maintain order, and perform these tasks while remaining in compliance with the law.

accreditation   The process of voluntary professional self-regulation that serves as a final approach to establishing minimum national standards in policing.

affirmative action   Originating in 1965, a court-ordered plan establishing specific goals and timetables for the employment of minorities and women for any private employer or government agency receiving federal funds.

Alice Stebbins Wells   A leader of the policewomen's movement, organized the International Association of Policewomen in 1915.

analysis   The second stage of the SARA model of problem-oriented policing, in which the police collect information about a problem to help identify its scope, nature, and cause.

assessment   The fourth stage of the SARA model of problem-oriented policing, in which the effectiveness of the response is evaluated through rigorous feedback that allows for revision if the response is not successful.

assessment center   A technique used in police departments to evaluate the ability of an applicant to handle the job being sought through promotion.

August Vollmer   Chief of police in Berkeley, California, from 1905 to 1932, known as the father of police professionalism for advocating higher education for police officers and promoting organizational reform within departments.

authorized strength   The maximum number of sworn officers any given law enforcement agency is authorized to employ.

behaviorally arrested   Occurs when taking a suspect into custody involves a number of different actions, such as a stop (in which the officer tells the individual not to leave), a verbal statement that the person is "under arrest," or physically restraining a person.

blue curtain   A code of silence among police officers whereby officers refuse to testify against corrupt officers, creating a veil of secrecy around police actions.

blue-ribbon commissions Commissions serving as a form of external accountability for police conduct that address a full range of police issues and bring together leading experts to help improve local departments.

bona fide occupational qualification Provides protection for employers who refuse to hire people not possessing established qualifications that are reasonably necessary to the normal operation of that particular business.

Boston Police Strike Occurred in 1919 when 1,117 officers went on strike and formed a police union after having received no pay raise in nearly twenty years. After violence and disorder erupted throughout Boston, the strike quickly collapsed and the striking officers were fired.

bribe Something offered or given to a person in the hope of influencing that individual's views or conduct. Police bribes can include monetary payoffs to protect illegal activity, sell information on criminal investigations, remove criminal files, or alter testimony in court.

broken windows hypothesis Developed by James Q. Wilson and George L. Kelling, argues that police should focus their resources on disorder problems that create fear of crime and lead to neighborhood decay.

bureaucracy A pyramidal model of government administration in which tasks are grouped into separate bureaus or departments and information flows up and down according to the hierarchical structure. Marked by diffuse authority, visible divisions of labor, and inflexible rules of operation, each employee answers to one supervisor, creating a uniform and clear chain of command.

call girl One who represents the upper end of the economic scale of prostitution by catering to a more affluent customer and generally making arrangements over the telephone. Since call girls do not actually walk the streets, their activities are not visible to either the public or the police.

campus police Special district police who serve college and university campuses.

citizen oversight An approach designed to provide independent citizen input for complaints filed against the police through agencies that independently review citizens' complaints, monitor the complaint process, scrutinize general police practices, review department policy and recommend policy changes, and audit the quality of complaint investigations.

civil service A nearly universal set of formal and legally binding procedures governing personnel decisions in police organizations, ensuring that such decisions are based on objective criteria and not on favoritism, bias, or political influence.

civilians Those who follow the pursuits of civil life and are not employed as sworn officers or officials.

clearance rate The traditional measure of success in criminal investigations for a police agency based on when the police have identified the offender, have sufficient evidence to charge him or her, and actually take the individual into custody.

"code of silence" Also known as the "blue curtain," a code of honor among police officers whereby officers refuse to testify against corrupt colleagues, creating a veil of secrecy around police actions.

collective bargaining A method of determining conditions of employment through bilateral negotiations according to the following principles: Employees have a legal right to form unions; employers must recognize employee unions; employees have a right to participate in negotiations over working conditions; and employers are required to negotiate with the union's designated representatives.

community partnership A collaborative partnership that stresses increased interaction between the police and the public to make the police more responsive to the community's needs and reduce community decay and disorder.

community policing A model of policing that stresses a two-way working relationship between the community and the police, in which the police become more integrated into the local community and citizens assume an active role in crime control and prevention.

COMPSTAT (Computer Comparison Statistics) An organizational model, first used by the New York City police in 1994, that allows police departments to blend timely intelligence, effective tactics, rapid deployment of personnel, and vigorous follow-up and assessment.

constable   A peace officer who is empowered to serve writs and warrants but has a smaller jurisdiction than a sheriff.

containment   A strategy used by police to confine the homeless problem to one area of a community to both minimize disorder and keep homeless people out of public view.

contingency theory   A theoretical framework for understanding the structures and practices of police organizations based on the underlying premise that these organizations are created and structured to achieve specific goals, such as crime control, and will ultimately fail if unable to adjust to environmental contingencies.

coroner   A medical examiner responsible for aiding criminal investigations by probing deaths not thought to be of natural causes.

corruption   A form of misconduct or deviant behavior by police officers that involves the misuse of authority in a manner designed to produce personal gain for themselves or for others.

county police   Municipal police that operate on a countywide basis and lack the non–law enforcement roles of the county sheriff. About 1 percent of local departments are county police.

counterpunching   Occurs when someone calls the police about another person to divert attention from his or her own behavior.

deadly force   The legal right of police officers to use force with the intent to kill if placed in a defense-of-life situation.

decentralize   To place greater decision-making responsibility on rank-and-file officers at the neighborhood level and to become more responsive to neighborhood residents.

decertification   The process of revoking a police officer's license to work in a given state; addresses the problem of an officer who is fired from one department for misconduct and is then hired by another, but does not prevent the fired officer from being hired in another state.

defense-of-life rule   States that police officers are allowed to use deadly force only in situations where their own lives or the life of another person are in danger.

deformalize   To eliminate many of the rules and policies that stifle creativity and discourage problem solving within police organizations.

delayerize   To decrease the amount of social and administrative distance between the beat officer and the chief of police.

despecialize   To replace specialized police units with neighborhood officers who are more knowledgeable about the problems their neighborhoods face.

differential response   The screening of 911 calls by the police to provide responses appropriate to the nature and severity of the calls.

discovery time   The interval between the commission of a crime and its discovery.

discretion   The freedom to act on one's own judgment.

discrimination   Differential treatment based on some extra-legal category such as race, ethnicity, or gender.

disparity   Differences or inequalities that are not necessarily caused by differential treatment.

domestic disturbance   A dispute requiring police response that involves two or more people engaged in an intimate relationship (married or divorced couples, live-in lovers, people on a first date, problems between adults and children, or adults and elderly parents).

domestic violence   A disturbance between two or more people engaged in an intimate relationship that has escalated to a degree involving actual or threatened violence.

early warning system   A management information system that systematically compiles and analyzes data on problematic police officer behavior, citizen complaints, police officer use of force reports, and other indicators to identify officers with recurring performance problems.

ethnicity   The cultural differences existing that characterize a group of people.

field training   A supplement to classroom training that allows for practical experience under the supervision of a training officer in on-the-job type situations.

field training officer (FTO)   An experienced police officer assigned to supervise recruits during field training.

fleeing-felon rule   Declared unconstitutional by the Supreme Court in 1985 (*Tennessee v. Garner*), allowed police the legal right to use deadly force in apprehending a felon attempting to escape.

foot patrol   Officers within a department who make neighborhood rounds on foot. While extremely expensive and able to cover only limited ground, foot patrol allows for enhanced police–community relations.

force factor   A framework for examining a police officer's use of force in relation to the actions of a citizen to help determine if the officer's actions were reasonable.

Fourteenth Amendment   Guarantees equal protection under the law by stating that all persons born or naturalized in the United States are citizens therein, and no state shall make or enforce laws that deprive citizens of life, liberty, or property, without due process of law; nor deny to any person within its jurisdiction the equal protection of the laws.

fragmented   Broken down into separate, decentralized parts.

functional specialization   A form of organizational structure in which employees are assigned specific duties based on their areas of expertise, thereby allowing less critical tasks to be delegated to paraprofessionals.

Garrity ruling   States that a police officer can be disciplined and even dismissed for refusing to answer questions by internal affairs, but the information disclosed cannot then be used against him or her in a criminal prosecution.

grass eater   A police officer who passively accepts gratuities offered to him or her.

gratuities   The most common form of police corruption, gifts or favors given to police officers, sometimes out of a sincere effort to thank the officers but often out of self-interest with an expectation of better police service.

hackers   Individuals who crack into computer networks for either the thrill of the experience, to make an illegal financial transaction, or to create computer viruses that have the potential to destroy computer data.

hate crime   A criminal offense against a person or property motivated in whole or in part by the offender's bias against a race, religion, disability, ethnic/national origin, or sexual orientation.

high-speed pursuit   A situation where a police officer attempts to stop a vehicle and the suspect knowingly flees at a high rate of speed.

honest law enforcement   An approach representative of low expectations for law enforcement that states police would continue to patrol neighborhoods, answer calls for service, intervene in problem situations, and try to apprehend offenders, but would not make unjustified claims that they are preventing crime.

hot spot   An area that receives a disproportionate number of calls for police service and/or has a very high crime rate.

human disorder   A form of societal neglect resulting from the disorderly actions of individuals in a neighborhood; examples include public drinking, street corner gangs, street harassment, street-level drug sale and use, noisy neighbors, and commercial sex.

injunctions   Court orders that prohibit a specified group from a specific course of action.

insiders   Current or former employees of a company with knowledge about the company's computer infrastructure, which allows them to steal proprietary data such as intellectual property, marketing strategies, client lists, and so on.

institutional theory   A theoretical framework for understanding the structures and practices of police organizations based on the premise that police organizations are social institutions that operate in relation to their external social and political environment.

J. Edgar Hoover   Former director of the Federal Bureau of Investigation from 1924 to 1972; increased the size and scope of the bureau's capabilities, but is best known for systematically misusing his power and exaggerating the bureau's effectiveness.

job stress   Conditions associated with one's work environment that are mentally or physically disruptive; the major cause of job dissatisfaction.

job stress coping mechanisms   Confidential assistance programs that utilize health professionals and/or peer support groups to help employees cope with personal or work-related problems.

Kansas City Gun Experiment   Designed to reduce gun-related crimes by removing guns from the streets of a high-crime precinct in Kansas City, represented a combination of problem-oriented policing (by focusing on a particular problem) and "hot spots" (by concentrating on particular areas of high criminal activity).

Kansas City Preventive Patrol Experiment   Conducted from 1972 to 1973, measured the impact of different levels of patrol on criminal activity, community perceptions, police officer behavior, and police department practices, while being the first independent and objective experiment to test the effectiveness of patrol that met the minimum standards of scientific research.

Kerner Commission   Created in 1967 to study issues of race relations; found that hostility between the police and ghetto communities was a major cause for disorder. Officially known as the National Advisory Commission on Civil Disorders.

lateral entry   Moving from one police department to another at either the same rank or a higher rank.

Lautenburg Amendment   A federal law passed in 1996 prohibiting anyone with a conviction for domestic violence from owning a firearm.

Law of Equal Employment Opportunity   Designed to eliminate employment discrimination by making it illegal to refuse employment to, discharge, or deny benefits and compensation to anyone on the basis of race, ethnicity, color, or sex.

legalistic style   An organizational style used in police departments that emphasizes aggressive crime fighting and attempts to control officer behavior through a rule-bound, "by-the-book" administrative approach.

legally arrested   Occurs when an individual is deprived of his or her liberty by legal authority and is under arrest or simply taken into custody. A police officer must have the intent to arrest, must communicate that intent to the person, and must actually take the person into custody.

local political control   A tradition, inherited from England during the colonial period, that places primary responsibility for public protection with local governments, both city and county.

local political culture   Values and traditions, communicated informally in a particular department, town, or community, that influence the organizational structure of policing and officer discretion in that area.

London Metropolitan Police   Created in 1829, represents the first example of an efficient, proactive police force. Introduced three important elements of policing: the mission of crime prevention, the strategy of preventative patrol, and an organizational structure similar to the military.

Mapp v. Ohio   A controversial Supreme Court decision that established Fourth Amendment protection against unreasonable searches and seizures by the police.

meat eater   A police officer who actively and aggressively demands gratuities.

Minneapolis Domestic Violence Study   A study conducted from 1981 to 1982 to determine the relative deterrent effect of arrest, mediation, and separation in misdemeanor domestic violence incidents; found that arrest produced lower rates of repeat violence than separation or mediation.

municipal police   Also known as *city police,* denote the most important component of American law enforcement. Representing the majority of all law enforcement agencies and sworn officers, municipal police are responsible for dealing with serious crime, difficult order maintenance problems, and a wide range of emergency services.

Newark Foot Patrol Experiment Conducted from 1978 to 1979 to test the effect of foot patrol on crime and public perception, concluded that added foot patrol did not affect serious crime, but did have a positive impact on public perception of the police.

O. W. Wilson Leader of the police professionalization movement from the late 1930s through the end of the 1960s. Developed a formula for efficient management of personnel by assigning patrol officers on the basis of a workload formula that reflected reported crime and calls for service.

occupational deviance Criminal and improper noncriminal behavior committed during the course of normal work activities or under the guise of a police officer's authority.

officially arrested Occurs only once the police make an official arrest report.

order maintenance Police intervention in incidents that do not involve actual criminal activity but often entail "interpersonal conflict" or "public nuisance."

organizational culture Values and traditions, communicated informally, that influence the organizational style of policing within a police department.

peace officer A status granted to individuals who have certain powers and providing certain legal protections not available to ordinary citizens. A peace officer can be a probation, parole, or corrections officer.

physical disorder A form of societal neglect resulting from physical decay within a neighborhood; examples include vandalism, dilapidation and abandonment of buildings, and trash buildup.

police aides Nonsworn personnel used by police departments to handle low-priority calls and routine assignments, freeing sworn officers for more critical tasks.

police brutality The use of excessive physical force by the police.

police officer A nonmilitary person who is employed by a government agency and has the authority to use coercive force when carrying out his or her duties.

police-to-population ratio The standard measure for the level of police protection in a community; usually expressed as the number of sworn officers per thousand population.

police–community relations Relations between the police and racial and ethnic minority communities.

political patronage The power a politician holds to appoint governmental or political positions based on friendship instead of merit.

preliminary investigation The first stage of investigating a crime, consisting of five steps: identifying and arresting any suspects, providing aid to any victims in need of medical attention, securing the crime scene to prevent loss of evidence, collecting all relevant physical evidence, and preparing a preliminary report.

proactive crime strategies Anticrime strategies initiated by the police themselves, as opposed to occurring in response to a citizen request for service.

problem-oriented policing A model of policing that stresses increased police response to identified crime problems.

promotion Advancement in rank or responsibility usually based on merit, but sometimes the result of personal favoritism.

race A group of people classified together on the basis of physical and biological similarities.

racial profiling The practice of making police stops solely on the basis of one's race or ethnicity and not because of criminal activity.

reactive crime strategies Anticrime strategies used by police when responding to a civilian's request for service.

reality shock The astonishment a new police officer experiences when encountering the unpleasant aspects of dealing with the public, the criminal justice system, and the department during the first weeks and months on the job.

residual deterrence Also called the *phantom effect,* involves assuming the police are patrolling an area from having seen them at another time or place, leading to the presumption that the police are present when there is no patrol in the area.

resource dependency theory   A theoretical framework for understanding the structures and practices of police organizations based on the premise that such organizations must obtain resources to survive, and that to obtain these resources they must engage in exchanges with other organizations in their environment.

response   The third stage of the SARA model of problem-oriented policing, in which data collected during the analysis stage are used to develop a strategy to address the problem and, ultimately, implement a response.

response time   The total amount of time between the commission of a crime and the moment a police officer arrives on the scene.

reverse discrimination   Discrimination focused on whites and/or males; in violation of the 1964 Civil Rights Act and the equal protection clause of the Fourteenth Amendment.

Robert Peel   Credited as the father of modern policing, fought to improve the basic structure of law enforcement and persuaded the English Parliament to establish the London Metropolitan Police in 1829.

scanning   The first stage of the SARA model of problem-oriented policing, in which officers take steps to identify possible problems and expose their underlying causes.

selective contact   A lack of cross-sectional contact and communication between police officers and a community that leads to misperceptions about public attitudes toward the police.

selective perception   The likelihood that police officers will remember traumatic or unpleasant incidents with citizens, even though only 2 to 5 percent of contacts involve hostility or conflict.

sheriff   Elected on a countywide basis in all but two states, an official serving all three components of the criminal justice system: law enforcement, courts, and corrections. Usually is directly involved in partisan politics in ways that municipal police chiefs are not.

social control   The capacity of a society to regulate itself according to desired principles and values without the use of repression or coerced conformity.

special district police   Police agencies designed to serve only specific government agencies. Examples include the Los Angeles School District police force and the Metropolitan Transit Police Force in the Washington, DC, subway system.

streetwalker   One who represents the lower end of the social and economic scale of prostitution by soliciting on the streets, thus being highly visible to both the police and the general public.

subjectively arrested   Occurs when someone having an encounter with the police believes he or she is not free to go, leading to the perception of having been arrested.

Title VII, 1964 Civil Rights Act   Makes it illegal to refuse to hire or to discharge any individual, or to otherwise discriminate against any individual with respect to employment on the basis of race, color, religion, sex, or national origin.

turnover   The number of employees hired by a company or department to replace workers who have left their jobs in a given period of time.

unfounding a crime   Occurs when a citizen reports a crime but a police officer fails to complete an official crime report.

verbal abuse   The use of inappropriate language, particularly racial and ethnic slurs, by police officers.

vice   Victimless crimes with no complaining party involving prostitution, gambling, or narcotics.

victimless crime   A crime that has no complaining party and often involves behavior that many people regard as legitimate, resulting in conflicting public attitudes about how vigorously the laws should be enforced.

The Watch   A policelike group, established in colonial times, requiring all adult males to patrol the city for crimes, fires, and disorder.

watchman style   An organizational style used in police departments that emphasizes peace-keeping without aggressive law enforcement and few controls over rank-and-file officers.

Wickersham Commission   Created in 1929 by President Herbert Hoover as the first national study of the American criminal justice system. Officially the National Commission on Law Observance and Enforcement.

zero-tolerance policing   Based on the belief that aggressive enforcement of disorder will motivate residents to better care for their community, a policy that calls for the police to focus primarily on disorder, minor crime, and the appearance of crime through interventions that vigorously enforce criminal and civil laws and are conducted for the purpose of restoring order to communities.

NAME INDEX

SUBJECT INDEX

A

ABA. *See* American Bar Association (ABA)
ABF. *See* American Bar Foundation (ABF)
Abortion, 187
Abuse of authority. *See* Brutality; Corruption;
    Discretion; Force
Academy of Criminal Justice Sciences
    (ACJS), 395, 398, 410
Accountability, 17, 48, 49, 218–219
    accreditation and, 363–364
    basic issues in, 352–354
    blue-ribbon commissions and, 374–375
    citizen complaints and, 358, 360–363
    citizen oversight and, 371–376
    criminal prosecution, 370–371
    definition of, 352
    early warning (EW) and, 362–363, 370
    external mechanisms of, 364–365
    force and, 354, 359, 363, 412
    internal affairs unit (IAU) and, 336, 357,
        359, 360–363
    internal mechanisms for, 356
    litigation and, 365–371
    officer rights versus, 450–451
    performance evaluations, 359–360
    in police role, 354–355
    supervision and, 356–360
    Three E's, 353
Accreditation, 77, 176, 363–364
ACJS. *See* Academy of Criminal Justice
    Sciences (ACJS)

ACLU. *See* American Civil Liberties Union
    (ACLU)
Active officers, 439
ADA. *See* Americans With Disabilities Act
    (ADA)
Affirmative action, 406–409
African Americans
    See also Minority groups
    abuse of discretion and, 248
    arrests and, 293–294
    attitudes toward police, 280, 281, 283, 285,
        286, 287, 299–301
    civil rights and, 41
    community policing and, 209, 437
    driving while black, 48, 273, 294
    drug offenses and, 179, 180, 294
    force and, 28, 45, 290, 369, 376
    juvenile arrests and, 145
    as police officers, 29, 36, 41, 44, 301, 302,
        392, 394, 396–397, 399, 402–404, 406,
        407, 433–434, 443
    racial profiling and, 48–49, 274, 278–279,
        294–297
    riots and, 36
Age Discrimination Employment Act
    of 1967, 402
AIDS, 141–143
Alabama, 186–187
Albuquerque, NM, 174, 374
Alcohol abuse, 12, 30, 31–32, 137, 138–139,
    448, 449